1978

The Stuart Editions

The Complete Poetry of
RICHARD CRASHAW

The Stuart Editions

J. Max Patrick, *series editor*

ALREADY PUBLISHED

The Prose of Sir Thomas Browne
EDITED WITH AN INTRODUCTION, NOTES, AND VARIANTS
BY NORMAN ENDICOTT

The Complete Poetry of Henry Vaughan
EDITED WITH AN INTRODUCTION, NOTES, AND VARIANTS
BY FRENCH FOGLE

An Anthology of Jacobean Drama, VOLUMES I & II
EDITED WITH AN INTRODUCTION, NOTES, AND VARIANTS
BY RICHARD C. HARRIER

The Complete Poetry of Ben Jonson
EDITED WITH AN INTRODUCTION, NOTES, AND VARIANTS
BY WILLIAM B. HUNTER, JR.

The Meditative Poem: An Anthology of Seventeenth-Century Verse
EDITED WITH AN INTRODUCTION AND NOTES
BY LOUIS L. MARTZ

Seventeenth-Century American Poetry
EDITED WITH AN INTRODUCTION, NOTES, AND COMMENTS
BY HARRISON T. MESEROLE

Short Fiction of the Seventeenth Century
SELECTED AND EDITED BY CHARLES C. MISH

The Complete Poetry of Robert Herrick
EDITED WITH AN INTRODUCTION AND NOTES
BY J. MAX PATRICK

The Prose of John Milton
SELECTED AND EDITED WITH AN INTRODUCTION,
NOTES AND TRANSLATIONS
BY J. MAX PATRICK

The Psalms of Sir Philip Sidney and the Countess of Pembroke
EDITED WITH AN INTRODUCTION BY J. C. A. RATHMELL

The Complete English Poetry of John Milton
ARRANGED IN CHRONOLOGICAL ORDER WITH AN
INTRODUCTION, NOTES AND VARIANTS
BY JOHN T. SHAWCROSS

The Complete Poetry of John Donne
EDITED WITH AN INTRODUCTION, NOTES, AND VARIANTS
BY JOHN T. SHAWCROSS

The Complete Plays of William Wycherley
EDITED WITH AN INTRODUCTION, NOTES, AND VARIANTS
BY GERALD WEALES

The Stuart Editions

The Complete Poetry of
RICHARD CRASHAW

*Edited with an
Introduction and Notes by
George Walton Williams*

New York: New York University Press

1972

GEORGE WALTON WILLIAMS is Professor of English at Duke University. He is the author of *Image and Symbol in the Sacred Poetry of Richard Crashaw* (University of South Carolina Press, 1963) and of articles on seventeenth-century poetry, on Shakespeare, and on textual criticism. He is the editor of *Romeo and Juliet* (Duke University Press, 1964) and of other Elizabethan and Jacobean plays.

This book was first published in 1970 in the Doubleday Anchor Seventeenth-Century Series.

Library of Congress Catalog Card Number 68-14177
ISBN: 8147-9154-9

Printed in the United States of America

ACKNOWLEDGMENTS

It is a pleasure to express my indebtedness to Phyllis S. Bowman who has worked closely with me and has been chiefly responsible for translating Crashaw's Latin poems; to Messrs. William C. Bradford and Thomas L. Berger who have been of great assistance in preparing and verifying the typescript; to the staffs of the Folger Shakespeare Library, the Huntington Library, the British Museum, the Edinburgh University Library, and the Duke University Library (especially Mr. James Harrison). I am grateful also to the Duke University Research Council which has generously contributed to research expenses. To my colleague, Professor William H. Willis, I offer particular appreciation for aid with the Greek texts and types.

I acknowledge with thanks the courtesy of the following libraries for permission to reproduce illustrations from volumes in their possession: the Folger Shakespeare Library for Plate II (and the illustrations in the text), the Edinburgh University Library for Plate III, and the Henry E. Huntington Library for Plates I and IV and the woodcut on page 61.

My concern with Richard Crashaw began innocuously enough in a term paper assigned by Professor Fredson Bowers in a graduate course at the University of Virginia in 1948. It is a great satisfaction to me that that concern after so long a time is finally brought to fruition here; I hope that it will be also to him, the grand original.

August 21, 1968   G. W. W.
Duke University

CONTENTS

SECULAR POEMS

CONTENTS   (xiii)

INTRODUCTION

Richard Crashaw may be considered the most un-English of all the English poets. As his native poetic genius developed, it absorbed continental influences, both sacred and secular, to such a degree that Crashaw eventually removed from Puritanism and England to Roman Catholicism and Rome. The spirit of the Counter Reformation flowed in him, and his poems disclose his acceptance of the artistic style of that movement which is called "baroque." He is, as T. S. Eliot has pointed out, the leading English representative of that style, a style which is fundamentally foreign to the spirit of English poetry. Had he written his mature poems in Latin, he would have moved easily into the company graced by Italian, Spanish, French, Dutch, and even Polish poets, but he chose, like his contemporary Milton, to write his culminating works in his native English whose richness he sensed and could not forego. By importing foreign spirit and style to domestic language he made his unique contribution to the canon of English literature.

Richard Crashaw was born in London during the winter of 1612–13.[1] His father was William Crashaw, an eminent preacher and a polemicist of strongly puritan leanings. When Richard was about two years old, the family moved to Agnes Burton, a small parish in Yorkshire, the county of several generations of Crashaws. The move was designed to provide the necessary leisure for William Crashaw to compile "A discoverye of popyshe Corruption." In November 1618, William Crashaw returned to London, to the "too great Parishe" of St. Mary Matfellon, in Whitechapel, then in the suburbs of the city.

Some time before Richard was seven, his mother died, and in 1619 his father remarried. The stepmother died in childbirth only fifteen

---

[1] Most of the material in this introduction derives from the standard edition of the poems, L. C. Martin, ed. *The Poems English Latin and Greek of Richard Crashaw* (Oxford, first edition 1927, second edition 1957); the standard biography, Austin Warren, *Richard Crashaw A Study in Baroque Sensibility* (Louisiana State University, 1939); and the major nineteenth-century edition, A. B. Grosart, ed. *The Complete Works of Richard Crashaw* (two vols., London, 1872–73). These works are cited by the name of the editors or author; citations to Martin's work are to the second edition (1957) throughout.

months later (in 1620), and Richard was again motherless. William Crashaw himself died in 1626 in London, leaving Richard, then fourteen, his only descendant. Young Richard was presumably attending school in London during these years; in 1629 he was admitted to the Charterhouse. In 1631 he went to Pembroke College, Cambridge, on a scholarship from the Watt Foundation.

When he reached Cambridge, Crashaw was evidently already reputed a poet, for he was called upon early in his college career to provide introductory verses for fairly important books published in Cambridge and London.[2] As a requirement of his scholarship he also prepared Greek and Latin epigrams on the New Testament reading each Sunday. In 1634 he presented a series of such epigrams to the Master of the College, Benjamin Laney; probably on Laney's encouragement, Crashaw then published his first volume of verse, and the only volume for which he could have been personally responsible, the *Epigrammatum Sacrorum Liber,* printed by the university press in 1634. In the same year, Crashaw received the degree of B.A.

In 1635, having been elected to a Fellowship at Peterhouse, Crashaw moved across the street to take up lodgings in that College. There he at once interested himself in refurbishing the college chapel with the work of his mind and hands. One of the first students placed under his tutelage in 1636 was Ferrar Collet, nephew of Nicholas Ferrar, the founder of the religious community at Little Gidding famous for such high Anglican spiritual devotions and exercises as night-long reading of the psalms, "cultivated yet ascetic piety," contemplation, and "an austere and heavenly rule of life."[3] From this time can be dated with certainty Crashaw's association with that community, though it is very likely that it had begun earlier.

In 1638 Crashaw proceeded M.A. and about the same time took holy orders. As a priest he was College Catechist and Curate of Little St. Mary's, the small parish church adjoining Peterhouse. The manner of his preaching is described by an early biographer: "Those thronged Sermons on each Sunday and Holiday [i.e. holy day], that ravished more like Poems . . . the Poet and Saint . . . scattering not so much Sentences as Extasies, his soul breathing in each word."[4] The matter of his preaching is recorded by puritan investigators: "Mr. Crashaw fellow of Peterhouse in a speech made in that Colledge Chappell *Die Annunciationis* 1639 is credibly reported to have turned himselfe to the picture of

---

[2] Burton Confrey in "A Note on Richard Crashaw," *MLN,* XXXVII (1922), 250–51, records that he was known as a poet in 1627. See also notes to poem No. 359.

[3] Basil Willey, *Richard Crashaw* (Cambridge, 1949), pp. 5, 11–12.

[4] Martin, p. 416.

the Virgine Mary and to have used these words *Hanc adoramus, colamus hanc* [We adore her, we worship her]. That is the rather probable because his practises in little St. Maryes, where he is Curat are superstitious."[5]

The investigators who discovered this popish corruption had been licensed by Parliament in 1640; they visited Cambridge in the early months of 1641 in order to survey the headquarters and breeding ground of high-church Anglicanism. Their visit must have been unsettling to Crashaw, who could have detected in it the first overt and official move against those things of the spirit that he held most dear. It may well have constituted the turning point in his life.

In his early years Crashaw had been influenced profoundly by the aggressive puritanism of his father whose writings he assimilated into his poetic subconscious. But William Crashaw's death when Richard was only fourteen removed that perhaps overpowering influence, and Richard's non-belligerent spirit, having fallen into company with Laudian and high-church ideas, began to realize that popish ways were not necessarily corruptions and that the Pope was not necessarily Anti-Christ. The puritan investigators were his father's spirit in arms, supported as never before by the power of the state.

The investigators objected to his "superstitious" practices: he held, they charged, "private masses"; before he officiated at the Communion, "he washeth his hands in the vestry"; he had made a special "carpet to tread upon when offices are performed at the Altar"; he "puts on a fresh paire of shoes" when he approaches the altar. But chiefly they objected to his adoration of the Virgin Mary.

The visit of the puritan investigators thus disrupted what was a singularly unified life—"a serenely happy life . . . : a fellowship in a college strongly Anglo-Catholic; a curacy in Little St. Mary's; frequent retreat to Little Gidding."[6] Soon after the visit, the war began between King and Parliament; Crashaw lent funds for the defense of the King, the same King whom he had praised only two summers before on the birth of his last son. In January 1643, his world about to come to an end, Crashaw fled from the little contentful kingdom at Peterhouse. Within a matter of weeks, Cromwell and an army of thirty thousand men occupied Cambridge and set to work at the orderly iconoclasm that the investigators' survey had shown was necessary. Very near Christmas, 1643, they visited and defaced the chapel at Peterhouse, which Crashaw had himself lovingly adorned, and Little St. Mary's Church where they "brake down 60 Superstitious Pictures, Some . . . Crucyfixes & God the father sitting in a

[5] Allan Pritchard, "Puritan Charges against Crashaw and Beaumont," *TLS*, July 2, 1964, p. 578.
[6] Warren, p. 46.

chayer."[7] One of their desecrations at Peterhouse, we may be sure, was the picture of the Virgin which Crashaw had venerated on the Feast of the Annunciation in 1639.

Twice motherless before he was nine, Crashaw sought constantly, as his poetry reflects, to achieve the maternal care, nourishment, and affection he had enjoyed only sporadically. He found it poetically in praising female saints—Mary Magdalene and Teresa (to whose writings he was introduced by his colleague Joseph Beaumont in 1638)—and in writing poems to and about female worthies—Mrs. M. R. and Alexias ("To [Mrs. M. R.] Councel," No. 65, and "Alexias," No. 84). He found it piously in Mary Collet, the "mother" superior of the monastic community at Little Gidding, to which he often went for prayer, vigils, and devotions. He found it politically in the Countess of Denbigh, and in Queen Henrietta Maria (whom he termed 'Maria' in poems). And he found it ecclesiastically and theologically in the Blessed Mary, Queen of Heaven, Mother of God. He was "styled By foes [—men like the puritan investigators—] the chaplaine of the virgine myld," and he justified the charge completely.

Crashaw fled from his *alma mater* presumably first to his conventual "mother" Mary Collet and the security of Little Gidding. But the nearness to Cambridge which before had been convenient now must have seemed dangerous, and Crashaw went to visit a friend in Lincolnshire. He gave to this friend copies of his poems written in his own hand: it was all he had to give.[8] From Lincolnshire probably he took ship for Holland, and in Leyden he rejoined Mary Collet. Perhaps in Leyden Crashaw hoped to be able to revive Little Gidding customs; but the place offended him, and he, it seems, offended Mary Collet's uncles who forbade him access to his "mother." Perhaps what gave offense to them was Crashaw's increasing inclination to render himself into the Communion of the Church of Rome.

In a letter written from Leyden in February 1644, Crashaw described rather ambiguously a major indecision in his life:

> But that I am not yet so desperate to your desires of further suspence, I assure you, or rather confes to you—for though t'will pleas you better perhaps, tis more a fault, I fear—a defect, at least a disproportion, of my weak soul to severer courses; I am not at present purposed for fixing.[9]

The context of the letter makes it clear that "fixing" is to be understood geographically, but the language of the letter makes it equally clear that

[7] Martin, p. xxv.

[8] J. E. Saveson, "Richard Crashaw," *TLS*, February 28, 1958, p. 115. The identity of the friend is not known.

[9] The letter—the only one of Crashaw's extant—was published first by E. C. Sharland, *Church Quarterly Review*, LXXIII (1912), 358; Martin, pp. xxvii–xxxi (punctuation mine).

religion is the concern of the "fixing."[10] Crashaw will not fix geographically in Leyden because the Reformed Church there is worse than the reformed church the puritans have made in Cambridge; in Leyden they have not only pulled down the saints, but they have set up "the plaine Pagan Pallas" as well. Perhaps before fixing in Rome and the Roman Church, he would attempt again to fix himself in England and the English Church.

Crashaw probably returned to England in the spring of 1644 and went to Oxford to the security offered by his political "mother," Queen Henrietta Maria, who had established her court there. He became a member of the University, renewed his Cambridge friendship with Abraham Cowley, and met the Countess of Denbigh, the First Lady of the Bedchamber. But this little kingdom was not to last either; the Queen fled to Paris in July 1644. It is possible that Crashaw remained at Oxford for another year; he is not heard of again until he has followed the Queen to Paris in 1645.[11] There and then no doubt he resolved to seek his final security in the Mother of God, and he fixed himself in the Church of Rome.

While in reduced circumstances in Paris, Crashaw was aided by his fellow poet Cowley, by the Countess of Denbigh, and by Thomas Car with whom he became an intimate friend and to whom he entrusted copies of his poems for a volume to be dedicated to the Countess "in hearty acknowledgment of his immortall obligation to her Goodnes and Charity." But Crashaw's real gift to her was spiritual: his poems were full of the convert's enthusiasm, urging her to join him without further delay in his new Church. Her gifts to him were her patronage and her intercession with the Queen for a letter recommending him to the Pope.

This letter the Queen wrote in September 1646, and with it Crashaw set out for his last home in Italy.[12] After Crashaw had been waiting patiently for a year for some favor from the Pope, the Queen wrote again to His Holiness, in November 1647, reminding him of Crashaw now "assaulted on the one hand by many grievous and dangerous infirmities, on the other hand with extream wants and necessities." Crashaw was finally

[10] The words "weak soul," "severer," "fixing"—all appear in the letter and also in the poem "To . . . the Countesse of Denbigh Perswading her to Resolution in Religion and to render her selfe without further delay into the Communion of the Catholick Church" (1652) at lines 8–10, 42; 26; 31. The poem is conceived as a remonstrance to a "fault." The letter includes the phrase "I desire to resolve my totall self" (Martin, p. xxx, ll. 22–23). Crashaw's poem was born not only of conviction but of personal experience also.

[11] It is possible that Crashaw's Lincolnshire visit (note 8) took place in this interim before the trip to Paris; the reconstruction in the text (based on Saveson) has more logic and orderliness, but these are not attributes to expect in England in the 1640s.

[12] P. G. Stanwood, "Crashaw at Rome," N&Q, CCXI (1966), 256–57.

appointed one of the followers of the Cardinal Palotto, a prelate of notable and upright character. After a year and a half in this service, Crashaw became a canon at the Santa Casa at Loreto on April 28, 1649, and going there in the summer, he caught a fever and died on August 21, 1649.

The Santa Casa was reputed to be the house in which the Virgin Mary had been born and in which she had received the Annunciation. Crashaw's pilgrimage from his first curacy at Mary's Little Church in Cambridge to his last canonship at Her Holy Shrine at Loreto was one marked by anguish and distress, irresolution and indefiniteness; but once at Loreto, Crashaw must have felt that the vexations, fulminations, and frantic heresies that he had heard in his father's library were now at last quieted in the embrace of his Mother, the Virgin mild. He would have approved Thomas Car's epitaph:

> Thus dying did he live, yet lived to dye
> In th' virgines lappe, to whom he did applye
> His virgine thoughtes and words.[13]

Crashaw was not a poet to press into print, and it is possible that his virgin thoughts and words would not have been produced in printed form without the editorial assistance of friends. The first of these was no doubt Benjamin Laney who assisted in the publication of the Latin epigrams in 1634. The volume contains the finest collection of Latin epigrams written by an Englishman, and the fact that they were all written before the poet's twenty-second birthday makes them even more remarkable. For brilliance of wit, precision, and structural sensitivity they are not excelled by any of the later work.

The second "editor" was "The Authors friend." (This was possibly "the author's intimate friend" in Lincolnshire to whom Crashaw delivered his poems before his going away. It is not even certain that Crashaw intended them for publication.) This friend had the poems printed in London as the *Steps to the Temple* and the *Delights of the Muses* (London: H. Moseley, 1646).[14] It is likely that the friend supplied the titles for this double volume of sacred and profane poems[15] and the "Preface" (see Appendix), full of biographical details, in which he refers to Crashaw as "this Learned young Gentleman (now dead to us)." ("Dead" geographically or theologically? Or both?) The *Delights* comprise in English and Latin many of the gratulatory, funerary, and academic poems dating from Crashaw's undergraduate days at Pembroke; many translations from Greek, Latin, and Italian; and a few occasional poems. The

---

[13] The image is typically Crashavian and occurs in "On Hope," ll. 45–47 (1646).

[14] See "Poet and Saint," *TLS*, June 1, 1946, p. 258.

[15] Grosart, I, xii.

Steps comprise in English nearly fifty translations from the Latin epigrams and fifteen longer poems. These fifteen include two psalm paraphrases (youthful work), one poem on Herbert's *Temple*, one accompanying the gift of the Book of Common Prayer, and the long translation from Marino's "Sospetto d'Herode" made in 1637. These items describe some of the sources of Crashaw's inspiration—the Old Testament ("Psalme 23," No. 2, contains an echo of William Crashaw's writing), the New Testament, George Herbert and the tradition of English sacred poetry (Donne and Southwell) and Anglican thought and practice, and the Italian concettists, notably Marino who taught Crashaw more in spirit than in technique. One poem which prefaces Shelford's *Treatises* (No. 67) in effect repudiates William Crashaw's discovery of popish corruption. Six poems praise feminine saints—two each to the Virgin Mary, Mary Magdalene, and Teresa of Avila. The *Steps*—"Stepps for happy soules to climbe heaven by"—incorporate and reflect the major concerns of Crashaw's life and present the themes, ideologies, and metaphors that define his work and give it its peculiar identity.

In 1648 the friend, who had evidently received new poems from Crashaw on the Continent, published a second edition of the work. To the *Delights* he added a few new Latin and English poems. To the *Steps* he added four Latin poems from old days at Cambridge, six translations from the Latin hymns of the medieval church, some ten new English poems, major revisions to six poems already published, and minor revisions to many of the others. The volume confirms the positions and attitudes of the earlier volume, and it intensifies the sensuousness and emphasizes the experiences of ecstatic mysticism already expressed.

Before he left Paris in 1646 for Rome, Crashaw conferred with Thomas Car about publishing a volume of his poems. He was moved no doubt partly by his wish to show his gratitude to the Countess of Denbigh and partly by the encouragement of Car, another "intimate Friend." Car described his assistance in the production of this volume, the *Carmen Deo Nostro:*

> CAR WAS but HE that enter'd as a friend
> With whom he [Crashaw] shar'd his thoughtes, and did commend
> (While yet he liv'd) this worke; . . . t'was his intent
> That what his riches pen'd, poore Car should print.

The "worke" consisted of a selection of 32 of Crashaw's already published sacred poems in English and a new poem addressed to the Countess of Denbigh "Perswading her to Resolution in Religion." It is arguable that in preparing the volume Crashaw once again made minor revisions in the poems that he had already extensively revised before the 1648 edition of the *Steps*. There is evidence also of the firm editorial hand of

Car in the sensible arrangement of the poems and in many details. The volume, dedicated to the Countess (who embraced the Roman Church in 1651) was published in Paris in 1652, six years after Crashaw had left Paris and three years after he was indeed dead to us.

One other unknown friend saw to the publication of a second version of Crashaw's *Letter* to the Countess of Denbigh in London in 1653(?).

The reputation of Crashaw as a writer of sacred English poetry rests on the 33 poems of the *Carmen Deo Nostro*. It is not an extensive canon, and Crashaw is not a major poet. He shows himself deficient in many respects, but he was a master of the voice which he chose for his own. It is a small voice, and among discriminating critics, few are sympathetic to it. It is the voice of the ecstatic vision, the sensuous transcended and made sublime, the suavity of pain, the long-sought joy of mystical death. It is a voice of confident and unquestioning faith. This voice is a small voice, yet no other English poet has ever sung so well with it.

CHRONOLOGY

1612–13   Richard Crashaw born in London.

1629   Admitted to the Charterhouse.

1631   Admitted to Pembroke College, Cambridge.

1634   *Epigrammatum Sacrorum Liber* published in Cambridge. Awarded B.A. degree.

1635   Accepted a Fellowship at Peterhouse, Cambridge.

1638   Awarded M.A. degree. Ordained priest(?).

1643   Fled from Cambridge.

1644   Crashaw on the Continent; in Leyden.

1645   Crashaw in Paris.

1646   *Steps to the Temple* and *Delights of the Muses* published in London. Crashaw in Rome.

1648   Second edition of *Steps* and *Delights* published in London.

1649   August 21. Crashaw's death at Loreto.

1652   *Carmen Deo Nostro* published in Paris.

1653(?)   *Letter to the Countess of Denbigh* published in London.

1670   Second edition of the Latin epigrams published in Cambridge; "Second" edition of *Steps, Delights,* and the *Carmen Deo Nostro* published in London.

A NOTE ON THE ARRANGEMENT OF THE BOOK

The customary method in editing an author in this series is to reprint the several volumes of his collected works. This is the method used in editing Crashaw's poems in Professor Martin's Oxford edition and in the Grove Press edition in paperback. As the results of this method are thus readily available in both scholarly and popular editions, the necessity of repeating the form is obviated. The first decision in arranging the poems in the present edition was then to abandon the traditional ordering by volumes. (In order to record the contents of the several volumes, however, the Tables of Contents of the original editions are provided, pp. 688–94.)

The second decision—originally Crashaw's—was to treat sacred and profane poems separately. The third decision was to provide (1) the Latin, Greek, and Italian originals that Crashaw translated into English poems and (2) English prose translations (prepared by Phyllis S. Bowman) of Crashaw's Latin poems.

As a consequence of these decisions the present edition is divided into "Sacred Poems" and "Secular Poems." Each of these major divisions has four parts: (1) poems in one English version, (2) poems in two English versions, (3) Latin, Greek, or Italian poems with Crashaw's English translations, (4) English translations of Crashaw's Latin poems. The ordering of the Sacred Poems in these four subdivisions follows the pattern of Thomas Car: the life of Christ followed by the major and minor saints, then miscellaneous poems. The scheme is most notable in the sequence of the Latin sacred epigrams, here arranged in gospel harmony through the life of Christ. The ordering of the Secular Poems follows the pattern indicated in the Contents; where possible the poems have been arranged in chronological order of composition. The translations into English are arranged by languages.

Poems in one version only are printed on *seriatim* pages; translated poems and poems in two versions are printed on facing pages in parallel texts. "Two versions" may be defined as the condition resulting from Crashaw's substantial reconsideration of the poem as a whole.

The Notes are arranged as follows: an introduction to the poem in general and critical comment on it are included in a headnote before the poem; glosses and comment immediately necessary for the understanding of the poem appear in the footnotes on the relevant pages. The numeral or other siglum immediately following the short title of the poem in the footnote indicates the copy-text for the poem; other sigla indicate other printings or revisions. An asterisk in the footnote indicates that there are further materials and textual variations in the Textual Notes.

KEY TO SOURCES FREQUENTLY CITED IN THE NOTES

Adams
: R. M. Adams, "Taste and Bad Taste in Metaphysical Poetry," *Hudson Review*, VIII (1955), 61–77.

Andrewes
: Lancelot Andrewes, *Ninety-six Sermons*. 2 vols. Oxford, 1841.

Claydon
: Sister Margaret Claydon, *Richard Crashaw's Paraphrases of the [Six Latin Hymns]*. Washington, 1964.

Daniel
: Hermann Adalbert Daniel, *Thesaurus Hymnologicus*. 5 vols. Halis, Lipsiæ, 1841–56.

Ellrodt
: Robert Ellrodt, *Les Poètes Métaphysiques Anglais*. Paris, 1960.

Esch
: Arno Esch, *Englische Religiöse Lyrik des 17. Jahrhunderts*. Tübingen, 1955.

Grosart
: A. B. Grosart, ed. *The Complete Works of Richard Crashaw*. 2 vols. London, 1872–73.

Martin
: L. C. Martin, ed. *The Poems English Latin and Greek of Richard Crashaw*. Oxford, 1957.

Martz
: Louis L. Martz, *The Poetry of Meditation*. New Haven, 1954.

Milhaupt
: Sister Maris Stella Milhaupt, *The Latin Epigrams of Richard Crashaw with Introduction, English Translation, and Notes*. Ann Arbor: University Microfilms, Inc., 1963 (#63–4900).

Praz
: Mario Praz, *The Flaming Heart*. [Anchor Books] Garden City, N. Y., 1958.

Turnbull
: W. B. Turnbull, ed. *The Complete Works of Richard Crashaw*. London, 1858.

Tuve
: Rosemond Tuve, *A Reading of George Herbert*. Chicago, 1952.

Wallerstein
: Ruth C. Wallerstein, *Richard Crashaw: A Study in Style and Poetic Development*. Madison, 1935.

Warren
: Austin Warren, *Richard Crashaw: A Study in Baroque Sensibility*. Louisiana State University, 1939.

White
: Helen C. White, *The Metaphysical Poets*. New York, 1936.

Williams
: George W. Williams, *Image and Symbol in the Sacred Poetry of Richard Crashaw*. Columbia, S. C., 1963.

SACRED POEMS

I

*Sacred Poems
in one English Version*

1   *The Authors Motto*

Live Jesus, Live, and let it bee
My life to dye, for love of thee.

The Authors Motto 46. This English "Motto" is placed as an *incipit* at the head of the poems in *Steps to the Temple* (1646). It is based on expressions in St. François de Sales, *Traité de l'Amour de Dieu,* XII.13, and is a full version of the Latin *finis* placed at the end of the poems in *Carmen Deo Nostro* (1652). See the *finis* and the note following poem No. 336, the last of the Sacred Poems.

Martin believes that this and the following psalm paraphrase are among Crashaw's earliest works—prior to 1630 (p. xcii). He finds traces of literary influence from William Crashaw in "Psalm 23" (p. 435). The poem is full of expressions of themes that are to become major in Crashaw's work: lines 5–6 continual spring (renewal and becoming), 10 abundance and material nourishment, 14 tears, 29 divine illumination, 50, 55–56 abundance (especially in regard to the overflowing cup), 70 medicinal liquors (associated with the wine of the Mass). The psalm prefigures the metaphor of the Good Shepherd (Luke 15:3–7, John 10:1–18; see also Crashaw's epigrams on these texts "In gregem" No. 204 and "O ego ut Angelicis," No. 213), and the paraphrase stresses pastoral feeding and the nourishment of the Mass. "The cheerfulness of this song offers a sharp contrast to the severe and almost sententious character of the psalm. . . . fantastic personifications . . . people Crashaw's lyric like the allegorical figures in a pageant. Nature, in this lyric, is instinct with human feelings. . . . Bold, ornate images spring up in quick succession" (Praz, p. 241).

> Happy me! o happy sheepe!
> Whom my God vouchsafes to keepe;
> Even my God, Even he it is,
> That points me to these wayes of blisse;
> On whose pastures cheerefull spring,   5
> All the yeare doth sit and sing,
> And rejoycing smiles to see
> Their greene backs were his liverie:
> Pleasure sings my soule to rest,
> Plenty weares me at her brest,   10
> Whose sweet temper teaches me
> Nor wanton, nor in want to be.
> At my feet the blubb'ring Mountaine
> Weeping, melts into a Fountaine,
> Whose soft silver-sweating streames   15
> Make high Noone forget his beames:
> When my waiward breath is flying,
> Hee calls home my soule from dying,
> Strokes and tames my rabid Griefe,
> And does wooe me into life: 20
> When my simple weaknesse strayes,
> (Tangled in forbidden wayes)
> Hee (my Shepheard) is my Guide,

Psalme 23. 46.
  8 *were:* i.e. wear.
  13 *blubb'ring:* weeping effusively.

Hee's before me, on my side,
And behind me, he beguiles   25
Craft in all her knotty wiles;
Hee expounds the giddy wonder
Of my weary steps, and under
Spreads a Path cleare as the Day,
Where no churlish rub saies nay   30
To my joy-conducted Feet,
Whil'st they Gladly goe to meet
Grace and peace, to meet new laies
Tun'd to my great Shepheards praise.
Come now all yee terrors, sally   35
Muster forth into the valley,
Where triumphant darknesse hovers
With a sable wing, that covers
Brooding Horror. Come thou Death,
Let the damps of thy dull Breath   40
Overshadow even the shade,
And make darknesse selfe afraid;
There my feet, even there shall find
Way for a resolved mind.
Still my Shepheard, still my God   45
Thou art with me, Still thy rod,
And thy staffe, whose influence
Gives direction, gives defence.
At the whisper of thy Word
Crown'd abundance spreads my Bord: 50
While I feast, my foes doe feed
Their rank malice not their need,
So that with the self-same bread
They are starv'd, and I am fed.
How my head in ointment swims!   55
How my cup orelooks her Brims!
So, even so still may I move
By the Line of thy deare Love;
Still may thy sweet mercy spread
A shady Arme above my head,   60
About my Paths, so shall I find
The faire Center of my mind

30 *rub:* impediment.
54 The catholic doctrine that wicked persons and "such as be void of a lively faith" who receive the bread and wine of the Mass do so to their condemnation not their salvation (see Article XXIX of the Thirty-nine Articles).

Thy Temple, and those lovely walls
Bright ever with a beame that falls
Fresh from the pure glance of thine eye,   65
Lighting to Eternity.
There I'le dwell for ever, there
Will I find a purer aire
To feed my Life with, there I'le sup
Balme and Nectar in my Cup,   70
And thence my ripe soule will I breath
Warme into the Armes of Death.

3   *Psalme 137.*

"[The musical spirit of Psalme 23] pervades also the version of Psalm
cxxxvii, which, with the variety of its verse, presents a pattern of very lively
motion. . . . The weak point of Crashaw's style is manifest in the manner in
which he renders that terrible close [of verse 9]. . . . [Crashaw's paraphrase in
lines 35–36] through its impropriety and circumlocution shows how incapable
the poet was of feeling the power of the original" (Praz, pp. 242–43).

On the proud bankes of great Euphrates flood,
    There we sate, and there we wept:
Our Harpes that now no Musicke understood,
    Nodding on the Willowes slept,
        While unhappy captiv'd wee   5
        Lovely Sion thought on thee.

They, they that snatcht us from our Countries brest
    Would have a Song carv'd to their Eares
In Hebrew numbers, then (o cruell jest!)
    When Harpes and hearts were drown'd in Teares: 10
        Come, they cry'd, come sing and play
        One of Sions songs to day.

Sing? play? to whom (ah) shall we sing or play,
    If not *Jerusalem* to thee?
Ah thee *Jerusalem!* ah sooner may   15
    This hand forget the mastery
        Of Musicks dainty touch, then I
        The Musicke of thy memory.

Psalme 137. 46. See note to preceding poem.

Which when I lose, o may at once my Tongue
   Lose this same busie speaking art   20
Unpearcht, her vocall Arteries unstrung,
   No more acquainted with my Heart,
     On my dry pallats roofe to rest
     A wither'd Leafe, an idle Guest.

No, no, thy good, Sion, alone must crowne   25
   The head of all my hope-nurst joyes.
But *Edom* cruell thou! thou cryd'st downe, downe
   Sinke Sion, downe and never rise,
     Her falling thou did'st urge and thrust,
     And haste to dash her into dust.   30

Dost laugh? proud *Babels* Daughter! do, laugh on,
   Till thy ruine teach thee Teares,
Even such as these, laugh, till a venging throng
   Of woes, to late doe rouze thy feares.
     Laugh, till thy childrens bleeding bones   35
     Weepe pretious Teares upon the stones.

4   Sampson *to his* Dalilah

Could not once blinding me, cruell, suffice?
When first I look't on thee, I lost mine eyes.

---

21 *Unpearcht:* as if his tongue were a bird which should fall from its perch (?).
Sampson to his Dalilah. 46. Judges 16:4–21.

DIVINE EPIGRAMS

The fifty epigrams which follow (nos. 5–54) are (all but two) translations by Crashaw of his Latin epigrams; for additional notes on each epigram, consult the Latin texts as indicated. They are arranged here in the order of the fuller Latin sequence. One more English translation appeared in two versions and is therefore included in the next section ("Song upon the Bleeding Crucifix," No. 71).

5   *On the Blessed Virgins bashfulnesse.*

That on her lap she casts her humble Eye,
'Tis the sweet pride of her Humility.
The faire starre is well fixt, for where, o where
Could she have fixt it on a fairer Spheare?
'Tis Heav'n 'tis Heaven she sees, Heavens God there lyes,   5
She can see heaven, and ne're lift up her eyes:
This new Guest to her Eyes new Lawes hath given,
'Twas once *looke up,* 'tis now *looke downe* to Heaven.

6   *Our Lord in his Circumcision*
to his Father.

The Feast of the Circumcision of Christ is celebrated on the first of January. By virtue of this date the Feast Day represents a time of beginning or becoming. The concept of growing informs the metaphoric structure of this epigram: from death to life, youth to maturity, hope to fulfillment, dawn to day, bud to tree, knife to spear. The bud of the purple rose, figured in the drops of blood shed by the Infant, grows to a full-blooming and full-bleeding tree, the cross. The image of growth is more thoroughly represented in the English version than in the Latin original. (Williams, pp. 50–51; White, p. 232.)

To thee these first fruits of my growing death
(For what else is my life?) lo I bequeath.
Tast this, and as thou lik'st this lesser flood
Expect a Sea, my heart shall make it good.

On the Blessed Virgins bashfulnesse. 46. See "In beatae Virginis verecundiam," No. 96.
  3–4 *starre . . . Spheare:* terms of Ptolemaic cosmology; each of the stars was fixed on a sphere, circumscribing the earth.
  7 *new Lawes:* the "new law" of the New Testament.
Our Lord in his Circumcision. 46.* See "Christus Circumcisus," No. 101. See also "New Year's Day," No. 56. Luke 2:21.

Thy wrath that wades heere now, e're long shall swim   5
The flood-gate shall be set wide ope for him.
Then let him drinke, and drinke, and doe his worst,
To drowne the wantonnesse of his wild thirst.
Now's but the Nonage of my paines, my feares
Are yet but in their hopes, not come to yeares.   10
The day of my darke woes is yet but morne,
My teares but tender and my death new-borne.
Yet may these unfledg'd griefes give fate some guesse,
These Cradle-torments have their towardnesse.
These purple buds of blooming death may bee,   15
Erst the full stature of a fatall tree.
And till my riper woes to age are come.
This knife may be the speares *Præludium.*

7   *To the Infant Martyrs.*

Goe smiling soules, your new built Cages breake,
In Heav'n you'l learne to sing ere here to speake,
Nor let the milky fonts that bath your thirst,
                         Bee your delay;
The place that calls you hence, is at the worst   5
                         Milke all the way.

8   *Upon the Infant Martyrs.*

To see both blended in one flood
The Mothers Milke, the Childrens blood,
Makes me doubt if Heaven will gather,
Roses hence, or *Lillies* rather.

8 an early statement of the theme of inebriation in love.
16 *Erst:* evidently Crashaw is using the word to mean "At some future time."
To the Infant Martyrs. 46. See "Ad Infantes Martyres," No. 112. Matthew 2:16–18. The subject of this and the next poem forms the theme of the "Sospetto d'Herode," No. 87.
Upon the Infant Martyrs. 46. See "In lactantes Martyres," No. 113.
4 *Roses . . . Lillies:* the same pair in Southwell, "St. Peter's Complaint," xciv.

9   Luke 2. *Quærit* Jesum *Suum* Maria.

This is one of the few English epigrams substantially longer than the Latin. The epigram is a comment on the visit to the Temple in Jerusalem when Jesus was twelve years old (Luke 2:41–50). The title, "Mary seeks her own Jesus," refers to the return of the Virgin to Jerusalem to find Jesus "about [his] Father's business."

And is he gone, whom these armes held but now?
      Their hope, their vow?
Did ever greife, and joy in one poore heart
      Soe soone change part?
Hee's gone. the fair'st flower, that e're bosome drest,   5
      My soules sweet rest.
My wombes chast pride is gone, my heav'en-borne boy;
      And where is joy?
Hee's gone. and his lov'd steppes to wait upon,
      My joy is gone.   10
My joyes, and hee are gone; my greife, and I
      Alone must ly.
Hee's gone. not leaving with me, till he come,
      One smile at home.
Oh come then. bring thy mother her lost joy: 15
      Oh come, sweet boy.
Make hast, and come, or e're my griefe, and I
      Make hast, and dy.
Peace, heart! the heavens are angry. all their sphaeres
      Rivall thy teares.   20
I was mistaken. some faire sphaere, or other
      Was thy blest mother.
What, but the fairest heaven, could owne the birth
      Of soe faire earth?
Yet sure thou did'st lodge heere. this wombe of mine   25
      Was once call'd thine.
Oft have these armes thy cradle envied,
      Beguil'd thy bed.
Oft to thy easy eares hath this shrill tongue
      Trembled, and sung.   30
Oft have I wrapt thy slumbers in soft aires,
      And stroak't thy cares.

Quærit Jesum. MS. See "Quærit Jesum," No. 116, which provides the Latin of lines 47–50.
   27 *envied:* three syllables.

Oft hath this hand those silken casements kept,
      While their sunnes slept.
Oft have my hungry kisses made thine eyes   35
      Too early rise.
Oft have I spoild my kisses daintiest diet,
      To spare thy quiet.
Oft from this breast to thine my love-tost heart
      Hath leapt, to part.   40
Oft my lost soule have I bin glad to seeke
      On thy soft cheeke.
Oft have these armes (alas!) show'd to these eyes
      Their now lost joyes.
Dawne then to me, thou morne of mine owne day,   45
      And lett heaven stay.
Oh, would'st thou heere still fixe thy faire abode,
      My bosome God:
What hinders, but my bosome still might be
      Thy heaven to thee?   50

10   *On the water of our Lords Baptisme.*

"The idea that the waters were cleansed through the baptism of Christ is
common in Christian literature . . . Andrewes (III, 245–46): 'Jordan had more
need come to him, than He to Jordan, to be cleansed. . . . He went into
[the waters] that they which should cleanse us, might by him first be
cleansed.'" (Milhaupt, pp. 125–26). The text is Matthew 3:13–17.

            Each blest drop, on each blest limme,
            Is washt it selfe, in washing him:
            Tis a Gemme while it stayes here,
            While it falls hence 'tis a Teare.

11   *To our Lord, upon the Water made Wine.*

         Thou water turn'st to Wine (faire friend of Life);
            Thy foe to crosse the sweet Arts of thy Reigne
         Distills from thence the Teares of wrath and strife,
            And so turnes wine to Water backe againe.

33 *casements:* eyelids.
On the water of our Lords Baptisme. 46. See "In aquam baptismi," No. 121.
To our Lord, upon the Water made Wine. 46. See "Ad Christum," No. 130. John 2:1–11.

12　Joh. 3. *But men loved darknesse rather then Light.*

> The worlds light shines; shine as it will,
> The world will love its Darknesse still:
> I doubt though when the World's in Hell,
> It will not love its Darknesse halfe so well.

13　*On St.* Peter *casting away his Nets at our*
　　Saviours call.

> Thou hast the art on't *Peter;* and canst tell
> 　To cast thy Nets on all occasions well.
> When Christ calls, and thy Nets would have thee stay:
> 　To cast them well's to cast them quite away.

14　Matthew 8. *I am not worthy that thou should'st come*
　　under my roofe.

> Thy God was making hast into thy roofe,
> 　Thy humble faith and feare keepes him aloofe:
> Hee'l be thy Guest, because he may not be,
> 　Hee'l come—into thy house? no, into thee.

15　Luc. 7. *She began to wash his feet with teares and*
　　wipe them with the haires of her head.

> Her eyes flood lickes his feets faire staine,
> Her haires flame lickes up that againe.
> This flame thus quench't hath brighter beames:
> This flood thus stained fairer streames.

But men loved darknesse. 46. See "Lux venit," No. 134. John 3:19.
On St. Peter casting away his Nets. 46. See "Relictis omnibus," No. 141. Luke 5:11.
I am not worthy. 46. See "Non sum dignus," No. 156. Matthew 8:8.
She began to wash. 46.* See "Coepit lacrymis rigare," No. 163. Luke 7:37–50. The first ap-
pearance of Mary Magdalene; see also "On the wounds of our crucified Lord," No. 45, and
"The Weeper," No. 74.

16   Luk. 11. *Upon the dumbe Devill cast out, and the
slanderous Jewes put to silence.*

Two Devills at one blow thou hast laid flat,
    A *speaking* Divell this, a *dumbe* one that.
Was't thy full victories fairer increase,
    That th' one spake, or that th' other held his peace?

17   Luke 11. *Blessed be the paps which Thou hast sucked.*

This little poem has provoked extravagant comment. William Empson (*Seven Types of Ambiguity*, p. 280): "This is to show the unearthly relation to earth of the Christ, and with a sort of horror, to excite adoration. . . . The second couplet is 'primitive' enough; a wide variety of sexual perversions can be included in the notion of sucking a long bloody teat which is also a deep wound. The sacrificial idea is aligned with incest, the infantile pleasures, and cannibalism. . . ." Adams (p. 69) continues this profitless explication: "Certainly in this poem Crashaw can hardly have intended anything but a nasty twist to the spiritual-carnal relation." A traditional view would point out that certainly Crashaw intended nothing of the sort. The bloody teat is the spear-wound in Christ's side, imaged here as near the breast, and it is mammary, not phallic ("a long . . . teat" is Empson's invention). The image of the nourishing breast of God is a devotional metaphor found in the Scriptures (Psalms 34:8 and I Peter 2:2–3), in St. Teresa ("when [Christ] desires to enrich and comfort [the soul] still more, He draws her . . . near to that sacred side and to those Divine breasts. Sustained by that Divine milk . . . , she can do nothing but rejoice" [Conceptions, IV]), in Donne (Sermons, X, 248), in Herbert ("Longing," "Whitsunday" [early version] *Lucus*, XXXIV), and in Vaughan ("Admission"). See further: Milhaupt, pp. 148–49; Williams, pp. 124–25; Ellrodt, I, 383–84. R. Goldfarb (*Explicator*, XIX [1961], 35) notes what is easy to overlook: that the poem is addressed not to the Virgin but to the faithful woman who speaks to Christ in Luke 11:27. "Thy teates" clearly refers to this (hypothetical) mother; "The Mother" must then refer again to her, and to maternity in general.

    Suppose he had been Tabled at thy Teates,
        Thy hunger feels not what he eates:
    Hee'l have his Teat e're long (a bloody one)
        The Mother then must suck the Son.

Upon the dumbe Devill. 46. See "Deus, post expulsum," No. 164. Luke 11:14.
Blessed be the paps. 46. See "Beatus venter," No. 165. Luke 11:27.

18   Marke 4. *Why are yee afraid, O yee of little faith?*

As if the storme meant him;
Or, 'cause Heavens face is dim,
His needs a cloud.
Was ever froward wind
That could be so unkind,   5
Or wave so proud?
The Wind had need be angry, and the Water black,
That to the mighty *Neptune's* self dare threaten wrack.

There is no storme but this
Of your owne Cowardise   10
That braves you out;
You are the storme that mocks
Your selves; you are the Rocks
Of your owne doubt:
Besides this feare of danger, there's no danger here;   15
And he that here feares Danger, does deserve his Feare.

19   *On the miracle of multiplyed loaves.*

This epigram and the next are two of the seven epigrams that Crashaw de-
voted to this miracle, regarding it as a type of the institution of the Eucharist
(as in "Psalme 23"). Notable in the epigrams are the ideas of abundance and
effortlessness; "food it selfe" (line 4) is the body of Christ. See Williams, pp.
15–17.

See here an easie Feast that knowes no wound,
That under Hungers Teeth will needs be sound:
A subtle Harvest of unbounded bread,
What would ye more? Here food it selfe is fed.

Why are yee afraid? 46. See "Quid timidi estis?", No. 170. Mark 4:40.
8 *Neptune's self:* a pagan term used to describe the Christian God.
On the miracle of the multiplyed loaves. 46. See "Quinque panes," No. 175. John 6:1–14.

20   *On the Miracle of Loaves.*

Now Lord, or never, they'l beleeve on thee,
Thou to their Teeth hast prov'd thy Deity.

21   Mar. 7. *The dumbe healed, and the people enjoyned*
silence.

Christ bids the dumbe tongue speake, it speakes; the sound
Hee charges to be quiet, it runs round:
If in the first he us'd his fingers Touch,
His hands whole strength here, could not be too much.

22   Math. 16:25. *Whosoever shall loose his life &c.*

Soe I may gaine thy death, my life I'le give.
(My life's thy death, and in thy death I live.)
Or else, my life, I'le hide thee in his grave,
By three daies losse æternally to save.

23   *It is better to go into Heaven with*
one eye, &c.

One Eye? a thousand rather, and a Thousand more
To fix those full-fac't Glories, o he's poore
Of Eyes that has but *Argus* store,
Yet if thou'lt fill one poore Eye, with thy Heaven and Thee,
O grant (sweet Goodnesse) that one Eye may be   5
All, and every whit of me.

On the Miracle of Loaves. 46. See "John. 6. Jam credunt," lines 1–2, No. 179. John 6:14, 26.
See note to preceding epigram.
    2 *to their Teeth:* a colloquial expression meaning "all the way."
The dumbe healed. 46. See "Tetigit linguam eius," No. 184. Mark 7:32–36.
Whosoever shall loose his life. MS. See "Quisquis perdiderit," No. 189.
It is better to go into Heaven. 46. See "Bonum intrare," No. 192. Matthew 18:9.

24   Luke 10. *And a certaine Priest comming that way*
looked on him and passed by.

Why dost Thou wound my wounds, o Thou that passest by
Handling and turning them with an unwounded eye?
The calm that cools thine eye does shipwrack mine, for o!
Unmov'd to see one wretched, is to make him so.

25   *I am the Doore.*

And now th'art set wide ope, The Speare's sad Art,
Lo! hath unlockt thee at the very Heart:
Hee to himselfe (I feare the worse)
     And his owne hope
Hath *shut* these Doores of Heaven, that durst   5
     Thus set them *ope*.

26   Luk. 15. *On the Prodigall.*

Tell me bright Boy, tell me my golden Lad,
Whither away so frolick? why so glad?
What all thy Wealth in counsaile? all thy state?
Are Husks so deare? troth 'tis a mighty rate.

And a certaine Priest. 46. See "Sacerdos quidam," No. 200. Luke 10:31.
I am the Doore. 46. See "Ego sum ostium," No. 205. See also for another 'door' image, "On
our crucified Lord," No. 44. John 10:7–9. The epigram conflates Christ's remark at John 10:9
with the later side-piercing at the Crucifixion. The Latin version includes the usual pun on
"clavi/claves" (nail, keys), omitted in English.
    3 *Hee:* the soldier of John 19:34.
On the Prodigall. 46. See "Congestis omnibus," No. 214. Luke 15:13.
    1 *golden:* an adjective applied also to Christ (Milhaupt, p. 90).

27   *Upon* Lazarus *his Teares.*

Rich *Lazarus!* richer in those Gems, thy Teares,
     Then *Dives* in the Roabes he weares:
He scornes them now, but o they'l sute full well
     With th' Purple he must weare in Hell.

28   Luke 16. Dives *asking a drop.*

A Drop, one drop, how sweetly one faire drop
     Would tremble on my pearle-tipt fingers top?
My wealth is gone, o goe it where it will,
     Spare this one Jewell; I'le be *Dives* still.

29   *Two went up into the Temple to pray.*

Two went to pray? o rather say
One went to brag, th'other to pray:

One stands up close and treads on high,
Where th'other dares not send his eye.

One neerer to Gods Altar trod,   5
The other to the Altars God.

Upon Lazarus. 46. See "In lacrymas Lazari," No. 215. Luke 16:19–31.
  1 *Lazarus:* the word means 'without help' in Hebrew.
  2 *Dives:* the word means 'rich' in Latin.
  3 *sute:* possibly a pun on the idea of clothing.
  4 *Purple:* flames; the red flames contrast with the white tears.
Dives asking a drop. 46. See "Dives implorat guttam," No. 216. Luke 16:24.
  1 Martin notes (p. 435) a comparable line in William Crashaw.
  2 *pearle-tipt:* continues the idea of gems.
Two went up. 46. See "Pharisaeus et Publicanus," No. 219. Luke 18:9–14. George MacDonald
(*England's Antiphon*, p. 241): "This appears to me perfect. . . . Artistically considered, the
poem could hardly be improved."

30   Marc. 10. *The blind cured by the word of our Saviour.*

> Thou spak'st the word (thy word's a Law)
> Thou spak'st and streight the blind man saw.
>
> To speake and make the blind man see,
> *Was never man Lord spake like Thee.*
>
> To speake thus, was to speake (say I)   5
> Not to his Eare, but to his Eye.

31   *Upon the Asse that bore our Saviour.*

> Hath onely Anger an Omnipotence
>   In Eloquence?
> Within the lips of Love and Joy doth Dwell
>   No miracle?
> Why else had *Baalams* Asse a tongue to chide   5
>   His Masters pride?
> And thou (Heaven-burthen'd Beast) hast ne're a word
>   To praise thy Lord?
> That he should find a Tongue and vocall Thunder,
>   Was a great wonder.   10
> But o me thinkes 'tis a farre greater one
>   That thou find'st none.

The blind cured. 46.* (See Textual Note for Scriptural citation.) See "Ad verbum Dei," No. 228.
    4 the line is a quotation from John 7:46.
Upon the Asse. 46. See "In Asinum Christi," No. 232. Matthew 21:7. The episode is recorded in Numbers 22.

32   Marke 12. (*Give to* Cæsar——) (*And to God*——)

> All we have is God's, and yet
> Cæsar challenges a debt,
> Nor hath God a thinner share,
> What ever Cæsar's payments are;
> All is God's; and yet 'tis true
> All wee have is Cæsar's too;
> All is Cæsar's; and what ods
> So long as Cæsar's self is Gods?

33   Matthew. 22. *Neither durst any man from that Day*
     aske him any more Questions.

> Midst all the darke and knotty Snares,
> Blacke wit or malice can or dares,
> Thy glorious wisdome breakes the Nets,
> And treads with uncontrouled steps.
> Thy quel'd foes are not onely now   5
> Thy triumphes, but thy Trophies too:
> They, both at once thy Conquests bee,
> And thy Conquests memorye.
> Stony amazement makes them stand
> Waiting on thy victorious hand,   10
> Like statues fixed to the fame
> Of thy renoune, and their owne shame.
> As if they onely meant to breath,
> To bee the Life of their owne Death.
> 'Twas time to hold their Peace when they,   15
> Had nere another word to say:
> Yet is their silence unto thee,
> The full sound of thy victory.
> Their silence speakes aloud, and is
> Thy well pronounc'd *Panegyris*.   20
> While they speake nothing, they speake all
> Their share, in thy Memoriall.
> While thy speake nothing, they proclaime
> Thee, with the shrillest Trumpe of fame.
>   To hold their peace is all the waies,   25
>   These wretches have to speake thy praise.

Give to Cæsar. 46. See "Date Cæsari," No. 239. Mark 12:17.
Neither durst any man. 46. See "Neque ausus fuit," No. 240. Matthew 22:46.
  17–26 Even the worthless silence of man proclaims God's glory.

34   Matthew 23. *Yee build the Sepulchres of the Prophets.*

Thou trim'st a Prophets Tombe, and dost bequeath
The life thou took'st from him unto his *Death.*
Vaine man! the stones that on his Tombe doe lye,
Keepe but the score of them that made him dye.

35   *The Widowes Mites.*

Two Mites, two drops, (yet all her house and land)
Falls from a steady Heart, though trembling hand:
The others wanton wealth foams high, and brave,
The other cast away, she onely gave.

36   Joh. 15. *Upon our Lords last comfortable discourse*
          with his Disciples.

All *Hybla's* honey, all that sweetnesse can
Flowes in thy Song (o faire, o dying Swan!)
Yet is the joy I take in't small or none;
It is too sweet to be a long-liv'd one.

37   *But now they have seen, and hated.*

Seene? and yet hated thee? they did not see,
They saw Thee not, that saw and hated thee:
No, no, they saw thee not, o Life, o Love,
Who saw ought in thee, that their hate could move.

Yee build the Sepulchres. 46. See "Ædificatis sepulchra," No. 241. Matthew 23:29.
The Widowes Mites. 46. See "Obulum Viduæ," No. 242. Mark 12:44.
    1 *Mites, drops:* the power of the drop is shown in this drop of a coin ("Gutta . . . nummi").
Upon our Lords last discourse. 46. See "In Cygnæam," No. 261. The Latin original refers to John 17, rather than John 15; both citations are acceptable, as the "last comfortable discourse" may be thought of as including chapters 15, 16, and 17.
    1 *Hybla's honey:* Hybla is a mountain in Sicily, noted in ancient times for its flowers and bees.
    2 *dying Swan:* the swan was thought to sing only at its death and to have then a lovely song.
But now they have seen. 46.* See "Viderunt, et oderunt me," No. 256. John 15:24.

38   Joh. 16. *Verily I say unto you, yee shall weep
and lament.*

Welcome my Griefe, my Joy; how deare's
To me my Legacy of Teares!
I'le weepe, and weepe, and will therefore
Weepe, 'cause I can weepe no more:
     Thou, thou (Deare Lord) even thou alone,   5
     Giv'st joy, even when thou givest none.

39   *On St.* Peter *cutting of* Malchus *his eare.*

Well *Peter* dost thou wield thy active sword,
     Well for thy self (I meane) not for thy Lord.
To strike at eares, is to take heed there bee
     No witnesse *Peter* of thy perjury.

40   Matthew. 27. *And he answered them nothing.*

O Mighty *Nothing!* unto thee,
Nothing, wee owe all things that bee.
God spake once when hee all things made,
Hee sav'd all when hee *Nothing* said.
The world was made of *Nothing* then;   5
'Tis made by *Nothyng* now againe.

41   *To* Pontius *washing his hands.*

Thy hands are washt, but o the waters spilt,
     That labour'd to have washt thy guilt:
The flood, if any can, that can suffice,
     Must have its Fountaine in thine Eyes.

Verily I say. 46. See "Vos flebitis," No. 257. John 16:20.
On St. Peter. 46. See "In Petrum," No. 262. John 18:10.
     4 *perjury:* i.e. Peter's threefold denial of his Lord.
And he answered. 46. See "Christus accusatus," No. 264. Matthew 27:12.
     5 *of Nothing:* i.e. *ex nihilo* [*nihil fit*] (nothing will come of nothing).
To Pontius. 46.* See "In Pontium," No. 265. Matthew 27:24.
     1 *spilt:* i.e. wasted, useless; Pilate's washing is the prototype of all (futile) shirking of
responsibility.

42   *To* Pontius *washing his blood-stained hands.*

Is murther no sin? or a sin so cheape,
     That thou need'st heape
A Rape upon't? till thy Adult'rous touch
     Taught her these sullied cheeks, this blubber'd face,
She was a Nimph, the meadowes knew none such,   5
     Of honest Parentage, of unstain'd Race,
The Daughter of a faire and well-fam'd Fountaine,
As ever Silver-tipt, the side of shady mountaine.

See how she weeps, and weeps, that she appeares
     Nothing but Teares;   10
Each drop's a Teare that weeps for her own wast;
     Harke how at every Touch she does complaine her:
Harke how she bids her frighted Drops make hast,
     And with sad murmurs, chides the Hands that stain her.
Leave, leave, for shame, or else (Good judge) decree,   15
What water shal wash this, when this hath washed thee.

43   *Upon the Thornes taken downe from our*
     Lords head bloody.

Know'st thou this, Souldier? 'tis a much chang'd plant, which yet
     Thy selfe did'st set,
'Tis chang'd indeed, did Autumn e're such beauties bring
     To shame his Spring?
O! who so hard an husbandman could ever find   5
     A soyle so kind?
Is not the soile a kind one (thinke ye) that returnes
     Roses for *Thornes?*

To Pontius washing his blood-stained hands. 46. See "Pontio lavanti," No. 266. Matthew 27:24.
Upon the Thornes. 46(52).* See "In spinas demtas," No. 267. Scripture does not mention the removal of the crown; cf. Matthew 27:31.
     3–4   *Autumn, Spring:* i.e. harvest, planting.
     5–6   This couplet may be paraphrased: 'What farmer as cruel as you would ever expect such a generous harvest?'

44   *On our crucified Lord Naked, and bloody.*

The scriptural text for this poem is Matthew 27:28–31, the Gospel for Palm Sunday, or Mark 15:17–20, the Gospel for the Tuesday before Easter. Adams (p. 67): "Nothing, from one point of view, could be more disgusting and grotesque. Yet how else to convey the combination of sacred, spiritual preciousness with the vulgar, social utility . . . more neatly than in a phrase like 'purple wardrobe'— . . . decorums wonderfully collide." See also Williams, p. 121 and notes, for seventeenth-century parallels.

> Th' have left thee naked Lord, O that they had;
> This Garment too I would they had deny'd.
> Thee with thy selfe they have too richly clad,
> Opening the purple wardrobe of thy side.
>> O never could bee found Garments too good   5
>> For thee to weare, but these, of thine owne blood.

45   *On the wounds of our crucified Lord.*

"If we resist the poet's imaginative unification of his feelings about Christ on the grounds that kissing wounds is unlovely and perverse, and counting out change is vulgar, we may seem to quarrel with the poet's central point, that love of Christ includes all extremes and reconciles all contraries" (Adams, p. 68). "The epigram . . . , juxtaposing the blood of Christ's feet nailed on the cross and the tears of Mary Magdalene, incorporates the imagery of white and red flowers and gems" (Williams, pp. 39–40). The tears of Mary (which the blood repays) are described in "She began to wash his feet," No. 13, Luke 7:37–50. For another treatment of the wounds see poems No. 72 and 270.

> O these wakefull wounds of thine!
>> Are they Mouthes? or are they eyes?
> Be they Mouthes, or be they eyne,
>> Each bleeding part some one supplies.
>
> Lo! a mouth, whose full-bloom'd lips   5
>> At too deare a rate are roses.
> Lo! a blood-shot eye! that weepes
>> And many a cruell teare discloses.

On our crucified Lord. 46(52).* There is no extant Latin original for this poem, but see for parallel ideas "Ego sum ostium," No. 205, and "Ego sum via," No. 251.
On the wounds of our crucified Lord. 46.* See "In vulnera," No. 271.
   5 *lips:* the medical term for the borders of a wound.

O thou that on this foot hast laid
    Many a kisse, and many a Teare,   10
Now thou shal't have all repaid,
    Whatsoe're thy charges were.

This foot hath got a Mouth and lippes,
    To pay the sweet summe of thy kisses:
To pay thy Teares, an Eye that weeps   15
    In stead of Teares such Gems as this is.

The difference onely this appeares,
    (Nor can the change offend)
The debt is paid in *Ruby*-Teares,
    Which thou in Pearles did'st lend.   20

46   *Upon our Saviours Tombe wherein*
              never man was laid.

Milhaupt (p. 248) suggests that the epigram may commemorate an occasion when the Annunciation and Good Friday fell on the same day, but such an occasion does not occur in the years Crashaw presumably was writing the series.

    How Life and Death in Thee
          Agree!
    Thou had'st a virgin Wombe
          And Tombe.
    A *Joseph* did betroth   5
          Them both.

---

9 *thou:* Mary Magdalene.
Upon our Saviours Tombe. 46(52).* See "[In tumulum Christi]," No. 273. Luke 23:50–53.

47   *Easter day.*

The epigram assembles the images of becoming: Heire, Tombe (here equiva-
lent to womb as in the preceding poem), the East (the dawn), the Nest, Morne,
bud, and birth. Line 9 seems to translate the second couplet of "In sepulchrum
Domini," No. 274.

    Rise, Heire of fresh Eternity,
        From thy Virgin Tombe:
    Rise mighty man of wonders, and thy world with thee
        Thy Tombe, the universall East,
        Natures new wombe,   5
    Thy Tombe, faire Immortalities perfumed Nest.

    Of all the Gloryes Make Noone gay
        This is the Morne.
    This rocke buds forth the fountaine of the streames of Day.
        In joyes white Annals live this houre,   10
        When life was borne,
    No cloud scoule on his radiant lids no tempest lowre.

    Life, by this light's Nativity
        All creatures have.
    Death onely by this Dayes just Doome is forc't to Dye;   15
        Nor is Death forc't; for may hee ly
        Thron'd in thy Grave;
    Death will on this condition be content to Dy.

48   *Upon the Sepulchre of our Lord.*

        Here, where our Lord once laid his Head,
        Now the Grave lies buried.

Easter day. 46. See "In resurrectionem Domini," No. 275. John 20:1–18.
    6 *perfumed Nest:* an oblique reference to the phoenix' nest, made of spicy twigs.
    9 *rocke:* the typological reference behind this image is obscured in the English, but
clear in "In sepulchrum Domini," No. 274; Williams (pp. 50, 122–23): "In the same way
that Moses' rod brought water from the rock and rescued the Israelites thirsting in the wilder-
ness (Numbers 20:11), here from the rock which has entombed Him, Christ . . . rises as a
fountain of light or unfolds as a white, perfumed bud."
Upon the Sepulchre. 46(52).* There is no extant Latin original for this poem, unless it is the
last couplet of "In resurrectionem Domini," translated immediately above. John 20:7.

49   Mat. 28. *Come see the place where the Lord lay.*

According to Matthew 28:1, "Mary Magdalene and the other Mary" came to the tomb on Easter morning. As the poem refers to tears, it is probable that Magdalene is the speaker, though her comments at lines 5–6 are more usually appropriated in Crashaw's verse to the Virgin Mary.

> Show me himselfe, himselfe (bright Sir) O show
>   Which way my poore Tears to himselfe may goe,
> Were it enough to show the place, and say,
>   Looke, *Mary,* here see, where thy Lord once lay,
> Then could I show these armes of mine, and say   5
>   Looke, *Mary,* here see, where thy Lord once lay.

50   *In Cicatrices Domini* Jesu.

The epigram depends on the customary conceit of Christ as Cupid, the god of love, and his traditional weapons—the bow, the dart, and the quiver. For another epigram using this conceit, see "[Non fugitivus Amor]," No. 117. The title means "On the wounds of the Lord Jesus"; the Latin refers to Luke 24 where Christ shows his wounds (verses 39–40) to the disciples. The "soldjers" seem to derive (in the Latin) from John 19:2–34. The removal of summary lines 11–12 to follow line 4 or line 6 would greatly improve the structure of the poem.

> Come, brave soldjers, come, and see
> Mighty love's Artillery.
> This was the conquering dart; and loe
> There shines his quiver, there his bow.
> These the passive weapons are,   5
> That made great Love a man of warre.
> The quiver, that he bore, did bide
> Soe neare, it prov'd his very side.
> In it there sate but one sole dart,
> A peircing one, his peirced heart.   10
> His weapons were nor steele, nor brasse:
> The weapon, that he wore, he was.

Come see the place. 46. See "Ecce locus," No. 278. Matthew 28:6.
In Cicatrices. MS. See "In cicatrices Domini adhuc superstites," No. 280 (lines 1–6). Luke 24:38–40.
    5 *passive:* "Love's passives are his activ'st part" ("An Apologie," No. 62, line 73).
    7 *quiver:* a container, not unlike the wardrobe of "On our crucified Lord," No. 44.

For bow his unbent hand did serve,
Well strung with many a broken nerve.
Strange the quiver, bow, and dart!   15
A bloody side, and hand, and heart!
But now the feild is wonne: and they
(The dust of Warre cleane wip'd away)
The weapons now of triumph be,
That were before of Victorie.   20

51   *On the still surviving markes of*
                  our Saviours wounds.

Milhaupt (p. 118): "This epigram is composed in the convention of 'Christ-our-charter,' common in medieval religious lyrics. Tuve (p. 43) finds the motif in Herbert's 'The Sacrifice' and mentions a sermon by Bishop John Fisher in which the wounds of Christ are compared to letters written on the parchment of his body. Andrewes (II, 180) describes the 'Liber charitatis': 'Every stripe as a letter, every nail as a capital letter, His *livores* [stripes] as black letters, His bleeding wounds as so many rubrics [red letters], to shew upon record his love toward us." See further Williams, pp. 116–18.

What ever story of their crueltie,
Or Naile, or Thorne, or Speare have writ in Thee,
    Are in another sence
      Still legible;
    Sweet is the difference: 5
      Once I did spell
    Every red letter
      A wound of thine,
    Now, (what is better)
      Balsome for mine.   10

52   Act. 5. *The sicke implore St. Peter's shadow.*

Under thy shadow may I lurke a while,
    Death's busie search I'le easily beguile:
Thy shadow *Peter*, must shew me the Sun,
    My light's thy shadowes shadow, or 'tis done.

On the still surviving markes. 46. See "In cicatrices quas Christus habet," No. 283. John 20:20.
The sicke implore. 46. See "Æger implorat," No. 297. Acts 5:15.
    1 *shadow:* the traditional view of benevolent and protective darkness; Psalms 17:8.

53   Act. 8. *On the baptized Æthiopian.*

Let it no longer be a forlorne hope
        To wash an Æthiope:
He's washt, His gloomy skin a peacefull shade
        For his white soule is made:
And now, I doubt not, the Eternall Dove,   5
        A black-fac'd house will love.

54   Act. 21. *I am ready not onely to be bound but to dye.*

Come death, come bands, nor do you shrink, my eares,
At those hard words mans cowardise calls feares.
Save those of feare, no other bands feare I;
Nor other death then this; the feare to dye.

On the baptized Æthiopian. **46.** See "Æthiops lotus," No. 303. Acts 8:26–39.
    3 *shade:* see preceding epigram.
I am ready. **46.** See "Nam ego non solum vinciri," No. 320. Acts 21:13.

T O

T H E   N A M E

A B O V E   E V E R Y   N A M E ,

T H E

N A M E   O F

I E S V S

A   H Y M N .

Praz (p. 255) suggests that this Hymn is "an exquisite string of variations on . . . *Jubilus de nomine Jesu*, attributed to Saint Bernard." Crashaw may well have received inspiration from the *Jubilus*—he may even have desired to emulate the Saint—but the variations are so extensive and have gone so far from the original as to eliminate the possibility of even Crashavian "translation." Martz (pp. 338–52) provides a detailed structural analysis of the Hymn, showing its dependence on Bishop Hall's *Arte of Divine Meditation* (1606). "The building of this action, unique in Crashaw's poetry, creates the pleasure of watching a mind mold its art upon an ancient model. . . . [The Hymn] is a masterwork in

Hymn to the Name of Jesus. 52(48).*

the poetry of meditation, and one of the very last in its kind" (pp. 62, 64). The steps in the scale of meditation as displayed in the Hymn are these (pp. 337–38): I *Modus recolligendi* (Introduction, 1–12); II *Gradus praeparatorii* (Preliminary self-address, 13–45); III *Gradus processorii, & mentis* (address to all creatures, 46–87); IV *Gradus processorii, & iudicii aut intellectus* (Justification of speaker's place, 88–114); V *Gradus processorii amoris, voluntatis, & affectus,* i–vi (Invocation of the Name, 115–50); VI *Gradus processorii amoris, voluntatis, & affectus,* vii (Appearance of the Name, 151–96); VII *Gradus terminatorii* (Conclusion, 197–239). The "text" for the poem is Phillipians 2:9–11; the hymn is evidently for the Feast of the Holy Name, "this Illustrious DAY." Wallerstein, pp. 40–48.

The device of the crowned dove has been identified by Praz as a medal of Pope Urban VI; the explanation of the device discloses that it has no more than a superficial relevance to the poem and that its presence here is probably due to the printer's convenience (I. Typotius, *Symbola . . . pontificum* [Prague, 1601–3], p. 25). Williams, p. 108.

I Sing the NAME which None can say
But touch't with An interiour RAY:
The Name of our New PEACE; our Good:
Our Blisse: and Supernaturall Blood:
The Name of All our Lives and Loves.   5
Hearken, And Help, ye holy Doves!
The high-born Brood of Day; you bright
Candidates of blissefull Light,
The HEIRS Elect of Love; whose Names belong
Unto The everlasting life of Song;   10
All ye wise SOULES, who in the wealthy Brest
Of This unbounded NAME build your warm Nest.
Awake, My glory. SOUL, (if such thou be,
And That fair WORD at all referr to Thee)
           Awake and sing   15
           And be All Wing;
Bring hither thy whole SELF; and let me see
What of thy Parent HEAVN yet speakes in thee.
           O thou art Poore
           Of noble POWRES, I see,   20
And full of nothing else but empty ME,
Narrow, and low, and infinitely lesse
Then this GREAT mornings mighty Busynes.
           One little WORLD or two
           (Alas) will never doe.   25
           We must have store.

8 *Candidates:* i.e. clothed in white robes (Lat. *candidatus*); the souls of the blessed or the angels in Heaven.

Goe, Soul, out of thy Self, and seek for More.
   Goe and request
Great Nature for the Key of her huge Chest
Of Heavns, the self involving Sett of Sphears   30
(Which dull mortality more Feeles then heares)
   Then rouse the nest
Of nimble Art, and traverse round
The Aiery Shop of soul-appeasing Sound:
And beat a summons in the Same   35
   All-soveraign Name
To warn each severall kind
And shape of sweetnes, Be they such
   As sigh with supple wind
   Or answer Artfull Touch,   40
That they convene and come away
To wait at the love-crowned Doores of
   This Illustrious Day.
Shall we dare This, my Soul? we'l doe't and bring
No Other note for't, but the Name we sing.   45
   Wake Lute and Harp
   And every sweet-lipp't Thing
   That talkes with tunefull string;
Start into life, And leap with me
Into a hasty Fitt-tun'd Harmony.   50
   Nor must you think it much
   T'obey my bolder touch;
I have Authority in Love's name to take you
And to the worke of Love this morning wake you.
   Wake; In the Name   55
Of Him who never sleeps, All Things that Are,
   Or, what's the same,
   Are Musicall;
   Answer my Call
   And come along;   60
Help me to meditate mine Immortall Song.
Come, ye soft ministers of sweet sad mirth,
Bring All your houshold stuffe of Heavn on earth;
O you, my Soul's most certain Wings,
Complaining Pipes, and prattling Strings,   65

---

30 *Sett of Sphears:* the Ptolemaic universe of concentric spheres, which in their spin-
ning produce a celestial harmony inaudible to "dull mortality."
 37 *severall:* separate.
 50 *hasty Fitt-tun'd:* tuned to a song (*Fitt*) in haste (because of urgency—"Start into life,
And leap with me").

Bring All the store
Of Sweets you have; And murmur that you have no more.
Come, nere to part,
Nature and Art!
Come; and come strong,   70
To the conspiracy of our Spatious song.
Bring All the Powres of Praise
Your Provinces of well-united Worlds can raise;
Bring All your Lutes and Harps of Heavn and Earth;
What e're cooperates to The common mirthe   75
Vessells of vocall Joyes,
Or You, more noble Architects of Intellectuall Noise,
Cymballs of Heav'n, or Humane sphears,
Solliciters of Soules or Eares;
And when you'are come, with All.   80
That you can bring or we can call;
O may you fix
For ever here, and mix
Your selves into the long
And everlasting series of a deathlesse Song;   85
Mix all your many Worlds, Above,
And loose them into One of Love.
Chear thee my Heart!
For Thou too hast thy Part
And Place in the Great Throng   90
Of This unbounded All-imbracing Song.
Powres of my Soul, be Proud!
And speake alowd
To All the dear-bought Nations This Redeeming Name,
And in the wealth of one Rich Word proclaim   95
New Similes to Nature.
May it be no wrong
Blest Heavns, to you, and your Superiour song,
That we, dark Sons of Dust and Sorrow,
A while Dare borrow   100
The Name of Your Delights and our Desires,
And fitt it to so farr inferior Lyres.
Our Murmurs have their Musick too,
Ye mighty Orbes, as well as you,
Nor yeilds the noblest Nest   105
Of warbling Seraphim to the eares of Love,

---

71 *conspiracy:* i.e. breathing together (Lat. *conspirare*).
87 *loose:* i.e. lose.

A choicer Lesson then the joyfull Brest
　　　　Of a poor panting Turtle-Dove.
And we, low Wormes have leave to doe
The Same bright Busynes (ye Third Heavens) with you.　110
Gentle Spirits, doe not complain.
　　　　We will have care
　　　　To keep it fair,
And send it back to you again.
Come, lovely Name! Appeare from forth the Bright　115
　　　　Regions of peacefull Light
Look from thine own Illustrious Home,
Fair King of Names, and come.
Leave All thy native Glories in their Gorgeous Nest,
And give thy Self a while The gracious Guest　120
Of humble Soules, that seek to find
　　　　The hidden Sweets
　　　　Which man's heart meets
When Thou art Master of the Mind.
Come, lovely Name; life of our hope!　125
Lo we hold our Hearts wide ope!
Unlock thy Cabinet of Day
Dearest Sweet, and come away.
　　　　Lo how the thirsty Lands
Gasp for thy Golden Showres! with long stretch't Hands　130
　　　　Lo how the laboring Earth
　　　　That hopes to be
　　　　All Heaven by Thee,
　　　　Leapes at thy Birth.
The'attending World, to wait thy Rise,　135
　　　　First turn'd to eyes;
And then, not knowing what to doe;
Turn'd Them to Teares, and spent Them too.
Come Royall Name, and pay the expence
Of All this Pretious Patience.　140
　　　　O come away
And kill the Death of This Delay.
O see, so many Worlds of barren yeares
Melted and measur'd out in Seas of Teares.
O see, The Weary liddes of wakefull Hope　145
(Love's Eastern windowes) All wide ope

110　*Third Heavens:* the outermost region of the cosmos, the empyrean (2 Corinthians 12:2–4).
129–30　*thirsty Lands Gasp:* a phrase from Psalm 143:6 (Book of Common Prayer).

With Curtains drawn,
To catch The Day-break of Thy DAWN.
O dawn, at last, long look't for Day!
Take thine own wings, and come away.   150
Lo, where Aloft it comes! It comes, Among
The Conduct of Adoring SPIRITS, that throng
Like diligent Bees, And swarm about it.
    O they are wise;
And know what SWEETES are suck't from out it.   155
    It is the Hive,
    By which they thrive,
Where All their Hoard of Hony lyes.
Lo where it comes, upon The snowy DOVE's
Soft Back; And brings a Bosom big with Loves.   160
WELCOME to our dark world, Thou
    Womb of Day!
Unfold thy fair Conceptions; And display
The Birth of our Bright Joyes.
    O thou compacted   165
Body of Blessings: spirit of Soules extracted!
O dissipate thy spicy Powres
(Clowd of condensed sweets) and break upon us
    In balmy showrs;
O fill our senses, And take from us   170
All force of so Prophane a Fallacy
To think ought sweet but that which smells of Thee.
Fair, flowry Name, In none but Thee
And Thy Nectareall Fragrancy,
    Hourly there meetes   175
An universall SYNOD of All sweets;
By whom it is defined Thus
    That no Perfume
    For ever shall presume
To passe for Odoriferous,   180
But such alone whose sacred Pedigree
Can prove it Self some kin (sweet name) to Thee.
SWEET NAME, in Thy each Syllable
A Thousand Blest ARABIAS dwell;

---

151 At this line the "Hymn" proper begins; it is preceded in 1648 by a blank line space after line 150.
    161–62 printed as one line in 1648 and probably so intended.
    184–87 *Arabias, Paradises:* references to the East from which Christianity arose. Arabia was thought to have been the location of Eden, as it was certainly the residence of the phoenix, and a sensuously perfumed land.

A Thousand Hills of Frankincense;   185
Mountains of myrrh, and Beds of spices,
And ten Thousand PARADISES
The soul that tasts thee takes from thence.
How many unknown WORLDS there are
Of Comforts, which Thou hast in keeping!   190
How many Thousand Mercyes there
In Pitty's soft lap ly a sleeping!
Happy he who has the art
                To awake them,
                And to take them   195
Home, and lodge them in his HEART.
O that it were as it was wont to be!
When thy old Freinds of Fire, All full of Thee,
Fought against Frowns with smiles; gave Glorious chase
To Persecutions; And against the Face   200
Of DEATH and feircest Dangers, durst with Brave
And sober pace march on to meet A GRAVE.
On their Bold BRESTS about the world they bore thee
And to the Teeth of Hell stood up to teach thee,
In Center of their inmost Soules they wore thee,   205
Where Rackes and Torments striv'd, in vain, to reach thee.
                Little, alas, thought They
Who tore the Fair Brests of thy Freinds,
                Their Fury but made way
For Thee; And Serv'd therein Thy glorious ends.   210
What did Their weapons but with wider pores
Inlarge thy flaming-brested Lovers
                More freely to transpire
                That impatient Fire
The Heart that hides Thee hardly covers.   215
What did their Weapons but sett wide the Doores
For Thee: Fair, purple Doores, of love's devising;
The Ruby windowes which inrich't the EAST
Of Thy so oft repeated Rising.
Each wound of Theirs was Thy new Morning;   220
And reinthron'd thee in thy Rosy Nest,
With blush of thine own Blood thy day adorning.
It was the witt of love o'reflowd the Bounds

198 *Freinds:* Christian saints and martyrs.
217-22 The passage is a brilliant succession of reds. The wounds of the martyrs are first
purple (royalty), then ruby (richness), and then rosy (becoming). The dawn of the new day
is suggested by the doors, the windows, and the nest, and by the Homeric adjective "rosy,"
traditional for the dawn (Williams, 46–47).

Of WRATH, and made thee way through All Those WOUNDS.
Wellcome dear, All-Adored Name! 225
      For sure there is no Knee
      That knowes not THEE.
Or if there be such sonns of shame,
      Alas what will they doe
      When stubborn Rocks shall bow 230
And Hills hang down their Heavn-saluting Heads
      To seek for humble Beds
Of Dust, where in the Bashfull shades of night
Next to their own low NOTHING they may ly,
And couch before the dazeling light of thy dread majesty. 235
They that by Love's mild Dictate now
      Will not adore thee,
Shall Then with Just Confusion, bow
      And break before thee.

56   *Hymn for New Year's Day*

See also "Our Lord in his Circumcision," No. 6. Luke 2:21, and "Hymn to the Name of Jesus," No. 55.

The second of the Christmas-tide hymns; see also the following "Hymn" and the "Nativity Hymn," No. 70. This apparently slight poem mediates between the two larger hymns. The first three stanzas describe the circumcision and recall in their blood-red coloring the dawn coloring of the Nativity; the remainder of the poem anticipates the sun worship of the "Epiphany Hymn" and its light/dark coloring, the last three stanzas and the distich describing exactly what happens in that "Hymn."

New Year's
Day.

Rise, thou best and brightest morning!
Rosy with a double Red;
    With thine own blush thy cheeks adorning
And the dear drops this day were shed.

230–32 Cf. Isaiah 40:4, 64:1–3.
Hymn for New Year's Day. 52 (46, 48).*
  2, 12 *Rosy, rose:* see also "[In circumcisionem]" ("Ah ferus"), No. 103.

All the purple pride that laces   5
The crimson curtains of thy bed,
   Guilds thee not with so sweet graces
Nor setts thee in so rich a red.

Of all the fair-cheek't flowrs that fill thee
None so fair thy bosom strowes,   10
   As this modest maiden lilly
Our sins have sham'd into a rose.

Bid thy golden God, the Sun,
Burnisht in his best beames rise,
   Put all his red-ey'd Rubies on;   15
These Rubies shall putt out their eyes.

Let him make poor the purple east,
Search what the world's close cabinets keep,
   Rob the rich births of each bright nest
That flaming in their fair beds sleep,   20

Let him embrave his own bright tresses
With a new morning made of gemmes;
   And wear, in those his wealthy dresses,
Another Day of Diadems.

When he hath done all he may   25
To make himselfe rich in his rise,
   All will be darknes to the Day
That breakes from one of these bright eyes.

And soon this sweet truth shall appear
Dear BABE, ere many dayes be done,   30
   The morn shall come to meet thee here,
And leave her own neglected Sun.

Here are Beautyes shall bereave him
Of all his eastern Paramours.
   His Persian Lovers all shall leave him,   35
And swear faith to thy sweeter Powres.

Nor while they leave him shall they lose the Sun,
But in thy fairest eyes find two for one.

5 *laces:* see also "Upon the birth of . . . Elizabeth," No. 339, line 51.
6 *curtains:* Psalm 104:2: "who stretchest out the heavens like a curtain."
21 *embrave:* make splendid.
30 *ere . . . done:* The Epiphany, January 6.
35 *Persian Lovers:* see the "Epiphanie Hymn."

The Hymn celebrates the Feast of the Epiphany (January 6), the Manifestation of Christ to the Gentiles. The text is Matthew 2:1–12. This Hymn (published in 1648) is a companion piece to the Nativity Hymn (No. 70) and the Circumcision Hymn ("New Year's Day," No. 56) (both published in 1646; second version 1648) and should be considered as one of a trio. The epigrams, "In Epiphanium Domini," No. 108, and "Accipe dona," No. 109, should also be consulted. "The relation between [the Nativity Hymn] and its companion piece on the [Epiphany] is one to invite speculation. The [former] contemplates the Child Jesus sleeping between the pure yet warm breasts of His Mother; the [latter] contemplates the God of the philosophers, the Logos, the *Lumen de Lumine.* Were the two attitudes, the corresponding two styles, designed as dramatic characterizations; or does the second ode represent some attempted and never consummated change in the character of Crashaw's religious life and his poetic method? Of the two types of mystics, the visionaries and the philosophers, Crashaw's temperament markedly allied him with the former; and the *via negativa,* with its denial of sensuous analogies, runs counter to the baroque belief that in my flesh shall I see God in His flesh. Whether, therefore, as experiment or imaginative projection of an attempt to impose upon one temperament

Hymn in the Glorious Epiphanie. 52 (48).*

the method natural to another, the ode on the Epiphany stands apart and alone in Crashaw's work" (Warren, p. 151). See also Wallerstein, pp. 143–45. Williams points to the images of color in the three poems: the Nativity Hymn (December 25) is full of imagery of white and red—dawn coloring, the becoming of a new day; the Circumcision Hymn (January 1) continues the coloring of red but concludes with coloring of light and dark; the Epiphany Hymn (January 6) develops the light and dark coloring extensively, signifying the fulfillment of the new day. The paradox on which the poem depends is the darkness of pagan sun worship, symbolized by the eclipse of the sun at the Crucifixion (see further, pp. 69–83). "The juxtaposition of the events of the . . . Epiphany with those of the Passion, of the Word made manifest with the Word rejected, is traditional and ubiquitous" (Tuve, p. 65).

IN THE GLORIOUS EPIPHANIE
OF OUR LORD GOD, A HYMN.
SUNG AS BY THE THREE KINGS

(1. Kinge.) Bright BABE! Whose awfull beautyes make
The morn incurr a sweet mistake;
(2.) For whom the'officious heavns devise
To disinheritt the sun's rise,
(3.) Delicately to displace   5
The Day, and plant it fairer in thy face;
(1.) O thou born KING of loves,
                    (2.) Of lights,
                    (3.) Of joyes!
(Cho.) Look up, sweet BABE, look up and see   10
                    For love of Thee
                    Thus farr from home
                    The EAST is come
To seek her self in thy sweet Eyes.
(1.) We, who strangely went astray,   15
                    Lost in a bright
                    Meridian night,
(2.) A Darkenes made of too much day,
                    (3.) Becken'd from farr
                    By thy fair starr,   20
Lo at last have found our way.
(Cho.) To THEE, thou DAY of night! thou east of west!
Lo we at last have found the way.
To thee, the world's great universal east.
The Generall and indifferent DAY.   25

15 *went astray:* in pagan sun worship.
17 *Meridian:* i.e. the noon of night, midnight; see "Hymn to Sixt hour," "Office of the Holy Crosse."
22 *east of west:* the kings have traveled westward to this rising sun.
25 *indifferent:* i.e. undiffering.

(1.) All-circling point. All centring sphear.
The world's one, round, Æternall year.
(2.) Whose full and all-unwrinkled face
Nor sinks nor swells with time or place;
(3.) But every where and every while   30
Is One Consistent solid smile;

    (1.) Not vext and tost
    (2.) 'Twixt spring and frost,
(3.) Nor by alternate shredds of light
Sordidly shifting hands with shades and night.   35
(Cho.) O little all! in thy embrace
The world lyes warm, and likes his place.
Nor does his full Globe fail to be
Kist on Both his cheeks by Thee.
Time is too narrow for thy YEAR   40
Nor makes the whole WORLD thy half-sphear.

    (1.) To Thee, to Thee
    From him we flee
(2.) From HIM, whom by a more illustrious ly,
The blindnes of the world did call the eye;   45
(3.) To HIM, who by These mortall clouds hast made
Thy self our sun, though thine own shade.
(1.) Farewell, the world's false light.

    Farewell, the white
    Ægypt! a long farewell to thee   50
    Bright IDOL; black IDOLATRY.
The dire face of inferior DARKNES, kis't
And courted in the pompous mask of a more specious mist.

    (2.) Farewell, farewell
    The proud and misplac't gates of hell, 55
    Pertch't, in the morning's way
And double-guilded as the doores of DAY.
The deep hypocrisy of DEATH and NIGHT
More desperately dark, Because more bright.

    (3.) Welcome, the world's sure Way! 60
    HEAVN's wholsom ray.
    (Cho.) Wellcome to us; and we
    (SWEET) to our selves, in THEE.
(1.) The deathles HEIR of all thy FATHER's day!

26 the concept of God devised by Hermes Trismegistus: "a circle whose center is every-
where, and whose circumference nowhere."
44 *Him:* the sun.
46 *Him:* the Babe. *mortall clouds:* cf. "Sospetto," xxiii.
49 *white:* white was the color of Upper Egypt.

(2.) Decently Born.   65
Embosom'd in a much more Rosy MORN,
The Blushes of thy All-unblemish't mother.
                    (3.) No more that other
                    Aurora shall sett ope
Her ruby casements, or hereafter hope   70
                    From mortall eyes
To meet Religious welcomes at her rise.
(*Cho.*) We (Pretious ones!) in you have won
A gentler MORN, a juster sun.
(1.) His superficiall Beames sun-burn't our skin;   75
                    (2.) But left within
(3.) The night and winter still of death and sin.
(*Cho.*) Thy softer yet more certaine DARTS
Spare our eyes, but peirce our HARTS.
(1.) Therefore with HIS proud persian spoiles   80
(2.) We court thy more concerning smiles.
                    (3.) Therfore with his Disgrace
We guild the humble cheek of this chast place;
(*Cho.*) And at thy FEET powr forth his FACE.
(1.) The doating nations now no more   85
Shall any day but THINE adore.
(2.) Nor (much lesse) shall they leave these eyes
For cheap Ægyptian Deityes.
(3.) In whatsoe're more Sacred shape
Of Ram, He-goat, or reverend ape,   90
Those beauteous ravishers opprest so sore
The too-hard-tempted nations.
                    (1.) Never more
By wanton heyfer shall be worn
(2.) A Garland, or a guilded horn.   95
The altar-stall'd ox, fatt OSYRIS now
                    With his fair sister cow,
(3.) Shall kick the clouds no more; But lean and tame,
(*Cho.*) See his horn'd face, and dy for shame.
And MITHRA now shall be no name.   100
(1.) No longer shall the immodest lust
Of Adulterous GODLES dust
(2.) Fly in the face of heav'n; As if it were
The poor world's Fault that he is fair.

96 *Osyris:* Egyptian god of the sun, represented as a bull or an ox.
97 *cow:* i.e. **Isis,** represented as a sacred cow.
99 *horn'd:* cuckolded (?).
100 *Mithra:* Persian god of the sun; compare "Out of Grotius," No. 83, lines 36–38.

(3.) Nor with perverse loves and Religious RAPES   105
Revenge thy Bountyes in their beauteous shapes;
And punish Best Things worst; Because they stood
Guilty of being much for them too Good.
(1.) Proud sons of death! that durst compell
Heav'n it self to find them hell;   110
(2.) And by strange witt of madnes wrest
From this world's EAST the other's WEST.
(3.) All-Idolizing wormes! that thus could crowd
And urge Their sun into thy cloud;
Forcing his sometimes eclips'd face to be   115
A long deliquium to the light of thee.
(Cho.) Alas with how much heavyer shade
The shamefac't lamp hung down his head
        For that one eclipse he made
        Then all those he suffered!   120
(1.) For this he look't so bigg; and every morn
With a red face confes't his scorn.
Or hiding his vex't cheeks in a hir'd mist
Kept them from being so unkindly kis't.
(2.) It was for this the day did rise   125
        So oft with blubber'd eyes.
For this the evening wept; and we ne'er knew
        But call'd it deaw.
        (3.) This dayly wrong
Silenc't the morning-sons, and damp't their song   130
(Cho.) Nor was't our deafnes, but our sins, that thus
Long made th'Harmonious orbes all mute to us.
        (1.) Time has a day in store
        When this so proudly poor
And self-oppressed spark, that has so long   135
By the love-sick world bin made
Not so much their sun as SHADE,
Weary of this Glorious wrong
From them and from himself shall flee
For shelter to the shadow of thy TREE;   140
(Cho.) Proud to have gain'd this pretious losse
And chang'd his false crown for thy CROSSE.
(2.) That dark Day's clear doom shall define
Whose is the Master FIRE, which sun should shine.

116 *deliquium:* lack.
119 *one eclipse:* at the Crucifixion.
130 *morning-sons:* the stars which sing in their spheres, Job 38:7.
133 *a day:* the Crucifixion, Luke 23:44–45.

That sable Judgment-seat shall by new lawes   145
Decide and settle the Great cause
                Of controverted light,
(*Cho.*) And natur's wrongs rejoyce to doe thee Right.
(3.) That forfeiture of noon to night shall pay
All the idolatrous thefts done by this night of day;   150
And the Great Penitent presse his own pale lipps
With an elaborate love-eclipse
                  To which the low world's lawes
                  Shall lend no cause
(*Cho.*) Save those domestick which he borrowes   155
From our sins and his own sorrowes.
(1.) Three sad hour's sackcloth then shall show to us
His penance, as our fault, conspicuous.
(2.) And he more needfully and nobly prove
The nations' terror now then erst their love.   160
(3.) Their hated loves changd into wholsom feares,
(*Cho.*) The shutting of his eye shall open Theirs.
(1.) As by a fair-ey'd fallacy of day
Mis-ledde before they lost their way,
So shall they, by the seasonable fright   165
Of an unseasonable night,
Loosing it once again, stumble'on true LIGHT
(2.) And as before his too-bright eye
Was Their more blind idolatry,
So his officious blindnes now shall be   170
Their black, but faithfull perspective of thee;
              (3.) His new prodigious night,
Their new and admirable light;
The supernaturall DAWN of Thy pure day.
                While wondring they   175
(The happy converts now of him
Whom they compell'd before to be their sin)
              Shall henceforth see
To kisse him only as their rod
Whom they so long courted as GOD,   180
(*Cho.*) And their best use of him they worship't be
To learn of Him at lest, to worship Thee.
(1.) It was their Weaknes woo'd his beauty;
              But it shall be

154 *no cause:* i.e. it was miraculous.
182 *lest:* i.e. least.

Their wisdome now, as well as duty, 185
To'injoy his Blott; and as a large black letter
Use it to spell Thy beautyes better;
And make the night it self their torch to thee.
(2.) By the oblique ambush of this close night
          Couch't in that conscious shade 190
The right-ey'd Areopagite
Shall with a vigorous guesse invade
And catche thy quick reflex; and sharply see
          On this dark Ground
          To descant THEE. 195
(3.) O prize of the rich SPIRIT! with what feirce chase
          Of his strong soul, shall he
          Leap at thy lofty FACE,
And seize the swift Flash, in rebound
From this obsequious cloud; 200
          Once call'd a sun;
          Till dearly thus undone,
(Cho.) Till thus triumphantly tam'd (o ye two
Twinne SUNNES!) and taught now to negotiate you.
(1.) Thus shall that reverend child of light, 205
(2.) By being scholler first of that new night,
Come forth Great master of the mystick day;
(3.) And teach obscure MANKIND a more close way
By the frugall negative light
Of a most wise and well-abused Night 210
To read more legible thine originall Ray,
(Cho.) And make our Darknes serve THY day;
Maintaining t'wixt thy world and ours
A commerce of contrary powres,
          A mutuall trade 215
          'Twixt sun and SHADE,

189–218 Dionysius the Areopagite, after witnessing the miracle of the eclipse, embraced Christianity; he was the mystic who devised the "via negativa" to God. His account of the eclipse (quoted in Williams, p. 80): "both of us at that time, at Heliopolis, being present, and standing together, saw the moon approaching the sun, to our surprise (for it was not appointed time for conjunction); and again from the ninth hour to the evening, supernaturally placed back again into a line opposite the sun. . . . So great are the supernatural things of that appointed time, and possible to Christ alone, the Cause of all, Who worketh great things and marvellous, of which there is not number."
204 *Twinne Sunnes:* the eyes of Christ.
208 *obscure:* darkened (the Latin meaning). *a more close way:* the negative way of mystical ascent is described by Dionysius in the opening chapter of his *Mystical Theology;* a section is quoted in Martz, *The Meditative Poem* (Anchor Books, Garden City, N.Y., 1963), p. 543.
210 *well-abused:* used [well and] fully (Lat. *abusus*).

By confederat BLACK and WHITE
Borrowing day and lending night.
(1.) Thus we, who when with all the noble powres
That (at thy cost) are call'd, not vainly, ours   220
        We vow to make brave way
Upwards, and presse on for the pure intelligentiall Prey;
        (2.) At lest to play
        The amorous Spyes
And peep and proffer at thy sparkling Throne;   225
(3.) In stead of bringing in the blissfull PRIZE
        And fastening on Thine eyes,
        Forfeit our own
        And nothing gain
But more Ambitious losse, at lest of brain;   230
(Cho.) Now by abased liddes shall learn to be
Eagles; and shutt our eyes that we may see.

The Close.

Therfore to THEE and thine Auspitious ray
        (Dread sweet!) lo thus
        At lest by us,   235
The delegated EYE of DAY
Does first his Scepter, then HIMSELF in solemne Tribute pay.
        Thus he undresses
        His sacred unshorn treses;
At thy adored FEET, thus, he layes down   240
        (1.) His gorgeous tire
        Of flame and fire,
(2.) His glittering ROBE, (3.) his sparkling CROWN,
(1.) His GOLD, (2.) his MIRRH, (3.) his FRANKINCENCE,
(Cho.) To which He now has no pretence.   245
For being show'd by this day's light, how farr
He is from sun enough to make THY starr,
His best ambition now, is but to be
Somthing a brighter SHADOW (sweet) of thee.
Or on heavn's azure forhead high to stand   250
Thy golden index; with a duteous Hand
Pointing us Home to our own sun
The world's and his HYPERION.

---

232 *Eagles:* in the bestiary tradition thought to have keen eyesight and to be able to look at the sun.
241 *tire:* attire.
253 *Hyperion:* the Græco-Roman god of the sun.

58   *To the Queen's Majesty*

MADAME.
'Mongst those long rowes of crownes that guild your race,
These Royall sages sue for decent place.
The day-break of the nations; their first ray;
When the Dark WORLD dawn'd into Christian DAY
And smil'd i'th' BABE's bright face, the purpling Bud   5
And Rosy dawn of the right Royall blood;
Fair first-fruits of the LAMB. Sure KINGS in this,
They took a kingdom while they gave a kisse.
But the world's Homage, scarse in These well blown,
We read in you (Rare Queen) ripe and full-grown.   10
For from this day's rich seed of Diadems
Does rise a radiant croppe of Royalle stemms,
A Golden harvest of crown'd heads, that meet
And crowd for kisses from the LAMB's white feet.
In this Illustrious throng, your lofty floud   15
Swells high, fair Confluence of all highborn Bloud!
With your bright head whole groves of scepters bend
Their wealthy tops; and for these feet contend.
So swore the LAMB's dread sire. And so we see't.
Crownes, and the HEADS they kisse, must court these FEET.   20
Fix here, fair Majesty! May your Heart ne're misse
To reap new CROWNES and KINGDOMS from that kisse.
Nor may we misse the joy to meet in you
The aged honors of this day still new.
May the great time, in you, still greater be   25
While all the YEAR is your EPIPHANY,
While your each day's devotion duly brings
Three K I N G D O M E S to supply this day's three KINGS.

To the Queen's Majesty. 52 (48).* The dedicatory poem, accompanying the Epiphany Hymn, addressed to Queen Henrietta Maria, wife of Charles I.
    7–14   The first royal worshipers were these three kings; now all kings and queens (as we observe in you) are worshipers.
    15–18   Your children (the Queen had seven) are distinguished in this throng of royal worshipers.
    22   *Crownes:* scil. heavenly.
    22   *that kisse:* at the Lamb's feet (line 14); this prostrate adoration Crashaw seems to have developed from contemplation of Mary Magdalene (Luke 7:38).
    28   *Three Kingdomes:* Great Britain, Ireland, France. A few months after the publication of this poem, King Charles had lost his head, and the Queen these kingdoms.

59   *Charitas Nimia*

CHARITAS

NIMIA.

OR

THE

DEAR BARGAIN.

Lord, what is man? why should he coste thee
So dear? what had his ruin lost thee?
Lord what is man? that thou hast overbought
      So much a thing of nought?

  Love is too kind, I see; and can   5
Make but a simple merchant man.
'Twas for such sorry merchandise
Bold Painters have putt out his Eyes.

  Alas, sweet lord, what wer't to thee
If there were no such wormes as we?   10
Heav'n ne're the lesse still heavn would be,
      Should Mankind dwell
      In the deep hell.
What have his woes to doe with thee?

    Let him goe weep   15
    O're his own wounds;
    SERAPHIMS will not sleep
Nor spheares let fall their faithfull rounds.

  Still would The youthfull SPIRITS sing;
And still thy spatious Palace ring.   20
Still would those beauteous ministers of light
      Burn all as bright,

Charitas Nimia. 52 (48).* The poem expresses the humility of man and his wonder at the goodness of his Creator. The text is Psalm 144:3–4 (Prayer Book version): "Lord, what is man, that thou hast such respect unto him? . . . Man is like a thing of nought." See Williams, pp. 31–32.
    5–8 the tradition of representing Cupid as blind.

And bow their flaming heads before thee;
Still thrones and Dominations would adore thee;
Still would those ever-wakefull sons of fire   25
        Keep warm thy prayse
        Both nights and dayes,
And teach thy lov'd name to their noble lyre.

  Let froward Dust then doe it's kind;
And give it self for sport to the proud wind.   30
Why should a peice of peevish clay plead shares
In the Æternity of thy old cares?
Why shouldst thou bow thy awfull Brest to see
What mine own madnesses have done with me?

  Should not the king still keepe his throne   35
Because some desperate Fool's undone?
Or will the world's Illustrious eyes
Weep for every worm that dyes?

        Will the gallant sun
        E're the lesse glorious run?   40
Will he hang down his golden head
Or e're the sooner seek his western bed,
        Because some foolish fly
        Growes wanton, and will dy?

  If I were lost in misery,   45
What was it to thy heavn and thee?
What was it to thy pretious blood
If my foul Heart call'd for a floud?

  What if my faithlesse soul and I
        Would needs fall in   50
        With guilt and sin?
What did the Lamb, that he should dy?
What did the lamb, that he should need,
When the wolf sins, himself to bleed?

        If my base lust   55
Bargain'd with Death and well-beseeming dust,
        Why should the white
        Lamb's bosom write
        The purple name
        Of my sin's shame?   60

Why should his unstaind brest make good
My blushes with his own heart-blood?

O my SAVIOUR, make me see
How dearly thou hast payd for me;

That lost again my LIFE may prove   65
As then in DEATH, so now in love.

60   *The Teare*

1   What bright soft thing is this?
  Sweet *Mary* thy faire Eyes expence?
   A moist sparke it is,
   A watry Diamond; from whence
The very Terme, I think, was found
The water of a *Diamond.*

2   O 'tis not a Teare,
  'Tis a starre about to drop
   From thine eye its spheare;
   The Sunne will stoope and take it up.
Proud will his sister be to weare
This thine eyes Jewell in her Eare.

3   O 'tis a Teare,
  Too true a Teare; for no sad eyne,
   How sad so e're
   Raine so true a Teare as thine;
Each Drop leaving a place so deare,
Weeps for it selfe, is its owne Teare.

4   Such a Pearle as this is,
  (Slipt from *Aurora's* dewy Brest)
   The Rose buds sweet lip kisses;
   And such the Rose it selfe when vext
With ungentle flames, does shed,
Sweating in too warme a Bed.

The Teare. 46 (48).* Evidently a preliminary sketch of the ideas that appear more fully in
"The Weeper," or, as Martin thinks (p. 434), "material not used in the longer poem." The
Magdalene's tears are recorded at Luke 7:38 and elsewhere. See further "The Weeper."
 1.6 *water:* the term for the transparency and luster of a diamond.
 2.5 *his sister:* scil. the Moon who will wear the tear as a star.

5   Such the Maiden Gemme
          By the wanton Spring put on,
            Peeps from her Parent stemme,
          And blushes on the manly Sun:
This watry Blossome of thy Eyne
Ripe, will make the richer Wine.

6   Faire Drop, why quak'st thou so?
          'Cause thou streight must lay thy Head
            In the Dust? o no;
          The Dust shall never bee thy Bed:
A pillow for thee will I bring,
Stuft with Downe of Angels wing.

7   Thus carryed up on high,
          (For to Heaven thou must goe)
            Sweetly shalt thou lye,
          And in soft slumbers bath thy woe;
Till the singing Orbes awake thee,
And one of their bright *Chorus* make thee.

8   There thy selfe shalt bee
          An eye, but not a weeping one,
            Yet I doubt of thee,
          Whither th'hadst rather there have shone
An eye of Heaven; or still shine here
In th'Heaven of *Mary's* eye, a *Teare.*

8.4 *Whither:* i.e. whether.

THE TERESA POEMS (Nos. 61, 62, 63).

"A Hymn," No. 61, and "An Apologie," No. 62, were published in 1646; they were joined in 1648 by "The Flaming Heart," No. 63; the three poems were reprinted in 1652 with the further addition of twenty-four lines concluding "The Flaming Heart." The poems were supplemented in 1648 by the "Song of divine Love," No. 64, which follows immediately in 1648 and 1652; it supplies a separate commentary on the state of ecstatic sacred love which the three Teresa poems celebrate.

The three Teresa poems record Crashaw's devotion to St. Teresa of Jesus of Avila, the Spanish saint, mystic, and administrator—"one of the extraordinary women of all time" (Warren, p. 139). "A Hymn" is a highly specialized biography of the saint describing her early quest for martyrdom, her mystical experiences in the years of her maturity, and her final blessedness in heaven. "An Apologie" addresses itself to Crashaw's spiritual indebtedness to the writings of Teresa and to the catholic value of those writings transcending national borders. "The Flaming Heart" comments on the picture of Teresa—"as she is usually expressed"—and concludes with Crashaw's most famous lines in English, the personal invocation to the Saint. "There is no passage in the 'Hymne' so magnificent as this; but as a poem, the 'Hymne' is much the best of the trio; it has a unity and sequence, a flow and a crescendo which Crashaw was rarely able to contrive. . . . These poems, particularly the 'Hymne,' flow with a passionate ease almost unparalleled in Crashaw's work" (Warren, pp. 143, 146).

61   *A Hymn to Sainte* Teresa

The heading of the poem notices first Teresa's remarkable administrative achievements but leaves them rapidly to luxuriate in her spiritual achievements, seeing in her youthful running away from home to obtain martyrdom a symbol of the desire to "dy in love's delicious fire" which was to mark the rest of Teresa's life. (Crashaw does not mention, incidentally, as Miss Jauernick has pointed out ["Crashaws Hymne auf St. Teresa," *Die Neueren Sprachen*, 14 N.F. (1965), p. 457], that Teresa's big brother Roderick ran away with his sister for the same purpose.) In this poem, Crashaw "unites two themes intensely dear to him—martyrdom and mysticism; . . . indeed, the two themes grow one: to live the mystical life is to die, not in a moment, but throughout a life—to die at the hand not of an enemy but of a lover" (Warren, p. 146). See also A. E. Farnham, "St. Teresa and the Coy Mistress," *Boston University Studies in English*, II (1956), 226–39.

Le Vray portraict de S.ᵗᵉ Terese, Fondatrice
des Religieuses, & Religieux reformez de
l'ordre de N.Dame du mont Carmel. Decedé
le 4 Octo. 1582. Canonisée le 12. Mars 1622.
J. Messager excudit.

A HYMN

TO

THE NAME AND HONOR

OF

THE ADMIRABLE

SAINTE

TERESA,

FOUNDRESSE

of the Reformation of the Discalced
CARMELITES, both
men and Women;

A

WOMAN

for Angelicall heigth of speculation, for
Masculine courage of performance,
more then a woman.

WHO

Yet a child, out ran maturity, and
durst plott a Martyrdome;

THE

HYMNE.

Love, thou art Absolute sole lord
Of LIFE and DEATH. To prove the word,
Wee'l now appeal to none of all
Those thy old Souldiers, Great and tall,
Ripe Men of Martyrdom, that could reach down   5
With strong armes, their triumphant crown,
Such as could with lusty breath
Speak lowd into the face of death
Their Great LORD's glorious name; to none
Of those whose spatious Bosomes spread a throne   10
For LOVE at larg to fill: spare blood and sweat;
And see him take a private seat,
Making his mansion in the mild
And milky soul of a soft child.
    Scarse has she learn't to lisp the name   15
Of Martyr; yet she thinks it shame
Life should so long play with that breath
Which spent can buy so brave a death.
She never undertook to know
What death with love should have to doe;   20
Nor has she e're yet understood
Why to show love, she should shed blood
Yet though she cannot tell you why,
She can LOVE, and she can DY.
    Scarse has she Blood enough to make   25
A guilty sword blush for her sake;
Yet has she'a HEART dares hope to prove
How much lesse strong is DEATH then LOVE.
    Be love but there; let poor six yeares
Be pos'd with the maturest Feares   30
Man trembles at, you straight shall find
LOVE knowes no nonage, nor the MIND.
'Tis LOVE, not YEARES or LIMBS that can
Make the Martyr, or the man.
    Love touch't her HEART, and lo it beates   35

A Hymn to Sainte Teresa. 52 (46, 48).*
  12 *private seat:* a residence withdrawn from public prominence.
  30 *pos'd:* placed against.
  31 *straight:* straightway.

High, and burnes with such brave heates;
Such thirsts to dy, as dares drink up,
A thousand cold deaths in one cup.
Good reason. For she breathes All fire.
Her weake brest heaves with strong desire   40
Of what she may with fruitles wishes
Seek for amongst her MOTHER's kisses.
    Since 'tis not to be had at home
She'l travail to a Martyrdom.
No home for her confesses she   45
But where she may a Martyr be.
    She'l to the Moores; And trade with them,
For this unvalued Diadem.
She'l offer them her dearest Breath,
With CHRIST's Name in't, in change for death.   50
She'l bargain with them; and will give
Them GOD; and teach them how to live
In him: or, if they this deny,
For him she'l teach them how to DY.
So shall she leave amongst them sown   55
Her LORD's Blood; or at lest her own.
    FAREWEL then, all the world! Adieu.
TERESA is no more for you.
Farewell, all pleasures, sports, and joyes,
(Never till now esteemed toyes)   60
Farewell what ever deare may bee,
MOTHER's armes or FATHER's knee
Farewell house, and farewell home!
SHE's for the Moores, and MARTYRDOM.
    SWEET, not so fast! lo thy fair Spouse   65
Whom thou seekst with so swift vowes,
Calls thee back, and bidds thee come
T'embrace a milder MARTYRDOM.
    Blest powres forbid, Thy tender life
Should bleed upon a barborous knife;   70
Or some base hand have power to race
Thy Brest's chast cabinet, and uncase
A soul kept there so sweet, o no;
Wise heavn will never have it so.

44   *travail to:* (1) labor to bring to birth, (2) travel to.
47   Against this line Crashaw has a reference to Chap. I of the *Vida* (PM MS.).
48   *unvalued:* invaluable.
65   *Spouse:* i.e. Christ.

THOU art love's victime; and must dy   75
A death more mysticall and high.
Into love's armes thou shalt let fall
A still-surviving funerall.
His is the DART must make the DEATH
Whose stroke shall tast thy hallow'd breath;   80
A Dart thrice dip't in that rich flame
Which writes thy spouse's radiant Name
Upon the roof of Heav'n; where ay
It shines, and with a soveraign ray
Beates bright upon the burning faces   85
Of soules which in that name's sweet graces
Find everlasting smiles. So rare,
So spirituall, pure, and fair
Must be th'immortall instrument
Upon whose choice point shall be sent   90
A life so lov'd; And that there be
Fitt executioners for Thee,
The fair'st and first-born sons of fire
Blest SERAPHIM, shall leave their quire
And turn love's souldiers, upon THEE   95
To exercise their archerie.
　　　O how oft shalt thou complain
Of a sweet and subtle PAIN.
Of intolerable JOYES;
Of a DEATH, in which who dyes   100
Loves his death, and dyes again.
And would for ever so be slain.
And lives, and dyes; and knowes not why
To live, But that he thus may never leave to DY.
　　　How kindly will thy gentle HEART   105
Kisse the sweetly-killing DART!
And close in his embraces keep
Those delicious Wounds, that weep
Balsom to heal themselves with. Thus
When These thy DEATHS, so numerous,   110
Shall all at last dy into one,

76　*mysticall and high*: i.e. a union of the soul with God, which leads to intuitive knowl-
edge of reality (R. G. Collmer, "Crashaw's 'Death More Misticall and High,'" *JEGP*,
LV[1956], 373–80). It will be noted that the Teresa poems and the "Song" all end in such a
death.
79–96　for the expansion of this matter see "The Flaming Heart."
94　Against this line Crashaw has a reference to Chap. XXIX of the *Vida* (PM MS.).
97　*complain*: scil. in her writings, the *Vida*, especially.
98　Against this line Crashaw has a reference to Chap. XX of the *Vida* (PM MS.).

And melt thy Soul's sweet mansion;
Like a soft lump of incense, hasted
By too hott a fire, and wasted
Into perfuming clouds, so fast   115
Shalt thou exhale to Heavn at last
In a resolving SIGH, and then—
O what? Ask not the Tongues of men,
Angells cannot tell: suffice,
Thy selfe shall feel thine own full joyes   120
And hold them fast for ever. There
So soon as thou shalt first appear,
The MOON of maiden starrs, thy white
MISTRESSE, attended by such bright
Soules as thy shining self, shall come   125
And in her first rankes make thee room;
Where 'mongst her snowy family
Immortall wellcomes wait for thee.
    O what delight, when reveal'd LIFE shall stand
And teach thy lipps heav'n with his hand;   130
On which thou now maist to thy wishes
Heap up thy consecrated kisses.
What joyes shall seize thy soul, when she
Bending her blessed eyes on thee
(Those second Smiles of Heav'n) shall dart   135
Her mild rayes through thy melting heart!
    Angels, thy old freinds, there shall greet thee
Glad at their own home now to meet thee.
    All thy good WORKES which went before
And waited for thee, at the door,   140
Shall own thee there; and all in one
Weave a constellation
Of CROWNS, with which the KING thy spouse
Shall build up thy triumphant browes.
    All thy old woes shall now smile on thee   145
And thy paines sitt bright upon thee
All thy sorrows here shall shine,
All thy SUFFRINGS be divine.
TEARES shall take comfort, and turn gemms
And WRONGS repent to Diademms.   150

122–82 Praz (pp. 260–61): "[though] a magnificent presentation of the beatific vision.
. . . There is still something detached and of a descriptive nature in this composition: the
poet does not yet possess the adequate lyric heat for the mystical experience."
124 *Mistresse:* the Virgin Mary.
129 *Life:* Christ.
138 *their own home:* they had previously visited Teresa at her home.

Ev'n thy DEATHS shall live; and new
Dresse the soul that erst they slew.
Thy wounds shall blush to such bright scarres
As keep account of the LAMB's warres.

Those rare WORKES where thou shalt leave writt   155
Love's noble history, with witt
Taught thee by none but him, while here
They feed our soules, shall cloth THINE there.
Each heavnly word by whose hid flame
Our hard Hearts shall strike fire, the same   160
Shall flourish on thy browes. and be
Both fire to us and flame to thee;
Whose light shall live bright in thy FACE
By glory, in our hearts by grace.

Thou shalt look round about, and see   165
Thousands of crown'd Soules throng to be
Themselves thy crown. Sons of thy vowes,
The virgin-births with which thy soveraign spouse
Made fruitfull thy fair soul, goe now
And with them all about thee bow   170
To Him, put on (hee'l say) put on
(My rosy love) That thy rich zone
Sparkling with the sacred flames
Of thousand soules, whose happy names
Heav'n keeps upon thy score. (Thy bright   175
Life brought them first to kisse the light
That kindled them to starrs.) and so
Thou with the LAMB, thy lord, shalt goe;
And whereso'ere he setts his white
Stepps, walk with HIM those wayes of light   180
Which who in death would live to see,
Must learn in life to dy like thee.

---

167   *Sons . . . vowes:* scil. those religious who have taken the vows of the Carmelites.
173   Against this line Crashaw has a reference to a Life of Teresa by Ribera (PM MS.).

62   *An Apologie for the fore-going Hymne.*

Martz thinks (*Meditative Poem*, p. 545) the last lines of the Heading "an editorial addition." "An Apologie" was needed, presumably, to excuse such pro-Spanish sentiments from an Englishman and to justify the "weak and worth-lesse song" of the poet attempting to praise in English "a saint already highly exalted in other tongues" (A. Warren, "Crashaw's Apologie," *TLS*, November 16, 1935, p. 746).

AN

APOLOGIE.

FOR

THE FORE-GOING HYMNE

as having been writt when the au-
thor was yet among the
protestantes.

Thus have I back again to thy bright name
(Fair floud of holy fires!) transfus'd the flame
I took from reading thee; tis to thy wrong
I know, that in my weak and worthlesse song
Thou here art sett to shine where thy full day   5
Scarse dawnes. O pardon if I dare to say
Thine own dear bookes are guilty. For from thence
I learn't to know that love is eloquence.
That hopefull maxime gave me hart to try
If, what to other tongues is tun'd so high,   10
Thy praise might not speak English too; forbid
(By all thy mysteryes that here ly hidde)
Forbid it, mighty Love! let no fond Hate
Of names and wordes, so farr præjudicate.
Souls are not SPANIARDS too, one freindly floud   15
Of BAPTISM blends them all into a blood.
CHRIST's faith makes but one body of all soules
And love's that body's soul, no law controwlls

An Apologie for the fore-going Hymne. 52 (48).*
    7 *bookes:* Crashaw certainly knew the *Vida* (published in Spanish in 1588, translated into English and published in various editions in 1611, 1623, 1642) and probably all of the major *Works*, published in many Spanish, French, and Latin editions from 1588; one small work appeared in Spanish in 1611. The editor of the *Steps to the Temple* (see Appendix) reports that Crashaw was "excellent" in Spanish and Latin. The sense of this "Apologie" would suggest that Crashaw read the works in Spanish (lines 21–24).

Our free traffique for heav'n, we may maintaine
Peace, sure, with piety, though it come from SPAIN.   20
What soul so e're, in any language, can
Speak heav'n like her's is my souls country-man.
O 'tis not spanish, but 'tis heav'n she speaks!
'Tis heav'n that lyes in ambush there, and breaks
From thence into the wondring reader's brest;   25
Who feels his warm HEART hatch'd into a nest
Of little EAGLES and young loves, whose high
Flights scorn the lazy dust, and things that dy.
  There are enow, whose draughts (as deep as hell)
Drink up al SPAIN in sack. Let my soul swell   30
With thee, strong wine of love! let others swimme
In puddles; we will pledge this SERAPHIM
Bowles full of richer blood then blush of grape
Was ever guilty of, Change we too 'our shape
(My soul,) Some drink from men to beasts, o then   35
Drink we till we prove more, not lesse, then men,
And turn not beasts, but Angels. Let the king
Me ever into these his cellars bring
Where flowes such wine as we can have of none
But HIM who trod the wine-presse all alone: 40
Wine of youth, life, and the sweet Deaths of love;
Wine of immortall mixture; which can prove
It's Tincture from the rosy nectar; wine
That can exalt weak EARTH; and so refine
Our dust, that at one draught, mortality   45
May drink it self up, and forget to dy.

29–46 Crashaw's fullest treatment of the theme of divine inebriation (see further, Williams, pp. 91–94) which stems from the Vulgate of Ps. 23: "calix meus inebrians, quam praeclarus est!" (My inebriating cup, how bright it is!). Yvor Winters (*In Defense of Reason,* [New York, 1947] pp. 131–33) draws a parallel between the rhythm and meter in religious passages and in contemporary tavern songs.

35 See the epigram "To our Lord, upon the Water made Wine."

37–38 *Let . . . bring:* a recollection of Song of Solomon 2:4: "Introduxit me in cellam vinariam, ordinavit in me charitatem" (He led me into the wine-cellar, he ordained in me love). St. Teresa has a full commentary on this text in *Conceptions of the Love of God,* VI (quoted in Williams, pp. 92–93): "His will is that [the soul] shall drink, and become inebriated with all the wines that are in the storehouse of God. Let her rejoice in those joys; . . . let her not fear to lose her life through drinking beyond the capacity of her weak nature; let her die in this paradise of delights."

40 *Him . . . alone:* a typological reference to Isaiah 63:3 of considerable richness, as Miss Tuve has shown (pp. 112–33); the text is the Epistle for Monday before Easter.

63   *The Flaming Heart.*

The title of this poem is generally thought to copy the title of Sir Toby
Mathew's English translation of the *Vida, The Flaming Hart or the Life of the
Glorious S. Teresa,* published in Antwerp in 1642; an earlier edition of this trans-
lation was published in London in 1623 though no copy is now known. "The
book and picture of the seraphicall saint" are certainly the *Vida* and the
portrait of the saint which usually accompanied it. It has been customary to
illustrate modern editions of Crashaw with a photograph of the Bernini statue of
St. Teresa in the ecstasy of transverberation (Santa Maria della Vittoria, Rome),
because it shares Crashaw's baroque exuberance fully; but it is most unlikely
that Crashaw ever saw that statue, and the saint was "usually expressed" in
the editions of her works as a rather dumpy nun, sensational in no way. Cra-
shaw's objections to the painter's technique may be understood by a glance at
the portraits of Teresa prefacing *Los Libros* (Salamanca, 1589), *Avisos Espiri-
tuales* (Barcelona, [1646]) here reproduced, or his own poems.

The poem is tripartite: lines 1–68 are facile "exercises" in contrasting the
Seraph and the Saint; in lines 69–84, "Crashaw's mood changes. He becomes
impassioned and eloquent as he contemplates the triumphant progress of Teresa"
(Warren, pp. 141–44); lines 85–108, the invocation to the Saint, by parallelism
and anaphora echo the Litany of the Book of Common Prayer (modern editions,
p. 55). (Surely it is remarkable that Crashaw should at the end of his life have
returned to English forms and Anglican ways to sustain this most Roman and
Counter Reformation ecstasy.) Praz (pp. 261–62): "in the ill-welded frag-
ment [lines 85–108] which stands by itself in its own halo of flame, without in-
timate connexion with what precedes, the intonation becomes very personal and
deeply felt . . . : the poet wants to tear himself from his own life, and his
yearning for ecstasy is so powerful and desperate that he almost seems to have
reached it. . . . In the whole course of seventeenth-century literature there is no
higher expression of that spiritualisation of sense which is condensed here in a
portentous, dizzy soaring of red-hot images."

The experience of the transverberation St. Teresa has vividly described:

It pleased our Blessed Lord, that I should haue sometimes, this follow-ing Vision. I saw an Angell very neer me, towards my left side, and he appeared to me, in a Corporeall forme; . . . He was not great; but rather little; yet withall, he was of very much beautie. His face was so inflamed, that he appeared to be of those most Superiour Angells, who seem to be, all in a fire; and he well might be of them, whome we call *Seraphins;* . . . I saw, that he had a long Dart of gold in his hand; and at the end of the iron below, me thought, there was a little fire; and I conceaued, that he thrust it, some seuerall times, through my verie Hart, after such a manner, as that it passed the verie inwards, of my Bowells; and when he drew it back, me thought, it carried away, as much, as it had touched within me; and left all that, which remained, wholy inflamed with a great loue of Almightye God. The paine of it, was so excessiue, that it forced me to utter those groanes; and the suauitie, which that extremitie of paine gaue, was also so very excessiue, that there was no desiring at all, to be ridd of it; nor can the Soule then, receaue anie contentment at all, in lesse, then God Almightie himself. (*The Flaming Hart* [1642], Chap. XXIX.)

THE

FLAMING HEART

UPON THE BOOK AND

Picture of the seraphicall saint

TERESA,

(AS SHE IS USUALLY EX-

pressed with a SERAPHIM

biside her.)

Well meaning readers! you that come as freinds
And catch the pretious name this peice pretends;
Make not too much hast to'admire
That fair-cheek't fallacy of fire.
That is a SERAPHIM, they say   5
And this the great TERESIA.
Readers, be rul'd by me; and make
Here a well-plac't and wise mistake,
You must transpose the picture quite,
And spell it wrong to read it right;   10
Read HIM for her, and her for him;
And call the SAINT the SERAPHIM.

The Flaming Heart. 52 (48).*
  2 *pretends:* holds forth (the Latin meaning).
  8 *wise mistake:* see *Epiphanie Hymne,* line 2.

Painter, what didst thou understand
To put her dart into his hand!
See, even the yeares and size of him   15
Showes this the mother SERAPHIM.
This is the mistresse flame; and duteous he
Her happy fire-works, here, comes down to see.
O most poor-spirited of men!
Had thy cold Pencil kist her PEN   20
Thou couldst not so unkindly err
To show us This faint shade for HER.
Why man, this speakes pure mortall frame;
And mockes with female FROST love's manly flame.
One would suspect thou meant'st to paint   25
Some weak, inferiour, woman saint.
But had thy pale-fac't purple took
Fire from the burning cheeks of that bright Booke
Thou wouldst on her have heap't up all
That could be found SERAPHICALL;   30
What e're this youth of fire weares fair,
Rosy fingers, radiant hair,
Glowing cheekes, and glistering wings,
All those fair and flagrant things,
But before all, that fiery DART   35
Had fill'd the Hand of this great HEART.
     Doe then as equall right requires,
Since HIS the blushes be, and her's the fires,
Resume and rectify thy rude design;
Undresse thy Seraphim into MINE.   40
Redeem this injury of thy art;
Give HIM the vail, give her the dart.
     Give Him the vail; that he may cover
The Red cheeks of a rivall'd lover.
Asham'd that our world, now, can show   45
Nests of new Seraphims here below.
     Give her the DART for it is she
(Fair youth) shootes both thy shaft and THEE
Say, all ye wise and well-peirc't hearts
That live and dy amidst her darts,   50
What is't your tastfull spirits doe prove

15 *size:* "rather little" as Teresa described him.
26 An accurate description of the usual engravings, not of Bernini.
28 *cheeks:* i.e. pages (see line 77).
42 *vail:* of the nun.
48 *shootes . . . Thee:* i.e. as if he were the shaft, not the target (see line 54).

In that rare life of Her, and love?
Say and bear wittnes. Sends she not
A SERAPHIM at every shott?
What magazins of immortall ARMES there shine!   55
Heavn's great artillery in each love-spun line.
Give then the dart to her who gives the flame;
Give him the veil, who kindly takes the shame.
    But if it be the frequent fate
Of worst faults to be fortunate;   60
If all's præscription; and proud wrong
Hearkens not to an humble song;
For all the gallantry of him,
Give me the suffring SERAPHIM.
His be the bravery of all those Bright things,   65
The glowing cheekes, the glistering wings;
The Rosy hand, the radiant DART;
Leave HER alone THE FLAMING HEART.
    Leave her that; and thou shalt leave her
Not one loose shaft but love's whole quiver.   70
For in love's feild was never found
A nobler weapon than a WOUND.
Love's passives are his activ'st part.
The wounded is the wounding heart.
O HEART! the æquall poise of love's both parts   75
Bigge alike with wounds and darts.
Live in these conquering leaves; live all the same;
And walk through all tongues one triumphant FLAME.
Live here, great HEART; and love and dy and kill;
And bleed and wound; and yeild and conquer still.   80
Let this immortall life wherere it comes
Walk in a crowd of loves and MARTYRDOMES.
Let mystick DEATHS wait on't; and wise soules be
The love-slain wittnesses of this life of thee.
O sweet incendiary! shew here thy art,   85
Upon this carcasse of a hard, cold, hart,
Let all thy scatter'd shafts of light, that play
Among the leaves of thy larg Books of day,
Combin'd against this BREST at once break in
And take away from me my self and sin,   90
This gratious Robbery shall thy bounty be;

61 *præscription:* right acquired through long possession.
   70 *quiver:* see the epigrams, "In Cicatrices Domini," No. 50, and "Stabat Mater," viii,
No. 78.

And my best fortunes such fair spoiles of me.
O thou undanted daughter of desires!
By all thy dowr of LIGHTS and FIRES;
By all the eagle in thee, all the dove;   95
By all thy lives and deaths of love;
By thy larg draughts of intellectuall day,
And by thy thirsts of love more large then they;
By all thy brim-fill'd Bowles of feirce desire
By thy last Morning's draught of liquid fire;   100
By the full kingdome of that finall kisse
That seiz'd thy parting Soul, and seal'd thee his;
By all the heav'ns thou hast in him
(Fair sister of the SERAPHIM!)
By all of HIM we have in THEE;   105
Leave nothing of my SELF in me.
Let me so read thy life, that I
Unto all life of mine may dy.

64   A SONG.

LORD, when the sense of thy sweet grace
Sends up my soul to seek thy face.
Thy blessed eyes breed such desire,
I dy in love's delicious Fire.
    O love, I am thy SACRIFICE.   5
Be still triumphant, blessed eyes.
Still shine on me, fair suns! that I
Still may behold, though still I dy.

                Second part.
    Though still I dy, I live again;
Still longing so to be still slain,   10
So gainfull is such losse of breath,
I dy even in desire of death.
    Still live in me this loving strife
Of living DEATH and dying LIFE.
For while thou sweetly slayest me   15
Dead to my selfe, I live in Thee.

101 *that finall kisse:* see St. Teresa, *Conceptions of the Love of God,* I, III.
A Song. 52 (48).*
Perhaps inspired by St. Teresa's *Interior Castle,* VI, Mansions.

65   *To* [Mrs. M. R.] *Councel Concerning her Choise*

The title in 1648 and 1652 is "To the Same Party Councel concerning her Choise." In both editions the poem follows "Ode on a prayer booke *Sent to* Mrs. M. R." (Printed here in Section II, No. 75). The identity of the lady has not been discovered, but she has evidently been "crossed" in love (line 46). The poet acts in behalf of his Lord to urge her to marry Him (to retire to a convent?). The poem anticipates Crashaw's similar urgings of the Countess of Denbigh (*Letter*, No. 75). The metaphor of matrimony that sustains this poem lacks the specific erotic references that are found in "Ode on a prayer booke," but there are many similarities.

TO

[Mrs. M. R.]

COUNCEL

CONCERNING HER

CHOISE.

Dear, heavn-designed SOUL!
    Amongst the rest
Of suters that beseige your Maiden brest,
        Why may not I
        My fortune try   5
And venture to speak one good word
Not for my self alas, but for my dearer LORD?
You'ave seen allready, in this lower sphear
Of froth and bubbles, what to look for here.
Say, gentle soul, what can you find   10
        But painted shapes,
        Peacocks and Apes,
        Illustrious flyes,
Guilded dunghills, glorious LYES.
        Goodly surmises   15
        And deep disguises,
Oathes of water, words of wind?
TRUTH biddes me say, 'tis time you cease to trust
Your soul to any son of dust.

To [Mrs. M. R.] *Councel.* 52 (48).*
    8 *lower sphear:* the terrestrial sphere below the moon (sublunary) marked by transience and decay; spheres above the moon were immutable.
    14–25 *dunghills, water, wind, fire:* the four elements, the three lowest of which provide "froth and bubbles" (line 9) and "dust" (line 19); only fire is pure enough for the upper spheres (line 25).

'Tis time you listen to a braver love,   20
       Which from above
       Calls you up higher
       And biddes you come
       And choose your roome
Among his own fair sonnes of fire,   25
       Where you among
       The golden throng
That watches at his palace doores
       May passe along
And follow those fair starres of yours;   30
Starrs much too fair and pure to wait upon
The false smiles of a sublunary sun.
Sweet, let me prophesy that at last t'will prove
       Your wary love
Layes up his purer and more pretious vowes,   35
And meanes them for a farre more worthy SPOUSE
Then this world of Lyes can give ye,
'Evn for Him with whom nor cost,
Nor love, nor labour can be lost;
Him who never will deceive ye.   40
Let not my lord, the Mighty lover
Of soules, disdain that I discover
       The hidden art
Of his high stratagem to win your heart;
       It was his heavnly art   45
       Kindly to crosse you
       In your mistaken love,
       That, at the next remove
       Thence he might tosse you
       And strike your troubled heart   50
Home to himself; to hide it in his brest
       The bright ambrosiall nest,
Of love, of life, and everlasting rest.
       Happy Mystake!
       That thus shall wake   55
Your wise soul, never to be wonne
Now with a love below the sun.
Your first choyce failes, o when you choose agen
May it not be amongst the sonnes of Men.

33 *t'will prove:* it will be proven that.
49–50 a metaphor from tennis.
54 *Happy Mystake:* see "The Flaming Heart," line 8.

66   *On Mr. G.* Herberts *booke, The Temple.*

The 'booke' was Herbert's *Temple: Sacred Poems and Private Ejaculations* (Cambridge, 1633). After Herbert's death in 1633, *The Temple* was seen through the press by Nicholas Ferrar, Herbert's close friend. It would certainly have been recommended to Crashaw by Ferrar soon after they also became close friends in 1634 (Martin, p. xxiv), in the unlikely event that Crashaw had not discovered it himself. It is generally agreed that the title of Crashaw's first English collection, *Steps to the Temple,* reveals his admiration of Herbert as well as his own fitting modesty. (The title may, of course, be the work of the editor of that collection; see "Preface" to 1646 in Appendix.) (Crashaw's poetic dependence on Herbert has been well noted by H. Swanston, "The Second 'Temple,'" *Durham University Journal,* LVI [1963], 14–22.) The identity of the Gentlewoman is not known.

On Mr. G. Herberts *booke intitu-*
led the Temple of Sacred Po-
ems, sent to a Gentle-
woman.

Know you faire, on what you looke?
Divinest love lyes in this booke:
Expecting fire from your eyes,
To kindle this his sacrifice.
When your hands unty these strings,   5
Thinke you have an Angell by th' wings.
One that gladly will bee nigh,
To wait upon each morning sigh.
To flutter in the balmy aire,
Of your well perfumed prayer.   10
These white plumes of his heele lend you,
Which every day to heaven will send you:
To take acquaintance of the spheare,
And all the smooth faced kindred there.

   And though *Herberts* name doe owe   15
   These devotions, fairest; know
   That while I lay them on the shrine
   Of your white hand, they are mine.

On Mr. G. Herberts booke. 46 (48).*
   4 *sacrifice:* the first poem in the section of *The Temple* named "The Church" is "The Altar"; the second is "The Sacrifice," a long poem dealing with Christ's sacrifice and passion.
   5 *strings:* the ribbons used to tie together the covers of the book in order to close the book (see G. W. Williams, "Crashaw and the Little Gidding Bookbinders," *N&Q,* CCI [1956], 9–10).
   11 *plumes:* i.e. the Angel's wings, the leaves of the book.
   15 *owe:* own.

67   *Upon the ensuing Treatises* [*of Mr.* Shelford]

This poem was first printed in Robert Shelford, *Five Pious and Learned Discourses* (Cambridge, 1635), and this version is the only one with manifest Crashavian authority. The truncation and (consequent?) change in title in 1646 are, I would suggest, editorial. The poem is not "On a Treatise of Charity," as titled in 1646 and 1648; it is rather on at least three of Shelford's five discourses: 1. A Sermon showing how we ought to behave our selves in God's house; 2. A Sermon preferring Holy Charity before Faith, Hope, and Knowledge; and 5. A Treatise showing the Antichrist not to be yet come. Many words and themes from the *Discourses* are repeated in the poem, particularly those from Sermon 1 concerning "Gods services," a subject in which Crashaw was intensely interested (see the Dedication to the *Epigrammata Sacra* and the "Description of a Religious House," No. 86).

Rise then, immortall maid! *Religion* rise!
Put on thy selfe in thine own looks: t' our eyes
Be what thy beauties, not our blots, have made thee,
Such as (ere our dark sinnes to dust betrayd thee)
Heav'n set thee down new drest; when thy bright birth   5
Shot thee like lightning, to th'astonisht earth.
From th' dawn of thy faire eyelids wipe away
Dull mists and melancholy clouds: take day
And thine owne beams about thee: bring the best
Of whatsoe're perfum'd thy *Eastern nest.*   10
Girt all thy glories to thee: then sit down,
Open this booke, faire Queen, *and take thy crown.*
These learned leaves shall vindicate to thee
Thy holyest, humblest, handmaid Charitie.
She'l dresse thee like thy self, set thee on high   15
Where thou shalt reach all hearts, command each eye.
Lo where I see thy Altars wake, and rise
From the pale dust of that strange sacrifice
Which they themselves were; each one putting on
A majestie that may beseem thy throne.   20
The holy youth of heav'n, whose golden rings
Girt round thy awfull Altars, with bright wings
Fanning thy fair locks (which the world beleeves
As much as sees) shall with these sacred leaves
Trick their tall plumes, and in that garb shall go   25
If not more glorious, more conspicuous tho.
　　　　　　　——Be it enacted then

Upon the ensuing Treatises [*of Mr. Shelford*] 1635. (46, 48).*
　　24, 25 *Leaves, plumes:* pages of the book, as in the preceding poem.

By the fair laws of thy firm-pointed pen,
Gods services no longer shall put on
A *sluttishnesse*, for *pure religion*:   30
No longer shall our Churches frighted stones
Lie scatter'd like the burnt and martyr'd bones
Of dead Devotion; nor faint marbles weep
In their sad ruines; nor Religion keep
A melancholy mansion in those cold   35
Urns. Like Gods Sanctuaries they lookt of old:
Now seem they Temples consecrate to *none*,
Or to a *new* God *Desolation*.
No more the hypocrite shall th'*upright* be
Because he's stiffe, and will confesse no knee: 40
While others bend their knee, no more shalt thou
(Disdainfull dust and ashes) bend thy brow;
Nor on Gods Altar cast *two scorching eyes*
Bak't in hot scorn, for *a burnt sacrifice*:
But (for a *Lambe*) thy tame and tender *heart*   45
New struck by love, still trembling on his dart;
Or (for two *Turtle doves*) it shall suffice
To bring a pair of meek and humble *eyes*.
This shall from hence-forth be the masculine theme
Pulpits and pennes shall sweat in; to redeem   50
Vertue to action, that life-feeding flame
That keeps Religion warme: not swell *a name*
Of faith, *a mountaine word*, made up of aire,
With those deare spoiles that wont to dresse the fair
And fruitfull Charities full breasts (of old)   55
Turning her out to tremble in the cold.
What can the poore hope from us, when we be
Uncharitable ev'n to *Charitie?*
Nor shall our zealous ones still have a fling
At that most horrible and horned thing,   60
Forsooth *the Pope*: by which black name they call
The Turk, the Devil, Furies, Hell and all,
And something more. O he is Antichrist:
Doubt this, and doubt (say they) that Christ is Christ.
Why, 'tis a point of Faith. What e're it be,   65
I'm sure it is no point of Charitie.
In summe, no longer shall our people hope,
To be a true Protestant, 's but to hate the Pope.

45, 47 *Lambe, Turtle doves:* traditional burnt offerings (Leviticus 5:6-7).

68   *On Hope*

First version 46 (48); second version 52.* See textual note.

This joint effort by Cowley and Crashaw was probably written when the poets were together at Cambridge; the system of alternating stanzas in 46, 48 may not be authorial. Cowley provided his own answering stanzas when he published his share of the joint poem in an edition of his own poems, *The Mistresse* (1647).

Abraham Cowley (1618–1647) published his first volume of poetry in 1633, his second in 1636, and his third in 1637. He went up to Trinity College, Cambridge, in 1637, and there continued his poetical activity. In 1643–44 he was ejected from Cambridge and retired to Oxford; he followed the Queen to Paris in 1646. He was thus in contact with Crashaw at Cambridge, possibly at Oxford, and in Paris. The association produced the slight piece "Upon two greene Apricockes sent to Cowley by Sir Crashaw," No. 365, praising Cowley's early 1633 volumes, the "brilliant controversy on *Hope*," and Cowley's splendid elegy on Crashaw (DNB; Martin, pp. xxxiii–xxxiv).

C. H. Miller ("The Order of Stanzas in Cowley and Crashaw's 'On Hope,'" *SP*, LXI [1964], 64–73) calls the dialogue "a striking and effective example of some dominant contrasts in seventeenth-century poetic themes and styles: in this poem the debate between the sacred and the profane is expressed in the conflict between Cowley's dry brilliant wit . . . and Crashaw's heady exuberant enthusiasm . . ." (p. 64). "Assuming the role of a worldly philosopher guided by 'Reasons light' . . . Cowley presents a logical argument in four closely interdependent steps. . . . Replying to these arguments as an enthusiastic Christian, . . . Crashaw transforms Cowley's human hope into the traditional theological virtue of hope" (pp. 69, 70). The "profane metaphors" of Cowley are "transformed into sacred symbols" (p. 73). "Because of this transformation Crashaw never meets Cowley's arguments . . . but rather transcends them" (p. 70).

On Hope,
By way of Question and Answer, betweene
A. Cowley, *and* R. Crashaw.

Cowley.

Hope, whose weake being ruin'd is
Alike, if it succeed, and if it misse.
Whom Ill, and Good doth equally confound,
And both the hornes of Fates dilemma wound.
     Vaine shadow! that doth vanish quite   5
     Both at full noone, and perfect night.
     The Fates have not a possibility
         Of blessing thee.
If things then from their ends wee happy call,
'Tis hope is the most hopelesse thing of all.   10

On Hope. 46(48, 52).*

Crashaw.

Deare Hope! Earths dowry, and Heavens debt,
The entity of things that are not yet.
Subt'lest, but surest being! Thou by whom
Our Nothing hath a definition.
    Faire cloud of fire, both shade, and light,   15
    Our life in death, our day in night.
Fates cannot find out a capacity
    Of hurting thee.
From thee their thinne dilemma with blunt horne
Shrinkes, like the sick Moone at the wholesome morne.   20

Cowley.

Hope, thou bold taster of delight,
Who, in stead of doing so, devour'st it quite
Thou bring'st us an estate, yet leav'st us poore,
By clogging it with Legacies before.
    The joyes, which wee intire should wed,   25
    Come deflour'd virgins to our bed.
Good fortunes without gaine imported bee,
    So mighty Custome's paid to thee.
For joy, like Wine kept close, doth better taste:
If it take ayre before, its spirits waste.   30

Crashaw.

Thou art Loves Legacie under lock
Of Faith: the steward of our growing stocke.
Our Crown-lands lye above, yet each meale brings
A seemly portion for the Sons of Kings.
    Nor will the Virgin-joyes wee wed   35
    Come lesse unbroken to our bed,
    Because that from the bridall cheeke of Blisse,
       Thou thus steal'st downe a distant kisse,
Hopes chaste kisse wrongs no more joyes maidenhead,
Then Spousall rites prejudge the marriage-bed.   40

12 the definition echoes Hebrews 11:1.
15 an echo of Exodus 13:21–22, the hope of the Israelites by which they were led through the wilderness. The replacement of this typological reference in 52 (lines 5–6 of Crashaw's poem) by a less specific remark gains a closer connection with Cowley and loses a reference richly symbolic.
19–20 compare the "Epiphanie Hymne," No. 56, lines 93–99.
27–28 i.e. the duty paid at Customs is so high that there is no profit left in selling the merchandise.
33 *Crown-lands:* the property of the Crown.

Crashaw.

Faire *Hope!* our earlier Heaven! by thee
Young *Time* is taster to Eternity.
Thy generous wine with age growes strong, not sower;
Nor need wee kill thy fruit to smell thy flower.
    Thy golden head never hangs downe,   45
    Till in the lap of Loves full noone
    It falls, and dyes: oh no, it melts away
      As doth the dawne into the day:
As lumpes of Sugar lose themselves, and twine
Their subtile essence with the soule of Wine.   50

Cowley.

Hope, Fortunes cheating Lotterie,
Where for one prize an hundred blankes there bee.
Fond Archer Hope, who tak'st thine ayme so farre,
That still, or short, or wide thine arrowes are.
    Thinne empty cloud, which th'eye deceives   55
    With shapes that our owne fancie gives:
    A cloud, which gilt, and painted now appeares,
      But must drop presently in teares.
When thy false beames o're Reasons light prevaile,
By *ignes fatui,* not North starres we sayle.   60

Crashaw.

Fortune? alas above the worlds low warres
Hope kicks the curl'd heads of conspiring starres.
Her keele cuts not the waves, where our winds stirre,
And *Fates* whole Lottery is one blanke to her.
    Her shafts, and shee fly farre above,   65
    And forrage in the fields of light, and love.
    Sweet *Hope!* kind cheat! faire fallacy! by thee
      Wee are not where, or what wee bee,
But what, and where wee would bee: thus art thou
Our absent presence, and our future now.   70

60 *ignes fatui:* false fires.
62 *conspiring starres:* stars in conjunction boding ill for men.

Cowley.

Brother of Feare! more gaily clad
The merrier Foole o'th' two, yet quite as mad.
Sire of Repentance! Child of fond desire,
That blows the Chymicks, and the Lovers fire,
Still leading them insensibly on,   75
With the strange witchcraft of *Anon*.
By thee the one doth changing Nature through
    Her endlesse Laborinths pursue,
And th'other chases woman, while she goes
More wayes, and turnes, then hunted Nature knowes.   80

Crashaw.

Faith's Sister! Nurse of faire desire!
Feares Antidote! a wise, and well stay'd fire
Temper'd 'twixt cold despaire, and torrid joy:
Queen Regent in young Loves minoritie.
    Though the vext Chymick vainly chases   85
    His fugitive gold through all her faces,
      And loves more fierce, more fruitlesse fires assay
      One face more fugitive then all they,
True *Hope's* a glorious Huntresse, and her chase
The God of Nature in the field of Grace.   90

69   *Upon the Powder Day.*

As the Latin epigram is included among the Sacred Epigrams, I have placed this English distich among the Sacred Poems; see other poems on this subject among the Secular Poems. The distich was removed from *Steps to the Temple* in 1646 to *The Delights of the Muses* in 1648. It celebrates the attempt by Guy Fawkes to explode the Houses of Parliament in 1605. The day is kept as almost a holy day in England.

How fit our well-rank'd Feasts doe follow,
All mischiefe comes after *All Hallow*.

71 *gaily clad:* i.e. in fool's parti-colored dress.
73 *fond:* foolish.
74, 85 *Chymick:* chemist; the reference is to the vain pursuit of gold in the laboratory, attempting by some as yet undiscovered method to convert inferior metals into gold.
Upon the Powder Day. 46. See "In die Conjurationis," No. 336.
   2 *All mischiefe:* i.e. Guy Fawkes Day, November 5. *All Hallow:* All Saints' Day, November 1.

II

Sacred Poems
in two English Versions

In this section, the poems are arranged with the
early version on the left-hand page and the
late version on the right-hand page.

First version 46; second version 52 (48).

The first of the Christmas-tide hymns, the "Nativity Hymn" is followed thematically and imagistically by the "Circumcision Hymn" ("New Year's Day") and by the "Epiphany Hymn" (Nos. 56, 57). The three Hymns should be considered as parts of a whole (see notes to the "Epiphany Hymn"). See also epigrams on the events of Christmas, one of which "In natales Domini Pastoribus nuntiatos," No. 100, would seem to have served as a "source" for the "Nativity Hymn," as it contains the name, Tityrus, and the shepherd-lamb conceit. The text of the poem is Luke 2:15–20; the "Hymn" is, in effect, the song of joy sung as "the shepherds returned, glorifying and praising God for all the things that they had heard and seen." Williams (pp. 51–56) has examined the poem in terms of its imagery of red and white which he sees as relevant to the coming of the dawn of a new day and the spring of a new year. Martz (pp. 165–67) draws the contrast between Crashaw's poem and Milton's "Nativity Ode," finding the former "a ritual love-song," the latter "a hymn in praise of the Power and Glory." Esch (pp. 117–23) suggests that the changes producing the second version are a milestone in Crashaw's poetic development. The fullest study of the two versions is that of Kerby Neill, "Structure and Symbol in Crashaw's *Hymn in the Nativity*," *PMLA*, LXIII (1948), 101–13.

Neill writes (pp. 101, 112–13) that in the two versions "Crashaw shows a growing sense of form, and the final version . . . has a conceptual unity that raises it to a level of poetry considerably above that of the 1646 version. He achieved this by substituting structural symbols for mere sense images, by emending a few lines, by dropping one stanza, and by adding two very important new stanzas that make the structural pattern of the poem much clearer. These changes had a considerable effect on the rest of the poem because they placed it in a new context. Miss Wallerstein [pp. 52, 10], who notes the 'steady pruning of the purely sensuous elements,' and who calls these additional stanzas 'the great stanzas which transmute the whole,' describes the final version of the poem as one of Crashaw's 'few perfectly realized poems.' . . . The first version apparently sets out to praise the Virgin and her Son. She is introduced at once . . . and . . . the conventional . . . praise of a lady is applied to her. . . . In the later versions [1648/52] the poem sets out to praise the Christ Child and *through Him* His mother. At once the poem becomes theological and the imagery symbolic . . . the shepherds have beheld the physical phenomena of the Nativity and penetrated to some of the inner mystery behind it."

IN THE HOLY NATIVITY OF OUR LORD GOD
A HYMN SUNG AS BY THE SHEPHEARDS.

Ton Createur te faict voir sa naissance,
Daignant souffrir pour toy des son enfance.

A Hymne of the Nativity, sung by
the Shepheards.

Chorus. Come wee Shepheards who have seene
   Dayes King deposed by Nights Queene.
  Come lift we up our lofty song,
   To wake the Sun that sleeps too long.

  Hee in this our generall joy,   5
   Slept, and dreampt of no such thing
  While we found out the fair-ey'd Boy,
   And kist the Cradle of our King;
  Tell him hee rises now too late,
  To shew us ought worth looking at.   10

  Tell him wee now can shew him more
   Then hee e're shewd to mortall sight,
  Then hee himselfe e're saw before,
   Which to be seene needs not his light:
  Tell him *Tityrus* where th'hast been,   15
  Tell him *Thyrsis* what th'hast seen.

Tityrus. Gloomy Night embrac't the place
   Where the noble Infant lay:
  The Babe lookt up, and shew'd his face,
   In spight of Darknesse it was Day.   20
  It was thy Day, Sweet, and did rise,
  Not from the East, but from thy eyes.

Thyrsis. Winter chid the world, and sent
   The angry North to wage his warres:
  The North forgot his fierce intent,
   And left perfumes, in stead of scarres: 25
  By those sweet Eyes persuasive Powers,
  Where he meant frosts, he scattered Flowers.

---

2 (46) *Nights Queene:* the Virgin, but it might also be the Moon.

THE

HYMN.

Chorus. Come we shepheards whose blest Sight
    Hath mett love's Noon in Nature's night;
      Come lift we up our loftyer Song
And wake the Sun that lyes too long.

To all our world of well-stoln joy   5
    He slept; and dream't of no such thing.
While we found out Heavn's fairer ey
    And Kis't the Cradle of our King.
Tell him He rises now, too late
To show us ought worth looking at.   10

Tell him we now can show Him more
    Then He e're show'd to mortall Sight;
Then he Himselfe e're saw before;
    Which to be seen needes not His light.
Tell him, Tityrus, where th'hast been   15
Tell him, Thyrsis, what th'hast seen.

Tityrus. Gloomy night embrac't the Place
    Where The Noble Infant lay.
The Babe look't up and shew'd his Face;
    In spite of Darknes, it was Day.   20
It was Thy day, Sweet! and did rise
Not from the East, but from thine Eyes.

      Chorus It was Thy day, Sweet

Thyrs. Winter chidde aloud; and sent
    The angry North to wage his warres.   25
The North forgott his feirce Intent;
    And left perfumes in stead of scarres.
By those sweet eyes' persuasive powrs
Where he mean't frost, he scatter'd flowrs.

      Chorus By those sweet eyes'   30

---

29 *flowrs:* the stable is decked with roses in "In stabulum," No. 99.

Both. We saw thee in thy Balmy Nest,
    Bright Dawne of our *Eternall Day;*   30
Wee saw thine Eyes break from the East,
    And chase the trembling shades away:
Wee saw thee (and wee blest the sight)
Wee saw thee by thine owne sweet Light.

Tityrus. I saw the curl'd drops, soft and slow   35
    Come hovering o're the places head,
Offring their whitest sheets of snow,
    To furnish the faire Infants Bed.
Forbeare (said I) be not too bold,
Your fleece is white, but 'tis too cold.   40

Thyrsis. I saw th'officious Angels bring,
    The downe that their soft brests did strow,
For well they now can spare their wings,

Both. We saw thee in thy baulmy Nest,
    Young dawn of our æternall DAY!
We saw thine eyes break from their EASTE
    And chase the trembling shades away.
We saw thee; and we blest the sight   35
We saw thee by thine own sweet light.

Tity. Poor WORLD (said I.) what wilt thou doe
    To entertain this starry STRANGER?
Is this the best thou canst bestow?
    A cold, and not too cleanly, manger?   40
Contend, ye powres of heav'n and earth.
To fitt a bed for this huge birthe.

        Cho.   Contend ye powers

Thyr. Proud world, said I; cease your contest
    And let the MIGHTY BABE alone.   45
The Phænix builds the Phænix' nest.
    LOVE's architecture is his own.
The BABE whose birth embraves this morn,
Made his own bed e're he was born.

        Cho.   The BABE whose.   50

Tit. I saw the curl'd drops, soft and slow,
    Come hovering o're the place's head;
Offring their whitest sheets of snow
    To furnish the fair INFANT's bed
Forbear, said I; be not too bold.   55
Your fleece is white But t'is too cold.

        Cho.   Forbear, sayd I

Thyr. I saw the obsequious SERAPHIMS
    Their rosy fleece of fire bestow.
For well they now can spare their wings   60

---

31 *baulmy:* 1) because Eastern, 2) to contrast with the perfumes of natural flowers, 3) because the Phoenix' nest is made of scented twigs.

44–49 the stanza recalls and improves upon Southwell's "The Nativity of Christ," lines 1–2: "Behold the father is his daughter's sonne, / The bird that built the nest is hatchd therein." The Phoenix is a traditional symbol of Christ resurrected, as the bird is unique and rises to new life from its own funeral pyre.

When Heaven it selfe lyes here below.
Faire Youth (said I) be not too rough,   45
Thy Downe though soft's not soft enough.

Tityrus. The Babe no sooner 'gan to seeke,
        Where to lay his lovely head,
    But streight his eyes advis'd his Cheeke,
        'Twixt Mothers Brests to goe to bed.   50
    Sweet choise (said I) no way but so,
    Not to lye cold, yet sleepe in snow.

All. Welcome to our wondring sight
        Eternity shut in a span!
    Summer in Winter! Day in Night!   55
Chorus.   Heaven in Earth! and God in Man!
    Great litle one, whose glorious Birth,
    Lifts Earth to Heaven, stoops heaven to earth.

    Welcome, though not to Gold, nor Silke,
        To more then *Caesars* Birthright is.   60
    Two sister-Seas of virgins Milke,
        With many a rarely-temper'd kisse,
    That breathes at once both Maid and Mother,
    Warmes in the one, cooles in the other.

Since HEAVN itself lyes here below.
Well done, said I: but are you sure
Your down so warm, will passe for pure?

Cho.   Well done sayd I

Tit. No no. your KING's not yet to seeke   65
    Where to repose his Royall HEAD
See see, how soon his new-bloom'd CHEEK
    Twixt's mother's brests is gone to bed.
Sweet choise, said we! no way but so
Not to ly cold, yet sleep in snow.   70

Cho.   Sweet choise, said we.

Both. We saw thee in thy baulmy nest,
    Bright dawn of our æternall Day!
We saw thine eyes break from their EAST
    And chase the trembling shades away.   75
We saw thee: and we blest the sight.
We saw thee, by thine own sweet light.

Cho.   We saw thee, &c.

Full Chorus. Wellcome, all WONDERS in one sight!
    Æternity shutt in a span.   80
Sommer in Winter. Day in Night.
    Heaven in earth, and GOD in MAN.
Great little one! whose all-embracing birth
Lifts earth to heaven, stoopes heav'n to earth.

WELLCOME. Though nor to gold nor silk.   85
    To more than Cæsar's birthright is;
Two sister-seas of Virgin-Milk,
    With many a rarely-temper'd kisse
That breathes at once both MAID and MOTHER,
Warmes in the one, cooles in the other.   90

---

63 *down . . . pure:* the angels cannot be impure, of course, but the color of their
wings is so generally associated with the rosy red color of human sin by Crashaw, that he
fancies they may be (see "In nocturnum & hyemale iter," No. 110, lines 79–80).
    86 *Cæsar's birthright:* see "Give to Caesar, and to God," No. 32.

Shee sings thy Teares asleepe, and dips   65
    Her Kisses in thy weeping Eye,
Shee spreads the red leaves of thy Lips,
    That in their Buds yet blushing lye.
Shee 'gainst those Mother-Diamonds tryes
The points of her young Eagles Eyes.   70

Welcome, (though not to those gay flyes
    Guilded i'th' Beames of Earthly Kings
Slippery soules in smiling eyes)
    But to poore Shepheards, simple things,
That use no varnish, no oyl'd Arts,   75
But lift clean hands full of cleare hearts.

Yet when young *Aprils* husband showres,
    Shall blesse the fruitfull *Maia's* Bed,
Wee'l bring the first-borne of her flowers,
    To kisse thy feet, and crowne thy head.   80
To thee (Dread Lambe) whose Love must keepe
The Shepheards, while they feed their sheepe.

To thee meeke Majesty, soft King
    Of simple Graces, and sweet Loves,
Each of us his Lamb will bring,   85
    Each his payre of silver Doves.
At last, in fire of thy faire Eyes,
Wee'l burne, our owne best sacrifice.

65–70 Praz (p. 249): "Similes and conceits form in these few lines a monstrous cluster:
the viewpoint shifts with such speed that what we see is a throbbing and dazzling chaos in-
stead of a definite pattern." Neill (p. 111): the stanza "was not part of the *welcome,* and as
it did not relate closely to the central theme, it was dropped."
78 *Maia's Bed:* scil. the flower beds of May.

WELCOME, though not to those gay flyes.
　　Guilded ith' Beames of earthly kings;
Slippery soules in smiling eyes;
　　But to poor Shepheards, home-spun things:
Whose Wealth's their flock; whose witt, to be 95
　　Well read in their simplicity.

Yet when young April's husband showrs
　　Shall blesse the fruitfull Maja's bed
We'l bring the First-born of her flowrs
　　To kisse thy FEET and crown thy HEAD. 100
To thee, dread Lamb! whose love must keep
　　The shepheards, more then they the sheep.

To THEE, meek Majesty! soft KING
　　Of simple GRACES and sweet LOVES.
Each of us his lamb will bring 105
　　Each his pair of sylver Doves;
Till burnt at last in fire of Thy fair eyes,
　　Our selves become our own best SACRIFICE.

99–100　a crown of flowers, not thorns.
　105–8　Williams (p. 56): "The final quatrain suggests the fulfillment of the New Cove-
nant, replacing the old tradition of animal sacrifice with the revealed experience of human
and personal sacrifice; and the last couplet, through its paraphrase of the Prayer of Conse-
cration in the Holy Eucharist, includes all sinners, inviting them to participate in the Obla-
tion, to reject the silver doves and to burn in the red fire [of divine love] of Christ's eyes."

71   *Office of the Holy Crosse*

First version 48; second version 52.*

The ritual for each of the seven hours of the day is fully suggested (with abbreviations) in 52. In 48, however, only the hymns (in proper order) are given; these are followed at the end by "Christs victory," which in 52 is divided into three antiphons. The present edition utilizes the extra space provided by parallel texts to include the Latin and English originals of the Hymns regularly and the Versicle and Response and Prayer once from *The Prymer in Englishe and Latin* (1557) in this pattern:

Left-hand page	*Right-hand page 52*
[*Prymer* versions of the hymn]	Versicle and Response
Hymn from 48	Hymn
	Antiphon
[*Prymer* versions for Matins only]	Versicle, Response, Prayer

The hours are followed by "The Recommendation" in both texts (preceded here by the *Prymer* versions on the left); then follow (in 48 only) a version of the "Prayer" and "Christs victory," i.e. the Antiphons of the Third, Sixth, and Ninth Hours. (For information on the *Prymer*, a collection of traditional prayers, psalms, and hymns written in English for private devotions of the laity, see William Maskell, "Dissertation on the Prymer," *Monumenta Ritualia Ecclesiae Anglicanae* (2nd ed.) [Oxford, 1882], III, i–lxvii.) The 48 version is a series of sacred poems on the canonical hours of the day; the 52 version would seem to have been designed for actual devotional use at those hours. The poem recalls in tone Herbert's "The Sacrifice."

Upon our B. Saviours Passion.

71 *Office of the Holy Crosse*

Tradidit semetipsum pro nobis oblationem, et hostiam Deo in odorem Suauitatis. ad Ephe.5

THE HOWRES
FOR THE HOUR OF MATINES.

The Versicle.

LORD, by thy Sweet and Saving SIGN,

The Responsory.

Defend us from our foes and Thine.

Ad matutinas de cruce.	Matins of the crosse.
Patris sapientia veritas diuina. Deus homo captus est hora matutina. A notis disci- pulis cito derelictus. Ac Iudeis vēditus tradictus afflictus.	He that is yᵉ great profoūd sapiēce. And diuine truth of yᵉ father on hie Which for mākind of his beneuolēce, Him self hath made both god & mā ioyntly. was sold & bought by yᵉ Jewes traiterously, And about midnight perturbed And taken. and of hys disciples anone forsaken.

1.

The wakefull dawning hast's to sing
The unknowne sorrowes of our King.
The Fathers Word, and Wisedome, made
Man, for Man, by Man's betray'd;
The World's Price set to sale, and by the bold
Merchants of Death and Sin, is bought and sold;
Of his best friends (yea of himselfe) forsaken,
By his worst foes (because he would) betrayd and taken.

Versus.	The versicle.
Adoramus te christe et benedicimus tibi.	We worship thee Christe with praise & benediction.
Responsorium.	**The answere.**
Quia p[er] sanctā crucē tuā redemisti mūdū.	For thou redeemedste the worlde from all affliction.

V. Thou shalt open my lippes, O LORD.
R. And my mouth shall shew forth thy Prayse.
V. O GOD make speed to save me.
R. O LORD make hast to help me.
GLORY be to the FATHER,
  and to the SON,
  and to the H. GHOST.
  As it was in the beginning, is now, and ever shall be, world without end. Amen.

THE HYMN.

The wakefull Matines hast to sing
The unknown sorrows of our king,
The FATHER's word and wisdom, made
MAN, for man, by man's betraid;
The world's price sett to sale, and by the bold
Merchants of Death and sin, is bought and sold.
Of his Best Freinds (yea of himself) forsaken,
By his worst foes (because he would) beseig'd and taken.

The Antiphona.

All hail, fair TREE
Whose Fruit we be.
What song shall raise
Thy seemly praise.
Who broughtst to light
Life out of death, Day out of night.

The Versicle.

Lo, we adore thee,
Dread LAMB! And bow thus low before thee,

The Responsor.

'Cause, by the covenant of thy CROSSE,
Thou'hast sav'd at once the whole world's losse.

Matines; The Hymn: Matthew 26:47–56.

Oremus.

Domine Iesu christe fili
dei, viui pone passionē,
crucē, et mortē tuā inter
iudiciū tuū et aīas nostras nūc
et in hora mortis nostre:
& largiri digneris
viuis mīam et gratiā, defunctis
veniam et requiē, ecclesie tue
sancte pacem et concordiā: et nobis
pecca-torib⁹ vitam & gloriā
sēpiternā. Qui viuis et regnas cui
deo patre in vnitate, per oīa
secula seculorum. . . . Amē.

Let us pray.

Lord Jesu Christe sōne of the
liuinge God, set thy holi passion,
crosse, and death betwene thy
iudgement and our soules, both
nowe and at the houre of deathe.
And more ouer vouchsafe to
graunte unto the liuing, mercy &
grace, to the dead pardon & reast,
to thy holy church peace & con-
cord, and to us pore sinners life &
ioy euerlasting: whiche liuest and
raignest with god the father in the
unitie of the holy gost, god world
without end. Amen.

Ad primam de
cruce.

Hora prima ductus est
Iesus ad Pilatum. Falsis
testimoniis multum accusatum.
In collo percutiunt manibus
ligatum. Vultum dei
cōspuūt lumen celi gratum.

The first hour of yᵉ crosse.

The fyrst houre in the morning
earely, Unto their iudge called
Pilate, the Jewes: Jesus with his
handes boūden they carie, Where
many a false wytnes dyd him
accuse. In the necke they him
smyte, hys body they bruse. They
spit and defiled ther hys godly face,
The light of heauē, repleate wᵗ al
grace.

2.

The early Morne blushes to say
It could not rise so soone as they,
Call'd *Pilat* up; to trie if he
Could lend them any crueltie.
Their hands with lashes arm'd, their tongues with lyes,
And loathsome spittle blotts those beauteous eyes,
The blisseful springs of joy, from whose al-chearing ray
The fair stars fill their wakefull fires, the Sun himselfe
(drinkes day.

The Prayer.

O Lord JESU-CHRIST, son of the living GOD! interpose, I
pray thee, thine own pretious death, thy CROSSE and Passion,
betwixt my soul and thy judgment, now and in the hour of my death.
And vouchsafe to graunt unto me thy grace and mercy; unto all
quick and dead, remission and rest; to thy church peace and concord;
to us sinners life and glory everlasting. Who livest and reignest
with the FATHER, in the unity of the HOLY GHOST, one GOD, world
without end. Amen.

FOR THE HOUR OF
PRIME.

The Versicle.

Lord by thy sweet and saving SIGN.

The Responsor.

Defend us from our foes and thine.

V. Thou shalt open.
R. And my mouth.
V. O GOD make speed.
R. O LORD make hast.
Glory be to.
As it was in.

THE HYMN.

The early PRIME blushes to say
She could not rise so soon, as they
Call'd Pilat up; to try if He
Could lend them any cruelty.
    Their hands with lashes arm'd, their toungs with lyes,
And loathsom spittle, blott those beauteous eyes,
The blissfull springs of joy; from whose all-chearing Ray
The fair starrs fill their wakefull fires the sun himselfe drinks Day.

Prime; The Hymn: Matthew 27:2, 11–14; 26:67–68.

Ad tertiam de cruce.

Crucifige clamitant hora
tertiarum. Illusus
induitur veste purpurarum.
Caput eius pungitur
corona spinarū. Crucem
portat humeris ad locum
penarum.

The thyrde houre of the crosse.

About three houres after the sōne
gan sprīg, Al the Jewes cried Jesus
to crucifi. And in scorn thei hī
clothed w^t purple clothīg And in
steade of a crowne on his head they
did tie. A crown of thorn that
prycked cruelly. And lad hym forth
to the place where he died. With a
great houdg crosse on his shulders
laid.

The Antiphona.
Victorious SIGN
That now dost shine,
Transcrib'd above
Into the land of light and love;
O let us twine
Our rootes with thine,
That we may rise
Upon thy wings, and reach the skyes.

The Versicle.
Lo we adore thee
Dread LAMB! and fall
Thus low before thee

The Responsor.
'Cause by the Convenant of thy CROSSE
Thou'hast sav'd at once the whole world's losse.

The Prayer.
O Lord JESU-CHRIST son of the living GOD! interpose,
I pray thee, thine own pretious death, thy CROSSE and
Passion, betwixt my soul and thy judgment, now and in the
hour of my death. And vouchsafe to graunt unto me thy
grace and mercy; unto all quick and dead, remission and rest; to
thy church peace and concord; to us sinners life and glory
everlasting. Who livest and reignest with the FATHER, in the
unity of the HOLY GHOST, one GOD, world without end.
Amen.

THE THIRD.

The Versicle.
Lord, by thy sweet and saving SIGN

The Responsor.
Defend us from our foes and thine.
V. Thou shalt open.
R. And my mouth.
V. O GOD make speed.
R. O LORD make hast.
V. Glory be to.
R. As it was in the.

Antiphona: Sign: i.e. the Cross, here imaged first as a tree and then as winged.

3.

The third hour's deafn'd with the cry
Of Crucify him, Crucify.
So goes the Vote (nor aske them why?)
Live *Barrabas* and let God dye.
But ther's wit in wrath, and they will try,
A Haile more cruell then their Crucify,
For while in sport he weares a spitefull Crown,
The serious showers a long his decent face run sadly down.

[*For the Antiphon, see first stanza of "Christs victory" below*]

THE HYMN

The Third hour's deafen'd with the cry
Of crucify him, crucify.
So goes the vote (nor ask them, Why?)
Live Barabbas! and let GOD dy.
But there is witt in wrath, and they will try
A HAIL more cruell then their crucify.
For while in sport he weares a spitefull crown,
The serious showres along his decent
    Face run sadly down.

The Antiphona.

CHRIST when he dy'd
Deceivd the CROSSE;
And on death's side
Threw all the losse.
The captive world awak't, and found
The prisoners loose, the Jaylor bound.

The Versicle.

Lo we adore thee
Dread LAMB, and fall
    thus low before thee

The Responsor.

'Cause by the convenant of thy CROSSE
Thou'hast sav'd at once the whole world's losse.

The Prayer.

O Lord JESU-CHRIST, son of the living GOD! interpose,
I pray thee, thine own pretious death, thy CROSSE
and Passion, betwixt my soul and thy judgment, now and in the
hour of my death. And vouchsafe to graunt unto me thy
grace and mercy; unto all quick and dead, remission and rest;
to thy church peace and concord; to us sinners life and glory
everlasting. Who livest and reignest with the FATHER, in the
unity of the HOLY GHOST, one GOD, world without end.
Amen.

Third; The Hymn: Matthew 27:15–30.

Ad sextā de cruce.	The syxt houre of yᵉ crosse.
Hora sexta Iesus est cruci conclauatus. Atq; cum latronibus pendens deputatus. Pre tormentis sitiens felle saturatus Agnus crimen diluit sic ludificatus.	The sixt hour springing before yᵉ midday, Jesu hand & foote to the cros thei nailed: With yᵉ shamefullest deth yᵗ they cōtrive mai And in despite betwene .ij. theeves him hanged. And for very paine whē that he thursted, His thurst for to quench, they profered hym gal, This lābe thus illuded bought our sīs al.

4.

Now is the Noone of sorrows Night,
High in his patience as their spight,
For the faint lambe, with weary limb,
Beares that huge tree which must beare him;
That fatall plant, so great of fame,
The fruit of sorrow and of shame,
Shall swell with both for him; and mix
All woes into one Crucifix.
Is tortur'd thirst it self too sweet a Cup?
Gall, and more bitter Mocks, shall make it up.
Are nailes blunt Pens of superficiall smart?
Contempt and scorn can send sure wounds to search the inmost heart.

[For the Antiphon, see second stanza of "Christs victory" below]

THE SIXT.

The Versicle.

Lord by thy sweet and saving SIGN,

The Responsor.

Defend us from our foes and thine.

V. Thou shalt open.
R. And my mouth.
V. O GOD make speed.
R. O LORD make hast.
V. Glory be
R. As it was in

THE HIMN.

Now is The noon of sorrow's night;
High in his patience, as their spite,
Lo the faint LAMB, with weary limb
Beares that huge tree which must bear Him.
That fatall plant, so great of fame
For fruit of sorrow and of shame,
Shall swell with both for HIM; and mix
All woes into one CRUCIFIX.
Is tortur'd Thirst, it selfe, too sweet a cup?
GALL, and more bitter mocks, shall make it up.
Are NAILES blunt pens of superficiall smart?
Contempt and scorn can send sure wounds to search the inmost Heart.

The Antiphona.

O deare and sweet Dispute
'Twixt death's and Love's farr different FRUIT!
Different as farr
As antidotes and poysons are.
By that first fatall TREE
Both life and liberty
Were sold and slain;
By this they both look up, and live again.

Sixt; The Himn: Matthew 27:31–44; John 19:16–17.
 2 *patience:* i.e. suffering (the Latin meaning).
 4 *Beares:* only John records that Christ bore the cross.
 10 *Gall:* the typological significance is rich: Christ fed His people with manna; they gave Him in return gall (Tuve, pp. 38–39).
 11 *Nailes:* imaged as writing implements; see "On the still surviving markes," No. 51.
Antiphona
 5 *first fatall Tree:* the Tree of Knowledge of good and evil in Eden; see Tuve, pp. 81–86.

Ad nonam de
cruce.

Hora nona dominus
Iesus expirauit.
Heli clamans spiritum
patri commendauit.
Latus eius lancea miles
perforauit. Terra
tūc contremuit et sol
obscurauit.

The ninth houre of yᵉ cros

Our merciful Lord Jesu Gods sōne,
Calling unto his father almighty:
Yelded his soule. And full upon
noone, The spyrit departed yᵉ
blessed body. The sunne waxed
dark thearth quoke wonderslye.
Great merueilous thinges to behold
and heare, And yet a knyght persed
hys hearte with a speare.

5.

The ninth with awful horror hearkened to those groans
Which taught attention even to rocks and stones.
Heare Father heare! thy Lamb at last complaines,
Of some more painefull thing than all his paines,
Then bowes his all obedient head, and dyes
His owne Love's and our great sins sacrifice.
The Sun saw that, And would have seen no more;
The center shooke; Her uselesse veile, th' inglorious Temple tore.

The Versicle.

Lo we adore thee
Dread LAMB! and bow thus low before thee;

The Responsor.

'Cause by the convenant of thy CROSSE.
Thou'hast sav'd the world from certain losse.

The Prayer.

O Lord JESU-CHRIST, son of the living GOD! interpose,
I pray thee, thine own pretious death, thy CROSSE and
Passion, betwixt my soul and thy judgment, now and in the
hour of my death. And vouchsafe to graunt unto me thy
grace and mercy; unto all quick and dead, remission and rest; to
thy church peace and concord; to us sinners life and glory ever-
lasting. Who livest and reignest with the FATHER, in the
unity of the HOLY GHOST, one GOD, world without end.
Amen.

THE NINTH.

The Versicle.

Lord by thy sweet and saving SIGN.

The Responsor.

Defend us from our foes and thine.
V.   Thou shalt open.
R.   And my mouth.
V.   O GOD make speed.
R.   O LORD make hast.
    Glory be to.
    As it was in.

THE HYMN.

The ninth with awfull horror hearkened to those groanes
Which taught attention ev'n to rocks and stones.
Hear, FATHER, hear! thy LAMB (at last) complaines.
Of some more painfull thing then all his paines.
Then bowes his all-obedient head, and dyes
His own love's, and our sin's GREAT SACRIFICE.
The sun saw That; And would have seen no more;
The center shook. Her uselesse veil th'inglorious Temple tore.

Ninth; The Hymn: Matthew 27:45–54.
  3–4   the pain of being abandoned by His Father; Psalm 22:1.
  7   *The Sun . . . no more:* the eclipse; see the "Epiphanie Hymne."

[For the Antiphon, see third stanza of "Christs victory" below]

Ad vesperas de
sancta cruce.

De cruce deponitur hora
vespertina. Fortitudo
latuit in mente diuina.
Talem mortem subijt
vite medicina. Heu
corona glorie iacuit
supina.

Euensong of the ho-
lye crosse.

The dead bodi of Christ that
blessed man, Frō the crosse was
loosed & takē away: At euensong
tyme, but alas where was than His
crown of glori & great strength that
day, Ful priuely within the godhead
it lay. Yet would he his cruel
deathe suffer thus, The true
midicine of life to brīg us.

The Antiphona.

O strange mysterious strife
Of open DEATH and hidden LIFE!
When on the crosse my king did bleed,
LIFE seem'd to dy, DEATH dy'd indeed.

The Versicle.

Lo we adore thee
Dread LAMB! and fall
thus low before thee

The Responsor.

'Cause by the convenant of thy CROSSE
Thou'hast sav'd at once the whole world's losse.

The Prayer.

O Lord JESU-CHRIST, son of the living GOD! interpose,
I pray thee, thine own pretious death, thy CROSSE
and Passion, betwixt my soul and thy judgment, now and in the
hour of my death. And vouchsafe to graunt unto me thy
grace and mercy; unto all quick and dead, remission and rest;
to thy church peace and concord; to us sinners life and glory
everlasting. Who livest and reignest with the FATHER, in
the unity of the HOLY GHOST, one GOD, world without end.
Amen.

EVENSONG.

The Versicle.

Lord, by thy sweet and saving SIGN

The Responsor.

Defend us from our foes and thine.

V. Thou shalt open.
R. And my mouth.
V. O GOD make speed.
R. O LORD make hast.
V. Glory be to.
R. As it was in the.

Evensong; The Hymn: John 19:31–37; Matthew 27:55–56.

6.

But there were rocks could not relent at this,
Lo, for their own hearts, they rend his,
Their deadly hate lives still, and hath
A wild reserve of wanton wrath.
Superfluous speare! But ther's a heart stands by
Will look no wounds be lost, no death's shall dye;
Gather now thy grief's ripe fruit, great Mother-maid,
Then sit thee down, and sing thine evensong in the sad tree's shade.

THE HYMN.

But there were Rocks would not relent at This.
Lo, for their own hearts, they rend his.
Their deadly hate lives still; and hath
A wild reserve of wanton wrath;
Superfluous SPEAR! But there's a HEART stands by
Will look no wounds be lost, no deaths shall dy.
Gather now thy Greif's ripe FRUIT. Great mother-maid!
Then sitt thee down, and sing thine Ev'nsong in the sad TREE's shade.

The Antiphona.

O sad, sweet TREE!
Wofull and joyfull we
Both weep and sing in shade of thee.
When the dear NAILES did lock
And graft into thy gracious Stock
The hope; the health,
The worth, the wealth
Of all the ransom'd WORLD, thou hadst the power
(In that propitious Hour)
To poise each pretious limb,
And prove how light the World was, when it weighd with HIM.
Wide maist thou spred
Thine Armes; And with thy bright and blisfull head
O'relook all Libanus. Thy lofty crown
The king himself is; Thou his humble THRONE.
Where yeilding and yet conquering he
Prov'd a new path of patient Victory.
When wondring death by death was slain,
And our Captivity his Captive ta'ne.

The Versicle.

Lo we adore thee
Dread LAMB! and bow thus low before thee;

---

5 *Superfluous:* because "Their deadly hate lives still." The spear is mentioned in the *Prymer* at Nones.
8 *Ev'nsong:* the "Stabat Mater Dolorosa," No. 78.
The Antiphona:
4 *Nailes . . . lock:* a pun in Latin: *clavi* (nails), *claves* (keys), see "Ego sum ostium," No. 205.
10–11 *poise:* i.e., weigh; the cross imaged as a scale.
14 *Libanus:* i.e. Lebanon.
19 Ephesians 4:8.

Ad completorium
de cruce.

Hora completorij datur
sepulture. Corpus
Christi nobile, spes
vite future. Cōditur
aromate cōplentur
scripture. Iugi sit
memoria mors hec
mihi cure.

Compline of the
crosse.

The hope of our lyfe euer to
endure, Of Jesᵘ the noble & blessed
bodi: At cōpline time was brought
to sepulture, Spiced & adorned
fragrant & swetely. Of scripture
complete wss [sic] thē the mistery,
Therfore Jesu graunt me thy
wounds tēder, And thy death
buselye styl to remembre.

7.

The Nightening houre comes last to call
Us to our owne lives Funerall,
A heartlesse taske! Yet hope takes head,
And lives in him, that here lyes dead:
Run *Mary*, run! Bring hither all the Blest
Arabia, for thy Royall *Phœnix* nest,
Power on thy noblest sweets, which when they touch
This sweeter body shall indeed be such.
But must thy bed, Lord, be a borrow'd grave,
Who lend'st to all things all the life they have?
O rather use this Heart, thus farre a fitter stone,
'Cause though a hard, and cold one, yet it is thine owne.

The Responsor.

'Cause by the convenant of thy CROSSE.
Thou'hast sav'd the world from certain losse.

The Prayer.

O lord JESU-CHRIST, son of the living, &c.

COMPLINE

The Versicle.

Lord by thy sweet and saving SIGN,

The Responsor.

Defend us from our foes and thine.
V. Thou shalt open.
R. And my mouth.
V. O GOD make speed.
R. O LORD make hast.
V. Glory be
R. As it was in

THE HIMN.

The Complin hour comes last, to call
Us to our own LIVE's funerall.
Ah hartlesse task! yet hope takes head;
And lives in Him that here lyes dead.
Run, MARY, run! Bring hither all the BLEST
ARABIA, for thy Royall Phoenix' nest;
Pour on thy noblest sweets, Which, when they touch
This sweeter BODY, shall indeed be such.
But must thy bed, lord, be a borrow'd grave
Who lend'st to all things All the LIFE they have?
O rather use this HEART, thus farr a fitter STONE,
'Cause, though a hard and cold one, yet it is thine owne. Amen.

Compline; The Himn: John 19:38–42; Matthew 27:57–61.
  5 *Mary:* more properly, Nicodemus; Mary (Magdalene) did not run with spices until
Easter morning; she is not mentioned in the *Prymer.*
  7–8 compare "Each blest drop, on each blest limme, / Is washt it self in washing him,"
"On the water of our Lords Baptisme," No. 10.

The Antiphona.

O Save us then
Merciful King of men;
Since thou would'st needs be thus
A Saviour, and at such rate for us,
Save us, o save us, Lord:
We now will own no shorter wish, nor
Name a narrower word,
Thy blood bidd's us be bold,
Thy wounds give us faire hold,
Thy sorrows chide our shame,
Thy Crosse, thy nature, and thy name
Advance our claime,
And cry with one accord,
Save them, o save them Lord.

Has horas canonicas
cum deuotione. Tibi
Christe recolo pia
ratione. Vt sicut tu
passus es penas in
agone Sic labori
consonans consors sim
corone.

O blessed Christ these houres
canonical, To the I offer with meke
deuotiō, For thou hast suffered
these paines all, In thy greuous
agony by like reason. So by the
remēbrance of thy passion, Make
me accordynge to my busines:
Partner of thy crown & glory
endles.

The recommendation of the precedent Poems.

These howers, and that which hovers o're my end
Into thy hands and heart Lord I commend,
Take both to thine account, that I and mine
In that hower, and in these may be all thine.
That as I dedicate my devoutest breath
To make a kind of life for my Lord's death,
So from his living, and life-giving death,
My dying life may draw a new, and never fleeting breath.

The Antiphona.

O save us then
Mercyfull KING of men!
Since thou wouldst needs be thus
A SAVIOUR, and at such a rate, for us;
Save us, o save us, lord.
We now will own no shorter wish, nor name a narrower word.
Thy blood bids us be bold.
Thy Wounds give us fair hold.
Thy Sorrows chide our shame.
Thy Crosse, thy Nature, and thy name
Advance our claim
And cry with one accord
Save them, o save them, lord.

A Prayer.

O Lord Jesus Christ, son of the living God,
interpose I pray thee, thine owne pretious death,
thy Crosse and Passion, betwixt my soule and thy
Judgement, now and in the hower of my death. And
vouchsafe to grant unto me thy grace and mercie,
remission and rest; To the Church, peace, and con-
cord; to us sinners, life, and glory everlasting;
Who livest and raignest with the Father, in the
unitie of the Holy Ghost, one God, world without
end: Amen.

Christs victory.

Christ when he dy'd
   Deceiv'd the crosse,
   And on death's side
   Threw all the losse;
The captive world awak't and found
The Prisoners loose, the Jaylor bound.

   O deare and sweet dispute
'Twixt death's and love's far different fruite,
   Different as farre
   As Antidots and Poysons are:
   By the first fatall Tree
   Both life and libertie
   Were sold and slaine,
By this they both looke up, and live againe.

O strange mysterious strife,
Of open death and hidden life!
When on the crosse my King did bleed,
Life seem'd to dye, Death dy'd indeed.

Christs victory. It can hardly be said that the three antiphons form a coherent poem.

SVM pulcher: at nemo tamen me diligit.
Sum nobilis: nemo est mihi qui seruiat.
Sum diues: a me nemo quicquam postulat.
Et cuncta possum: nemo me tamen timet.
Æternus exsto: quæror a paucissimis.
Prudensque sum: sed me quis est qui consulit?
Et sum via: at per me quotusquisque ambulat?
Sum veritas: quare mihi non creditur?
Sum vita: verum rarus est qui me petit.
Sum vera lux: videre me nemo cupit.
Sum misericors: nullus fidem in me collocat.
TV, si peris, non id mihi imputes, Homo:
Salus tibi est a me parata: hac vtere.
I. Mёßager excud.

THE RECOMMENDATION.

These Houres, and that which hover's o're my END,
Into thy hands, and hart, lord, I commend.

Take Both to Thine Account, that I and mine
In that Hour, and in these, may be all thine.

That as I dedicate my devoutest BREATH
To make a kind of LIFE for my lord's DEATH,

So from his living, and life-giving DEATH,
My dying LIFE may draw a new, and never fleeting BREATH.

72   *Song upon the Bleeding Crucifix*

First version 46; second version 52 (48).*

See "In vulnera Dei pendentis," No. 270. This is the only one of the early English translations of the Latin epigrams to appear in two distinct versions. Esch (pp. 100–5) finds the changes in the second version show Crashaw's intention to move away from "Epigrammstruktur," i.e. episodic structure, towards the totality of the poem as a unit. M. E. Rickey (*Rhyme and Meaning in Crashaw* [University of Kentucky, 1961], pp. 63–64) finds that the changes make possible a symmetry of rhyme repetition. G. W. Williams ("Textual Revision in Crashaw's 'Upon the Bleeding Crucifix,'" *Studies in Bibliography*, I (1948–49), 191–93) remarks that "the progressive change of name is significant. The emphasis has been shifted from the wounds [1646] through the body

On the bleeding wounds of our crucified Lord

[1]

Jesu, no more, it is full tide
    From thy hands and from thy feet,
From thy head, and from thy side,
    All thy *Purple Rivers* meet.

[2]

Thy restlesse feet they cannot goe,
    For us and our eternall good
As they are wont; what though?
    They swim, alas! in their owne flood.

[3]

Thy hand to give thou canst not lift;
    Yet will thy hand still giving bee;
It gives, but o it self's the Guift,
    It drops though bound, though bound 'tis free.

[4]

But o thy side! thy deepe dig'd side
    That hath a double *Nilus* going,
Nor ever was the *Pharian* tide
    Halfe so fruitfull, halfe so flowing.

[5]

What need thy faire head beare a part
    In Teares? as if thine eyes had none?
What need they helpe to drowne thine heart,
    That strives in Torrents of its owne?

72   *Song upon the Bleeding Crucifix*

[1648] to the crucifix [1652], and . . . the poem has been made consciously
cruciform in the later version [1648/52]. No major change has occurred in the
thought of the poem, but the deceptively simple transposition in lines two and
three of the first stanza and the consequential rearrangement of the order of
the following four stanzas evidence a certain intention to provide the 1648 ver-
sion with an articulated structure" in Herbert's manner. "Furthermore, the
words [—head, feet, hands, side—] parallel the movement of the hand in making
the sign of the cross." He continues (*Image and Symbol,* pp. 17–20) to point
out the cumulative progression in water imagery in the latter part of the poem:
Nile, red sea, one [river] all ore, overflowed rivers, deluge, Well of living
Waters.

UPON THE BLEEDING CRUCIFIX A SONG.

I.

Jesu, no more! It is full tide.
From thy head and from thy feet,
From thy hands and from thy side
All the purple Rivers meet.

II.

What need thy fair head bear a part
In showres, as if thine eyes had none?
What need They help to drown thy heart,
That strives in torrents of it's own?

III.

Thy restlesse feet now cannot goe
For us and our eternall good,
As they were ever wont. What though?
They swimme. Alas, in their own floud.

IV.

Thy hands to give, thou canst not lift;
Yet will thy hand still giving be.
It gives but o, it self's the gift.
It gives though bound; though bound 'tis free.

V.

But o thy side, thy deep-digg'd side!
That hath a double Nilus going.
Nor ever was the pharian tide
Half so fruitfull, half so flowing.

IV. 1–3 *hands to give:* a typological commonplace (Tuve, p. 46, note); the hand (i.e. body
of Christ) is the gift of the Eucharist.

[6]

Water'd by the showres they bring,
  The thornes that thy blest browes encloses
(A cruell and a costly spring)
  Conceive proud hopes of proving Roses.

[7]

Not a haire but payes his River
  To this *Red Sea* of thy blood,
Their little channels can deliver
  Something to the generall flood.

[8]

But while I speake, whither are run
  All the Rivers nam'd before?
I counted wrong; there is but one,
  But o that one is one all o're.

[9]

Raine-swolne Rivers may rise proud
  Threatning all to overflow,
But when indeed all's overflow'd
  They themselves are drowned too.

[10]

This thy Bloods deluge (a dire chance
  Deare Lord to thee) to us is found
A deluge of deliverance,
  A deluge least we should be drown'd.

Nere was't thou in a sence so sadly true,
The well of living Waters, Lord, till now.

VI.

No hair so small, but payes his river
To this red sea of thy blood
Their little channells can deliver
Somthing to the Generall floud.

VII.

But while I speak, whither are run
All the rivers nam'd before?
I counted wrong. There is but one;
But o that one is one all ore.

VIII.

Rain-swoln rivers may rise proud,
Bent all to drown and overflow.
But when indeed all's overflow'd
They themselves are drowned too.

IX.

This thy blood's deluge, a dire chance
Dear LORD to thee, to us is found
A deluge of Deliverance;
A deluge least we should be drown'd.

N'ere wast thou in a sense so sadly true,
The WELL of living WATERS, Lord, till now.

IX   there is a recollection here of the deliverance of Noah (a type of Christ) in the Deluge.
DISTICH: *Well of living Waters:* John 4:14. Williams (p. 20): "The bleeding upon the cross
is the . . . greatest gift of all; such generosity . . . can only be described in terms of . . .
the summation of abundance."

73   *Hymn in the Assumption*

First version 46; second version 52 (48).*
   As has often been noted, the doctrine of the bodily Assumption of the Virgin
Mary is the only article of faith in Crashaw's poems that is Roman but not
Anglican dogma. But the doctrine was received by many Anglicans in Cra-
shaw's time; hence the writing of a poem on the Assumption cannot be regarded
as firm assurance that the writer had embraced the Roman Church. See Anth.
Stafford, *The Femall Glorie* (London, 1635) and A. M. Allchin, "Our Lady in
Seventeenth-century Anglican Devotion and Theology," in E. L. Mascall, *The*

On the Assumption

Harke shee is called, the parting houre is come,
Take thy farewel poore world, heaven must go home.
A peece of heavenly Light purer and brighter
Then the chast stars, whose choice Lamps come to light her.
While through the christall orbs clearer then they   5
Shee climbes, and makes a farre more milky way;
Shee's call'd againe, harke how th'immortall Dove
Sighs to his silver mate: rise up my Love,
Rise up my faire, my spotlesse one,
The Winter's past, the raine is gone: 10
The Spring is come, the Flowers appeare,
No sweets since thou art wanting here.
    Come away my Love,
    Come away my Dove
      cast off delay: 15
    The Court of Heav'n is come,
    To wait upon thee home;
      Come away, come away.

73   *Hymn in the Assumption*

Blessed Virgin Mary (London, 1963), pp. 53–76. Esch (pp. 126–28) praises
the addition of lines 17–26 (52), a "divisio," or amplification, term by term of
lines 10–11, and the deletion of lines 31–40 (46) which add nothing new to the
poem and merely repeat in lines 38–40 the solemn request of lines 42–45
(52). He notes also the change in line 3 from "Light" to "earth," "with which
oxymoron not only the union of heaven and earth in the virgin but also the
central metaphoric motif of the poem are underscored at the start of the poem."
This union is suggested again at the end in lines 64–65.

IN THE GLORIOUS ASSUMPTION OF OUR BLESSED LADY.

THE HYMN.

Hark! she is call'd, the parting houre is come.
Take thy Farewell, poor world! heavn must goe home.
A peice of heav'nly earth; Purer and brighter
Then the chast starres, whose choise lamps come to light her
While through the crystall orbes, clearer then they   5
She climbes; and makes a farre more milkey way.
She's calld. Hark, how the dear immortall dove
Sighes to his sylver mate rise up, my love!
Rise up, my fair, my spotlesse one!
The winter's past, the rain is gone.   10
    The spring is come, the flowrs appear
No sweets, but thou, are wanting here.
        Come away, my love!
        Come away, my dove! cast off delay,
        The court of heav'n is come   15
        To wait upon thee home; Come come away!
        The flowrs appear.
Or quickly would, wert thou once here.
The spring is come, or if it stay,
'Tis to keep time with thy delay.   20
The rain is gone, except so much as we
Detain in needfull teares to weep the want of thee.
    The winter's past.
    Or if he make lesse hast,
His answer is, why she does so.   25
If sommer come not, how can winter goe?

5 *orbs:* the Ptolemaic spheres.
8–12 *rise up . . . here:* compare Song of Solomon 2:10–14 (in italics in 1648).

Shee's call'd againe, and will shee goe;
When heaven bids come, who can say no? 20
Heav'n calls her, and she must away,
Heaven will not, and she cannot stay.
Goe then, goe (glorious) on the golden wings
Of the bright youth of Heaven, that sings
Under so sweet a burden: goe, 25
Since thy great Sonne will have it so:
And while thou goest, our song and wee,
Will as wee may reach after thee.
Haile holy Queen of humble hearts,
Wee in thy praise will have our parts. 30
And though thy dearest looks must now be light
To none but the blest heavens, whose bright
Beholders lost in sweet delight
Feed for ever their faire sight
With those divinest eyes, which wee 35
And our darke world no more shall see.
Though, our poore joyes are parted so,
Yet shall our lips never let goe
Thy gracious name, but to the last,
Our Loving song shall hold it fast. 40
      Thy sacred Name shall bee
      Thy selfe to us, and wee
      With holy cares will keepe it by us,
         Wee to the last,
         Will hold it fast, 45
      And no Assumption shall deny us.
      All the sweetest showers,
      Of our fairest Flowers,
      Will wee strow upon it:
      Though our sweetnesse cannot make 50
      It sweeter, they may take
      Themselves new sweetnesse from it.
Mary, men and Angels sing,
Maria Mother of our King.
Live rarest Princesse, and may the bright 55

    Come away, come away.
The shrill winds chide, the waters weep thy stay;
The fountains murmur; and each loftyest tree
Bowes low'st his heavy top, to look for thee.   30
    Come away, my love.
    Come away, my dove &c.
She's call'd again. And will she goe?
When heavn bidds come, who can say no?
Heavn calls her, and she must away.   35
Heavn will not, and she cannot stay.
Goe then; goe GLORIOUS.
    On the golden wings
Of the bright youth of heavn, that sings
Under so sweet a Burthen. Goe,   40
Since thy dread son will have it so.
And while thou goest, our song and we
Will, as we may, reach after thee.
HAIL, holy Queen of humble hearts!
We in thy prayse will have our parts.   45

    Thy pretious name shall be
    Thy self to us; and we
With holy care will keep it by us.
    We to the last
    Will hold it fast   50
And no ASSUMPTION shall deny us.
    All the sweetest showres
    Of our fairest flowres
Will we strow upon it.
    Though our sweets cannot make   55
    It sweeter, they can take
Themselves new sweetnes from it.
MARIA, men and Angels sing
MARIA, mother of our KING.
    LIVE, rosy princesse, LIVE. And may the bright   60

Crown of an incomparable Light
Embrace thy radiant browes, o may the best
Of everlasting joyes bath thy white brest.
Live our chaste love, the holy mirth
Of heaven, and humble pride of Earth: 60
Live Crowne of Women, Queen of men:
Live Mistris of our Song, and when
Our weak desires have done their best;
Sweet Angels come, and sing the rest.

Crown of a most incomparable light
Embrace thy radiant browes. O may the best
Of everlasting joyes bath thy white brest.
LIVE, our chast love, the holy mirth
Of heavn; the humble pride of earth. 65
Live, crown of woemen; Queen of men.
Live mistresse of our song. And when
Our weak desires have done their best,
Sweet Angels come, and sing the rest.

74   *The Weeper*

First version 46; second version 52 (48).*

The chief example of Crashaw's adulation of the tears of Mary Magdalene, this poem is one of a vast group of poems in honor of the saint who was the pattern of the Christian penitent and became extremely popular in the religious poetry of the sixteenth and seventeenth centuries. Crashaw wrote at least a dozen poems in which she figures prominently. Medieval hagiology combined several scriptural Marys into one Magdalene who wept for the death of her brother Lazarus (John 11:33), when she anointed Christ's feet (Luke 7:38), and on the resurrection morning (John 20:11) (Williams, p. 87).

This poem has received the burden of criticism aimed at Crashaw's poetry, for it is certainly true that it contains the largest collection of images that may be thought of as typically Crashavian and in them the most striking examples of the grotesque. Furthermore, the existence of "The Teare" and the two quite different versions of "The Weeper" encourage the hypotheses that structurally it is rather loose. Praz (pp. 218–31) discusses at length its sources in Latin, English, and Italian poetry and thought. He terms it (pp. 218–19) "indeed little more than a rosary of epigrams or madrigals clumsily linked together, without progression: the stanzas might be arranged in a different order . . . and the poem might be augmented indefinitely, or reduced . . . : the unit is not the poem, but the stanza, the madrigal, the epigram, . . ." This view is shared by Warren (p. 128): "The poem is a series of metaphors, in which the poet perpetually returns to his initial image—tears . . . the variations lack much variety: they do not change timbre or increase in resonance; and though they are all ingenious, even their ingenuity is not climactic." Warren finds that (in distinction to Praz, p. 229) the poem is improved in the second version: the changes in arrangement work toward a more sequential effect (p. 128); and here he is followed by Esch (pp. 105–17) who suggests that the second version is a decided improvement, and that with the added stanzas on love (xv–xviii) Crashaw sought to give the poem a structural center (p. 114). The most thoughtful voice in praise of the thematic coherence and structural integrity of the poem (second version) has been that of S. Manning ("The Meaning of 'The Weeper,'" *ELH*, XXII [1955], 34–47); he finds an orderly spiritual progression from beginning to end (pp. 46–47): "Crashaw generalizes in I–V upon Magdalene's spiritual state: she is on the way to perfection, having repented of her sins. In VI–XVIII he traces the steps by which she arrived at this spiritual state. The center of the poem is XIX, where she is extolled as both the penitent sinner and the follower of Christ: this sums up the preceding stanzas and gives rise to further development in XX–XXVII in temporal terms, with an air of timelessness from its continuity. Finally [XXVIII–XXXI], having addressed the eyes up to this point, Crashaw turns to the tears, and they, in answer, confirm that Magdalene has renounced all earthly things for Christ. And so the poem ends on a note of quiet triumph." It is not clear that this view has received general agreement; some readers will no doubt prefer to hold with John Peter ("Crashaw and 'The Weeper,'" *Scrutiny*, XIX [1952–53], 258–73): "We are obliged to admit that the eyes and tears of the weeper have in the poem the function almost of pretexts, that their connection with the imagery lavished upon them is at best a tenuous one, and that in consequence the effect is to direct us, not to a relation or fusion (which might be profound or revealing), but simply to the imagery *per se*. Crashaw's persistent returns to his point of departure, the eyes

74   *The Weeper*

or the tears, would seem to indicate an awareness on his part that the gap between tenor and vehicle had somehow to be closed, and the imagery forced into some kind of dependence. . . . The fact is simply that . . . in so many passages in the poem we have been too involved in something quite different and even inconsonant. . . . And that something, we realize, was mere ingenuity— an ingenuity which is the more distraction for regarding itself (as it plainly does) as adroit and rather brilliant" (p. 270).

Williams (pp. 98–104) examines the first twenty-one stanzas of the poem in terms of the symbolic values of the imagery of liquidity. The image of the liquid tear includes springs, rills, crystal, snow, milk, cream, pearls, dew, balsam, blossom, water, showers, fountain, rain, floods, wells, fountains, baths, and oceans—all the variants of white liquids that Crashaw uses (see also pp. 44– 45). The whiteness of these liquids is a mark of their purity; the fact that they flow from the heart of the weeper is a mark of her genuine and effective contrition. As this line of imagery dries up after stanza XXI, it is difficult to agree with Manning that the poem is structurally coherent. On the other hand, Peter supposes that self-conscious ingenuity cannot validly be used to the honor of the Magdalene and the greater glory of God. If it is accepted that the Unworthiness of the Ministers hinders not the effect of the Sacraments (Article XXVI), then it follows that Peter's view is also untenable—though it is probably nearer the truth than Manning's. It must finally be said that for a small body of sensitive readers whose devotion includes these grotesques, this poem is successful because of its absurdities. It is the first poem in *Steps to the Temple*—the first of the "Steps for happy soules to climbe heaven by" (Preface).

Adams (pp. 69–70): "The Magdalene's grief is grotesque, it distorts her out of all resemblance to humanity. . . . her tears, as they transcend ordinary grief, transcend ordinary ugliness and absurdity. . . . The whole technique of loosely, floridly extended metaphor seems to culminate in [stanza XIX], which is ridiculous, of course . . . ; the art is developed beyond and in defiance of nature. But its absurdity can be seen as true to a sort of feeling. . . . A Christian poet, at least, can scarcely be blamed for assuming, and asking his readers to assume for the moment, a definition of reality which includes more than the humanly demonstrable; and how to suggest such a reality if not through the feelings imagined as appropriate to it?"

SAINTE

MARY

MAGDALENE

OR

THE WEEPER

Loe where a WOUNDED HEART with Bleeding EYES conspire.
Is she a FLAMING Fountain, or a Weeping fire?

Distich: the contrast between tears and fire appears in the epigram (No. 15) on Luke 7:37–38: "Her eyes flood . . . Her haires flame"; it is repeated in stanza XVII, but the distich promises an extensive use of fire and the poem does not include it (Williams, pp. 102–3, 84–86) (St. Teresa, *The Way of Perfection*, xix).

THE WEEPER

1   Haile *Sister Springs,*
    Parents of Silver-forded rills!
    Ever bubling things!
    Thawing Christall! Snowy Hills!
    Still spending, never spent; I meane
    Thy faire Eyes sweet *Magdalene.*

T H E

W E E P E R.

I.

Hail, sister springs!
   Parents of sylver-footed rills!
     Ever bubling things!
     Thawing crystall! snowy hills,
Still spending, never spent! I mean
Thy fair eyes, sweet MAGDALENE!

I. 1 *springs, Parents, Ever bubling:* these terms all suggest the true contrition of the sinner, rising from within (Psalm 119:136).
    4 *crystall, snowy:* the thawing of two hard, cold, pure liquids symbolizes the softening and warming of the hard and cold eye and heart of the sinner (Psalm 58:7).
    5 *Still:* always. "These exuberant exclamations cannot be fused with each other . . . it is through their very effect of heterogeneity . . . , that Crashaw implies the nature of the coherence that they possess; and that coherence is clearly one of tone" (Peter, p. 264).

2   Heavens thy faire Eyes bee,
   Heavens of ever-falling stars,
    Tis seed-time still with thee
   And stars thou sow'st whose harvest dares
  Promise the earth; to countershine
  What ever makes Heavens fore-head fine.

3   But wee are deceived all,
   Stars they are indeed too true,
    For they but seeme to fall
   As Heavens other spangles doe:
  It is not for our Earth and us,
  To shine in things so pretious.

4   Upwards thou dost weepe,
   Heavens bosome drinks the gentle streame.
    Where th' milky rivers meet,
   Thine Crawles above and is the Creame.
  Heaven, of such faire floods as this,
  Heaven the Christall Ocean is.

5   Every morne from hence,
   A briske Cherub something sips
    Whose soft influence
   Adds sweetnesse to his sweetest lips.
  Then to his Musicke, and his song
  Tastes of this breakefast all day long.

6   When some new bright guest
   Takes up among the stars a roome,
    And Heaven will make a feast,
   Angels with their Bottles come;
  And draw from these full Eyes of thine,
  Their Masters water, their owne Wine.

II.

Heavens thy fair eyes be;
Heavens of ever-falling starres.
'Tis seed-time still with thee
And starres thou sow'st, whose harvest dares
Promise the earth to counter shine
Whatever makes heavn's forhead fine.

III.

But we'are deceived all.
Starres indeed they are too true;
For they but seem to fall,
As Heavn's other spangles doe.
It is not for our earth and us
To shine in Things so pretious.

IV.

Upwards thou dost weep.
Heavn's bosome drinks the gentle stream.
Where th' milky rivers creep,
Thine floates above; and is the cream.
Waters above th'Heavns, what they be
We'are taught best by thy TEARES and thee.

V.

Every morn from hence
A brisk Cherub somthing sippes
Whose sacred influence
Addes sweetnes to his sweetest Lippes.
Then to his musick. And his song
Tasts of this Breakfast all day long.

II. 2 *ever-falling:* the tears of the Weeper fall downward onto Christ's feet, but—III.3—
they but seem to fall; in fact they go up (Manning, pp. 38–39).
IV. 1 *Upwards:* a poetic commonplace (Praz, pp. 220–21, note).
   3 *milky-rivers:* the Milky Way, regarded as the pathway to heaven.
   5–6 *Waters:* the supracelestial waters of Genesis 1:6–7 and Psalm 148:4 (Manning, p.
38). In 46, stanza 4, line 6, 'Christall' is a pun.
V. 2 *A brisk Cherub:* the figure is intended to be slightly amusing or whimsical (See fur-
ther Adams, pp. 66–67).
   4 *sweetnes:* compare "Musick's Duel," No. 382, lines 75–80 (Manning, p. 39; Peter, p.
266).

7   The dew no more will weepe,
The Primroses pale cheeke to decke,
The deaw no more will sleepe,
Nuzzel'd in the Lillies necke.
Much rather would it tremble heere,
And leave them both to bee thy Teare.

8   Not the soft Gold which
Steales from the Amber-weeping Tree,
Makes sorrow halfe so Rich,
As the drops distil'd from thee.
Sorrowes best Jewels lye in these
Caskets, of which Heaven keeps the Keyes.

9   When sorrow would be seene
In her brightest Majesty,
(For shee is a Queen)
Then is shee drest by none but thee.
Then, and onely then shee weares
Her richest Pearles, I meane thy Teares.

10   Not in the Evenings Eyes
When they red with weeping are,
For the Sun that dyes,
Sits sorrow with a face so faire.
Nowhere but heere did ever meet
Sweetnesse so sad, sadnes so sweet.

11   Sadnesse all the while
Shee sits in such a Throne as this,
Can doe nought but smile,
Nor beleeves shee sadnesse is.
Gladnesse it selfe would bee more glad
To bee made so sweetly sad.

VI.

Not in the evening's eyes
When they Red with weeping are
For the Sun that dyes,
Sitts sorrow with a face so fair,
No where but here did ever meet
Sweetnesse so sad, sadnesse so sweet.

VII.

When sorrow would be seen
In her brightest majesty
(For she is a Queen)
Then is she drest by none but thee.
Then, and only then, she weares
Her proudest pearles; I mean, thy TEARES.

VIII.

The deaw no more will weep
The primrose's pale cheek to deck,
The deaw no more will sleep
Nuzzel'd in the lilly's neck;
Much reather would it be thy TEAR,
And leave them Both to tremble here.

VIII. 1 *deaw:* a heaven-sent and therefore gracious liquid.

12   There is no need at all
  That the Balsame-sweating bough
   So coyly should let fall,
  His med'cinable Teares; for now
 Nature hath learn't t' extract a dew,
 More soveraigne and sweet from you.

13   Yet the poore drops weepe,
  Weeping is the ease of woe,
   Softly let them creepe
  Sad that they are vanquish't so,
 They, though to others no releife
 May Balsame bee for their own grief.

14   Golden though hee bee,
  Golden *Tagus* murmurs though,
   Might hee flow from thee
  Content and quiet would he goe,
 Richer far does he esteeme
 Thy silver, then his golden streame.

IX.

There's no need at all
That the balsom-sweating bough
So coyly should let fall
His med'cinable teares; for now
Nature hath learn't to'extract a deaw
More soveraign and sweet from you.

X.

Yet let the poore drops weep
(Weeping is the ease of woe)
Softly let them creep,
Sad that they are vanquish't so.
They, though to others no releife,
Balsom maybe, for their own greife.

XI.

Such the maiden gemme
By the purpling vine put on,
Peeps from her parent stemme
And blushes at the bridegroome sun.
This watry Blossom of thy eyn,
Ripe, will make the richer wine.

XII.

When some new bright Guest
Takes up among the starres a room,
And Heavn will make a feast,
Angels with crystall violls come
And draw from these full eyes of thine
Their master's Water: their own Wine.

XIII.

Golden though he be,
Golden Tagus murmures tho;
Were his way by thee,
Content and quiet he would goe.
So much more rich would he esteem
Thy sylver, then his golden stream.

IX. 2 *balsom:* a medicinal and restorative liquid.
XII. 5–6 *draw . . . Wine:* an echo of the miracle at the wedding feast at Cana, John 2:1–11.
The 46 version (st. 6) has "Bottles," a close echo of Psalm 56:8.
XIII. 2 *Tagus:* a river in Spain noted for its golden sand. *murmures:* i.e. complains.

15   Well does the *May* that lyes
        Smiling in thy cheekes, confesse,
          The *April* in thine eyes,
        Mutuall sweetnesse they expresse.
        No *April* e're lent softer showres,
        Nor *May* returned fairer flowers.

XIV.

Well does the May that lyes
Smiling in thy cheeks, confesse
The April in thine eyes.
Mutuall sweetnesse they expresse.
No April ere lent kinder showres,
Nor May return'd more faithfull flowres.

XV.

O cheeks! Bedds of chast loves
By your own showres seasonably dash't;
Eyes! nests of milky doves
In your own wells decently washt,
O wit of love! that thus could place
Fountain and Garden in one face.

[XVI.]

O sweet Contest; of woes
With loves, of teares with smiles disputing!
O fair, and Freindly Foes,
Each other kissing and confuting!
While rain and sunshine, Cheekes and Eyes
Close in kind contrarietyes.

XVII.

But can these fair Flouds be
Freinds with the bosom fires that fill thee!
Can so great flames agree
Æternall Teares should thus distill thee!
O flouds, o fires! o suns o showres!
Mixt and made freinds by loue's sweet powres.

XVIII.

Twas his well-pointed dart
That digg'd these wells, and drest this Vine;
And taught the wounded HEART
The way into these weeping Eyn.
Vain loves avant! bold hands forbear!
The lamb hath dipp't his white foot here.

XIV. 1 *May:* i.e. flowers.
XVII compare the opening distich.

16   Thus dost thou melt the yeare
        Into a weeping motion,
          Each minute waiteth heere;
        Takes his teare and gets him gone;
      By thine eyes tinct enobled thus
      Time layes him up: he's pretious.

XIX.

And now where're he strayes,
Among the Galilean mountaines,
Or more unwellcome wayes,
He's follow'd by two faithfull fountaines;
Two walking baths; two weeping motions;
Portable, and compendious oceans.

XX.

O Thou, thy lord's fair store!
In thy so rich and rare expenses,
Even when he show'd most poor,
He might provoke the wealth of Princes.
What Prince's wanton'st pride e're could
Wash with Sylver, wipe with Gold.

XXI.

Who is that King, but he
Who calls't his Crown to be call'd thine,
That thus can boast to be
Waited on by a wandring mine,
A voluntary mint, that strowes
Warm sylver shoures where're he goes!

XXII.

O pretious Prodigall!
Fair spend-thrift of thy self! thy measure
(Mercilesse love!) is all.
Even to the last Pearle in thy treasure.
All places, Times, and objects be
Thy teare's sweet opportunity.

XIX For the conventional background of the hyperbole of the images in this stanza see Martin, p. 449; analogues will also be found in Song of Solomon 7:4 and Jeremiah 9:1. In the volume of Andrewes' *Sermons* for which Crashaw prepared the introductory verses, Bishop Andrewes writes "Mary Magdalene wept enough to have made a bath" (I, 369). Williams (p. 103): "The fountains suggest that penitence must come from the heart of the sinner; the baths suggest that that penitence goes far toward washing the sinner of his sins; the motions suggest that the sinner must be vigorous and constant in his penance; and the oceans suggest that as man's sins are great, so must his contrition be." The ideas of "faithfull," "walking," and "Portable" are summed up in the verb "follow'd," suggesting that the sinner's devotion— even as far as the more unwelcome ways of the crucifixion or the painful death of a martyr —are in the footsteps of the Lamb: "Thou with the Lamb, thy lord, shalt goe; / And whereso'ere he setts his white / Stepps, walk with Him" ("Hymn to St. Teresa," No. 60, lines 178–80).
XX. 1 *store:* accumulated wealth.
    4 *provoke:* call forth (the Latin meaning).

17   Time as by thee he passes,
Makes thy ever-watry eyes
   His Hower-Glasses.
By them his steps he rectifies.
The sands he us'd no longer please,
For his owne sands hee'l use thy seas.

18   Does thy song lull the Ayre?
Thy teares just Cadence still keeps time.
   Does thy sweet breath'd *Prayer*
Up in clouds of Incense climbe?
Still at each sigh, that is each stop:
A bead, that is a teare doth drop.

19   Does the Night arise?
Still thy teares doe fall, and fall.
   Does night loose her eyes?
Still the fountaine weeps for all.
Let night or day doe what they will
Thou hast thy taske, thou weepest still.

20   Not, so long she liv'd,
Will thy tombe report of thee
   But *so long she greiv'd,*
Thus must we date thy memory.
Others by Dayes, by Monthes, by Yeares
Measure their Ages, Thou by Teares.

19 (46), 3 *loose:* i.e. lose.

XXIII.

Does the day-starre rise?
Still thy starres doe fall and fall.
Does day close his eyes?
Still the FOUNTAIN weeps for all.
Let night or day doe what they will,
Thou hast thy task; thou weepest still.

XXIV.

Does thy song lull the air?
Thy falling teares keep faithfull time.
Does thy sweet-breath'd praire
Up in clouds of incense climb?
Still at each sigh, that is, each stop,
A bead, that is, A TEAR, does drop.

XXV.

At these thy weeping gates,
(Watching their watry motion)
Each winged moment waits,
Takes his TEAR, and gets him gone.
By thine Ey's tinct enobled thus
Time layes him up; he's pretious.

XXVI.

Not, so long she lived,
Shall thy tomb report of thee;
But, so long she greived,
Thus must we date thy memory.
Others by moments, months, and yeares
Measure their ages; thou, by TEARES.

XXIV. 1 *song:* i.e. the Magdalene's sighs (Manning, pp. 44–45).
5 *stop:* i.e. a rest (in music); musicians of the lutenist school regarded the rest as a convenient device to represent a sigh.
6 *bead:* i.e. of a rosary.

21   Say watry Brothers
      Yee simpering sons of those faire eyes,
        Your fertile Mothers.
      What hath our world that can entice
      You to be borne? what is't can borrow
      You from her eyes swolne wombes of sorrow.

22   Whither away so fast?
      O whither? for the sluttish Earth
        Your sweetnesse cannot tast
      Nor does the dust deserve your Birth.
      Whither hast ye then? o say
      Why yee trip so fast away?

23   We goe not to seeke
      The darlings of *Aurora's* bed,
        The Roses modest cheeke
      Nor the Violets humble head.
      No such thing; we goe to meet
      A worthier object, *Our Lords* feet.

---

xxviii. 4 *tice:* entice.

xxxi. 6 *Feet:* literally, the feet of Luke 7:38; symbolically, the feet nailed to the cross. In this stanza the idea is particularly contrasted with Crown'd Heads, and the feet are, of course, "worthier" than the heads. (The same contrast occurs in the poem "To the Queen's Majesty," No. 57). The emphasis on Christ's feet is found everywhere in Crashaw—see stanza xviii, for

XXVII.

So doe perfumes expire.
So sigh tormented sweets, opprest
With proud unpittying fire.
Such Teares the suffring Rose that's vext
With ungentle flames does shed,
Sweating in a too warm bed.

XXVIII.

Say, ye bright brothers,
The fugitive sons of those fair Eyes
Your fruitfull mothers!
What make you here? what hopes can tice
You to be born? what cause can borrow
You from Those nests of noble sorrow?

XXIX.

Whither away so fast?
For sure the sordid earth
Your Sweetnes cannot tast
Nor does the dust deserve your birth.
Sweet, whither hast you then? ô say
Why you trip so fast away?

XXX.

We goe not to seek,
The darlings of Auroras bed,
The rose's modest Cheek
Nor the violet's humble head.
Though the Feild's eyes too WEEPERS be
Because they want such TEARES as we.

XXXI.

Much lesse mean we to trace
The Fortune of inferior gemmes,
Preferr'd to some proud face
Or pertch't upon fear'd Diadems.
Crown'd Heads are toyes. We goe to meet
A worthy object, our lord's FEET.

---

example—as a fit object for the adoring prostration of the humble sinner, and the feet leave a
path which the devout will follow (see note to st. XIX—a comment that might equally be ap-
plied to st. XXI; see also textual note to st. I.2).

75   *Ode on a Prayer-book*

First version 46; second version 52 (48).*
   A. F. Allison ("Some Influences in Crashaw's Poem 'On a Prayer Booke sent
to Mrs. M. R.,' " *RES*, XXIII [1947], 34–42) considers this poem as influenced
by St. Teresa's *Vida* and her account of the mystical life in *The Interior Castle*.
Indeed, the 1652 edition places this poem and its companion piece "To the same
Party Councel" (titled in the present edition "To [Mrs. M. R.] Councel," No.
65) immediately after the Teresa poems and "The Song." This location in 1652
disrupts the exact ordering of poems, unless the two poems are also considered as
"Teresa poems"; they should normally have come at the end of the volume
after the poems on St. Alexis and with the miscellaneous poems, not interrupt-
ing the sequence from major to minor saints.
   Allison terms this poem "Crashaw's most successful description of the mystical
progress of the soul" (p. 34). That progress falls into three sections, all repre-

On a prayer booke sent
to Mrs. M. R.

Loe here a little volume, but large booke,
   (Feare it not, sweet,
   It is no hipocrit)
Much larger in it selfe then in its looke.

It is in one rich handfull, heaven and all   5
   Heavens royall Hoasts incampt, thus small;
   To prove that true, schooles use to tell,
A thousand Angells in one point can dwell.

It is loves great Artillery,
   Which here contracts it selfe and comes to lye   10
   Close coucht in your white bosome, and from thence

75   *Ode on a Prayer-book*

sented in the "Ode": Purgation (lines 1–64), Illumination (lines 65–86), Union (lines 87–124). The first two sections are indebted to *The Interior Castle* (and are in spirit like "To [Mrs. M. R.] Councel") for material, but for the third section, Teresa's borrowings from the Song of Solomon are "too restrained to provide . . . the material for a magnificent peroration." Crashaw borrows from "the most notoriously licentious verses of . . . Thomas Carew . . . 'A Rapture' " (pp. 40–41). The "Prayer-Book" is identified in a contemporary manuscript as the *Book of Common Prayer* (Martin, p. 126). See further Esch, pp. 123–26; Williams, pp. 94–95, 111–12.

PRAYER.

AN ODE, WHICH WAS

Præfixed to a little Prayer-book

givin to a young

GENTLE-WOMAN.

Lo here a little volume, but great Book!
A nest of new-born sweets;
     Whose native fires disdaining
     To ly thus folded, and complaining
     Of these ignoble sheets,   5
     Affect more comly bands
     (Fair one) from thy kind hands
     And confidently look
     To find the rest
Of a rich binding in your BREST.   10
It is, in one choise handfull, heaven; and all
Heavn's Royall host; incamp't thus small
To prove that true, schooles use to tell,
Ten thousand Angels in one point can dwell.

It is love's great artillery   15
Which here contracts it self, and comes to ly
Close couch't in your white bosom: and from thence

---

6 *Affect:* aspire to. *bands:* the sturdy cloth strips across the spine to which the sheets of a volume are sewn; the Little Gidding bookbinders specialized in comely bands, but the hands of Mrs. M. R. supporting the book under its spine would in effect parallel the binders' bands (Williams, "Richard Crashaw and the Little Gidding Bookbinders," *N&Q*, CCI [1956], 9–10).
14 *Ten . . . dwell:* a scholastic truism.

As from a snowy fortresse of defence
Against the ghostly foe to take your part:
And fortifie the hold of your chast heart.

It is the Armory of light,   15
Let constant use but keep it bright,
   Youl find it yeelds
To holy hands, and humble hearts,
   More swords and sheilds
Then sinne hath snares, or hell hath darts.   20

      Onely bee sure,
      The hands bee pure,
That hold these weapons and the eyes
Those of turtles, chast, and true,

      Wakefull, and wise   25
Here is a friend shall fight for you,
Hold but this booke before your heart,
Let prayer alone to play his part.

But o', the heart
That studyes this high art,   30
Must bee a sure house keeper,
And yet no sleeper.

Deare soule bee strong,
Mercy will come ere long,
And bring her bosome full of blessings,   35
Flowers of never fading graces;
To make immortall dressings
For worthy souls whose wise embraces
Store up themselves for him, who is alone
The spouse of Virgins, and the Virgins son.   40

But if the noble Bridegrome when hee comes
   Shall find the wandring heart from home,
      Leaving her chast abode,
        To gad abroad:

As from a snowy fortresse of defence,
Against your ghostly foes to take your part,
And fortify the hold of your chast heart.   20

It is an armory of light
Let constant use but keep it bright,
    You'l find it yeilds
To holy hands and humble hearts
    More swords and sheilds   25
Then sin hath snares, or Hell hath darts.

    Only be sure
    The hands be pure
That hold these weapons; and the eyes
Those of turtles, chast and true;   30

    Wakefull and wise;
Here is a freind shall fight for you,
Hold but this book before your heart
Let prayer alone to play his part.

    But o the heart   35
    That studyes this high ART
    Must be a sure house-keeper;
    And yet no sleeper.

Dear soul, be strong.
    MERCY will come e're long   40
And bring his bosom fraught with blessings,
Flowers of never fading graces
To make immortall dressings
For worthy soules, whose wise embraces
Store up themselves for HIM, who is alone   45
The SPOUSE of Virgins and the Virgin's son.

But if the noble BRIDEGROOM, when he come,
Shall find the loytering HEART from home;
    Leaving her chast aboad
    To gadde abroad   50

19 *ghostly:* spiritual.
30 *turtles:* turtledoves.
30–31 *chast, true, Wakefull, wise:* Williams (*Image and Symbol*, p. 109) quotes *Batman
uppon Bartholome:* "The Turtle is a chast Birde [*chast*] . . . and if he leeseth his make
[loseth his mate], he seekth not companye of any other [*true*], . . . but . . . groneth alwaye
[*Wakefull*]; and loveth . . . solitarye place [*wise*, i.e. from contemplation]."

Amongst the gay mates of the god of flyes;   45
    To take her pleasures, and to play
    And keep the divells holy day,
To dance in the Sunneshine of some smiling
    but beguiling
Spheare of sweet, and sugred lies,   50
    Some slippery paire,
    Of false perhaps as faire
Flattering but forswearing eyes,

Doubtles some other heart
    Will git the start,   55
    And stepping in before,
Will take possession of the sacred store
    Of hidden sweets, and holy joyes,
    Words which are not heard with eares,
(These tumultuous shops of noise)   60
    Effectuall whispers whose still voyce,
The soule it selfe more feeles then heares.

Amorous Languishments, Luminous trances,
    Sights which are not seen with eyes,
Spirituall and soule peircing glances.   65
    Whose pure and subtle lightning, flies
Home to the heart, and setts the house on fire;
And melts it downe in sweet desire:
    Yet doth not stay
To aske the windowes leave, to passe that way.   70

Delicious deaths, soft exhalations
Of soule; deare, and divine annihilations.
    A thousand unknowne rites
    Of joyes, and rarifyed delights.

An hundred thousand loves and graces,   75
    And many a misticke thing,
    Which the divine embraces
Of the deare spowse of spirits with them will bring.
    For which it is no shame,
That dull mortality must not know a name.   80

Among the gay mates of the god of flyes;
To take her pleasure and to play
And keep the devill's holyday;
To dance ith' sunshine of some smiling
        But beguiling   55
Spheare of sweet and sugred Lyes,
        Some slippery Pair
Of false, perhaps as fair,
Flattering but forswearing eyes;

Doubtlesse some other heart   60
        Will gett the start
Mean while, and stepping in before
Will take possession of that sacred store
Of hidden sweets and holy joyes,
Words which are not heard with Eares   65
(Those tumultuous shops of noise)
Effectuall wispers, whose still voice
The soul it selfe more feeles then heares;

Amorous languishments; luminous trances;
Sights which are not seen with eyes;   70
Spirituall and soul-peircing glances
Whose pure and subtil lightning flyes
Home to the heart, and setts the house on fire
And melts it down in sweet desire
        Yet does not stay   75
To ask the windows leave to passe that way;

Delicious Deaths; soft exalations
Of soul; dear and divine annihilations;
        A thousand unknown rites
Of joyes and rarefy'd delights;   80

A hundred thousand goods, glories, and graces,
        And many a mystick thing
        Which the divine embraces
Of the deare spouse of spirits with them will bring
        For which it is no shame   85
That dull mortality must not know a name.

51 *mates . . . flyes:* i.e. young courtiers or gallants who associate with this god, who is Beelzebub.
54–59 the description of the human lover recalls that in the "Councel" to the same young gentlewoman.

Of all this hidden store
Of blessings, and ten thousand more;
   If when hee come
Hee find the heart from home,
     Doubtles hee will unload   85
Himselfe some other where,
     And powre abroad
     His precious sweets,
On the faire soule whom first hee meets.

O faire! ô fortunate! ô rich! ô deare!   90
   O happy and thrice happy shee
   Deare silver breasted dove
     Who ere shee bee,
     Whose early Love
     With winged vowes,   95
Makes haste to meet her morning spowse:
And close with his immortall kisses.
     Happy soule who never misses,
     To improve that precious houre:
       And every day,   100
       Seize her sweet prey;
     All fresh and fragrant as hee rises,
     Dropping with a balmy showre
     A delicious dew of spices.

O let that happy soule hold fast   105
Her heavenly armefull, shee shall tast
At once, ten thousand paradises;
     Shee shall have power,
     To rifle and deflower,
The rich and roseall spring of those rare sweets,   110
Which with a swelling bosome there shee meets,
Boundlesse and infinite————————
————————————bottomlesse treasures,
     Of pure inebriating pleasures,
Happy soule shee shall discover,   115
     What joy, what blisse,
     How many heavens at once it is,
To have a God become her lover.

Of all this store
Of blessings and ten thousand more
    (If when he come
    He find the Heart from home)   90
    Doubtlesse he will unload
    Himself some other where,
    And poure abroad
    His pretious sweets
On the fair soul whom first he meets.   95

O fair, o fortunate! O riche, o dear!
O happy and thrice happy she
    Selected dove
    Who ere she be,
    Whose early love   100
    With winged vowes
Makes hast to meet her morning spouse
And close with his immortall kisses.
Happy indeed, who never misses
To improve that pretious hour,   105
        And every day
        Seize her sweet prey
All fresh and fragrant as he rises
Dropping with a baulmy Showr
A delicious dew of spices;   110

O let the blissfull heart hold fast
Her heavnly arm-full, she shall tast
At once ten thousand paradises;
    She shall have power
    To rifle and deflour   115
The rich and roseall spring of those rare sweets
Which with a swelling bosome there she meets
        Boundles and infinite
        Bottomles treasures
Of pure inebriating pleasures.   120
Happy proof! she shal discover
        What joy, what blisse,
How many Heav'ns at once it is
To have her GOD become her LOVER.

---

103 *close with:* come to terms with (a legal phrase).

76   *Letter to the Countess of* Denbigh.

First version 52; second version 53 (?).

The first version supplements the dedication of *Carmen Deo Nostro* (1652), the title page of which reads: "Carmen Deo Nostro, . . . Most humbly Presented. To My Lady The Countesse of Denbigh by Her most devoted Servant. R. C. In hearty acknowledgment of his immortall obligation to her Goodnes & Charity." The second version is from a separate pamphlet consisting of the

NON VI.

'Tis not the work of force but skill
To find the way into man's will.
'Tis love alone can hearts unlock.
Who knowes the Word, *he needs not knock.*

TO THE
Noblest and best of Ladyes, the
Countesse of Denbigh.
Perswading her to Resolution in Religion,
and to render her selfe without further
delay into the Communion of
the Catholick Church.

What heav'n-intreated Heart is This?
Stands trembling at the gate of blisse;
Holds fast the door, yet dares not venture
Fairly to open it, and enter.

76 *Letter to the Countess of* Denbigh

Letter only, printed in London probably in 1653. Crashaw must have left the first version in Paris with Car in 1646 and must have produced the second version in Italy (1646–49) without further conference with Car. Such a supposition would suggest that (as Martin states, p. xxxiv) Crashaw had indeed planned the 1652 version with Car before he left Paris and that the *Letter* was conceived as a quite separate work.

These two versions of a letter of advice to the Countess form the central exhibits in a group of sacred poems to ladies; the group includes the two preceding versions of the "Ode on a Prayer-book sent to Mrs. M. R.," the poem of *"Councel"* to the same party, and the poem accompanying the gift of *The Temple* (No. 66). To these one might add the poems—mostly secular and political—to the Queen. The saints honored—the Virgin, Mary Magdalene, Teresa (and Alexias)—contribute substantially to the feminine quality of Crashaw's poetry.

Susan, first Countess of Denbigh, was the sister of Sir George Villiers, Duke of Buckingham. Her father and her husband were both extremely influential at court and active in support of Charles I; the Earl of Denbigh lost his life in the King's army in 1643. The Countess, surviving her husband many years, became first lady of the bedchamber to Queen Henrietta Maria and followed her in her flight first to Oxford, then to Paris. Always "unstable in her ecclesiastical allegiance," in Paris, at Easter 1651, she became a Roman Catholic (DNB; Martin, pp. xxxi–xxxiii; Warren, pp. 54–55).

Esch (p. 134) regards the first version as a tender, religious seduction poem; Crashaw does not wish to convince by argument, he makes a direct appeal to the amorous emotions of the Countess. In the second version, Crashaw has dissociated the problem of irresolution "in matters of religion" from its personal application and has elevated it to a logical inquiry, using the personal case merely as an exemplum. The theme is then conveyed through a clearer explanation.

A Letter
From
MR. CRASHAW
to the
Countess of DENBIGH,
Against Irresolution and Delay in matters
of RELIGION.

What Heav'n-beseiged Heart is this
Stands Trembling at the Gate of Blisse:
Holds fast the Door, yet dares not venture
Fairly to open and to enter?

2 Martin (p. 446): "The main idea . . . is anticipated in [epigram No. 321]."
3-4 *venture, enter:* a correct rhyme in Crashaw's day.

Whose DEFINITION is a doubt   5
Twixt life and death, twixt in and out.
Say, lingering fair! why comes the birth
Of your brave soul so slowly forth?
Plead your pretences (o you strong
In weaknes) why you choose so long   10
In labor of your selfe to ly,
Nor daring quite to live nor dy?
Ah linger not, lov'd soul! a slow
And late consent was a long no,
Who grants at last, long time tryd   15
And did his best to have deny'd.
What magick bolts, what mystick Barres
Maintain the will in these strange warres!
What fatall, yet fantastick, bands
Keep The free Heart from it's own hands!   20
So when the year takes cold, we see
Poor waters their owne prisoners be.
Fetter'd, and lockt up fast they ly
In a sad selfe-captivity.
The'astonisht nymphs their flood's strange fate deplore,   25
To see themselves their own severer shore.
Thou that alone canst thaw this cold,
And fetch the heart from it's strong Hold;
Allmighty LOVE! end this long warr,
And of a meteor make a starr.   30
O fix this fair INDEFINITE.
And 'mongst thy shafts of soveraign ligh.
Choose out that sure decisive dart
Which has the Key of this close heart,
Knowes all the corners of't, and can controul   35
The self-shutt cabinet of an unsearcht soul.
O let it be at last, love's houre.
Raise this tall Trophee of thy Powre;
Come once the conquering way; not to confute
But kill this rebell-word, IRRESOLUTE   40
That so, in spite of all this peevish strength
Of weaknes, she may write RESOLV'D AT LENGTH,
Unfold at length, unfold fair flowre
And use the season of love's showre,

---

30 *meteor* . . . *starr:* meteors were sublunary, hence indefinite, irregular, transient;
stars were above the moon, hence finite, regular, fixed, and permanent. See also "Description
of a Religious House," No. 86, lines 37–39.

Whose Definition is, A Doubt 5
'Twixt Life and Death, 'twixt In and Out,
Ah! linger not, lov'd Soul: A slow
And late Consent was a long No.
Who grants at last, a great while try'de,
And did his best to have Deny'de. 10
    What Magick-Bolts, what mystick Barrs
Maintain the Will in these strange Warrs?
What Fatall, yet fantastick, Bands
Keep the free Heart from his own Hands?
Say, lingring Fair, why comes the Birth 15
Of your brave Soul so slowly forth?
Plead your Pretences, (O you strong
In weaknesse) why you chuse so long
In Labour of your self to ly,
Not daring quite to Live nor Die. 20
    So when the Year takes cold we see
Poor Waters their own Prisoners be:
Fetter'd and lock'd up fast they lie
In a cold self-captivity.
Th'astonish'd Nymphs their Floud's strange Fate deplore, 25
To find themselves their own severer Shoar.
      Love, that lends haste to heaviest things,
    In you alone hath lost his wings.
    Look round and reade the World's wide face,
    The field of Nature or of Grace; 30
    Where can you fix, to find Excuse
    Or Pattern for the Pace you use?
    Mark with what Faith Fruits answer Flowers,
    And know the Call of Heav'n's kind showers:
    Each mindfull Plant hasts to make good 35
    The hope and promise of his Bud.
Seed-time's not all; there should be Harvest too,
Alas! and has the Year no Spring for you?
      Both Winds and Waters urge their way,
    And murmure if they meet a stay, 40
    Mark how the curl'd Waves work and wind,
    All hating to be left behind.
Each bigge with businesse thrusts the other,
And seems to say, Make haste, my Brother.

Meet his well-meaning Wounds, wise heart!   45
And hast to drink the wholesome dart.
That healing shaft, which heavn till now
Hath in love's quiver hid for you.
O Dart of love! arrow of light!
O happy you, if it hitt right,   50
It must not fall in vain, it must
Not mark the dry regardles dust.
Fair one, it is your fate; and brings
Æternall worlds upon it's wings.
Meet it with wide-spread armes; and see   55
It's seat your soul's just center be.

Disband dull feares; give faith the day.
To save your life, kill your delay.
It is love's seege; and sure to be
Your triumph, though his victory.   60
'Tis cowardise that keeps this feild

46 *hast to drink:* the idea of divine inebriation fused with erotic transverberation.
48 *love's quiver:* Cupid was equipped with a quiver; see "In cicatrices Domini," No. 50, and "The Flaming Heart," No. 63, line 70.

The aiery nation of neat Doves, 45
That draw the Chariot of chast Loves,
Chide your delay: yea those dull things,
Whose wayes have least to doe with wings,
Make wings at least of their own Weight,
And by their Love controll their Fate. 50
So lumpish Steel, untaught to move
Learn'd first his Lightnesse by his Love.
  What e're Love's matter be, he moves
By th'even wings of his own Doves,
Lives by his own Laws, and does hold 55
In grossest Metalls his own Gold.
  All things swear friends to Fair and Good,
Yea Suitours; Man alone is wo'ed,
Tediously wo'ed, and hardly wone:
Only not slow to be undone. 60
As if the Bargain had been driven
So hardly betwixt Earth and Heaven;
Our God would thrive too fast, and be
Too much a gainer by't, should we
Our purchas'd selves too soon bestow 65
On him, who has not lov'd us so.
When love of Us call'd Him to see
If wee'd vouchsafe his company,
He left his Father's Court, and came
Lightly as a Lambent Flame, 70
Leaping upon the Hills, to be
The Humble King of You and Me.
Nor can the cares of his whole Crown
(When one poor Sigh sends for him down)
Detain him, but he leaves behind 75
The late wings of the lazy Wind,
Spurns the tame Laws of Time and Place,
And breaks through all ten Heav'ns to our embrace.
  Yield to his Siege, wise Soul, and see
Your Triumph in his Victory. 80
Disband dull Feares, give Faith the day:
To save your Life, kill your Delay.
'Tis Cowardise that keeps this Field;

47–52 *yea . . . Love:* the scholastic thesis that stones, steel, and other dull and lumpish
objects demonstrated their love of God by falling (Williams, pp. 109–10).
  54 *wings . . . Doves:* Venus' chariot was drawn by doves.
  70 *Lambent flame:* a pun on 'Lamb'; Psalms 104:4, Song of Solomon 2:8 (G. W.
Williams, "Crashaw's 'Letter . . .'" *Explicator,* VI [1948], No. 7, #48).

And want of courage not to yeild.
Yeild then, o yeild, that love may win
The Fort at last, and let life in.
Yeild quickly. Lest perhaps you prove   65
Death's prey, before the prize of love.
This Fort of your fair selfe, if't be not won,
He is repulst indeed; But you'are undone.

And want of Courage not to Yield.
　　Yield then, O yield, that Love may win　　　　　85
The Fort at last, and let Life in.
Yield quickly, lest perhaps you prove
Death's Prey, before the Prize of Love.
This Fort of your Fair Self if't be not wone,
He is repuls'd indeed, but You'r undone.　　　　　90

III

Sacred Poems
Translated into English from
Latin and Italian

In this section the Latin and Italian originals are on the left-hand page, and Crashaw's English versions face them on the right-hand page.

HYMNS OF THE MEDIEVAL CHURCH.

The six poems that follow (Nos. 77–82) are Crashaw's translations or free paraphrases of some of the great hymns of the western Church. They were all published in 1648 and reprinted in 1652. The closest study of them is by Sister Margaret Claydon, *Richard Crashaw's Paraphrases;* it examines the language and the details of translation, but it does not lose sight of the variations of style and devotion. These hymns, she writes (pp. 136–37), "differ among themselves, representing early and late medieval poetry, emotional and intellectual schools of devotion, personal prayers or meditations, and doctrinal sequences.

77   *Hymnus de Passione Domini*

The Latin version places the emphasis on the cross throughout; the English introduces an addressee, the "languishing Soul," before turning to the cross, and thence to the Crucified. The result is a shift from the doctrinal and universal to the affective and particular. This paraphrase is perhaps the freest of all of the six Latin hymns. See further, Claydon, pp. 111–31.

1.   Vexilla regis prodeunt,
     Fulget crucis mysterium,
     Quo carne carnis conditor
     Suspensus est patibulo.

2.   Confixa clavis viscera
     Tendens manus vestigia,
     Redemptionis gratia
     Hic immolata est hostia.

HYMNS OF THE MEDIEVAL CHURCH.

Nevertheless, the resultant translations all exhibit an affective, subjective, dramatic, dynamic emphasis. . . . Crashaw has heightened the total emotional tone by structural means. By the increased use of adjectives he has effected a movement towards *stasis;* by changes in mood, tense, voice, introduction of personification and terms of address (all dramatic means), he has brought in a counter movement towards *dynamism.* He has thus created a tension between static and dynamic meanings which is lacking in the original poems."

77   *Vexilla Regis*

VEXILLA REGIS,
THE
HYMN
OF THE HOLY
CROSSE.

I.

Look up, languishing Soul! Lo where the fair
BADG of thy faith calls back thy care,
    And biddes thee ne're forget
    Thy life is one long Debt
Of loue to Him, who on this painfull TREE
Paid back the flesh he took for thee.

II.

Lo, how the streames of life, from that full nest
Of loues, thy lord's too liberall brest,
    Flow in an amorous floud
    Of WATER wedding BLOOD.
With these he wash't thy stain, transfer'd thy smart,
And took it home to his own heart.

Vexilla Regis: 52 (48).*
Heading: *Vexilla Regis:* Banners of the King (i.e. Badg of . . . Faith).
II Crashaw's stanza depends on #3 of the Latin.
    3-4 a reference to John 19:34.
    5 *wash't, transfer'd:* the two liquids represent the Sacraments of Baptism and Eucharist: with the water, Christ washed the stain (in Baptism); with the blood, he assumed the sin (Holy Eucharist) (Williams, p. 96).

3. Quo vulneratus insuper
   Mucrone diro lanceæ,
   Ut nos lavaret crimine
   Manavit unda sanguine.

4. Impleta sunt quæ concinit
   David fideli carmine
   Dicens: in nationibus
   Regnavit a ligno Deus.

5. Arbor decora et fulgida
   Ornata regis purpura,
   Electa digno stipite
   Tam sancta membra tangere.

6. Beata cuius brachiis
   Pretium pependit sæculi,
   Statera facta sæculi
   Prædamque tulit tartaris.

III.

But though great LOVE, greedy of such sad gain
Usurp't the Portion of THY pain,
    And from the nailes and spear
    Turn'd the steel point of fear,
Their use is chang'd, not lost; and now they move
Not stings of wrath, but wounds of love.

IV.

Tall TREE of life! thy truth makes good
What was till now ne're understood,
    Though the prophetick king
    Struck lowd his faithfull string,
It was thy wood he meant should make the THRONE
For a more then SALOMON.

V.

Larg throne of love! Royally spred
With purple of too Rich a red.
    Thy crime is too much duty;
    Thy Burthen, too much beauty;
Glorious, or Greivous more? thus to make good
Thy costly excellence with thy KING's own BLOOD.

VI.

Even ballance of both worlds! our world of sin,
And that of grace heavn way'd in HIM,
    Us with our price thou weighed'st;
    Our price for us thou payed'st;
Soon as the right-hand scale rejoyc't to prove
How much Death weigh'd more light then love.

III Crashaw's stanza depends on ##2 and 3 of the Latin.

IV. 3 *king:* i.e. David.

    5 *he meant:* evidently refers to Psalm 96:10, where David sings "Say among the heathen that the Lord reigneth." Manuscripts of the Psalter add "from the cross" (*a ligno*); it is clear that Fortunatus, author of the original Latin hymn, and Crashaw have these versions in mind (Claydon, p. 119).

VI the cross is traditionally imaged as a balance (see "Office of the Holy Crosse," No. 71), but the idea of using scales to decide the outcome of a conflict is classical also.

    5 *scale:* i.e. weighing pan.

7.　O crux ave spes unica
　　Hoc passionis tempore,
　　Auge piis iustitiam
　　Reisque dona veniam.

8.　Te summa Deus Trinitas
　　Collaudet omnis spiritus,
　　Quos per crucis mysterium
　　Salvas, rege per sæcula.

VII.

Hail, our alone hope! let thy fair head shoot
Aloft; and fill the nations with thy noble fruit.
    The while our hearts and we
    Thus graft our selves on thee;
Grow thou and they. And be thy fair increase
The sinner's pardon and the just man's peace.

[VIII]

Live, o for ever live and reign
The LAMB whom his own love hath slain!
And let thy lost sheep live to'inherit
That KINGDOM which this CROSSE did merit.
    AMEN.

78   *Sancta* Maria *Dolorum or The Mother of Sorrows*

This poem, "one of Crashaw's masterpieces, metaphorizes much which in the 'Stabat Mater' is prose statement. What are isolated motifs in [the Latin hymn] become recurrent and ritual in Crashaw; and the relations between Christ and His Mother form a perpetual and reciprocal movement. . . . Then to this drama of the two who are one is added a third, the compassionate poet . . . the intent is to draw the third . . . more and more closely into the union. The stanzas vary in metaphorical concentration . . . ; but the poem as a whole nowhere lapses much in temperature—indeed, better, perhaps, than any poem of Crashaw's, moves climactically. This is the most successful of Crashaw's paraphrases, for, though he has appropriated the substance [of the Latin] poem, he has completely reshaped it [and] translated it into his own sensibility as well as into English" (Warren, pp. 156–57). See further Praz (pp. 238–39) who emphasizes the comparison between the crude sublimity of the Latin and the fireworks of the English; and Martz (pp. 115–17) who relates those fireworks to the meditative tradition; and Claydon (pp. 11–30) who demonstrates the syntactic, grammatic, and metaphoric methods used to achieve a more dynamic and dramatic poem.

78 *Sequentia de Septem Doloribus Beatæ Virginis*

A
Patheticall descant upon the
devout Plainsong
OF
STABAT MATER
DOLOROSA.

SANCTA MARIA
D O L O R V M.

Sancta Maria Dolorum: 52 (48).*
Heading: the remarks about the "Patheticall descant, etc." sound editorial.
  Sancta Maria Dolorum: Holy Mary, of Sorrows [the Mother], see I 4.

1. Stabat mater dolorosa
   Iuxta crucem lacrymosa,
   Dum pendebat filius.
   Cuius animam gementem,
   Contristantem et dolentem
   Pertransivit gladius.
2. O quam tristis et afflicta
   Fuit illa benedicta
   Mater Unigeniti!
   Quae moerebat et dolebat,
   Et tremebat, dum videbat
   Nati poenas inclyti.
3. Quis non potest contristari,
   Matrem Christi contemplari
   Dolentem cum filio.
   In me sistat dolor tui,
   Crucifixo fac me frui
   Dum sum in exilio.

4. Hunc dolorem fac me moestum,
   Nec me facias alienum
   Ab hoc desiderio.
   Illum corde, illum ore,
   Semper feram cum dolore
   Et mentis martyrio.

I.

In shade of death's sad TREE
    Stood Dolefull SHEE.
Ah SHE! now by none other
Name to be known, alas, but SORROW'S MOTHER.
    Before her eyes
    Her's, and the whole world's joyes,
Hanging all torn she sees; and in his woes
And Paines, her Pangs and throes.
Each wound of His, from every Part,
All, more at home in her owne heart.

II.

    What kind of marble than
    Is that cold man
    Who can look on and see,
Nor keep such noble sorrowes company?
    Sure ev'en from you
    (My Flints) some drops are due
To see so many unkind swords contest
    So fast for one soft Brest.
While with a faithfull, mutuall, floud
Her eyes bleed TEARES, his wounds weep BLOOD.

III.

    O costly intercourse
    Of deaths, and worse,
    Divided loves. While son and mother
Discourse alternate wounds to one another;
    Quick Deaths that grow
    And gather, as they come and goe:
His Nailes write swords in her, which soon her heart
    Payes back, with more then their own smart;
Her SWORDS, still growing with his pain,
Turn SPEARES, and straight come home again.

II probably depends on ##3 and 5 of the Latin.
    10 "the Virgin's tears cannot atone for the sins of the world as blood, but they can
demonstrate the whiteness of contrition for the world in general. Similarly, the blood of Christ
weeps in white penitence for the red sins of the world which He has assumed" (Williams, pp.
96–97). The line anticipates IX 10.
III probably depends on ##1 and 2 of the Latin.
    7 *swords:* a reference to the prophecy of Simeon (Luke 2:35) "et tuam ipsius animam
pertransibit gladius" (Yea, a sword shall pierce through thy own soul also)—compare ##1,
4 of the Latin.

5. Quis est homo, qui non fleret,
   Matrem Christi si videret
   In tanto supplicio?
   Quis tam fortis degustaret
   Poenas matris, cum clamaret
   In tanto iudicio?

6. Pro peccatis suæ gentis
   Vidit Christum in tormentis,
   Et flagellis subditum;
   Vidit suum dulcem natum,
   Morientem, desolatum,
   Cum emisit spiritum.

7. Eia mater, fons amoris,
   Me sentire vim doloris
   Fac, ut tecum lugeam.
   Fac, ut ardeat cor meum
   In amando Christum deum,
   Et sibi complaceam.

8. Sancta mater, istud agas
   Crucifixi fige plagas
   Cordi meo valide.
   Tui nati vulnerati,
   Tam dignati pro me pati,
   Poenas mecum divide.

9. Alma salus, advocata
   Morte Christi dosolata,
   Miserere populi;
   Virgo dulcis, virgo pia,

IV.

She sees her son, her GOD,
Bow with a load
Of borrowd sins; And swimme
In woes that were not made for Him.
Ah hard command
Of love! Here must she stand
Charg'd to look on, and with a stedfast ey
See her life dy:
Leaving her only so much Breath
As serves to keep alive her death.

V.

O Mother turtle-dove!
Soft sourse of love
That these dry lidds might borrow
Somthing from thy full Seas of sorrow!
O in that brest
Of thine (the noblest nest
Both of love's fires and flouds) might I recline
This hard, cold, Heart of mine!
The chill lump would relent, and prove
Soft subject for the seige of love.

VI.

O teach those wounds to bleed
In me; me, so to read
This book of loves, thus writ
In lines of death, my life may coppy it

IV   probably depends on ##4 and 6 of the Latin.
    3 *swimme:* see "Upon the Bleeding Crucifix," III, 4.
V   depends on #7 of the Latin.
    3 *these . . . lidds:* these words introduce the poet, who has been mentioned as early as #3 in the Latin ("In me . . .").
    9 *relent:* soften, liquefy (the Latin meaning).

Virgo clemens, O Maria,
Audi preces servuli.

10. Fac me vere tecum flere,
Crucifixo condolere,
Donec ego vixero.
Iuxta crucem tecum stare,
Te libenter sociare,
Cum planctu desidero.

11. Virgo virginum præclara,
Iam non mihi sis amara,
Fac me tecum plangere.
Fac, ut portem Christi mortem
Passionis eius sortem
Et plagas recolere.

With loyall cares.
O let me, here, claim shares;
Yeild somthing in thy sad præogative
(Great Queen of greifes) and give
Me too my teares; who, though all stone,
Think much that thou shouldst mourn alone.

VII.

Yea let my life and me
Fix here with thee,
And at the Humble foot
Of this fair TREE take our eternall root.
That so we may
At least be in loves way;
And in these chast warres while the wing'd wounds flee
So fast 'twixt him and thee,
My brest may catch the kisse of some kind dart,
Though as at second hand, from either heart.

VIII.

O you, your own best Darts
Dear, dolefull hearts!
Hail; and strike home and make me see
That wounded bosomes their own weapons be.
Come wounds! come darts!
Nail'd hands! and peirced hearts!
Come your whole selves, sorrow's great son and mother!
Nor grudge a yonger-Brother
Of greifes his portion, who (had all their due)
One single wound should not have left for you.

IX.

Shall I, sett there
So deep a share
(Dear wounds) and onely now
In sorrows draw no Dividend with you?
O be more wise
If not more just, mine eyes!

VI probably depends on #8 of the Latin.
   3 *book of loves:* the *liber charitatis;* see poem No. 51.
VII depends on #10 of the Latin.
   7 *wing'd wounds:* A. F. Allison ("Crashaw and St. François de Sales," *RES,* XXIV [1948], 295–302) finds influences in this passage and in the following stanza from St. François' *Traité de l'amour de Dieu,* VI, 13–14.
VIII depends on #11 of the Latin.
IX continues the dependence on #11 of the Latin.
   4 *draw no Dividend:* a metaphor from commerce, fully exploited in these stanzas (Williams, pp. 128–29).

12. Fac me plagis vulnerari,
     Cruce fac inebriari
     Et cruore filii.
     Inflammatus et accensus
     Per te, virgo, sim defensus
     In die iudicii.

13. Fac me cruce custodiri
     Morte Christi præmuniri
     Confoveri gratia.
     Quando corpus morietur,
     Fac, ut animæ donetur
     Paradisi gloria.

Flow, tardy founts! and into decent showres
 Dissolve my Dayes and Howres.
And if thou yet (faint soul!) deferr
To bleed with him, fail not to weep with her.

x.

 Rich Queen, lend some releife;
 At least an almes of greif
To'a heart who by sad right of sin
Could prove the whole summe (too sure) due to him.
 By all those stings
 Of love, sweet bitter things,
Which these torn hands transcrib'd on thy true heart
 O teach mine too the art
To study him so, till we mix
Wounds; and become one crucifix.

xi.

 O let me suck the wine
 So long of this chast vine
 Till drunk of the dear wounds, I be
A lost Thing to the world, as it to me.
 O faithfull freind
 Of me and of my end!
Fold up my life in love; and lay't beneath
 My dear lord's vitall death.
Lo, heart, thy hope's whole Plea! Her pretious Breath
Powr'd out in prayrs for thee; thy lord's in death.

---

x depends on line 1 of #12 of the Latin.
 7 *torn hands transcrib'd:* the wounds as writing implements (Williams, p. 118).
xi depends on ##12 and 13 of the Latin.
 1, 3 *suck . . . drunk:* the concept of divine nourishment fused with that of intoxication.

79   *Rhythmus ad Sacram Eucharistiam*

The difference between the headings for this poem in 52 and 48, where it is called "A Hymne to Our Saviour by the Faithful Receiver of the Sacrament," shows clearly the doctrinal differences in the countries of origin of the editions, the differences in the theology of the editors, and possibly the differences in Crashaw's religious affiliations. The Hymn is rightly an adoration—not of the Saviour as 48 would have it thought—of the Sacrament, a form of worship prohibited by number xxviii of the Thirty-nine Articles: "The Sacrament of the Lord's Supper was not by Christ's ordinance . . . [to be] worshipped." The hymn is written by St. Thomas Aquinas, the great Dominican philosopher-theologian, who contrasts his own faith sustained by hearing with the faith of St. Thomas Didymus, the Doubter (John 20:24–29), sustained by sight and touch. The identity of the names gives the generally austere Latin poem a pleasant intimacy which is maintained in Crashaw's poem. The concepts of faith in the two Thomases and in Crashaw derive from passages in John 20:29 "Thomas, because thou hast seen me, thou hast believed: blessed are they that have not seen and yet have believed" and in Mark 9:24 "Lord I believe; help thou my unbelief." The Anglican collect for St. Thomas's Day (the Gospel is the passage from John) presents doubt as a means of confirming faith. The doubt of Thomas is the subject of several epigrams—as is the doubt of Matthew 28:17. (See further Esch, pp. 143–51, and Claydon, pp. 31–51.) Claydon points out (pp. 50–51) that in the Latin the emphasis is always on the addressee while in the English, it has shifted to the speaker. The paragraph divisions of the English correspond roughly to the stanzas of the Latin, but lines 27–32 and 33–36 should perhaps be one stanza and lines 51–56 a separate stanza. Such an ordering would reflect the Latin exactly. See also "Lauda Sion Salvatorem," the next hymn. See S. L. Bethell, "The *Adoro Te Devote* of St. Thomas Aquinas and Crashaw's English version *The Hymn in Adoration of the Blessed Sacrament Compared*," *Comparative Literature Studies* (Cardiff), VI–VII (1942), 38–42.

1.   Adoro te devote, latens deitas
      Quae sub his figuris vere latitas
      Tibi se cor meum totum subiicit
      Quia te contemplans totum deficit.

79   *Adoro Te.*
The Hymn of St. Thomas *in Adoration of the Blessed Sacrament*

THE HYMN OF SAINTE THOMAS
IN ADORATION OF THE BLESSED SACRAMENT.

ADORO TE

With all the powres my poor Heart hath
Of humble love and loyall Faith,
Thus lowe (my hidden life!) I bow to thee
Whom too much love hath bow'd more low for me.
Down down, proud sense! Discourses dy.   5
Keep close, my soul's inquiring ey!
Nor touch nor tast must look for more
But each sitt still in his own Dore.

Adoro Te: 52 (48).*
Engraving: Ecce panis angelorū: Behold the bread of angels. The object pictured is the
ciborium in which the consecrated elements of the Mass are reserved. Christ's body feeds
men on earth and angels in heaven; see "Lauda Sion Salvatorem," XI.

2. Visus, tactus, gustus in te fallitur
Sed auditu solo tuto creditur:
Credo quidquid dixit Dei filius:
Nil hoc verbo veritatis verius.

3. In cruce latebat sola deitas
Ad hic latet simul et humanitas:
Ambo tamen credens atque confitens
Peto quod petivit latro pœnitens.

4. Plagas sicut Thomas non intueor
Deum tamen meum te confiteor:
Fac me tibi semper magis credere,
In te spem habere et diligere.

5. O memoriale mortis domini,
Panis vivus, vitam praestans homini:
Praesta meæ menti de te vivere
Et te illi semper dulce sapere.

Your ports are all superfluous here,
Save That which lets in faith, the eare.   10
Faith is my skill. Faith can beleive
As fast as love new lawes can give.
Faith is my force. Faith strength affords
To keep pace with those powrfull words.
And words more sure, more sweet, then they   15
Love could not think, truth could not say.

O let thy wretch find that releife
Thou didst afford the faithfull theife.
Plead for me, love! Alleage and show
That faith has farther, here, to goe   20
And lesse to lean on. Because than
Though hidd as GOD, wounds writt thee man,
Thomas might touch; None but might see
At least the suffring side of thee;
And that too was thy self which thee did cover,   25
But here ev'n That's hid too which hides the other.

Sweet, consider then, that I
Though allow'd nor hand nor eye
To reach at thy lov'd Face; nor can
Tast thee GOD, or touch thee MAN;   30
Both yet beleive and wittnesse thee
My LORD too and my GOD, as lowd as He.
Help lord, my Faith, my Hope increase;
And fill my portion in thy peace.
Give love for life; nor let my dayes   35
Grow, but in new powres to thy name and praise.

O dear memoriall of that Death
Which lives still, and allowes us breath!
Rich, Royall food! Bountyfull BREAD!
Whose use denyes us to the dead;   40
Whose vitall gust alone can give
The same leave both to eat and live;

17–26 probably depends on #3, lines 1–2 of the Latin.
18 *theife:* of Luke 23:39–43, who also demonstrated his faith when it must have seemed totally futile.
21 *than:* i.e. then.
25 *thy self:* i.e. the blood; see "On our Crucified Lord, Naked and Bloody," No. 44.
27–36 probably depends on #3, lines 3–4, and #4 of the Latin.
32 *My Lord . . . God:* Thomas's acceptance, John 20:28.

6. Pie pellicane, Iesu domine
   Me immundum munda tuo sanguine
   Cuius una stilla salvum facere
   Totum mundum quit ab omni scelere

7. Iesum quem velatum nunc adspicio
   Oro: fiat illud quod tam sitio,
   Ut te revelata cernens facie
   Visu sim beatus tuæ gloriæ.

Live ever Bread of loves, and be
My life, my soul, my surer selfe to mee.

O soft self-wounding Pelican!   45
Whose brest weepes Balm for wounded man.
Ah this way bend thy benign floud
To'a bleeding Heart that gaspes for blood.
That blood, whose least drops soveraign be
To wash my worlds of sins from me.   50
Come love! Come Lord! and that long day
For which I languish, come away.
When this dry soul those eyes shall see,
And drink the unseal'd sourse of thee.
When Glory's sun faith's shades shall chase,   55
And for thy veil give me thy FACE.
                    AMEN.

---

45 *Pelican:* the emblem of Christ's sacrifice; the pelican is traditionally held to feed her young with her own blood, thus dying that they may live (Williams, p. 108; Claydon, p. 45).

49–50 compare *Lauda Sion,* x; "St. Thomas praises the blood because it will wash the world clean from sin; Crashaw . . . praises it because it will wash the worlds of sin clean from Crashaw" (Williams, p. 24); "It is deplorable that the scope of religion should have been so narrowed" (Bethell, *ibid.,* p. 42).

51–56 depend on #7 of the Latin.

54 *unseal'd sourse:* open and continually flowing spring.

56 *Face:* I Corinthians 13:12 "Now we see through a glass, darkly; but then face to face."

80   *De Venerabili Sacramento in Festo Corporis* Christi

This hymn, also by St. Thomas, is the companion piece to the preceding, "Adoro Te"; both contemplate the Blessed Sacrament—"This soveraign subject" —and move in meditation from that subject to a final prayer (lines 45–56, stanzas xiii–xiv), ending with a petition for communion in Heaven before Christ's "Face." The original contemplation fixes on "this day . . . this bright day," evidently the day of the institution of the Lord's Supper; stanzas iv–v express the significance of the new covenant; stanzas vi–x "expound the dogma of the Holy Eucharist, following generally in outline the articles in the third part of [St. Thomas's] *Summa Theologica*" (Claydon, p. 53). The remaining stanzas return to Sion, the original addressee, and include the whole church in the final prayer. (See Claydon, pp. 52–77.)

1. Lauda Sion salvatorem,
    Lauda ducem et pastorem
      In hymnis et canticis:
    Quantum potes, tantum aude,
    Quia maior omni laude,
      Nec laudare sufficis.

2. Laudis thema specialis
    Panis vivus et vitalis
      Hodie proponitur,
    Quem in sacrae mensa coenæ
    Turbæ fratrum duodenæ
      Datum non ambigitur.

3. Sit laus plena, sit sonora
    Sit iucunda, sit decora,
      Mentis iubilatio:
    Dies enim sollemnis agitur
    In qua mensæ prima recolitur
      Huius institutio.

80   *Lauda Sion Salvatorem. The Hymn for the Blessed Sacrament*

LAUDA SION SALVATOREM.

THE HYMN.

FOR

THE BL.

SACRAMENT.

I.

Rise, Royall SION! rise and sing
Thy soul's kind shepheard, thy hart's KING.
Stretch all thy powres; call if you can
Harpes of heavn to hands of man.
This soveraign subject sitts above
The best ambition of thy love.

II.

Lo the BREAD of LIFE, this day's
Triumphant Text, provokes thy prayse.
The living and life-giving bread,
To the great twelve distributed
When LIFE, himself, at point to dy
Of love, was his own LEGACY.

III.

Come, love! and let us work a song
Lowd and pleasant, sweet and long;
Let lippes and Hearts lift high the noise
Of so just and solemn joyes,
Which on his white browes this bright day
Shall hence for ever bear away.

Lauda Sion Salvatorem (Praise, O Sion, thy Saviour): 52 (48).*
II   the institution of the Eucharist, Matthew 26:26–29, or perhaps more specifically I Co-
rinthians 11:23–26, the Epistle for Maundy Thursday–"this day's Triumphant Text."
III   this invitation recalls the "Hymn to the Name of Jesus" and the "O Gloriosa Domina."
   3   *lippes and Hearts:* cf. "O Gloriosa Domina," line 31.

4. In hac mensa novi regis
   Novum pascha novæ legis
       Phase vetus terminat.
   Vetustatem novitas,
   Umbram fugat veritas,
       Noctem lux eliminat.

5. Quod in cœna Christus gessit
   Faciendum hoc expressit
       In sui memoriam.
   Docti sacris institutis,
   Panem, vinum in salutis,
       Consecramus hostiam.

6. Dogma datur Christianis,
   Quod in carnem transit panis
   Et vinum in sanguinem.
   Quod non capis, quod non vides,
   Animosa firmat fides
       Praeter rerum ordinem.

7. Sub diversis speciebus,
   Signis tantum et non rebus,
       Latent res eximiæ.
   Caro cibus, sanguis potus:
   Manet tamen Christus totus
       Sub ultraque specie.

IV.

Lo the new LAW of a new LORD
With a new Lamb blesses the Board.
The aged Pascha pleads not yeares
But spyes love's dawn, and disappeares.
Types yeild to TRUTHES; shades shrink away;
And their NIGHT dyes into our Day.

V.

But lest THAT dy too, we are bid
Ever to doe what he once did.
And by a mindfull, mystick breath
That we may live, revive his DEATH;
With a well-bles't bread and wine,
Transsum'd, and taught to turn divine.

VI.

The Heavn-instructed house of FAITH
Here a holy Dictate hath
That they but lend their Form and face,
Themselves with reverence leave their place
Nature, and name, to be made good
By'a nobler Bread, more needfull BLOOD.

VII.

Where nature's lawes no leave will give,
Bold FAITH takes heart, and dares beleive.
In different species, names not things
Himself to me my SAVIOUR brings,
As meat in That, as Drink in this;
But still in Both one CHRIST he is.

IV. 1 *new Law:* the new covenant of Grace transcending the old covenant of the Law; see Hebrews 7–10.
  2 *blesses:* the characteristic Christian gesture: I Corinthians 11:24 (*Eucharist* is in Greek 'giving thanks'); Matthew 14:19; Luke 24:30, 35.
  3 *Pascha:* the Paschal, or Passover, Lamb; so I Corinthians 5:7: "Etenim Pascha nostrum immolatus est Christus" (Christ our Passover is sacrificed for us). The Jewish Passover, the institution of blood symbolic of Mosaic Law (Exodus 12), "disappears" (Hebrews 8:13) like the night before the day—at the foundation of the new institution of blood symbolic of Christian Love.
  4 *Types:* the Old Testament anticipations of New Testament events, see further stanza XII.
v. 2 *Ever to doe:* "this do ye . . . in remembrance of me" (I Corinthians 11:25).
  4 *revive his Death:* "For as often as ye eat this bread, and drink this cup, ye do shew the Lord's death till he come" (I Corinthians 11:26).
VI The Doctrine of Transubstantiation (but cf. Art. XXVIII).

8. A sumente non concisus,
    Non confractus, non divisus,
        Integer accipitur
    Sumit unus, sumunt mille,
    Quantum isti, tantum ille,
        Nec sumptus consumitur.

9. Sumunt boni, sumunt mali
    Sorte tamen inaequali
        Vitæ vel interitus.
    Mors est malis, vita bonis:
    Vide, paris sumptionis
        Quam sit dispar exitus.

10. Fracto demum sacramento
    Ne vacilles, sed memento
    Tantum esse sub fragmento
        Quantum toto tegitur:
    Nulla rei fit scissura,
    Signi tantum fit fractura
    Qua nec status nec statura
        Signati minuitur.

11. Ecce panis angelorum,
    Factus cibus viatorum,
    Vere panis filiorum,
        Non mittendus canibus.

VIII.

The Receiving Mouth here makes
Nor wound nor breach in what he takes.
Let one, or one THOUSAND be
Here Dividers, single he
Beares home no lesse, all they no more,
Nor leave they both lesse then before.

IX.

Though in it self this SOVERAIN FEAST
Be all the same to every Guest,
Yet on the same (life-meaning) Bread
The child of Death eates himself Dead.
Nor is't love's fault, but sin's dire skill
That thus from LIFE can DEATH distill.

X.

When the blest signes thou broke shall see,
Hold but thy Faith intire as he
Who, howsoe're clad, cannot come
Lesse then whole CHRIST in every crumme.
In broken formes a stable FAITH
Untouch't her pretious TOTALL hath.

XI.

Lo the life-food of ANGELLS then
Bow'd to the lowly mouths of men!
The children's BREAD; the Bridegroom's WINE.
Not to be cast to dogges, or swine.

VIII The stanza recalls the miracles of the feeding of the multitudes.

IX. 4 *child . . . Dead:* I Corinthians 11:27–29: "For he that eateth . . . unworthily, eateth
. . . damnation to himself." See Article XXVIII, and Epigram, No. 11.

X. 3–4 *cannot . . . crumme:* the epitome of Crashaw's theme of great power in small particles (drops, tears, etc.), these lines, at once great poetry and great dogma, translate the decree of the Council of Trent: "Totus enim et integer Christus sub panis specie et sub quavis ipsius speciei parte . . . exsistit" (For Christ whole and unbroken exists in the species of bread and in every part whatever of that species). (See also Southwell, "Of the Blessed Sacrament of the Aulter"; Williams, p. 24.)

XI. 1 *life-food of Angells:* see the engraving (and note) to preceding poem.

In figuris præsignatur,
Quum Isaac immolatur,
Agnus Paschæ deputatur,
    Datur manna patribus.

12. Bone pastor, panis vere,
Iesu, nostri miserere.
Tu nos pasce, nos tuere,
Tu nos bona fac videre
    In terra viventium.

Tu qui cuncta seis et vales,
Qui nos pascis hic mortales,
Tuos ibi commensales,
Cohaeredes et sodales
    Fac sanctorum civium.

XII.

Lo, the full, finall, SACRIFICE
On which all figures fix't their eyes.
The ransom'd ISACK, and his ramme;
The MANNA, and the PASCHAL Lamb.

XIII.

JESU MASTER, Just and true!
Our FOOD, and faithfull SHEPHARD too!
O by thy self vouchsafe to keep,
As with thy selfe thou feed'st thy SHEEP.

XIV.

O let that love which thus makes thee
Mix with our low Mortality,
Lift our lean Soules, and sett us up
Convictors of thine own full cup,
Coheirs of SAINTS. That so all may
Drink the same wine; and the same WAY.
Nor change the PASTURE, but the PLACE;
To feed of THEE in thine own FACE.

AMEN.

XII. 2 *figures:* types.
 3–4 *Isack . . . ramme, Manna, Paschal Lamb:* three types of Christ: Isaac, carrying the wood for the burnt offering of himself (Genesis 22:1–18), anticipates Christ carrying his own cross; manna, given to feed the Israelites in the wilderness (Exodus 16:1–15), anticipates the body of Christ given to feed mankind; Paschal Lamb, the means of deliverance from captivity in Egypt (Exodus 12), anticipates the Lamb of God, the deliverance from sin. See further Tuve, pp. 121–22, 162; Williams, p. 105.
XIV. 4 *Convictors:* co-victors (as Coheirs).
 4–7 *cup . . . Pasture:* the wine and bread of the Eucharist—the blood and body of Christ—are the food of angels (Williams, p. 98).
 7–8 *Pasture . . . Face:* a commonplace pun; as Christ is the "Food, and . . . Shephard too," he is both pasture for the sheep and pastor of them.

81   *Prosa de Mortuis*

The "Dies Irae" is generally regarded as the masterpiece of the medieval hymns, impressive in its solemnity. Crashaw by introducing himself in the first line has robbed the opening of its universality and much of its dignity and so set a tone of intimacy out of keeping with the intent of the Latin. The first part of the poem which in the Latin is a general description of the *eschaton* is made almost sentimental in the English by being referred to the "my soul" of the opening line. The private application, coming in the Latin at stanza #7, is there set in proper perspective against the horrors of that day; in the English redaction there is no such contrast. It is safe to say that Crashaw's spirit—thou much concerned to contemplate eternal salvation through love—has little interest in Christ as judge. The attributes of a judge are properly "sure," "sharp," "angry," "dread," "Just," "merciful"; but these are virtues which have no particular attractiveness to Crashaw. He has therefore attempted to see the Judge as "my Freind" and has called him "soft" and "Dear," attributes for which there is ample Christian tradition but which are none the less out of keeping with the other proper attributes as expressed in the poem. See also Claydon, pp. 78–99.

81 *Dies Iræ Dies Illa.*

THE

HYMN.

OF THE

CHURCH,

IN MEDITATION OF

THE DAY OF

JUDGMENT.

Dies Iræ Dies Illa: 52 (48).* The wording of the heading is from (Vulgate) Zephaniah 1:15.
Other Apocalyptic visions are to be found in Matthew 24–25, in the Pauline epistles, and in
the Revelation.

1. Dies iræ, dies illa,
   Solvet sæclum in favilla,
   Teste David cum Sibylla.

2. Quantus tremor est futurus,
   Quando iudex est venturus,
   Cuncta stricte discussurus?

3. Tuba mirum spargens sonum,
   Per sepulcra regionum,
   Coget omnes ante thronum.

4. Mors stupebit et natura,
   Cum resurget creatura,
   Iudicanti responsura.

5. Liber scriptus proferetur,
   In quo totum continetur,
   Unde mundus iudicetur.
6. Iudex ergo cum sedebit,
   Quidquid latet, apparebit,
   Nil inultum remanebit.

7. Quid sum miser tunc dicturus,
   Quem patronum rogaturus,
   Cum vix iustus sit securus?

I.

Hears't thou, my soul, what ‑serious things
Both the Psalm and sybyll sings
Of a sure judge, from whose sharp Ray
The world in flames shall fly away.

II.

O that fire! before whose face
Heavn and earth shall find no place.
O those eyes! whose angry light
Must be the day of that dread Night.

III.

O that trump! whose blast shall run
An even round with the circling Sun.
And urge the murmuring graves to bring
Pale mankind forth to meet his king.

IV.

Horror of nature, hell and Death!
When a deep Groan from beneath
Shall cry we come, we come and all
The caves of night answer one call.

V.

O that Book! whose leaves so bright
Will sett the world in severe light.
O that Judge! whose hand, whose eye
None can indure; yet none can fly.

VI.

Ah then, poor soul, what wilt thou say?
And to what Patron chuse to pray?
When starres themselves shall stagger; and
The most firm foot no more then stand.

I. 2 *Psalm, sybyll:* i.e. both sacred and pagan; St. Augustine cites in the *De Civitate Dei*
the Erythraean Sibyl's prediction of the end of the world (Claydon, p. 80).
III. 1 *trump:* Zephaniah 1:16.
   3 *urge:* force (the Latin meaning).
v. 1 *Book:* Revelation 13:8.
VI. 3 *starres . . . shall stagger:* Matthew 24:29.

8. Rex tremendæ maiestatis,
    Qui salvandos salvas gratis,
    Salva me fons pietatis.

9. Recordare, Iesu pie,
    Quod sum causa tuæ viæ:
    Ne me perdas illa die.

10. Quærens me sedisti lassus.
    Redemisti crucem passus:
    Tantus labor non sit cassus.

11. Iuste iudex ultionis,
    Donum fac remissionis
    Ante diem rationis.

12. Ingemisco tanquam reus,
    Culpa rubet vultus meus:
    Supplicanti parce Deus.

Pſal. 137. 2.
*In conſpectu Angelorum psallam tibi et adorabo
ad Templum ſanctam tuum*

PLATE II.
Engraved frontispiece to the *Steps to the Temple*
(London, 1670).

EFFIGIES R. P. LANCELOTI ANDREWES EPISCOPI WINTONIENSIS.

See heer a Shadow from that setting SUNNE,
Whose glorious course through this Horizon runn
Left the dimm face of our dull Hemisphære,
All one great Eye, all drown'd in one great Teare.
Whose rare industrious Soule led his free thought
Through Learning's Universe, and (vainly) sought
Room for her spacious Self; untill at length
She found ÿ way home: with an holy strength

Snatcht herself hence to Heav'n; fill'd a bright place
Midst those immortal Fires, and on the face
Of her Great MAKER, fixt a flaming eye,
Where still She reads true, pure Divinitie.
And now ÿ graue Aspect hath deign'd to shrink
Into this lesse appearance. If you think
'Tis but a dead face, Art doth heer bequeath
Look on the following leaues & see him breath.

HONI·SOIT·QVI·MAL·PENSE.

ΟΡΘΟΤΟΜΕΙΝ ΚΑΙ ΟΡΘΟΠΟΔΕΙΝ.

Are to be sold by R. Badger dwelling
in Stationer's Hall. 1632.

John Payne Fecit

PLATE III.
John Payne's engraved frontispiece of Lancelot Andrewes.
See Poem Number 359.

PLATE IV.
William Marshall's engraved title page of *Saturni Ephemerides*,
by Henry Isaacson, 1633.
See Poem Number 360.

VII.

But thou giv'st leave (dread Lord) that we
Take shelter from thy self, in thee;
And with the wings of thine own dove
Fly to thy scepter of soft love.

VIII.

Dear, remember in that Day
Who was the cause thou cams't this way.
Thy sheep was stray'd; And thou wouldst be
Even lost thy self in seeking me.

IX.

Shall all that labour, all that cost
Of love, and ev'n that losse, be lost?
And this lov'd soul, judg'd worth no lesse
Then all that way, and wearynesse?

X.

Just mercy then, thy Reckning be
With my price, and not with me:
'Twas pay'd at first with too much pain,
To be pay'd twice; or once, in vain.

XI.

Mercy (my judge) mercy I cry
With blushing Cheek and bleeding ey,
The conscious colors of my sin
Are red without and pale within.

XII.

O let thine own soft bowells pay
Thy self; And so discharge that day.
If sin can sigh, love can forgive.
O say the word my Soul shall live.

---

x. 2 *my price:* i.e. Christ (Williams, p. 127).

xi. 2 *bleeding ey:* i.e. weeping red tears (*red without*) to represent the ashy white contrition of the heart (*pale within*).

xii. 1 *bowells:* the seat of the sympathetic emotions; "soft bowells . . . discharge," however, by the process of elimination, has quite a different meaning; it may be thought not in the best taste to introduce scatology into eschatology—the stanza has no Latin original.

13. Qui Mariam absolvisti,
    Et latronem exaudisti,
    Mihi quoque spem dedisti,

14. Preces meæ non sunt dignæ,
    Sed tu bonus fac benigne,
    Ne perenni cremer igne.

15. Inter oves locum præsta,
    Et ab hœdis me sequestra,
    Statuens in parte dextra.

16. Confutatis maledictis,
    Flammis acribus addictis;
    Voca me cum benedictis.

17. Oro supplex et acclinis,
    Cor contritum, quasi cinis:
    Gere curam mei finis.

XIII.

Those mercyes which thy MARY found
Or who thy crosse confes't and crown'd,
Hope tells my heart, the same loves be
Still alive; and still for me.

XIV.

Though both my Prayres and teares combine,
Both worthlesse are; For they are mine.
But thou thy bounteous self still be;
And show thou art, by saving me.

XV.

O when thy last Frown shall proclaim
The flocks of goates to folds of flame,
And all thy lost sheep found shall be,
Let come ye blessed then call me.

XVI.

When the dread ITE shall divide
Those Limbs of death from thy left side,
Let those life-speaking lipps command
That I inheritt thy right hand.

XVII.

O hear a suppliant heart; all crush't
And crumbled into contrite dust.
My hope, my fear! my Judge, my Freind!
Take charge of me, and of my END.

XVI. 1 *Ite:* classical goddess of death.
XVII. 2 *contrite:* a bilingual pun; *contritum* means "crumbled into dust."

82   *[De Beata Virgine]*

This is the smallest and most intimate of the Latin hymns Crashaw translated.
Miss Wallerstein thought (pp. 142–43) it the best English poem of the six. If it
is, then that distinction lies in its smallness and intimacy and in Crashaw's af-
finity for the themes of Mariolotry and maternity. He is more at home in the
bosom of Mary than, for example, in the contemplation of Christ the judge in
"Dies Iræ." Furthermore, the aspirant adoration with which the poem begins is
one of Crashaw's characteristic postures, and the united choral effort with
which the poem ends is one of his favorite methods of praise. Claydon (p. 102)
cites parallel passages from the Mass of Our Lady, the "Salve, Sancta Parens,"
no. 2. See Claydon, pp. 100–10.

HYMNUS

1.   O gloriosa domina,

     Excelsa supra sydera:

     Qui te creavit provide,

     Lactasti sacro ubere.

82 *O Gloriosa Domina*

S. MARIA MAIOR.
Dilectus meus mihi et ego illi,
qui pascitur inter lilia. Cant. 2.
I. Messager sc.

THE

HIMN

O GLORIOSA DOMINA.

Hail, most high, most humble one!
Above the world, below thy Son;
Whose blush the moon beauteously marres
And staines the timerous light of starres.
He that made all things, had not done   5
Till he had made Himself thy son
The whole world's host would be thy guest
And board himself at thy rich Brest.
O boundles Hospitality!
The Feast of all things feeds on thee.   10

O Gloriosa Domina (O Lady, Full of Glory): 52 (48).*
  1–10 depend on stanza #1.
  3–4 *Whose . . . starres:* i.e. Mary's blush mars the moon and stains the stars; Mary's blush is the blush of modesty which, being perfect, mars and stains in a celestial not a human manner—it shows that the moon and stars are inadequate, but it does so "beauteously."
  5–6 see "The Phaenix builds the Phaenix' nest," "Nativitie Hymn," No. 68, line 46, and note (Williams, pp. 53–54).
  7 *host:* a pun—the bread or wafer of the Mass; but in "host . . . guest" there is a Latin pun on the word *hospes* which has both meanings. (As in Epigram No. 201.)
  10 *Feast of all things:* i.e. "the whole world's host."

2. Quod Eva tristis abstulit,

    Tu reddis almo germine:

    Intrent ut astra flebiles,

    Celi fenestra facta es.

3. Tu regis alti ianua,
    Et porta lucis fulgida:
    Vitam datam per virginem,
    Gentes redemptæ plaudite.

4. Gloria tibi domine,
    Qui natus es de virgine:
    Cum patre et sancto spiritu,
    In sempiterna secula.
                        Amen.

11–26 depend on stanza #2 (see Claydon, pp. 104–5).
12–16 *E're* . . . *bitt:* Eve's unnatural (unmotherly) haste bore children of death rather than of life (the paradox of a mother who should give life, giving death); this gift is unkind (cruel, unnatural), it is a "hasty Grave" and a "Quick . . . Tomb" (a living burial—the quick are the dead).
17 *Better Fruit:* in contrast to Eve's apple, but also the fruit of the second tree, the cross; see "Office of the Holy Crosse," No. 70, Sixth Hour, Antiphona, and Tuve, pp. 81–86.
18–34 *womb, window, Dawn, door, sourse, fountain:* all metaphors of becoming.
19 *window:* a symbol of the virginity of Mary: the glass permits the passage of light but is not broken in the process.

The first Eve, mother of our FALL,
E're she bore any one, slew all.
Of Her unkind gift might we have
The inheritance of a hasty GRAVE;
Quick burye'd in the wanton TOMB   15
 Of one forbidden bitt;
Had not a Better FRUIT forbidden it.
 Had not thy healthfull womb
 The world's new eastern window bin
And given us heav'n again, in giving HIM. 20
Thine was the Rosy DAWN that sprung the Day
Which renders all the starres she stole away.
 Let then the Aged world be wise, and all
Prove nobly, here, unnaturall.
'Tis gratitude to forgett that other   25
And call the maiden Eve their mother.
 Yee redeem'd Nations farr and near,
Applaud your happy selves in her,
(All you to whom this love belongs)
And keep 't alive with lasting songs.   30
 Let hearts and lippes speak lowd; and say
Hail, door of life: and sourse of day!
The door was shutt, the fountain seal'd;
Yet LIGHT was seen and LIFE reveald.
The door was shutt, yet let in day,   35
The fountain seald, yet life found way.
 Glory to thee, great virgin's son
In bosom of thy FATHER's blisse.
 The same to thee, sweet SPIRIT be done;
As ever shall be, was, and is.   40
   AMEN.

---

26 *maiden Eve:* i.e. Mary.

27–36 depend on stanza #3.

31 *hearts and lippes . . . say:* the invitation to join in the choral song of praise may be paralelled in the "Hymn to the Name of Jesus," No. 55 and in the "Lauda Sion"; in the latter (III) occurs the phrase "lippes and Hearts."

35 *door . . . day:* St. Augustine writes "What means this closed gate in the House of the Lord [Ezekiel 44:2], except that Mary is to be ever inviolate?" (see further Williams, p. 122).

36 *fountain . . . way:* from Song of Solomon 4:12.

83　　　　　　*Tragœdia* Christus *Patiens*

Martin (pp. xc–xcii) dates this poem before 1635, early in Crashaw's career. It thus is contemporary with (or before) the Sacred Epigrams in Latin, and it concerns itself in giving the biography of Christ (the speaker) as do those Epigrams. It is the opening speech of the tragedy. The same themes are present here in simple and straightforward language which Crashaw will handle later with greater color and floridity. Yet here it is possible to see the beginnings of the later manner. For example, the slaughter of the innocents (lines 19–30) lacks

Actus Primus.

IESUS.

O Qui futuræ fortis immense arbiter

Rerum potente fata moliris manu,

Supreme mundi genitor, & genitor meus

Mundo prioris, omnia æquavi hactenus

Imperia factis: si quid ulterius iubes

Paratus asto: cuncta quæ timeo feram:

Hác lege veni. Quem tamen finem gravi

Statuis labori. Nulla me vidit dies

Secura: crevit ipse dum fertur labos,

Maloque patuit semper in peius via.

Paterna summi templa deservi ætheris

Nec natus exul. pauperem pressi casam

Stabulique prima turpis incunabula

Male notus infans: parvus, infelix, miser

Iam dignus hostis rege Iudaeo fui.

Nondum annus alter ierat, ætati parum

Nimium tyranno, dirus Ephratias nurus

Orbavit ensis: turba puerorum cadit,

83   *Out of* Grotius *his Tragedy of* Christes *sufferinges.*

almost entirely the characteristic Crashavian manner of the four epigrams on the same subject, but Crashaw has managed to add the mothers' breasts though in a merely naturalistic context. It may be argued that the translation is an academic assignment; it is difficult to account otherwise for such close attention to the original in both spirit and rendering (compare Crashaw's "Psalme 23," No. 2).

O thou the span of whose Omnipotence
Doth graspe the fate of thinges, and share th' events
Of future chance! the world's grand sire; and mine
Before the world. Obedient lo! I joyne
An æquall pace thus farre; thy word, my deedes   5
Have flow'd together. if ought further needes
I shrinke not. but thus ready stand to beare
(ffor else why came I?) ev'n what e're I feare.
Yett o what end? where does the period dwell
Of my sad labours? no day yett could tell   10
My soule shee was secure. Still have I borne
A still increasing burden; worse hath torne
His way through bad, to my successive hurt.
I left my glorious Fathers star-pav'd Court.
E're borne was banish't: borne was glad t' embrace   15
A poore (yea scarce a) roofe. whose narrow place
Was not so much as cleane: a stable kind;
The best my cradle and my birth could find.
Then was I knowne; and knowne unluckily
A weake, a wretched child; ev'n then was I   20
For Juryes king an enemy, even worth
His feare; the circle of a yeares round growth
Was not yett full, (a time that to my age
Made litle, not a litle to his rage)

Christ's sufferings: MS.*
   3, 4 *mine, joyne:* a correct rhyme in Crashaw's day—and still today in some speech patterns.
   11, 12 *Still:* i.e. always.
   21 *Juryes king:* i.e. the king of Jewry (Herod, king of Judæa).

Dum quæror unus, meque dilapso fuga

Cruentus error perdidit tantum nefas.

Centum per orbem cognitus miraculis

Patrem probavi. Livor adversum furit,

Et ipsa virtus peius Herode nocet.

Pater quid istud? Semper agnoscor tuus,

Semper recusor. Persa me coluit magus,

Et ante parvos jacuit infantis pedes,

Suoque Mithrae prætulit sidus meum.
At Abrahami gens ab æternis tibi
Seposita sæclis, priscaque Isacidum domus,
Excussit omnem mente degeneri Deum.
Hinc contumaces bella Pharisæi movent
Pierate fallax turba: at hinc in me trahit
Legum magistros dira pontificum cohors:
Illinc profani secta Sadoci minax
Regalis aulæ purpura invisum premit.
Fidei quid ultra restat? ad nutus meos
Natura rerum cessit & fassa est Deum.
Undæ liquentis ebrios potus bibit

Galilæa pubes. depuli alienam famem;

Meam subegi: bisque vicenos dies

Ieiuna nullis ora violavi cibis.

Inter secantes dexteras crevit Ceres:

Satiatus ingens populus, & toto tamen

Plus est relictum. flabra compressit notus,

Et æstuantis ira detumuit freti.

Durata siccos unda transmisit pedes.

Ferale morbi virus & membris grave

Arti negatum cedere humanæ malum

Vox medica vicit. longa caligo fugit,

When a wild sword ev'n from their brests, did lop   25
The Mothers Joyes in an untimely crop.
The search of one child (cruell industry!)
Was losse of multitudes; and missing mee
A bloud drunke errour spilt the costly ayme
Of their mad sin; (how great! and yett how vayne!)   30
I cal'd a hundred miracles to tell
The world my father. then does envy swell
And breake upon mee: my owne virtues height
Hurtes mee far worse then Herods highest spite;
A riddle! (father) still acknowledg'd thine   35
Am still refus'd; before the Infant Shrine
Of my weake feet the Persian Magi lay
And left their Mithra for my star: this they.
But Isaacks issue, the peculiar heyres
Of thy old goodnesse, know thee not for theires,   40
Basely degenerous. Against mee flocke
The stiffe neck'd Pharisees that use to mocke
Sound goodnesse with her shadow which they weare,
And 'gainst religion her owne colours beare.
The bloud hound brood of Priests against mee draw   45
Those Lawlesse tyrant masters of the Law.
Profane Sadocus too does fiercely lead
His court-fed impes against this hated head.
What would they more? th' ave seene when at my nod
Great Natures selfe hath shrunke and spoke mee god.   50
Drinke fayling there where I a guest did shine
The Water blush'd, and started into Wine.
Full of high sparkeling vigour: taught by mee
A sweet inebriated extasy.
And streight of all, this approbation gate,   55
Good wine in all poynts. but the easy rate;
Other mens hunger with strange feasts I quell'd,
Mine owne with stranger fastings, when I held
Twice twenty dayes pure abstinence, To feed
My minds devotion in my bodyes need.   60
A subtle inundation of quicke food
Sprang in the spending fingers, and o'reflow'd
The peoples hunger, and when all were full
The broken meate was much more then the whole.

38 *Mithra:* Persian god of the sun; see "Epiphany Hymn," No. 57, line 100.
47–48 *Sadocus . . . impes:* the Saducees, followers of Sadok.
52 *blush'd:* perhaps the origin of the famous "erubuit" of the epigram.
55 *gate:* got.

Meæque cæcus dexteræ debet diem.

Auditur ille qui nec audivit prius,

Silentiumque rumpit in laudes meas.

Quid illa sanctis semper adversa & Deo

Hostilis Erebi dira pallentis lues

Non pulsa nostris legibus mortalium

Habitata linquit pectora & vocem tremit?

Post opera tanta non satis Christo fuit

Prodesse vivis. victor ingenti manu

Fregi silentum regna, & infernum chaos.

Terris & astris & triumphato mari

Restabat orcus: per sepulchrales specus,

Per operta terris iura & umbrarum domos

Imperia misi.

The Wind in all his roaring brags stood still 65
And listned to the whisper of my will;
The wild waves couch'd; the sea forgott to sweat
Under my feet, the waters to bee wett.
In death-full desperate ills where art and all
Was nothing, there my voyce was med'cinall. 70
Old clouds of thickest blindnesse fled my sight
And to my touch darke Eyes did owe the light.
Hee that ne're heard now speakes, and finds a tongue
To chaunt my prayses in a new-strung song.
Even hee that belches out a foaming flood 75
Of hot defiance 'gainst what e're is good,
Father and Heyre of darkenesse, when I chide
Sinkes into Horrours bosome, glad tc hide
Himselfe in his owne hell; and now lets loose
Mans brest (his tenement) and breakes up house. 80
Yett here's not all, nor was't enough for mee;
To freind the living world, even death did see
Mee ranging in his quarters; and the land
Of deepest silence answered my command.
Heav'n, Earth, and Sea, my triumphs. what remain'd 85
Now but the Grave? the Grave it selfe I tam'd.

&c:.

79–80 *lets loose . . . house:* i.e. gives up the lease on the place he is renting and breaks up housekeeping.

84   *Alexias*

Crashaw's three "Alexias" elegies are based on selections from F. Remond's seven Latin elegies, "Uxoris Sancti Alexii Querimoniae" (The Laments of the Wife of St. Alexis). St. Alexius, who is thought to have lived in the fifth century, was one of the popular legendary saints of the sixteenth and seventeenth centuries. His achievements lay in mortification of the flesh, poverty, contrition, and continual prayer. Though a patrician Roman, he rejected the wealth and distinction of his parents and the company of his bride, whom he married to please them, and fled on his wedding day to the Far East where he lived for seventeen years. His piety revealed by a miracle of the Virgin, he returned to Rome and lived in a hole under the steps of his own palace for seventeen years.

ELEGIA PRIMA.

Illa ego Romanae virgo laus magna iuuentæ
    Quæ toties fueram mille negata procis,
En iaceo miseranda nouo sine coniuge coniux,
    Pæne relicta prius quam bene iuncta viro.
Succedit tantis etiam noua cura querelis,
    Vulneret (heu!) teneros quo vagas orbe pedes.
Si mihi nota foret regio qua liber oberrat,
    Inciperet certus mitior esse dolor.
Illi missa graves narraret epistola curas,
    Audiret meas forsitan ille preces.
Nectuntur scribendo moræ: prior ipsa volarem,
    Atque meæ fierem nuntia tristitiæ.
Cedere nam didici furtim, te, o Alexi, magistro,
    Et fugere e patria sola peulla domo.
Ipse daret pedibus celeres amor anxius alas,
    Præcipitique irem per loca vasta fuga.
Nullaque virgineos tardare pericula gressus,
    Dicere nec possent, parua puella mane. . . .
Meque docebit amor, fuerit si fracta carina,
    Indociles undis arte movere manus. . . .
Si tamen in me eritis crudeles vos quoque pisces,
    Naufraga si duro sum peritura mari,
Me manibus perijsse tuis, amor alme, iuuabit:
    Castus honorati funeris auctor eris.
Deque meo pontus faciet sibi nomine nomen,
    Et felix inter sidera sidus ero.

84   *Alexias*
The Complaint of the Forsaken Wife of Sainte Alexis

Another miracle disclosed his location to the Pope who found him there dead (Warren, pp. 136–39; Catholic Encyclopedia [1911]). Crashaw's selection from Remond omits many details of the saint's biography (that would have made the laments somewhat more coherent) and in consequence shifts the emphasis to the distinctly feminine. So the first Elegy concludes in a funeral tribute paid to the wife and the third includes a substantial section on the constancy of St. Cecilia. The theme of the elegies appears to be in effect "femal constancy," and the language throughout recalls amorous complaints of rejected lovers of the Petrarchan tradition.

THE FIRST ELEGIE.

I late the roman youth's loud prayse and pride,
Whom long none could obtain, though thousands try'd,
Lo here am left (alas), For my lost mate
T'embrace my teares, and kisse an unkind FATE.
Sure in my early woes starres were at strife,   5
And try'd to make a WIDOW ere a WIFE.
Nor can I tell (and this new teares doth breed)
In what strange path my lord's fair footsteppes bleed.
O knew I where he wander'd, I should see
Some solace in my sorrow's certainty.   10
I'd send my woes in words should weep for me,
(Who knowes how powrfull well-writt praires would be?)
Sending's too slow a word, my selfe would fly.
Who knowes my own heart's woes so well as I?
But how shall I steal hence? ALEXIS thou   15
Ah thou thy self, alas, hast taught me how.
Love too, that leads the way, would lend the wings
To bear me harmlesse through the hardest things.
And where love lends the wing, and leads the way,
What dangers can there be dare say me nay?   20
If I be shipwrack't, Love shall teach to swimme.
If drown'd; sweet is the death indur'd for HIM,

Alexias: 52 (48).*
First
    5   *starres . . . at strife:* a malevolent conjunction of planets.
    8   *lord's . . . bleed:* this language recalls the Lord's footsteps in the "Hymn to St. Teresa," No. 61, lines 178–82.
    17   *Love . . . wings:* the travels of lovers were frequently to be made with assistance from Cupid's wings.

Navita præteriens illa plorabit in unda,
  Firmabitque mea vota marina fide;
Et dicet, perijt quondam hic Romana puella,
  Dum toto amissum quæreret orbe virum.
Vivat tantus amor: semper sis, o bona virgo,
  Tam dilecta Deo, quam bene fida viro.

ELEGIA QUINTA.

Ast ego quot Soles numero? si credis amanti,
  Quolibet in spatio sæcula mille traho.
Iam didici stellas, iam Lunæ tempora novi.
  Eois iam sum doctior Astrologis.
Surge, age, pacato sidus mihi noscere cælo,
  Æthereasque novo lumine vince faces:
Quale Magos olim Christi ad cunabula reges
  Duxit, & optatam constitit ante casam:
Nascere, & ambiguum radijs mihi percute Alexim:
  Ibo nec incertas pes teret usque vias.

The noted sea shall change his name with me;
I, 'mongst the blest STARRES a new name shall be.
And sure where lovers make their watry graves   25
The weeping mariner will augment the waves.
For who so hard, but passing by that way
Will take acquaintance of my woes, and say
Here 't was the roman MAID found a hard fate
While through the world she sought her wandring mate.   30
Here perish't she, poor heart, heavns, be my vowes
As true to me, as she was to her spouse.
O live, so rare a love! live! and in thee
The too frail life of femal constancy.
Farewell; and shine, fair soul, shine there above   35
Firm in thy crown, as here fast in thy love.
There thy lost fugitive thou'hast found at last.
Be happy; and for ever hold him fast.

THE SECONDE ELEGIE.

Though All the joyes I had fleed hence with Thee,
Unkind! yet are my TEARES still true to me.
I'am wedded ore again since thou art gone;
Nor couldst thou, cruell, leave me quite alone.
ALEXIS' widdow now is sorrow's wife.   5
With him shall I weep out my weary life.
Wellcome, my sad sweet Mate! Now have I gott
At last a constant love that leaves me not.
Firm he, as thou art false, Nor need my cryes
Thus vex the earth and teare the beauteous skyes.   10
For him, alas, n'ere shall I need to be
Troublesom to the world, thus, as for thee.
For thee I talk to trees; with silent groves
Expostulate my woes and much-wrong'd loves.
Hills and relentlesse rockes, or if there be   15
Things that in hardnesse more allude to thee;
To these I talk in teares, and tell my pain;
And answer too for them in teares again.
How oft have I wept out the weary sun!
My watry hour-glasse hath old times outrunne.   20
O I am learned grown, Poor love and I
Have study'd over all astrology.

38 *hold . . . fast:* see "Ode on a Prayer-book," No. 75, lines 111–12.
Second
15 *relentlesse rockes:* see "Office of the Holy Crosse," Evensong, Hymn, No. 71.

ELEGIA SECUNDA.

Crudelis regio, quæ te fovet usque latentem:
    Illa meis facta est terra beata malis.
Ah! percat quisquis, si fas est dicere, primus
    Inuiti docuit terga domare salis;
Intactum qui fregit iter, montesque subegit,
    Virgineam pedibus qui violauit humum.
Septeni colles, & Tybridis Ostia, tutus
    Exigui limes tunc erat imperij.
Tunc erat Urbs vix nota sibi, paruoque Quiriti
    Extremi Æthiopes porta Capena fuit.
Dictator numerabat oves pressoque senator
    Fessus aratro, humili sub lare iura dabat.
Nunc quoque sic utinam, clausis regionibus, esses
    Mecum sub vili pauper Alexi casa?
Cur fugis e patria non ullo pulsus ab hoste?
    Si tibi cura mei est, o fugitive redi.
Si tibi cura mei nulla est, miserere parentum;
    Quem trahis, ipse iubet spiritus esse pium.
Non hæc sperabant meritæ solatia vitæ
    Et pater infelix, & miseranda parens. . . .
Ast ego quid merui? vel quo rea crimine dicor?
    Nullum in me crimen, præter amare, vides.
Si tibi virginitas, iuuenis castissime, sancta est,
    Virgineo possum vivere nupta thoro.
Vivere si possum cum coniuge virgine virgo,
    Cur fugis aspectus dure marite meos?
Este mihi testes Superi, nil firmius opto,
    Quam vita exacta cælibe posse mori.
Connubij non vincla venus, non fœdera nectit;
    Nec facit amplexus concubitusque virum.
Cælicolum Regina potens, & gloria terræ
    Ipsa simul coniux, virgo parensque fuit.

I' am perfect in heavn's state, with every starr
My skillfull greife is grown familiar.
Rise, fairest of those fires; whate're thou be   25
Whose rosy beam shall point my sun to me.
Such as the sacred light that erst did bring
The EASTERN princes to their infant king.
O rise, pure lamp! and lend thy golden ray
That weary love at last may find his way.   30

THE THIRD ELEGIE.

Rich, churlish LAND! that hid'st so long in thee,
My treasures, rich, alas, by robbing mee.
Needs must my miseryes owe that man a spite
Who e're he be was the first wandring knight.
O had he nere been at that cruell cost   5
NATURE's virginity had nere been lost.
Seas had not bin rebuk't by sawcy oares
But ly'n lock't up safe in their sacred shores.
Men had not spurn'd at mountaines; nor made warrs
With rocks; nor bold hands struck the world's strong barres.   10
Nor lost in too larg bounds, our little Rome
Full sweetly with it selfe had dwell't at home.
My poor ALEXIS, then in peacefull life,
Had under some low roofe lov'd his plain wife.
But now, ah me, from where he has no foes   15
He flyes; and into willfull exile goes.
Cruell return. O tell the reason why
Thy dearest parents have deserv'd to dy.
And I, what is my crime I cannot tell.
Unlesse it be a crime to'have lov'd too well.   20
If Heates of holyer love and high desire
Make bigge thy fair brest with immortall fire,
What needes my virgin lord fly thus from me,
Who only wish his virgin wife to be?
Wittnesse, chast heavns! no happyer vowes I know   25
Then to a virgin GRAVE untouch't to goe.
Love's truest Knott by Venus is not ty'd;
Nor doe embraces onely make a bride.
The QUEEN of angels, (and men chast as You)
Was MAIDEN WIFE and MAIDEN MOTHER too.   30

28 *Eastern princes:* see "Epiphanie Hymne," No. 57.
Third
  8 *ly'n:* [had] lain.
18 *parents . . . dy:* in some versions the parents live until the body is discovered.

Cæcilia antiquæ potuit nova gloria gentis
    O quam dissimilem ducere virgo virum!
Coniugis in thalamum prima cum nocte veniret,
    Protinus exclamat, Valleriane cave:
Valleriane cave, custos fortissimus adstat,
    Qui mihi libati corporis ultor erit.
Est mihi virginitas summo iurata Tonanti;
    Peruigil in lectum fert sua vota sopor.
Gorgone tuta, meo caream Alite? telaque vibrans,
    Fingitur a vobis Pallas, inermis ero?
Crede mihi, Paridis non est hæc fabula vestri,
    Cum Menelaœo rapta Lacena thoro est.
Sum tua, tu meus es, Christum cole; sim modo virgo.
    Tu pater, & coniux, & mihi frater eris.
Sic ait. Ille sacro lustratus fonte, meretur
    Optato ætherei militis ore frui.
Sanguis utrumque iterum fœcunda in morte maritat:
    Ornat utrique manum palma, corona caput,
Noster Hymen tali caleat face, teda iugalis
    Sentiet haud flammas dire Cupido tuas.
Femina, virque iugo sacri subiguntur amoris.
    O quanta existit vis in amore pari!
Ast ego te rerum pulcherrime, semper amavi:
    Sic placidi redeant in mea vota dies.
O! quoties cum me peteret male sana procorum
    Turba, meus, dixi, solus Alexis erit.
Altera vera fuit, fuit, heu! vox altera mendax;
    Et solus, sed non diceris esse meus.

CECILIA, Glory of her name and blood
With happy gain her maiden vowes made good.
The lusty bridegroom made approach: young man,
Take heed (said she) take heed, VALERIAN!
My bosome's guard, a SPIRIT great and strong,   35
Stands arm'd, to sheild me from all wanton wrong.
My Chastity is sacred; and my sleep
Wakefull, her dear vowes undefil'd to keep.
PALLAS beares armes, forsooth, and should there be
No fortresse built for true VIRGINITY?   40
No gaping gorgon, this. None, like the rest
Of your learn'd lyes. Here you'l find no such jest.
I'am yours, O were my GOD, my CHRIST so too,
I'd know no name of love on earth but you.
He yeilds, and straight Baptis'd, obtains the grace   45
To gaze on the fair souldier's glorious face.
Both mixt at last their blood in one rich bed
Of rosy MARTYRDOME, twice Married.
O burn our hymen bright in such high Flame.
Thy torch, terrestriall love, have here no name.   50
How sweet the mutuall yoke of man and wife,
When holy fires maintain love's Heavnly life!
But I, (so help me heavn my hopes to see)
When thousands sought my love, lov'd none but Thee.
Still, as their vain teares my firm vowes did try,   55
ALEXIS, he alone is mine (said I)
Half true, alas, half false, proves that poor line.
ALEXIS is alone; But is not mine.

31–48 the legend of St. Cecilia is an appropriate one for Alexias to cite: Cecilia's
"Spirit" (line 35) was an angel, not a "gaping gorgon" (line 41); when Valerian asked to see
the angel, Cecilia sent him to the Pope, who baptized him, and sent him back a Christian to
his bride; then he saw the angel (line 46); Valerian later suffered martyrdom, and when
Cecilia died, also a martyr, her body was placed next to his (Catholic Encyclopedia [1911]).
The double burial is treated again by Crashaw in "An Epitaph upon a Young Married Cou-
ple," No. 354.
57–58 like many prayers addressed to the classical gods, this one is granted only par-
tially.

85   *In amorem divinum*

Quid totis Te, Dius amor, sit amare medullis,
Expertus nisi sit, dicere nemo potest:
Quid vero sit amare, iterumque abs te redamari,
Sit licet expertus, dicere nemo potest.

86   *[Domus non auratæ descriptio.]*

It is possible that the absence of the phrase "And Condition of Life" from
the Protestant heading in 48 is more significant than it would at first appear.
The poem is about the religious life, even the monastic life, not about the re-
ligious house. Though the life and the house are interdependent, Crashaw has
emphasized the former. Martin has pointed (p. 452) to the parallel between
the "kingdomes of contentfull Cells" (line 35) and "a little contenfull King-
dom" (p. xxix, line 32), which phrase Crashaw used in his long letter to the
Ferrars to describe his "beloved Patrimony" at Peterhouse. There is much in
the poem to recall the religious regimen maintained at Peterhouse and at Little
Gidding. It is perhaps significant that this poem in 48 is followed immediately

Non isthic aurata domus, luxuque fluentes
Sunt epulæ, spondave sopor pretiosus eburna,
Aut in carbaseo Tyrius velamine murex.
Non gemma vibrante nitor, non persona cantu
Limina, non prono famulantum examina collo,
Atque avidas quicquid trahit in certamina gentes;
Sed nemora, & nudæ rupes, neglictaque squalent
Confraga: Sunt epulæ viles, jussæque quietis
Hora brevis: Duro velantur corpora texto:
Et labor in pretio, & vitam mors longa fatigat.

85   *In amorem divinum.* (Hermannus Hugo.)

    Æternall love! what 'tis to love thee well,
    None, but himselfe, who feeles it, none can tell.
    But oh, what to be lov'd of thee as well,
    None, not himselfe, who feeles it, none can tell.

86   *Description of a Religious House and Condition of Life*

by two poems on Peterhouse, "Votiva Domus Petrensis" and "Ejusdem . . .
Gemitus." Puritans offended by the beauty and holiness of Peterhouse and the
discipline of Little Gidding would be offended by a poem on the "Condition of
Life." It will be noted that the Condition in the poem requires obedience and
poverty; the third vow of the monastic life—celibacy—is not mentioned, but
there are no indications that the life is other than celibate.

DESCRIPTION

OF

A RELIGIOUS HOUSE

AND CONDITION

OF LIFE

(OUT OF BARCLAY.)

    No roofes of gold o're riotous tables shining
    Whole dayes and suns devour'd with endlesse dining;
    No sailes of tyrian sylk proud pavements sweeping;
    Nor ivory couches costlyer slumbers keeping;
    False lights of flairing gemmes; tumultuous joyes;   5
    Halls full of flattering men and frisking boyes;
    Whate're false showes of short and slippery good
    Mix the mad sons of men in mutuall blood.
    But WALKES and unshorn woods; and soules, just so
    Unforc't and genuine; but not shady tho.   10

In amorem divinum (*On divine love*) MS.* The epigram aptly describes the unutterable ex-
perience of mystical union.
Description of a Religious House: 52 (48).*
   3 *sailes of tyrian sylk:* (women's?) dresses of costly silks from Tyre.
   7 *slippery:* see the "Ode on a Prayer-Book," No. 75, line 57.

At neque crudeles Diræ, vilique flagello
Sævit cura ferox; falso non abditus ore
Ipse sua insanus furit in præcordia livor.
Alma quies, parvisque habitat Concordia tectis,
Et semper niveo veri de pectore risus.
Ipsa suæ meminit stirpis, seseque deisq;
Mens fruitur fœlix, & novit in astra reverti.

Our lodgings hard and homely as our fare.
That chast and cheap, as the few clothes we weare.
Those, course and negligent, As the naturall lockes
Of these loose groves, rough as th'unpolish't rockes.
A hasty Portion of præscribed sleep;   15
Obedient slumbers? that can wake and weep,
And sing, and sigh, and work, and sleep again;
Still rowling a round sphear of still-returning pain.
Hands full of harty labours; Paines that pay
And prize themselves; doe much, that more they may,   20
And work for work, not wages; let to morrow's
New drops, wash off the sweat of this daye's sorrows.
A long and dayly-dying life, which breaths
A respiration of reviving deaths.
But neither are there those ignoble stings   25
That nip the bosome of the world's best things,
And lash Earth-laboring souls.
No cruell guard of diligent cares, that keep
Crown'd woes awake; as things too wise for sleep.
But reverent discipline, and religious fear,   30
And soft obedience, find sweet biding here;
Silence, and sacred rest; peace, and pure joyes;
Kind loves keep house, ly close, and make no noise,
And room enough for Monarchs, while none swells
Beyond the kingdomes of contentfull Cells.   35
The self-remembering Soul sweetly recovers
Her kindred with the starrs; not basely hovers
Below: But meditates her immortall way
Home to the originall sourse of Light and intellectuall Day.

16–17 *wake . . . sleep again:* the keeping of vigils and the observation of the canonical hours for prayer, e.g. the "Office of the Holy Crosse," No. 71.
34 *Monarchs:* Charles I did indeed visit Little Gidding.

87   *Sospetto d' Herode*

In this his longest poem, Crashaw has translated Book One, "The Suspicion of Herod," from Marino's four-book religious epic *La Strage de gli innocenti* (*The Slaughter of the Innocents*). Crashaw probably intended to translate all the books, winning at last to Book Three where the Slaughter actually occurs and Book Four where the Innocents are received into Limbo, but to do so he had first to pass through the tedium of the Meeting of the Fallen Angels in Book Two, a journey his nature could not accomplish. Warren supposes that the later Books "offer so much that was congenial to his temperament and his taste that Crashaw . . . began his translation with full intention of completing it. . . . Doubtless the 'Sospetto' cost Crashaw more labor than anything else he wrote; he rose ambitiously to its dimensions and produced, by emulation, an effect of largeness and strength which he was never to repeat" (pp. 120–21). Praz considers (pp. 233, 238) the Italian poem an inferior work, a flabby and "late scion of the decayed epic tradition" and the English poem "admirable." He points to many places where Crashaw has sharpened, enlivened, and made coherent the images suggested by Marino, at the same time increasing their number and complexity (pp. 232–38). He has, furthermore, as in no other of his longer translations, followed the metrical pattern of his original exactly—the *ottava rima*.

Libro Primo.

Argomento.

L'iniquo Rè de le tartaree grotte
Preuedendo 'l suo mal s'affligge, e rode
Quindi esce fuor da la perpetua notte.
Furia crudele à insospettir Herode.
Egli, che nel suo cor stima interrotte
Le quieti al regnar, di ciò non gode,
Ma per opporsi à la crudel Fortuna
I Satrapi à consiglio alfin raduna.

1.

Musa non più d'Amor cantiam lo sdegno
Del crudo Rè, che mille Infanti afflitti,
(Ahi, che non pote auidità di regno?)
Fè dal materno sen cader trafitti.
E voi reggete voi l'infermo Ingegno
Nuntij di Christo, e testimoni inuitti,
Che deste fuor de le squarciate gole
Sangue invece di voce, e di parole.

87   *Sospetto d' Herode.* (*The Suspicion of* Herod.)

The translation was evidently made in 1637, and served as "a kind of apprenticeship for Crashaw" (Praz, p. 232). He learned in it, we may suppose, how to improve upon a model. He had translated smaller pieces by Marino already, and he must have approached this impressive religious work in a spirit of devotion to its subject and admiration for the "vast reputation" of the courtier-knight-poet. He discovered he could out-Marino Marino. He learned also much of the disciplines of translation and of concerted and continuous work, and he discovered he wanted no more of them. The influence of Marino on Crashaw's poetry has perhaps been overestimated (see L. Pettoello, "A Current Misconception Concerning the Influence of Marino's Poetry on Crashaw's," *MLR*, LII [1957], 321–28), but the influence on his spirit cannot be (see J. V. Mirollo, *Poet of the Marvelous* [New York, 1963], pp. 248–50).

Crashaw's poem was influential in its own time, for it is reasonably clear that Milton's *Paradise Lost* owes some inspiration for the figure of Satan and his journey up to Earth to this translation. The text for the event (which does not occur in this Book) is Matthew 2:13–18. See further G. Pozzi, ed. *Dicerie Sacre e La Strage* . . . (Torino, 1960).

Libro Primo.

Argomento.

Casting the times with their strong signes,
Death's Master his owne death divines.
Strugling for helpe, his best hope is
Herod's suspition may heale his.
Therefore he sends a fiend to wake
The sleeping Tyrant's fond mistake;
Who feares (in vaine) that he whose Birth
Meanes Heav'n, should meddle with his Earth.

1.

Muse, now the servant of soft Loves no more,
Hate is thy Theame, and *Herod,* whose unblest
Hand (o what dares not jealous Greatnesse?) tore
A thousand sweet Babes from their Mothers Brest:
The Bloomes of Martyrdome. O be a Dore
Of language to my infant Lips, yee best
Of Confessours: whose Throates answering his swords,
Gave forth your Blood for breath, spoke soules for words.

Sospetto d' Herode (The Suspicion of Herod): 46 (48).*
Sospetto: Suspicion, or Fear; *Libro Primo:* Book One.
Argomento: Argument.
1. 5–8 *Dore . . . words:* underlying this conceit is the Latin meaning of *infant,* "not able to speak"; the martyrs could not speak words, they spoke souls; similarly the poet prays for help from them (as saints) to help his speechlessness.

2.

Antonio, e tù del gran Ibero honore,
Germoglio altier d'Imperadori, e Regi,
Chi non s'abbaglia al tuo souran splendore,
S'al Sole istesso l'*ALBA* tua pareggi.
O de più grandi Heroi specchio, e valore,
Che d'inuitta virtù ti glorij, e pregi.
Non dispreggiar di sacre rime ordito,
Questo picciol d'honor serto fiorito.

3.

Nè fregìar di tai fior sì degna fronte,
La mia Musa deuota arrossir deue,
Di que'fior che nutrisce il chiaro fonte,
In cui d'acqua vital vena sì beue;
Fior di cui mai non spoglia il Sacro monte,
O di Sirio, ò di Borea arsura, ò neue;
Da cui suggendo alte dolcezze ascose,
Formano eterno mele Api ingegnose.

4.

Tu che con tanto pregio, e gloria tanta
Di Partenope bella il fren regesti;
Ch'Athene, ò Roma Heroe di te non vanta
Più degno, onde memoria al mondo resti.
Si che lieta non pur celebra, e canta
La mia Sirena i tuoi famosi gesti,
Ma di tutto il Thirren l'onda sonora,
Il tuo nome immortal mormora ancora.

2.

Great *Anthony! Spains* well-beseeming pride,
Thou mighty branch of Emperours and Kings.
The Beauties of whose dawne what eye may bide,
Which with the Sun himselfe weigh's equall wings.
Mappe of Heroick worth! whom farre and wide
To the beleeving world Fame boldly sings:
    Deigne thou to weare this humble Wreath that bowes,
    To be the sacred Honour of thy Browes.

3.

Nor needs my Muse a blush, or these bright Flowers
Other then what their owne blest beauties bring.
They were the smiling sons of those sweet Bowers,
That drinke the deaw of Life, whose deathlesse spring,
Nor *Sirian* flame, nor *Borean* frost deflowers:
From whence Heav'n-labouring Bees with busie wing,
    Suck hidden sweets, which well digested proves
    Immortall Hony for the Hive of Loves.

4.

Thou, whose strong hand with so transcendent worth,
Holds high the reine of faire *Parthenope*,
That neither *Rome*, nor *Athens* can bring forth
A Name in noble deedes Rivall to thee!
Thy Fames full noise, makes proud the patient Earth,
Farre more then matter for my Muse and mee.
    The *Tyrrhene* Seas, and shores sound all the same,
    And in their murmures keepe thy mighty Name.

---

2. 1 *Anthony:* Fifth Duke of Alba (1585–1639), Viceroy of Naples under Philip II of Spain, "famous for many great Actions in the service of his Master in the Wars of Italy, Flanders, and Portugal, to whom our Authour Marino, was rather a Friend, then a Domestique servant, though after his [Anthony's] return to Naples . . . he [Marino] continued in the family of that great Man employ'd in his most important affairs" (T. R., *The Slaughter of the Innocents* [London, 1675], p. 20).

3. 1 *Flowers:* verses; as other verses are inspired by the pagan Helicon, these are the sons of those who are inspired by (drunk from) a deathless spring yielding the dew of life (Christ).
    5 *Sirian:* of Sirius, the dog star, the rising of which is associated with the summer, the dog days; the adjective means "hot." *Borean:* of Boreas, the north wind.
    6 *Bees:* angels.

4. 2 *reine . . . Parthenope:* i.e. rules in Naples; Parthenope, a Siren, was traditionally associated with the city; her tomb was there.

5.

Sotto gli abissi, in mezzo al cor del Mondo
Nel punto vniuersal de l'vniuerso,
Dentro la bolgia del più cupo fondo
Stassi l'antico spirito peruerso.
Con mordaci ritorte vn groppo immondo
Lo stringe di cento aspidi à trauerso.
Di tai legami in sempiterno il cinse
Il gran Campion, che'n Paradiso il vinse.

6.

Guidice di tormento, e Rè di pianto,
D'inestinguibil foco hà trono, e vesta;
Vesta, già ricco, e luminoso manto,
Hor di fiamme, e di tenebre contesta.
Porta (e sol questo è del suo regno il vanto)
Di sette corna alta corona in testa.
Fan d'ogn'intorno al suo diadema regio,
Hidre verdi, e Ceraste horribil fregio.

7.

Ne gli occhi, oue mestitia alberga, e morte,
Luce fiammeggia torbida, e vermiglia.
Gli sguardi obliqui, e le pupille torte
Sembran Comete, e lampadi le ciglia.
E da le nari, e da le labra smorte
Caligine, e fetor vomita, e figlia,
Iracondi, superbi, e disperati,
Tuoni i gemiti son, folgori i fiati.

8.

Che la vista pestifera, e sanguigna,
Con l'alito crudel, ch'auampa, e fuma,
La pira accende horribile, e maligna,
Che 'nconsumabilmente altrui consuma.
Con amaro stridor batte, e digrigna
I denti aspri di rugine, e di schiuma;
E de'membri d'acciaio entro le fiamme
Fà con l'estremo suo sonar le squamme.

5.

Below the Botome of the great Abysse,
There where one Center reconciles all things;
The worlds profound Heart pants; There placed is
Mischifes old Master, close about him clings
A curl'd knot of embracing Snakes, that kisse
His correspondent cheekes: these loathsome strings
   Hold the perverse Prince in eternall Ties
   Fast bound, since first he forfeited the skies,

6.

The Judge of Torments, and the King of Teares:
Hee fills a burnisht Throne of quenchlesse fire:
And for his old faire Roabes of Light, hee weares
A gloomy Mantle of darke flames, the Tire
That crownes his hated head on high appeares;
Where seav'n tall Hornes (his Empires pride) aspire.
   And to make up Hells Majesty, each Horne
   Seav'n crested *Hydra's* horribly adorne.

7.

His Eyes, the sullen dens of Death and Night,
Startle the dull Ayre with a dismall red:
Such his fell glances as the fatall Light
Of staring Comets, that looke Kingdomes dead.
From his black nostrills, and blew lips, in spight
Of Hells owne stinke, a worser stench is spread.
   His breath Hells lightning is: and each deepe grone
   Disdaines to thinke that Heav'n Thunders alone.

8.

His flaming Eyes dire exhalation,
Unto a dreadfull pile gives fiery Breath;
Whose unconsum'd consumption preys upon
The never-dying Life, of a long Death.
In this sad House of slow Destruction,
(His shop of flames) hee fryes himselfe, beneath
   A masse of woes, his Teeth for Torment gnash,
   While his steele sides sound with his Tayles strong lash.

---

5. 2 *one Center:* i.e. the center of the Earth, in the Ptolemaic cosmogony the center of all things.

9.

Tre rigorose Vergini vicine
Sonno assistenti a l'infernal Tiranno,
E con sferze di vipere, e di spine
Intente sempre à stimularlo stanno,
Crespi han di serpi innanellato il crine,
C'horrida intorno al volto ombra lor fanno
Scettro ei sostien di ferro, e mentre regna
Il suo regno, e se stesso abhorre, e sdegna.

10.

Misero, e come il tuo splendor primiero
Perdesti, ò già di luce Angel più bello.
Eterno haurai dal punitor seuero
A l'ingiusto fallir giusto flagello.
De'fregi tuoi vagheggiatore altero,
De l'altrui seggio vsurpator rubello,
Trasformato, e caduto in Flegetonte,
Orgoglioso Narciso, empio Fetonte.

11.

Questi da l'ombre morte à l'aria viva,
Inuido pur di nostro stato humano,
Le luci onde per dritto in giù s'apriua
Cauernoso spiraglio, alzò lontano.
E proprio là ne la famosa riua,
Oue i christalli suoi rompe il Giordano,
Cose vide e comprese, onde nel petto
Rinouando dolor, crebbe sospetto.

12.

Membra l'alta cagion de'gran conflitti
Esca, ch'accese in Ciel tante fauile.
Volge frà se gli oracoli, e gli editti,
E di sacri Indouini, e di Sibille.
Osserva poi vaticinati, e scritti
Mille prodigi inusitati, e mille;
E mentre pensa, e teme, e si ricorda,
L'andate cose à le presenti accorda.

9.

Three Rigourous Virgins waiting still behind,
Assist the Throne of th'Iron-Sceptred King.
With whips of Thornes and knotty vipers twin'd
They rouse him, when his ranke Thoughts need a sting.
Their lockes are beds of uncomb'd snakes that wind
About their shady browes in wanton Rings.
  Thus reignes the wrathfull King, and while he reignes
  His Scepter and himselfe both he disdaines.

10.

Disdainefull wretch! how hath one bold sinne cost
Thee all the Beauties of thy once bright Eyes?
How hath one blacke Eclipse cancell'd, and crost
The glories that did guild thee in thy Rise?
Proud Morning of a perverse Day! how lost
Art thou unto thy selfe, thou too selfe-wise
  Narcissus? foolish Phaeton? who for all
  Thy high-aym'd hopes, gaind'st but a flaming fall.

11.

From Death's sad shades, to the Life-breathing Ayre,
This mortall Enemy to mankinds good,
Lifts his malignant Eyes, wasted with care,
To become beautifull in humane blood.
Where Jordan melts his Chrystall, to make faire
The fields of Palestine, with so pure a flood,
  There does he fixe his Eyes: and there detect
  New matter, to make good his great suspect.

12.

He calls to mind th'old quarrell, and what sparke
Set the contending Sons of Heav'n on fire:
Oft in his deepe thought he revolves the darke
Sibills divining leaves: hee does enquire
Into th'old Prophesies, trembling to marke
How many present prodigies conspire,
  To crowne their past predictions, both hee layes
  Together, in his pondrous mind both weighes.

10. 7 *Narcissus:* youth who fell in love with his own image. *Phaeton:* the son of the sun, who, hoping to drive his father's chariot, was destroyed in flames by Zeus.
11. 5 *Jordan . . . Chrystall:* the Jordan River flows with heavenly streams.
    8 *suspect:* suspicion.
12.4 *Sibills:* pagan prophetess (see "Dies Iræ," I, 2).

13.

Vede da Dio mandato in Galilea
Nuntio celeste à Verginella humile,
Che la 'nchina e saluta, e come a Dea,
Le reca i gigli de l'eterno Aprile.
Vede nel ventre de la Vecchia hebrea,
Feconda in sua sterilità senile,
Adorar palpitando il gran concetto
Prima santo, che nato, vn pargoletto.

14.

Vede d'Atlante i ghiacci adamantini
Sciorsi in riui di nettare, e d'argento,
E verdeggiar di Scithia i gioghi alpini,
E i diserti di Libia in vn momento.
Vede l'elci, e le querce, e gli orni, e i pini
Sudar di mele, e stillar manna il vento.
Fiorir d'Engaddo à mezzo verno i dumi,
Correr balsamo i fonti, e latte i fiumi.

15.

Vede de la felice, e santa notte
Le tacit'ombre, e i tenebrosi horrori
Da le voci del Ciel percosse, e rotte,
E vinti da gli angelici splendori.
Vede per selue, e per seluagge grotte
Correr Bifolchi poi, correr Pastori
Portando lieti al gran Messia venuto
De' rozzi doni il semplice tributo.

13.

Heavens Golden-winged Herald, late hee saw
To a poore *Galilean* virgin sent:
How low the Bright Youth bow'd, and with what awe
Immortall flowers to her faire hand present.
Hee saw th'old *Hebrewes* wombe, neglect the Law
Of Age and Barennesse, and her Babe prevent
    His Birth, by his Devotion, who began
    Betimes to be a Saint, before a Man.

14.

Hee saw rich Nectar thawes, release the rigour
Of th'Icy North, from frost-bcount *Atlas* hands
His Adamantine fetters fall: greene vigour
Gladding the *Scythian* Rocks, and *Libian* sands.
Hee saw a vernall smile, sweetly disfigure
Winters sad face, and through the flowry lands
    Of faire *Engaddi* hony-sweating Fountaines
    With *Manna*, Milk, and Balm, new broach the Mountaines.

15.

Hee saw how in that blest Day-bearing Night,
The Heav'n-rebuked shades made hast away;
How bright a Dawne of Angels with new Light
Amaz'd the midnight world, and made a Day
Of which the Morning knew not: Mad with spight
Hee markt how the poore Shepheards ran to pay
    Their simple Tribute to the Babe, whose Birth
    Was the great businesse both of Heav'n and Earth.

13. 4 *flowers:* Gabriel is usually represented bringing a lily to Mary, the *"Galilean* virgin."
    5 *old Hebrewes:* Elizabeth, Luke 1:5–25.
    6 *prevent:* come before (the Latin meaning); i.e. the embryo John leaped in his mother's womb, Luke 1:41.
14. 1 *Hee saw:* the prospect offered here recalls Milton's Satan's view of Paradise.
    4 *Scythian . . . Libian:* Scythia comprised the area roughly northward of Bethlehem, as Lybia (i.e. Africa) was the area roughly southward of Bethlehem; much of Scythia is arid ("Rocks").
    7 *Engaddi:* a town in Judah (the name in Hebrew means "fountain of God"); the most important reference is in Song of Solomon 1:14; the stanza describes the miraculous spring in the entire geographical region.
15. 4–5 *Day . . . knew not:* see the "Epiphanie Hymn," No. 57.

16.

Vede aprir l'vscio à triplicato Sole
La reggia oriental, che si disserra.
Scardinata cader vede la mole
Sacra à la bella Dea, ch'odia la guerra
Gl'Idoli, e i simulacri, oue si cole
Sua Deità, precipitati à terra,
E la terra tremarne, e scoppiar quanti
V'hà d'illecito amor nefandi amanti.

17.

Vede dal Ciel con peregrino raggio
Spiccarsi ancor miracolosa stella,
Che verso Betthelem dritto il viaggio,
Segnando và folgoreggiante, e bella;
E quasi precursor diuin Messaggio,
Fidata scorta, e luminosa ancella,
Tragge di là da gli odorati Eoi,
L'inclito stuol de' trè presaghi Heroi.

18.

Ai nuoui mostri, à i non pensati mali
L'auersario del ben gli occhi conuerte,
Nè men, ch'à Morte, à se stesso mortali
Già le piaghe anteuede espresse, e certe.
Scotesi, e per volar dibatte l'ali,
Che 'n guisa hà pur di due gran vele aperte,
Ma 'l duro fren, che l'incatena, e fascia,
Da l'eterna prigion partir no'l lascia.

19.

Poiche da' bassi effetti egli raccolse
L'alto tenor de le cagion superne,
Tinte di sangue, e di venen trauolse
Quasi bragia infernal, l'empie lucerne.
S'ascose il viso entro le branche, e sciolse
Ruggito, che 'ntronò l'atre cauerne,
E de la coda, onde se stesso attorse,
La cima per furor tutta si morse.

16.

Hee saw a threefold Sun, with rich encrease,
Make proud the Ruby portalls of the East.
Hee saw the Temple sacred to sweet Peace,
Adore her Princes Birth, flat on her Brest.
Hee saw the falling Idols, all confesse
A comming Deity. Hee saw the Nest
 Of pois'nous and unnaturall loves, Earth-nurst;
 Toucht with the worlds true *Antidote* to burst.

17.

He saw Heav'n blossome with a new-borne light,
On which, as on a glorious stranger gaz'd
The Golden eyes of Night: whose Beame made bright
The way to *Beth'lem,* and as boldly blaz'd,
(Nor askt leave of the Sun) by Day as Night.
By whom (as Heav'ns illustrious Hand-maid) rais'd
 Three Kings (or what is more) three Wise men went
 Westward to find the worlds true *Orient.*

18.

Strucke with these great concurrences of things,
Symptomes so deadly, unto Death and him;
Faine would hee have forgot what fatall strings,
Eternally bind each rebellious limbe.
Hee shooke himselfe, and spread his spatious wings:
Which like two Bosom'd sailes embrace the dimme
 Aire, with a dismall shade, but all in vaine,
 Of sturdy Adamant is his strong chaine.

19.

While thus Heav'ns highest counsails, by the low
Footsteps of their Effects, hee trac'd too well,
Hee tost his troubled eyes, Embers that glow
Now with new Rage, and wax too hot for Hell.
With his foule clawes hee fenc'd his furrowed Brow,
And gave a gastly shreeke, whose horrid yell
 Ran trembling through the hollow vaults of Night,
 The while his twisted Tayle hee gnaw'd for spight.

---

16. 5 *falling Idols:* "This General fall of Idols, in Egypt was prophesied by Isaiah (cap. 9.v.1.) but it is remarkable in Ecclesiastique writers (as Eusebius, &c.) that Joseph, and the Virgin Mary, either by design, or curiosity, bringing the Child Jesus into one of the stately Temples in Hermopolis . . . all the idols immediately fell down, and were broken in pieces . . ." (T. R., *ibid.,* p. 20).

20.

Così freme frà sè. Ma d'altra parte
Stassi intra due, non ben ancor sicuro.
Studia il gran libro, e de l'antiche carte
Interpretar s'ingegna il senso oscuro,
Sà, nè sà però come, ò con qual arte,
L'alto natal del gran parto futuro
D'ogni vil macchia inuiolato, e bianco
Douer'vscir di virginello fianco.

21.

Onde creder non vuol del gran mistero
La merauiglia à i chiari ingegni ascosa.
Come possa il suo fiore hauere intero
Sì che Vergine sia Donna, ch'è sposa.
E poi, che 'l vero Dio diuenga huom vero
Strana gli sembra, e non possibil cosa.
Che lo spirto s'incarni, e che vestita
Gir di spoglia mortal deggia la vita.

22.

Che l'incompreso, & inuisibil lume
Si riueli, à Pastor mentre, che nasce:
Che l'Infinito Omnipottente Nume
Fatto sia prigionier di poche fasce,
Che latte bea con pueril costume
Chi di celeste nettare si pasce.
Che 'n rozza stalla, in vil capanna assiso
Stia chi trono hà di stelle il Paradiso.

23.

Che 'l sommo Sol s'offuschi in picciol velo;
E che 'l Verbo diuin balbo vagisca,
Che del foco il Fattor tremi di gelo,
E che 'l riso de gli Angeli languisca,
Che serua sia la Maestà del Cielo,
E che l'Immensità s'impicciolisca,
Che la Gloria à soffrir venga gli affanni,
E che l'Eternità soggiaccia à gli anni.

20.

Yet on the other side, faine would he start
Above his feares, and thinke it cannot be.
Hee studies Scripture, strives to sound the heart,
And feele the pulse of every Prophecy.
Hee knowes (but knowes not how, or by what Art)
The Heav'n expecting Ages, hope to see
    A mighty Babe, whose pure, unspotted Birth,
    From a chast Virgin wombe, should blesse the Earth.

21.

But these vast Mysteries his senses smother,
And Reason (for what's Faith to him?) devoure.
How she that is a maid should prove a Mother,
Yet keepe inviolate her virgin flower;
How Gods eternall Sonne should be mans Brother,
Poseth his proudest Intellectuall power.
    How a pure Spirit should incarnate bee,
    And life it selfe weare Deaths fraile Livery.

22.

That the Great Angell-blinding light should shrinke
His blaze, to shine in a poore Shepheards eye.
That the unmeasur'd God so low should sinke,
As Pris'ner in a few poore Rags to lye.
That from his Mothers Brest hee milke should drinke,
Who feeds with Nectar Heav'ns faire family.
    That a vile Manger his low Bed should prove,
    Who in a Throne of stars Thunders above.

23.

That hee whom the Sun serves, should faintly peepe
Through clouds of Infant flesh: that hee the old
Eternall Word should bee a Child, and weepe.
That hee who made the fire, should feare the cold;
That Heav'ns high Majesty his Court should keepe
In a clay-cottage, by each blast control'd.
    That Glories selfe should serve our Griefs, and feares:
    And free Eternity, submit to yeares.

20. 3 *studies Scripture:* Isaiah 7 and Malachi 3 notably; Satan quotes Scripture in the temptation of Jesus, Matthew 4:6.

21. 2 *Reason . . . devoure:* Milton's Satan has the same difficulty, attempting to reason rightly with fallen reason; also stanza 24.

23. 3 *Word . . . weepe:* "The *Word* an infant? The *Word,* and not . . . able to speak a word" (Andrewes, I, 92).

24.

Et oltre poi, c'humiliato, e fatto
Al taglio vbidiente, ancor se stesso
Del gran Legislator sopponga al patto,
Dal marmoreo coltel piagato anch'esso;
E 'l Redentore immacolato intatto
Del marchio sia de' peccatori impresso,
Questo la mente ancor dubbia gl'inuolue
Nè ben de' suoi gran dubbi il nodo ei solue.

25.

Mentre à machine noue alza l'ingegno,
L'ombra del fosco cor stampa nel viso.
Del viso l'ombra in quell oscuro regno
E d'interna mestitia espresso auiso,
Come suol di letitia aperto segno
Essere in Cielo il lampo, in Terra il riso.
Da queste cure stimulato, e stretto
Vn disperato ohimè svelse dal petto.

26.

Ohimè (muggiando) ohimè (dicea) qual veggio
D'insoliti portenti alto concorso?
Che fià questo? ah l'intendo, ah per mio peggio
M'auanza ancor l'angelico discorso.
Che non poss'io torre a Natura il seggio,
E mutare à le Stelle ordine, e corso,
Perche tanti del Ciel sinistri auspici
Diuenisser per me lieti, e felici?

27.

Che può più farmi ho mai chi la celeste
Reggia mi tolse, e i regni miei lucenti?
Bastar doueagli almen per sempre in queste
Confinarmi d'horror case dolenti,
Habitator d'ombre infelici, e meste,
Tormentator de le perdute genti,
Oue per fin di sì maluaggia sorte
Non m'è concessa pur speme di morte.

24.

And further, that the Lawes eternall Giver,
Should bleed in his owne lawes obedience:
And to the circumcising Knife deliver
Himselfe, the forfeit of his slaves offence.
That the unblemisht Lambe, blessed for ever,
Should take the marke of sin, and paine of sence.
   These are the knotty Riddles, whose darke doubt
   Intangles his lost Thoughts, past getting out.

25.

While new Thoughts boyl'd in his enraged Brest,
His gloomy Bosomes darkest Character,
Was in his shady forehead seen exprest.
The forehead's shade in Griefes expression there,
Is what in signe of joy among the blest
The faces lightning, or a smile is here.
   Those stings of care that his strong Heart opprest,
   A desperate, *Oh mee,* drew from his deepe Brest.

26.

Oh mee! (thus bellow'd hee) *oh mee!* what great
Portents before mine eyes their Powers advance?
And serves my purer sight, onely to beat
Downe my proud Thought, and leave it in a Trance?
Frowne I; and can great Nature keep her seat?
And the gay starrs lead on their Golden dance?
   Can his attempts above still prosp'rous be,
   Auspicious still, in spight of Hell and me?

27.

Hee has my Heaven (what would he more?) whose bright
And radiant Scepter this bold hand should beare.
And for the never-fading fields of Light
My faire Inheritance, hee confines me here,
To this darke House of shades, horrour, and Night,
To draw a long-liv'd Death, where all my cheere
   Is the solemnity my sorrow weares,
   That Mankinds Torment waits upon my Teares.

---

27. 3 *Light:* Satan's name before his fall was Lucifer, the light-bearer; see stanza 30.

28.

Volse à le forme sue semplici, e prime
Natura soura alzar corporea, e bassa,
E de' membri del Ciel capo sublime
Far di limo terrestre indegna massa.
I' no 'l soffersi, e d'Aquilon le cime
Salsi, oue d'Angel mai volo non passa.
E se quindi il mio stuol vinto cadeo,
Il tentar l'alte imprese è pur trofeo.

29.

Ma che non satio ancor voglia, e pretenda
Gli antichi alberghi miei spopular d'alme?
Che 'n sè con nodo indissolubil prenda
Per farmi ira maggior, l'humane salme?
Che poscia vincitor sotterra scenda
Ricco di ricche, e gloriose palme?
Che vibrando qua giù le fulgid'armi
Ne le miserie ancor venga à turbarmi?

30.

Ah non se' tu la creatura bella,
Principe già de' fulguranti Amori,
Del Matutino Ciel la prima stella,
La prima luce de gli alati Chori?
Che come suol la Candida facella
Scintillar frà le lampadi minori,
Così ricco di lumi alti celesti
Frà la plebe de gli Angeli splendesti.

31.

Lasso, ma che mi val fuor di speranza
A lo stato primier volger la mente,
Se con l'amara, e misera membranza
Raddoppia il ben passato il mal presente?
Tempo è d'opporsi al fatto, e la possanza
Del nemico fiaccar troppo insolente.
Se l'Inferno si lagna, il Ciel non goda,
Se la forza non val, vaglia la fronda.

28.

Darke, dusty Man, he needs would single forth,
To make the partner of his owne pure ray:
And should we Powers of Heav'n, Spirits of worth
Bow our bright Heads, before a King of clay?
It shall not be, said I, and clombe the *North*,
Where never wing of *Angell* yet made way
What though I mist my blow? yet I strooke high,
And to dare something, is some victory.

29.

Is hee not satisfied? meanes he to wrest
Hell from me too, and sack my Territories?
Vile humane Nature means he now t'invest
(O my despight!) with his divinest Glories?
And rising with rich spoiles upon his Brest,
With his faire Triumphs fill all future stories?
Must the bright armes of Heav'n, rebuke these eyes?
Mocke mee, and dazle my darke Mysteries?

30.

Art thou not *Lucifer?* hee to whom the droves
Of Stars, that guild the Morne in charge were given?
The nimblest of the lightning-winged Loves?
The fairest, and the first-borne smile of Heav'n?
Looke in what Pompe the Mistresse Planet moves
Rev'rently circled by the lesser seaven,
Such, and so rich, the flames that from thine eyes,
Oprest the common-people of the skyes.

31.

Ah wretch! what bootes thee to cast back thy eyes,
Where dawning hope no beame of comfort showes?
While the reflection of thy forepast joyes,
Renders thee double to thy present woes.
Rather make up to thy new miseries,
And meet the mischiefe that upon thee growes.
If Hell must mourne, Heav'n sure shall sympathize
What force cannot effect, fraud shall devise.

---

28. 5　*North:* traditionally the source of evil and woe.
　　7–8　*yet . . . victory:* this apostate voice is heard also in the epigram on Rev. 12:7, "Arma viri!" No. 330, and in *Paradise Lost.*
30. 5–6　*Mistresse Planet . . . lesser seaven:* Marino means the Moon (*la candida facella*); the lesser seven may be the Pleiades, but the cosmology of the passage is not clear (see Williams, p. 130 note).

32.

Ma qual forza tem'io? già non perdei
Con l'antico candor l'alta natura.
Armisi il mondo, e 'l Ciel: de' cenni miei
Gli elementi, e le stelle hauran paura.
Son qual fui, sia che può, come potrei
Se non curo fattor, curar fattura?
S'armi Dio, che farà? vò' quella guerra,
Che non mi lece in Ciel, mouergli in terra.

33.

Lodaro i detti, e solleuar la fronte
Le trè forici, e rigide sorelle,
E tutte in lui di Stige, e d'Acheronte
Rotar le serpi, e scosser le facelle.
Eccoci (disser) preste, eccoci pronte
D'ogni tua voglia essecutrici ancelle.
Sommo Signor di questo horribil chiostro,
Tuo fia l'imporre, e l'vbidir fia nostro.

34.

Prouasti in Ciel ne la magnanim'opra
Cio che sà far con le compagne Aletto.
Nè perc'hoggi qua giù t'accoglia, e copra
Ombroso albergo, e ferrugineo tetto,
Men superbir dei tù; che se là sopra
Al Monarca tonante eri soggetto,
Quì siedi Rè, che libero, & interno
Hai de la Terra, e de l'Abisso impero.

35.

Se valer potrà nulla industria, ò senno,
Virtu d'herbe, e di pietre, ò suon di carmi,
Inganno, Ira, & Amor, che spesso fenno
Correr gli huomini al sangue, e trattar l'armi,
Tu ci vedrai (sol che ti piaccia) à vn cenno
Trar le stelle dal Ciel, l'ombre dai marmi,
Por sossoura la terra e 'l mar profondo,
Crollar, spiantar da le radici il Mondo.

32.

And yet whose force feare I? have I so lost
My selfe? my strength too with my innocence?
Come try who dares, *Heav'n, Earth,* what ere dost boast,
A borrowed being, make thy bold defence.
Come thy Creator too, what though it cost
Mee yet a second fall? wee'd try our strengths.
 Heav'n saw us struggle once, as brave a fight
 Earth now should see, and tremble at the sight.

33.

Thus spoke th'impatient Prince, and made a pause,
His foule Hags rais'd their heads, and clapt their hands.
And all the Powers of Hell in full applause
Flourisht their Snakes, and tost their flaming brands.
Wee (said the horrid sisters) wait thy lawes,
Th'obsequious handmaids of thy high commands.
 Be it thy part, Hells mighty Lord, to lay
 On us thy dread commands, ours to obey.

34.

What thy *Alecto*, what these hands can doe,
Thou mad'st bold proofe upon the brow of Heav'n,
Nor should'st thou bate in pride, because that now,
To these thy sooty Kingdomes thou art driven.
Let Heav'ns Lord chide above lowder then thou
In language of his Thunder, thou art even
 With him below: here thou art Lord alone
 Boundlesse and absolute: Hell is thine owne.

35.

If usuall wit, and strength will doe no good,
Vertues of stones, nor herbes: use stronger charmes,
Anger, and love, best hookes of humane blood.
If all faile wee'l put on our proudest Armes,
And pouring on Heav'ns face the Seas huge flood
Quench his curl'd fires, wee'l wake with our Alarmes
 Ruine, where e're she sleepes at Natures feet;
 And crush the world till his wide corners meet.

---

34. 1 *Alecto:* one of the Erinyes, or avenging deities; the snake was one of the attributes
of these angry goddesses.

36.

Risponde il fiero, O miei sostegni, o fidi
De la mia speme, e del mio regno appoggi,
Ben le vostr'arti, e 'l valor vostro io vidi
Chiaro lasù ne gli stellanti poggi.
Ma, perche molto in tutte io mi confidi,
Huopo d'vna però mi sia sol hoggi.
Crudeltà chieggio sola e sol costei
Può trar di dubbio i gran sospetti miei.

37.

Era costei de le tre Dee del male
Suora ben degna, e fera oltra le fere,
E sen gia d'hor in hor battendo l'ale
A riueder quelle malnate schiere.
Vaga di rinforzar l'esca immortale
Al foco onde bollian l'anime nere,
Nel più secreto baratro profondo
Del sempre tristo, e lagrimoso mondo.

38.

Vlularo trè volte i caui spechi,
Trè volte rimbombar l'ombre profonde,
E fin ne' gorghi più riposti, e ciechi
Tonar del gran Cocito i sassi, e l'onde.
Vdì quel grido, e i suoi dritt'occhi in biechi
Torse colei da le tartaree sponde,
E per risposta al formidabil nome
Fè sibilar le serpentine chiome.

39.

Casa non hà la region di Morte
Più de la sua terribile, & oscura.
Stan sempre ai gridi altrui chiuse le porte
Scabre; e di selce adamantina, e dura.
Son di ferro le basi, e son di forte
Diaspro impenetrabile le mura.
E di sangue macchiate, e tutte sozze
Son di teste recise, e membra mozze.

36.

Reply'd the proud King, O my Crownes Defence!
Stay of my strong hopes, you of whose brave worth,
The frighted stars tooke faint experience,
When 'gainst the Thunders mouth wee marched forth:
Still you are prodigal of your Love's expence
In our great projects, both 'gainst Heav'n and Earth.
 I thanke you all, but one must single out,
 Cruelty, she alone shall cure my doubt.

37.

Fourth of the cursed knot of Hags is shee,
Or rather all the other three in one;
Hells shop of slaughter shee do's oversee,
And still assist the Execution.
But chiefly there do's shee delight to be,
Where Hells capacious Cauldron is set on:
 And while the black soules boile in their owne gore,
 To hold them down, and looke that none seethe o're.

38.

Thrice howl'd the Caves of Night, and thrice the sound,
Thundring upon the bankes of those black lakes
Rung, through the hollow vaults of Hell profound:
At last her listning Eares the noise o'retakes,
Shee lifts her sooty lampes, and looking round
A gen'rall hisse, from the whole Tire of snakes
 Rebounding, through Hells inmost Cavernes came,
 In answer to her formidable Name.

39.

Mongst all the Palaces in Hells command,
No one so mercilesse as this of hers.
The Adamantine Doors, for ever stand
Impenetrable, both to prai'rs and Teares,
The walls inexorable steele, no hand
Of *Time*, or Teeth of hungry *Ruine* feares.
 Their ugly ornaments are the bloody staines,
 Of ragged limbs, torne sculls, and dasht out Braines.

37. 8 *seethe:* boil.
38. 5 *lampes:* eyes.

40.

V'hà la Vendetta in su la soglia, e 'n mano
Spada brandisce insanguinata ignuda.
Hauui lo Sdegno, e col Furor insano
E la Guerra, e la Strage anhela, e suda.
Con le minaccie sue fremer lontano
S'ode la Rabbia impetuosa, e cruda.
E nel mezzo si vede in vista accerba
La gran falce rotar Morte superba.

41.

Per le pareti abhominandi ordigni,
Onde talhor sono i mortali offesi,
De la fiera magion fregi sanguigni,
In vece v'hà di cortinaggi appesi.
Rote, ceppi, catene, haste, macigni,
Chiodi, spade, securi, & altri arnesi,
Tutti nel sangue horribilmente intrisi
Di fratelli suenati, e padri vccisi.

42.

In mensa detestabile, e funesta
L'ingorde Arpie con la vorace Fame,
E l'inhumano Erisitton di questa
Cibano ad hor, ad hor l'auide brame.
E con Tantalo, e Progne i cibi appresta
Attreo feroce, e Licaone infame.
Medusa entro 'l suo teschio a la crudele
Porta in sangue stemprato a bere il fele.

40.

There has the purple *Vengeance* a proud seat,
Whose ever-brandisht Sword is sheath'd in blood.
About her *Hate, Wrath, Warre,* and *slaughter* sweat;
Bathing their hot limbs in life's pretious flood.
There rude impetuous Rage do's storme, and fret:
And there, as Master of this murd'ring brood,
 Swinging a huge Sith stands impartiall *Death,*
 With endlesse businesse almost out of Breath.

41.

For Hangings and for Curtaines, all along
The walls, (abominable ornaments!)
Are tooles of wrath, Anvills of Torments hung;
Fell Executioners of foule intents,
Nailes, hammers, hatchets sharpe, and halters strong,
Swords, Speares, with all the fatall Instruments
 Of sin, and Death, twice dipt in the dire staines
 Of Brothers mutuall blood, and Fathers braines.

42.

The Tables furnisht with a cursed Feast,
Which *Harpyes,* with leane *Famine* feed upon,
Unfill'd for ever. Here among the rest,
Inhumane *Erisi-cthon* too makes one;
Tantalus, Atreus, Progne, here are guests:
Wolvish *Lycaon* here a place hath won.
 The cup they drinke in is *Medusa's* scull,
 Which mixt with gall and blood they quaffe brim full.

---

42. 2 *Harpyes:* fantastic birds with women's faces; voracious creatures.
 4 *Erisi-cthon:* a creature who tore up the earth.
 5 *Tantalus:* a criminal king, who stole from the gods. *Atreus:* the murderer of his brother and the founder of the ill-omened house of Atreus, the father of Agamemnon and Menelaus. *Progne:* (usually Procne) a violent lady who killed her son and served him up to his father in a dish.
 6 *Lycaon:* an impious king, he attempted to murder Zeus.
 7 *Medusa:* one of the Gorgons, a being with hair of serpents; whoever looked on her was turned to stone.

43.

Le spauentose Eumenidi sorelle
Son sempre seco; e sempre in man le ferue
Furial face, intorno hà Iezabelle,
Scilla, Circe, Medea ministre, e serue.
Son de l'iniqua Corte empie donzzelle
Le Parche inessorrabili, e proterue,
Da le cui man fur le sue vesti ordite
Di negre fila di recise vite.

44.

Circonda il tetto intorno intorno vn bosco,
C'hà sol d'infauste piante ombre nocenti,
Ogni herba è peste, & ogni fiore e tosco.
Sospir son l'aure, e lacrime i torrenti.
Pascon quiui per entro, à l'aer fosco
Minotauri, e Ciclopi horridi armenti
Di Draghi, e Tigri, e van per tutto à schiere
Sfinge, Hiene, Ceraste, Hidre, e Chimere.

45.

Di Diomede i destier, di Fereo i cani,
E di Therodamante hauui i leoni,
Di Busiri gli altari empi, e profani,
Di Silla le seuere aspre prigioni,
I letti di Procuste horrendi, e strani,
Le mense immonde, e rie de' Lestrigoni,
E del crudo Sciron, del fiero Scini
Gl'infami scogli, e dispietati pini.

43.

The foule Queens most abhorred Maids of Honour
Medæa, Jezabell, many a meager Witch
With *Circe, Scylla,* stand to wait upon her.
But her best huswifes are the *Parcæ,* which
Still worke for her, and have their wages from her.
They prick a bleeding heart at every stitch.
    Her cruell cloathes of costly threds they weave,
    Which short-cut lives of murdred *Infants* leave.

44.

The house is hers'd about with a black wood,
Which nods with many a heavy headed tree.
Each flowers a pregnant poyson, try'd and good,
Each herbe a Plague. The winds sighes timed-bee
By a black Fount, which weeps into a flood.
Through the thick shades obscurely might you see
    Minotaures, Cyclopses, with a darke drove
    Of *Dragons, Hydraes, Sphinxes,* fill the Grove.

45.

Here *Diomed's* Horses, *Phereus* dogs appeare,
With the fierce Lyons of *Therodamas.*
Busiris ha's his bloody Altar here,
Here *Sylla* his severest prison has.
The *Lestrigonians* here their Table reare;
Here strong *Procrustes* plants his Bed of Brasse.
    Here cruell *Scyron* boasts his bloody rockes,
    And hatefull *Schinis* his so feared Oakes.

43. 2 *Medæa:* a witch-queen who murdered her own children. *Jezabell:* the wife of King Ahab of Israel, she caused the death of many prophets.
    3 *Circe:* an enchantress capable of turning men into beasts. *Scylla:* a sea-monster capable of eating six men at a time.
    4 *Parcæ:* the Fates who weave the thread of life.
44. 7–8 *Minotaures, Cyclopses, Hydraes, Sphinxes:* animal monsters in Greek myths.
45. 1 *Diomed's Horses:* which ate human flesh.
    2 *Therodamas:* king of Scythia who fed his lions human flesh (Pozzi, p. 481).
    3 *Busiris:* Egyptian King who killed all foreigners on the Altar of Zeus in Egypt.
    4 *Sylla:* (usually Sulla) dictator of Rome in the first century B.C., he invented the proscription lists by which many thousands died during his dictatorship—a reign of horror.
    5 *Lestrigonians:* cannibalistic giants living in Italy.
    6 *Procrustus:* possessor of a bed (or two beds) on which he made strangers lie, chopping them off if too long, stretching them out if too short.
    7 *Sycron:* a robber who occupied a rocky ledge above the ocean, fought with travelers, and threw them over.
    8 *Schinis:* Pozzi has been unable to locate any appropriate figure of the name (p. 482); perhaps Sinis is intended by Marino, the robber who destroyed his victims by tying them to a tree (a pine or fir) which then sprang up into the air (he is one of the robbers, like Scyron, whom Theseus destroys); Pozzi terms Marino's "Scini" "una sua colossale confusione," and Crashaw's translation of Marino's "pini" (pines) as "Oaks" may be thought to be in the same notable tradition.

46.

Quanti mai seppe imaginar flagelli
L'implacabil Mezzentio, ò Gerione.
Ocho, Ezzellino, Falari, e con quelli
Il sempre formidabile Nerone.
V'hà tutti, hauui le fiamme, hauui i coltelli
Di Nabucco, & Acabbe, e Faraone
Tale è l'albergo, e quinci esce veloce
La quarta Furia à la terribil voce.

47.

A costei la sua mente aperse à pena
L'Imperador de la tremenda Corte,
Ch'ella di Dite in men, che non balena
Abbandonò le ruginose porte,
E la faccia del Ciel pura, e serena
Tutta macchiando di pallor di morte,
Sol con la vista auuenenati al suolo
Fè piombar gli augelletti à mezzo 'l volo.

48.

Tosto, che fuor de la vorago oscura.
Venne quel mostro à vomitar l'Inferno,
Parvero i fiori intorno, e la verdura
Sentir forza di peste, ira di Verno.
Potria col ciglio instupidir Natura,
Inhorridire il bel pianeta eterno,
Irrigidir le stelle, e gli elementi,
Se non gliel ricoprissero i serpenti.

49.

Già da l'ombrose sue riposte caue.
De la notte compagno, aprendo l'ali,
Lente, e con grato furto il sonno graue
Togliea la luce à i pigri occhi mortali;
E con dolce tirannide, e soaue
Sparse le tempie altrui d'acque lethali,
I tranquilli riposi, e lusinghieri
S'insignorian de' sensi, e de' pensieri.

46.

What ever Schemes of Blood, fantastick frames
Of Death *Mezentius*, or *Geryon* drew;
Phalaris, Ochus, Ezelinus, names
Mighty in mischiefe, with dread *Nero* too,
Here are they all, Here all the swords or flames
Assyrian Tyrants, or *Egyptian* knew.
    Such was the House, so furnisht with the Hall,
    Whence the fourth *Fury,* answer'd *Pluto's* call.

47.

Scarce to this Monster could the shady King,
The horrid summe of his intentions tell;
But shee (swift as the momentary wing
Of lightning, or the words he spoke) left Hell.
Shee rose, and with her to our world did bring,
Pale proofe of her fell presence. Th'aire too well
    With a chang'd countenance witnest the sight,
    And poore fowles intercepted in their flight.

48.

Heav'n saw her rise, and saw Hell in the sight.
The field's faire Eyes saw her, and saw no more,
But shut their flowry lids for ever. Night
And Winter strow her way; yea, such a sore
Is shee to Nature, that a generall fright,
An universall palsie spreading o're
    The face of things, from her dire eyes had run,
    Had not her thick Snakes hid them from the Sun.

49.

Now had the Night's companion from her den,
Where all the busie day shee close doth ly,
With her soft wing, wipt from the browes of men
Day's sweat, and by a gentle Tyranny,
And sweet oppression, kindly cheating them
Of all their cares, tam'd the rebellious eye
    Of sorrow, with a soft and downy hand,
    Sealing all brests in a *Lethæan* band.

---

46. 2 *Mezentius:* mythical king of the Etruscans, expelled for his cruelty. *Geryon:* a monster with three bodies.
    3 *Phalaris:* ruler of Agrigentum proverbial as a cruel and inhuman tyrant. *Ochus:* (usually Artaxerxes III) achieved his crown by treason and murder and then extirpated his family.

50.

Quando le negre piume agili, e preste
Spiega l'Erinne, e 'n Betthelem ne viene,
Che 'n Betthelem lo scettro, à le moleste
Cure inuolato, il Rè crudel sostiene.
E qual già con facelle empie, e funeste
Di Thebe apparue à le sanguigne cene,
Ricerca, e spia de la magion reale,
Con sollecito piè, camere, e sale.

51.

La reggia allhor del buon Dauid reggea
Ligio d'Augusto Herode, huom gia canuto,
Non legittimo Rè, mà d'Idumea
Stirpe, e del Regno occupator temuto.
Già 'l Diadema Real de la Giudea
La progenie di Giuda hauea perduto,
E del giogo seruil gli aspri rigori
Sostenendo piangea gli antichi honori.

52.

Scorso l'arbergo tutto, à le secrete
Ritirate sen va del gran palagio,
Là doue in placidissima quiete
Tra molli piume il Rè posa à grand'agio.
Non vuole à lui, qual proprio vscì di Lete,
Mostrarsi il Mostro perfido, e maluagio,
Ma dispon cangiar faccia, e girle auante
Fatta pallida imago, ombra vagante.

53.

Ciò che di Furia hauea spoglia in vn tratto,
E di forma mortal si vela, e cinge.
Giusippo à l'aria, al volto, à ciascun'atto
Quale, e quanio ei si fu simula, e finge.
Al Rè dal sonno oppresso, e sourafatto
S'accosta, e 'l cor con fredda man gli stringe;
Poi la voce mentita, e mentitrice
Scioglie trà 'l sonno, e la vigilia, e dice.

50.

When the *Erinnys* her black pineons spread,
And came to *Bethlem*, where the cruell King
Had now retyr'd himselfe, and borrowed
His Brest a while from care's unquiet sting.
Such as at *Thebes* dire feast shee shew'd her head,
Her sulphur-breathed Torches brandishing,
  Such to the frighted Palace now shee comes,
  And with soft feet searches the silent roomes.

51.

By *Herod* leige to Cesar now was borne
The Scepter, which of old great *David* swaid.
Whose right by *David's* linage so long worne,
Himselfe a stranger to, his owne had made:
And from the head of *Judahs* house quite torne
The Crowne, for which upon their necks he laid
  A sad yoake, under which they sigh'd in vaine,
  And looking on their lost state sigh'd againe.

52.

Up, through the spatious Pallace passed she,
To where the Kings proudly-reposed head
(If any can be soft to *Tyranny*
And selfe-tormenting sin) had a soft bed.
She thinkes not fit such he her face should see,
As it is seene by Hell; and seene with dread.
  To change her faces stile she doth devise,
  And in a pale Ghost's shape to spare his Eyes.

53.

Her selfe a while she layes aside, and makes
Ready to personate a mortall part.
Joseph the Kings dead Brothers shape she takes,
What he by Nature was, is she by Art.
She comes toth' King and with her cold hand slakes
His Spirits, the Sparkes of Life, and chills his heart,
  Lifes forge; fain'd is her voice, and false too, be
  Her words, sleep'st thou fond man? sleep'st thou? (said she).

50. 2 *King:* Herod.

51 "M[arc] Antony having crucify'd Antigonus . . . gave the Crown of Judea to Herod (an Idumean, by descent, and of no regal line) which Augustus afterward confirm'd" (T. R., *ibid.*, p. 20).

53. 3 *Joseph:* "brother to Herod commanded his Army against Antigonus, and as he be-seiged Jericho, was driven into streights by Pappus (Antigonus his Lieutenant) his Army routed, himself slain and his Head, cut off, was sold to Herod by the Enemy for 50 talents" (T. R., *ibid.*, p. 21).

54.

Mal accorto tù dormi, e qual nocchiero,
Che per l'Egeo, di nembi oscuri, e densi
Cinto, à l'onda superba, al vento fiero
Obliato il timon, pigro non pensi,
Te ne stai neghittoso, e 'l cor guerriero
Ne l'otio immergi, e nel riposo i sensi,
E non curi, e non sai ciò, che vicino
Ti minacci di reo forte destino.

55.

Sai, che de' Reggi Hebrei dal ceppo antico
Quasi d'arido stel frutto insperato,
Ammirabil fanciul, benche mendico,
Là trà le bestie, e 'l fien pur dianzi è nato
Del nouo germe, à te fatal nemico
Troppo amico si mostra il vulgo ingrato,
Gli applaude, il segue, e già con chiara fama
Tuo successor, suo regnatore il chiama.

56.

O quai machine volge, o quai disegna
Moti seditiosi; il foco hà in seno,
Il ferro in man; già d'occultar s'ingegna
Ne le regie viuande anco il veneno.
Ne v'hà pur vn, che l'ire à fren ritegna
Del rio trattato, ò che te 'l scopra almeno.
Hor và poi tù con l'armi, e con le leggi,
Popolo sì fellon difendi, e reggi.

57.

Quell'io, che già, per stabilirti in mano
De la verga reale il nobil peso,
Posi in non cale, e vita, e sangue; in vano
Dunque il sangue, e la vita hò sparso, e speso?
Per più lieue cagion contro il germano
Proprio, e i propri tuoi figli han l'armi preso,
Hor giaci, o frate ad altre cure intento
Nel maggior huopo irresoluto, e lento?

54.

So sleeps a Pilot, whose poore Barke is prest
With many a mercylesse o're mastring wave;
For whom (as dead) the wrathfull winds contest,
Which of them deep'st shall digge her watry Grave.
Why dost thou let thy brave soule lye supprest,
In Death-like slumbers; while thy dangers crave
   A waking eye and hand? looke up and see
   The fates ripe, in their great conspiracy.

55.

Know'st thou not how of th' Hebrewes royall stemme
(That old dry stocke) a despair'd branch is sprung
A most strange Babe! who here conceal'd by them
In a neglected stable lies, among
Beasts and base straw: Already is the streame
Quite turn'd: th' ingratefull Rebells this their young
   Master (with voyce free as the Trumpe of *Fame*)
   Their new King, and thy Successour proclaime.

56.

What busy motions, what wild Engines stand
On tiptoe in their giddy Braynes? th' have fire
Already in their Bosomes; and their hand
Already reaches at a sword: They hire
Poysons to speed thee; yet through all the Land
What one comes to reveale what they conspire?
   Goe now, make much of these; wage still their wars
   And bring home on thy Brest more thanklesse scarrs.

57.

Why did I spend my life, and spill my Blood,
That thy firme hand for ever might sustaine
A well-pois'd Scepter? does it now seeme good
Thy Brothers blood be-spilt life spent in vaine?
'Gainst thy owne sons and Brothers thou hast stood
In Armes, when lesser cause was to complaine:
   And now crosse Fates a watch about thee keepe,
   Can'st thou be carelesse now? now can'st thou sleep?

---

57. 1 *spend my life:* see preceding note.

58.

Sù sù perche ti stai? qual ti ritarda
O viltate, ò follia? destati desta,
Sorgi misero homai, scuotiti, e guarda
Quale spada ti pende in sù la testa.
Sueglia il tuo spirto addormentato, ond'arda
Di Regio sdegno, e l'ire, e l'armi appresta.
Teco di ferro, e sangue, ombra fraterna,
Inuisibil m'haurai ministra eterna.

59.

Così gli parla, e poi l'anfesibene
De le schiume di Cerbero nodrita,
Ch'al manco braccio auuiluppata tiene;
Venonosa, e fischiante al cor gl'irrita;
E gli spira in vn soffio entro le vene
Fiamma, c'hauiua ogni virtu sospita;
Ciò fatto entra nel buio, e si nasconde
Trà l'ombre più secrete, e più profonde.

60.

Rompesi il sonno, e di sudor le membra
Sparso dal letto infausto il Rè si scaglia,
Che, benche ricco, e morbido, gli sembra
Siepe di spine, e campo di battaglia.
Ciò che d'hauer veduto egli rimembra
E ciò ch'vdì, ne la memoria intaglia.
Pien d'affanno, e d'angoscia à voto sfida,
Imperuersa, minaccia, & armi grida.

61.

Come se larga man pascolo accresce
D'esca à la fiamma, ò mantice l'alluma,
Ferue concauo rame, e mentre mesce
Il bollor col vapor, mormora, e fuma.
Gonfiasi l'onda insuperbita, & esce
Sù 'l giro estremo, e si conuolue, e spuma,
Versasi al fine intorno e nocer tenta
A quel medesmo ardor, che la fomenta.

58.

Where art thou man? what cowardly mistake
Of thy great selfe, hath stolne King *Herod* from thee?
O call thy selfe home to thy selfe, wake, wake,
And fence the hanging sword Heav'n throws upon thee.
Redeeme a worthy wrath, rouse thee, and shake
Thy selfe into a shape that may become thee.
  Be *Herod,* and thou shalt not misse from mee
  Immortall stings to thy great thoughts, and thee.

59.

So said, her richest snake, which to her wrist
For a beseeming bracelet shee had ty'd
(A speciall Worme it was as ever kist
The foamy lips of *Cerberus*) shee apply'd
To the Kings Heart, the Snake no sooner hist,
But vertue heard it, and away shee hy'd,
  Dire flames diffuse themselves through every veine,
  This done, Home to her Hell shee hy'd amaine.

60.

Hee wakes, and with him (ne're to sleepe) new feares:
His Sweat-bedewed Bed had now betrai'd him,
To a vast field of thornes, ten thousand Speares
All pointed in his heart seem'd to invade him:
So mighty were th'amazing Characters
With which his feeling Dreame had thus dismay'd him,
  Hee his owne fancy-framed foes defies:
  In rage, *My armes, give me my armes,* hee cryes.

61.

As when a Pile of food-preparing fire,
The breath of artificiall lungs embraves,
The Caldron-prison'd waters streight conspire,
And beat the hot Brasse with rebellious waves:
He murmures, and rebukes their bold desire;
Th'impatient liquor, frets, and foames, and raves;
  Till his o'reflowing pride suppresse the flame,
  Whence all his high spirits, and hot courage came.

62.

Così confuso, e stupido quand'ode
Nouo solleuator sorger nel Regno;
Sentesi l'alma il dispietato Herode;
Gia di timor gelata, arder di sdegno.
Tarlo d'ingiuria impatiente il rode
Nè troua loco à l'inquieto ingegno,
E de la notte, ou'altri posa, e tace,
Quasi guerra importuna, odia la pace.

63.

Già per mille profetici presagi
Questo dubbio nel cor gli entrò da prima.
Poi da che vide i tributarij Magi
Nel suo Regno passar da strano clima,
A rodergli i pensier crudi, e maluagi
Ritornò di timor tacita lima.
Hor, che i sospetti in lui desta, e rinoua
Il fantasma infernal, posa non troua.

64.

Tosto, che spunti in Oriente il giorno
(Che l'aria ancora è nubilosa; e nera)
Vuol, che s'aduni entro 'l real soggiorno
De' consiglieri Principi la schiera.
Và de' sergenti, e de gli Araldi intorno.
La sollecita turba Messagiera,
Et à capi, e ministri in ogni banda
Rapporta altrui, chi manda, e che comanda.

65.

Di che pauenti Herode? e quale acceso
Hai di sangue nel cor fero desire?
Humana forma il Rè de' Reggi hà preso
Non per signoreggiar, ma per seruire.
Non à furarti il Regno in Terra è sceso,
Ma te de' regni suoi brama arricchire.
Vano, e folle timor, c'habbia colui,
Che 'l suo ne dona, ad vsurpar l'altrui.

62.

So boyles the fired *Herods* blood-swolne brest,
Not to be slakt but by a Sea of blood.
His faithlesse Crowne he feeles loose on his Crest,
Which on false Tyrants head ne're firmly stood.
The worme of jealous envy and unrest,
To which his gnaw'd heart is the growing food
    Makes him impatient of the lingring light.
    Hate the sweet peace of all-composing Night.

63.

A Thousand Prophecies that talke strange things,
Had sowne of old these doubts in his deepe brest.
And now of late came tributary Kings,
Bringing him nothing but new feares from th'East,
More deepe suspicions, and more deadly stings,
With which his feav'rous cares their cold increast.
    And now his dream (Hels firebrand) stil more bright,
    Shew'd him his feares, and kill'd him with the sight.

64.

No sooner therefore shall the Morning see
(Night hangs yet heavy on the lids of Day)
But all his Counsellours must summon'd bee,
To meet their troubled Lord without delay.
Heralds and Messengers immediately
Are sent about, who poasting every way
    To th'heads and Officers of every band;
    Declare who sends, and what is his command.

65.

Why art thou troubled *Herod?* what vaine feare
Thy blood-revolving Brest to rage doth move?
Heavens King, who doffs himselfe weake flesh to weare,
Comes not to rule in wrath, but serve in love.
Nor would he this thy fear'd Crown from thee Teare,
But give thee a better with himselfe above.
    Poore jealousie! why should he wish to prey
    Upon thy Crowne, who gives his owne away?

63. 3 *came . . . Kings:* Matthew 2:1–2.
64. 3 *summon'd:* Matthew 2:3.

66.

Già per regnar, per guerreggiar non nasce
Fanciullo ignudo, e pouerel negletto,
Cui Donna imbelle ancor di latte pasce,
In breue culla, in pochi panni stretto.
I guerrier son Pastor, l'armi son fasce,
Il palagio real rustico tetto,
Pianti le trombe; i suoi destrier son due
Pigri animali, vn Asinello, vn Bue.

Il fine del Libro Primo.

66.

Make to thy reason man; and mocke thy doubts,
Looke how below thy feares their causes are;
Thou art a Souldier *Herod;* send thy Scouts
See how hee's furnish't for so fear'd a warre.
What armour does he weare? A few thin clouts.
His Trumpets? tender cryes. his men to dare
    So much? rude Shepheards. What his steeds? alas
    Poore Beasts! a slow Oxe, and a simple Asse.

Il fine del libro primo.

Il . . . primo: The end of the first book.

IV

Sacred Poems
in Latin and Greek

In this section, Crashaw's sacred poems in Latin and Greek are on the right-hand page, and the English prose translations, prepared especially for this edition, are on the left-hand page.

88   *Psalm 1.*

O thou, blest over and over!
whom no slippery error nor wanton disorder
with its pitiful mockery has involved.
When the fanatic flock everywhere grow shrill
with their accursed plots, having joined neither in ear (happy man!)
in spirit (happy man!) nor in word,
you pay no attention to their wicked mutterings.
But you, fiercely devoted to those delights
based on simple culture and sober devotion,
wish [to meditate] continually in the law of the Lord.
   [You are] like the fruit tree, planted by the waters of faith,
   which neither the violent Sirius with his savage breath
   nor the wrath of the relentless storm
         destroys.
But you, ungodly dust, wicked sport
of any wind at all. With what countenance will you
as claimant stand in the judgment? How much of the might of your
storm will remain then and what will it be like? O how you will be
by the iron will, the victim of the cruel frown,   [destroyed
to be struck by lightning ah far, far from
the light of the holy presence, far from the golden places,
where the long true peace will always
caress the pious in its eternal bosom
and rise above on shadowy wing, and rains of living nectar
shower the blessed with perpetual dew.
   Thus, o thus, like an avenger [the Lord] remains watchful
   and will remain grim with wrath against the ungodly;
      and into the hearts of the righteous
        [thus He] steals with gentle affection.

88   *Psalmus 1.*

O te te nimis, & nimis beatum!
Quem non lubricus implicavit error;
Nec risu misero procax tumultus.
Tu cùm grex sacer undique execrandis
Strident consiliis, nec aure (felix!)   5
(Felix!) non animo, vel ore mixtus,
Haud intelligis impios susurros.
Sed tu deliciis ferox repôstis
Cultu simplice, sobriâque curâ
Legem numinis usque, & usque voluis.   10
    Læta sic fidas colit arbor undas:
    Quam nec immiti violentus aurâ
    Seirius frangit, neque contumacis
       Ira procellæ.
At tu, profane pulvis, & lusus sacer   15
Cujusvis auræ; fronte quâ tandem feres
Vindex tribunal? quanta tum, & qualis tuæ
Moles procellæ stabit? ô quàm ferreo
Frangêre nutu, præda frontis asperæ,
Sacrique fulminandus ah procul, procul   20
A luce vultûs, aureis procul à locis,
Ubi longa gremio mulcet æterno pios
Sincera semper pax, & umbrosâ super
Insurgit alâ, vividique nectaris
Imbres beatos rore perpetuo pluit.   25
    Sic ille sic ô vindice stat vigil,
    Et stabit irâ torvus in impios,
      Seseque sub mentes bonorum
      Insinuat facili favore.

Psalmus 1: MS.* Martin (p. 453) divides the poem into four metrical schemes: lines 1–10 Phalæcian hendecasyllables; 11–14 a Sapphic stanza; 15–25 six-footed iambics; 26–29 an Alcaic stanza. The first fourteen lines paraphrase verses 1–3, the last fifteen verses 4–6. Like the English psalms, this psalm cannot be traced to a specific text.
    13 *Seirius:* the hot wind.

SACRED EPIGRAMS

These short pieces are the crown of Crashaw's early work. They have recently been most capably translated and edited by Sister Maris Stella Milhaupt, *The Latin Epigrams of Richard Crashaw*. The following translations are often indebted to her good work, but where she has happily achieved her aim of gracious and easy idiom, we have attempted literal closeness at the price of angularity and awkward English. Grosart's translations aspire to English poetry (or rhymed verse) and so leave the original Latin too far behind for our purposes.

Crashaw was admitted to Pembroke on July 6, 1631; he was graduated on March 12, 1635. During his undergraduate years he was on a scholarship from the Watt Foundation, one of the requirements of which was that he should compose Latin and Greek epigrams every Sunday on the Scripture readings for the day. Accordingly, the extant epigrams begin in the summer of 1631 and continue in weekly series through January 1635. It is possible, thanks to the researches of Sister Maris Stella, to date almost all of them within a week. The dating of the epigrams in the *Epigrammata Sacrorum Liber* (1634) is as follows: the first eighteen are undated, perhaps composed at the Charterhouse; the remainder in almost uninterrupted weekly sequence run from August 24, 1631, to May 15, 1634. The other major source of epigrams is Archbishop Tanner's Manuscript (Bodleian MS. Tanner 465); after some undated epigrams, the series resumes on May 18, 1634, and continues through January 11, 1635. The *Poemata et Epigrammata* (Cambridge, 1670) offers a few additional epigrams not dated in the sequence (and all the Greek versions). The epigrams are reprinted in Martin and in Milhaupt in the chronological order of their composition and may there be studied readily in that sequence. In the present edition, the epigrams are arranged in a Scriptural order, based on W. A. Stevens and E. D. Burton *A Harmony of the Gospels* (Boston, 1900). This ordering makes possible for the first time the examination of all the epigrams on one topic at one place. The ordering here is of greatest interest, it is supposed, in the familiar chronology of the events at Christ's birth, death, and ascension; the miracles and teachings that fall between (about one third of the collection) are perhaps not chronologically disposed in the minds of all Christian readers, but there is yet a convenience in finding together all the epigrams on any one miracle. (See below the special indices of Scriptural citations and of events, miracles, and teachings in the epigrams.)

It is evident at once that the epigrams treat themes and topics that are to be of major importance to Crashaw's later and mature work. They include metaphors and conceits that will in later years adorn that work. It would be surprising if Crashaw had not improved on these images, of course, yet some of them appear here in what seems to be almost full flower. The epigrams are distinctive, however, for their brief and brittle wit and the consummate control of the line and the paired distichs. Even persons not trained in Latin can observe, for example, in the first epigram, on the Voice and the Word, how the syntax of the sentence breaks down into units of the line and how the paired lines and phrases balance and answer to one another. Similarly, in the second epigram the repetitions of "Infantis" and "Infans" and of *"signum"* connect the lines and provide

EPIGRAMMATA SACRA

a terse unity to the distich and to the epigram. If there is a fault in this virtue it lies in Crashaw's too frequent using of the line as a unit rather than the distich, but it is a small fault. The brilliant firmness of structure that the four-line epigrams exhibit is not so obvious in the longer poems included among them, and the English poems of later date simply do not have the splendid discipline of mind that can see a poem as a whole and as the sum of its parts.

Leicester Bradner writes (*Musæ Anglicanæ* [New York, 1940], p. 92): "By far the greatest writer of the conventional sacred epigram in England was Richard Crashaw"; and Warren continues (p. 89): "Nor will a diligent search through the neglected volumes of Renaissance Neo-Latinity discover any master of whom Crashaw is not peer."

The reader should refer to the notes in Martin's edition for sources and parallels in classical and Renaissance Latin and for discussions on emendations and Latin versification, and to the notes in Sister Maris Stella's edition for exact dating and relationships to the Anglican liturgy.

EPIGRAM-
MATUM
SACRORUM
LIBER.

CANTABRIGIÆ,
Ex Academiæ celeberrimæ
typographeo. 1634.

89   John 1:1–18. *John the Voice; Christ the Word.*

John reveals Christ. This does not seem strange:
  one was the voice, obviously the other was the word.

Christ is before John. This does seem strange:
  the word does not usually exist before its voice.

90   Luke 1:18. *Zacharias not believing at all.*

                                                [thing;
That you will be the father of a speechless [babe] seems a strange
    meanwhile you yourself have become a speechless father.
                                    [(too anxiously),
And while you were asking *for a sign* of the promised One
    now—except *by a sign*—you can ask for nothing.

91   Luke 1:20–38. *To the blessed Virgin.*
            Concerning the salutation of the angel.

Nor does Cæsar's bird now say *his* HAIL;
    your HAIL comes on whiter wing.

But let the bird be quiet also which says *your* HAIL;
    my HAIL comes on [even] whiter wing.

What more shining spokesman should say *my* HAIL to me
    than that shining one who says *yours* to you?

89   *Vox Joannes; X^{us} Verbum.*

Monstrat Joannes Christum. haud res mira videtur:
Vox unus, verbum scilicet alter erat.

Christus Joanne est prior. hæc res mira videtur:
Voce suâ verbum non solet esse prius.

90   *Luc. 1:18. Zacharias minùs credens.*

Infantis fore te patrem, res mira videtur;
Infans interea factus es ipse pater.

Et dum promissi *signum* (nimis anxie) quæris,
Jam nisi *per signum* quærere nulla potes.

91   *Beatæ Virgini. De salutatione Angelicâ.*

Χαῖρε *suum* neque Cæsareus jam nuntiet ales;
Χαῖρε *tuum* pennâ candidiore venit.

Sed taceat, qui Χαῖρε *tuum* quoque nuntiat, ales;
Χαῖρε *meum* pennâ candidiore venit.

Quis dicat mihi Χαῖρε *meum* magè candidus autor,   5
Quàm tibi qui dicit candidus ille *tuum?*

89. MS. See also the later epigrams where John's Voice is again mentioned: "In Baptistam vocem," No. 120, and "Ego sum vox," No. 126, 127. The four epigrams are divided, as they emphasize the different aspects of John's Voice. Here the emphasis is on the priority of the Word (the Logos); in the later epigrams, John is preaching the word and crying in the wilderness. The appropriate texts are, furthermore, for different holy days: this one is for Christmas.

90. 34.* The poem depends on the double meanings of *infans* (1) speechless, (2) an infant, and of *signum* (1) gesture, (2) omen. The dumbness of Zacharias is mentioned at Luke 1:20–22, 64.

91. 34.* "There is no English equivalent for the Greek χαῖρε, which is both a . . . greeting and an imperative meaning *be well* and *rejoice*" (Milhaupt, p. 188).

Virgin, you ask what can be whiter than that shining one?
The Virgin who asks can be.

That shining one will give *your* HAIL to you (Virgin);
you still more shining give me *my* HAIL.

Hear how *my* HAIL should differ from *your* HAIL:
he *speaks* yours, you *give birth* (behold!) to mine.

92   Luke 1:38. *To the Blessed Virgin, believing.*

You wonder (indeed what else would you do?) but also you believe
you believe these sweet miracles of your womb. [these things:

Lo, your reward, o Queen, is most worthy of your faith.
You were a faithful daughter of God; *you will be* [His] *mother.*

93   *God in the womb of the virgin.*

Behold your father, Nature! here is your father, he is here:
He, whom the womb of his mother holds, he is your father.

The mighty Son whom neither you nor she [can] *contain wholly*
(believe it) *is cramped by the fragile tissues.*

What reverence for your womb do you have, o Queen,
while God lies here, in too small a heaven.

The quick organs swell with divine movement
(no more holy air moves the heavenly poles).

How well under the same roof are conceived by you
prayers and [He] (to whom prayers ought to be conceived), God!

What other prayers ask of the clouds and the halls of heaven above,
your prayers will find at home.

Virgo, rogas, quid candidius quàm candidus ille
Esse potest? Virgo, quæ rogat, esse potest.

Χαῖρε *tuum* (Virgo) donet tibi candidus ille;
Donas candidior tu mihi Χαῖρε *meum.*   10

Χαῖρε *meum* de Χαῖρε *tuo* quid differat, audi:
Ille tuum *dicit,* tu *paris* (ecce) meum.

92   Luc. 1. *Beatæ Virgini credenti.*

Miraris (quid enim faceres?) sed & hæc quoque credis:
Hæc uteri credis dulcia monstra tui.

En fidei, Regina, tuæ dignissima merces!
Fida Dei fueras filia; *mater eris.*

93   *Deus sub utero virginis.*

Ecce tuus, Natura, pater! pater hic tuus, hic est:
Ille, uterus matris quem tenet, ille pater.

Pellibus exiguis arctatur Filius ingens,
     Quem tu non totum (crede) *nec ipsa capis.*

Quanta uteri, Regina, tui reverentia tecum est,   5
     Dum jacet hîc, cœlo sub breviore, Deus!

Conscia divino gliscunt præcordia motu
     (Nec vehit æthereos sanctior aura polos)

Quàm bene sub tecto tibi concipiuntur eodem
     Vota, & (vota cui concipienda) Deus!   10

Quod nubes alia, & tanti super atria cœli
     Quærunt, invenient hoc tua vota domi.

---

92. 34.* The paradox of this poem—a favorite one—reappears in the "Hymn in the Holy
Nativity," No. 70, and elsewhere.

O happy this soul which so touches its own joys!
For which its own fire is beneath its heart.

Let her love her body (it is allowable) and not prefer the stars:
what is a bond for others, she considers home.

You will lie alone, and not alone; on whatever couch you recline,
you and your child lie on that couch.

Indeed, while you lie, a chaste wife, with your husband—
this is more strange—you are yourself a couch.

94   Luke 2:7. *There was no room for them in the inn.*

Is there no place for him? Do you mean you banish him? Him?
He is *God* whom you banish thus; he is *God.*

O madness! the savage miracles of human madness!
There is no place for him *without whom there is no place.*

95   *On the easy parturition of the Blessed Virgin.*

Still she was not made a mother without pain; [even though]
that Boy came so gently from his mother's womb.

Whatever that one hour of birth spared,
she was in travail with him her whole lifetime.

That one time he was the joys of birth for his mother;
every day he was the groans of birth.

O felix anima hæc, quæ tam sua gaudia tangit!
Sub conclave suo cui suus ignis adest.

Corpus amet (licet) illa suum, neque sydera malit: 15
Quod vinc'lum est aliis, hoc habet illa domum.

Sola jaces, neque sola; toro quocunque recumbis,
Illo estis positi túque tuúsque toro.

Immo ubi casta tuo posita es cum conjuge conjunx,
(Quod mirum magìs est) es tuus ipsa torus.   20

94   Luc. 2:7. *Non erat iis in diversorio locus.*

Illi non locus est? Illum ergò pellitis? Illum?
Ille *Deus*, quem sic pellitis; ille *Deus*.

O furor! humani miracula sæva furoris!
Illi non locus est, *quo sine nec locus est.*

95   *In partum B. Virg^s. non difficilem.*

Nec facta est tamen illa Parens impunè; quòd almi
Tam parcens uteri venerit ille Puer.

Una hæc nascentis quodcunque pepercerit hora,
Toto illum vitæ tempore parturijt.

Gaudia parturientis erat semel ille parenti;
Quotidie gemitus parturientis erat.

93. 34.
94. 34.
95. MS. It was held that Mary had an easy parturition because, having been immaculately conceived herself, she was free of birth sin and hence of the specific curse on Eve: "in sorrow thou shalt bring forth children." See *Summa Theologica*, Part III, Q.xxxv, Art. 6; E. L. Mascall, *The Blessed Virgin Mary* [London, 1963], p. 61.

96   *On the bashfulness of the blessed Virgin.*

You ask why the Virgin should keep her eyes on her lap
thus? in what better place might she keep them, pray tell?

O where better than on heaven should she keep her eyes?
She looks down, *but even so she nevertheless still sees heaven.*

97   *On the bashfulness of the Blessed Virgin.*

This is (believe it) the modesty not of the mother but of the Son,
that the virgin casts her eyes down at her lap.

There now God is. Now therefore the eye of the Virgin
in order to see heaven must be cast down.

98   Matthew 1:23. *God with us.*

Is *God with us?* This is your [saying], [yes] yours, poor me:
God is *with you,* o asses and oxen.

He is not with us: for a golden house claims us:
God is with us, and will he lie in a stable?

So in order [for this saying] to become *ours,* sweetest Jesus,
We should be given *to the stables* or *a house* be given to you.

96   *In beatæ Virginis verecundiam.*

In gremio, quæris, cur sic sua lumina Virgo
Ponat? ubi meliùs poneret illa, precor?

O ubi, quàm cœlo, meliùs sua lumina ponat?
Despicit, *at cœlum sic tamen illa videt.*

97   *In Beatæ Virginis verecundiam.*

Non est hoc matris, sed (crede) modestia nati,
Quòd virgo in gremium dejicit ora suum.

Illîc jam Deus est. oculus jam Virginis ergò,
Ut cælum videat, dejiciendus erit.

98   Matth. 1:23. *Deus nobiscum.*

Nobiscum Deus est? vestrum hoc est (hei mihi!) vestrum:
Vobiscum Deus est, ô asini atque boves.

Nobiscum non est: nam nos domus aurea sumit:
Nobiscum Deus est, & jacet in stabulo?

Hoc igitur *nostrum* ut fiat (dulcissime Jesu)
Nos dandi *stabulis,* vel tibi danda *domus.*

---

96. 34. See Crashaw's English translation, "On the Blessed Virgins bashfulness," No. 5, and the next poem. Milhaupt (p. 112) suggests that the poem is inspired by a picture; the text for the Annunciation (the Sunday where this epigram fits into the series) does not include any mention of the infant Jesus.

97. MS. See the preceding poem, of which Milhaupt suggests this is an early draft (p. 210).

98. 34.

99   Luke 2:7. *On the stable where the Master was born.*

Is that home *a stable?* it is not, golden Boy, it is not:
is that home where you will be born a *stable?*

That home is the most beautiful house in the whole world;
scarcely may one call it smaller than your heaven.

Do you see how that house glows with its own gold everywhere?
Do you see how it smiles amid roses in bloom?

Or if it is not gold, and that not a rose smiling there,
it is easy to prove [the glow and the smile to come] from Your eyes.

99   *In stabulum ubi natus est Dominus.*

Illa domus *stabulum?* non est (Puer auree) non est:
Illa domus, quâ tu nasceris, est *stabulum?*

Illa domus toto domus est pulcherrima mundo;
Vix cœlo dici vult minor illa tuo.

Cernis ut illa suo passim domus ardeat auro?
Cernis ut effusis rideat illa rosis?

Sive aurum non est, nec quæ rosa rideat illic;
Ex oculis facile est esse probare tuis.

99   Ὄικος δδ' ἐστ' αὔλη. οὐ μή. τεὸς οἶκος, Ἰησοῦ,
Ἐν θ' ᾧ τὸ τίκτη αὔλιον οὐ πέλεται.

Οἴκων μὲν πάντων μάλα δὴ κάλλιστος ἐκεῖνος·
Οὐρανοῦ οὐδὲ τεοῦ μικρότερος πέλεται.

Ἤνιδε κεῖνο νεῷ δῶμ' ἐμπυρίζετο χρύσῳ,
Ἤνιδε κεῖνο νεοῖς δῶμα ῥόδοισι γελᾷ.

Ἦν ῥόδον οὔχι γελᾷ, ἦν οὐδὲ τε χρύσον ἐκεῖθεν·
Ἔκ σου δ' ὀφθαλμῶν ἐστὶν ἐλεγχέμεναι.

99. 34. The Greek version of this epigram as of all the others is found in the 1670 edition.

100   Luke 2:8–14. *On the birth of the Lord
made known to the Shepherds.*

The youth in royal purple brings such great joys to you
on wings of stars, Good Tityrus, to you.

O well would I watch you to whom such great joys are brought,
that while you are keeping watch you do not think you are keeping
[awake.
Whom did heaven want to be revealed to shepherds in this way,
was it a Shepherd or a lamb? He was Shepherd and lamb.

When God Himself will be the Shepherd, who will not be a lamb?
Who will not be a shepherd, when God will be the Lamb?

101   Luke 2:21. *Christ, circumcised, to the Father.*

Lo, receive these first fruits of our death, Father, [to you]
from whom I have received life, I have dedicated my life;

your wrath, Father, will have tasted of this shower:
at a later time this whole side will flow forth in its own streams.

Then let [your wrath] thirst and thirst, let it drink and drink forever:
Then it will be able to enjoy the whole splendid spring.

Meanwhile now let the *knife* foreshadow the *spear:*
the hope of my [whole] being will be in the torments [that are to
[come].

100   *In natales Domini Pastoribus nuntiatos.*

Ad te sydereis, ad te, Bone Tityre, pennis
Purpureus juvenis gaudia tanta vehit.

O bene te vigilem, cui gaudia tanta feruntur,
Ut neque, dum vigilas, te vigilare putes.

Quem sic monstrari voluit pastoribus æther,
Pastor, an Agnus erat? Pastor, & Agnus erat.

Ipse Deus cùm Pastor erit, quis non erit agnus?
Quis non pastor erit, cùm Deus Agnus erit?

101   *Christus circumcisus ad Patrem.*

Has en primitias nostræ (Pater) accipe mortis;
(Vitam ex quo sumpsi, vivere dedidici)

Ira (Pater) tua de pluviâ gustaverit istâ:
Olim ibit fluviis hoc latus omne suis.

Tunc sitiat licèt & sitiat, bibet & bibet usqué:
Tunc poterit toto fonte superba frui.

Nunc *hastæ* interea possit præludere *culter:*
Indolis in pœnas spes erit ista meæ.

---

100. MS. This epigram seems to lie behind the "Nativity Hymn," No. 70, in that it includes
the "pastoral" shepherd, Tityrus, and the shepherd/lamb conceit with which also the longer
poem concludes. Lines 3–4 are a difficult sentence to translate. Part of the difficulty lies in
the various meanings of the punning words as in the Vulgate: "Et pastores erant . . . vigi-
lantes, et custodientes vigilias noctis . . ." See also the margin of the King James Bible. The
lines may refer to the amazement of the shepherd as equivalent to sleep.
101. 34. See Crashaw's English, "Our Lord in his Circumcision," No. 6.

102   Luke 2:21. *On the blood of the Lord's circumcision.*
To the guests who celebrate this day with us.

Hark guest! are you drinking? Mary and Mary's little boy
send this new wine from their wine-press to be drunk.

Indeed there is only one single drop (which alone, nevertheless,
is equal to the whole world), which trembles in its little orb.

O drink from this; however much or whatever kind you have drunk
(believe me), you have drunk nothing so sweet ere now.

O drink and drink; still there remains more to be drunk:
It remains because no thirst can reduce it.

Surely here the extent of thirst is the extent of drinking:
however much you wish to drink these wines, *you drink.*

103   Luke 2:21. *On the Circumcision.*

Ah cruel knife! which first commanded such fair lilies
to change into such cruel roses.

Which first stained this virgin ivory with purple
and introduced into His nature the purple stain.

Indeed whatever stream rushes hence
hereafter will come from this seed of the purple font.

Indeed the boy accepts this first talon of death:
today the fates and violence lay hand [on him].

See, his blood begins to be poured forth, and see
how there was scarcely enough blood to be able to be poured forth.

He draws from a new jar wine scarcely [ready]
and calls wild passions into youthful limbs.

102   *In sanguinem circumcisionis Dominicæ.*
   Ad convivas, quos hæc dies apud nos solennes habet.

Heus conviva! bibin'? Maria hæc, Mariæque puellus,
 Mittunt de prælo musta bibenda suo.

Una quidem est (toti quæ par tamen unica mundo)
 Unica gutta, suo quæ tremit orbiculo.

O bibite hinc; quale aut quantum vos cunque bibistis,
 (Credite mî) nil tam suave bibistis adhuc.

O bibite & bibite; & restat tamen usquè bibendum:
 Restat, quod poterit nulla domare sitis.

Scilicet hîc, mensura sitis, mensura bibendi est:
 Hæc quantum cupias vina bibisse, *bibis*.

103   *[In circumcisionem.]*

Ah ferus, ah culter! qui tam bona lilia primus
 In tam crudeles jussit abire rosas.

Virgineüm hoc qui primus ebur violavit ab ostro;
 Inque sui instituit muricis ingenium.

Scilicet hinc olim quicunque cucurrerit amnis,   5
 Ex hoc purpurei germine fontis erit.

Scilicet hunc mortis primum puer accipit unguem:
 Injiciunt hodie fata, furorque manus.

Ecce illi sanguis fundi jam cæpit; & ecce,
 Qui fundi possit, vix bene sanguis erat.   10

Excitat è dolio vix dum bene musta recenti,
 Atque rudes furias in nova membra vocat.

---

102. 34. The "wine-press" recalls Isaiah 63:3; see also "An Apologie," No. 62, lines 39–40.

Outrageous! how even now He girds on too much pain!
And weapons not to be shaken by a tender hand.

Outrageous! how now He dares to play at youthful deaths!
And to die in the small measure of life that a child [has]!

Outrageous! how impatiently He reveals the foreshadowing of tragic
        and refuses now to walk in his own sock.   [fate

Indeed this hand reflects on buskins for these feet!
Does this mind reflect on threats with flattery?

Is this so harsh rattle suited for this small hand?
Is this hand fit enough for Giant's cheeks?

Are crosses so to be mixed with the cradle? And with [his] mother's
        are there to be mingled death and crime and madness?   [breast

As he smiles at his father so silently too he observes the knife;
with the same glance he caresses his mother and returns to the weapons.

Gods of heaven! this rage is in his eyes! this cruel look is on his face!
He gives to Mars the countenance that Love would prefer for himself.

Delights of pains! Cruel smiles! tender soldiers!
Gentle madness! sweet terror! lovable fear!

sad jollity for the boy precocious in punishments!
Harsh beginnings! and rough basic training!

Now a sparing and a slighter wound for this slight body,
and may blood flow for a slighter time from a slight wound:

Hereafter when the sinews and fiercer breath of life
will give abundant substance to death;

at some time later he will try the mature showers [of blood];
then will he dare a strong complete death.

Pray tell, for what will he have blood except to harden against cruel
        and except to be able to pour forth?   [treatment

Improbus! ut nimias jam nunc accingitur iras!
　Armaque non molli sollicitanda manu!

Improbus! ut teneras audet jam ludere mortes!　　15
　Et vitæ ad modulum, quid puerile mori!

Improbus! ut tragici impatiens præludia fati
　Ornat, & in socco jam negat ire suo!

Scilicet his pedibus manus hæc meditata cothurnos!
　Hæc cum blanditiis mens meditata minas?　　20

Hæc tam dura brevem decuêre crepundia dextram?
　Dextra Gigantæis hæc satis apta genis?

Sic cunis miscere cruces? cumque ubere matris
　Commisisse neces, & scelus, & furias?

Quo ridet patri, hoc tacite quoque respicit hastam;　　25
　Quoque oculo matrem mulcet, in arma redit.

Dii Superi! furit his oculis! hoc asper in ore est!
　Dat Marti vultus, quos sibi mallet Amor.

Deliciæ irarum! torvi, tenera agmina, risus!
　Blande furor! terror dulcis! amande metus!　　30

Præcocis in pænas pueri lascivia tristis!
　Cruda rudimenta! & torva tyrocinia!

Jam parcum breviusque brevi pro corpore vulnus,
　Proque brevi brevior vulnere sanguis eat:

Olim, cùm nervi, vitæque ferocior haustus　　35
　Materiam morti, luxuriemque dabunt;

Olim maturos ultrò conabitur imbres;
　Robustum audebit tunc, solidumque mori.

Ergò illi, nisi qui in sævos concreverit usus,
　Nec nisi quem possit fundere, sanguis erit?　　40

Well done, cruel Boy! Well done, yet most gentle in all things!
    You can be so cruel only to yourself, Boy!

Well done, cruel to yourself! Well done most gentle in all things to me.
    Well done gentle Lion! but yet cruel Lamb!

Be reverenced, Boy! be reverenced for this honor of such harsh praise!
    O be reverenced for this talented genius for punishment!

    Ah cruel knife! under which, so expert in griefs,
    you hasten thus to become a man of sorrow, Boy.

    Ah cruel knife! under which, Golden Boy, you grow,
    advancing under this ferule, as it were, of death.

104   Luke 2:22–39. *The infant Christ is presented
            to his Father in the temple.*

Let the lamb go, and let him play at the feet of his butting father (he
    and far off let the turtle dove live with her mate.   [may);

    Here there is no need to go through the *Lamb, the mediator,*
    nor that the fragile bird should suffer for a fate not her own.
                                        [presents, these which
    Heretofore we have played with these trifles as if they were mere
    were to be accepted by a hand forgiving much.

    This is the Gift of which we say to you with our whole heart,
    Take it Father: take this for yourself on its own merits.

    This is the Gift, this it is, which surely should dare
    to be worthy of God himself: of course it is *God himself.*

Euge puer trux! Euge tamen mitissime rerum!
Quique tibi tantùm trux potes esse, puer!

Euge tibi trux! Euge mihi mitissime rerum!
Euge Leo mitis! trux sed & Agne tamen!

Macte puer! macte hoc tam duræ laudis honore!   45
Macte ô pænarum hac indole, & ingenio!

Ah ferus ah culter! sub quo, tam docte dolorum,
In tristem properas sic, puer, ire virum.

Ah ferus, ah culter! sub quo, puer auree, crescis
Mortis proficiens hac quasi sub ferulâ.   50

104   Luc. 2. *Christus infans Patri sisitur in templo.*

Agnus eat, ludátque (licet) sub patre petulco;
Cúmque sua lcngùm conjuge turtur agat.

Conciliatorem nihil hîc opus ire per *agnum:*
Nec tener ut volucris non sua fata ferat.

Hactenus exigua hæc, quasi munera, lusimus; hæc quæ
Multum excusanti sunt capienda manu.

Hoc Donum est; de quo, toto tibi dicimus ore,
Sume Pater: meritis hoc tibi sume suis.

Donum hoc est, hoc est; quod scilicet audeat ipso
Esse Deo dignum: scilicet *ipse Deus.*

---

103. MS.* The *oystrum* (line 3) (oyster) and *murex* (4) from which purple dyes are made.
Soccus (18) is the low shoe worn by the comic actor; *cothurnus* (19) the high shoe worn
by tragedians (see Milton, "L'Allegro," "Il Penseroso"). *Ferula* (50) is the rod used to pun-
ish schoolboys.
104. 34. The lamb and turtle dove, the usual sacrificial animals for the poor, are not needed
at this presentation (Leviticus 5:6–7).

105   Luke 2:27–32. *Now lettest thou [thy servant] depart.*

Did my arms then finally hold my hopes?
Do my eyes then drink in your eyes?

Then let them drink; and let them be able to hope for new youth:
O let them not be able to remember their old age!

Nay rather let death cover me with its gentle shadow
(if still there can be a shadow under these eyes).

Ah, it is enough. I have seen You, Golden Boy, seen You:
I want to see nothing after you, except you, o Christ.

106   Luke 2:27–32. *Now lettest thou [thy servant] depart.*

Go, my eyes (for what more do you want?):
go slowly after the eyelids have been closed.

Nay, see still yet again and again;
receive these lights of all lights.

And now go; and shut yourself up well within safe walls:
keep safe these lights of all lights.

This is the first [wish], that I could see you (Christ): second,
having seen you, to have been able to die straightway.

107   Luke 2:35. *A sword shall pierce through thy own soul.*

Since your tragedy has no *sword,* Christ,
what will be your *sword,* blessed Virgin?

For no wounds were given to you otherwise, Virgin,
than those which were given by your wounds, Christ.

Perhaps since he was then a rather thick-sighted old man,
what Simeon believed [to be] a *sword,* was a *spear.*

105   Luc. 2. *Nunc dimittis.*

Spésne meas tandem ergò mei tenuêre lacerti?
Ergò bibunt oculos lumina nostra tuos?

Ergò bibant; possíntque novam sperare juventam:
O possint senii non meminisse sui!

Immo mihi potiùs mitem mors induat umbram
(Esse sub his oculis si tamen umbra potest)

Ah satis est. Ego te vidi (puer auree) vidi:
Nil post te, nisi te (Christe) videre volo.

106   Luc. 2. *Nunc dimittis.*

Ite mei (quid enim ulteriùs, quid vultis?) ocelli:
Leniter obductis ite superciliis.

Immo & adhuc & adhuc, iterúmque iterúmque videte;
Accipite hæc totis lumina luminibus.

Jámque ite; & tutis ô vos bene claudite vallis:
Servate hæc totis lumina luminibus.

Primum est, quòd potui te (Christe) videre: secundum,
Te viso, rectà jam potuisse mori.

107   Luc. 2. *Tuam ipsius animam pertransibit gladius.*

Quando habeat *gladium* tua, Christe, tragœdia nullum,
Quis fuerit *gladius*, Virgo beata, tuus?

Námque nec ulla aliàs tibi sunt data vulnera, Virgo,
Quàm quæ à vulneribus sunt data, Christe, tuis.

Forsan quando senex jam caligantior esset,
Quod Simeon *gladium* credidit, *hasta* fuit.

105. 34. The "Nunc dimittis," the opening words of Luke 2:29–32, is Simeon's song of praise, sung in the services of Morning and Evening Prayer (Milhaupt, p. 108).
106. 34. See preceding note. The words *lumina luminibus* are an echo from the Nicene Creed, *lumen de lumine*, "Light of Light."
107. 34. Crashaw's exercise of wit imagines that the old gentleman in an ecstatic vision mistook the spear that pierced Christ's side (John 19:34) for a sword and that it is the contemplation of the spear-thrust and side-wound that pierces Mary's soul. But Crashaw concludes that any one of Christ's sufferings would serve equally well.

Rather it was neither *spear* nor *nail* nor *thorn:*
Alas for me still, *thorn, nail, spear* it was.

For from whatever evils your tragedy grew, Christ,
all these are your *sword,* blessed Virgin.

108   Matthew 2:1–12. *On the epiphany of the Lord.*

The day is not content with the light of the usual torch of Aurora;
see how it twinkles adorned with new beams.

Hurry Persian sage: run about through the lofty courts of the kings,
through the gold and marble houses:

ask what Queen the royal robe warmed at her delivery;
which house echoed with a Prince's cry.

Are you listening, Persian seer? *He who performed so many works in*
is crying in the stalls of Bethlehem.   [*heaven,*

109   Matthew 2:11. *The Gifts of the Persian Sages.*

Receive these gifts, Boy; the first fruits of inadequate praise.
Receive them, not to be received on their own merits.

Receive these gifts, sweet Boy, and while you receive them,
you also will make worthy those, Boy, that you receive.

Whether by your eye or by your right hand you honor them;
you will make them worthy of your hand and eye.

Not only are you kind to the givers but to the gifts themselves;
not only giving do you give but also receiving.

Immo neque *hasta* fuit, neque *clavus,* sed neque *spina:*
Hei mihi, *spina* tamen, *clavus,* & *hasta* fuit.

Nam queiscunque malis tua, Christe, tragœdia crevit,
Omnia sunt *gladius,* Virgo beata, tuus.

108   *In Epiphaniam Domini.*

Non solitâ contenta dies face lucis Eoæ,
    Ecce micat radiis cæsariata novis.

Persa sagax, propera: discurre per ardua Regum
    Tecta, per auratas marmoreásque domus:

Quære ô, quæ intepuit Reginæ purpura partu;
    Principe vagitu quæ domus insonuit.

Audin' Persa sagax? *Qui tanta negotia cœlo*
    Fecit, Bethlemiis vagiit in stabulis.

109   *[Dona magorum.]*

Accipe dona, Puer; parvæ libamina laudis.
    Accipe, non meritis accipienda suis.

Accipe dona, Puer dulcis. dumque accipis illa,
    Digna quoque efficies, quæ, puer, accipias.

Sive oculo, sive illa tuâ dignabere dextrâ;
    Dextram, oculumque dabis posse decere tuum.

Non modò es in dantes, sed & ipsa in dona benignus;
    Nec tantùm donans das, sed & accipiens.

108. 34.
109. MS.*

110   Matthew 2:13–15. *On the dark and stormy Journey*
of the infant Lord.

Does the night hold these tender wayfarers, the Mother with her Son,
of whom not any day is worthy?

For why alas will the night and the storm kiss
the lips of the Boy? or the cheeks of the mother?

Lilies should kiss them, a rose should; and whatever
the gentle west wind which glows with undying violets breathes.

They deserved either that there should be no night or, if there be one,
that it should pass clearer than our day.

But see how the night and winter have enclosed these tender ones:
and who knows what the night, what the storm may be contriving?

Ah may the winter not plan to rage with its south winds
and [with the] black terrors that evil night usually brings.

Ah may the course of this night not pass with ungentle southeast winds.
May the brisk breeze not herald the harsh south winds!

Alas how many many real dangers the shadows have with them!
How many many monsters worship lady night!

How many wandering illusions which come in false shapes!
Grim eye! wing the color of the Stygian god!
[images,
Whether these monsters appear in their real shapes or in flickering
for the virgin, there are enough fears from those, enough from these.

Therefore come, come, make a louder noise with your whole bow,
Cynthia, bang your full quiver far off.

May these monsters or those be the marks for your arrows:
may [those arrows have] more certain aim [than] the shaft of your
[brother.

110   Matth. 2. *In nocturnum & hyemale iter infantis Domini.*

Ergò viatores teneros, cum Prole Parentem,
   Nox habet hos, queîs est digna nec ulla dies?

Nam quid ad hæc Pueri vel labra, genásve Parentis?
   Heu quid ad hæc facient oscula, nox & hyems?

Lilia ad hæc facerent, faceret rosa; quicquid & halat   5
   Æterna Zephyrus qui tepet in viola.

Hi meruêre, quibus vel nox sit nulla; vel ulla
   Si sit, eat nostrâ puriùs illa die.

Ecce sed hos quoque nox & hyems clausêre tenellos:
   Et quis scit, quid nox, quid meditetur hyems?   10

Ah nè quid meditetur hyems sævire per Austros!
   Quæque solet nigros nox mala ferre metus!

Ah nè noctis eat currus non mollibus Euris!
   Aspera nè tetricos nuntiet aura Notos!

Heu quot habent tenebræ, quot vera pericula secum!   15
   Quot noctem dominam, quantáque monstra colunt!

Quot vaga quæ falsis veniunt ludibria formis!
   Trux oculus! Stygio concolor ala Deo!

Seu veris ea, sive vagis stant monstra figuris;
   Virginei satìs est hinc, satìs indè metûs.   20

Ergò veni; totóque veni resonantior arcu,
   (Cynthia) prægnantem clange procul pharetram.

Monstra vel ista, vel illa, tuis sint meta sagitis:
   Nec fratris jaculum certior aura vehat.

110. 34.*
   22 (*Cynthia*): the Moon; Crashaw is asking the Moon (and later the stars) to shine
and give light to the travelers; when they come, they are compared unfavorably to those
travelers.

Therefore come: come with your whole face blazing more brightly,
    worthy to have sustained Apollo's shining.

You know well how the sister of Phoebus should shine:
    if you do not, Cynthia, learn from these cheeks.

O how much more lovely would your torch be in them!
How much night would prefer to have its day from them!

How much more shyly would this moon cast its silent fires!
And how cautiously would she stand with her awe-struck horses.

Moon, the rose of your day is not so blushing:
    nor does your torch tremble with so virginal a bloom.

Therefore come: but also gather your band of stars, Cynthia:
    They have the eyes of the Boy, which they may imitate.

Here [a light] in an eye, there in a star; but each twinkles with equal
    The face of the heavens, and the heavenly face of the Boy.   [fire,

See how well the story of either one would fit the other!
How well their equivalent glories [would fit] in the hands of the other!

If that [starry] eye of the sky should stand in this heaven of his brow
    or this star of the Boy in the heavenly brow.

If this star of the Boy should gleam in the brow of heaven
    He would believe this eye was no less His own.

If that eye of the sky should stand in this heaven of His brow,
    it would think it was no less in its own skies.

The heaven and the stars can alternate such beautiful interchanges
with the brow of the Little One and with the eyes of the Little One.

Indeed the stars might wish it: they might wish a permanent treaty to
            to begin their turn in a changed home.   [be sealed

And the Heaven itself (despite such unequal numbers) might wish
    such favorable agreements to be made for changed eyes.

Ergò veni; totóque veni flagrantior ore,   25
  Dignáque Apollineas sustinuisse vices.

Scis bene quid deceat Phoebi lucere sororem:
  Ex his, si nescis, (Cynthia) disce genis.

O tua, in his, quantò lampas formosior iret!
  Nox suam, ab his, quantò malit habere diem!   30

Quantùm ageret tacitos hæc luna modestior ignes!
  Atque verecundis sobria staret equis!

Luna, tuæ non est rosa tam pudibunda diei:
  Nec tam virgineo fax tua flore tremit.

Ergò veni; sed & astra, tuas age (Cynthia) turmas: 35
  Illa oculos pueri, quos imitentur, habent.

Hinc oculo, hinc astro; at parili face nictat utrumque;
  Ætheris os, atque os æthereum Pueri.

Aspice, quàm bene res utriusque deceret utrumque!
  Quàm bene in alternas mutua regna manus!   40

Ille oculus cœli hôc si staret in æthere frontis;
  Sive astrum hoc Pueri, fronte sub ætherea.

Si Pueri hoc astrum ætherea sub fronte micaret,
  Credat & hunc oculum non minùs esse suum.

Ille oculus cœli, hoc si staret in æthere frontis,   45
  Non minùs in cœlis se putet esse suis.

Tam pulchras variare vices cum fronte Puelli,
  Cúmque Puelli oculis, æther & astra queant.

Astra quidem vellent; vellent æterna pacisci
  Fœdera mutatæ sedis inire vicem.   50

Æther & ipse (licèt numero tam dispare) vellet
  Mutatis oculis tam bona pacta dari.

Indeed with how much better stars would the sky move,
if only it could have these eyes for its stars!

Indeed in how much better a sky would the stars twinkle,
if they could have this brow as their own sky.
[wish and the stars:
The heaven and stars would wish this: but in vain would the heaven
lo the brow of The Boy refuses, the eyes refuse.

Ah let it refuse, let them refuse: for what heaven would these eyes
or what greater stars should this brow want? [prefer?

What if some star should gleam softly with a lovely light?
[or what] if the way to heaven is three or four times [as] milky [as it is]?

This eye is more lovely which smiles in this rosy face;
this brow is three and four times [as] milky.

Therefore let them refuse, and let the stars keep their own heaven:
the stars should not be given away from their skies.

Therefore they refuse, and, lo, they hide themselves behind their cloud,
behind the little cloud of the closing eyelid.

And not content to be enclosed by the ramparts of their heaven,
they seek a place to hide in the bosom of the Mother.
[touches of its frost
Only in such [a place to be] where that [virgin] snow warms with
and chaste winter turns to spring without icy cold.

Clearly this day is worthy to be colored with such a beautiful evening
and *it is fitting for these suns so to set.*

May the purple evening which closes Olympus close [this day];
may you be pleased with your purple colored couch, Phoebe,

while adulterous Thetis lengthens the wanton night for you,
put your shameful couch amid the Hesperian roses.

Quippe iret cœlum quantò melioribus astris,
Astra sua hos oculos si modò habere queat!

Quippe astra in cœlo quantum meliore micarent,   55
Si frontem hanc possint coelum habuisse suum.

Æther & astra velint: frustra velit æther, & astra:
Ecce negat Pueri frons, oculíque negant.

Ah neget illa, negent illi: nam quem æthera mallent
Isti oculi? aut frons hæc quæ magìs astra velit?   60

Quid si aliquod blandâ face lenè renideat astrum?
Lactea si cœli térque quatérque via est?

Blandior hic oculus, roseo hôc qui ridet in ore;
Lactea frons hæc est térque quatérque magís.

Ergò negent, cœlúmque suum sua sydera servent: 65
Sydera de cœlis non bene danda suis.

Ergò negant; séque ecce sua sub nube recondunt,
Sub tenera occidui nube supercilii:

Nec claudi contenta sui munimine cœli,
Quærunt in gremio Matris ubi lateant.   70

Non nisi sic tactis ubi nix tepet illa pruinis,
Castáque non gelido frigore vernat hyems.

Scilicet iste dies tam pulchro vespere tingi
Dignus; & *hos soles sic decet occidere.*

Claudat purpureus qui claudit vesper Olympum;   75
Puniceo placeas tu tibi (Phœbe) toro;

Dum tibi lascivam Thetis auget adultera noctem
Pone per Hesperias strata pudenda rosas.

71–72 The oxymoron of warm snow is more fully developed in the "Nativity Hymn,"
No. 70, lines 51–70.
75 Such an evening as it can be imagined came to the pagan gods.
76 *Phoebe:* the Moon.
78 The Hesperian roses grew in the gardens of the Hesperides, in the Western Isles;
the Moon sets in the western sea.

Of course those roses, which guilty purple painted,
  guilt and shame made them be roses.

To these suns [are well suited] the snowy nights and the chaste bed
  which virgin Thetis spreads over the pure sea;
            [lilies are well suited
To these [suns], holy flowers [are well suited]; to these [suns], such pure
  and roses [which need] not blush for themselves.

To these [suns], this bosom was well suited; where behold, lying all
  they bathe themselves in the milky ocean. [night long,

And let them bathe: and finally let them be released in the morning
  so that day itself may drink from this source.

111   Matthew 2:13–23. *Christ in Egypt.*

You, O Nile, show him to your people by a greater flood:
  Say he is your source (*completely unknown*).

Now, Nile, you are increasing your size: now flood yourself:
  Now you yourself may be the *flood of* your own *joy.*

112   Matthew 2:16–18. *To the infant martyrs.*

Pour out your laughing souls; pour them out to heaven:
  There your tongue will learn to speak—o how well!

Do not seek your milk and [your] mothers' fountains:
  what awaits you is the whole *milky way.*

Illas nempe rosas, quas conscia purpura pinxit;
Culpa pudórque suus queîs dedit esse rosas.   80

Hos soles, niveæ noctes, castúmque cubile,
Quod purum sternit per mare virgo Thetis;

Hos, sancti flores; hos, tam sincera decebant
Lilia; quæque sibi non rubuêre rosæ.

Hos, decuit sinus hic; ubi toto sydere proni   85
Ecce lavant sese lacteo in oceano.

Atque lavent: tandémque suo se mane resolvant,
Ipsa dies ex hoc ut bibat ore diem.

111   Matth. 2. *Christus in Ægypto.*

Hunc tu (Nile) tuis majori flumine monstra:
Hunc (*nimis ignotum*) dic caput esse tibi.

Jam tibi (Nile) tumes: jam te quoque multus inunda:
Ipse tuæ jam sis *lætitiæ fluvius.*

112   Matth. 2. *Ad Infantes Martyres.*

Fundite ridentes animas; effundite cœlo:
Discet ibi vestra (ô quàm bene!) lingua loqui.

Nec vos lac vestrum & maternos quærite fontes:
Quæ vos expectat *lactea* tota *via* est.

79–80 For the close association between red and shamefulness, see also line 84 below
and "Videte lilia agrorum," No. 153, and the "Nativity Hymn," No. 70, lines 62–63.
86 See the "Nativity Hymn," No. 70, lines 87–90.
111. 34. In Crashaw's time the source of the Nile was unknown.
112. 34. This epigram and the three following (see also the two English epigrams "On the
Infant Martyrs," No. 7, 8) exhibit one of Crashaw's favorite themes. In the first two (which
are those translated), he discusses milk and blood, lilies and roses; in the second two,
Crashaw treats the theme of life and death.

113   Matthew 2:16–18. *On the nursing martyrs.*

Whoever saw the wounds of the children and the breasts of the mothers
flow together in their streams, ah, through the boys:

Whoever saw the boys so, doubted whether he should call them
the *lilies* of heaven or the *roses.*

114   Matthew 2:16–18. *On the young martyrs.*

Ah, [he] who fell thus to such an early death
had only enough of life so he could die.

But God has so used his death,
he has only enough of death so he can live forever.

115   Matthew 2:16–18. *On the blessed Martyrs.*

Happy souls! you sped, hurrah, you made haste. And you
mastered the high road by a shorter way.

Not overburdened by too many storms, the skiff
bore you thither through the little sea of your blood;

while the scarcely trustworthy force of the inexhaustible sea
carries us toiling under such slow rowing.

Us the delay, us the idleness of a long death wears out.
We serve as an extravagant plaything of death.

We are abandoned to old age, affliction, and broad seas.
We are dropped into pitfalls, we are laid low by madness.

113   Matth. 2. *In lactentes Martyres.*

Vulnera natorum qui vidit, & ubera matrum,
    Per pueros fluviis (ah!) simul ire suis;

Sic pueros quisquis vidit, dubitavit, an illos
    Lilia cœlorum diceret, anne *rosas.*

114   *In tenellos Martyres.*

Ah qui tam propero cecidit sic funere, vitæ
    Hoc habuit tantùm, possit ut ille mori.

At cujus Deus est sic usus funere, mortis
    Hoc tantùm, ut possit vivere semper, habet.

115   [*In felices Martyres.*]

Felices! properâstis jo, properâstis. & altam
    Vicistis gyro sub breviore viam.

Vos per non magnum vestri mare sanguinis illuc
    Cymba tulit nimiis non operosa notis;

Quò nos tam lento sub remigio luctantes   5
    Ducit inexhausti vis malè fida freti.

Nos mora, nos longi consumit inertia lethi.
    In ludum mortis, luxuriemque sumus.

Nos ævo, & senio, & latis permittimur undis.
    Spargimur in casus,—porrigimur furiis.   10

---

113. 34. See preceding note and "Upon the Infant Martyrs," No. 8.
114. 34. It is to be doubted that the long poem which follows states the matter better than this little quatrain.

We are wretched from excess and we vanish after a time.
The fates scrutinize us and judge our works.

We are the natural disposition of fate, the ambition of sins;
the zeal and purpose of death are we.

The ground of a long death is revealed in a long life.

The years do not number life for us, however many we have lived:
ours is a short life although we may have lived long.

The fact that [we] lead a long life is not to live long:
a long history is often acted out in a short life.

God did not send you shortness of life
so much as he refused to let your death have more power over you.

Whatever is cut off from old age adds to life;
and so the more quickly we die, the shorter that [old age] is.

116   Luke 2:41–50. *The blessed Virgin seeks her Jesus.*

Ah, may you return, sweet boy, may you return to your poor parent;
Ah do not give yourself back to your heavens so quickly.

Heaven would our arms be for you,
if our arms could hold you, their *God.*

117   Luke 2:41–50. *No runaway Love.*

Holy Virgin, do not suffer these laments too much.
Your son will not wish, will not be able to be away long.

For what would hold him? or what kisses would he want more?
what would keep him away from his natural home in your bosom?

Nos miseri sumus ex amplo; spatioque perimus.
In nos inquirunt fata; probantque manus.

Ingenium fati sumus, ambitioque malorum;
Conatus mortis, consiliumque sumus.

In vitæ multo multæ patet area mortis . . . 　　　　15

Non vitam nobis numerant, quot viximus, anni:
Vita brevis nostra est; sit licèt acta diu.

Vivere non longum est, quod longam ducere vitam:
Res longa est vitâ sæpe peracta brevi. 　　　　　20

Nec vos tam vitæ Deus in compendia misit,
Quàm vetuit vestræ plus licuisse neci.

Accedit vitæ quicquid decerpitur ævo.
Atque illò breviùs, quò citiùs morimur.

116　　　　　Luc. 2. *Quærit Jesum suum beata Virgo.*

Ah, redeas miseræ, redeas (puer alme) parenti;
Ah, neque te cœlis tam citò redde tuis.

Cœlum nostra tuum fuerint ô brachia, si te
Nostra suum poterunt brachia ferre *Deum.*

117　　　　　*[Non fugitivus Amor.]*

Ne, pia, ne nimium, Virgo, permitte querelis:
Haud volet, haud poterit natus abesse diu.

Nam quid eum teneat? vel quæ magis oscula vellet?
Vestri illum indigenam quid vetet esse sinûs?

115. MS.* Line 16 is missing in the MS. Milhaupt translates the last line (p. 240) "and the sooner we die, the less we die." See also the epigram "In S. Lucam Medicum," No. 324, and the secular "Humanæ vitæ descriptio," No. 414.

116. 34. This epigram introduces a series of four treating the same event. It is translated in effect by the concluding lines (47–50) of the English poem "Quærit Jesum," No. 9.

117. MS. These lines recall in subject matter though not in tone or point of view the complaints of Mary uttered in lines 1–46 of the English poem "Quærit Jesum," No. 9. This poem, however, adds the idea of Cupid, the runaway (see "Out of the Greek Cupids Cryer," No. 372).

Indeed what lips may be considered more suited for those cheeks?
or what hand is more worthy for this neck?

What would the boy desire for himself more eagerly than those arms?
Or in what embrace could he be more sweetly?

O what vine more loving binds to itself the tender elm,
dying in each other's embraces?

Whom would he clasp in unexpected embrace more impatiently?
or what face would observe [him] with so many glances?

Upon what kisses so ready would the boy rise so often?
With what jewel more noble would [anyone] mark [his] cheek?

Where might the grape mature more sweetly in breezes so springlike,
or hang beneath ridges so sunny?

In what shade would weariness come to him so pleasing?
Under what murmur would he sleep so pleasantly?

O where will he reign in a cell so dear,
so pure as in this bosom both motherly and virginal?

Would he flee from these? Would he not wish such great joys?
Could he fail to hasten to this bosom?

Would he spurn so fair an inheritance [as] this bosom?
having been made heir to such [and] so many delights?

No indeed, do not suffer these laments of yours, holy one.
Why should you doubt? *This is no runaway Love.*

Quippe illis quæ labra genis magis apta putentur? 5
 Quæve per id collum dignior ire manus?

His sibi quid speret puer ambitiosiùs ulnis?
 Quóve sub amplexu dulciùs esse queat?

O quæ tam teneram sibi vitis amicior ulmum
 Implicet, alternis nexibus immoriens? 10

Cui circum subitis eat impatientior ulnis?
 Aut quæ tam nimiis vultibus ora notet?

Quæ tam prompta puer toties super oscula surgat?
 Quâ signet gemmâ nobiliore genam?

Illa ubi tam vernis adolescat mitiùs auris, 15
 Tamve sub apricis pendeat uva jugis?

Illi quâ veniat languor tam gratus in umbrâ?
 Commodiùs sub quo murmure somnus agat?

O ubi tam charo, tam casto in carcere regnet,
 Maternoque simul, virgineoque sinu? 20

Ille ut ab his fugiat? nec tam bona gaudia vellet?
 Ille ut in hos possit non properare sinus?

Ille sui tam blanda sinûs patrimonia spernet?
 Hæres tot factus tam bene deliciis?

Ne tantum, ne, Diva, tuis permitte querelis: 25
 Quid dubites? *Non est hic fugitivus Amor.*

118   Luke 2:46–47. *The boy Jesus in the midst of the doctors.*

The man is deceived who hangs on every bearded chin
as if smooth cheeks could not have any wisdom at all.

Obviously Apollo would be poorly judged from his beard,
and a winter of the mind often accompanies a snowy head.

Let that man learn that he can also be taught by this young teacher
not to think that *whiteness of the head* is the *head.*

119   Luke 2:48–49. *Lo we sought you, etc.*

In sorrow I seek and seek for thee: now you too go about
the Father's business: the Father is your only care:

Indeed to many pains and to death in many names,
to mourning and to tears—woe is me!—am *I mother.*

120   Matthew 3:3. *On the voice of the Baptist.*

So much the Baptist had to speak, so many streams of thought,
that indeed he will have been a Voice, nothing else.

But lo at last he said one *Word:*
but with one *Word* he had said everything.

118   Luc. 2. *Puer Jesus inter Doctores.*

Fallitur, ad mentum qui pendit quemque profundum,
   Ceu possint læves nil sapuisse genæ.

Scilicet è barba malè mensuratur Apollo;
   Et bene cum capitis stat nive, mentis hyems.

Discat, & à tenero disci quoque posse magistro:
   Canitiem capitis nec putet esse *caput.*

119   Luc. 2:49. *Ecce quærebamus te, &c.*

Te quæro misera, & quæro: tu nunc quoque tractas
   Res Patris: Pater est unica cura tibi:

Quippe quòd ad poenas tantùm & tot nomina mortis,
   Ad luctum & lacrymas (hei mihi!) *mater ego.*

120   *In Baptistam Vocem.*

Tantum habuit Baptista loqui, tot flumina rerum,
   Ut bene Vox fuerit, prætereaque nihil.

Ecce autem *Verbum* est unum tantùm ille loquutus:
   Uno sed *Verbo* cuncta loquutus erat.

---

118. 34.
   3 Apollo was generally represented in classical art without a beard.
   6 *Caput* probably has connotations of the "head of the class."
119. 34.
120. MS. See also the first epigram "Vox Joannes," No. 89, and the two later ones, Nos. 126 and 127. Milhaupt, finding that this epigram sequentially falls on St. John the Baptist's Day (June 24) has assigned the proper text to it. At this point in the present arrangement of epigrams, the "public ministry" of John begins. Jesus' ministry follows with his baptism and temptation.

121   Matthew 3:13–15. *On the water of the Lord's baptism.*

O blessed [water], which may thus go over the holy limbs!
o blessed [water]! while it washes him, the water is washed itself.

Indeed whatever drop passes over the holy limbs,
while it remains here, is a jewel; while it falls hence, a tear.

122   Matthew 3:16–17. *On the holy dove sitting
near Christ's head.*

Over whom does the *sacred bird* hover on starry wing?
On whom will it place its foot whiter than snow?

O Christ, for your head it steers by every breeze,
where the sweeter shadow of your thick hair plays.

There what does it not tell you in secret whisper
(in a whisper not imitating mortal sounds)?

This bird alone is not unworthy to sleep in this nest:
this nest alone is quite worthy of this bird.

121   Joann. 3. *In aquam baptismi Dominici.*

Felix ô, sacros cui sic licet ire per artus!
Felix! dum lavat hunc, ipsa lavatur aqua.

Gutta quidem sacros quæcunque perambulat artus,
Dum manet hîc, gemma est; dum cadit hinc, lacryma.

122   *In S. Columbam ad Christi caput sedentem.*

Cui *sacra* sydereâ *volucris* suspenditur alâ?
Hunc nive plùs niveum cui dabit illa pedem?

Christe, tuo capiti totis se destinat auris,
Quà ludit densæ blandior umbra comæ.

Illîc arcano quid non tibi murmure narrat?
(Murmure mortales non imitante sonos)

Sola *avis hæc* nido hoc non est indigna cubare:
Solus *nidus hic* est hâc bene dignus ave.

122   Πῆ ταχυεργὸς ἄγει πτέρυγ' ἀστερόεσσαν ἐρετμὸς;
      Ἢ τινὶ κεῖνα φέρει τὴν πόδα χιονέην;

Χριστὲ τεῇ κεφαλῇ πάσαις πτερύγεσσιν ἐπείγει·
Πῆ σκιά τοι δασιόις παῖζε μάλα πλοκάμοις.

Ποῖά σοι ἀρρήτῳ ψιθυρίσματι κεῖν' ἀγορεύει;
Ἄρρητ', οὐκ ἠχῆς ἴσα μὲν ἀνδρομέης.

Μοῦνα μὲν ἠδ' ὄρνις καλιᾶς ἐστ' ἄξια ταύτης·
Ἄξια δ' ὄρνιθος μοῦνα μὲν ἡ καλιά.

121. 34. See "On the water of our Lords Baptism," No. 10. Crashaw's citation, John 3, does not mention the baptising of Christ, though verse 23 mentions the baptising of others.
122. 34. Crashaw's interest in the whiteness of feet is seen here in the dove's foot.

123   Matthew 4:3. [*Command*] *that this stone*
                    be made bread.

And it was: that stone (why not say it?) was bread, Christ:
                but it was *your* bread.

Indeed since the greatest will of the Father has turned out so,
        it is your bread, not to have had bread.

124   Matthew 4:5. *Christ carried by the devil.*

Come now, will he—oh, a load more suitable for the wings of angels—
        will he be willing to be carried on such a Stygian bird?

        Blackguard! do not rejoice yet. Obviously from this
            you are no less a Demon, he no less a God.

125 Matthew 4:6. *If thou be the Son of God, cast thyself down.*

If Christ should not cast himself down from the pinnacle of the Temple,
            you do not believe that he is the Son of God.

But soon he casts you down from the human heart: poor you,
        do you not believe that he is the Son of God?

123   Matth. 4. *Hic lapis fiat panis.*

Et fuit: ille lapis (quidni sit dicere?) panis,
Christe, fuit: panis sed *tuus* ille fuit.

Quippe, Patris cùm sic tulerit suprema voluntas,
Est panis, panem non habuisse, tuus.

123   Ἄρτος ἔην τοι δῆτ' (εἰπεῖν θέμις ἐστὶν) ἐκεῖνος
Χριστέ τοι ἄρτος ἔην καὶ λίθος· ἀλλὰ τεός.

Ἦν οὕτως τοῦ πατρὸς ἐῇ μεγάλου τὸ θέλημα
Ἄρτος ὅτ' οὐκ ἦν τοι, Χριστὲ, τοι ἄρτος ἔην.

124   Mat. 4. *Christus à dæmone vectus.*

Ergò ille, Angelicis ô sarcina dignior alis,
Præpete sic Stygio sic volet ille vehi?

Pessime! nec lætare tamen. tu scilicet inde
Non minùs es Dæmon, non minùs ille Deus.

125   Matth. 4. *Si Filius Dei es, dejice te.*

Ni se dejiciat Christus de vertice Templi,
Non credes quòd sit Filius ille Dei.

At mox te humano de pectore dejicit: heus tu,
Non credes quòd sit Filius ille Dei?

123. 34. The nature of Christ's bread suggests John 4:32, 34.
124. MS.
125. 34.

126   John 1:23. *I am the voice, etc.*

I am the voice, you say: you are the voice, Saint John?
If you are *the voice,* why was your father *silent?*

How strange that silence of your father was!
He did not have a *voice* even then while he fathered [one].

127   John 1:23.

I am the voice, you say: Are you the voice, Saint John?
If you are the voice, why was your mother barren?

How strange was that unfruitfulness of your mother!
It is even rarer for a woman to be barren of voice.

128   John 1:29. *The Lamb of God which taketh away the sins
                    of the world.*

Alas [will he] who must pass—grim sights—before so many mouths of
        beside so many lairs of wolves, will he be a Lamb?   [lions,

Against so many horrible leopards (as many as my sins),
        against so many beasts bold in claw and in tooth?
                                                  [fighters?
[Would it were] better! who indeed will argue with those [wild]
        Whom neither their arms nor their wrath makes equals.

126   Joann. 1:23. *Ego sum vox, &c.*

Vox ego sum, dicis: tu vox es, sancte Joannes?
Si *vox* es, genitor cur tibi *mutus* erat?

Ista tui fuerant quàm mira silentia patris!
Vocem non habuit tunc quoque cùm genuit.

127   Joh. 1:23.

Vox ego sum, dicis. tu vox es, sancte Johannes?
Si vox es, sterilis cur tibi mater erat?

Quàm fuit ista tuæ mira infæcundia matris!
In vocem sterilis rarior esse solet.

128   Joh. 1. *Agnus Dei, qui tollit peccata mundi.*

Ergò tot heu (torvas facies) tot in ora leonum,
In tot castra lupûm qui meat, Agnus erit?

Hic tot in horribiles, quot sunt mea crimina, pardos?
Hic tot in audaces ungue, vel ore feras?

Ah melius! pugiles quis enim commiserit istos?
Quos sua non faciunt arma, vel ira pares.

---

126. 34. See the earlier epigrams "Vox Joannes," No. 89, and "In Baptistam vocem," No. 120. The text for this and the following epigram is from the Gospel for the Fourth Sunday in Advent. The dumbness of Zacharias (see also "Zacharius minus credens," No. 90) is referred to in Luke 1:20–22, 64.
127. MS. See preceding note. The barrenness of Elizabeth is referred to in Luke 1:7.
128. MS.

129   John 2:1–11. *Waters turned into wine.*

Whence comes [this] redness to your waters, [as it is] not its own purple?
    What rose so strange changes these wondering waters?

       O guests, acknowledge God, the spirit present:
    the chaste nymph has seen [her] God *and blushed.*

130   John 2:1–11. *To Christ about the water*
               turned into wine.

   [Miraculous] signs your enemy has contrary to your signs:
       you turn sad water into wine for me.

      But he, bringing tears and quarrels from wine,
   wines again he changes—poor me!—into sad *waters.*

131   John 3:1–21. *On Nicodemus.*

It was night and you, Teacher badly taught, were seeking Christ,
      In Christ to lay down your shadows.

    But while that good man refreshes you with many a word
    and leads you through the hidden paths to the heights,

    the sun comes and reveals itself in the first bloom of day
    and plays like a golden ripple over the wavering waters.

The Sun rises. But still and still yet, o good man, you are ignorant.
    The sun rises. But night is still with you even yet.

    It was not that of heaven; it was your night.

129   Joann. 2. *Aquæ in vinum versæ.*

Unde rubor vestris, & non sua purpura lymphis?
Quæ rosa mirantes tam nova mutat aquas?

Numen (convivæ) præsens agnoscite Numen:
Nympha pudica Deum vidit, *& erubuit.*

130   Joann. 2. *Ad Christum, de aqua in vinum versa.*

Signa tuis tuus hostis habet contraria signis:
In vinum tristes tu mihi vertis aquas.

Ille autem è vino lacrymas & jurgia ducens,
Vina iterum in tristes (hei mihi!) mutat *aquas.*

131   Joh. iii.

Nox erat, & Christum (Doctor malè docte) petebas,
In Christo tenebras depositure tuas.

Ille autem multo dum te bonus irrigat ore,
Atque per arcanas ducit in alta vias,

Sol venit, & primo pandit se flore diei,
Ludit et in dubiis aureus horror aquis.

Sol oritur. sed adhuc, & adhuc tamen (ô bone) nescis.
Sol oritur. tecum nox tamen est & adhuc.

Non cæli illa fuit; nox fuit illa tua.

---

129. 34. The fourth line of the epigram is the most admired and celebrated line in Crashaw's entire corpus. There are many analogues in early Latin verse, and many noble attempts at English translation. One of the best is Crashaw's own at "Out of Grotius," No. 83, line 52. This epigram is dated by Milhaupt at January 20, 1633. See also the note at "Quinque panes," No. 175.
130. 34. See "To our Lord, upon the Water made Wine," No. 11.
131. MS. The last distich lacks a line.

132   John 3:4. *How can a man be born who is old?*

[flourishing years
Tell me, whence does a new phoenix leap forth into [new and]
and with golden wings beat the fires [that it has] eluded?

What trick of serpents winds their way back through the ages
and orders their worn-out body to flourish [as new]?

Why with its dying beak does the savage bird preying on its own old age
gather more time with its impetuous mouth?

Nay indeed, what Lucina attends the second labors
whence an old man may have a second birth?

Do you not know, Pharisee? that is enough. You will learn to believe:
he who is properly ignorant has half of his faith.

133   John 3:16. *God so loved the world that he gave his Son
to death.*

Ah it is too much indeed to give him for our life:
why does an ocean do what a little drop would do?

From this [gift] my life has a place whence it can abound;
death has a place whence it can fully and grandly die.

134   John 3:19. *Light is come into the world but men loved
darkness rather than light.*

Behold God comes with his light and shines in the world:
yet still the world continues to love its darkness.

But for this reason the world will be condemned to the Stygian shades:
does the world still continue to love its darkness?

132 Joann. 3:4. *Quomodo potest homo gigni qui est senex?*

> Dic, Phœnix unde in nitidos novus emicat annos;
> Plaudit & elusos aurea penna rogos?
>
> Quis colubrum dolus insinuat per secula retro,
> Et jubet emeritum luxuriare latus?
>
> Cur rostro pereunte suam prædata senectam
> Torva ales, rapido plus legit ore diem?
>
> Immo, sed ad nixus quæ stat Lucina secundos?
> Natales seros unde senex habeat.
>
> Ignoras, Pharisæe? sat est: jam credere disces:
> *Dimidium fidei, qui bene nescit, habet.*

133 Joann. 3:16. *Sic dilexit mundum Deus, ut Filium morti traderet.*

> Ah nimis est, illum nostræ vel tradere vitæ:
> Guttula quod faceret, cur facit oceanus?
>
> Unde & luxuriare potest, habet hinc mea vita:
> Amplè & magnificè mors habet unde mori.

134 Joann. 3:19. *Lux venit in mundum, sed dilexerunt homines magìs tenebras quàm lucem.*

> Luce suâ venit ecce Deus, mundóque refulget;
> Pergit adhuc tenebras mundus amare suas.
>
> At Stygiis igitur mundus damnabitur umbris:
> Pergit adhuc tenebras mundus amare suas?

132. 34.
  7 *Lucina:* the goddess of childbirth.
  10 the last line is in distinguishing type because it is an adaptation of a line from Horace (Martin, p. 429).
133. 34. Milhaupt (p. 161) suggests that the "more abundant life" is an echo of John 10:10.
134. 34. See "But men loved darknesse," No. 12.

135   John 4:47. *He besought him that he would come down and heal his son.*

You who ask that he should go with you for the healing of your son and
       Ah you do not know, I believe, that Love is winged.   [for you,

     That he should go with you? How your desires delay themselves!
     That he should go? He would arrive there so much the later.

      Lest he should come late, Christ refuses to go with you:
      Of course, to go [will] delay Christ's journey.

      To be sure, on Christ's paths, whatever is passed by dies:
   to be sure, on Christ's paths even to hurry indeed is a delay.

       Here is Christ to whom you make your petitions
but—believe me—the same Christ who will grant these petitions is there.

136   Luke 4:24. *The Lord not accepted in his own country.*

     Look at these blood-relations! Christ is an exile in his own
     country! *and nowhere else was he such a stranger.*

   The robber who at the last hung [beside Him] in blood brotherhood,
       O how much more *a blood-relation* was he!

137   Luke 4:29. *On the Jews trying to cast Christ down headlong.*

      Tell me why [have you] so much confidence in your crime?
To have wished for the very crime that the Devil was unable to commit?

To have wished to accomplish the crime that the Devil was unable to
      That was, I believe, *to tempt the Devil himself.*   [commit!

135   Joh. *4. Rogavit eum, ut descenderet,*
                & sanaret filium suum.

Ille ut eat tecum, in natique, tuique salutem?
     Qui petis; ah nescis (credo) quòd Ales Amor.

Ille ut eat tecum? quàm se tua vota morantur!
     Ille ut eat? tantò seriùs esset ibi.

Ne tardus veniat, Christus tecum ire recusat:
     Christi nempe ipsum hoc ire moratur iter.

Christi nempe viis perit hoc quodcunque meatur:
     Christi nempe viis vel properare mora est.

Hîc est, cui tu vota facis tua, Christus: at idem
     (Crede mihi) dabit hæc qui rata, Christus ibi est.

136   Luc. *4. Dominus apud suos vilis.*

En consanguinei! patriis en exul in oris
     Christus! *& haud alibi tam peregrinus erat.*

Qui socio demum pendebat sanguine latro,
     O *consanguineus* quàm fuit ille magìs!

137   Luc. *4:29. In Judæos Christum præcipitare*
                   conantes.

Dicite, quæ tanta est sceleris fiducia vestri?
     Quod nequiit dæmon, id voluisse scelus?

Quod nequiit dæmon scelus, id voluisse patrare!
     Noc *tentare ipsum dæmona* (credo) fuit.

---

135. MS. For other epigrams on this subject see the two "Absenti Centurionis" and "Christus
absenti," Nos. 157 and 158.

136. 34. Bradner (*Musæ Anglicanæ*, p. 94): "It would be hard to exceed the bitter irony of
the play upon words in the second couplet. What is sometimes in Crashaw only a trick of
rhetoric becomes in epigrams such as this the expression of an intense sincerity."

137. 34. The Devil tempted Christ to cast himself down; see "Si Filius Dei es, dejice te,"
No. 125.

138   Matthew 4:19. *The fishermen called.*

Play now, you fish, anywhere in the safe sea:
we too are fish (but of a different kind).

Not to have been caught is your one hope of safety:
our one hope of safety is to have been caught.

139   Mark 1:16–18. *To St. Andrew the fisherman.*

How well you can catch and trick the fish!
There you slyly school a hundred to swim into your traps.

Alas good fisherman! Christ has stretched his nets.
Reverse your skill, and now you too learn to be caught.

140   Luke 5:9. *For he was astonished at the draught*
of the fishes.

While you were seized with amazement at your catch of fish, Peter
—as I see it—you yourself were caught by your own fish.

I understand the story. Christ caught you, a catch for himself: and from
all of those, there was one piece of bait for you.

141   Luke 5:11. *Forsaking everything, they followed him.*

You threw away the nets at the Master's nod, Peter.
Never had they been cast so well before.

Of course this is rightly to throw your nets, Peter,
indeed to throw them away when Christ ordered.

138   Matth. 4:19. *Piscatores vocati.*

Ludite jam pisces secura per æquora: pisces
Nos quoque (sed varia sub ratione) sumus.

Non potuisse capi, vobis spes una salutis:
Una salus nobis est, potuisse capi.

139   Marc. 1:16. *Ad S. Andream piscatorem.*

Quippe potes pulchrè captare & fallere pisces!
Centum illîc discis lubricus ire dolis.

Heus bone piscator! tendit sua retia Christus:
Artem inverte, et jam tu quoque disce capi.

140   Luc. 5:9. *Pavor enim occupaverat eum super*
               capturam piscium.

Dum nimiùm in captis per te, Petre, piscibus hæres,
Piscibus (ut video) captus es ipse tuis.

Rem scio. te prædam Christus sibi cepit: & illi
Una in te ex istis omnibus esca fuit.

141   Luc. 5. *Relictis omnibus sequuti sunt eum.*

Ad nutum Domini abjecisti retia, Petre.
Tam bene non unquam jacta fuere priùs.

Scilicet hoc rectè jacere est tua retia, Petre,
Nimirum, Christus cùm jubet, abjicere.

138. 34.*
139. 34. Milhaupt (pp. 100–1) suggests the text should be Matthew 4:18–22, part of the Gospel for St. Andrew's Day.
140. MS.
141. MS. See "On St. Peter casting away his nets," No. 13, and the epigram just below on the call to Matthew.

142   Mark 1:30–31 and   { *the woman with fever* }
             Luke 14:1–6. On {   } *healed.*
                              { *the man with dropsy* }

In the holy writ read recently [Christ] stopped a serious fever:
Now in the reading he gives a dry body to the man with dropsy.

How these miracles touch each other in brotherly turn
and through each other's help loyally love!

Indeed how well he drowned the fires in these floods!
how well he put down those waters with these fires!

143   Matthew 8:1–4. *The Leper begging the Master.*

[I believe
I believe that you can do these things, if only you wished: but because
Christ, that you can do them, I believe that you will want to do them.

Only you, you put on affectionate smiles for me, *my Sun;*
My snow will not be able to bear your rays.

144   Mark 2:1–13. *The paralytic recovering.*

The scribes are not hesitant to call Christ *blasphemous*
because he readily forgives the sins of this wretch.

As soon as the Paralytic heard this crime, impatient
in anger, *he took up his bed and went forth.*

142   Marc. 1. & Luc. 14. *In* $\left\{\begin{array}{c} febricitantem \\ \& \\ hydropicum \end{array}\right\}$ *sanatos.*

Nuper lecta gravem extinxit pia pagina febrem:
Hydropi siccos dat modò lecta sinus.

Hæc vice fraternâ quàm se miracula tangunt,
Atque per alternum fida juvamen amant!

Quippe ignes istos his quàm bene mersit in undis!
Ignibus his illas quàm bene vicit aquas!

143   Matth. 8. *Leprosus Dominum implorans.*

Credo quòd ista potes, velles modó: sed quia credo,
Christe, quòd ista potes, credo quòd ista voles.

Tu modò, tu faciles mihi, *Sol meus,* exere vultus;
Non poterit radios *nix mea* ferre tuos.

144   Marc. 2. *Paralyticus convalescens.*

Christum, quòd misero facilis peccata remittit,
Scribæ *blasphemum* dicere non dubitant.

Hoc scelus ut primùm Paralyticus audiit; irâ
Impatiens, *lectum sustulit atque abiit.*

---

142. MS. Both passages from Holy Writ are appointed to be read on the seventeenth Sunday
after Trinity (Milhaupt, p. 228), one at Morning Prayer, the other at the Communion. See
another treatment of the cure of the dropsical man at "Hydropicus sanatur," No. 208.
143. 34.
144. 34.

145   Matthew 9:9. *Matthew from the receipt of custom.*

Ah it is enough, too much: do not keep this office any longer
and [bow your] neck shamefully to your master, avarice.

Flee now; now, Matthew, flee the power of the cruel tyrant:
go happily in flight to the *good cross.* *

* *Of Christ, that is.*

146   Luke 5:28. *Leaving everything, he followed him.*

When Matthew left these riches at Christ's command,
At that moment he began truly to have his own riches.

That is the good use of evil riches, the only use;
that a man has evil riches which he may lose well.

147   Matthew 9:11. *Why eateth your Master with publicans?*

Do you mean he joins *those* sinners?
Do you mean he does not deny his sacred side *to them?*

You, Pharisee, ask why Jesus has done this?
let me say truly: He was *Jesus,* not a *Pharisee.*

148   Matthew 9:11. *Why eateth your Master
with sinners, etc.*

Is it thus, wicked man, that you shrink from your brother's diseases,
when your disease (even more serious) holds you?

A disease which dared seek such a doctor for itself was great;
that one which dared scorn such a doctor was Greater.

145   Matth. 9:9. *A telonio Matthæus.*

Ah satìs, ah nimis est: noli ultrà ferre magistrum,
Et lucro domino turpia colla dare.

Jam fuge; jam (Matthæe) feri fuge regna tyranni:
Inque *bonam* felix i fugitive *crucem.

Christi scilicet.

146   Luc. 5:28. *Relictis omnibus sequutus est eum.*

Quas Matthæus opes, ad Christi jussa, reliquit,
Tum primùm verè cœpit habere suas.

Iste malarum est usus opum bonus, unicus iste;
Esse malas homini, quas bene perdat, opes.

147   Matth. 9:11. *Quare cum Publicanis manducat
Magister vester?*

Ergò *istis* socium se peccatoribus addit?
Ergò *istis* sacrum non negat ille latus?

Tu, Pharisæe, rogas Jesus cur fecerit istud?
Næ dicam: *Jesus,* non *Pharisæus,* erat.

148   Mat. 9. *Quare comedit Magister vester
cum peccatoribus &c.*

Siccine fraternos fastidis, improbe, morbos,
Cùm tuus, (& gravior) te quoque morbus habet?

Tantum ausus medicum morbus sibi quærere, magnus;
Tantum ausus medicum spernere, Major erat.

---

145. 34. Milhaupt (p. 96) glosses the phrase "i in bonam crucem" as a Christian reverse of the classical objurgation "I in malem crucem" (go to the bad cross, i.e. go and be hanged!). Fugitive slaves were usually crucified; legends report that Matthew died a martyr.

146. 34. See above the earlier responses to the call.

147. 34.

148. MS.

149   John 5:1–16. *The man placed near the pool of Bethesda.*

What new Tantalus here leans toward the receding waves,
   whom health so fleeting fails so many times?

Whence [comes] this fortunate shipwreck? and healing storms?
   and life, which a precious tempest has given?

150   Mark 3:1–5. *The withered hand is healed.*

                                                     [right hand
O happy man! now you watch the birthday celebrations of your own
which a little while ago was a deplorable corpse when you looked at it.

Surely that hand which recently was of no use in outer functions
   now will be the [right] *hand of your faith.*

151   Mark 3:1–5. *On the withered hand by which
            the compassion of Christ was moved.*

Grasp Christ, poor man; and with Christ grasp health:
But [your] hand is crippled, you will say: grasp anyway.

This very act is a hand upon Christ; this is to grasp Christ:
not to have had a hand by which you might grasp Christ.

152   Matthew 4:24. *And they brought unto him
all sick people, and those which were possessed with devils,
and those which were lunatick . . . and he healed them.*

Gather to yourself both the furies and the fevers, grim Dragon,
   and those diseases night and Hell call their own:

now make each Erinnys of yours shake her snakes;
gather, gather them boldly to yourself so that——*you may die.*

149   Joann. 5. *Ad Bethesdæ piscinam positus.*

Quis novus hic refugis incumbit Tantalus undis,
   Quem fallit toties tam fugitiva salus?

Unde hoc naufragium felix? medicæque procellæ?
   Vitáque, tempestas quam pretiosa dedit?

150   Marc. 3. *Manus arefacta sanatur.*

Felix! ergò tuæ spectas natalia dextræ,
   Quæ modò spectanti flebile funus erat.

Quæ nec in externos modò dextera profuit usus,
   Certè erit illa tuæ jam *manus & fidei.*

151   Marc. 3. *In manum aridam quâ*
          Christo mota est miseratio.

Prende (miser) Christum; & cum Christo prende salutem:
   At manca est (dices) dextera: prende tamen.

Ipsum hoc, in Christum, manus est: hoc prendere Christum est,
   Quâ Christum prendas, non habuisse manum.

152   Matth. 4:24. *Attulerunt ei omnes malè affectos,*
          dæmoniacos, lunaticos—& sanavit eos.

Collige te tibi (torve Draco) furiásque facésque,
   Quásque vocant pestes nox Erebúsque suas:

Fac colubros jam tota suos tua vibret Erinnys;
   Collige, collige te fortiter, ut—*pereas.*

149. 34. Each time Tantalus in Hades attempted to lower his head to drink, the waters receded; each time the infirm man attempted to enter the healing waters of Bethesda, someone else stepped down before him.

150. 34.

151. 34.

152. 34.

153   Matthew 6:28–29. *Consider the lilies of the fields—*
not even Solomon, etc.

White king of the field, who has the ivory pomp of flowers
and a long toga of the fleece of crusted snow;

Solomon in his purple is said to be unlike you. So be it.
Of course—and this is better—he was like roses.

154   Matthew 6:34. *Take therefore no thought*
for the morrow.

Go, poor fellow, do not waste your time on your worries
and continue to be undone by evils not yet born.

One day is enough for my complaints, it is tortured for enough hours:
One day is damp enough with its own tears for me.

I have no leisure to wait for sorrows to come:
I am unwilling, I am unwilling *today to be tomorrow's wretch.*

155   Luke 6:36–43. *On the beam of the Pharisee.*

Let them yield who will give glasses capable of focusing
in the eye clearly whatever is slender and tiny.
[Pharisee's *eye,*
[Here is] a work of [more] remarkable skill! See the *beam* is in the
by which he can see *nothing at all* (I speak the truth.)

153   Mat. 6:29. *Videte lilia agrorum—nec Solomon &c.*

Candide rex campi, cui floris eburnea pompa est,
    Deque nivis fragili vellere longa toga;

Purpureus Solomon impar tibi dicitur. esto.
    Nempe (quod est melius) par fuit ille rosis.

154   Matth. 6:34. *Nè soliciti estote in crastinum.*

I Miser, ínque tuas rape non tua tempora curas:
    Et nondum natis perge perire malis.

Mî querulis satìs una dies, satìs angitur horis:
    Una dies lacrymis mî satìs uda suis.

Non mihi venturos vacat expectare dolores:
    Nolo ego, nolo *hodie crastinus esse miser.*

155   Matth. 15. *In trabem Pharisaicam.*

Cedant, quæ, rerum si quid tenue atque minutum est,
    Posse acie certâ figere, vitra dabunt.

Artis opus miræ! Pharisæo en *optica trabs* est,
    Ipsum (vera loquor) quâ videt ille *nihil.*

---

153. 34. The shamefulness of the color red is to be noted also in "In nocturnum & hyemal
iter," No. 110.
154. 34.
155. 34. Milhaupt (p. 165) corrects the text for the epigram. Matthew 15:1–14 concerns th
blindness of the Pharisees, but Matthew 7:1–5 contains the same event as does Luke 6
The passage in Luke is chosen by Milhaupt because it fits into the sequence appropriately.

156   Matthew 8:8. *I am not worthy that thou shouldest come under my roof.*

God will come into your house: but your modesty and the soaring faith in your lowly breast do not in any way permit that.

Therefore *since you do not receive him,* you will receive him: therefore God will enter *you,* not *your house.*

157   Matthew 8:13. *The Lord, though absent, cures the absent son of the Centurion.*

What unexpected health glides in on silent wings! On wings which your voice gave it, Christ.

What long hands your voice has! This voice was the cure, *absent and present* it was the cure.

158   Matthew 8:13. *Christ cures the absent man.*

Could the voice just now sent forth already reach its goals? O gods! This was not to go but to have gone.

The miracle was health itself—you may well believe— when the very path to health is the miracle.

159   Luke 7:11–15. *The son of the widow is delivered to his mother from the bier.*

Lo they return, and new joys atone for the brief tears: and twice has she been made a mother, for one child.

Happy you, who are more of a mother through the death of a son! *to have lost* [a son] was for you again *to have borne* [him].

156   Matth. 8. *Non sum dignus ut sub tecta mea venias.*

> In tua tecta Deus veniet: tuus haud sinit illud
> Et pudor, atque humili in pectore celsa fides.

> Illum ergò accipies *quoniam non accipis:* ergò
> In *te* jam veniet, non *tua tecta,* Deus.

157 Matth. 8:13. *Absenti Centurionis filio Dominus absens medetur.*

> Quàm tacitis inopina salus illabitur alis!
> Alis, quas illi vox tua, Christe, dedit.

> Quàm longas vox ista manus habet! hæc medicina
> *Absens, & præsens* hæc medicina fuit.

158   Matth. 8:13. *Christus absenti medetur.*

> Vox jam missa suas potuit jam tangere metas?
> O superi! non noc ire sed isse fuit.

> Mirac'lum fuit ipsa salus (bene credere possis)
> Ipsum, mirac'lum est, quando salutis iter.

159   Luc. 7. *Viduæ filius è feretro matri redditur.*

> En redeunt, lacrymásque breves nova gaudia pensant:
> Bísque illa est, uno in pignore, facta parens.

> Felix, quæ magìs es nati per funera mater!
> *Amisisse,* iterum cui *peperisse* fuit.

156. 34. See "I am not worthy," No. 14.

157. 34. See above "Rogavit eum"; Crashaw has confused this curing of the Centurion's *servant* (in Matthew and Luke) with the curing of the nobleman's *son.* In the title *filio* (son) should be *servo* (servant).

158. 34. See preceding note.

159. 34.

160   Luke 7:15. *The son is delivered to his mother
           from the bier.*

Is it true then that by such a sudden turn this doleful dread could
     change into a gleaming white toga for the day of birth?

I had believed that the groans which I [heard] were those *of a grieving
     mother*: they were the groans *of one giving birth.*

161   Luke 7:19. *John sends men to ask Christ whether
           it is he.*

You who so impatiently hastened to identify Christ,
     even then when the bars of your womb held you,

do you keep asking who is Christ? and do you ask it of him?
     Any mute person can tell you this.

162   Matthew 11:2–6. *The delegation of the Baptist
           to Christ.*

I pray, who are you? The Baptist sends that [question] to his Master.
     Christ has such [an answer] which they report back to him.

By whom the blind man sees, the dumb loosens [his tongue] in words,
     the lame walks, the dead lives: I pray, who is he?

163   Luke 7:37–50. *She began to wash his feet with tears
           and did wipe* [them] *with the hairs of her head.*

The wave most calm washes the holy dust:
     the bright flame of yellow hair washes this wave.

That wave moves more purely through this dust; and at the same time
     that fire will burn more purely through these waters.

160   Luc. 7:15. *Filius è feretro matri redditur.*

Ergóne tam subitâ potuit vice flebilis horror
In natalitia candidus ire toga?

Quos vidi, matris gemitus hos esse *dolentis*
Credideram; gemitus *parturientis* erant.

161   Luc. 7:19. *Mittit Joannes qui quærant à Christo,*
                an is sit.

Tu qui adeò impatiens properâsti agnoscere Christum,
Tunc cùm claustra uteri te tenuêre tui,

Tu, quis sit Christus, rogitas? & quæris ab ipso?
Hoc tibi vel mutus dicere quisque potest.

162   Mat. 11. *Legatio Baptistæ ad Christum.*

Oro, quis es? legat ista suo Baptista Magistro.
Illi quæ referant, talia Christus habet.

Cui cæcus cernit, mutus se in verba resoluit,
It claudus, vivit mortuus; Oro, quis est?

163   Luc. 7:37. *Cœpit lacrymis rigare pedes ejus,*
                & capillis extergebat.

Unda sacras sordes lambit placidissima: flavæ
Lambit & hanc undam lucida flamma comæ.

Illa per has sordes it purior unda; simúlque
Ille per has lucet purior ignis aquas.

160. 34.
161. 34.* "Crashaw's use of *claustra* [bars, cage] strengthens the parallel between the two incidents: John was in prison when he sent his disciples to Christ" (Milhaupt, p. 156). See Matthew 11:2; Luke 1:41.
162. MS.
163. 34. See "She began to wash," No. 15.

164   Luke 11:14. *God, after the dumb devil was cast out,*
      closed the mouths of the slanderous Jews.

Almost at one thrust, you shatter a pair of demons:
  this demon indeed is *mute;* but that one *speaks.*

Of course—what laurel tree does not rise for you?—
no more does this one *in speaking* than that one *in silence* praise you.

165   Luke 11:27. *Blessed is the womb and the paps*
            [which thou hast sucked].

And what if Jesus should indeed drink from your breast?
  what does it do to your thirst because he drinks?

And soon He will lay bare his breast—alas, not milky!—
  from her son then the *mother* will drink.

166   Luke 8:4–15. *The word among thorns.*

Often the word of God falls among thorn-bushes; and the
bold thorn springs up with the unlucky body—unhappily joined.

Indeed I believe so: for so obviously do You, Very God,
    the Word also, fall among thorns, O Christ.

167   Matthew 13:24. *On the sacred grain field.*

See how it begs for its sickle with bowed head:
Give your sickle to the grain, gracious Father.

You do not give the sickle? Do you delay the harvest, Christ?
This very thing is the sickle: this delay will be the harvest.

164   Luc. 11. *Deus, post expulsum Dæmonem mutum,*
         maledicis Judæis os obturat.

Unâ penè operâ duplicem tibi Dæmona frangis:
     Iste quidem Dæmon *mutus;* at ille *loquax.*

Scilicet in laudes (quæ non tibi laurea surgit?)
     Non magìs hic *loquitur,* quàm *tacet* ille tuas.

165   Luc. 11:27. *Beatus venter & ubera, &c.*

Et quid si biberet Jesus vel ab ubere vestro?
     Quid facit ad vestram, quòd bibit ille, sitim?

Ubera mox sua & Hic (ô quàm non lacteal) pandet:
     E nato *Mater* tum bibet ipsa suo.

166   Luc. 8. *Verbum inter spinas.*

Sæpe Dei verbum sentes cadit inter; & atrum
     Miscet spina procax (ah malè juncta!) latus.

Credo quidem: nam sic spinas ah scilicet inter
     Ipse Deus Verbum tu quoque (Christe) cadis.

167   Matth. 13:24. *In segetem sacram.*

Ecce suam implorat, demisso vertice, falcem:
     Tu segeti falcem da (Pater alme) suam.

Tu falcem non das? messem tu (Christe) moraris?
     Hoc ipsum falx est: hæc mora messis erit.

164. 34. See "Upon the dumbe Devill," No. 16.
165. 34. See "Blessed be the paps," No. 17.
166. 34. Warren (p. 87): "Christ followed his parable of the Sower with an exegesis, according to which the seed is the Word, the thorns among which some of it fell, the 'cares . . . of this world.' Crashaw, choosing to take the seed figuratively and the thorns literally, derives the 'Verbum inter spinas'—the Logos crowned with thorns."
167. 34.

168   Matthew 8:23–27. *Christ in the storm.*

That which boils around you in such a great tempest, Christ,
is not the wrath of the sea, Christ, but its ambition.

This is that ambition: it asks you in such a loud voice
that it may at your words of command, Christ, be silent.

169   Matthew 8:25. *And the disciples came and awoke him.*

Ah, what madness was it to dispel this sleep, so rare?
O you men, over whom even Christ's deep slumber watches!

If sleep held him, dreams frighten you,
dreams redoubled with senseless fears.

The sleep of Christ harmed nothing, believe me. The sleep
which harmed was the sleep of your faith.

170   Mark 4:40. *Why are ye so fearful?*

As if the wild wind would work its fury *on him!*
As if the channel knew it held rocks *for him!*

You are your rocks, you are the wind and wave:
He who feared shipwreck with him *deserved* it.

171   Matthew 9:20–22.

You err. And you depict Love as naked, Painter, badly: you do not
show unadorned love merely by showing him without a garment.

When [Christ] so reveals himself at the finger of a faithful person, is
he not then—even when clothed—then also unadorned love?

168   Matt. 8. *Christus in tempestate.*

Quòd fervet tanto circum te, Christe, tumultu,
Non hoc ira maris, Christe, sed ambitio est.

Hæc illa ambitio est, hoc tanto te rogat ore,
Possit ut ad monitus, Christe, tacere tuos.

169   Mat. 8. *& accedentes discipuli excitavérunt eum.*

Ah, quis erat furor hos (tam raros) solvere somnos?
O vos, queîs Christi vel sopor invigilat!

Illum si somnus tenuit, vos somnia terrent,
Somnia tam vanos ingeminata metus.

Nil Christi nocuit somnus (mihi credite.) Somnus,
Qui nocuit, vestræ somnus erat fidei.

170   Marc. 4:40. *Quid timidi estis?*

Tanquam *illi* insanus faceret sua fulmina ventus!
Tanquam *illi* scopulos nôrit habere fretum!

Vos vestri scopuli, vos estis ventus & unda:
Naufragium cum illo qui metuit, *meruit.*

171   Mat. 9.

Falleris. & nudum malè ponis (Pictor) Amorem:
Non nudum facis hunc, cùm sine veste facis.

Nonne hic est (dum sic digito patet ille fideli)
Tunc, cùm vestitus, tunc quoque nudus amor?

168. 34.
169. MS.
170. 34. See "Why are yee afraid," No. 18.
171. MS. The epigram contrasts the naked Cupid and the clothed Christ, the hem of whose garment was touched by the faithful.

172　　　Matthew 9:23. *On the minstrels and the people*
　　　　　　making a noise around the dead girl.

Silly ones, why are you so noisy? for although *she sleeps,**
still she may not be recalled from her sleep in this way.

That slumber awaits only the whispers of Christ:
she sleeps; but she is *not asleep to everyone.*

*Verse 24. for the maid is not dead, but sleepeth.

173　　　Matthew 9:24. *And they laughed him to scorn.*

In such great grief, was there time to laugh at Christ?
Was that laugh more foolish or the grief?

In such great grief this laugh of yours, foolish ones,
believe me, deserved to be your greatest grief.

174　Matthew 9:27–34. *On the blind men confessing Christ,*
　　　　　　the Pharisees denying him.

Do not cast your eyes on me, wild Pharisee:
Look at that blind man! even that blind man sees Christ.

You, Pharisee, cannot see Christ in Christ:
He sees though blind; blind you are, though you [think you] see.

172   Matth. 9. *In tibicines & turbam tumultuantem*
            circa defunctam.

Vani, quid strepitis? nam, quamvìs *dormiat illa,
Non tamen è somno est sic revocanda suo.

Expectat solos Christi sopor iste susurros:
Dormit; nec *dormit omnibus* illa tamen.

* Vers. 24. Non enim mortua est puella, sed dormit.

173   Matth. 9. *Et ridebant illum.*

Luctibus in tantis, Christum ridere vacabat?
Vanior iste fuit risus, an iste dolor?

Luctibus in tantis hic vester risus, inepti,
(Credite mî) meruit maximus esse dolor.

174   Matth. 9. *In cæcos Christum confitentes,*
            Pharisæos abnegantes.

Ne mihi, tu (Pharisæe ferox) tua lumina jactes:
En cæcus! Christum cæcus at ille videt.

Tu (Pharisæe) nequis in Christo cernere Christum:
Ille videt cæcus; cæcus es ipse videns.

---

172. 34. "Non dormio omnibus" (I am not asleep to everyone) is a proverbial expression: Cipius was pretending to be asleep, but when a slave stole one of his cups, he "woke up" and with this expression retrieved his property (Martin, p. 429).
173. 34.
174. 34.

175   John 6:1–14. *Five loaves of bread for five thousand men.*

Behold the easy tables, and the wounds of a feast restored to life,
and whatever calls [men's] mouths to an endless banquet!

The swollen Ceres is astounded that she grows by a secret harvest.
At last what is left? *Food itself is fed.*

176   John 6:9–14. *The miracle of the five loaves.*

Behold a wave of food comes; it comes strong in its sacred
nature and nourishing into countless mouths.

Whenever was there such holy abundance of an unending feast?
The *hunger* of the people it feeds, and their *faith.*

177   John 6:10–15. *To the guests at the miraculous dinner
of the five loaves.*

Eat your bread: but also, O guest, eat Christ:
He clearly is the bread of your bread.

You will depart filled with this bread *from Christ,* O guest,
rightly, if then you hunger more *for Christ,* himself the bread.

175   Joann. 6. *Quinque panes ad quinque hominum millia.*

En mensæ faciles, redivivâque vulnera cœnæ,
Quæque indefessâ provocat ora dape!

Aucta Ceres stupet arcanâ se crescere messe.
Denique quid restat? *Pascitur ipse cibus.*

176   Joann. 6. *Miraculum quinque panum.*

Ecce vagi venit unda cibi; venit indole sacrâ
Fortis, & in dentes fertilis innumeros.

Quando erat invictæ tam sancta licentia cœnæ?
Illa *famem* populi pascit, & illa *fidem.*

177   Joann. 6. *Ad hospites cœnæ miraculosæ*
                    quinque panum.

Vescere pane tuo: sed & (hospes) vescere Christo:
Est panis pani scilicet ille tuo.

Tunc pane hoc CHRISTI rectè satur (hospes) abibis,
Panem ipsum CHRISTUM si magìs esurias.

---

175. 34. See "On the miracle of multiplyed loaves," No. 19. The 'easy tables' describe the
effortlessness of the miracle; the personification of the goddess ("Aucta Ceres stupet") is
like that in the epigram "Aquæ in vinum versæ," No. 129, ("Nympha pudica . . . vidit")
and in the *Letter* to the Countess of Denbigh, No. 76 ("Th'astonish'd Nymphs . . . de-
plore"), line 25. See also "Pisces multiplicati," No. 186, and "Murmurabant Pharisæi," No.
212.
176. 34. Milhaupt (p. 111) translates the key words as "famine . . . faith"; other pairs (less
suitable) are "belly . . . belief," "craw . . . creed," etc.
177. 34. The reference to eating Christ is John 6:48–59.

178   John 6:14. *They said this is of a truth a prophet.*

After so many miracles for them *to see,* so many *to touch,*
you gave the people, Christ, also these for them *to taste.*

Now *soothsayer, king,* and whatever holy names they could think of,
Christ was [all of them]: I should like to say [their] stomach was.

For whatever Christ was to them in the fullness of their stomachs
all that was, by its true name, their stomach.

179   John 6:14–26.

[God with
Now they believe. You are God. (He is God who [can be proved to be]
the palate as a witness; in short, and with the very teeth as the judge.)

Of course they understand these miracles:
By which their belly can profit and their fat body overflow.

You performed these miracles of yours for the people. They believe.
Pious race! and consecrated to its stomach!

180   Matthew 14:23–33. *Seeing the wind boisterous, he was
afraid, and beginning to sink, he cried, etc.*

O Peter, you will fall if you doubt: o have faith: the sea itself
does not break faith with the faithful, Peter.

Everything else sinks, pressed down by its own *weight:* only you,
Peter, are submerged by the *burden* of your *lightness.*

178   Joann. 6. *Dicebant, Verè hic est propheta.*

Post tot quæ *videant,* tot quæ miracula *tangant,*
Hæc & quæ *gustent* (Christe) dabas populo.

Jam *Vates, Rex,* & quicquid pia nomina possunt,
Christus erat: vellem dicere, venter erat.

Namque his, quicquid erat Christus, de ventre repleto
Omne illud vero nomine venter erat.

179   Joh. 6:14. 26.

Jam credunt. Deus es. (Deus est, qui teste palato,
Quique ipso demum est judice dente Deus.)

Scilicet hæc sapiunt miracula: de quibus alvus
Proficere, & possit pingue latus fluere.

Hæc sua fecisti populo miracula. credunt.
Gens pia! & in ventrem relligiosa suum!

180   Matth. 14. *Videns ventum magnum, timuit, & cùm
cœpisset demergi, clamavit, &c.*

Petre, cades, ô, si dubitas: ô fide: nec ipsum
(Petre) negat fidis æquor habere fidem.

Pondere pressa suo subsidunt cætera: solum
(Petre) tuæ mergit te *levitatis onus.*

---

178. 34.
179. MS. See "On the Miracle of the Loaves," No. 20.
180. 34. As in English, *levitas* has the two meanings of lightness: not heavy and not dependable.

181   Matthew 15:21–28. *Christ rather obstinate toward the
woman of Canaan.*

In order to set a price for a gift, you refuse to bestow it:
as long as she begs as a suppliant, you still say no continuously.

But this also was to give: to refuse to give.
He gives often, who gives things denied often.

182   Matthew 15:21–28. *On the woman of Canaan
contending with the Master.*

[bravely.

See, he is yielding. Now at this moment he will give in. Press on, still
Now, if your hand does not fail you, now he will fall.

He wants this too much. He favors your triumph.
In silence your enemy directs your actions.

He makes the hands which he lets [strike him], he is beneath every blow;
and he feels the strength in you and he loves it,

even so far is your enemy not at all cruel nor iron-hearted!
Even so far is this soldier not savage Love!

What an easy victory rises from that enemy
who comes to fight only that he can be overcome!

183   Matthew 15:28. *The woman of Canaan.*

Whatever the old legend said about the Amazon girls,
Believe it: lo you see *Amazonian faith.*

A woman, and of such strong faith? now I believe that faith is
more than grammatically of the *feminine gender.*

181   Matth. 15:21. *Christus mulieri Canaaneæ difficilior.*

    Ut pretium facias dono, donare recusas:
      Usquè rogat supplex, tu tamen usquè negas.

    Hoc etiam donare fuit, donare negare.
      Sæpe dedit, quisquis sæpe negata dedit.

182   Mat. 15. *In mulierem Canaanæam cum Dn⁰ decertantem.*

    Cedit io. jam, jamque cadet. modò fortiter urge.
      Jam, tua nî desit dextera, jamque cadet.

    Nimirum hoc velit ipse. tuo favet ipse triumpho:
      Ipse tuas tacitus res tuus hostis agit.

    Quas patitur, facit ille manus. ictu ille sub omni est;
      Atque in te vires sentit, amatque suas,

    Usque adeò haud tuus hic ferus est, neque ferreus hostis!
      Usque adeò est miles non truculentus Amor!

    Illo quàm facilis victoria surgit ab hoste,
      Qui, tantùm ut vinci possit, in arma venit!

183   Matth. 15. *Mulier Canaanitis.*

    Quicquid Amazoniis dedit olim fama puellis
      Credite: *Amazoniam* cernimus ecce *fidem.*

    Fœmina, tam fortis fidei? jam credo fidem esse
      Plus quàm grammaticè *fœminei generis.*

181. 34.
182. MS. Crashaw envisions the discussion as involving physical force.
183. 34.

184   Mark 7:32–36. *He touched his tongue etc.—and he spake*
plain and he charged them that they should tell no man:
but so much the more a great deal they published it.

Christ, you command the mute lips to speak; the mute lips speak:
you command the healthy lips to keep silent; and they do not keep silent.

If then you used a *finger*, loosing the sealed lips;
don't you need to use your *whole hand* now, o Christ?

185   Mark 7:32–36.

Christ, you used voice and hand together for loosing the tongue:
you used mere words for stopping it.

But clearly the tongue is a horse let out with slack reins:
the voice sets it loose, but nothing but the whole hand will stop it.

186   Mark 8:1–9. *The fishes multiplied.*

What secret nets pass from your silent word
by which you do not so much catch fish, as the [whole] Ocean?

187   Matthew 16:24. *If any man will come after me, let him*
take up [his] cross & follow me.

Therefore *I follow*, see *I follow!* and indeed I have my cross, Christ:
of course it is small; but, look, I do not manage it very well.
                                        [not be considered small.
[Can] I not manage it? not this little [cross]? On that account it must
It is a great cross not to bear a small cross well.

184 Marc. 7:33, 36. *Tetigit linguam ejus, &c.—& loquebatur—*
& præcepit illis nè cui dicerent: illi verò eò magìs
prædicabant.

Christe, jubes muta ora loqui; muta ora loquuntur:
Sana tacere jubes ora; nec illa tacent.

Si *digito* tunc usus eras, muta ora resolvens;
Nónne opus est *totâ* nunc tibi, Christe, *manu?*

185   Marc. 7:33. & 36.

Voce, manuque simul linguæ tu, Christe, ciendæ:
Sistendæ nudis vocibus usus eras.

Sanè at lingua equus est pronis effusus habenis:
Vox ciet, at sistit non nisi tota manus.

186   Marc. 8. *Pisces multiplicati.*

Quæ secreta meant taciti tibi retia verbi,
Queîs non tam pisces, quàm capis Oceanum?

187   Matth. 16:24. *Si quis pone me veniet, tollat*
crucem & sequatur me.

Ergò *sequor, sequor* en! quippe & mihi crux mea, Christe, est:
Parva quidem; sed quam non satìs, ecce, rego.

Non rego? non parvam hanc? ideo neque parva putanda est.
Crux magna est, parvam non bene ferre crucem.

---

184. 34. See "The dumbe healed," No. 21.
185. MS.
186. MS. Crashaw has written this epigram (as Milhaupt shows, p. 262) on the Gospel
account of the Feeding of the Four Thousand. All the other epigrams on the miraculous feed-
ing are headed John 6 and describe the feeding of the Five Thousand. This epigram is fur-
ther distinguished by including the image of nets and fishing; it thus recalls the miracles of
the Heavy Draught of Fishes in John 21:1–14 (as Grosart thought) or in Luke 5:4–11 when
not only fishes but fishermen and fishers of men are caught.
187. 34.

188   Mark 8:34. *Let him take up his cross, etc.*

Therefore put down your cross: that we may take up our cross:
   if you want us to take up our cross, put yours down.

That, that one which doubles you up with its heavy beam, that
   indeed is our [cross], or that bore our crosses.

189   Matthew 16:25. *Whosoever will lose his life for my sake,
               shall find it.*

Go, Life; Go, I shall lose you: your death was devised for me, O Christ:
   (Your death is life for me; my life is death to you).

Or I shall hide you in Christ's tomb, my Life.
   That third day is not at all far off.

190   Luke 9:32–33. *It is good for us to be here.*

Why do you want to stay here yet, sleepy Peter?
You do not see such good dreams elsewhere, Peter.

191   Matthew 17:27. *On the well-endowed fish.*

If you want a fish, Christ, behold he comes and brings
his own purchase money: indeed it is worth so much to have died for you.

Christ, you do not need a market-place; you do not need
   to pay money: *the fish will buy himself for you.*

188   *Tollat crucem suam—&c.*

Ergò tuam pone; ut nobis sit sumere nostram:
Si nostram vis nos sumere, pone tuam.

Illa illa, ingenti quæ te trabe duplicat, illa
Vel nostra est, nostras vel tulit illa cruces.

189   Matth. 16:25. *Quisquis perdiderit animam suam
meâ causâ, inveniet eam.*

I Vita; I, perdam: mihi mors tua, Christe, reperta est:
(Mors tua vita mihi est; mors tibi, vita mea)

Aut ego te abscondam Christi (mea Vita) sepulchro.
Non adeò procul est *tertius ille dies.*

190   *Bonum est nobis esse hîc.*

Cur cupis hîc adeo, dormitor Petre, manere?
Somnia non alibi tam bona, Petre, vides.

191   Matth. 17:27. *In piscem dotatum.*

Tu piscem si, Christe, velis, venit ecce, suúmque
Fert pretium: tanti est vel periisse tibi.

Christe, foro tibi non opus est; addicere nummos
Non opus est: *ipsum se tibi piscis emet.*

---

188. MS. Text supplied by Milhaupt appropriate to the sequence.
189. 34.* See "Whosoever shall loose his life," No. 22.
190. MS. This epigram celebrates Peter's going to sleep and his subsequent comment at the Transfiguration. The Transfiguration was not a feast day in the Anglican Kalendar in Crashaw's time, though it is found in the Sarum Missal, where the Gospel is Matthew 17:1–9; but Crashaw is following Luke, the only account that mentions Peter's being "heavy with sleep."
191. 34.

192   Matthew 18:9. *It is good to enter into heaven*
with one eye, etc.

With one eye? ah rather a hundred for me, a hundred thousand:
For who is there in heaven who will be *Argus* enough?

Or if only one eye is alloted to me,
May *I* become, *all in all,* that one eye.

193   John 8:52. *Now we know that thou hast a devil.*

You ought to know either God or at least the demon better,
evil people, who say God has demons.

You could have failed to recognize God, o blind people: but I pray you
could you not have recognized your own father?

194   John 8:59. *Then they took up stones.*

Stones? against him? What did such detestable furies want?
Did they want something for their stones?

I recognize the nature and the traces of their ancient father:
they wanted bread from their stones.

195   Luke 10:3. *I send you forth, as lambs in the midst*
of wolves.

These too? Will you savage [beasts] tear apart these lambs?
At least here, here you can not be [like] the wolves.

But with wicked ones there is no leniency. But therefore you will learn
that he who is now a Lamb is sometimes a Lion.

192   Matth. 18. *Bonum intrare in cœlos cum uno oculo, &c.*

Uno oculo? ah centum potiùs mihi, millia centum:
Nam quis ibi, in cœlo, quis satìs *Argus* erit?

Aut si oculus mihi tantùm unus conceditur, unus
Iste oculus fiam *totus & omnis ego.*

193   Joann. 8:52. *Nunc scimus te habere dæmonium.*

Aut Deus, aut saltem dæmon tibi notior esset.
(Gens mala) quæ dicis dæmona habere Deum.

Ignorâsse Deum poteras, ô cæca: sed oro,
Et patrem poteras tam malè nôsse tuum?

194   Joann. 8:59. *Tunc sustulerunt lapides.*

Saxa? illi? quid tam fœdi voluêre furores?
Quid sibi de saxis hi voluêre suis?

Indolem, & antiqui agnosco vestigia patris:
Panem de saxis hi voluêre suis.

195   *Mitto vos, sicut agnos in medio luporum.*

Hos quoque? an hos igitur sævi lacerabitis agnos?
Hîc saltem, hîc vobis non licet esse lupis.

At sceleris nulla est clementia. at ergò scietis,
Agnus qui nunc est, est aliquando Leo.

192. 34. See "It is better to go into Heaven," No. 23. Argus is a mythological figure with one hundred eyes.
193. 34.
194. 34. The "ancient father" is Satan; Matthew 4:3. See also "Hic lapis fiat panis," No. 123.
195. MS.

196   Matthew 11:25. *On the wise men of [that] time.*

Is it true then that Folly gives delights, and applauds herself from on high
   that she wishes to be approached with this adulation?

Indeed has she become so difficult and serious finally?
Can it be that ever anyone can *have insight* in this matter?

Was she so great in order that you could have a wiser downfall?
Was it a matter of so great a brain, to have died?

There is no need at all for genius; no need at all for this *Art of madness:*
   You could obviously be wretched more easily.

197   Matthew 11:25. *On the wisdom of [that] age.*

Do not be curious of the height lest a lofty fall drag back your weary
   footsteps (this the teachers of yore wished).

But I tell myself: *Do not be curious of the depth:*
I would not wish to have studied out for myself [the way] to hell.

198   Matthew 11:30. *My burden is light.*

Whichever one of you wishes to be unburdened, receive Christ's burden:
   It will be a wing for your shoulders, not a burden.

Or do you ask how heavy the burden of Christ may be: Listen [to me]:
apparently so heavy that it may press you down to the highest heavens.

196   Matth. 11:25. *In seculi sapientes.*

Ergóne delitias facit, & sibi plaudit ab alto
Stultitia, ut velit hâc ambitione peti?

Difficilísne adeò facta est, & seria tandem?
Ergò & in hanc etiam quis *sapuisse* potest?

Tantum erat, ut possit tibi doctior esse ruina?
Tanti igitur cerebri res, periisse, fuit?

Nil opus ingenio; nihil hâc opus *Arte furoris:*
Simpliciùs poteris scilicet esse miser.

197   Matth. 11:25. *In sapientiam seculi.*

Noli altum sapere (hoc veteres voluêre magistri)
Nè retrahat lassos alta ruina gradus.

Immo mihi dico, *Noli sapuisse profundum:*
Non ego ad infernum me sapuisse velim.

198   Matth. 11. *Onus meum leve est.*

Esse levis quicunque voles, onus accipe Christi:
Ala tuis humeris, non onus, illud erit.

Christi onus an quæris quàm sit grave? scilicet, audi,
Tam grave, ut ad summos te premat usque polos.

196. 34.
197. 34.
198. 34.*

199   Luke 10:23. *Blessed the eyes which see.*

When the sweetest Christ was walking on our shores
and ordered the blind to have a new day—

are they called blessed who then had eyes?
I call them blessed who did not have [them].

200   Luke 10:31. *A certain priest coming down that same way
saw him and passed by [on the other side].*

Ah! do you see and touch my wounds with unmoved eyes?
O grief! o wounds to my wounds!

The calmness of your face—how savage it is! its serenity—how sad!
Who sees a wretch, unruffled, himself makes a wretch.

201   Luke 10:39. *But Mary sitting at his feet heard
his word.*

See—for indeed it is strange—how the hostess hangs on the guest!
She prepares [food] for this mouth; she takes food from this mouth.

Are you indeed busy with the feast to be served, Sister,
And, *Martha,* she says, do you allow this sacred feast to be wasted?

202   John 9. *The man born blind.*

Happy is he who could after the clouds of such a long night
([a day] worthy of so long a night!) see the day:

Happy that eye, happy on two counts it must be considered:
Because it sees and because first of all it sees *God.*

199   Luc. 10:23. *Beati oculi qui vident.*

Cum Christus nostris ibat mitissimus oris,
     Atque novum cæcos jussit habere diem,

Felices, oculos qui tunc habuêre, vocantur?
     Felices, & qui non habuêre, voco.

200   Luc. 10:32. *Sacerdos quidam descendens eâdem viâ,*
                 vidit & præteriit.

Spectásne (ah!) placidísque oculis mea vulnera tractas?
     O dolor! ô nostris vulnera vulneribus!

Pax oris quàm torva tui est! quàm triste serenum!
     Tranquillus miserum qui videt, ipse facit.

201   Luc. 10:39. *Maria verò assidens ad pedes ejus,*
                 audiebat eum.

Aspice (namque novum est) ut ab hospite pendeat hospes!
     Huic ori parat; hoc sumit ab ore cibos.

Túne epulis adeò es (soror) officiosa juvandis,
     Et sinis has (inquit) *Martha*, perire dapes?

202   Joann. 9. *Cæcus natus.*

Felix, qui potuit tantæ post nubila noctis
     (O dignum tantâ nocte!) videre diem:

Felix ille oculus, felix utrinque putandus;
     Quòd videt, & primùm quòd videt ille *Deum.*

199. 34.*
200. 34. See "And a certaine Priest," No. 24. Crashaw's citation is in error.
201. 34.
202. 34.

203 John 9:22. *The [Jews] agreed that if any man did confess that he was Christ, he should be put out of the synagogue.*

Unlucky man, whoever you are, *accused* of worshiping Christ!
O unlucky defendant! how heavy is your guilt!

Therefore you will be *condemned* to the highest, to the highest heavens:
O unlucky defendant! how heavy is your punishment!

204 John 10:1–18. *On the flock of Christ, the Shepherd.*

O flock, o too much blessed in such a great Shepherd!
O where are pastures worthy of such a flock?

Lest there should be no pastures worthy of such a flock, Christ
himself is *Shepherd* for it, and himself is *pasture* for his flock.

205 John 10:7–9. *I am the door.*

Now you lie open. A heavy spear has thrown back the bolt of your heart.
And the nails as keys unlock you on all sides.

Ah I fear that the wicked hand which dared so to open
these gates of heaven has closed them for itself.

203 Joann. 9:22. *Constituerunt ut si quis confiteretur eum esse Christum, synagogâ moveretur.*

Infelix, Christum *reus* es quicunque colendi!
O reus infelix! quàm tua culpa gravis!

Tu summis igitur, summis *damnabere* cœlis:
O reus infelix! quàm tua pœna gravis!

204 Joann. 10. *In gregem Christi Pastoris.*

O grex, ô nimiùm tanto Pastore beatus!
O ubi sunt tanto pascua digna grege?

Nè non digna forent tanto grege pascua, Christus
Ipse suo est *Pastor, pascuum* & ipse gregi.

205 Joh. 10. *Ego sum ostium.*

Jamque pates. cordisque seram gravis hasta reclusit,
Et clavi claves undique te reserant.

Ah, vereor, sibi ne manus impia clauserit illas,
Quæ cæli has ausa est sic aperire fores.

---

203. 34.
204. 34. The pun on "pastor/pascuum" (shepherd/pasture) is traditional; see "Hymn for the Blessed Sacrament," No. 80, XIII–XIV.
205. MS. See "I am the Doore," No. 25, and the comparable epigram "Ego sum via," No. 251.

206   John 10:22–23.
*Christ walked [in the Temple] in Solomon's porch and
it was winter.*

Was it winter? No, no: ah it was not, [not] near that face:
if it was; it was not the year's own winter.

Winter would wish to be more lovely than springtime for you,
overflowing with unbudded roses by itself.

But only these *hailstones** which your people brandish prevent
winter from denying its own nature so well for you.

* Verse 31. They took up stones.

207   Luke 13:11.
*The Master cures the woman, bowed together, and the ruler
of the synagogue [is] indignant.*

She who had crept about bent over in her own lap
and was nothing but a *demon's knot,*—poor woman!—

was loosed at the touch of the Master's finger: but there is
[still] one knot tighter than [hers]; your heart, Pharisee.

208   Luke 14:1–6. *The man with dropsy is healed.*

May the man who was his own sea, drowned in his watery disease,
now rejoice, happy and light!

Indeed, once more Christ has changed water into wine, I believe;
and now that man *is drunk from his own waters.*

206 Joann. 10:22. *Christus ambulabat in porticu Solomonis,*
& hyems erat.

Bruma fuit? non, non: ah non fuit, ore sub isto:
Si fuit; haud anni, nec sua bruma fuit.

Bruma tibi vernis velit ire decentior horis,
Per sibi non natas expatiata rosas.

At, tibi nè possit se tam bene bruma negare,
Sola hæc, quam vibrat gens tua, *grando* vetat.

* Vers. 31. sustulerunt lapides.

207 Luc. 13:11. *Mulieri incurvatæ medetur Dominus,*
indignante Archisynagogo.

In proprios replicata sinus quæ repserat, & jam
Dæmonis (infelix!) nil nisi *nodus* erat,

Solvitur ad digitum Domini: sed strictior illo
Unicus est nodus; cor, Pharisæe, tuum.

208 Luc. 14. *Hydropicus sanatur.*

Ipse suum pelagus, morbóque immersus aquoso
Qui fuit, ut lætus nunc micat atque levis!

Quippe in vina iterum Christus (puto) transtulit undas;
Et nunc iste *suis ebrius est ab aquis.*

206. 34.
207. 34.
208. 34. See also "In febricitentem et hydropicum sanatos," No. 142, for another treatment
of this miracle.

209   Luke 14:4. *The man with dropsy healed now thirsts for Christ.*

Thirst is driven thence; but here another thirst rises:
here he thirsts the more while there he thirsts the less.

O happy disease that will be able to disdain death!
He thirsts for water from the very *source of life.*

210   Luke 14:5. *The Sabbath* $\begin{cases} Jewish, \\ and \\ Christian. \end{cases}$

How much the same thing is distinguished by different practice!
Our sabbaths save the *man;* yours the *ox.*

Therefore—and what is more just than this agreement?—let
men observe our sabbaths, *oxen* your sabbaths.

211   Luke 14:19. *I have bought yokes of oxen.*

I call you to the feast, which the master's orders wished;
You mention *oxen* to me, clod—I don't know which ones.

Goodby, indeed, neither a worthy nor a useful guest for us!
The feast would, I think, rather have your oxen [than you].

212   Luke 15:2. *The Pharisees murmured, saying, This man receiveth sinners and eateth with them.*

Ah in sorrow may he die, whoever he is! he, of course, who doesn't
the brute, allow these [sinners] to be with their own guest!

When Christ is present as a guest with them,
O Christ is not their guest, but rather their *very food.*

209   Luc. 14:4. *Hydropicus sanatus, Christum jam sitiens.*

Pellitur indè sitis; sed & hinc sitis altera surgit:
Hinc sitit ille magìs, quò sitit indè minús.

Fælix ô, & mortem poterit qui temnere morbus!
Cui *vitæ* ex ipso *fonte* sititur aqua!

210   Luc. 14:5. *Sabbatum* $\left\{ \begin{array}{c} \textit{Judaicum,} \\ \textit{\&} \\ \textit{Christianum.} \end{array} \right.$

Res eadem vario quantum distinguitur usu!
Nostra *hominem* servant sabbata; vestra *bovem.*

Observent igitur (pacto quid justius isto?)
Sabbata nostra *homines,* sabbata vestra *boves.*

211   Luc. 14:19. *Juga boum emi.*

Ad cœnam voco te (domini quod jussa volebant)
Tu mihi, nescio quos, dicis (inepte) *boves.*

Imò vale, nobis nec digne nec utilis hospes!
Cœna tuos (credo) malit habere boves.

212   Luc. 15:2. *Murmurabant Pharisæi, dicentes, Recipit*
        peccatores & comedit cum illis.

Ah malè, quisquis is est, pereat! qui scilicet istis
Convivam (sævus!) non sinit esse suum.

Istis cùm Christus conviva adjungitur, istis
O non conviva est Christus, at *ipse cibus.*

209. 34.
210. 34.
211. 34.
212. 34. The conclusion of this epigram suggests that of "Quinque panes," No. 175.

213   Luke 15:4–7. *What man of you, having a hundred sheep,*
if he lose one of them, etc.

O, that I may bring great joys to the band of angels,
search for me through the fields with anxious step.

A thousand sheep of yours play in the protected mountains
which you can call yours without any doubt in your voice.

I alone wandered where my wandering took me,
I alone shall have been the greater pleasure for you.

[Those things] do not bring joys which have not also brought fear;
and they please more which offer real dangers.

From those which you kept safe your enjoyment will be broader.
From me whom you brought back, your enjoyment will be sweeter.

214   Luke 15:13. *Having gathered all together, he took his*
journey into a far country.

Tell me, golden lad, whither are you hurrying so many coins?
To what end is this fortune being [so] quickly amassed?

Why do whole inheritances belch forth fleeting wealth for you?
Indeed, couldn't husks be bought for less?

213   Luc. 15:4. *Quis ex vobis si habeat centum oves, &*
         perdiderit unam ex illis . . . &c.

O ut ego angelicis fiam bona gaudia turmis,
Me quoque sollicito quære per arva gradu.

Mille tibi tutis ludunt in montibus agni,
Quos potes haud dubiâ dicere voce tuos.

Unus ego erravi, quò me meus error agebat,
Unus ego fuerim gaudia plura tibi.

Gaudia non faciunt, quæ nec fecêre timorem;
Et plus, quæ donant ipsa peric'la, placent.

Horum, quos retines, fuerit tibi latior usus.
De me, quem recipis, dulcior usus erit.

Ἐις μὲν ἐγὼ, ᾗ μου πλάνη περιῆγεν, ἄλημι·
Ἐις δὲ τοι σῶς ἔσομαι γηθοσύναι πλέονες.

Ἀμνὸς ὁ μή ποιῶν φόβον, οὐ ποιεῖ δέ τε χάρμα.
Μείζων τῶν μὲν, ἐμοῦ χρεῖα δὲ γλυκυτέρη.

214   Luc. 15:13. *Congestis omnibus peregrè profectus est.*

Dic mihi, quò tantos properas, puer auree, nummos?
Quorsum festinæ conglomerantur opes?

Cur tibi tota vagos ructant patrimonia census?
Non poterunt siliquæ nempe minoris emi?

---

213. 70 (MS.)* There are two slightly varying versions of this epigram (see Textual Notes).
The Greek quatrain translates lines 5–8 of the Latin.
214. 34. See "On the Prodigall," No. 26.

215   Luke 16:19–31. *On the tears of Lazarus scorned by Dives.*

O happy man! O Lazarus, richer in your tears
than he who goes laden with purple riches!

When a new purple [robe] of gleaming fire clothes him,
how he will wish for your tears to be his!

216   Luke 16:24. *The rich man begs for a drop.*

O if one single drop should quiver and shake on his finger tip for me!
o if one drop should relieve my flames!

Let the fickle flood of my wealth run wherever it wishes:
Should this one droplet be given to me, *I will be a rich man* [still].

217   Luke 17:11–19. *The ungrateful lepers.*

[as they went.
While they were leaving Christ—ah, [a real] illness!—they were healed
indeed the *illness* itself was thus a remedy.

But the sound ones abandoned Christ—ah, unsound mind!
indeed the *remedy* itself was thus an illness.

218   Luke 17:11–19. *The ungrateful lepers.*

The law orders the [unclean] *lepers* to go far from the company of men.
But why did the *clean* go far away from Christ?

The disease did not go away, but it merely changed its seat in them;
and the sore which was on the body now lies in the mind.

So thus by a fitting turn the situation is changed, and as before they
had men far away from them, now they have God.

215   Luc. 16. *In lacrymas Lazari spretas à Divite.*

Felix ô! lacrymis (ô Lazare) ditior istis,
    Quàm qui purpureas it gravis inter opes!

Illum cùm rutili nova purpura vestiet ignis,
    Ille tuas lacrymas quàm volet esse suas!

216   Luc. 16. *Dives implorat guttam.*

O Mihi si digito tremat & tremat unica summo
    Gutta! ô si flammas mulceat una meas!

Currat opum quocunque volet levis unda mearum:
    Una mihi hæc detur gemmula, *Dives ero.*

217   Luc. 17. *Leprosi ingrati.*

Dum linquunt Christum (ah morbus!) sanantur euntes:
    Ipse etiam *morbus* sic medicina fuit.

At sani Christum (mens ah malesana!) relinquunt:
    Ipsa etiam morbus sic *medicina* fuit.

218   Luc. 17. *Leprosi ingrati.*

Lex jubet ex hominum cœtu procul ire *leprosos:*
    At *mundi* à Christo cur abiêre procul?

Non abit, at sedes tantùm mutavit in illis;
    Et lepra, quæ fuerat corpore, mente sedet.

Sic igitur dignâ vice res variatur; & à se
    Quàm procul antè homines, nunc habuêre Deum.

215. 34. See "Upon Lazarus his Teares," No. 27.
216. 34. See "Dives asking a Drop," No. 28.
217. 34. Close verbal parallel in lines 2, 4.
218. 34.

219   Luke 18:9–14. *Pharisee & Publican.*

Behold two men approach the temple (but with different intentions):
    that one standing far off looks at the ground with anxious eye;

This one goes in and with religious zeal reaches the innermost chambers.
    This one has more of the *temple;* that one has more of *God.*

220   Luke 18:9–14. *Not as this publican.*

That fellow? rude clot! How glad I am, you say,
    that I know he is so different from me!

but *that churl* moves away from the holy altars in greater grace:
    go now, and you may boast that he is *not like you.*

221   Luke 18:9–14. *Not as this publican.*

While you confess the sins of that poor man
which he not gently marks with [his own] angry finger;

this good is enough for a double weapon against his sins.
    Meanwhile what will there be for yours, my Pharisee?

219   Luc. 18. *Pharisæus & Publicanus.*

En duo Templum adeunt (diversis mentibus ambo:)
   Ille procul trepido lumine signat humum:

It gravis hic, & in alta ferox penetralia tendit.
   Plus habet hic *templi;* plus habet ille *Dei.*

219   Ἄνδρες, ἰδοὺ, (ἑτέροισι νόοις) δύω ἵρον ἐσῆλθον·
     Τήλοθεν ὀρρωδεῖ κεῖνος ὁ φρικαλέος,

   Ἀλλ' ὁ μὲν ὡς σοβαρὸς νηοῦ μυχὸν ἐγγὺς ἱκάνει·
     Πλεῖον ὁ μὲν νηοῦ, πλεῖον ὁ δ' εἶχε θεοῦ.

220   Luc. 18:11. *Nec velut hic Publicanus.*

Istum? vile caput! quantum mihi gratulor, inquis,
   Istum quòd novi tam mihi dissimilem!

Vilis at *iste* abiit sacris acceptior aris:
   I nunc, & jactes hunc tibi *dissimilem.*

221   Luc. 18. *Nec sicut iste Publicanus.*

Tu quoque dum istius miseri peccata fateris,
   Quæ nec is irato mitiùs ungue notat;

Hic satis est gemino bonus in sua crimina telo.
   Interea quid erit, mi Pharisæe, tuis?

---

219. 34. See "Two went up into the Temple," No. 29. This epigram stands first in 1634;
Crashaw evidently thought it his best.
220. 34.
221. MS.

222   Luke 18:13. *The publican, standing afar off,*
                    smote his breast.

Lo this frightened sinner seeks the temple as a stranger;
   And the only thing he dares do [is] beat his sad breast.

Faithful wretch, knock on these doors bravely:
   You will find God *in that nearer temple.*

223   Matthew 20:20. *St. John to his mother.*

O mother, why do you ask for *the right hand* or *the left* for me,
      why I pray, mother, unfriendly in your office?

I do not want Christ's *right hand* for myself, nor his *left:*
   I do not like to be so far from his holy *bosom.*

224   Matthew 20:20. *Concerning the request for the*
                    sons of Zebedee.

May you, John, and you, James, have what you wish:
   May the *right* hand be yours, the *left* yours.

I hope there is another seat in heaven, not unsuitable:
   even if it is neither the *left* hand nor the *right* hand.

I do not wish to seek *this* or *that* part of heaven for myself:
   O give *heaven,* [*just*] *heaven* to me, dear Father.

225   Luke 18:39.

Be silent, wicked mob. My desires draw so near to me,
   and do you expect my tongue to keep silent about my [plight]?

Then, then I should be silent when my [Lord] speaks to me.
   If you do not know, that voice holds my eyes.

222   Luc. 18:13. *Publicanus procul stans percutiebat pectus suum.*

Ecce hic peccator timidus petit advena templum;
Quódque audet solum, pectora mœsta ferit.

Fide miser; pulsáque fores has fortiter: illo
Invenies *templo* tu *propiore* Deum.

223   Matth. 20:20. *S. Joannes matri suæ.*

O Mihi cur *dextram*, mater, cur, oro, *sinistram*
Poscis, ab officio mater iniqua tuo?

Nolo *manum* Christi *dextram* mihi, nolo *sinistram:*
Tam procul à sacro non libet esse *sinu.*

224   Matth. 20:20. *De voto filiorum Zebedæi.*

Sit tibi (Joannes) tibi sit (Jacobe) quod optas:
Sit tibi *dextra* manus; sit tibi *læva* manus.

Spero, alia in cœlo est, & non incommoda, sedes:
Si neque *læva* manus; si neque *dextra* manus.

Coeli *hanc* aut *illam* nolo mihi quærere partem:
O, *cœlum*, *cœlum* da (Pater alme) mihi.

225   Luc. 18:39.

Tu mala turba tace. mihi tam mea vota propinquant,
Tuque in me linguam vis tacuisse meam?

Tunc ego, tunc taceam, mihi cùm meus Ille loquetur.
Si nescis, oculos vox habet ista meos.

222. 34.
223. 34. The epigram recalls John 13:23, which describes John "leaning on Jesus' bosom."
224. 34. Close verbal parallel in lines 2, 4.
225. MS. There is sufficient variation between this and the next poem to justify including both.

O take pity on my night. Take pity, by that
day which smiles so happily in your face.

O take pity on my night; take pity by that
day which would wish to be night unless it saw you.

O take pity on my night; take pity by that
day which this night of my faith has.

Jesus, that day of the soul asks for this [day] of the eyes.
Give that, I pray; and do not take this from me.

226   Luke 18:39. *The blind man implores Christ.*

Be silent wicked mob. My desires now draw so near me,
do you expect my tongue to be silent about my [plight]?

Then, then I should be silent, when my [Lord] speaks to me:
If you do not know, that voice holds my eyes.

O take pity on my night, take pity: by that
day that smiled on you at its first rising.

O take pity on my night, take pity: by that
day which would wish to be night unless it saw you.

O take pity on my night, take pity: by that
day which this very night of faith has in you.

This day of the soul so bright asks for that of the eyes:
I beg you to give that; and do not take this from me.

O noctis miserere meæ. miserere, per illam,   5
Quæ tam læta tuo ridet in ore diem.

O noctis miserere meæ. miserere, per illam
Quæ, nisi te videat, nox velit esse, diem.

O noctis miserere meæ. miserere, per illam,
Hæc mea quam (fidei) nox habet ipsa, diem.   10

Illa dies animi (Jesu) rogat hanc oculorum.
Illam (oro) dederis; hanc mihi ne rapias.

226   Luc. 18. *Cæcus implorat Christum.*

Improba turba tace. Mihi tam mea vota propinquant,
Et linguam de me vis tacuisse meam?

Tunc ego tunc taceam, mihi cùm meus ille loquetur:
Si nescis, oculos vox habet ista meos.

O noctis miserere meæ, miserere; per illam   5
In te quæ primo riserit ore, diem.

O noctis miserere meæ, miserere; per illam
Quæ, nisi te videat, nox velit esse, diem.

O noctis miserere meæ, miserere; per illam
In te quam fidei nox habet ipsa, diem.   10

Hæc animi tam clara dies rogat illam oculorum:
Illam, oro, dederis; hanc mihi nè rapias.

226   Νύκτ' ἐλέησον ἐμήν. ἐλέησον. ναί τοι ἐκεῖνο
Χριστὲ ἐμοῦ ἦμαρ, νὺξ δ γ' ἐμεῖο ἔχει.

'Οφθαλμῶν μὲν ἐκεῖνο, Θεός, δέεται τόδε γνώμης.
Μή μοι τοῦτ' αἴρῃς, δός μοι ἐκεῖνο φάος.

226. 70. See note above. The Greek quatrain translates the last two distichs of the Latin.

227   Luke 18:41. *What wilt thou that I shall do unto thee?*

You ask what I want, Christ? oh how I want to see, Christ.
Oh how I wish to see you, sweet Christ.

But I do see, and even now I gaze at you with the eyes of faith:
I have faith which has never been eyeless.

But *although I do see* [by faith], still, oh, I wish to see, Christ:
and *since I see,* Christ, I wish to see.

228   Mark 10:52. *The blind man is healed by the word of God.*

O Christ, you had spoken—o sacred license of the word!—
and now a new day has flooded the face of the blind man.

Now I believe, *No one has spoken like you,** o Christ:
To our ears? Nay rather *to our eyes* have you spoken, o Christ.

* John 7:46. Never man spake like this man.

229   Matthew 20:34. *Having received sight, the blind men
follow Christ.*

Lo with the touch of his hand, Christ placed new stars.
The faithful stars follow their homeland, the hand.

This hand is heaven for them, I think. These stars,
I suspect, are those which one day he will bear in his hand.*

* Revelation 1:16.

227   Luc. 18:41. *Quid vis tibi faciam?*

Quid volo (Christe) rogas? quippe ah volo, Christe, videre:
Quippe ah te (dulcis Christe) videre volo.

At video; fideique oculis te nunc quoque figo:
Est mihi, quæ nunquam est non oculata, fides.

Sed *quamvìs videam,* tamen ah volo (Christe) videre:
Sed *quoniam video* (Christe) videre volo.

228   Marc. 10:52. *Ad verbum Dei sanatur cæcus.*

Christe, loquutus eras (ô sacra licentia verbi!)
Jámque novus cæci fluxit in ora dies.

Jam, credo, **Nemo est, sicut Tu,* Christe, *loquutus:*
Auribus? immo *oculis,* Christe, loquutus eras.

* Joann. 7:46.

229   Matth. 20:34. *Cæci receptis oculis Christum sequuntur.*

Ecce manu impositâ Christus nova sidera ponit.
Sectantur patriam sidera fida manum.

Hæc manus his, credo, cœlum est. Hæc scilicet astra
Suspicor esse, olim quæ geret ille *manu.

* Revel. 1:16.

229   Χεὶρ ἐπιβαλλομένη Χριστοῦ ἐπέβαλλεν ὀπωπῶν
        Ἄστρα. ὀπηδεύει κεῖνά γε χειρὶ Θεοῦ.

Χεὶρ ἀυτη τούτοις πέλεν οὐρανός. ἄστρα γὰρ ὀιμαι,
Ἐν χερὶ ταῦτ᾽ ὄισει Χριστὸς ἔπειτα ἑῇ.

227. 34.
228. 34.* See "The blind cured," No. 30, and Textual Note to that poem.
229. 70.

230   Luke 19:4. *Zachæus in the sycamore tree.*

Why, O tree, do you boast of strange fruits?
What are you doing with leaves not your own, Sycamore?

Indeed [he], who now is swaying back and forth from your high branch
there, soon will be a cluster on the heavenly vine.

231   Matthew 21:7. *The master is carried on an ass.*

Then does he honor such a common beast as you, little ass,
O quite unworthy of your burden?

Ah! does the patience of Christ not struggle at all against these surprises?
It was *to bear* this too, that *he is borne* thus.

232   Matthew 21:7. *On the Ass the bearer of Christ.*

That one* once learned to rebuke his master:
and why shouldn't you learn to praise yours?

It is not less strange that you could now have *kept silent*
than it was that he could then have *spoken.*

* BALAAM'S *ass.*

230   Luc. 19:4. *Zachæus in Sycomoro.*

Quid te, quid jactas alienis fructibus, arbor?
Quid tibi cum foliis non (Sycomore) tuis?

Quippe istic ramo qui jam tibi nutat ab alto,
Mox è divinâ vite racemus erit.

230   Τίπτ' ἐπικομπάζεις κενεόν; ξεινῷ δὲ τε καρπῷ,
Καὶ φύλλοις σεμνὴ μὴ, συκόμωρε, τεοῖς;

Καί γαρ ὁδ' ἐκκρημνὴς σοῦ νῦν μετέωρος ἀπ' ἔρνους,
'Αμπέλου ὁ κλαδὼν ἔσσεται οὐρανίου.

231   Matth. 21:7. *Dominus asino vehitur.*

Ille igitur vilem te, te dignatur asellum,
O non vecturâ non bene digne tuâ?

Heu quibus haud pugnat Christi patientia monstris?
Hoc, quòd sic *fertur,* hoc quoque *ferre* fuit.

232   Matth. 21:7. *In Asinum Christi vectorem.*

*Ille suum didicit quondam objurgare magistrum:
Et quid ni discas tu celebrare tuum?

Mirum non minùs est, te jam potuisse *tacere,*
Illum quàm fuerat tum potuisse *loqui.*

* BALAAMI *Asinus.*

230. 70.
231. 34.
232. 34. See "Upon the Asse," No. 31.

233   Luke 19:41. *The master weeping over the Jews.*

Learn, you wretched ones, learn [to recognize] the approaching flames;
        o do not let my tears have been wasted so!

    Still they could not have been wasted: believe me, this water
        will either put out your flames or create them.

234   Luke 19:41. *On the Master weeping.*

        For you Jews, for you, this wave is rolled forth;
        which since you reject it, *will be a fire* for you,

    Quick the torches, Roman, the torches! that field of fury,
        only for these waters, will be a fiery harvest.

235   Luke 19:41. *He beheld the city and wept over it.*

    In truth do you scorn my tears, faithless city? Scorn [them].
    Scorn my [tears]. O thus you make them yours.

        There will be a time when finally our scorned tear
        will be able to scorn your tears—not unjustly.

236   Mark 11:13–4, 20–1. *The tree withering at
                    Christ's command.*

        He commands: go far from my boughs, my glory:
        no breeze may call our tresses any more.

    Go; but o do not grieve: for neither the wrath of the lightning
    nor the cruel wing of the south wind torments you: *He commands.*

        O voice! o indeed thus also sweeter than any Zephyr!
        I cannot enjoy a nobler Autumn.

233   Luc. 19:41. *Dominus flens ad Judæos.*

Discite vos miseri, venientes discite flammas;
     Nec facite ô lacrymas sic periisse meas.

Nec periisse tamen poterunt: mihi credite, vestras
     Vel reprimet flammas hæc aqua, vel faciet.

234   Luc. 19:41. *In lacrymantem Dominum.*

Vobis (Judæi) vobis hæc volvitur unda;
     Quæ vobis, quoniam spernitis, *ignis erit.*

Eia faces (Romane) faces! seges illa furoris,
     Non nisi ab his undis, ignea messis erit.

235   Luc. 19. *Vidit urbem, & flevit super eam.*

Ergò meas spernis lacrymas, urbs perfida? Sperne.
     Sperne meas. quas ô sic facis esse tuas.

Tempus erit, lacrymas poterit cùm lacryma demum
     Nostra (nec immeritò) spernere spreta tuas.

236   Marc. 11:13. *Arbor Christi jussu arescens.*

Ille jubet: procul ite mei, mea gloria, rami:
     Nulla vocet nostras amplìus aura comas.

Ite; nec ô pigeat: nam vos neque fulminis ira,
     Nec trucis ala Noti verberat: *Ille jubet.*

O vox! ô Zephyro vel sic quoque dulcior omni!
     Non possum Autumno nobiliore frui.

233. 34.
234. 34. The "torches" are those with which the Romans will fire the city.
235. 34.
236. 34.

237   Matthew 22:15. *On the Pharisees entangling Christ*
in his talk.

O how those unfounded loathings of your wretched desire mock you
who hope for evil from this mouth, Pharisee!

Thus who would hope for night from the arms of Aurora
whence the young Sun is wont to go his first rosy rays?

So would you seek Acheron from that place where milky Cynthia
laves her starry horses in the glittering stream.

Thus would you ask violets for wolf's bane: thus for poison, the naiad,
who bubbling in a glassy whirlpool shakes the river bed.

In short (to make this moral clear by a closer example)
thus would anyone hope for good from you, Pharisee.

238   Mark 12:14–17. *Is it lawful to give tribute unto Caesar?*

After so many battles of the scribes against you, Christ, at last
Caesar himself comes: Caesar comes into battle.
[Caesar as the sword:
These terrible [scribes] do not fight with Caesar's sword, but with
but, Caesar, you yourself are indeed being conquered.

Enter this also in your triumphs, Augustus:
Who was so worthy to be conquered except Caesar?

239   Mark 12:17. *Render unto Caesar.*

All things are owed to God: yet Caesar has his things as well;
God has no less thereby if Caesar has his own things.

God has no less thereby if everything else is rendered to Caesar's throne,
when Caesar himself is rendered to God.

237   Mat. *22. In Pharisæos Christi verbis insidiantes.*

O quàm te miseri ludunt vaga tædia voti,
  Ex ore hoc speras qui, Pharisæe, malum!

Sic quis ab Auroræ noctem speraverit ulnis,
  Unde solet primis Sol tener ire rosis?

Sic Acheronta petas illinc, unde amne corusco
  Lactea sydereos Cynthia lavit equos.

Sic violas aconita roges: sic toxica nympham,
  Garrula quæ vitreo gurgite vexat humum.

Denique (ut exemplo res hæc propiore patescat)
  A te sic speret quis (Pharisæe) bonum.

238   Marc. *12. Licétne Cæsari censum dare?*

Post tot Scribarum (Christe) in te prælia, tandem
  Ipse venit Cæsar: Cæsar in arma venit.

Pugnant terribiles non Cæsaris ense, sed ense
  Cæsare: quin Cæsar vinceris ipse tamen.

Hoc quoque tu conscribe tuis, Auguste, triumphis.
  Sic vinci dignus quis nisi Cæsar erat?

239   Marc. *12. Date Cæsari.*

Cuncta Deo debentur: habet tamen & sua Cæsar;
  Nec minus indè Deo est, si sua Cæsar habet.

Non minus indè Deo est, solio si cætera dantur
  Cæsareo, Cæsar cùm datur ipse Deo.

237. MS.
238. 34.
239. 34. See "Give to Caesar," No. 32.

240　Matthew 22:46. *Neither durst any man from that day forth ask him any more questions.*

O Christ, you escape the evil treachery, the Pharisaical nets:
and you shatter the pitiful traps with your holy word.

Therefore at last *they are quiet* and keep an unaccustomed silence:
in no other way could they *speak* your [praise] so well.

241　　　Matthew 23:29. *Ye build the tombs of the Prophets.*

What good is that labor in caring for the tombs of the saints?
It does not allow the death of the saint to die.

Foolish man, as many stones as you place on the tombs of the Prophets,
so many witnesses you make of the stones by which they died.

242　　　　　　Mark 12:44. *The Widow's Mite.*

A small drop of money (support of her old age)
falls from the fingers of the unhesitating old woman.

From the others, many coins foam up [as] from a whirlpool.
Those *cast away* to be sure; she *gave*.

240　Matth. 22:46. *Neque ausus fuit quisquam ex illo die eum amplius interrogare.*

Christe, malas fraudes, Pharisaica retia, fallis:
Et miseros sacro discutis ore dolos.

Ergò *tacent* tandem, atque invita silentia servant:
Tam bene non aliter te potuêre *loqui.*

241　Matth. 23:29. *Ædificatis sepulchra Prophetarum.*

Sanctorum in tumulis quid vult labor ille colendis?
Sanctorum mortem non sinit ille mori.

Vane, Prophetarum quot ponis saxa sepulchris,
Tot testes lapidum, queis periêre, facis.

242　Marc. 12:44. *Obolum Viduæ.*

Gutta brevis nummi (vitæ patrona senilis)
E digitis stillat non dubitantis anûs:

Istis multa vagi spumant de gurgite census,
Isti *abjecerunt* scilicet; Illa *dedit.*

242　Κερματίοιο βραχεῖα ῥάνις, βιότοιο τ᾽ ἀφαυρῆς
Ἕρκος, ἀποστάζει χειρὸς ἀπὸ τρομέρας.

Τοῖς δὲ ἀνασκιρτᾷ πολὺς ἀφρὸς ἀναίδεος ὄλβου·
Οἱ μὲν ἀπόρριπτον· κεῖνα δέδωκε μόνον.

240. 34. See "Neither durst any man," No. 33.
241. 34.* See "Yee build the Sepulchres," No. 34. The Latin epigram (not the English) is a dramatic dialogue; the second line is a response from the foolish Pharisee to the poet's question.
242. 34. See "The Widows Mites," No. 35. *Gurgite* (line 3) can mean also "spendthrift"; here both meanings are implied.

243   John 12:37. *Though he had done so many miracles*
yet they believed not in him.

Do not so many miracles of yours warrant faith in you, o Christ?
(O sweet powers of your word, your hand!)

Do they not warrant [it]? do not men believe after so many miracles?
The man who did not believe was himself a miracle.

244   John 12:37. *Though he had done so many miracles,*
yet they believed not.

On whatever great wing that love of yours may rise,
with whatever effort your lofty hand may flourish,

the world is present and thunders in opposition. It repays miracles
with miracles, but it is indeed still the supreme authority for sin.

Nay rather—o may the power of this rash word be not imprudent—
it attacked all your [miracles] indeed for one reason:

It pitted this one miracle against yours, so many and so great:
not to have Faith in yours, so many and so great.

245   Luke 21:25. *Signs of the coming of Christ.*

So come; whatever fears may accompany the signs [of your coming],
whatever sorrows call us, o Christ, come.

Christ, come, though their own labor carry off the stars snatched away
and not allow them to come and go their tangled paths,

and though in turn the world may reel under an astonishing covenant
and discordant Nature not unwind her toil, now wandering wildly.

243   Joann. 12:37. *Cùm tot signa edidisset, non credebant*
in eum.

Non tibi, Christe, fidem tua tot miracula præstant:
(O verbi, ô dextræ dulcia regna tuæl)

Non præstant? neque te post tot miracula credunt?
Mirac'lum, qui non credidit, ipse fuit.

244   Joh. 12:37. *Cùm tot signa edidisset, non credebant.*

Quantâ amor ille tuus se cunque levaverit alâ,
Quo tua cunque opere effloruit alta manus;

Mundus adest, contráque tonat. signisque reponit
Signa. (adeo sua sunt numina vel sceleri.)

Imò (ô nec nimii vis sit temeraria verbi)
Ille uno sensu vel tua cuncta premit.

Tot, tantisque tuis miràclum hoc objicit unum,
Tot tantisque tuis non adhibere fidem.

245   [*Signa adventus Christi.*]

Ergò veni; quicunque ferant tua signa timores:
Quæ nos cunque vocant tristia, Christe, veni.

Christe, veni. suus avulsum rapiat labor axem,
Nec sinat implicitas ire redire vias.

Mutuus attonito titubet sub fædere mundus,   5
Nec Natura vagum dissona volvat opus.

243. 34.
244. MS.*
245. MS. Milhaupt has proposed the text on the Second Coming as appropriate to the se-
quence for the Second Sunday of Advent.

Christ, come, though the sun may not wish to pass again through rosy
risings any longer and may feebly drive his uncertain horses.

Christ, come, though Cynthia herself may endure her own night,
blushing from more than quaking of the Thessalian [witch],
[deplorable void,
though the evil locks of the [falling] stars may rejoice through the
their hair freshly dressed with a weird flower,

though under the reluctant sun the wicked power of unexpected and
lawless night may steal the expected day,

though ungovernable day, unaware of the agreement of Eos,
may move through the whisperings of forsaken night.

Christ, come, though Father Ocean may thunder and not wish his limits,
the wandering mountains, to move under a new scepter.

Christ, come. Whatever fear dares, let it dare more.
Let the Fates do what they will. Only you, Christ, come.

Christ, come. With whatever payment for sins you come,
However great the cost of your coming, come.

Of such great [worth] it is to have been able to see you and your eyes!
Oh of such worth it is to have been able indeed to enjoy you so!

Whatever [the cost] is, Father, all will be paid by your face;
whatever it is, let it come: *Only you, Christ, come.*

246   Luke 21:27. *They shall see the son of man coming*
                  in a cloud.

Yea, *come*, O Christ, make ready your heavenly chariot
and be present gleaming in a triumphant cloud.

Do you seek a cloud? Our sighs—ah!—will be [your] cloud:
or the sun itself will give itself [to be] your cloud.

Christe, veni. roseos ultrà remeare per ortus
Nolit, & ambiguos Sol trahat æger equos.

Christe, veni. ipsa suas patiatur Cynthia noctes,
Plus quàm Thessalico tincta tremore genas.　　　　10

Astrorum mala cæsaries per inane dolendùm
Gaudeat, horribili flore repexa caput.

Sole sub invito subitæ vis improba noctis
Corripiat solitam, non sua jura, diem.

Importuna dies, nec Eöi conscia pacti,　　　　15
Per desolatæ murmura noctis eat.

Christe, veni. tonet Oceanus pater; & sua nolit
Claustra. vagi montes sub nova sceptra meent.

Christe, veni. quodcunque audet metus, audeat ultrà.
Fata id agant, quod agent. tu modò, Christe, veni.　　　　20

Christe, veni. quâcunque venis mercede malorum.
Quanti hoc constiterit cunque venire, veni.

Teque, tuosque oculos tanti est potuisse videre!
Oh tanti est te vel sic potuisse frui!

Quicquid id est, Pater, omne tuo pensabitur ore;　　　　25
Quicquid id est, veniat: *Tu modò, Christe, veni.*

246　　Luc. 21:27. *Videbunt Filium hominis venienten in nube.*

Immo *veni:* aërios (ô Christe) accingere currus,
Inque triumphali nube coruscus ades.

Nubem quæris? erunt nostra (ah!) suspiria nubes:
Aut sol in nubem se dabit ipse tuam.

The "Thessalian witch" is Medea (line 10); the "locks of the stars" describe the tail of a
comet (lines 11–12). "Eos" (line 15) is the Greek name for Aurora, the dawn; her agree-
ment was that the day followed her.
246. 34. The cloud appears in the Ascension epigrams also.

247   Luke 22:26. *He that is greatest among you, let him be as the one who is least.*

Oh good man, do you wish to be the greatest disciple of Christ?
But indeed for that reason you must become less.

This path must be followed to holy success—believe me—this reasoning:
that *you may* not be less, *wish to be.*

248   John 13:9. *Lord, not my feet only, but also my head, etc.*

Behold my head and my face! which work more than enough for their
uncleanness! Add your streams hither, you say.

It is not necessary. For these must be washed by their own
streams, Peter—when the third cock crows.

249   John 13:23. *To St. John, the beloved disciple.*

Enjoy yourself: hide your head in his majestic bosom, for then it
would never wish to be placed on a bed of everlasting roses;

Enjoy yourself: and while he carries you in his holy *bosom* thus,
o it will be enough for me to have been able to ride on his *back.*

250   John 13:34. *Where he teaches love.*

Just as the expiring swan, sweeter in its final word,
lives on in [its] verses and dying songs;

so may you, above the clashes of hatred and your funeral rites, Jesus,
complete love complete in pure love, sing.

247   Luc. 22:26. *Qui maximus est inter vos, esto sicut*
                    qui minimus.

O bone, discipulus Christi vis maximus esse?
At verò fies hâc ratione minor.

Hoc sanctæ ambitionis iter (mihi crede) tenendum est,
Hæc ratio; Tu, nè *sis* minor, *esse velis.*

248   Joh. 13. *Domine, non solùm pedes, sed & caput, &c.*

En caput! atque suis quæ plus satìs ora laborant
Sordibus! huc fluvios huc (ais) adde tuos.

Nil opus est. namque hæc (modò tertius occinat ales)
E fluviis fuerint, Petre, lavanda suis.

249   *Sancto Joanni, dilecto discipulo.*

Tu fruere; augustóque sinu caput abde (quod ô tum
Nollet in æterna se posuisse rosa)

Tu fruere: & sacro dum te sic *pectore* portat,
O sat erit *tergo* me potuisse vehi.

250   Joh. 13:34. *Ubi amorem præcipit.*

Sic magis in numeros, morituraque carmina vivit
Dulcior extremâ voce caducus olor;

Ut tu inter streditus odii, & tua funera, Jesu,
Totus amor liquido totus amore sonas.

---

247. 34.
248. MS.
249. 34. Milhaupt (p. 138) provides the text for St. John's Day (December 27) appropriate
in the sequence, John 21:20. That verse includes a reference (see margin of King James
Bible) to the principal entry, John 13:23. See also "D. Joannes in exilio," No. 325.
250. 34.* Tradition held that the swan sang only at its death and then most sweetly (see
Pseudodoxia Epidemica, III, xxvii, 1). See "In Cygnæam," No. 261.

251   John 14:6. *I am the way. To the Jews who scorn Christ.*

O but still not [a way] to be trodden on: do you press on. wicked foot?
Wicked foot, I pray was this how to walk the way to heaven?

Ah, fierce Jew, may that wicked foot [of yours] die
which so makes the *path* to *heaven* be *worn down.*

252   John 14:27. *My peace I give unto you.*

Wars call: arms, o comrades, let us make ready our arms
and swords: ah! that is, of course, our necks.

Why do I prepare for wars when Christ would give me peace?
Because Christ gives me peace, I prepare for wars.

He gave—for what creator more certain could give?—
he gave peace: but he gave peace that was *his.*

253   John 15:1–8. *Christ the vine to his Father, the husbandman.*

See your vine spreads, your vine spreads with its scarlet shoot
and it covers the earth with scorned leaves.

You come help your vine, my great Vine-dresser;
Grant a support. Grant me a support. What kind? *A cross.*

254   John 15:1. *On Christ, the Vine.*

The vine loves the elm; indeed there is even in the tree a flame
which sweet love keeps warm in its green heart:

that one of all trees, o *Vine,* you have loved that one
—whatever one it was—which was *the tree of the cross.*

251   Joann. 15. *Ego sum via. Ad Judæos spretores Christi.*

O sed nec calcanda tamen: pes improbe pergis?
Improbe pes, ergò hoc cœli erat ire viam?

Ah pereat (Judæe ferox) pes improbus ille,
Qui *cœli tritam* sic facit esse *viam*.

252   Joann. 14. *Pacem meam do vobis.*

Bella vocant: arma (ô socii) nostra arma paremus
Atque enses: nostros scilicet (ah!) jugulos.

Cur ego bella paro, cùm Christus det mihi pacem?
Quòd Christus pacem dat mihi, bella paro.

Ille dedit (nam quis potuit dare certior autor?)
Ille dedit pacem: sed dedit ille *suam*.

253   Joann. 15. *Christus Vitis ad Vinitorem Patrem.*

En serpit tua, purpureo tua palmite vitis
Serpit, & (ah!) spretis it per humum foliis.

Tu viti succurre tuæ, mi Vinitor ingens:
Da fulcrum; fulcrum da mihi: quale? *crucem*.

254   Joann. 15:1. *In Christum Vitem.*

Ulmum vitis amat (quippe est & in arbore flamma,
Quam fovet in viridi pectore blandus amor:)

Illam ex arboribus cunctis tu (*Vitis*) amâsti,
Illam, quæcunque est, quæ *crucis arbor* erat.

251. 34. See also "Ego sum ostium," No. 205, Milhaupt provides the text.
252. 34.
253. 34. It will be noted that the leaves of the vine growing all over the ground are *spretis* (unwanted, or scorned), the same word used in the title of epigram 251 to describe the Jews' attitude to Christ.
254. 34. "From the practice of training vines on elm trees derived a common symbol of love between the sexes" (Milhaupt, p. 149).

255   John 15:1. *I am the true vine.*

Indeed I believe. But also the enemy Caiaphas himself believed you
and Judas himself believed, I think.

If you were not the true vine, Jesus,
whence could they have had such a great thirst for your blood?

256   John 15:24. *They have both seen and hated me.*

He saw? and hated still? Ah, he saw not you, Jesus.
He saw not you who saw and hated still.

He saw not, he saw not you, sweetest of all things,
who saw anything in you which he could refuse to love.

257   John 16:20. *Ye shall weep and lament.*

Therefore welcome my griefs that to me are my joys:
How dear, o God, is *my weeping* to me!

I should weep, if I could not weep: *You alone, sweet Jesus,
give joy even then when you deny it.*

258   John 16:26. *I say not unto you that I will pray the
Father for you.*

Ah nevertheless, *you yourself, ask:* of course the Father cannot be harsh
to you when you ask nor is he wont to be.

With every look he fixes his loves on you
and into your bosom is poured his every word.

255   Joh. 15. *Ego vitis vera.*

Credo quidem. sed & hoc hostis te credidit ipse
Caiaphas, & Judas credidit ipse, reor.

Unde illis, Jesu, vitis nisi vera fuisses,
Tanta tui potuit sanguinis esse sitis?

256   Joh. 15:24. *Vidérunt, & odérunt me.*

Vidit? & odit adhuc? Ah, te non vidit, Jesu.
Non vidit te, qui vidit, & odit adhuc.

Non vidit, te non vidit (dulcissime rerum)
In te qui vidit quid, quod amare neget.

257   Joann. 16:20. *Vos flebitis & lamentabimini.*

Ergò mihi salvete mei, mea gaudia, luctus:
Quàm charum (ò Deus) est hoc mihi *flere meum!*

Flerem, ne flerem: *Solus tu (dulcis Jesu)*
Lætitiam donas tunc quoque quando negas.

258   Joann. 16:26. *Non dico, me rogaturum Patrem pro vobis.*

Ah tamen *Ipse roga:* tibi scilicet ille roganti
Esse nequit durus, nec solet esse, Pater.

Ille suos omni facie te figit amores;
Inque tuos toto effunditur ore sinus.

---

255. MS.*
256. MS.* See "But now they have seen," No. 37. The epigram plays tricks with *vidit* (he saw). The subject is singular, though the text is plural.
257. 34. See "Verily I say," No. 38.
258. 34. Uniquely of the longer epigrams, this epigram is carefully structured: it begins with a distich depending directly on the text quoted as title (lines 1–2). The next five distichs (lines 3–12) comment on the propriety of Jesus' prayers to God and conclude with a restatement of the opening distich.

Indeed, looking at your eyes, he sees himself in them:
and in your bosom, Jesus, he comforts himself.

From you he judges himself and learns his divinity,
and from you his own echo is returned to him.

He binds himself to you and you to himself, equally each to the other.
So much is he yours that he may not be more his own.

Therefore ask: *you yourself, ask;* of course the Father cannot
be harsh to you when you ask nor is he wont to be.

Should *I* ask him? alas, he must not be asked with this mouth,
a mouth which does not make prayers pure enough.

If I should ask him, who knows with what tempests
he may rise and what wrath may thunder on this wretched head?

Perhaps even a thunderbolt may come upon me from that countenance:
certainly, often many a thunderbolt has come from that countenance.

Perhaps he may pierce me with one point of an angry word
or one nod, and *I am ruined:*

Not I, I should not ask: of course the Father can be harsher
to me when I ask and he is wont to be.

Yes, I shall ask: however, not with my mouth: yes, I shall ask
with my mouth, Jesus, that is, with *your mouth.*

259   John 16:33. *I have overcome the world.*

You are my leader against the world, fairest Jesus?
But you my leader yourself lie fallen (poor me!)

If you, my leader are yourself fallen, is there any hope of salvation?
Indeed, if you do not fall, for me there is no salvation.

Quippe, tuos spectans oculos, se spectat in illis;   5
Inque tuo (Jesu) se fovet ipse sinu.

Ex te metitur sese, & sua numina discit:
Indè repercussus redditur ipse sibi.

Ille tibi se, te ille sibi par nectit utrinque:
Tam tuus est, ut nec sit magìs ille suus.   10

Ergò roga: *Ipse roga:* tibi scilicet ille roganti
Esse nequit durus, nec solet esse, Pater.

Illum ut *ego* rogitem? Hôc (eheu) non ore rogandum;
Ore satìs puras non faciente preces.

Illum ego si rogitem, quis scit quibus ille procellis   15
Surgat, & in miserum hoc quæ tonet ira caput?

Isto etiam forsan veniet mihi fulmen ab ore:
(Sæpe isto certè fulmen ab ore venit)

Ille unâ irati forsan me cuspide verbi,
Uno me nutu figet, & *interii:*   20

Non ego, non rogitem: mihi scilicet ille roganti
Durior esse potest, & solet esse, Pater.

Immo rogabo: nec ore meo tamen: immo rogabo
Ore meo (Jesu) scilicet *ore tuo.*

259   Joann. 16:33. *Ego vici mundum.*

Tu contra mundum dux es meus, optime Jesu?
At tu (me miserum!) dux meus ipse jaces.

Si tu, dux meus, ipse jaces, spes ulla salutis?
Immo, ni jaceas tu, mihi nulla salus.

The next five distichs (lines 13–22) comment on the impropriety of the poet's prayers to
God and conclude with a revision of the opening distich. The poem ends with a distich
resolving the dilemma: the poet will make his prayers to God through the intercessory mouth
of Jesus.

259. 34. The epigram is military; *dux* might be translated "captain." It contains interesting
repetitions and parallels.

260   John 16:33. *About the fight of Christ against the world.*

Are you, poor man, you—so the world says—setting your hands
against my mighty power, when your hand has been stripped of weapons?

Go, lictor, and put chains on those bold hands.
The lictor put on the chains *and* [thereby] *gave the weapons.*

261   John 17. *On the singing swan of the Lord Jesus.*

[your songs!
What sweetness, oh how many honeycombs, Christ, do you pour into
Sweet and dying swan—ah madness!

Yet spare [me], if these voices are less my joys:
indeed [you sing with] a sweet voice but a dying one.

262   John 18:10. *On Peter the ear-slayer.*

However much this fierce sword of yours flashes, Peter,
you are now fighting for yourself, my good man, not for the Lord.

Obviously you are raging against this poor ear most relentlessly,
lest it be a witness of your treachery.

263   Matthew 26:65. *Caiaphas resents Christ acknowledging
himself.*

You berate Christ because he does not deny he is Christ:
This was his crime: that he was *himself.*

Should I trust you as a priest? That is a new [kind of] priest
by whom God is not allowed to be God with impunity.

260   Joann. 16:33. *De Christi contra mundum pugna.*

Tune, miser? tu (Mundus ait) mea fulmina contra
Ferre manus, armis cùm tibi nuda manus?

I lictor; manibúsque audacibus injice vinc'la:
Injecit lictor vincula, & *arma dedit.*

261   *In* (Joh. 17.) *Cygnæam D*. *Jesû cantionem.*

Quæ mella, ô quot, Christe, favos in carmina fundis!
Dulcis, & (ah furias!) ah moribundus olor!

Parce tamen; minus hæ si sunt mea gaudia voces:
Voce quidem dulci, sed moriente canis.

262   Joann. 18:10. *In Petrum auricîdam.*

Quantumcunque ferox tuus hic (Petre) fulminat ensis,
Tu tibi jam pugnas (ô bone) non Domino.

Scilicet in miseram furis implacidissimus aurem,
Perfidiæ testis nè queat esse tuæ.

263   Matth. 26:65. *Indignatur Caiphas Christo se confitenti.*

Tu Christum, Christum quòd non negat esse, lacessis:
Ipsius hoc crimen, quod fuit *ipse,* fuit.

Téne Sacerdotem credam? Novus ille Sacerdos,
Per quem impunè Deo non licet esse Deum.

---

260. 34. "In love's feild was never found / A nobler weapon than a Wound" ("The Flaming Heart," No. 63, lines 71–72). A "lictor" is a Roman official.
261. MS. See "Upon our Lords last discourse," No. 36. The "Swan song" is "our Lords last comfortable discourse with his disciples," John 15–17. The song has "a dying fall" (Milhaupt, p. 230). See also "Ubi amorem præcipit," No. 250. The English epigram is headed John 15 and is therefore in a different position in the sequence.
262. 34. See "On St. Peter," No. 39.
263. 34.

264   Matthew 27:12. *The accused Christ answers nothing.*

> *He says nothing:* o precious silence of that holy tongue!
> o of what great weight was that *nothing!*

> He who once *said* the *word* and *made* all things,
> *saying no word,* now *remakes* all things.

265   Matthew 27:24. *On Pontius poorly washed.*

> That water washes your hands, most false judge:
> ah! but that water does not wash away your crime.

> No water will wash away your crime: or if any should wash it,
> o it will want to come from your eyes.

266   Matthew 27:24. *To Pontius washing.*

> Is not murder enough, that you add this outrage to it
> and be the ravisher of virgin water?

> Indeed this nymph so pure, *the daughter of a noble spring,*
> mourns, now profaned by your adultery.

> The chaste drop hastes away with shamed murmur,
> she thinks she will not be enough for her own tear.

> Stop, ah stop defiling these shining dews:
> or say what water will wash these pitiful waters.

267   *On the thorns taken from Christ's head [and]*
> *stained with blood.*

> Take the sprouts you planted, Soldier—or don't you recognize them?
> How changed in color is this harvest of your field!

> O what soil is so kind to so hard a farmer?
> He sows thorns: and it returns roses.

264   Matth. 27:12. *Christus accusatus nihil respondit.*

Nil ait: ô sanctæ pretiosa silentia linguæ!
Ponderis ô quanti res *nihil* illud erat!

Ille olim, *verbum* qui *dixit,* & omnia *fecit,*
Verbum non dicens omnia nunc *reficit.*

265   Matth. 27:24. *In Pontium malè lautum.*

Illa manus lavat unda tuas, vanissime Judex:
Ah tamen illa scelus non lavat unda tuum.

Nulla scelus lavet unda tuum: vel si lavet ulla,
O volet ex oculis illa venire tuis.

266   *Pontio lavanti.*

Non satìs est cædes, nisi stuprum hoc insuper addas,
Et tam virgineæ sis violator aquæ?

Nympha quidem pura hæc & *honesti filia fontis*
Luget, adulterio jam temerata tuo.

Casta verecundo properat cum murmure gutta,
Nec satìs in lacrymam se putat esse suam.

Desine tam nitidos stuprare (ah, desine) rores:
Aut dic, quæ miseras unda lavabit aquas.

267   *In spinas demtas è Christi capite cruentatas.*

Accipe (an ignoscis?) de te sata germina, Miles.
Quàm segeti est messis discolor illa suæ!

O quæ tam duro gleba est tam grata colono?
Inserit hic spinas: reddit & illa rosas.

264. 34. See "And he answered," No. 40.
265. 34. See "To Pontius," No. 41.
266. 34. See "To Pontius washing his . . . hands," No. 42.
267. MS. See "Upon the Thornes," No. 43.

268　　　　　Mark 14:65. *And they spat upon him.*

What so foully will not the wrath of this cruel sea dare!
　　Lo, it spits on your eyes, our stars.

Perhaps here someone blinded you with spittle, Jesus,
　who owes to your spittle the fact that he himself sees.

269　　　　　*On the day of the Master's Passion.*

Should I be so gloomy? away with fasts! I have
　sweet wine in my jar—nor is it ashamed to be there.

I have what the parent grape produced on the
virginal vine sprout in chaste bunches—*not placed in the press.*

At last see the spear drinks before me from its cask
　　(Indeed it aged enough in thirty years).

Now it goes, and oh with what fragrance does that burning torrent steam!
　as hence a stinging odor rushes out like a heavenly breeze!

What rose so fresh flutters though Falernian glasses?
　What wines of Massica sparkle with such a star?

I did not know; but behold, that is the *wine of love:*
　how should I, how should I be equal to such glasses?

I am overcome: oh I am almost completely mingled with these aromas:
　　I am not, I am not equal to such glasses.

But why do I fear the great strength of invincible wine?
　See there is what cuts the strength of the wine, water.*

* John 19:34. And forthwith came there out blood and water.

268   *Et conspuebant illum.*

Quid non tam fœdè sævi maris audeat ira!
Conspuit ecce oculos (sydera nostra) tuos.

Forsan & hîc aliquis sputo te excæcat, Jesu,
Qui debet sputo, quòd videt ipse, tuo.

269   *In die Passionis Dominicæ.*

Tamne ego sim tetricus? valeant jejunia: vinum
Est mihi dulce meo (nec pudet esse) cado.

Est mihi quod castis, *neque prelum passa,* racemis
Palmite virgineo protulit uva parens.

Hoc mihi (ter denis sat enim maturuit annis)   5
Tandem ecce è dolio præbibit hasta suo.

Jámque it; & ô quanto calet actus aromate torrens!
Acer ut hinc aurâ divite currit odor!

Quæ rosa per cyathos volitat tam viva Falernos?
Massica quæ tanto sydere vina tremunt?   10

O ego nescibam; atque ecce est *Vinum* illud *amoris:*
Unde ego sim tantis, unde ego par cyathis?

Vincor: & ô istis totus propè misceor auris:
Non ego sum tantis, non ego par cyathis.

Sed quid ego invicti metuo bona robora vini?   15
Ecce est, quæ validum diluit, *unda, merum.

* Joh. 19. & continuò exivit sanguis & aqua.

268. MS. Text from Milhaupt. For the blind man cured by Christ's spittle see "Cæcus natus,"
No. 202.
269. 34. Christ and the wine press form one of the traditional icons of the Church (Tuve,
p. 133 and *passim*).

270   *On the wounds of God hanging [on the cross].*

O streams of blood from head, side, hands, and feet!
O what rivers rise from the purple fountain!

His foot is not strong enough to walk for our safety (as once it was)
but it swims; ah—it swims in its own streams.

His hand is held fast; *but it gives, though held fast:* his good right hand
gives holy dews, and it is dissolved into its own gift.

O side, o torrent! for what Nile goes forth in greater
flood where it is carried headlong by the rushing waters?

His head drips and drips with thousands and thousands of drops
at once: do you see how the cruel shame reddens his cheeks?

The thorns cruelly watered by this rain flourish
and hope forthwith to change into new roses.

Each hair is a slender channel for a tiny rill,
a little stream, from this *red sea,* as it were.

O too much *alive* [are] the *waters* in those precious streams!
Never was he more truly the *fountain of life.*

271   *On the wounds of the Lord hanging [on the cross].*

Whether I call your wounds *eyes* or *mouths*—
surely everywhere are mouths—alas!—everywhere are eyes.

Behold the mouths! o blooming with lips too red!
Behold the eyes! ah wet with cruel tears!

Magdala, you who were accustomed to bring tears and kisses to the
sacred foot, take yours in turn from the sacred foot.

The foot has its own *mouths,* to give your kisses back:
This clearly is the *eye* by which it returns your tears.

270   *In vulnera Dei pendentis.*

O Frontis, lateris, manuúmque pedúmque cruores!
O quæ purpureo flumina fonte patent!

In nostram (ut quondam) pes non valet ire salutem,
Sed natat; in fluviis (ah!) natat ille suis.

Fixa manus; *dat, fixa:* pios bona dextera rores   5
Donat, & in donum solvitur ipsa suum.

O latus, ô torrens! quis enim torrentior exit
Nilus, ubi pronis præcipitatur aquis?

Mille & mille simul cadit & cadit undique guttis
Frons: viden' ut sævus purpuret ora pudor?   10

Spinæ hôc irriguæ florent crudeliter imbre,
Inque novas sperant protinus ire rosas.

Quisque capillus it exiguo tener alveus amne,
Hôc quasi de *rubro* rivulus *oceano.*

O nimiùm *vivæ* pretiosis amnibus *undæ!*   15
Fons vitæ nunquam verior ille fuit.

271   *In vulnera pendentis Domini.*

Sive *oculos,* sive *ora* vocem tua vulnera; certè
Undique sunt ora (heu!) undique sunt oculi.

Ecce ora! ô nimiùm roseis florentia labris!
Ecce oculi! sævis ah madidi lacrymis!

Magdala, quæ lacrymas solita es, quæ basia sacro
Ferre pedi, sacro de pede sume vices.

Ora pedi sua sunt, tua quò tibi basia reddat:
Quò reddat lacrymas scilicet est *oculus.*

270. 34. See the two English versions of this poem, "Song Upon the bleeding Crucifix," No.
72. The Latin version shares the inadequacies of the 1646 version. Stanzas 8–10 in that ver-
sion have no originals here.
271. 34. See "On the wounds of our Crucified Lord," No. 45. Crashaw imagines Mary Mag-
dalene standing at the foot of the cross, weeping over the feet as at Luke 7:37.

272   *On the tears of the suffering Christ.*

Cruel grief! can you [do] this? do you also flood those eyes [with tears]?
O how this flood makes furrows in your cheeks not deserving [them]!

> O I [am worthier] to weep your tears, I am worthier of this
> to have as my share whatever dew falls on you.

Is this possible? for me to weep your tears for you? ah, my good Jesus,
if I could only weep my own tears for me.

> Weep my tears? no, no, yours. If only I could do this:
> I could not fail to weep my own tears.

> To weep yours is to weep mine. Your tear, Christ,
> is mine. Or if it is your tear, the cause [of it] is mine.

273   Luke 23:50–53. *On the tomb of Christ.*

> This circle moves in an orbit, similar and how equal to itself!
> How well the end loves its beginning!

> To the virgin marriage-couch how beautifully fits
> the virgin tomb (where no one has lain)!

> That this matter might move with equal step on all sides;
> that [couch] was betrothed to a Joseph as was that [tomb].

274   John 19:41–42. *On the sepulchre of the Lord.*

Now let them yield, let those miracles of the rock of old [time] yield,
whence fresh water had flowed all at once like a river.

> You blessed rock, when the third day will dawn,
> will proudly flow in a sacred font of flames.

272   *In lacrymas Christi patientis.*

Sæve dolor! potes hoc? oculos quoque perpluis istos?
   O quàm non meritas hæc arat unda genas!

O lacrymas ego flere tuas, ego dignior istud,
   Quod tibi cunque cadit roris, habere meum.

Siccine? me tibi flere tuas? ah, mi bone Jesu,
   Si possem lacrymas vel mihi flere meas!

Flere meas? immò immò tuas. hoc si modò possem:
   Non possem lacrymas non ego flere meas.

Flere tuas est flere meas. tua lacryma, Christe,
   Est mea. vel lacryma est si tua, causa mea est.

273   *[In tumulum Christi.]*

Circulus hic similem quàm par sibi pergit in orbem!
   Principiumque suum quàm bene finis amat!

Virgineo thalamo quàm pulchrè convenit ille
   (Quo nemo jacuit) virgineus tumulus!

Undique ut hæc æquo passu res iret; & ille
   Josepho desponsatus, & ille fuit.

274   Joh. 19. *In Sepulchrum Domini.*

Jam cedant, veteris cedant miracula saxi,
   Unde novus subito fluxerat amne latex.

Tu, felix rupes, ubi se lux tertia tollet,
   Flammarum sacro fonte superba flues.

272. MS.
273. MS. See "Upon the Saviours Tomb," No. 46.
274. See "Easter Day," No. 47.

275   John 20:1–18. *On the resurrection of the Lord.*

Behold, you are born! and with you, your world, golden King,
    is born with you from the *virgin** tomb.

With you nature hastes into a second birth
    and a new world has in you a new life.

From your life, gracious Sun, everything takes life:
    to be sure nothing, except death, is forced henceforth to die.

But surely not even death: indeed so that it may be buried in your tomb,
    Christ, death itself will wish to die.

* John 19:41. Wherein was never man yet laid.

276   John 20:1. [*The first day of the week*] *cometh Mary*
    Magdalene early [*when it was yet dark*]
    unto the sepulcher.

You came before the rosy dawn, holy
    Magdalene; *but already then your Sun had risen.*

And now, rightly, the old sun does not make its vain risings
    and does not consider its rays of much worth.

Nay, somewhere, I believe, he, a new star, now twinkles in the skies,
    and the little one considers itself a small torch in the night.

O how he wishes to be a herald, as it were, of such a great day!
    and to be the new *Morning Star* for the new *Sun!*

277   Mark 16:1–2. *On the day of the Master's resurrection.*
    Magdalene came to the tomb bearing spices.

Nay even you too adore the ashes of your phoenix;
    You too bring *sad treasures,* my mind.

If they are not scented and not any amomum perfumes you
    —how rich a harvest is scented by Magdalene's hand—

275   *In resurrectionem Domini.*

Nasceris, en! tecúmque tuus (Rex auree) mundus,
    Tecum *virgineo nascitur è tumulo.

Tecum in natales properat natura secundos,
    Atque novam vitam te novus orbis habet.

Ex vita (Sol alme) tua vitam omnia sumunt:
    Nil certè, nisi mors, cogitur indè mori.

At certè neque mors: nempe ut queat illa sepulchro
    (Christe) tuo condi, mors volet ipsa mori.

* Joann. 19:41. ἐν ᾧ οὐδέπω οὐδεὶς ἐτέθη.

276   Joann. 20:1. *Primo mane venit ad sepulchrum*
                    Magdalena.

Tu matutinos prævertis, sancta, rubores,
    Magdala; *sed jam tum Sol tuus ortus erat.*

Jámque vetus meritò vanos Sol non agit ortus,
    Et tanti radios non putat esse suos.

Quippe aliquo (reor) ille, novus, jam nictat in astro,
    Et se nocturnâ parvus habet faculâ.

Quàm velit ô tantæ vel nuntius esse diei!
    Atque novus *Soli Lucifer* ire novo!

277   *In die Resurrectionis Dominicæ. Venit ad sepulchrum*
           Magdalena ferens aromata.

Quin & tu quoque busta tui Phœnicis adora;
    Tu quoque fer *tristes* (mens mea) *delitias.*

Si nec aromata sunt, nec quod tibi fragrat amomum;
    (Qualis Magdalinâ est messis odora manu)

275. 34. See "Easter Day," No. 47.
276. 34.

this is what surpasses the spices, what surpasses the amomum:
  this sweet little, jeweled tearlet for you.

And a tear is something: nor has Magdala wept in vain:
  she realized this: that her tears were not nothing.

With these—even then when the Master's head would lie in amomum—
  she made the feet be the envy of the head.

Now too when his bosom is drenched with so much perfume,
  she takes more from her eyes to compensate.

Christ, the tears are fitting: it is right that with this *dew* should be
  moistened this *eternal morning of life and your day.*

278   Matthew 28:6. *See the place where the Lord lay.*

Him, Him, oh rather, bright one, show me [Him], I beg;
  To Him, To Him, o I pray that my tears may go [to Him].

If it is enough to show the *place* and tell us,
  Behold, Mary, see here, here your Lord did lie;

I myself can show my arms and say,
  Behold, Mary, see here, here your Lord did lie.

279   Matthew 28:11–16. *They gave large money unto the
                   soldiers.*

Are you giving bribes so the soldier will be unwilling to say those things?
  You give what is able to speak even when he is silent.

Those things that you cause one, under the persuasion of a bribe, to
                                                              [silence,
  You cause to be spoken more clearly and more shamefully.

Est quod aromatibus præstat, quod præstat amomo: 5
Hæc tibi mollicula, hæc gemmea lacrymula.

Et lacryma est aliquid: neque frustra Magdala flevit:
Sentiit hæc, lacrymas non nihil esse suas.

His illa (& tunc cùm Domini caput iret amomo)
Invidiam capitis fecerat esse pedes.   10

Nunc quoque cùm sinus huic tanto sub aromate sudet,
Plus capit ex oculis, quo litet, illa suis.

Christe, decent lacrymæ: decet isto *rore* rigari
Vitæ hoc *æternum mane, tuúmque diem.*

278   Matth. 28. *Ecce locus ubi jacuit Dominus.*

Ipsum, Ipsum (precor) ô potiùs mihi (candide) monstra:
Ipsi, Ipsi, ô lacrymis oro sit ire meis.

Si monstrare *locum* satìs est, & dicere nobis,
En, Maria, hîc tuus en, hîc jacuit Dominus;

Ipsa ulnas monstrare meas, & dicere possum,
En, Maria, hîc tuus en, hîc jacuit Dominus.

278   Φαίδιμε, μοὶ αὐτὸν μᾶλλόν μοι δείκνυθι αὐτόν.
Αὐτός μου, δέομαι, αὐτὸς ἔχῃ δάκρυα.

'Ει δὲ τόπόν μοι δεικνύναι ἅλις ἐστί, καὶ εἰπεῖν
�ͅΩδε τεὸς Μαριὰμ (ἤνιδε) κεῖτο ἄναξ.

'Αγκοίνάς μου δεικνύναι δύναμαι γε, καὶ εἰπεῖν
῍Ωδε τεὸς Μαριὰμ (ἤνιδε) κεῖτο ἄναξ.

279   Matth. 28. *Dederunt nummos militibus.*

Ne miles velit ista loqui, tu munera donas?
Donas, quod possit, cùm tacet ipse, loqui.

Quæ facis à quoquam, pretio suadente, taceri;
Clariùs, & dici turpiùs ista facis.

---

277. 34. Amomum is a spicy extract from an aromatic plant.
278. 34. See "Come see the place," No. 49.
279. 34.

280   Luke 24:38–40. *On the wounds of the Master*
                    still present.

You see the weapons: the bows, the quiver and the light darts;
        and—by whatever name—the soldier was Love.

Love used these things: but also he was these things himself: both his
        dart and he himself the quiver for his darts.

Now they brightly gleam, and with the dust of war swept away,
        they hang as great names in the memorial temple.

But there will be a time when Love will give over to wrath
these weapons, the quiver, and the fruit of the quiver, the little arrows.

Alas! with what spirit, with what an expression will [your] guilty hand
        when every hand recognizes its own crime?   [stand

Wicked soldier, you will see there the wounds you inflicted
        through whatever skill your madness tricked you with.

Whether at your finger's prodding the *thorny laurel* drank
        from his temples, or the spear drank from the holy side,

        or the nails grew cruelly red under your blow,
        or the scourge was ashamed to act at your command.

Wicked soldier, you will see there the wounds you inflicted.
        To see the wound you inflicted will be your wound.

The blow [you gave], avenger for itself, will requite *nails* and *spear:*
        and as it requites them, it will be *nail* and *spear* to itself.

        Who will arouse such *dire*, such *righteous* wrath?
        your very wounds, O Christ, will fight for you.

281   Luke 24:38–39. *Why are ye troubled? Behold my hands
            and feet, that it is I myself.*

        Behold me and my marks, once my wounds! Surely
        unless you believe, they are my wounds even yet.

        O now indeed may my wounds heal your faith:
        o now may your faith heal my wounds.

280   Luc. 24. *In cicatrices Domini adhuc superstites.*

Arma vides; arcus, pharetrámque, levésque sagittas,
  Et quocunque fuit nomine miles Amor.

His fuit usus Amor: sed & hæc fuit ipse; suúmque
  Et jaculum, & jaculis ipse pharetra suis.

Nunc splendent tantùm, & deterso pulvere belli   5
  E memori pendent nomina magna tholo.

Tempus erit tamen, hæc iræ quando arma, pharetrámque
  Et sobolem pharetræ spicula tradet Amor.

Heu! quâ tunc animâ, quo stabit conscia vultu,
  Quum scelus agnoscet dextera quæque suum?   10

Improbe, quæ dederis, cernes ibi vulnera, miles,
  Quâ tibi cunque tuus luserit arte furor.

Seu digito suadente tuo *mala Laurus* inibat
  Temporibus; sacrum seu bibit hasta latus:

Sive tuo clavi sævùm rubuêre sub ictu;   15
  Seu puduit jussis ire flagella tuis.

Improbe, quæ dederis, cernes ibi vulnera, miles:
  Quod dederis vulnus, cernere, vulnus erit.

Plaga sui vindex *clavós*que rependet & *hastam:*
  Quóque rependet, erit *clavus* & *hasta* sibi.   20

Quis tam *terribiles,* tam *justas* moverit iras?
  Vulnera pugnabunt (Christe) vel ipsa tibi.

281   Luc. 24:39. *Quid turbati estis? Videte manus meas &*
                  pedes, quia ego ipse sum.

En me, & signa mei, quondam mea vulnera! certè,
  Vos nisi credetis, vulnera sunt & adhuc.

O nunc ergò fidem sanent mea vulnera vestram:
  O mea nunc sanet vulnera vestra fides.

---

280. 34. See "In cicatrices," No. 50. The first three distichs only are translated by the English.
281. 34.

282   John 20:20. *On the marks of the wounds which the Lord shows to strengthen the faith of his followers.*

With these eyes (not yet met together like closed windows)
your love watches over us.

Your love sees us with these eyes: and with them
our faith rejoices to see your love, Christ.

283   John 20:20. *On the wounds which Christ has still surviving in him.*

Whatever the spiked *thorn,* or the sharp-pointed *nail,*
or the *spear* had written with crimson letters,

still lives with you: but now they are not your wounds:
no, but they are the medicine for my wounds.

284   John 20:25. *Unless I shall put my finger, etc.*

Then will the impious finger again [drive] the nails? again [thrust] the
again run through the whole sad work?   [spear?

So that, Thomas, you may believe that Christ *lives,*
would you, ah cruel one, make Christ *die?*

285   John 20:27. *Christ to Thomas.*

O harsh faith! did you wish to prolong my sorrows?
O cruel fingers! have you discovered God in this way?

You wish to touch my wounds *lest you doubt,* but alas,
you make those wounds worse *while you doubt.*

282   Joann. 20:20. *In vulnerum vestigia quæ ostendit*
             Dominus, ad firmandam suorum fidem.

His oculis (nec adhuc clausis coïère fenestris)
Invigilans nobis est tuus usus amor.

His oculis nos cernit amor tuus: his & amorem
(Christe) tuum gaudet cernere nostra fides.

283   Joann. 20. *In cicatrices quas Christus habet in se adhuc*
                 superstites.

Quicquid *spina* procax, vel stylo *clavus* acuto,
   Quicquid purpureâ scripserat *hasta* notâ,

Vivit adhuc tecum: sed jam tua vulnera non sunt:
Non, sed vulneribus sunt medicina meis.

284   Joann. 20. *Nisi digitum immisero, &c.*

Impius ergò iterum clavos? iterum impius hastam?
Et totum digitus triste revolvet opus?

Túne igitur Christum (Thoma) quò *vivere* credas,
Tu Christum faceres (ah truculente!) *mori?*

285   Joann. 20. *Christus ad Thomam.*

Sæva fides! voluisse meos tractare dolores?
Crudeles digiti! sic didicisse Deum?

Vulnera, *nè dubites*, vis tangere nostra: sed eheu,
Vulnera, *dum dubitas*, tu graviora facis.

---

282. 34.
283. 34. See "On the still surviving marks," No. 51.
284. 34.
285. 34. Bradner (*Musæ Anglicanæ*, p. 93): "Here . . . is the . . . elaboration of conscious art . . . , using questions, word-play, and paradox, but the art is employed solely to arouse in the reader a religious response to the dramatic situation in the Bible."

286   Matthew 28:17. *But some doubted.*

Indeed the quaking earth *shakes*∗; but
the very fact that the earth shakes forbids you to shake [in your faith].

Those guards themselves, if you ask them, will speak [of] that
in this very way, *that they cannot speak.*∗

∗ Verse 2. there was a great earthquake.
∗ Verse 4. the keepers did shake, and became as dead men.

287   Luke 24:44–53. *On the Master's ascension.*

Lo! He goes through the open gates of his heaven:
he goes to heaven and pours forth a new heaven from his face.

The sun is scattered before his feet and now leaning nearer
with its full brightness, drinks the face of its own Sun.

But Phoebe, denying that she owes her light to her brother,
now becomes golden from a better Phoebus.

You give these *triumphs* yourself, Father, *for you, the conquered:*
How else would you celebrate a triumph, who else was sufficient?

288   Luke 24:44–53. *On the day of the Master's Ascension.*

Still, O Christ, do we hold You, our loves?
Alas how much we suffer the envy of heaven for this!

We may suffer envy: the heavens have their own stars;
which adorn the flickering fires like so many curly-haired faces;

Phoebe and Phoebus and so many fleecy clouds of painted mist;
fleecy clouds which the sun has varicolored with his rosy needle.

286   Matth. 28:17. *Aliqui verò dubitabant.*

Scilicet & tellus *dubitat* tremebunda: sed ipsum hoc,
    Quòd tellus dubitat, vos dubitare vetat.

Ipsi custodes vobis, si quæritis, illud
    Hoc ipso dicunt, *dicere quòd nequeunt.*

* Vers. 2. σεισμὸς ἐγένετο μέγας.
* Vers. 4. ἐσείσθησαν οἱ τηροῦντες καὶ ἐγένοντο ὡσεὶ νεκροί.

287   *In ascensionem Dominicam.*

Vadit (Io!) per aperta sui penetralia cœli:
    It cœlo, & cœlum fundit ab ore novum.

Spargitur ante pedes, & toto sidere pronus
    Jam propiùs Solis Sol bibit ora sui.

At fratrì debere negans sua lumina Phœbe,
    Aurea de Phœbo jam meliore redit.

Hos, *de te victo,* tu das (Pater) ipse *triumphos:*
    Unde triumphares, quis satìs alter erat?

288   *In die Ascensionis Dominicæ.*

Usque etiam nostros Te (Christe) tenemus amores?
    Heu cœli quantam hinc invidiam patimur!

Invidiam patiamur: habent sua sydera cœli;
    Quæque comunt tremulas crispa tot ora faces;

Phœbênque & Phœbum, & tot pictæ vellera nubis;
    Vellera, quæ roseâ Sol variavit acu.

---

286. 34. The epigram puns on the meanings of *dubitare:* to quake (of the earth), to waver (of a person). The guards "did shake" from fear of the angel.
287. 34.

Was it so great that they allowed us to be sustained by this one torch?
Let there be one here: there are (and may be) there a thousand torches.

We are powerless! for because you do not ascend to it,
heaven itself indeed descends* for you, Christ.

* Acts 1. A cloud received him and took him up.

289   Acts 1:9. *On the cloud which carried off the Master.*

O this black [cloud]! Why indeed does it show its shining breast to me?
a breast more shining than the cheeks of Cygnus [the swan]?

But even if it is whiter, more golden than Phoebus
and however shining in itself, it is black to me.

A black cloud for me! no blacker one than this brings the south wind
or the weapons [of lightning] proclaiming the angry God.

Black, it may be! though it brings no storm clouds and no night.
If it does not bring night, behold it steals away the day.

290   *Raise our eyes.*

Lift our eyes, o lift our eyes with you, your stars.
Ah what, indeed, what would they do here without their sun?

That, O Heaven, which without their sun your stars would do,
these would do here on earth without their sun.

Those without their sun would be blinded by their own rain:
these would be blinded by their own tears without their sun.

Quantum erat, ut sinerent hâc unâ˜ nos face ferri?
Una sit hîc: sunt (& sint) ibi mille faces.

Nil agimus: nam tu quia non ascendis ad illum,
Æther *descendit (Christe) vel ipse tibi.

* Act. 1. Nubes susceptum eum abstulit.

288   Νῦν ἔτι ἡμέτερον σε, Χριστὲ, ἔχομεν τὸν ἔρωτα;
      Οὐρανοῦ οὖν ὅσσον τὸν φθόνον ὡς ἔχομεν·

'Αλλὰ ἔχωμεν. ἔχει ἑὰ μὲν τὰ δ' ἀγάλματα αἰθήρ·
"Αστρατε, καὶ Φοῖβον, καὶ καλὰ τῶν νεφέλων.

"Οσσον ἔην, ἡμῖν ὄφρ' εἴη ἐν τόδε ἄστρον;
"Αστρον ἐν ἡμῖν ᾖ· εἰσι τοι ἄστρ' ἕκατον.

Πάντα μάτην. ὅτι Χριστὲ συ οὐκ ἀνάβαινες ἐς αὐτὸν,
Αὐτὸς μὲν κατέβη οὐρανὸς εἰς σε τεός.

289   Act. 1. *In nubem, quæ Dnũ abstulit.*

O Nigra hæc! Quid enim mihi candida pectora monstrat?
Pectora Cygnǽis candidiora genis.

Sit verò magis alba, suo magis aurea Phæbo,
Quantumcunque sibi candida; nigra mihi est.

Nigra mihi nubes! et quâ neque nigrior Austros,
Vel tulit irati nuncia tela Dei.

Nigra! licèt nimbos, noctem neque detulit ullam.
Si noctem non fert, at rapit, ecce, diem.

290   *[Tolle oculos nostros.]*

Tolle oculos, tolle ô tecum (tua sydera) nostros.
Ah quid enim, quid agant hîc sine sole suo?

Id, quod agant sine sole suo tua sydera, Cælum:
Id terræ hæc agerent hîc sine sole suo.

Illa suo sine sole suis cæca imbribus essent:
Cæca suis lacrymis hæc sine sole suo.

288. 34. The Greek translation omits lines 4 and 6 of the Latin.
289. MS.
290. MS. The phrase *sine sole suo* (without their sun) appears in every line but the first.

291   *The disciples lament Christ's departure.*

He has gone away. Now o you evils, whichever ones remain to us,
    now keep back those weapons prepared for our deaths.

Keep them back. Those for whom you formerly prepared these weapons,
    [already] have perished at the departure of their Lord.

292   Acts 2:1–19. *On the descent of the Holy Spirit.*

What cloud most sweet brings the golden rain clouds?
    What shining storm drives the gentle rain?

I know. This cloud took away our fires:
    this cloud now returns to us with equal fire.

O kind and mindful cloud! which did not wish us
    to be able to complain of it so harshly any more!

Well done! for by no other dew could the breath
    of heaven be replaced which earth gave just now.

293   Acts 2:1–19. *On the descent of the Holy Spirit.*

Catch, o catch in your bosoms the *grape-harvest of heaven* [which] falls;
    and the holy grape is poured forth from the heavenly heights.

Too happy are [you] by whom such good new wines are drunk;
    into whose bosoms streams the cold and shining downpour!

Behold [your] head! how it sparkles and twinkles with a star of nectar!
    and the living crown rejoices in its rosy locks.

To those—o Gods! who would not be drunk in this way?—
    to those lest they stagger, *their wines give a torch.*

291   *Abscessum Christi queruntur discipuli.*

Ille abiit. jamque ô quæ nos mala cunque manetis,
Sistite jam in nostras tela parata neces.

Sistite. nam quibus hæc vos olim tela paratis,
Abscessu Domini jam periêre sui.

292   *In descensum Spiritûs Sancti.*

Quæ vehit auratos nubes dulcissima nimbos?
Quis mitem pluviam lucidus imber agit?

Agnosco. nostros hæc nubes abstulit ignes:
Hæc nubes in nos jam redit igne pari.

O nubem gratam, & memorem! quæ noluit ultrà
Tam sævè de se nos potuisse queri!

O bene! namque alio non posset rore rependi,
Cælo exhalatum quod modò terra dedit.

293   Act. 2. *In Spiritûs sancti Descensum.*

Ferte sinus, ô ferte: cadit *vindemia cœli;*
Sanctáque ab æthereis volvitur uva jugis.

Felices nimiùm, queîs tam bona musta bibuntur;
In quorum gremium lucida pergit hyems!

En caput! en ut nectareo micat & micat astro!
Gaudet & in roseis viva corona comis!

Illis (ô Superi! quis sic neget ebrìus esse?)
Illis, nè titubent, *dant sua vina faces.*

291. MS.
292. MS. The same cloud which took Christ up is seen as descending with the Holy Spirit.
293. 34. The drunkenness of the apostles, repudiated in verse 15, is the divine inebriation of heavenly love. The torch (line 8) is from the flames of fire (verse 3).

294   Acts 2:1–11. *On the descent of the Holy Spirit.*

Now the clash of heaven thundered round: the violent
storm mixed with flames brought threats of arms.

The cruel Jew shouts: Behold vengeance is coming to the wicked,
behold vengeance is coming mindful of a thunderbolt well-deserved.

But then a gentler fire settles like a peaceful star,
and the friendly flame licks the hair unharmed;

because this seemed to be a false thunderbolt to the Jews,
the thunderbolt was real by its very name.

295   Acts 2:3. *On the Holy Spirit descending with tongues
of fire.*

Away with them who feign pious hearts with a false face,
whom the fiery tongue blesses [even] in their hearts of clay.

My petitions ask this rather, my incense strives [for this],
that I may have a heart of fire, a tongue of clay.

294   *In descensum Spiritûs sancti.*

Jam cœli circùm tonuit fragor: arma, minásque
Turbida cum flammis mista ferebat hyems.

Exclamat Judæus atrox; Venit ecce nefandis,
Ecce venit meriti fulminis ira memor.

Verùm ubi composito sedit fax blandior astro,
Flammáque non læsas lambit amica comas;

Judæis, fulmen quia falsum apparuit esse,
Hoc ipso verum nomine fulmen erat.

294   Οὐρανοῦ ἐκτύπησε βρόμος· πόλεμον καὶ ἀπειλὰς
      Ἦγε τρέχων ἄνεμος σὺν φλογὶ σμερδαλέῃ.

Αὖεν ᾿Ιουδαῖος. μιαρὰ στυγερῶν τὰ κάρηνα
     ᾿Εφθασε τῆς ὀργῆς τὸ πρέπον οὐρανίης.

᾿Αλλὰ γαληναίῳ ὅτε κεῖται ἥσυχον ἄστρῳ
     Φλέγμα, καὶ ἀβλήτους λεῖχε φιλὸν πλοκαμούς,

᾿Εκθαμβεῖ. ὅτι γὰρ κείνοις οὔκ ἦεν ἀληθής,
     Νυνὶ ἐτεὸν διότι τῷδε κεραυνὸς ἔη.

295   *In Sanctum igneis linguis descendentem Spiritum.*

Absint, qui ficto simulant pia pectora vultu,
Ignea quos luteo pectore lingua beat.

Hoc potius mea vota rogant, mea thura petessunt,
Ut mihi sit mea mens ignea, lingua luti.

294. 34.
295. MS.

296   Acts 5:15. *The shadow of St. Peter cures the sick.*

Cheerfully they gather—*yes, yes, it is pleasing to go beneath his shadows*—
and the *shade* prevents them from becoming *shades*—can you believe it?

O powerful shadow of Peter! what miracles does it not perform?
Now too, O Pope, that [shadow] sustains your glory.

297   Acts 5:15. *The sick man begs for St. Peter's shadow.*

Peter, let me hide a little while under your shadow, Peter:
thus my fates will seek me and not find me.

Your shadow will let me be able to see my sun
and my light will be thus the shadow of your shadow.

298   Acts 7:54–60. *To the Jewish slaughterers of Stephen.*

In vain do the hurtling stones mock at him, in vain: not even
the harsh tempest—alas how savage!—of a hailstorm harms him.

He can bear those things; he can disregard them: but those
which are in your heart, those stones harm him.

299   Acts 7:54–60. *To the Jewish slaughterers of St. Stephen.*

Why do you give your anger to the unwilling stones, ah wretched ones?
Why do you hurl so many into this tragic task?

Unwilling they give themselves to Stephen's death; but
of their own will they make his tomb after he is slain.

296   Act. 5:15. *Umbra S. Petri medetur ægrotis.*

Conveniunt alacres (*sic, sic juvat ire sub umbras*)
Atque *umbras* fieri (creditis?) *umbra* vetat.

O Petri umbra potens! quæ non miracula præstat?
Nunc quoque, Papa, tuum sustinet illa decus.

297   Act. 5. *Æger implorat umbram D. Petri.*

Petre, tua lateam paulisper (Petre) sub umbra:
Sic mea me quærent fata, nec invenient.

Umbra dabit tua posse meum me cernere solem;
Et mea lux umbræ sic erit umbra tuæ.

298   Act. 7:16. *Ad Judæos mactatores Stephani.*

Frustra illum increpitant, frustra vaga saxa: nec illi
Grandinis (heu sævæ!) dura procella nocet.

Ista potest tolerare; potest nescire: sed illi,
Quæ sunt in vestro pectore, saxa nocent.

299   Act. 7. *Ad Judæos mactatores S. Stephani.*

Quid datis (ah miseri!) saxis nolentibus iras?
Quid nimis in tragicum præcipitatis opus?

In mortem Stephani se dant invita: sed illi
Occiso faciunt sponte suâ tumulum.

---

296. 34. The epigram turns on the benificent power of darkness.
297. 34. See "The sicke implore," No. 52.
298. 34.
299. 34.*

300   Acts 7:54–60. *St. Stephen to his friends preparing*
a funeral for him.

I pray let no marbles rise for my tomb: these stones
which knew my death may be my tomb.

Thus it will not be necessary for anyone to mark this tomb with a verse
(saying) *he died for his Master.*

Let this tomb be mine, which death itself gave [me]; and
let this be a *witness* of my *witness.*

301   Acts. 7:54–60. *To the crown of Stephen.*

Behold your stones! There is nothing more precious than those
whether they give a value to your head or take [one] from it.

Of course this is the reason for your diadem: this is
why it is right for you to wear a crown in your hair.

However valueless each stone is in itself,
by so much will it be the more costly jewel for your head.

302   Acts 8:18. *He offered them money.*

To what end do you offer these coins here? Why, wicked Simon?
That is not *Judas* here, but *Peter* is with you.

Did you wish *to buy God?* Rather, I pray, do this, Simon,
if you can, you yourself first *sell your demon.*

300   Act. 7. S. *Stephanus amicis suis, funus sibi curantibus.*

Nulla (precor) busto surgant mihi marmora: bustum
Hæc mihi sint mortis conscia saxa meæ.

Sic nec opus fuerit, notet ut quis carmine bustum,
Pro Domino (dicens) *occidit ille suo.*

Hic mihi sit tumulus, quem mors dedit ipsa; meíque
Ipse hic *martyrii* sit mihi *martyrium.*

301   Εἰς τὸν τοῦ Στεφάνου στέφανον.

Ecce tuos lapides! nihil est pretiosius illis;
Seu pretium capiti dent, capiantᵛe tuo.

Scilicet hæc ratio vestri diadematis: hoc est,
Unde coronatis vos decet ire comis.

Quisque lapis quantò magis in se vilis habetur,
Ditior hôc capiti est gemma futura tuo.

302   Act. 8:18. *Obtulit eis pecunias.*

Quorsum hos hîc nummos profers? quorsum, impie Simon?
Non ille hîc *Judas,* sed tibi *Petrus* adest.

Vis *emisse Deum?* potiùs (precor) hoc age, Simon,
Si potes, ipse priùs *dæmona vende tuum.*

---

300. 34.* *Martyrium* means both "witness" and "martyr"; one who witnesses (or testifies) be-
comes a martyr.
301. MS.* *Stephanos* means "crown."
302. 34.

303   Acts 8:26–39. *The Ethiopian washed.*

The *black* man comes forth from the holy waves—how well washed!
Indeed it was not in vain *to wash an Ethiopian.*

What a snow-white heart the shadow of pitch-black skin will protect!
Now the holy Dove will wish even a black house.

304   Acts 9:3–9. *On Saul blinded by too much light.*

What are these shades of light? what is this night of day?
A new night which the shadow of too much light makes!

Whether Saul was blind I can scarcely say;
I do know this, that Saul was *captured by light.*

305   Acts 9:3–9. *On St. Paul at once enlightened
and blinded.*

Christ, what twofold glory of a *double weapon* do you have
which at once takes his eyes from him and gives them?

A holy day of the soul was lurking in this night of the eyes;
so that Paul could see you, he was blind.

306   Acts 9:29. *The Greek disputants plot death for St. Paul.*

Hurrah for argument! *thus he disputes:* Hurrah for the sophist!
Yes it was right for him so to clench the fist of Logic.

What does this argument prove against the case, little Greek?
It proves that you can prove nothing against the case.

303   Act. 8. *Æthiops lotus.*

Ille *niger* sacris exit (quàm lautus!) ab undis:
  Nec frustra *Æthiopem* nempe *lavare* fuit.

Mentem quàm niveam piceæ cutis umbra fovebit!
  Jam *volet & nigros sancta Columba lares.*

304   Act. 9:3. *In Saulum fulgore nimio excæcatum.*

Quæ lucis tenebræ? quæ nox est ista diei?
  Nox nova, quam nimii luminis umbra facit!

An Saulus fuerit cæcus, vix dicere possum;
  Hoc scio, quòd *captus lumine* Saulus erat.

305   Act. 9. *In D. Paulum illuminatum simul & excæcatum.*

Quæ, Christe, ambigua hæc *bifidi* tibi gloria *teli* est,
  Quod simul huic oculos abstulit, atque dedit?

Sancta dies animi, hac oculorum in nocte, latebat;
  Te ut possit Paulus cernere, cæcus erat.

306   Act. 9:29. *Græci disputatores Divo Paulo mortem*
                         machinantur.

Euge argumentum! *sic disputat:* euge sophista!
  Sic pugnum Logices stringere, sic decuit.

Hoc argumentum in causam quid (Græcule) dicit?
  Dicit, te in causam dicere posse nihil.

---

303. 34. See "On the baptized Æthiopian," No. 53 (and in the Secular Poems, "Upon the faire Ethiopian," No. 363). The successful washing of the Ethiopian in baptism may be compared with Pilate's unsuccessful washing. The futility of washing an Ethiopian was proverbial (Jeremiah 13:23; Tilley, *Proverbs,* E 186).

304. 34.

305. 34.

306. 34. Martin (p. 430) refers to an epigram of John Owen in which the clenched fist is the symbol of logic, the open hand that of rhetoric.

307   Acts 10:39.

What evil man hung life on the stump of death?
O poor farmer! was this [good] grafting?

Nay, who hung death on this tree of life?
O good farmer! this was [good] grafting.

308   Acts 12:1–2. *To Herod slaying St. James.*

You do not know how much James owes you for this blow.
and how your anger raged against his sacred head.

Surely you gave him a crown with this very sword,
with which sword you had cut off his sacred head.

What could fully pay for a cut-off head
was only this crown so savage and sacred.

309   Acts 12:3–7. *The chains fall off voluntarily.*

You who covered Peter with irons, heartless keeper,
will learn from your iron to be more gentle.

Lo it softened, and relaxed its own bonds without asking:
Go, ninny, and *put chains on your chains.*

307   Act. x:39.

Quis malus appendit de mortis stipite vitam?
O malus Agricola! hoc inseruisse fuit?

Immò quis appendit vitæ hac ex arbore mortem?
O bonus Agricola! hoc inseruisse fuit.

308   *Herodi D. Jacobum obtruncanti.*

Nescis Jacobus quantum hunc tibi debeat ictum
Quæque tua in sacrum sæviit ira caput.

Scilicet ipso illi donâsti hoc ense coronam,
Quo sacrum abscideras scilicet ense caput.

Abscissum pensare caput quæ possit abundè,
Sola hæc tam sæva & sacra corona fuit.

308   "Εν μὲν, 'Ιάκωβε, κεφαλὴν τοι ξίφος ἀπῆρεν,
       "Εν τόδε καὶ στέφανον ξίφος ἔδωκε τεόν.

Μοῦνον ἀμείβεσθαι κεφαλήν, 'Ιάκωβε, δύναιτο
Κεῖνος ὁδ' ὡς καλὸς μαρτυρίου στέφανος.

309   Act. 12. *Vincula sponte decidunt.*

Qui ferro Petrum cumulas, durissime custos,
A ferro disces mollior esse tuo.

Ecce fluit, nodisque suis evolvitur ultro:
I fatue, & *vinc'lis vincula pone tuis.*

307. MS.
308. 70. The Greek translates the two final distichs of the Latin.
309. 34.

310   Acts 12:6–7. *On St. Peter set free by the Angel.*

Death and Herod draw nigh to you, when the winged messenger
brings joys which you think dreams are bringing.

What so great a thing did he give you, I ask? He loosed the chains.
Death and Herod, would they not have given the same to you?

311   Acts 12:7–10. *On the chains of Peter, fallen away*
voluntarily, and the open doors.

Iron does not remember to be iron: the chains
dissimulate for Peter: the prison knows not that it has doors.

How very free will he be *whom the prison frees! whom*
the chains themselves *set loose,* how very safe will he be.

312   Acts 12:10. *On the doors opening for St. Peter*
of their own will.

What did it avail to have closed those doors, good doorman?
It is even apparent now that they are their own *keys* for Peter.

You say they open of their own will: but clearly this very fact is Peter's
key: that Peter has no need at all of a key.

313   Acts 12:22–23. *On Herod, eaten of worms.*

He is *God, God:* this is the shout of the people as one:
only the worms (base tribe) say they refuse to believe it.

But quickly the wretches quickly now confess they have erred.
They taste the flesh, they think [it] *ambrosia.*

310   Act. 12:6, 7. *In D. Petrum ab Angelo solutum.*

Mors tibi, & Herodes instant: cùm nuncius ales
Gaudia fert, quæ tu somnia ferre putas.

Quid tantum dedit ille (rogo) tibi? Vincula solvit.
Mors tibi, & Herodes nonne dedisset idem?

311 Act. 12. *In vincula Petro sponte delapsa, & apertas fores.*

Ferri non meminit ferrum: se vincula Petro
Dissimulant: nescit carcer habere fores.

Quàm bene liber erit, *carcer quem liberat!* ipsa
Vincula quem solvunt, quàm bene tutus erit!

312   Act. 12. *In fores Divo Petro sponte apertas.*

Quid juvit clausisse fores (bone janitor) istas?
Et Petro *claves* jam liquet esse suas.

Dices, Sponte patent: Petri ergò hoc scilicet ipsum
Est clavis, Petro clave quòd haud opus est.

313   Act. 12:23. In Herodem σκωληκόβρωτον.

Ille *Deus, Deus:* hæc populi vox unica: tantùm
(Vile genus) vermes credere velle negant.

At citò se miseri, citò nunc errâsse fatentur;
Carnes degustant, *Ambrosiám*que putant.

310. MS.
311. 34.
312. 34. To Peter Christ gave the keys of the kingdom of heaven (Matthew 16:19).
313. 34. The acclamation of Herod here and in the next epigram is to be contrasted with that of Paul at epigram 315.

314   Acts 12:22–23.

Hurrah, a *God!* on all sides the people roar with full applause.
Surely the voice does not bespeak a man. Hurrah, a God!

But yet what [sort of] god he may be, you tell us, worms
you are the crowd intimate with him; he cherishes you in his bosom.

315 Acts 14:8–18. *The people of Lystra worship St. Paul,
healing the lame man with a word, as Mercury.*

What Tagus is this, what new wave of Pactolus rolls forth?
This is not the voice of a man: *he is a God, a God.*

Hail, honored too greatly for a mortal dwelling!
A son worthy of God, worthy of God the thunderer.

O hail! but why, kind sir, did you want to hide your [virtues]?
Surely indeed your tongue proclaims you a God.

I do not wonder at all at this praise: *A man deserves to be considered
who persuaded a lame man to have swift feet.* [eloquent

316   Acts 16:21. *They teach customs, which are not
lawful for us to receive, being Romans.*

O Rome, have your Caesar and his weapons given you this? Is it
therefore *not permitted* to the Romans alone to be pious?

Ah better that for you no Caesar in tragic arms
high on a panting horse had thundered,

314   Act. 12:23.

Euge Deus! (pleno populus fremit undique plausu.)
Certè non hominem vox sonat. euge Deus!

Sed tamen iste Deus qui sit, vos dicite, vermes,
Intima turba illi; vos fovet ille sinu.

315   Act. 14. D. Paulum, verbo sanantem claudum, pro
Mercurio Lystres adorant.

Quis Tagus hic, quæ Pactoli nova volvitur unda?
Non hominis vox est hæc: Deus ille, Deus.

Salve, mortales nimiùm dignate penates!
Digna Deo soboles, digna tonante Deo!

O salve! quid enim (alme) tuos latuisse volebas?
Te dicit certè vel tua lingua Deum.

Laudem hanc haud miror: Meruit facundus haberi,
Qui claudo promptos suasit habere pedes.

316   Act. 16:21. Annunciant ritus, quos non licet
nobis suscipere, cùm simus Romani.

Hoc Cæsar tibi (Roma) tuus dedit, armáque? solis
Romanis igitur non licet esse piis?

Ah, meliùs, tragicis nullus tibi Cæsar in armis
Altus anhelanti detonuisset equo;

314. MS. See notes to preceding and following poems.
315. 34. The Tagus (in Spain) and the Pactolus (in Asia Minor) were famed for their golden sands; Crashaw cites these two wonders from West and East to show the extent of Paul's miracle. Mercury, pictured with winged feet, would naturally have given a lame man "swift feet."

And that the symbol *of your master's bird* feared throughout the world
was not wont to come fiercely on your standards:

How sad that a triumph should remain for you over yourself, Rome,
that because of such great ambition you should become *nothing*.

You conquer not for yourself but for crime: what a sad laurel [wreath]!
A laurel? [rather] a shade more suited to the locks of Cerberus!

Scarcely does Father Pluto himself in his crown so repulsive,
scarcely does he seat himself so black on his throne.

From so many triumphs of Caesar this remains for you, Rome:
you are *Caesar's* or (what is the same) you are *egregiously* wretched.

317   Acts 17:16–34. *On the real Athenian.*

You know the very bridal chambers of nature and the deepest bonds
of things, and whatever the first shadows do;

why the withdrawing sea hesitates, why the wandering stars revolve;
but Christ is a theme foreign to your studies.

To know in this way is, in short, not to know those things more verbosely.
Who merely knows those things alone, does not know even them.

318   Acts 19:12. *From his body were brought [unto the sick]*
handkerchiefs, etc.

Linens touched by the hand of Paul imperiously overcome diseases
and bind fast the harsh bonds of death.

Whence comes this praise and glory for blessed flax?
These strands, I believe, were from the *distaff of Lachesis.*

Nec *domini volucris* facies horrenda per orbem   5
  Sueta tibi in signis torva venire tuis:

Quàm miser ut staret de te tibi (Roma) triumphus,
  Ut tantâ fieres ambitione *nihil.*

Non tibi, sed sceleri vincis: proh laurea tristis!
  Laurea, Cerbereis aptior umbra comis!   10

Tam turpi vix ipse pater diademate Pluto,
  Vix sedet ipse suo tam niger in solio.

De tot Cæsareis redit hoc tibi (Roma) triumphis:
  Cæsareè, aut (quod idem est) *egregiè* misera es.

317   Act. 17. *In Atheniensem merum.*

Ipsos naturæ thalamos sapis, imaque rerum
  Concilia, & primæ quicquid agunt tenebræ.

Quid dubitet refluum mare. quid vaga sydera volvant.
  Christus at est studiis res aliena tuis.

Sic scire, est tantùm nescire loquaciùs illa.
  Qui nempe illa sapit sola, nec illa sapit.

318   Act. 19:12. *Deferebantur à corpore ejus sudaria, &c.*

Imperiosa premunt morbos, & ferrea fati
  Jura ligant, Pauli lintea tacta manu.

Unde hæc felicis laus est & gloria lini?
  Hæc (reor) è *Lachesis* pensa fuêre *colo.*

---

316. 34. Caesar's bird was the eagle of his legions.

317. MS.* Martin (p. 453): The title "seems to have been suggested by Juvenal, Sat. vi. 187 where *mera Cecropis* [i.e. a mere Cecropian, or a pure Athenian] . . . is applied not to a native of Athens but to [a foreigner who assumes] Athenian characteristics."

318. 34. Lachesis was the classical Fate who assigned to a man his fate.

319   Acts 21:13. *I am ready not to be bound only*
                 but also to die.

I shall endure not only prison but also death for thee, o Christ,
   Paul said, practiced in the art of clever double-meanings.
                                            [*bound* for you,
He might say this otherwise: I shall be ready not only to be willing *to be*
      o Christ, but also indeed *to be set free.**

* Philippians 1:23. having a desire to depart.

320   Acts 21:13. *For I* [*am ready*] *not to be bound only, etc.*

Why do you throw out death [as an object fit] for our fear? why chains?
   There is no fear in them, nor comes my fear from that.

      The chains I would fear are the chains of fear alone:
      The only death I must fear is to have feared to die.

321   Acts 26:28. *Almost thou persuadest me*
                 to be a Christian.

   Almost? What is this *almost?* a harsh nearness to salvation!
      O how evil you are in the proximity to good!
                                       [*shipwrecked;*
   Ah! he who perishes with the harbor [to] *witness it, he is twice*
      not so much the sea as his own land overcomes him.

These hopes which are *barely* out of reach are *more cruelly* out of reach:
   I was almost happy is the declaration of an unhappy man.

319   Act. 21:13. *Non solùm vinciri sed & mori paratus sum.*

Non modò vincla, sed & mortem tibi, Christe, subibo,
  Paulus ait, docti callidus arte doli.

Diceret hoc aliter: Tibi non modò velle *ligari,*
  Christe, sed & **solvi* nempe paratus ero.

* Phil. 1:23. τὴν ἐπιθυμίαν ἔχων εἰς τὸ ἀναλύσαι.

320   Act. 21. *Nam ego non solum vinciri—&c.*

Quid mortem objicitis nostro, quid vinêla timori?
  Non timor est illinc, non timor inde meus.

Vincula, quæ timeam, sunt vincula sola timoris:
  Sola timenda mihi est mors, timuisse mori.

321   Act. 26:28. *Penè persuades mihi ut fiam Christianus.*

Penè? quid hoc *penè* est? Vicinia sæva salutis!
  O quàm tu malus es proximitate boni!

Ah! portu qui teste perit, bis naufragus ille est;
  Hunc non tam pelagus, quàm sua terra premit.

Quæ nobis spes *vix* absunt, *crudeliùs* absunt:
  Penè fui felix, Emphasis est miseri.

319. 34. Milhaupt (p. 92): "Latin *solvi* . . . has two meanings: to release, and to die. Cf. Andrewes (II, 350–51): 'First, by *solvite,* that is, dissolving, is meant death. . . . Second upon the loosing the soul from the body, . . . there follows an universal loosening of all the bonds and knots here.' "
320. MS. See "I am ready," No. 54.
321. 34. The third line is distinguished because it is a Latin proverb.

322   Acts 28:3.

Paul, fear nothing. This viper does not bear venom:
he wants to study the goodness of your hand.

He brings kisses not bites; as a suppliant, not an enemy.
He comes not to be feared but rather to be pitied.

323   *To St. Luke, the physician.*

I ask you for no medicines for me, Luke,
even though you yourself may be a doctor and I may be sick.

Indeed, while I hold you as my example of faith,
you, doctor, you yourself are my medicine for me.

324   *On St. Luke the physician.*

This life, which my sins make wretched for me,
this life, Physician, your remedy makes long.

Is this to have lived for a long time? Believe me, this is not
to have lived for a long time but to have feared for a long time to die.

322   **Acts 28:3.**

> Paule, nihil metuas. non fert hæc vipera virus:
> Virtutem vestræ vult didicisse manûs.

> Oscula, non morsus; supplex, non applicat hostis.
> Nec metuenda venit, sed miseranda magìs.

323   *Ad D. Lucam medicum.*

> Nulla mihi (Luca) de te medicamina posco,
> Ipse licèt medicus sis, licèt æger ego:

> Quippe ego in exemplum fidei dum te mihi pono,
> Tu, medice, ipse mihi es tu medicina mea.

323   'Ουδὲν ἐγώ, Λουκᾶ, παρά σου μοι φάρμακον αἰτῶ,
>   Κᾶν σὺ δ' ἰατρὸς ἔης, κᾶν με ἐγὼ νοσερός.

> 'Αλλ' ἐν ὅσῳ παράδειγμα πέλεις μοι πίστιος, αὐτός,
>   Αὐτὸς ἰατρὸς, ἐμοὶ γ' ἐσσὶ ἀκεστορίη.

324   *In S. Lucam Medicum.*

> Hanc, mihi quam miseram faciunt mea crimina vitam,
> Hanc, medici, longam vestra medela facit.

> Hocné diu est vixisse? diu (mihi credite) non est
> Hoc vixisse; diu sed timuisse mori.

322. MS.

323. 34. This and the following epigram were written for St. Luke's Day (October 18), but as they fit into no historical sequence they are placed here at the end of Acts, Luke's second treatise. The reference to Luke as a physician is Colossians 4:14; see also Luke 4:23 (a unique record).

324. MS. See note to preceding poem. For another comment on bitter drugs see the secular "On taking Physicke," No. 370; see the epigram on the Innocents, "[In felices Martyres]," No. 115, for a comparable view of a long life.

You, dear physician, offer cures in your leaves
even for bitter drugs (which are the greatest evils)

This is to avoid death well: to avoid by enduring.
And to have lived for a long time is this: quickly to be able to die.

325   Revelation 1:9–10. *St. John in exile.*

An Exile is he [who was the] *Love of Christ:* yet the exile found Christ:
even there he has found his familiar bosom.

Ah, point out to us the lands for a long, ah an endless
exile, if the bosom of Christ is the exile.

326   *To Domitian. About St. John at the Lateran gate.*

Is it true you would go unpunished? But still you shall not go unpunished,
having dared so to dishonor me and my gods.

Burn him in oil, Lictor. The lictor prepares to burn him in oil:
but the one whom the lictor believed to be burned was anointed.

Thus also did the slipperiness of oil fail you?
Is it thus that your Pallas helps you, Domitian?

327   *On St. John whom Domitian put in boiling oil*
           (unharmed).

That fire—which running in a flickering flame through the whole world
is not indeed called John, but *Love* itself—

Is it that fire you are struggling to put out, good Domitian?
To *give* it *oil* is not [the way], Domitian.

Tu foliis, Medice alme, tuis medicamina præbes,
Et medicaminibus (quæ mala summa) malis.

Hoc mortem bene vitare est; vitare ferendo.
Et vixisse diu est hoc; citò posse mori.

325   Rev. 1:9. *D. Joannes in exilio.*

Exul, *Amor Christi* est: Christum tamen invenit exul:
Et solitos illìc invenit ille sinus.

Ah longo, æterno ah terras indicite nobis
Exilio, Christi si sinus exilium est.

326   *Domitiano. De S. Johanne ad portam Lat.*

Ergò ut inultus eas? Sed nec tamen ibis inultus,
Sic violare ausus meque, meosque Deos.

Ure oleo, Lictor. Oleo parat urere Lictor:
Sed quem uri Lictor credidit, unctus erat.

Te quoque sic olei virtus malefida fefellit?
Sic tua te Pallas, Domitiane, juvat?

327   *In D. Joannem, quem Domitianus ferventi oleo*
                        (illæsum) indidit.

Illum (qui, toto currens vaga flammula mundo,
Non quidem Joannes, ipse sed audit *amor*)

Illum ignem extingui, bone Domitiane, laboras?
Hoc non est *oleum*, Domitiane, *dare.*

325. 34. For John in Christ's bosom see John 13:23. See also "Sancto Joanni, dilecto discipulo," No. 249.

326. MS. This and the following epigrams have no Scriptural authority but are based on the tradition of the early Church (*Catholic Encyclopedia* quoting Tertullian). They are placed here (like those on Luke) in conjunction with the appropriate book of the Bible. Martin (p. 454): "*tua* Pallas [*your* Pallas] . . . because Domitian affected a special cult of Minerva [her Roman counterpart] . . . , and . . . because Pallas was the creator of the olive tree [and hence of oil]." Milhaupt (p. 241) explains *unctus* (anointed) as an allusion to wrestlers who oiled themselves to prevent their opponents from holding them.

327. 34.

328
On the day of all saints.
Revelation 7:3. *Hurt not the earth, neither the sea,*
nor the trees till we have sealed the servants of our God
in their foreheads.

Nowhere let the harsh wind vent its roars; nowhere
let the forest tremble with its curly hair ruffled.

May gentle Thetis peacefully gliding along bear kisses to the Earth;
may the friendly earth open its embrace to Thetis:

Everywhere may golden peace, poured forth, fly on holy wings,
until each good brow has been marked by its own sign.

Ah, why must signs be sought from elsewhere thus?
It is enough that each good brow has been marked by its own tears.

329
On the heavenly company of all the saints.

Happy souls! whom virtue, owed to heaven,
has now introduced to your heavenly realms.

The unsparing use of [your] distinguished blood gave this [reward],
and [your] hope which has overflowed your paths [full of] obstructions.

O spring! o ever golden fields of long light!
day not cut in half by alternating night!

O what a *palm* smiles in your hand! what a *crown* on your brow!
O *whiteness* of virginal toga not to be sullied!

There you see the faces of unfailing peace:
You see the eyes of the sweet Lamb: you—*But what do I do?*

328   *In diem omnium Sanctorum.*
Rev. 7:3. *Nè lædite terram, neque mare, neque arbores,*
quousque obsignaverimus servos Dei nostri
in frontibus suis.

Nusquam immîtis agat ventus sua murmura; nusquam
   Sylva tremat, crispis sollicitata comis.

Æqua Thetis placidè allabens ferat oscula Terræ;
   Terra suos Thetidi pandat amica sinus:

Undique Pax effusa piis volet aurea pennis,
   Frons bona dum signo est quæque notata suo.

Ah quid in hoc opus est signis aliunde petendis?
   Frons bona sat lacrymis quæque notata suis.

329   *In cœtum cœlestem omnium Sanctorum.*

Felices animæ! quas cœlo debita virtus
   Jam potuit vestris inseruisse polis.

Hoc dedit egregii non parcus sanguinis usus,
   Spésque per obstantes expatiata vias.

O ver! ô longæ semper seges aurea lucis!
   Nocte nec alternâ dimidiata dies!

O quæ *palma* manu ridet! quæ fronte *corona!*
   O *nix* virgineæ non temeranda togæ!

Pacis inocciduæ vos illîc ora videtis:
   Vos Agni dulcis lumina: vos—*Quid ago?*

---

328. 34. The text is from the Epistle for All Saints Day (November 1).
329. 34. This epigram is perhaps the high point of Crashaw's personal intrusion into what are
corporate actions. It is a little startling to discover the poet asserting himself in this context.

330   Revelation 12:7.

To arms, men! You starry princes lead the heavenly
throng in any rank you wish. To arms, men!

Let every hand stand by its arrows (unaccustomed to them as it is),
let it stand by the cruelly flashing gleam of its sword.

The Dragon is at hand in full force and grows in size in his total wrath.
And the Dragon brings whatever indeed the Dragon can bring.

What shapes there are with him (the evil offspring of deepest night)!
How many black gods he leads with him into battle!

Now he makes ready to fight—how cruel! and now he fights. and lo
scarcely could I say *he fights*. Now he has fallen.

Ah still it is too much that he added wraths to these brows;
that he could plant wrinkles on these cheeks.

This is a savage glory and the fierceness of haughty fate:
the fact that the death of great sin was also great:

that, though beaten, he may not lie contemptible in the victory:
that it deserved to be a labor of much lightning;

that he could say this among his flames,
I bore arms in vain: but still I bore arms.

331   Revelation 12:9. *On the Dragon falling.*

Go, vainly ferocious beast; far off the golden stars
now very safe in their sky are laughing at your threats.

Were you, then, getting ready to go above the starry sky?
There is no need for such a long climb to the pit.

330   Apocal. xii:7.

Arma, viri! (ætheriam quocunque sub ordine pubem
    Siderei proceres ducitis) Arma viri!

Quæque suis, (nec queîs solita est) stet dextra sagittis,
    Stet gladii sævâ luce corusca sui.

Totus adest, totisque movet se major in iris.   5
    Fertque Draco, quicquid vel Draco ferre potest.

Quas secum facies (imæ mala pignora noctis)!
    Quot secum nigros ducit in arma Deos!

Jam pugnas parat (heu sævus!) jam pugnat. & ecce
    Vix potui, *Pugnat,* dicere. jam cecidit.   10

His tamen ah nimium est quòd frontibus addidit iras;
    Quòd potuit rugas his posuisse genis:

Hoc torvum decus est, tumidique ferocia fati,
    Quòd magni sceleris mors quoque magna fuit.

Quòd neque, si victus, jaceat victoria vilis: 15
    Quòd meruit multi fulminis esse labor.

Quòd queat ille suas hoc inter dicere flammas,
    Arma tuli frustra; sed tamen arma tuli.

331   Rev. 12:9. *In Draconem præcipitem.*

I Frustra truculente; tuas procul aurea rident
    Astra minas, cœlo jam bene tuta suo.

Túne igitur cœlum super ire atque astra parabas?
    Ascensu tanto non opus ad barathrum.

---

330. MS. Grosart (II, lxxxvii) calls attention to this poem as "very Miltonic." It retains for
Satan a heroism in folly which does suggest one way of approaching *Paradise Lost.* This view
is expressed in Crashaw's poems only in these lines; they do not seem to be ironic.
331. 34.*

332   *Faith which alone justifies, does not exist
without hope and love.*

Martin (pp. 425–26) traces the title and the poem to a *cause célèbre* in
June 1634 at Cambridge when Crashaw's friend, John Tournay, preached a
sermon which seemed "to avouch the insufficiency of faith to justification, and
to impugn the doctrine of our 11th article" of the Thirty-nine Articles.

For neither does it exist so *alone*. O what bitter critic
maliciously denies the closely joined hands on the common scepters.
Take away Faith; the name of Love will do nothing nor shall it now even
[be [the name of Love]:
And either it shall be, or what will Faith do without Love?
But profane Love, Go, die; go through the great shades, dear boy:
not so vain is thy spirit in Elysian places.
How good that your *quiver* truly excels this, and [*your*] *bow*.
Lest there should be no pyre for you in the last funeral piles,
How good that your *fire* truly provides these torches for you
which you can bear to your funeral rites!
You are cruel, ah, you whoever break such sweet chains;
which bind and by which Love himself is bound.
O cruel separation of the well-united sisters
who held their hands so closely entwined!
For who so different live in such mutual flesh?
Or where are those two who are so nearly one and the same?
They encompass each other in each other's arms,
without and above, below and within they go.
Not as does the persistent Nymph, now entwined with Bacchus her
[tree-husband; [she]
hides the vigorous wines in her curving branches.
After her mate has been taken, indeed the turtledove keeps her moanings
and bitterly lives in the manner of a widow.
But let Love be taken from Faith: she will not mourn,
she will not be impatient or ill: *now she will die.*
Did the palm tree, from whom harsh winter far off stole the shade of her
forthwith stretch out on her young face?   [mate,
She turned her head full circle and nodded to all the winds,
as if the breeze would ruffle her husband's hair.

332   *Fides quæ sola justificat, non est sine*
                Spe & Dilectione.

Crashaw is not interested in the usual controversy of faith or works but in the impossibility of separating Hope and Love from Faith—a theological point on which there is little dispute.

Nam neque tam *sola* est. O quis malè censor amarus
    Tam socias negat in mutua sceptra manus?
Deme Fidem; nec aget, nec erit jam nomen Amoris:
    Et vel erit, vel aget quid sine Amore Fides?
Ergò Amor, I, morere; I magnas, Puer alme, per umbras: 5
    Elysiis non tam numen inane locis.
O bene, quòd *pharetra* hoc saltem tua præstat & *arcus*,
    Nè tibi in extremos sit pyra nulla rogos!
O bene, quòd tuus has saltem tibi providet *ignis*,
    In tua quas possis funera ferre, faces!   10
Durus es, ah, quisquis tam dulcia vincula solvis;
    Quæ ligat, & quibus est ipse ligatus Amor.
O bene junctarum divortia sæva sororum,
    Tam penitus mixtas quæ tenuêre manus!
Nam quæ (tam varia) in tam mutua viscera vivunt?   15
    Aut ubi, quæ duo sunt, tam propè sunt eadem?
Alternis sese circùm amplectuntur in ulnis:
    Extráque & suprà, subter & intus eunt.
Non tam Nympha tenax, Baccho jam mista marito,
    Abdidit in liquidos mascula vina sinus.   20
Compare jam dempto, saltem sua murmura servat
    Turtur; & in viduos vivit amara modos.
At Fidei sit demptus Amor; non illa dolebit,
    Non erit impatiens, ægráque: *jam moritur.*
Palma, marem cui tristis hyems procul abstulit umbram,   25
    Protinus in viridem procubuit faciem?
Undique circumfert caput, omnibus annuit Euris;
    Siqua maritalem misceat aura comam:

Fides quæ sola justificat. 48.
    19 *Nympha tenax:* Ariadne, wife of Bacchus.

Ah poor thing, she waits long and dies slowly
and at last is stripped of all her leaves.
But without Love, Faith does not continue
to live long enough so that one may say Faith is going to die.
She is now already dead: unless [you imagine that] at last
this bodily house, with the soul gone, is not dead.
If you take this soul of Love from this body of Faith,
then your Faith is indeed *alone* but sadly *alone*.
From this Hector whom the chariot of Achilles even now knows,
would you hope for that Hector whom his father recently knew?
Do you call these sad bits of skin, the pieces of Oetaean madness,
foolishly by the name and deeds of Hercules?
Or will this grim sad corpse of Faith
be enough against these monsters of evils, more than Nemaean.
Yes, Love itself desires Faith even as his own loves;
thus in Love Faith itself acknowledges Faith.

Therefore

That Faith which *alone* takes pride in an empty court,
whom Hope despairs of, whom Love will not love;
this Faith *alone* so sadly, so desolately alone (because it is near us)
alone let it be as long as it may.   [*alone*.
[Faith] which is *alone* apart from its friends, apart also from itself, is
Let me not have Faith which is much too much to itself.

Ah misera, expectat longùm, lentúmque expirat,
 Et demum totis excutitur foliis.   30
At sine Amore Fides, nec tantum vivere perstat
 Quo dici possit vel moritura Fides.
Mortua jam nunc est: nisi demum mortua non est
 Corporea hæc, animâ deficiente, domus.
Corpore ab hoc Fidei hanc animam si demis Amoris,   35
 Jam tua *sola* quidem est, sed malè *sola* Fides.
Hectore ab hoc, currus quem jam nunc sentit Achillis,
 Hectora eum speres quem modò sensit herus?
Tristes exuvias, Oetæi frusta furoris,
 (Vanus) in Alcidæ nomen & acta vocas?   40
Vel satis in monstra hæc, plùs quàm Nemeæa, malorum
 Hoc Fidei torvum & triste cadaver erit?
Immo, Fidem usquè suos velut ipse Amor ardet amores;
 Sic in Amore fidem comprobat ipsa Fides.

ERGO

Illa Fides vacua quæ *sola* superbiet aulâ,   45
 Quam Spes desperet, quam nec amabit Amor;
Sola Fides hæc, tam miserè, tam desolatè
 Sola, (quod ad nos est) *sola* sit usque licet.
A sociis quæ *sola* suis, à se quoque *sola* est.
 Quæ sibi tam nimia est, sit mihi nulla Fides.   50

37–38 *Hectore . . . Hectora:* Crashaw draws a contrast between the dead Hector at the wheels of Achilles' chariot and the heroic Hector.

39 *exuvias, Oetæi:* Hercules (grandson of Alcaeus), poisoned by the coat of Nessus, tore it off his body, tearing off at the same time much of his own skin; he then mounted his funeral pyre atop Mount Oeta whence he was translated to heaven.

41 *monstra . . . Nemeæa:* Hercules destroyed the fierce Nemean lion as the first of his twelve labors.

333   *Baptism does not take away future sins.*

You, who were but recently that child Achilles whom your
    prudent *mother** dipped into the waters of the heavenly Styx,
        are sent forth from there healed but not free from danger:
            you still live unprotected against new wounds.
A thousand ways lie open; and more than being wounded in the heel,
        you will fear the thousand darts of the black god.
    But if it is true safety, to *remember* former safety;
        if actually this really is to be [pious], to *have been* pious;
            if that ship which overcame the south winds
            for you in former times, still rides upon the main;
            and while you observe your wretched friends
            on the shore and the sad society of sinners,
        it still will bear sweet repose with furled sails,
                waiting until you can return:
therefore then you should give wines, boy; give [a toast] to life *"To live!"*;
            Leave this gloom to the old men;
        let us give its cold to the cowering winter, my friends:
        and let here eternal roses hold these new realms.
        Ah not so shall we surmount winds so harsh; nor is
            this the way to rescue *a damaged vessel.*

    Therefore it is right to quench these waves in other waves;
        to sink this shipwreck with another shipwreck:
        so that that eye recently wrecked by evil waves
            can now be better wrecked by its own tears.

* The Church.

333   *Baptismus non tollit futura peccata.*

Quisquis es ille tener modò quem tua* *mater* Achilles
    In Stygis æthereæ provida tinxit aquis,
Sanus, sed non securus dimitteris illinc:
    In nova non tutus vulnera vivis adhuc.
Mille patent aditus; & plùs quàm calce petendus   5
    Ad nigri metues spicula mille dei.
Quòd si est vera salus, veterem *meminisse* salutem;
    Si nempe hoc verè est esse, *fuisse* pium;
Illa tibi veteres navis quæ vicerat Austros,
    Si manet in mediis usquè superstes aquis;   10
Ac dum tu miseros in littore visis amicos,
    Et peccatorum triste sodalitium,
Illa tibi interea tutis trahet otia velis,
    Expectans donec tu rediisse queas:
Quin igitur da vina, puer; da *vivere* vitæ;   15
    Mitte suum senibus, mitte supercilium;
Donemus timidæ, ô socii, sua frigora brumæ:
    Æternæ teneant hîc nova regna rosæ.
Ah non tam tetricos sic eluctabimur Euros;
    Effractam non est sic revocare *ratem*.   20

Has undas aliis decet ergò extinguere in undis;
    Naufragium hoc alio immergere naufragio:
Possit ut ille malis oculus modò naufragus undis,
    Jam lacrymis meliùs naufragus esse suis.

* Ecclesia.

Baptismus non tollit futura peccata. 48.
    1 *mater Achilles:* some legends tell that Achilles' mother, Thetis, dipped her son into the River Styx to make him immortal; she held him by the heel, however, and in the heel he was mortally wounded at Troy. In the allegory of the poem, Achilles' mother represents the Church, a curious conceit indeed. This poem would, like its predecessor, appear to be addressed to a theological principle or controversy.

334   *Peterhouse praying for its House of God.*

This poem and the next are requests for contributions to the building of the
New Chapel at Peterhouse. The work was begun by Matthew Wren in 1632,
and the chapel was still under construction in 1635, Crashaw himself assisting in

As now the *coming day* is still in the prayers of the world
   and in the songs of birds when it trembles on the first point,
     and the early *light* plays from the rosy *sunrise;*
when *Phoebus* is no longer absent nor fully present rejoicing in the
                          [reins of Eos' [horses],
     and far off soothes the vague sounds of birds:

So are *we*, whom just now a *holy day* [begins to] inspire with its
   distinguished rays; through the halls of our heaven
     (the *sacred House* is *our heaven*) now the not yet
fixed flare of the *still trembling day* pours forth in its *soft little light:*
now the impatience of too much prayer arouses *us*
and presses with a more intimate *hope* of its own.——

      ——*What* love of such a great
   undertaking moves our hearts! How the *slow hopes*
  gape with *long desire!* O sweetest *House* in the world!
House full of God! Ah, *Who will be, Who will he be* (we say)
(O Good Man, o mighty in merit, o closest to *God himself*,
  whom he calls into *his Gifts!*) by whom as avenger
  may these *holy half-lights* cast out all *shadows?*——

      ——*When,*
when will it be that that *tender flower* alas of trembling *day,*
which just as from its *rising* now plays around the *high altars,*
   and far off nods to us like a *dim star,*
may reveal itself in *full leaf* and, rejoicing in a *full lamp*
(as when the golden *Sun* gleams from the highest point of heaven),
  be fully able to enter the *inspired House* with a *full-grown*
  star and caress the *holy walls* with no hesitating face?

334   *Votiva Domus Petrensis Pro Domo Dei.*

the embellishment of organ, vestry, altar, and gallery (Martin, p. xxii). The two poems are obviously set pieces.

Ut magìs in Mundi votis, Aviúmque querelis
Jam *veniens* solet esse *Dies,* ubi cuspide primâ
Palpitat, & roseo *Lux prævia* ludit ab *ortu;*
Cùm nec abest *Phœbus,* nec Eois lætus habenis
Totus adest, volucrúmque procul vaga murmura mulcet: 5

Nos ità; quos nuper radiis afflavit honestis
Relligiosa Dies; nostríque per atria Cœli
(*Sacra Domus nostrum* est *Cœlum*) jam *luce tenellâ*
Libat adhuc *trepidæ* Fax nondum firma *Diei:*
Nos ità jam exercet nimii impatientia *Voti,*   10
Spéque sui *propiore* premit.——

               ——*Quis* pectora tanti
Tendit amor Cœpti! *Desiderio* quàm *longo*
Lentæ spes inhiant! *Domus* ô dulcissima rerum!
Plena Deo *Domus!* Ah, *Quis erit, Quis* (dicimus) *Ille,*
(O Bonus, ô Ingens meritis, ô Proximus *ipsi,*   15
Quem vocat in *sua Dona, Deo!*) quo vindice totas
Excutiant *Tenebras* hæc *Sancta Crepuscula?*——

               ——*Quando,*
Quando erit, ut tremulæ *Flos* heu *tener* ille *Diei,*
Qui velut ex *Oriente* suo jam *Altaria* circûm
Lambit, & *ambiguo* nobis procul annuit *astro,*   20
Plenis se pandat *foliis,* & *Lampade totâ*
Lætus (ut è medio cûm *Sol* micat aureus axe)
Attonitam penetrare *Domum* bene possit *adulto*
Sidere, nec dubio *Pia Mœnia* mulceat ore?

Votiva Domus Petrensis Pro Domo Dei. 48.*
    4 *Eois . . . habenis:* the horses of Eos (Aurora), the dawn.

When will it be that the beautiful *vaults* may bloom with their own
fair flowers and the *fretted roof* tremble with a rosy smile?
[the vaults] *which* too conscious, as it were, of their *unformed front*
now purify themselves with constant *teardrops.*

When will it be that by the clear *window* with better *light*
through *panes of glass* the *holy page* may live?

When will it be that a noble murmur will stir the organ's *nerves*
with skilled and never-failing sound while we
celebrate the *sacred hymn;* and an untrustworthy *pipe* will not
make the evil noises of ill-fitting bellows?

In short, whatever it is which this *sacred work* requires, [may]
that propitious auspicious *hand* (o may it be *yours*) to whom
this *Dawn* owes her *Day* [accomplish it]. The altar *itself* begs *you,*
the *altar itself* makes *prayers to you.* Now *you* hear *hers,*
she will hear *yours.* It is doubtful [when you] stretch forth *your hand*
whether *you give* more or *take away* more: dare only to be *blessed,*
and gain this loss for yourself.——

——You know yourself which
wheel makes winged *wealth* [fly away]; therefore *fix* it here forever in the
[*rock of Peter*
as the foundations of [his] *House;* thus take away her *wheel*
from *Fortune.* You know yourself how the
fleet *wing* carries wanton *riches* by the wandering winds;
come, take those *wings* away from flying *riches*
and let them have their nest near *our altars:*
that at last having acquired *wings* of *better oarage* they may
take themselves *and their Master with them* above the Heavens.

O happy the man who could use with such great foresight
the *wings of fortune* and the lightness *of his own wealth,*
and so added the *wings of the eagle** to his riches.

* Proverbs 23:5.

Quando erit, ut *Convexa* suo quoque pulchra sereno   25
Florescant, roseóque tremant *Laquearia* risu?
Quæ nimiùm *informis* tanquam sibi conscia *frontis*
Perpetuis jam se lustrant *lacrymantia* guttis.

Quando erit, ut claris meliori *luce Fenestris*
Plurima per *vitreos* vivat *Pia Pagina vultus?*   30

Quando erit, ut *Sacrum* nobis *celebrantibus Hymnum*
Organicos facili, & nunquam fallente susurro
Nobile murmur agat *nervos;* pulmonis iniqui
Fistula nec monitus faciat male-fida sinistros?

Denique, quicquid id est, quod *Res* hîc *Sacra* requirit,   35
Fausta illa, & felix (sitque ô *Tua*) *Dextra,* suam cui
Debeat hæc *Aurora Diem, Tibi* supplicat *Ipsa,*
Ipsa Tibi facit *Ara preces. Tu* jam *Illius* audi,
Audiet *Illa tuas.* Dubium est (modò porrige *dextram*)
Des magìs, an *capias:* aude tantùm esse *beatus,*   40
Et damnum hoc lucrare Tibi.——

                ——Scis Ipse volucres
Quæ *Rota* volvat *opes;* has ergò hîc *fige* perennis
Fundamenta Domus *Petrensi* in *Rupe;* suámque
Fortunæ sic deme *Rotam.* Scis Ipse procaces
Divitias quàm prona vagos vehat *ala* per Euros,   45
Divitiis illas, agè, deme volucribus *alas,*
Fácque suus *Nostras* illis sit nidus ad *Aras:*
Remigii ut tandem *pennas melioris* adeptæ,
Se rapiant *Dominúmque suum* super æthera *secum.*

Felix ô qui sic potuit bene providus uti   50
Fortunæ pennis & *opum* levitate *suarum,*
Divitiísque suis *Aquilæ** *sic* addidit *Alas.*

* *Proverbs* 23:5.

---

28 *guttis:* it would seem that the unfinished roof was leaking.

335   *The Groans of the same [Peterhouse] on
the difficult travail for the rest of the work.*

O too happy is *that* [*Phoenix*] and the noble name
of our envy! who, rising from an easy *death*
a fragrant *mother*, restores anew the fibers of her own *shining youth*
and [*completes*] her own fate by means of the *hurried fires*.
She, not at all worn out by the passage of birthdays,
by so many *slow* months and such painful *delays*, she *flies* with *one*
leap, as it were, into a new age and decks her *whole head* in handsome
feathers and *comes forth again* from a rosy rising.
At the same moment *she* will ascend her spicewood funeral pyres
and happily drink all *Phoebus*, and at that instant with conquering wings
will beat the ground and *her ashes.——*
——Alas, we are borne
by a *different* fate; and an *older Phoenix under its Apollo*,
our *Mother*, of *Peter*[*house*], still hangs poised on *fickle breezes*
and seeks *a hiding place* in which she may leave her *helpless relics*
and, revived by the spoils even of her *old age*,
[where she] may press upward through every difficulty [*bearing*] a
[*fitting appearance* and *expression*.
But now alas in the *very throes* of a better day
she suffers a long deprivation.
But now alas in the *long* effort of a *slow life* meanwhile
she dies! *With uncertain expression the walls* stand
like a lovely part of her, and their brothers in vain invite [other] *walls*
to alliance, but the *stones* do not respond to
these *stones*. The interrupted *works* mourn and pray
for *hands.——*
——Take pity, take pity on your pious *mother*,
o whoever [of you] is *pious*. Take pity on *that mother*
whom so many holy *mothers* consider as their *own*.
Whoever you are, o *to you*, believe me, *to you* so many *gaping mouths*
speak from the broken ramparts. Believe me, *you ought to honor your*
[*mother,*
[her] *walls broken* by such long old age and idleness just as if
she showed white *hairs*. Take pity on the one who asks.
Formerly she prayed with [*breasts*] *full for thee;* now she prays *for herself*
with *empty breasts*, lest you should be lacking in her *old age*.
So may *a long youth* smile *on you*, never to yield to *querulous old age*.

335

EJUSDEM
In cæterorum Operum difficili Parturitione
GEMITUS.

O Felix nimis *Illa,* & nostræ nobile Nomen
Invidiæ *Volucris!* facili quæ *funere* surgens
Mater odora sui *nitidæ* nova fila *juventæ,*
Et *festinatos* peragit sibi fata per *ignes.*
Illa, haud natales tot *tardis* mensibus horas   5
Tam miseris tenuata *moris, saltu* velut *uno*
In nova secla *rapit* sese, & *caput omne* decoras
Explicat in frondes, roseóque *repullulat* ortu.
Cinnameos simul *Illa* rogos conscenderit, omnem
Læta bibit *Phœbum,* & jam jam victricibus alis   10
Plaudit humum, *Cinerés*que *suos.*——
                    ——*Heu! dispare* Fato
Nos ferimur; *Seniorque suo* sub *Apolline Phœnix*
Petrensis Mater, dubias librata per *auras*
Pendet adhuc, quærítque *sinum* in quo ponat *inertes*
Exuvias, spoliìsque suæ *Reparata Senectæ*   15
Ore Pari surgat, *Simili*que per omnia *Vultu.*
At nunc heu *nixu* secli melioris in *ipso*
Deliquium patitur!–
At nunc heu *Lentæ longo* in molimine *Vitæ*
Interea moritur! *Dubio* stant *Mœnia vultu*   20
Parte sui Pulchra, & fratres in fœdera *Muros*
Invitant frustrà, nec respondentia *Saxis*
Saxa suis. Mœrent *Opera* intermissa, *manúsque*
Implorant.——
                ——*Succurre Piæ,* succurre *Parenti,*
O Quisquis *pius* es. *Illi* succurre *Parenti,*   25
Quam sibi tot sanctæ *Matres* habuere *Parentem.*
Quisquis es, ô *Tibi,* crede, *Tibi* tot *hiantia* ruptis
Mœnibus *Ora* loqui! *Matrem Tibi,* crede, *verendam*
Muros tam longo *laceros* senióque sitúque
Ceu *Canos* monstrare suos. Succurre roganti.   30
Per *Tibi Plena* olim, per jam *Sibi Sicca* precatur
Ubera, nè desis *Senio.* Sic *longa Juventus*
Te foveat, *querulæ* nunquam cessura *Senectæ.*

Ejusdem Gemitus. 48.*
    26 *Matres:* i.e. churches staffed by alumni (Grosart).

336   *On the day of the powder conspiracy.*

This distich was published first in the *Epigrammatum Sacrorum Liber* (1634), but as it is not Scriptural it has been removed from the sequence of Sacred Epigrams. The English version "Upon the Powder Day," No. 69 (which see),

> With what well arranged feasts does the year race along!
> After *All Saints, all sin* follows.

Live Jesus!

The "finis" of *Carmen Deo Nostro* (1652), this is a part of the "Motto" (No. 1) with which Crashaw opened the *Steps to the Temple* (1646); it was a phrase coined by St. François de Sales who used it as his motto in many editions of

336 *In die Conjurationis sulphuræ.*

appeared first in *Steps to the Temple* (1646) but was removed to the *Delights of the Muses* in 1648. As Crashaw thought of it as a sacred poem, it is included here.

Quàm bene dispositis annus dat currere festis!
Post *Omnes Sanctos, Omne scelus* sequitur.

VIVE JESU.

his works (A. F. Allison, "Crashaw and St. François de Sales," *RES*, XXIV [1948], 295–302, esp. p. 296); the English *incipit* is the full version, which the Latin is intended to suggest. 52.

In die. 34.

SECULAR POEMS

V

Secular Poems
in one English Version

ROYAL AND POLITICAL

337   *Upon the Kings Coronation.*

Like the several poems on the Gunpowder Plot, which are presumably
written on the anniversaries of the deliverance, this "ode" cannot positively be
dated as of February 2, 1626, the date on which Charles II was crowned,
though the reference to "but now" (line 1), suggesting the funeral of James,
May 5, 1625, makes such a dating possible. If this "ode" is to be dated 1626,
Crashaw was fourteen years old. (See next poem.)

Strange Metamorphosis! It was but now
The sullen heaven had vail'd its mournfull brow
With a black maske: the clouds with child by greife
Traveld th' Olympian plaines to find releife.
But at the last (having not soe much powe'r   5
As to refraine) brought forth a costly shower
Of pearly drops, and sent her numerous birth
(As tokens of her greife) unto the earth.
Alas, the earth, quite drunke with teares, had reel'd
From of her center, had not Jove upheld   10
The staggering lumpe: each eye spent all its store,
As if heereafter they would weepe noe more.
Streight from this sea of teares there does appear
Full glory flaming in her owne free sphaere.
Amazed Sol throwes of his mournfull weeds   15
Speedily harnessing his fiery steeds,
Up to Olympus stately topp he hies,
From whence his glorious rivall hee espies.
Then wondring starts, and had the curteous night
Withheld her vaile, h' had forfeited his sight.   20
The joyfull sphaeres with a delicious sound
Affright th' amazed aire, and dance a round
To their owne Musick, nor (untill they see
This glorious Phaebus sett) will quiet bee.
Each aery Siren now hath gott her song,   25

Upon the Kings Coronation. MS.*
    4 *Traveld:* probably a pun on "travailed."
   18 *rivall:* i.e. King Charles.

To whom the merry lambes doe tripp along
The laughing meades, as joyfull to behold
Their winter coates cover'd with flaming gold.
Such was the brightnesse of this Northerne starre,
It made the Virgin Phoenix come from farre   30
To be repaird: hither she did resort,
Thinking her father had remov'd his court.
The lustre of his face did shine soe bright,
That Rome's bold Eagles now were blinded quite,
The radiant darts, shott from his sparkling eyes,   35
Made every mortall gladly sacrifice
A heart burning in love; all did adore
This rising sunne. Their faces nothing wore,
But smiles, and ruddy joyes, and at this day
All melancholy clowds vanisht away.   40

338   *Upon the Kings coronation.*

This "ode" copies many of the manners of the preceding one, and indeed both
of them seem to be entirely conventional and are probably academic exercises.
Both poems contain, for examples, the dance of the spheres, the phoenix, and
the ocean of tears. This one refers (line 25) to Cynthia, a name Crashaw uses
for Queen Henrietta Maria, and to a "constellation," "those three great starres,"
"Each little beame" (lines 29–31). These, one supposes, are the members of the
royal family, the children evidently of Charles and Henrietta; as there are three
of them the poem must follow the birth of James on October 14, 1633, and pre-
cede the birth of Elizabeth on December 28, 1635 (see next poem). It is there-
fore to be dated February 1634 or 1635. Martin (pp. lxvi–lxx) discusses the
authorship of the poem by an analysis of its imagery.

Sound forth, cælestiall Organs, lett heavens quire
Ravish the dancing orbes, make them mount higher
With nimble capers, and force Atlas tread
Upon his tiptoes, e're his silver head
Shall kisse his golden burthen. Thou, glad Isle,   5
That swim'st as deepe in joy, as Seas, now smile;
Lett not thy weighty glories, this full tide

28 *winter coates:* the coronation took place on February 2.
29 *this Northerne starre:* Charles had been born in Scotland.
30 *Phoenix:* probably Queen Henrietta Maria who was married to Charles (by proxy)
in Paris on May 1, 1625, and arrived in England June 12.
34 *Rome's . . . Eagles:* Henrietta Maria's mother was Mary di Medici.
Upon the Kings coronation. MS.*
5 *burthen:* the heavens; Atlas is represented as holding the heavens on his back.

Of blisse, debase thee; but with a just pride
Swell: swell to such an height, that thou maist vye
With heaven itselfe for stately Majesty.   10
Doe not deceive mee, Eyes: doe I not see
In this blest earth heavens bright Epitome,
Circled with pure refined glory? heere
I veiw a rising sunne in this our sphære,
Whose blazing beames, maugre the blackest night,   15
And mists of greife, dare force a joyfull light.
The gold, in which he flames, does well præsage
A precious season, and a golden age.
Doe I not see joy keepe his revels now,
And sitt triumphing in each cheerfull brow?   20
Unmixt felicity with silver wings
Broodeth this sacred place. hither peace brings
The choicest of her olive-crownes, and praies
To have them guilded with his courteous raies.
Doe I not see a Cynthia, who may   25
Abash the purest beauties of the Day?
To whom heavens lampes often in silent night
Steale from their stations to repaire their light.
Doe I not see a constellation,
Each little beame of which would make a sunne?   30
I meane those three great starres, who well may scorne
Acquaintance with the Usher of the morne.
To gaze upon such starres each humble eye
Would be ambitious of Astronomie.
Who would not be a Phænix, and aspire   35
To sacrifice himselfe in such sweet fire?
Shine forth, ye flaming sparkes of Deity,
Yee perfect Emblemes of Divinity.
Fixt in your sphæres of glory, shed from thence
The treasures of our lives, your influence.   40
For if you sett, who may not justly feare,
The world will be one Ocean, one great teare.

---

23 *olive-crownes:* the olive is traditionally the wreath of peace.
25 *Cynthia:* the goddess of the Moon (appropriate after the remarks on the King as the sun, line 14), a name Crashaw uses for the Queen; see the following poem and "Upon the Duke of Yorke His Birth," line 79.
31 *three great starres:* the royal children: Charles (b. 1630), Mary (b. 1631), James (b. 1633).

339   *Upon the birth of the Princesse* Elizabeth.

The Princess Elizabeth, the fourth child of Charles and Henrietta to survive, was born on December 28, 1635; this poem and the Latin "In Serenissimæ Reginæ partum hyemalem," No. 391 both record the event. The poem follows faithfully the conventions of gratulatory verse: hyperbolic praise in imagery of stars, jewels, flowers compared with unassuming modesty.

Bright starre of Majesty, oh shedd on mee
A precious influence, as sweet as thee.
That with each word, my loaden pen letts fall,
The fragrant spring may be perfum'd withall.
That Sol from them may suck an honied shower,   5
To glutt the stomack of his darling flower.
With such a sugred livery made fine,
They shall proclaime to all, that they are thine.
Lett none dare speake of thee, but such as thence
Extracted have a balmy Eloquence.   10
But then, alas, my heart! oh how shall I
Cure thee of thy delightfull tympanie?
I cannot hold, such a spring tide of joy
Must have a passage, or 'twill force a way.
Yet shall my loyall tongue keepe this command: 15
But give me leave to ease it with my hand.
And though these humble lines soare not soe high,
As is thy birth; yet from thy flaming eye
Drop downe one sparke of glory, and they'l prove
A præsent worthy of Apollo's love.   20
My quill to thee may not præsume to sing:
Lett th' hallowed plume of a Seraphick wing
Bee consecrated to this worke, while I
Chant to my selfe with rustick melodie.
    Rich, liberall heaven, what, hath your treasure store   25
Of such bright Angells, that you give us more?
Had you, like our great Sunne, stamped but one
For earth, 't had beene an ample portion.

Upon the Birth of the Princesse Elizabeth. MS.*
    12 *tympanie:* in this context, a swelling of the heart from joy.
    21–24 *My quill . . . melodie:* the passage recalls Crashaw's frequent invitations to other voices to assist him in sacred songs; "quill" and "rustick" are traditional terms of the pastoral poet.

Had you but drawne one lively coppy forth,
That might interpret our faire Cynthia's worth,   30
Y' had done enough to make the lazy ground
Dance, like the nimble sphæres, a joyfull round.
But such is the cælestiall Excellence
That in the princely patterne shines, from whence
The rest pourtraicted are, that 'tis noe paine   35
To ravish heaven to limbe them o're againe.
Wittnesse this mapp of beauty; every part
Of which doth show the Quintessence of art.
See! nothing's vulgar, every atome heere
Speakes the great wisdome of th' artificer.   40
Poore earth hath not enough perfection,
To shaddow forth th' admired Paragon.
Those sparkling twinnes of light should I now stile
Rich diamonds, sett in a pure silver foyle;
Or call her cheeke a bed of new blowne roses;   45
And say that Ivory her front composes;
Or should I say, that with a scarlet wave
Thoses plumpe soft rubies had bin drest soe brave;
Or that the dying lilly did bestow
Upon her neck the whitest of his snow;   50
Or that the purple violets did lace
That hand of milky doune: All these are base;
Her glories I should dimme with things soe grosse,
And foule the cleare text with a muddy glosse.
Goe on then, Heaven, and limbe forth such another,   55
Draw to this sister miracle a brother;
Compile a fift glorious Epitome
Of heaven, and earth, and of all raritie;
And sett it forth in the same happy place,
And I'le not blurre it with my Paraphrase.   60

30 *Cynthia:* the Queen (see preceding poem).
   36 *limbe:* limn (i.e. portray). *o're againe:* perhaps Crashaw in these lines is thinking
specifically of the first princess as well as of her royal parents.
   56–57 *sister miracle a brother . . . a fift:* the fifth child was a daughter, Anne (born
1637).

340   *On the Gunpowder-Treason.*

The Gunpowder Treason was a plot by Guy Fawkes and several Roman Catholic associates to blow up the Houses of Parliament when James and his two sons were present. The plot was revealed and the conspirators were apprehended. The day of delivery, November 5, 1605, is kept as a holy day in England. See also the English and Latin epigrams on the day, printed with the Sacred poems (Nos. 69, 336).

I sing Impiety beyond a name:
Who stiles it any thinge, knowes not the same.

> Dull, sluggish, Ile! what more than Lethargy
> Gripes thy cold limbes soe fast, thou canst not fly,
> And start from of thy center? hath heavens love   5
> Stuft thee soe full with blisse, thou can'st not move?
> If soe, oh Neptune, may she farre be throune
> By thy kind armes to a kind world unknowne:
> Lett her survive this day, once mock her fate,
> And shee's an Island truely fortunate.   10
> Lett not my suppliant breath raise a rude storme
> To wrack my suite. oh keepe pitty warme
> In thy cold breast, and yearely on this day
> Mine eyes a tributary streame shall pay.
> Do'st thou not see an exhalation   15
> Belch'd from the sulph'ry lungs of Phlegeton?
> A living Comet, whose pestiferous breath
> Adulterates the Virgin aire? with death
> It labours, Stif'led nature's in a swound,
> Ready to dropp into a chaos, round   20
> About horror's displai'd; It doth portend,
> That earth a shoure of stones to heaven shall send,
> And crack the Christall globe; the milky streame
> Shall in a silver raine runne out, whose creame
> Shall choake the gaping earth, which then shall fry   25
> In flames, and of a burning fever dy.
> That wonders may in fashion be, not rare,
> A winters thunder with a groane shall scare,

On the Gunpowder-Treason. MS.*
  16 *Phlegeton:* a fiery river in Hell.

And rouze the sleepy ashes of the dead,
Making them skip out of their dusty bed.   30
Those twinckling eyes of heaven, which ev'n now shin'd,
Shall with one flash of lightning be struck blind.
The sea shall change his youthfull greene, and slide
Along the shore in a grave purple tide.
It does præsage, that a great Prince shall climbe,   35
And gett a starry throne before his time.
To usher in this shoale of Prodigies,
Thy infants, Æolus, will not suffice.
Noe, Noe, a giant wind, that will not spare
To tosse poore men like dust into the aire;   40
Justle downe mountaines: Kings courts shall be sent,
Like bandied balles, into the firmament.
Atlas shall be tript upp, Jove's gate shall feele
The weighty rudenes of his boysterous heele.
All this it threats, and more Horror, that flies   45
To th' Empyræum of all miseries.
Most tall Hyperbole's cannot descry it;
Mischeife, that scornes expression should come nigh it.
All this it only threats. the Meteor ly'd;
It was exhal'd, a while it hung, and dy'd.   50
Heaven kickt the Monster doune. doune it was throune,
The fall of all things it praesag'd, its owne
It quite forgott. the fearfull earth gave way,
And durst not touch it, heere it made noe stay.
At last it stopt at Pluto's gloomy porch;   55
He streightway lighted upp his pitchy torch.
Now to those toiling soules it gives its light,
Which had the happines to worke i' th' night.
They banne the blaze, and curse its curtesy,
For lighting them unto their misery.   60
Till now hell was imperfect; it did need
Some rare choice torture; now 'tis hell indeed.
Then glutt thy dire lampe with the warmest blood,
That runnes in violett pipes: none other food
It can digest. then watch the wildfire well,   65
Least it breake forth, and burne thy sooty cell.

35–36 *great Prince . . . time:* perhaps the untimely death of Prince Henry is intended.
42 *bandied:* struck as in tennis.
65 *wildfire:* the anniversary is still marked by the lighting of bonfires.

341 *Upon the gunpowder treason.*

Reach me a quill, pluckt from the flaming wing
Of Pluto's Mercury, that I may sing
Death to the life. My inke shall be the blood
Of Cerberus, or Alecto's viperous brood.
Unmated malice! Oh unpeer'd despight!   5
Such as the sable pinions of the night
Never durst hatch before: Extracted see
The very Quintessence of villanie.
I feare to name it; least that he, which heares,
Should have his soule frighted beyond the sphæres.   10
Heaven was asham'd, to see our mother Earth
Engender with the Night, and teeme a birth
Soe foule, one minutes light had it but seene,
The fresh face of the morne had blasted beene.
Her rosy cheekes you should have seene noe more   15
Dy'd in vermilion blushes, as before:
But in a vaile of clouds mufling her head
A solitary life she would have led.
Affrighted Phæbus would have lost his way,
Giving his wanton palfreys leave to play   20
Olympick games in the'Olympian plaines,
His trembling hands loosing the golden raines.
The Queene of night gott the greene sicknes then,
Sitting soe long at ease in her darke denne,
Not daring to peepe forth, least that a stone   25
Should beate her headlong from her jetty throne.
Joves twinckling tapers, that doe light the world,
Had beene puft out. and from their stations hurl'd.
Æol kept in his wrangling sonnes, least they
With this grand blast should have bin bloune away.   30
Amazed Triton with his shrill alarmes
Bad sporting Neptune to pluck in his armes,
And leave embracing of the Isles, least hee

Upon the gunpowder treason ("Reach me a quill"). MS.* See note above.
  2 *Pluto's Mercury:* the (imaginary) messenger of the ruler of Hell.
  4 *Cerberus:* three-headed dog at gates of Hell. *Alecto:* one of the classical Furies.
  23 *the greene sicknes:* a malady of young maids in which they grow pale, slightly green,
and faint.

Might be an actor in this Tragædy:
Nor should wee need thy crisped waves, for wee   35
An Ocean could have made t' have drowned thee.
Torrents of salt teares from our eyes should runne,
And raise a deluge, where the flaming sunne
Should coole his fiery wheeles, and never sinke
Soe low to give his thirsty stallions drinke.   40
Each soule in sighes had spent its dearest breath,
As glad to waite upon their King in death.
Each winged Chorister would swan-like sing
A mournfull Dirge to their deceased King.
The painted meddowes would have laught noe more   45
For joye of their neate coates; but would have tore
Their shaggy locks, their floury mantles turn'd
Into dire sable weeds, and sate, and mourn'd.
Each stone had streight a Niobe become,
And wept amaine; then rear'd a costly tombe,   50
T' entombe the lab'ring earth. for surely shee
Had died just in her delivery.
But when Joves winged Heralds this espied,
Upp to th' Almighty thunderer they hied,
Relating this sad story. streightway hee   55
The monster crusht, maugre their midwiferie.
And may such Pythons never live to see
The light's faire face, but still abortive bee.

342   *Upon the gunpowder treason.*

Grow plumpe, leane Death; his Holinesse a feast
Hath now præpar'd, and you must be his guest.
Come grimme destruction, and in purple gore
Dye sev'n times deeper than they were before
Thy scarlet robes. for heere you must not share   5
A common banquett. noe, heere's princely fare.
And least thy bloodshott eyes should lead aside
This masse of cruelty, to be thy guide

---

41 *sighes:* thought to represent the wasting of breath in death.
49 *Niobe:* a nymph who wept so much at the death of her children that Zeus turned her into a stone from which a fountain flowed.
Upon the gunpowder treason ("Grow plumpe"). MS.* See note above.
6 *princely fare:* a grim pun—the princes were to have been in the building.

Three coleblack sisters, (whose long sutty haire,
And greisly visages doe fright the aire;   10
When Night beheld them, shame did almost turne
Her sable cheekes into a blushing morne,
Too see some fowler than herselfe) these stand,
Each holding forth to light the aery brand,
Whose purer flames tremble to be soe nigh,   15
And in fell hatred burning, angry dy.
Sly, lurking treason is his bosome freind,
Whom faint, and palefac't feare doth still attend.
These need noe invitation. onely thou,
Black dismall horror, come; make perfect now   20
Th' Epitome of hell: oh lett thy pinions
Be' a gloomy Canopy to Pluto's minions.
In this infernall Majesty close shrowd
Your selves, you Stygian states; a pitchy clowd
Shall hang the roome, and for your tapers bright,   25
Sulphureous flames, snatch'd from æternall night.
But rest, affrighted Muse; thy silver wings
May not row neerer to these dusky Kings.
Cast back some amorous glances on the cates,
That heere are dressing by the hasty fates.   30
Nay. stopp thy clowdy eyes. it is not good,
To droune thy selfe in this pure pearly flood.
But since they are for fire workes, rather prove
A Phænix, and in chastest flames of love
Offer thy selfe a Virgin sacrifice   35
To quench the rage of hellish deities.
        But dares destruction eate these candid breasts,
The Muses, and the Graces sugred neasts?
Dares hungry death snatch of one cherry lipp?
Or thirsty treason offer once to sippe   40
One dropp of this pure Nectar, which doth flow
In azure channells warme through mounts of snow?
The roses fresh, conserved from the rage,
And cruell ravishing of frosty age,
Feare is afraid to tast of: only this,   45
He humbly crav'd to banquett on a kisse.
Poore meagre horror streightwaies was amaz'd,

9 *sutty:* sooty.
24 *Stygian states:* regions of the river Styx in Hades.
37–42 members of the royal family (?).

And in the stead of feeding, stood, and gaz'd.
Their appetites were gone at th' very sight;
But yet their eyes surfett with sweet delight.   50
Only the Pope a stomack still could find;
But yett they were not powder'd to his mind.
Forthwith each God stept from his starry throne,
And snatch'd away the banquett. every one
convey'd his sweet delicious treasury   55
To the close closet of æternity:
Where they will safely keepe it, from the rude,
And rugged touch of Pluto's multitude.

---

51 *stomack:* only the Pope would be so devilish as to destroy such beauty.
52 *powder'd:* sprinkled with seasoning or spice.

343   *An Epitaph*
Upon Mr. Ashton *a conformable*
Citizen.

A manuscript version of this epitaph notes that Mr. Ashton was a "Citizen of London," but no identification has as yet been made (Martin, p. 443). If that description is correct, it would suggest that Crashaw wrote the poem while he was still "in this Towne" (London), i.e. before 1631.

The modest front of this small floore
Beleeve mee, Reader can say more
Then many a braver Marble can;
Here lyes a truly honest man.
One whose Conscience was a thing,   5
That troubled neither Church nor King.
One of those few that in this Towne,
Honour all Preachers; heare their owne,
Sermons he heard, yet not so many,
As left no time to practise any.   10
Hee heard them reverendly, and then
His practice preach'd them o're agen.
For every day his deedes put on
His Sundayes repetition.
His *Parlour-Sermons* rather were   15
Those to the Eye, then to the Eare.
His prayers tooke their price and strength
Not from the lowdnesse, nor the length.
Hee was a Protestant at home,
Not onely in despight of *Rome.*   20
He lov'd his *Father;* yet his zeale
Tore not off his Mothers veile.
To th' Church hee did allow her Dresse,
True *Beauty,* to true *Holinesse.*

An Epitaph upon Mr. Ashton. 46 (48).*
    Title: *conformable:* amiable, compliant (presumably not pejorative here).
    8–18   an interesting picture of the churchgoer.
    19–24   He loved God, his Father, but was not so zealous (i.e. puritanical) as to prohibit beauty to holiness. This emphasis on the adornment of worship is constant in Crashaw's works; see dedication to the *Epigrammata Sacra,* etc.

Peace, which hee lov'd in Life, did lend   25
Her hand to bring him to his end;
When Age and Death call'd for the score,
No surfets were to reckon for.
Death tore not (therefore) but sans strife
Gently untwin'd his thread of Life.   30
What remaines then, but that Thou
Write these lines, Reader, in thy Brow,
And by his faire Examples light,
Burne in thy Imitation bright.
So while these Lines can but Bequeath   35
A Life perhaps unto his Death,
His better Epitaph shall bee,
His Life still kept alive in Thee.

344   *An Epitaph.*
               Upon Doctor Brooke.

Samuel Brooke, Master of Trinity College, Cambridge, died September 16,
1631. Crashaw had matriculated at Cambridge on July 6 preceding. Having,
one may suppose, only the slightest acquaintance with this very prominent fig-
ure, all Crashaw could do was make the obvious pun on the name of the de-
ceased and fill it with tears. See "In Rev. Dr. Brooke Epitaphium," No. 395.

A *Brooke* whose streame so great, so good,
Was lov'd, was honour'd as a flood:
Whose Bankes the Muses dwelt upon,
More then their owne Helicon;
Here at length, hath gladly found
A quiet passage under ground;
Meane while his loved bankes now dry,
The Muses with their teares supply.

An Epitaph. 46 (48).

345   *Upon the Death of Mr.* Herrys.

William Herrys, fellow of Pembroke College, Cambridge, died on October
15, 1631 (see the Latin "Epitaphium in Dominum Herrisium," No. 397).
Crashaw's early reputation is demonstrated clearly by the fact that he provided
the "official" epitaph for Herrys's monument at Pembroke after having been in
the College only four months. Perhaps this commission spurred him to the writ-
ing of six other mortuary notices—perhaps they were trials; or perhaps—revers-
ing the matter—Crashaw's many Herrysian elegies won him the commission for
the "official" epitaph. The number of elegies on Herrys and the presence of the
epitaph are evidently related. One manuscript describes this poem as an "Al-
legory."

A Plant of noble stemme, forward and faire,
As ever whisper'd to the Morning Aire
Thriv'd in these happy Grounds, the Earth's just pride,
Whose rising Glories made such haste to hide
His head in Cloudes, as if in him alone   5
Impatient Nature had taught motion
To start from Time, and cheerfully to fly
Before, and seize upon Maturity.
Thus grew this gratious plant, in whose sweet shade
The Sunne himselfe oft wisht to sit, and made   10
The Morning Muses perch like Birds, and sing
Among his Branches: yea, and vow'd to bring
His owne delicious Phœnix from the blest
Arabia, there to build her Virgin nest,
To hatch her selfe in, 'mongst his leaves the Day   15
Fresh from the Rosie East rejoyc't to play.
To them shee gave the first and fairest Beame
That waited on her Birth: she gave to them
The purest Pearles, that wept her Evening Death,
The balmy *Zephirus* got so sweet a Breath   20
By often kissing them. And now begun
Glad Time to ripen expectation.
The timourous Maiden-Blossomes on each Bough,
Peept forth from their first blushes: so that now
A Thousand ruddy hopes smil'd in each Bud,   25
And flatter'd every greedy eye that stood
Fixt in Delight, as if already there
Those rare fruits dangled, whence the Golden Yeare

Upon the Death of Mr. Herrys. 46 (48).
  8 *Maturity:* he had just received his A.M., and was about twenty-five.

His crowne expected, when (ô Fate, ô Time
That seldome lett'st a blushing youthfull Prime   30
Hide his hot Beames in shade of silver Age;
So rare is hoary vertue) the dire rage
Of a mad storme these bloomy joyes all tore,
Ravisht the Maiden Blossoms, and downe bore
The trunke. Yet in this ground his pretious Root   35
Still lives, which when weake Time shall be pour'd out
Into Eternity, and circular joyes
Dance in an endlesse round, againe shall rise
The faire son of an ever-youthfull Spring,
To be a shade for Angels while they sing,   40
Meane while who e're thou art that passest here,
O doe thou water it with one kind Teare.

346   *Upon the Death of the most desired Mr.* Herrys.

Death, what dost? ô hold thy Blow,
What thou dost, thou dost not know.
Death thou must not here be cruell,
This is Natures choycest Jewell.
This is hee in whose rare frame,   5
Nature labour'd for a Name,
And meant to leave his pretious feature,
The patterne of a perfect Creature.
Joy of Goodnesse, Love of Art,
Vertue weares him next her heart.   10
Him the Muses love to follow,
Him they call their vice-*Apollo.*
Apollo golden though thou bee,
Th'art not fairer then is hee.
Nor more lovely lift'st thy head,   15
Blushing from thine Easterne Bed.
The Gloryes of thy youth ne're knew,
Brighter hopes then he can shew.
Why then should it e're be seene,
That his should fade, while thine is Greene?   20
And wilt Thou, (ô cruell boast!)
Put poore Nature to such cost?

Upon the death of the most desired Mr. Herrys. 46 (48).* See note above.

O 'twill undoe our common Mother,
To be at charge of such another.
What? thinke we to no other end,   25
Gracious Heavens do use to send
Earth her best perfection,
But to vanish and be gone?
Therefore onely give to day,
To morrow to be snatcht away?   30
I've seen indeed the hopefull bud,
Of a ruddy Rose that stood
Blushing, to behold the Ray
Of the new-saluted Day;
(His tender toppe not fully spread)   35
The sweet dash of a shower now shead,
Invited him no more to hide
Within himselfe the purple pride
Of his forward flower, when lo
While he sweetly 'gan to show   40
His swelling Gloryes, *Auster* spide him,
Cruell *Auster* thither hy'd him,
And with the rush of one rude blast,
Sham'd not spitefully to wast
All his leaves, so fresh, so sweet,   45
And lay them trembling at his feet.
I've seene the Mornings lovely Ray,
Hover o're the new-borne Day:
With rosie wings so richly Bright,
As if he scorn'd to thinke of Night,   50
When a ruddy storme whose scoule,
Made Heavens radiant face looke foule;
Call'd for an untimely Night,
To blot the newly blossom'd Light.
But were the Roses blush so rare,   55
Were the Mornings smile so faire
As is he, nor cloud, nor wind
But would be courteous, would be kind.
Spare him Death, ô spare him then,
Spare the sweetest among men.   60
Let not pitty with her Teares,
Keepe such distance from thine Eares.

23 *common Mother:* i.e. Nature.
41 *Auster:* the South Wind.

But o thou wilt not, canst not spare,
Haste hath never time to heare.
Therefore if hee needs must go,   65
And the Fates will have it so,
Softly may he be possest,
Of his monumentall rest.
Safe, thou darke home of the dead,
Safe o hide his loved head.   70
Keepe him close, close in thine armes,
Seal'd up with a thousand charmes.
For pitties sake o hide him quite,
From his Mother Natures sight:
Lest for Griefe his losse may move,   75
All her Births abortive prove.

347   *Another* [*on Mr.* Herrys].

If ever Pitty were acquainted
With sterne Death, if e're he fainted,
Or forgot the cruell vigour,
Of an Adamantine rigour,
Here, o here we should have knowne it,   5
Here or no where hee'd have showne it.
For hee whose pretious memory,
Bathes in Teares of every eye:
Hee to whom our sorrow brings,
All the streames of all her springs: 10
Was so rich in Grace and Nature,
In all the gifts that blesse a Creature;
The fresh hopes of his lovely Youth,
Flourisht in so faire a grouth;
So sweet the Temple was, that shrin'd   15
The Sacred sweetnesse of his mind:
That could the Fates know to relent,
Could they know what mercy meant;
Or had ever learnt to beare,
The soft tincture of a Teare: 20
Teares would now have flow'd so deepe,
As might have taught Griefe how to weepe.

Another. 46 (48). See note above.

Now all their steely operation,
Would quite have lost the cruell fashion.
Sicknesse would have gladly been,   25
Sick himselfe to have sav'd him:
And his Feaver wish'd to prove
Burning, onely in his Love.
Him when wrath it selfe had seene,
Wrath its self had lost his spleene.   30
Grim Destruction here amaz'd,
In stead of striking would have gaz'd.
Even the Iron-pointed pen,
That notes the Tragicke Doomes of men
Wet with teares still'd from the eyes,   35
Of the flinty Destinyes;
Would have learn't a softer style,
And have been asham'd to spoyle
His lives sweet story, by the hast,
Of a cruell stop ill plac't.   40
In the darke volume of our fate,
Whence each leafe of Life hath date,
Where in sad particulars,
The totall summe of Man appeares,
And the short clause of mortall breath,   45
Bound in the period of death,
In all the Booke if any where
Such a tearme as this, *spare here*
Could have been found 'twould have been read,
Writ in white Letters o're his head: 50
Or close unto his name annext,
The faire glosse of a fairer Text.
In briefe, if any one were free,
Hee was that one, and onely he.
    But he, alas! even hee is dead   55
And our hopes faire harvest spread
In the dust. Pitty now spend
All the teares that griefe can lend.
Sad mortality may hide,
In his ashes all her pride;   60
With this inscription o're his head
All hope of never dying, here lyes dead.

37 *a softer style:* the Iron-pointed pen recalls the nails of the Crucifixion, specifically
the phrase "vel stylo clavus acuto"; see the epigram "Quicquid spina," No. 283. ("style" and
"spoyle" rhyme.)

348   [*Mr.* Herrys,] *His Epitaph.*

Passenger who e're thou art,
Stay a while, and let thy Heart
Take acquaintance of this stone,
Before thou passest further on.
This stone will tell thee that beneath,   5
Is entomb'd the Crime of Death;
The ripe endowments of whose mind,
Left his Yeares so much behind,
That numbring of his vertues praise,
Death lost the reckoning of his Dayes;   10
And believing what they told,
Imagin'd him exceeding old.
In him perfection did set forth,
The strength of her united worth.
Him his wisdomes pregnant growth   15
Made so reverend, even in Youth,
That in the Center of his Brest
(Sweet as is the Phænix nest)
Every reconciled Grace,
Had their Generall meeting place.   20
In him Goodnesse joy'd to see
Learning, learne Humility.
The splendor of his Birth and Blood,
Was but the Glosse of his owne Good:
The flourish of his sober Youth,   25
Was the Pride of Naked Truth.
In composure of his face,
Liv'd a faire, but manly Grace.
His Mouth was Rhetoricks best mold,
His Tongue the Touchstone of her Gold.   30
What word so e're his Breath kept warme,
Was no word now but a charme.
For all persuasive Graces thence
Suck't their sweetest Influence.
His vertue that within had root,   35
Could not chuse but shine without.
And th'heart-bred lustre of his worth,

His Epitaph. 46 (48). See note above.

At each corner peeping forth,
Pointed him out in all his wayes,
Circled round in his owne Rayes: 40
That to his sweetnesse, all mens eyes
Were vow'd Loves flaming Sacrifice.

Him while fresh and fragrant Time
Cherisht in his Golden Prime;
E're *Hebe's* hand had overlaid   45
His smooth cheekes, with a downy shade:
The rush of Death's unruly wave,
Swept him off into his Grave.

Enough, now (if thou canst) passe on,
For now (alas) not in this stone   50
(Passenger who e're thou art)
Is he entomb'd, but in thy Heart.

349   *Upon the Death of a Gentleman* [*Mr.* Chambers].

Faithlesse and fond Mortality,
Who will ever credit thee?
Fond and faithlesse thing! that thus,
In our best hopes beguilest us.
What a reckoning hast thou made,   5
Of the hopes in him we laid?
For Life by volumes lengthened,
A Line or two, to speake him dead.
For the Laurell in his verse,
The sullen Cypresse o're his Herse.   10
For so many hoped yeares
Of fruit, so many fruitlesse teares.
For a silver-crowned Head,
A durty pillow in Death's Bed.
For so deare, so deep a trust,   15
Sad requitall, thus much dust!
Now though the blow that snatcht him hence,
Stopt the Mouth of Eloquence,
Though shee be dumbe e're since his Death,
Not us'd to speake but in his Breath,   20
Leaving his death ungarnished

---

45 *Hebe's hand:* Hebe was a general assistant to all the gods.
Upon the Death of a Gentleman [*Mr. Chambers*]. 46 (48).* Two manuscript versions of
this epitaph identify the gentleman as Mr. Chambers, Fellow of Queens' College, Cam-
bridge. Michael Chambers was buried in the College Chapel on February 16, 1634.

Therefore, because hee is dead,
Yet if at least shee not denyes,
The sad language of our eyes,
We are contented: for then this 25
Language none more fluent is.
Nothing speakes our Griefe so well
As to speake Nothing, Come then tell
Thy mind in Teares who e're Thou be,
That ow'st a Name to misery. 30
Eyes are vocall, Teares have Tongues,
And there be words not made with lungs;
Sententious showers, ô let them fall,
Their cadence is Rhetoricall.
Here's a Theame will drinke th' expence, 35
Of all thy watry Eloquence,
Weepe then, onely be exprest
Thus much, *Hee's Dead*, and weepe the rest.

350   *An Elegy upon the death of Mr.* Stanninow
        fellow of Queenes Colledge.

Hath aged winter, fledg'd with feathered raine,
To frozen Caucasus his flight now tane?
Doth hee in downy snow there closely shrowd
His bedrid limmes, wrapt in a fleecy clowd?
Is th' earth disrobed of her apron white, 5
Kind winter's guift, and in a greene one dight?
Doth she beginne to dandle in her lappe
Her painted infants, fedd with pleasant pappe,
Which their bright father in a pretious showre
From heavens sweet milky streame doth gently poure? 10
Doth blith Apollo cloath the heavens with joye,
And with a golden wave wash cleane away
Those durty smutches, which their faire fronts wore,
And make them laugh, which frown'd and wept before?
If heaven hath now forgot to weepe; o then 15
What meane these shoures of teares amongst us men?
These Cataracts of greife, that dare ev'n vie

25 *then:* i.e. than.
27-28 *Nothing . . . Nothing:* reminiscent of the epigram "Neither durst any man from that Day," No. 33.
An Elegy upon the death of Mr. Stanninow. MS. James Stanenough, Fellow of Queens' College, Cambridge, was buried in the College Chapel March 5, 1635. One of his poems is published in Isaacson's Chronology; see Crashaw's poem "On the Frontispiece," No. 360.

With th' richest clowds their pearly treasurie?
If winter's gone, whence this untimely cold,
That on these snowy limmes hath laid such hold?   20
What more than winter hath that dire art found,
These purple currents hedg'd with violets round
To corrallize, which softly wont to slide
In crimson waveletts, and in scarlet tide?
If Flora's darlings now awake from sleepe,   25
And out of their greene mantletts dare to peepe:
O tell me then, what rude outragious blast
Forc't this prime flowre of youth to make such hast
To hide his blooming glories, and bequeath
His balmy treasure to the bedd of death?   30
'Twas not the frozen zone; One sparke of fire,
Shott from his flaming eye, had thaw'd it's ire,
And made it burne in love: 'Twas not the rage,
And too ungentle nippe of frosty age:
'Twas not the chast, and purer snow, whose nest   35
Was in the modest Nunnery of his brest:
Noe. none of these ravish't those virgin roses,
The Muses, and the Graces fragrant posies.
Which, while they smiling sate upon his face,
They often kist, and in the sugred place   40
Left many a starry teare, to thinke how soone
The golden harvest of our joyes, the noone
Of all our glorious hopes should fade,
And be eclipsed with an envious shade.
Noe, 'twas old doting Death, who, stealing by,   45
Dragging his crooked burthen, look't awry,
And streight his amorous syth (greedy of blisse)
Murdred the earth's just pride with a rude kisse.
A winged Herald, gladd of soe sweet a prey,
Snatch't upp the falling starre, soe richly gay,   50
And plants it in a precious perfum'd bedd,
Amongst those Lillies, which his bosome bredd.
Where round about hovers with silver wing
A golden summer, an æternall spring.
Now that his root such fruit againe may beare,   55
Let each eye water't with a courteous teare.

19 *winter's gone:* the poem was evidently written in a March that was unusually mild
and springlike.
23 *corrallize:* i.e. coralize, turn into coral (hence to make beautiful).
46 *burthen:* the scythe (?)

351   *Death's Lecture*

DEATH'S LECTURE AT THE FUNERAL OF
A YOUNG GENTLEMAN [MR. STANNINOW].

Dear Reliques of a dislodg'd SOUL, whose lack
Makes many a mourning paper put on black!
O stay a while, ere thou draw in thy head
And wind thy self up close in thy cold bed.
Stay but a little while, untill I call   5
A summons worthy of thy funerall.
Come then, YOUTH, BEAUTY, and blood!
     All ye soft powres,
Whose sylken flatteryes swell a few fond howres
Into a false æternity. Come man;   10
Hyperbolized NOTHING! know thy span;
Take thine own measure here: down, down, and bow
Before thy self in thine idæa; thou
Huge emptynes! contract thy self; and shrinke
All thy wild circle to a Point. O sink   15
Lower and lower yet; till thy leane size
Call heavn to look on thee with narrow eyes.
Lesser and lesser yet; till thou begin
To show a face, fitt to confesse thy Kin,
Thy neighbourhood to NOTHING.   20
Proud lookes, and lofty eyliddes, here putt on
Your selves in your unfaign'd reflexion,
Here, gallant ladyes! this unpartiall glasse
(Though you be painted) showes you your true face.
These death-seal'd lippes are they dare give the ly   25
To the lowd Boasts of poor Mortality
These curtain'd windows, this retired eye
Outstares the liddes of larg-look't tyranny.
This posture is the brave one; this that lyes
Thus low, stands up (me thinkes,) thus and defies   30
The world. All-daring dust and ashes! only you
Of all interpreters read Nature True.

Death's Lecture. 52 (46, 48).* See note above.
   2 *mourning paper:* see note to next poem, lines 7–12.

352   *An Elegie on the death of Dr.* Porter.

Stay, silver-footed Came, strive not to wed
Thy maiden streames soe soone to Neptunes bed:
Fixe heere thy wat'ry eyes upon these towers.
Unto whose feet in reverence of the powers
That there inhabite, thou on every day   5
With trembling lippes an humble kisse do'st pay.
See all in mourning now; the walles are jett,
With pearly papers carelesly besett
Whose snowy cheekes, least joy should be exprest,
The weeping pen with sable teares hath drest.   10
Their wronged beauties speake a Tragædy,
Somewhat more horrid than an Elegy.
Pure, and unmixed cruelty they tell,
Which poseth mischeife's selfe to Parallel.
Justice hath lost her hand, the law her head;   15
Peace is an Orphan now; her father's dead,
Honesties nurse, Vertues blest Guardian,
That heavenly mortall, that Seraphick man.
Enough is said. now, if thou canst crowd on
Thy lazy crawling streames, pri'thee be gone,   20
And murmur forth thy woes to every flower,
That on thy bankes sitts in a verdant bower,
And is instructed by thy glassy wave
To paint its perfum'd face with colours brave.
In vailes of dust their silken heads they'le hide,   25
As if the oft departing sunne had dy'd.
Goe learne that fatall Quire, soe sprucely dight
In downy Surplisses, and vestments white,
To sing their saddest Dir'ges, such as may
Make their scar'd soules take wing, and fly away.   30
Lett thy swolne breast discharge thy strugling groanes

An Elegie on the death of Dr Porter. MS.* George Porter, Fellow of Queens' College, Cambridge, died in 1635.
    1 *Came:* i.e. Cam, the river on which Cambridge stands (see Milton, "Lycidas," 103).
    4 *Unto those feet:* the emphasis on feet is common in the sacred poems.
    7-12 an allusion to the custom of posting papers (containing memorial verses) on the death of prominent persons; by the terms of his scholarship, Crashaw "published" in this manner his Latin epigrams "on ye skreene before dinner" (Warren, p. 215, note 11).
    15 *Justice . . . head:* Dr. Porter was Regius Professor of Civil Law.
    27 *learne:* i.e. teach.

To th' churlish rocks; and teach the stubborne stones
To melt in gentle drops, lett them be heard
Of all proud Neptunes silver-sheilded guard;
That greife may crack that string, and now untie   35
Their shackled tongues to chant an Elegie.
Whisper thy plaints to th' Oceans curteous eares,
Then weepe thyselfe into a sea of teares.
A thousand Helicons the Muses send
In a bright Christall tide, to thee they tend,   40
Leaving those mines of Nectar, their sweet fountaines,
They force a lilly path through rosy mountaines.
Feare not to dy with greife; all bubling eyes
Are teeming now with store of fresh supplies.

353   · Upon the death of a freind.

Crashaw is described in the "Preface" to 1646 as having "skill in . . .
Musicke"; the subject of this elegy was also a musician. That joint interest lies
behind many lines in the poem including probably such references as "too
deepe," "Quavering" (a quaver is an eighth note), "striking . . . touch," and
"part."

Hee's dead: Oh what harsh musicks there
Unto a choyce, and curious eare!
Wee must that Discord surely call,
Since sighs doe rise, and teares doe fall.
Teares fall too low, sighes rise too high,   5
How then can there be Harmony?
But who is he? him may wee know
That jarres, and spoiles sweet consort soe?
O Death, 'tis thou: you false time keepe,
And stretch'st thy dismall voice too deepe.   10
Long time to Quavering age you give,
But to Large youth short time to Live.
You take upon you too too much,
In striking where you should not touch.
How out of tune the world now lies,   15
Since youth must fall, when it should rise!
Gone be all Consort, since alone

---

43 *bubling:* see "The Weeper," line 1; the tears of the bereaved will keep the river full
of water.
Upon the death of a freind. MS.*

He, that once bore the best part, 's gone.
Whose whole life Musick was; wherein
Each vertue for a part came in.   20
And though that Musick of his life be still
The Musick of his name yett soundeth shrill.

354   *An Epitaph upon a Young Married Couple*

AN EPITAPH UPON
A YOUNG MARRIED COUPLE DEAD AND BURYED TOGETHER.

To these, whom DEATH again did wed,
This GRAVE's their second Marriage-bed.
For though the hand of fate could force
'Twixt SOUL and BODY a Divorce,
It could not sunder man and WIFE,   5
'Cause They Both lived but one life.
Peace, good Reader. Doe not weep.
Peace, The Lovers are asleep.
They, sweet Turtles, folded ly
In the last knott love could ty.   10
And though they ly as they were dead,
Their Pillow stone, their sheetes of lead,
(Pillow hard, and sheetes not warm)
Love made the bed; They'l take no harm
Let them sleep: let them sleep on,   15
Till this stormy night be gone,
Till the'Æternall morrow dawn;
Then the curtaines will be drawn
And they wake into a light,
Whose day shall never dy in Night.   20

22 *shrill:* loud (not pejorative).
An Epitaph upon a Young Married Couple. 52 (46, 48).*
    5 *sunder:* "Let no man put asunder" (Book of Common Prayer, Marriage Service).
    9 *Turtles:* i.e. turtle-doves.

AMOROUS

Wishes.
To his (supposed) Mistresse.

This poem appeared in truncated form in *Witt's Recreations* (1641), the version there consisting of only thirty lines, a miscellaneous selection of the tercets (Martin, pp. 443–44). This version exhibits such errors (notably at line 13: "Might you heare") as suggest that it is a subsequent and not an early form of the 1646 version. It demonstrates further that the poem was in existence in 1641, and Martin indeed suggests that it was written before 1634 (p. xc).

The poem is evidently one of the major secular poems in the canon, as it occupies the final position in the *Delights of the Muses* in 1646, and its musical charm has been pointed out often. The command of metrics and rhyme in the expanding tercets is especially notable.

> Who ere shee bee,
> That not impossible shee
> That shall command my heart and mee;
>
> Where ere shee lye,
> Lock't up from mortall Eye,   5
> In shady leaves of Destiny:
>
> Till that ripe Birth
> Of studied fate stand forth,
> And teach her faire steps to our Earth;
>
> Till that Divine   10
> *Idæa*, take a shrine
> Of Chrystall flesh, through which to shine:
>
> Meet you her, my wishes,
> Bespeake her to my blisses,
> And bee yee call'd my absent kisses.   15
>
> I wish her Beauty,
> That owes not all his Duty
> To gaudy Tire, or glistring shoo-ty.

Wishes to his (supposed) Mistresse. 46 (48).
  16–105 the wishes themselves.
  18 *Tire:* attire. *shoo-ty:* shoestring.

Something more than
Taffata or Tissew can,   20
Or rampant feather, or rich fan.

More then the spoyle
Of shop, or silkewormes Toyle
Or a bought blush, or a set smile.

A face thats best   25
By its owne beauty drest,
And can alone commend the rest.

A face made up
Out of no other shop,
Then what natures white hand sets ope.   30

A cheeke where Youth,
And Blood, with Pen of Truth
Write, what the Reader sweetly ru'th.

A Cheeke where growes
More then a Morning Rose: 35
Which to no Boxe his being owes.

Lipps, where all Day
A lovers kisse may play,
Yet carry nothing thence away.

Lookes that oppresse   40
Their richest Tires but dresse
And cloath their simplest Nakednesse.

Eyes, that displaces
The Neighbour Diamond, and out faces
That Sunshine by their owne sweet Graces.   45

Tresses, that weare
Jewells, but to declare
How much themselves more pretious are.

33 *ru'th:* i.e. rueth, pitieth.
36 *Boxe:* rouge box.

Whose native Ray,
Can tame the wanton Day   50
Of Gems, that in their bright shades play.

Each Ruby there,
Or Pearle that dare appeare,
Bee its owne blush, bee its owne Teare.

A well tam'd Heart   55
For whose more noble smart,
Love may bee long chusing a Dart.

Eyes, that bestow
Full Quivers on loves Bow;
Yet pay lesse Arrowes then they owe.   60

Smiles, that can warme
The blood, yet teach a charme,
That Chastity shall take no harme.

Blushes, that bin
The burnish of no sin,   65
Nor flames of ought too hot within.

Joyes, that confesse,
Vertue their Mistresse,
And have no other head to dresse.

Feares, fond and flight,   70
As the coy Brides, when Night
First does the longing lover right.

Teares, quickly fled,
And vaine, as those are shed
For a dying Maydenhead.   75

Dayes, that need borrow,
No part of their good Morrow,
From a fore spent night of sorrow.

60   *owe:* i.e. own.
64–65   *Blushes . . . sin:* blushes of modesty not of shame.
70   *flight:* fleeting (Martin, p. 444).

Dayes, that in spight
Of Darkenesse, by the Light   80
Of a cleere mind are Day all Night.

Nights, sweet as they,
Made short by lovers play,
Yet long by th' absence of the Day.

Life, that dares send   85
A challenge to his end,
And when it comes say *Welcome Friend*.

Sydnæan showers
Of sweet discourse, whose powers
Can Crowne old Winters head with flowers,   90

Soft silken Houres,
Open sunnes; shady Bowers,
Bove all; Nothing within that lowres.

What ere Delight
Can make Dayes forehead bright;   95
Or give Downe to the Wings of Night.

In her whole frame,
Have Nature all the Name,
Art and ornament the shame.

Her flattery,   100
Picture and Poesy,
Her counsell her owne vertue bee.

I wish, her store
Of worth, may leave her poore
Of wishes; And I wish—No more.   105

Now if Time knowes
That her, whose radiant Browes
Weave them a Garland of my vowes;

88 *Sydnæan:* like Sir Philip Sydney.
107 *That her:* That not impossible shee.

Her whose just Bayes,
My future hopes can raise,   110
A trophie to her present praise;

Her that dares bee,
What these Lines wish to see:
I seeke no further, it is shee.

'Tis shee, and heere   115
Lo I uncloath and cleare,
My wishes cloudy Character.

May shee enjoy it,
Whose merit dare apply it,
But Modesty dares still deny it.   120

Such worth as this is,
Shall fixe my flying wishes
And determine them to kisses.

Let her full Glory,
My fancyes, fly before yee,   125
Bee ye my fictions; But her story.

356   *Loves Horoscope.*

This poem offers a delicate paradox based on the conceit of astrological influences from the stars in their spheres. These influences are rejected, however, in favor of the power of a particular "Beauty," whose frowns and smiles (not the stars') control the fate of Love. The "new Astrology" (line 16) might seem to recall Donne's "new philosophy," but the context of the poem is entirely Ptolemaic. The influence of the stars is regularly used by Crashaw in addressing the royal family. The poem has a simple but logical structure—a pleasure to find in Crashaw.

Love, brave vertues younger Brother,
    Erst hath made my Heart a Mother,
    Shee consults the conscious Spheares,
    To calculate her young sons yeares.
    Shee askes if sad, or saving powers,   5
    Gave Omen to his infant howers,
    Shee asks each starre that then stood by,
    If poore Love shall live or dy.

Loves Horoscope. 46 (48).
    4 *sons yeares:* i.e. how long he will live.

Ah my Heart, is that the way?
   Are these the Beames that rule thy Day?   10
   Thou know'st a Face in whose each looke,
   Beauty layes ope loves Fortune-booke,
   On whose faire revolutions wait
   The obsequious motions of Loves fate.
   Ah my Heart, her eyes and shee,   15
   Have taught thee new Astrology.
   How e're Loves native houres were set,
   What ever starry Synod met,
   'Tis in the mercy of her eye,
   If poore Love shall live or dye.   20

If those sharpe Rayes putting on
   Points of Death bid Love be gone
   (Though the Heavens in counsell sate,
   To crowne an uncontrouled Fate,
   Though their best Aspects, twin'd upon   25
   The kindest Constellation,
   Cast amorous glances on his Birth,
   And whisper'd the confederate Earth
   To pave his pathes with all the good
   That warmes the Bed of youth and blood)   30
   Love ha's no plea against her eye
   Beauty frownes, and Love must dye.

But if her milder influence move;
   And guild the hopes of humble Love:
   (Though heavens inauspicious eye   35
   Lay blacke on loves Nativitye;
   Though every Diamond in *Joves* crowne
   Fixt his forehead to a frowne,)
   Her Eye a strong appeale can give,
   Beauty smiles and love shall live.   40

O if Love shall live, o where
   But in her Eye, or in her Eare,
   In her Brest, or in her Breath,
   Shall I hide poore Love from Death?
   For in the life ought else can give,   45
   Love shall dye although he live.

13 *revolutions:* as if Beauty were a sphere herself.
17 *native:* natal.
25 *Aspects:* a technical term meaning (from the way the planets look) the influence they shed. *twin'd:* (see poem No. 369 B, lines 60–62).

Or if Love shall dye, o where
But in her Eye, or in her Eare,
In her Breath, or in her Breast,
Shall I Build his funerall Nest?   50
While Love shall thus entombed lye,
Love shall live, although he dye.

357   *On Marriage.*

I would be married, but I'de have no Wife,
I would be married to a single Life.

358   *Epithalamium.*

This epithalamium probably celebrates the marriage of Sir John Branston and
Alice Abdy in 1635 in London. The groom and the poet were boys together
(the groom was one year older) in the same parish in London (Whitechapel),
and it is easy to believe that they knew one another. The groom's brother (one
year younger than the poet) came up to Cambridge in 1632, thus perhaps con-
tinuing the association among the young men (Martin, p. 462). The twelve-line
stanza of this poem is the most enterprising stanza Crashaw ever attempted;
the varying line lengths and the mismatched final couplet (long and short
lines) are of particular interest.

1.   Come virgin Tapers of pure waxe
        made in the Hive of Love, all white
     as snow, and yet as cold, where lackes
        Hymens holy heate and light;
            where blooming kisses
                their beds yet keepe
            and steepe their blisses
                in Rosy sleepe;
     where sister budds yet wanting brothers
     kisse their owne lipps in Lieu of others;
     help me to mourne a matchlesse maydenhead
            that now is dead:

On Marriage. 46 (48).
Epithalamium. MS.*

2. A fine thin negative thing it was
   a nothing with a dainty name,
which pruned her plumes in selfe loves glasse,
   made up of fancy and fond fame;
     within the shade
       of its owne winge
     it sate and played
       a selfe crownd King;
A froward flower, whose peevish pride
within it selfe, it selfe did hide,
flying all fingers, and even thinking much
     of its owne touch:

3. This bird indeed the phænix was
   late chaced by loves revengefull arrowes,
whose warres now left the wonted passe
   and spared the litle lives of sparrowes;
     to hunt this foole
       whose froward pride,
     Loves noble schoole,
       and Courts denyed,
And froze the fruite of faire desire
which flourisheth in mutuall fire,
'gainst nature, who 'mong all the webbs she spunn
     nere wove A Nunne:

4. She of Cupids shafts afraid
   left her owne balme-breathing East,
and in a westerne bosome made
   a softer, and a sweeter neast;
     there did she rest
       in the sweet shade,
     of a soft breast,
       whose beauties made
Thames oft stand still, and lend a glasse
while in her owne she saw heavens face,
and sent him full of her faire names report
     to Thetis Court:

4.9 *Thames:* Alice Abdy was a Londoner.
12 *Thetis:* a water goddess.

5. And now poore Love was at a stand
   the Christall castle which she kept
was proofe against the proudest hand;
   there in safest hold she slept;
      his shafts expence
         left there noe smart,
      but bounding thence
         broached his owne heart;
At length a fort he did devise
built in noble Brampstons eyes
and ayming thence, this matchlesse maydenhead
         was soone found dead:

6. Yet Love in death did wayte upon her,
   granting leave she should expire
in her fumes, and have the honour
   t' exhale in flames of his owne fire;
      her funerall pyle
         the marriage bedd,
      in a sighed smile
         she vanished.
So rich a dresse of death nere famed
the Cradles where her kindred flamed;
so sweet her mother phænixes of th' East
         nere spiced their neast:

7. With many pretty peevish tryalls
   of angry yeelding, faint denyings
melting No's, and milde denyalls
   dying lives, and short lived dyings;
      with doubtfull eyes,
         halfe smiles, halfe teares,
      with trembling joyes,
         and jocund feares;
Twixt the pretty twylight strife
of dying maide and dawning wife;
twixt raine, and sun-shine, this sweet maydenhead
         alas is dead:

6.3 *fumes:* the aromatic smoke of the phoenix' pyre.

8. Happy he whose wakefull joyes
    kept the prize of this rich losse,
happy she whose watry eyes
    kisse noe worse a weeping Crosse;
        thrice happy he
           partakes her store,
        thrice happy she
           hath still the more.
Thinke not sweet Bride, that faint shewer slakes
the fires he from thy faire eyes takes,
Thy dropps are salt, and while they thinke to tame,
        sharpen his flame:

9. Blessed Bridegroome ere the raine be layd
    use good weather while it proves,
those dropps that wash away the maide
    shall water your warme planted loves;
        faire youth make haste
           ere it be drye
        the sweet brine taste
           from her moist eye;
Thy lipps will find such deaw as this is
best season for a lovers kisses,
and those thy morning starres will better please
        bathed in those seas:

10. Nor may thy Vine, faire oake, embrace thee
    with ivy armes, and empty wishes,
but with full bosome enterlace thee,
    and reach her Clusters to thy kisses;
        safe may she rest
           her laden boughes,
        on thy firme breast,
           and fill thy vowes,
up to the brimm, till she make even
their full topps with the faire eyed heaven,
And heaven to guild those glorious Hero's birth
        stoope and kisse earth:

8.11–12 *salt . . . sharpen:* i.e. make more spicy.

11. Long may this happy heaven tyed band
    exercise its most holy art,
keeping her heart within his hand
    keeping his hand upon her heart;
        but from her eyes
            feele he noe Charmes,
        finde she noe joy
            but in his armes;
May each maintaine a well fledged neast
of winged loves in eithers breast
Be each of them a mutuall sacrefice
    of eithers eyes:

12. May their whole life a sweet song prove
    sett to two well composed parts,
by musickes noblest master, Love,
    playd on the strings of both their harts;
        whose mutuall sound
            may ever meete
        in a just round,
            not short though sweet;
Long may heaven listen to the songe,
and thinke it short though it bee long;
oh prove't a well sett song indeed, which showes
    sweet'st in the Close.

11.5, 8 *but:* except.

MISCELLANEOUS

359   Upon Bishop *Andrewes* his Picture before his Sermons.

Lancelot Andrewes (1555–1626), was Master of Pembroke College (c. 1589–1605), Bishop of Winchester, and Chairman of the Committee appointed by King James to translate the Bible. His major works include his Private Prayers and the *XCVI Sermons* preached before the King. Those sermons were collected by Archbishop Laud and the Bishop of Ely and published in folio in 1629, second edition 1631 (second issue 1632), third edition 1635, fourth edition 1641. For the 1632 issue John Payne engraved the handsome portrait (see Plate III) with these verses below (also engraved on the plate). Bishop Andrewes was one of the most influential men of his day, as a prelate, a preacher, and a writer. Echoes of his sermons are to be found throughout Crashaw's poems. It is likely that Crashaw's reputation as a youthful poet of high church sympathies recommended him to Laud and Andrewes's friends and secured for him this privileged and honorific appointment. See the Latin poems on the same subject, Nos. 403, 404.

> See heer a Shadow *from that setting* SUNNE,
> *Whose glorious course through this Horizon runn*
> *Left the dimm face of our dull Hemisphære,*
> *All one great* Eye, *all drown'd in one great* Teare.
> *Whose rare industrious Soule, led his free thought*   5
> *Through* Learning's *Universe, and (vainly) sought*
> *Roome for her spacious Self; untill at length*
> *She found the way home: with an holy strength*
> *Snatch't herself hence to Heav'n; fil'd a bright place*
> *'Midst those immortall Fires, and on the face*   10
> *Of her Great MAKER, fixt a flaming eye,*
> *Where still she reads true, pure* Divinitie.
> *And now that grave Aspect hath deign'd to shrink*
> *Into this lesse appearance. If you think*
> *'Tis but a dead face Art doth heer bequeath,*   15
> *Look on the following leaves and see him breath.*

Upon Bishop Andrewes his Picture. 32 (46, 48).*

   5 *industrious:* Andrewes was known as an indefatigable scholar (see DNB).
  16 the comment quoted by the writer of the Preface to *Steps to the Temple.*

360   *On the Frontispiece of* Isaacsons
Chronologie explained.

Henry Isaacson (1581–1657), student at Pembroke College while Lancelot Andrewes was the Master, was thereafter "an inmate of the Bishop's house, and remained with him as his amanuensis and intimate friend, until his death" (S. Isaacson, ed. *The Life and Death of Lancelot Andrewes by Henry Isaacson* [London, 1829], p. x). He was the author of a biography of Andrewes (published 1650) and of the Chronology, *Saturni ephemerides sive Tabula historico-chronologica containing, A Chronological Series or Succession of the four Monarchyes, . . . as also A Succession of the Kings and Rulers over most Kingdomes and Estates of the World . . . with A Compend of the History of the Church of God from the Creation* (London, 1633). This universal history was prefaced by commendatory verses by—among others—J. Stanenough of Cambridge, the subject of Crashaw's elegy, who speaks of Isaacson as "ingeniosissimum sibique amicissimum virum" (most ingenious and most friendly man). Isaacson, though termed "Londoner" on the title page of the volume, kept up his Cambridge associations. The poem should be read with the frontispiece (see Plate IV) in view; for a further explanation of the plate, see Martin, pp. 410–11. It is evident that the choice of Crashaw's verses for Andrewes's *Sermons* in 1632 recommended the poet to Isaacson for his volume a year later.

Let hoary TIME's vast Bowels be the Grave
To what his Bowels birth and being gave;
Let Nature die, if (PHÆNIX-like) from death
Revived Nature take a second breath;
If on TIMES right hand, sit faire HISTORIE;   5
If, from the seed of empty Ruine, she
Can raise so faire an HARVEST: Let Her be
Ne're so farre distant, yet CHRONOLOGIE
(Sharpe sighted as the EAGLES eye, that can
Out-stare the broad-beam'd Dayes Meridian)   10
Will have a PERSPICILL to finde her out,
And, through the NIGHT of error and dark doubt,
Discerne the DAWNE of Truth's eternall ray,
As when the rosie MORNE budds into Day.
    Now that TIME's Empire might be amply fill'd,   15
BABELS bold *Artists* strive (below) to build
Ruine a Temple; on whose fruitfull fall
HISTORY reares her PYRAMIDS more tall

On the Frontispiece of Isaacsons Chronologie. 33 (46, 48).*
  11 *Perspicill:* telescope.

Then were th' *Ægyptian* (by the life, these give,
Th' *Ægyptian Pyramids* themselves must live:)   20
On these she lifts the WORLD; and on their base
Shewes the two termes and limits of TIME's race:
That, the CREATION is; the JUDGEMENT, this;
That, the World's MORNING, this her MIDNIGHT is.

361   [*With Some Poems sent to a Gentlewoman. I.*]

This and the following poem preface a manuscript collection of Crashaw's
poems, apparently a gift to a lady sometime shortly before 1635. Both poems
show an interest in bookmaking and are thus related to the complimentary poems
accompanying the "Ode on a Prayer Book," No. 75 and "On Mr. G. Herberts
booke," No. 66 (see further, Williams, "Crashaw and the Little Gidding Book-
binders," *N&Q*, CCI [1956], 9–10).

At th' Ivory Tribunall of your hand
(Faire one) these tender leaves doe trembling stand.
Knowing 'tis in the doome of your sweet Eye
Whether the Muse they cloth shall live or die.
Live shee, or dye to Fame; each Leafe you meet   5
Is her Lifes wing, or her death's winding-sheet.

362   [*With Some Poems sent to a Gentlewoman. II.*]

Though now 'tis neither May nor June
And Nightingales are out of tune,
Yett in these leaves (Faire one) there lyes
(Sworne servant to your sweetest Eyes)
A Nightingale, who may shee spread   5
In your white bosome her chast bed,
Spite of all the Maiden snow
Those pure untroden pathes can show,
You streight shall see her wake and rise
Taking fresh Life from your fayre Eyes;   10
And with clasp't winges proclayme a spring
Where Love and shee shall sit and sing,
For lodg'd so ne're your sweetest throte

At th' Ivory Tribunall. MS.*
Though now 'tis neither May nor June. MS.* See note to preceding poem.
   1–2 Nightingales sing in England in May and June.
   9 *streight:* straightway.

What Nightingale can loose her noate?
Nor lett her kinred birds complayne   15
Because shee breakes the yeares old raigne,
For lett them know shee's none of those
Hedge-Quiristers whose Musicke owes
Onely such straynes as serve to keepe
Sad shades and sing dull Night asleepe.   20
No shee's a Priestesse of that Grove
The holy chappell of chast Love
Your Virgin bosome. Then what e're
Poore Lawes divide the publicke yeare,
Whose revolutions wait upon   25
The wild turnes of the wanton sun;
Bee you the Lady of Loves Yeere:
Where your Eyes shine his suns appeare:
There all the yeare is Loves long spring.
There all the yeare Loves Nightingales   30
    shall sitt and sing.

363   *Upon* The Faire Ethiopian *sent*
                  to a Gentlewoman.

The Faire Ethiopian, a translation of Heliodorus' romance *Æthiopicorum
Libri Decem* by William l'Isle, was published in London in 1631. Crashaw be-
gan a comparable translation (see further "The beginning of Heliodorus," No.
371). Charicleia, the daughter of the Ethiopian King and Queen, was born having
a fair white skin (line 1); this extraordinary circumstance caused the Queen to
conceal her and spirit her out of the country (line 2). After many remarkable
adventures (line 3), during which she is supported by the love of a young
Thessalian nobleman (line 2), Charicleia is returned in a melodramatic fashion
to her father. The poem turns on the compliment to the Gentlewoman, in com-
parison to whose "white hand" the fair Charicleia will appear black. See for an-
other Ethiopian, the epigram "On the baptized Æthiopian," No. 53.

Lo here the faire *Chariclia!* in whom strove
    So false a Fortune, and so true a Love.
Now after all her toyles by Sea and Land,
    O may she but arrive at your white hand,
Her hopes are crown'd, onely she feares that than,   5
    Shee shall appeare true Ethiopian.

14 *loose:* i.e. lose.
18 *Hedge-Quiristers:* birds (choristers) that sing in hedges. *owes:* owns.
25 *revolutions wait:* see note to "Love's Horoscope," line 13.
Upon The Faire Ethiopian. 46 (48).

364   *With a Picture sent to a Friend.*

The Preface to *Steps to the Temple* informs us of Crashaw's "skill in Poetry,
Musicke, Drawing, Limming, . . . (exercises of his curious invention and sudden
fancy)." The poem evidently accompanied a painting by Crashaw himself.

> I Paint so ill, my peece had need to bee
>   Painted againe by some good Poesie.
> I write so ill, my slender Line is scarce
>   So much as th' Picture of a well-lim'd verse.
> Yet may the love I send be true, though I   5
>   Send nor true Picture, nor true Poesie:
> Both which away, I should not need to feare,
>   My Love, or *Feign'd* or *painted* should appeare.

365   *Upon two greene Apricockes sent to*
                    Cowley *by Sir* Crashaw.

> Take these, times tardy truants, sent by me,
> To be chastis'd (sweet friend) and chidd by thee.
> Pale sons of our *Pomona!* whose wan cheekes
> Have spent the patience of expecting weekes,
> Yet are scarce ripe enough at best to show   5
> The redd, but of the blush to thee they ow.
> By thy comparrison they shall put on
> More summer in their shames reflection,
> Than ere the fruitfull *Phœbus* flaming kisses
> Kindled on their cold lips. O had my wishes   10
> And the deare merits of your Muse, their due,
> The yeare had found some fruit early as you;
> Ripe as those rich composures time computes
> Blossoms, but our blest tast confesses fruits.
> How does thy April-Autumne mocke these cold   15

With a Picture. 46 (48).
Upon two greene Apricockes. 48.* For the friendship between Cowley and Crashaw see "On
Hope," No. 68.
  3 *Pomona:* goddess of fruits.
  12 *early as you:* Cowley was unusually precocious.
  15 *April-Autumne:* spring (of youth)–harvest (of poetry).

Progressions 'twixt whose termes poor time grows old?
With thee alone he weares no beard, thy braine
Gives him the morning worlds fresh gold againe.
'Twas only Paradice, 'tis onely thou,
Whose fruit and blossoms both blesse the same bough.　　　20
Proud in the patterne of thy pretious youth,
Nature (methinks) might easily mend her growth.
Could she in all her births but coppie thee,
Into the publick yeares proficiencie,
No fruit should have the face to smile on thee　　　25
(Young master of the worlds maturitie)
But such whose sun-borne beauties what they borrow
Of beames to day, pay back againe to morrow,
Nor need be double-gilt. How then must these,
Poore fruites, looke pale at thy Hesperides!　　　30
Faine would I chide their slownesse, but in their
Defects I draw mine owne dull character.
Take them, and me in them acknowledging,
How much my summer waites upon thy spring.

366　　　　　　*Upon* Ford's *two Tragedyes*
　　　　Loves Sacrifice *and* The Broken Heart.

Thou cheat'st us *Ford*, mak'st one seeme two by Art.
What is *Loves Sacrifice*, but *the broken Heart?*

367　　　　　*On a foule Morning, being then to*
　　　　　　take a journey.

Where art thou Sol, while thus the blind-fold Day
Staggers out of the East, looses her way
Stumbling on Night? Rouze thee Illustrious Youth,
And let no dull mists choake the Lights faire growth.
Point here thy Beames; o glance on yonder flockes,　　　5

30 *Hesperides:* the daughters of Hesperus; by metonymy, the garden in the Isles of the
Blest which they guarded; by further metonymy, the golden apples that grew there.
　33–34 a notable compliment from an older to a younger man.
Upon Ford's two Tragedyes. 46 (48).
　"The two tragedies in question were both published in 1633" (Martin, p. 442).
On a foule morning. 46 (48).*

And make their fleeces Golden as thy lockes.
Unfold thy faire front, and there shall appeare
Full glory, flaming in her owne free spheare.
Gladnesse shall cloath the Earth, we will instile
The face of things, an universall smile.   10
Say to the Sullen Morne, thou com'st to court her;
And wilt command proud *Zephirus* to sport her
With wanton gales: his balmy breath shall licke
The tender drops which tremble on her cheeke;
Which rarifyed, and in a gentle raine   15
On those delicious bankes distill'd againe
Shall rise in a sweet Harvest; which discloses
Two ever blushing beds of new-borne Roses.
Hee'l fan her bright locks, teaching them to flow
And friske in curl'd *Mæanders:* Hee will throw   20
A fragrant Breath suckt from the spicy nest
O'th pretious *Phœnix,* warme upon her Breast.
Hee with a dainty and soft hand, will trim
And brush her Azure Mantle, which shall swim
In silken Volumes; wheresoe're shee'l tread,   25
Bright clouds like Golden fleeces shall be spread.
     Rise then (faire blew-ey'd Maid) rise and discover
Thy silver brow, and meet thy Golden lover.
See how hee runs, with what a hasty flight
Into thy Bosome, bath'd with liquid Light.   30
Fly, fly prophane fogs, farre hence fly away,
Taint not the pure streames of the springing Day,
With your dull influence, it is for you,
To sit and scoule upon Nights heavy brow;
Not on the fresh cheekes of the virgin Morne,   35
Where nought but smiles, and ruddy joyes are worne,
Fly then, and doe not thinke with her to stay;
Let it suffice, shee'l weare no maske to day.

---

9 *instile:* i.e. instyle, to entitle (we will name the face "one great smile").

368   *To the Morning.*
               Satisfaction for sleepe.

What succour can I hope the Muse will send
Whose drowsinesse hath wrong'd the Muses friend?
What hope *Aurora* to propitiate thee,
Unlesse the Muse sing my Apology?
    O in that morning of my shame! when I   5
Lay folded up in sleepes captivity;
How at the sight did'st Thou draw back thine Eyes,
Into thy modest veyle? how did'st thou rise
Twice di'd in thine owne blushes, and did'st run
To draw the Curtaines, and awake the Sun?   10
Who rowzing his illustrious tresses came,
And seeing the loath'd object, hid for shame
His head in thy faire Bosome, and still hides
Mee from his Patronage; I pray, he chides:
And pointing to dull *Morpheus,* bids me take   15
My owne *Apollo,* try if I can make
His *Lethe* be my *Helicon:* and see
If *Morpheus* have a Muse to wait on mee.
Hence 'tis my humble fancy finds no wings,
No nimble rapture starts to Heaven and brings   20
Enthusiasticke flames, such as can give
Marrow to my plumpe *Genius,* make it live
Drest in the glorious madnesse of a Muse,
Whose feet can walke the milky way, and chuse
Her starry throne; whose holy heats can warme   25
The Grave, and hold up an exalted arme
To lift me from my lazy Urne, to climbe
Upon the stooped shoulders of old Time;
And trace Eternity—But all is dead,
All these delicious hopes are buried,   30
In the deepe wrinckles of his angry brow,
Where mercy cannot find them: but o thou

To the Morning. 46 (48).* Martin prints a title for this poem from a manuscript (p. 183):
"To ye Deane on occasion of sleeping chappell."
   2 *friend:* evidently the Dean.
   9 *Twice di'd:* twice as rosy as usual.
   17 *Lethe:* river of forgetfulness in Hades. *Helicon:* river of the Muses.

Bright Lady of the Morne, pitty doth lye
So warme in thy soft Brest it cannot dye.
Have mercy then, and when he next shall rise   35
O meet the angry God, invade his Eyes,
And stroake his radiant Cheekes; one timely kisse
Will kill his anger, and revive my blisse.
So to the treasure of thy pearly deaw
Thrice will I pay three Teares, to show how true   40
My griefe is; so my wakefull lay shall knocke
At th' Orientall Gates; and duly mocke
The early Larkes shrill Orizons to be
An Anthem at the Dayes Nativitie.
And the same rosie-fingerd hand of thine,   45
That shutts Nights dying eyes, shall open mine.
   But thou, faint God of sleepe, forget that I
Was ever knowne to be thy votery.
No more my pillow shall thine Altar be,
Nor will I offer any more to thee   50
My selfe a melting sacrifice; I'me borne
Againe a fresh Child of the Buxome Morne,
Heire of the Suns first Beames; why threat'st thou so?
Why dost thou shake thy leaden Scepter? goe,
Bestow thy Poppy upon wakefull woe   55
Sicknesse, and sorrow, whose pale lidds ne're know
Thy downy finger, dwell upon their Eyes,
Shut in their Teares; Shut out their miseryes.

55 *Poppy:* a soporific, extracted from the plant.

VI

Secular Poems
in two English Versions

In this section, the poems are arranged with the early version on the left-hand page and the late version on the right-hand page.

369   *A Panegyricke* [upon the Royal Family]

First version 46; second version 40 (48).*

The first version of this panegyric was evidently one in the series of gratu-
latory poems that Crashaw wrote on the royal family while at Pembroke. The
first version (i.e. on the left-hand pages) names the royal children through
James, Duke of York; it is therefore to be dated between October 1633 and
December 1635 and is contemporary with "Upon the Kings coronation," No.
338. The first version had some currency, for it appears (Martin, p. 176) in
two manuscripts; it is printed in the 1646 *Steps to the Temple*. This version re-
quests a younger sister for the Princess Mary (lines 51–58), and two years
later, the Princess Elizabeth was born. Elizabeth is celebrated in "Upon the
birth of the Princesse Elizabeth," No. 339, a poem which requests a younger
brother for her (lines 55–58); five years later, Prince Henry, Duke of Glou-
cester, was born (July 8, 1640). The second version (i.e. on the right-hand
pages) celebrates the birth of Henry and the birth of Elizabeth, five years
earlier. (The lines on Elizabeth, 63–68, have an immediacy to them which sug-
gests that they were written in 1635 and not in 1640, but they do not seem to
have given separate currency to the poem a second time.) The birth of Henry,
the "new-born Prince," was celebrated by the poets at Cambridge in the gratu-
latory volume, *Voces Votivæ Ab Academicis Cantabrigiensibus* . . . (Cam-
bridge, 1640). For this volume Crashaw supplied a Latin poem, "In Reginam,
Et sibi & Academiæ semper parturientem," No. 393, and refurbished the old
"Panegyricke Upon the Duke of Yorke his Birth" by adding lines 76–114. The
second version (1640) was reprinted in the 1648 edition of *Delights of the
Muses*.

Upon the Duke of Yorke *his Birth
A Panegyricke*

Brittaine, the mighty Oceans lovely Bride,
Now stretch thy self (faire Ile) and grow, spread wide
Thy bosome and make roome; Thou art opprest
With thine owne Gloryes: and art strangely blest
Beyond thy selfe: for lo! the Gods, the Gods   5
Come fast upon thee, and those glorious ods,
Swell thy full gloryes to a pitch so high,
As sits above thy best capacitye.
   Are they not ods? and glorious? that to thee
Those mighty *Genii* throng, which well might bee   10
Each one an Ages labour, that thy dayes
Are guilded with the Union of those Rayes,
Whose each divided Beame would be a Sun,

369   *A Panegyricke* [upon the Royal Family]

[369 A]   *To the Queen,*
       An Apologie for the length of the following Panegyrick.

>   When you are Mistresse of the song,
>   Mighty Queen, to thinke it long,
>   Were treason 'gainst that Majestie
>   Your vertue wears. Your modestie
>   Yet thinks it so. But ev'n that too   5
>   (Infinite, since part of You)
>   New matter to our Muse supplies,
>   And so allows what it denies.
>   Say then, dread Queen, how may we do
>   To mediate 'twixt your self and You,   10
>   That so our sweetly temper'd song
>   Nor be too short, nor seem too long?
>   Needs must your Noble praises strength
>   That made it long, excuse the length.

[369 B]   *To the Queen,*
             Upon her numerous Progenie,
                    A Panegyrick.

Britain! the mighty Oceans lovely bride!
Now stretch thy self, fair Isle, and grow; spread wide
Thy bosome, and make room. Thou art opprest
With thine own glories, and art strangely blest
Beyond thy self: For (lo) the Gods, the Gods   5
Come fast upon thee; and those glorious ods
Swell thy full honours to a pitch so high
As sits above thy best capacitie.
  Are they not ods? and glorious? that to thee
Those mightie Genii throng, which well might be   10
Each one an ages labour? that thy dayes
Are gilded with the union of those rayes
Whose each divided beam would be a Sunne

A Panegyricke
     6 *ods:* persons "singular in . . . merit, or eminence; unique, remarkable; . . . rare."

To glad the Spheare of any Nation.
Or if for these thou mean'st to find a seat,   15
Th'ast need ô *Brittaine* to be truly Great.
And so thou art, their presence makes thee so,
They are thy Greatnesse; Gods where e're they go
Bring their Heaven with them, their great footsteps place
An everlasting smile upon the face   20
Of the glad Earth they tread on. While with thee
Those Beames that ampliate Mortalitie,
And teach it to expatiate, and swell
To Majesty, and fulnesse, deigne to dwell.
Thou by thy selfe maist sit, (blest Isle) and see   25
How thy Great Mother Nature doats on thee:
Thee therefore from the rest apart she hurl'd
And seem'd to make an Isle, but made a world.

Great *Charles!* thou sweet Dawne of a glorious day,
Center of those thy Grandsires, shall I say   30
Henry and *James*, or *Mars* and *Phoebus* rather?
If this were Wisdomes God, that Wars sterne father,
'Tis but the same is said, *Henry* and *James*
Are *Mars* and *Phoebus* under divers Names.
O thou full mixture of those mighty soules,   35
Whose vast intelligences tun'd the Poles
Of Peace and Warre; Thou for whose manly brow
Both Lawrels twine into one wreath, and wooe
To be thy Garland: see (sweet Prince) o see
Thou and the lovely hopes that smile in thee   40
Are ta'ne out and transcrib'd by thy Great Mother,
See, see thy reall shadow, see thy Brother,
Thy little selfe in lesse, read in these Eyne
The beames that dance in those full starres of thine.
From the same snowy Alablaster Rocke   45
These hands and thine were hew'n, these cherries mocke
The Corall of thy lips. Thou art of all
This well-wrought Copy the faire Principall.

To glad the sphere of any nation?
Sure, if for these thou mean'st to find a seat   15
Th'hast need, O Britain, to be truly *Great*.
    And so thou art; their presence makes thee so:
They are thy greatnesse. Gods, where-e're they go,
Bring their Heav'n with them: their great footsteps place
An everlasting smile upon the face   20
Of the glad earth they tread on. While with thee
Those beams that ampliate mortalitie,
And teach it to expatiate, and swell
To majestie and fulnesse, deign to dwell,
Thou by thy self maist sit, blest Isle, and see   25
How thy great mother Nature dotes on thee.
Thee therefore from the rest apart she hurl'd,
And seem'd to make an Isle, but made a World.
    Time yet hath dropt few plumes since Hope turn'd Joy,
And took into his arms the princely Boy,   30
Whose birth last blest the bed of his sweet Mother,
And bad us first salute our Prince a brother.
    Bright Charles! thou sweet dawn of a glorious day!   *The Prince.*
Centre of those thy Grandsires (shall I say,
Henry and James? or, Mars and Phebus rather?   35
If this were Wisdomes God, that Warres stern father,
'Tis but the same is said: Henry and James
Are Mars and Phebus under diverse names.)
O thou full mixture of those mighty souls
Whose vast intelligences tun'd the Poles   40
Of peace and warre; thou, for whose manly brow
Both lawrels twine into one wreath, and woo
To be thy garland: see, sweet Prince, O see,
Thou, and the lovely hopes that smile in thee,   *The D. of York.*
Art ta'n out and transcrib'd by thy great Mother: 45
See, see thy reall shadow; see thy Brother,
Thy little self in lesse: trace in these eyne
The beams that dance in those full starres of thine.
From the same snowie Alabaster rock
Those hands and thine were hew'n; those cherries mock   50
The corall of thy lips: Thou wert of all
This well-wrought *copie* the fair *principall*.

22 *ampliate:* extend the dignity of.
30 *Boy:* the infant Henry, Duke of York.
35 *Henry:* Henri IV of France, a distinguished warrior, whose life and reign were
marked by wars from 1580 to 1598. *James:* James I of England, a philosopher, poet, and
man of letters.

Justly, Great Nature, may'st thou brag and tell
How even th'ast drawne this faithfull Paralell,   50
And matcht thy Master-Peece: o then go on
Make such another sweet comparison.
See'st thou that *Mary* there? o teach her Mother
To shew her to her selfe in such another:
Fellow this wonder too, nor let her shine   55
Alone, light such another starre, and twine
Their Rosie Beames, so that the Morne for one
Venus, may have a Constellation.

So have I seene (to dresse their Mistresse *May*)
Two silken sister flowers consult, and lay   60
Their bashfull cheekes together, newly they
Peep't from their buds, shew'd like the Gardens eyes
Scarce wakt: like was the Crimson of their joyes,
Like were the Pearles they wept, so like that one
Seem'd but the others kind reflection.   65

55 *Fellow:* produce a companion for.

Justly, great Nature, didst thou brag, and tell
How ev'n th'hadst drawn that faithfull parallel,
And matcht thy master-peice. O then go on,　　　　　　55
Make such another sweet comparison.
Seest thou that Marie there? O teach her Mother　　*L. Mary.*
To shew her to her self in such another.
Fellow this wonder too; nor let her shine
Alone; light such another starre, and twine　　　　　60
Their rosie beams, that so the morn for one
Venus may have a Constellation.

These words scarce waken'd Heaven, when (lo) our vows
Sat crown'd upon the noble Infants brows.
Th'art pair'd, sweet Princesse: In this well-writ book　*L. Elizab.*
Read o're thy self; peruse each line, each look.　　　66
And when th'hast summ'd up all those blooming blisses,
Close up the book, and clasp it with thy kisses.
So have I seen (to dresse their mistresse May)
Two silken sister-flowers consult, and lay　　　　　70
Their bashfull cheeks together: newly they
Peep't from their buds, show'd like the garden's Eyes
Scarce wak't: like was the crimson of their joyes;
Like were the tears they wept, so like, that one
Seem'd but the others kind reflexion.　　　　　　　75

And now 'twere time to say, Sweet Queen, no more.
Fair source of Princes, is thy pretious store
Not yet exhaust? O no. Heavens have no bound,
But in their infinite and endlesse Round
Embrace themselves. Our measure is not theirs;　　　80
Nor may the pov'rtie of mans narrow prayers
Span their immensitie. More Princes, come:
Rebellion, stand thou by; Mischief, make room:
Warre, Bloud, and Death (Names all averse from Joy)　84
Heare this, We have another bright-ey'd Boy:　　　*The new-*
That word's a warrant, by whose vertue I　　　　*born Prince.*
Have full authoritie to bid you Dy.
Dy, dy, foul misbegotten Monsters; Dy:
Make haste away, or e'r the world's bright Eye
Blush to a cloud of bloud. O farre from men　　　　90
Fly hence, and in your Hyperborean den
Hide you for evermore, and murmure there

63 *vows:* prayers.

But stay, what glimpse was that? why blusht the day?
Why ran the started aire trembling away?
Who's this that comes circled in rayes, that scorne
Acquaintance with the Sunne? what second Morne
At mid-day opes a presence which Heavens eye   70
Stands off and points at? is't some Deity
Stept from her Throne of starres deignes to be seene?
Is it some Deity? or is't our Queene?
'Tis shee, 'tis shee: her awfull Beauties chase
The Dayes abashed Glories, and in face   75
Of Noone weare their owne Sunshine, ô thou bright
Mistresse of wonders! *Cynthia's* is the Night,
But thou at Noone dost shine, and art all Day,
(Nor does the Sunne deny't) our *Cynthia,*
Illustrious sweetnesse! In thy faithfull wombe,   80
That Nest of *Heroes,* all our hopes finde roome.

Where none but Hell may heare, nor our soft aire
Shrink at the hatefull sound. Mean while we bear
High as the brow of Heaven, the noble noise   95
And name of these our just and righteous joyes,
Where Envie shall not reach them, nor those eares
Whose tune keeps time to ought below the spheres.
　But thou, sweet supernumerary Starre,
Shine forth; nor fear the threats of boyst'rous Warre.   100
The face of things has therefore frown'd a while
On purpose, that to thee and thy pure smile
The world might ow an universall calm;
While thou, fair Halcyon, on a sea of balm
Shalt flote; where while thou layst thy lovely head,   105
The angry billows shall but make thy bed:
Storms, when they look on thee, shall straight relent;
And Tempests, when they tast thy breath, repent
To whispers soft as thine own slumbers be,
Or souls of Virgins which shall sigh for thee.   110
　Shine then, sweet supernumerary Starre;
Nor feare the boysterous names of Bloud and Warre:
Thy Birthday is their Death's Nativitie;
They've here no other businesse but to die.   114

　But stay; what glimpse was that? why blusht the day?   *To the*
Why ran the started aire trembling away?   *Queen.*
Who's this that comes circled in rayes that scorn
Acquaintance with the Sun? what second morn
At midday opes a presence which Heavens eye
Stands off and points at? Is't some Deity   120
Stept from her throne of starres, deignes to be seen?
Is it some Deity? or i'st our Queen?
　'Tis she, 'tis she: Her awfull beauties chase
The Day's abashed glories, and in face
Of noon wear their own Sunshine. O thou bright   125
Mistresse of wonders! Cynthia's is the night;
But thou at noon dost shine, and art all day
(Nor does thy Sun deny't) our Cynthia.
　Illustrious sweetnesse! in thy faithfull wombe,
That nest of Heroes, all our hopes find room.   130

---

104 *Halcyon:* kingfisher, which was thought to nest on the ocean and to charm the
winds and waves to calmness.
129–38 see Wallerstein further for comment on the image of the phoenix, pp. 129–32.

Thou art the Mother *Phœnix,* and thy Breast
Chast as that Virgin honour of the East,
But much more fruitfull is; nor does, as shee,
Deny to mighty Love a Deity.   85
Then let the Easterne world bragge and be proud
Of one coy *Phœnix,* while we have a brood
A brood of *Phœnixes,* while we have Brother
And Sister *Phœnixes,* and still the Mother;
And may we long; long may'st thou live, t'encrease   90
The house and family of *Phœnixes.*
Nor may the light that gives their Eye-lids light,
E're prove the dismall Morning of thy Night:
Ne're may a Birth of thine be bought so deare,
To make his costly cradle of thy Beere.   95
O mayst thou thus make all the yeare thine owne,
And see such Names of joy sit white upon
The brow of every Moneth; and when that's done
Mayest in a son of his find every son
Repeated, and that son still in another,   100
And so in each child often prove a Mother:
Long mayest thou laden with such clusters leane
Upon thy Royall Elme (faire Vine) and when
The Heavens will stay no longer, may thy glory
And Name dwell sweet in some eternall story!   105

Pardon (bright excellence) an untun'd string,
That in thy Eares thus keeps a murmuring.
O speake a lowly Muses pardon; speake
Her pardon or her sentence; onely breake
Thy silence; speake; and she shall take from thence   110
Numbers, and sweetnesse, and an influence
Confessing thee: or (if too long I stay)
O speake thou and my Pipe hath nought to say:
For see *Appollo* all this while stands mute,
Expecting by thy voyce to tune his Lute.   115

But Gods are gratious: and their Altars, make
Pretious their offerings that their Altars take.
Give then this rurall wreath fire from thine eyes.
This rurall wreath dares be thy sacrifice.

Thou art the Mother-Phenix, and thy brest
Chast as that Virgin honour of the East,
But much more fruitfull is; nor does, as she,
Deny to mightie Love a Deitie.
Then let the Eastern world brag and be proud   135
Of one coy Phenix, while we have a brood,
A brood of Phenixes; while we have Brother
And Sister-Phenixes, and still the Mother.
    And may we long! Long mayst Thou live t'increase
The house and family of Phenixes.   140
Nor may the life that gives their eye-lids light
E're prove the dismall morning of thy night:
Ne're may a birth of thine be bought so dear
To make his costly cradle of thy beer.
    O mayst thou thus make all the year thine own,   145
And see such names of joy sit white upon
The brow of every moneth! And when th'hast done,
Mayst in a son of His find every son
Repeated, and that son still in another,
And so in each child often prove a Mother.   150
Long mayst Thou, laden with such clusters, lean
Upon thy Royall Elm, fair Vine! And when
The Heav'ns will stay no longer, may thy glory
And name dwell sweet in some Eternall story!

    Pardon, bright Excellence, an untun'd string,   155
That in thy eares thus keeps a murmuring.
O speake a lowly Muses pardon, speake
Her pardon, or her sentence; onely break
Thy silence. Speak, and she shall take from thence
Numbers, and sweetnesse, and an influence   160
Confessing Thee. Or if too long I stay,
O speak Thou, and my Pipe hath nought to say:
For see Apollo all this while stands mute,
Expecting by thy voice to tune his Lute.

    But Gods are gracious; and their Altars make   165
Pretious the off'rings that their Altars take.
Give then this rurall wreath fire from thine eyes,
This rurall wreath dares be thy Sacrifice.

144 *beer:* i.e. bier.
167 *rurall:* unsophisticated; a modest disclaimer.

370   *In praise of Lessius*

First version: "On taking Physicke" 46, "To the Reader" 34; second version: "Temperance" 52.*

Leonard Lessius (Leys) (1554–1623), a Jesuit theologian and Professor of Philosophy at Louvain, published *Hygiasticon seu vera ratio valetudinis bonae et vitae* (Antverpiæ, 1613–14). An English translation of this work, *Hygiasticon: Or the Right course of preserving Life and Health unto extream old Age* (Cambridge, 1634), by T. S., appeared in two editions in 1634 with a third in 1636. (In this publication was included also George Herbert's English translation of Lessius' Latin translation of Luigi Cornaro's Italian *Trattato de la vita sobria* [Padua, 1558], another treatise on temperate diet. Both Herbert and the Ferrars at Little Gidding practiced such a regimen of diet (see F. E. Hutchinson, ed. *The Works of George Herbert* [Oxford, 1959], pp. 564–66). Crashaw wrote the commendatory verses ("To the Reader") for the second edition of

[370 A]   *On taking Physicke*

> Goe now with some dareing drugg,
> Baite thy disease, and while they tugg
> Thou to maintaine their cruell strife,
> Spend the deare treasures of thy life:
> Goe, take phisicke, doat upon   5
> Some bigg-named composition,
> The oraculous doctors mistick bills,
> Certain hard words made into pills;
> And what at length shalt get by these?
> Onely a costlyer disease.   10
> Goe, poore man, thinke what shall bee
> Remedie 'gainst thy remedie.
> That which makes us have no need
> Of Phisick, thats Phisick indeed.

[370 B]   *To the Reader, upon this*
             Books intent.

> Heark hither, Reader: wouldst thou see
> Nature her own Physician be?
> Wouldst see a man all his own wealth,
> His own musick, his own health?
> A man, whose sober soul can tell   5
> How to wear her garments well;

370 *In praise of Lessius*

1634. The lines at the beginning ("On taking Physicke") appear as a unit in one manuscript (Martin, p. 156). The lines were originally, I would suggest, a separate poem, and Crashaw has later prefixed them to another poem on a comparable theme. The joint between the two poems is hardly smooth, nor is the thought in the second version ("Temperance") altogether coherent. The 1646 *Delights of the Muses* prints (as one poem) lines 1–14 and 1–32 ("Goe now . . . Live to be old and still a man?"); it is difficult to argue for any authority for this abrupt truncation. There is a sort of conclusion to this version, but the final eight lines found in the earlier printing of 1634 and the later of 1652 (and 48) are clearly a superior conclusion. The heading of 52 in calling attention to the cheapness of this method is responding to the idea of economy mentioned in "On taking Physicke"; that idea hardly occurs elsewhere in the poem.

TEMPERANCE. OR THE CHEAP PHYSITIAN
UPON THE TRANSLATION OF LESSIUS.

Goe now; and with some daring drugg
Bait thy disease. And whilst they tugge,
Thou to maintain their pretious strife
Spend the dear treasures of thy life.
Goe, take physick: Doat upon   5
Some big-nam'd composition.
Th'Oraculous Doctor's mystick bills;
Certain hard Words made into pills,
And what at last shalt' gain by these?
Only a costlyer disease.   10

That which makes us have no need
Of physick, that's Physick indeed.
Hark hither, Reader! wilt thou see
Nature her own physitian be?
Wilt' see a man, all his own wealth,   15
His own musick, his own health;
A man whose sober soul can tell
How to wear her garments well.

18 *garments:* the garments of the soul are the body.

Her garments that upon her sit
(As garments should do) close and fit?
A well-cloth'd soul, that's not opprest
Nor choakt with what she should be drest?   10
Whose soul's sheath'd in a crystall shrine,
Through which all her bright features shine;
As when a piece of wanton lawn,
A thinne aeriall vail, is drawn
O're Beauties face; seeming to hide,   15
More sweetly shows the blushing bride?
A soul, whose intellectuall beams
No mists do mask, no lazie steams?
A happie soul, that all the way
To heav'n rides in a summers day?   20
Wouldst see a man, whose well-warm'd bloud
Bathes him in a genuine floud?
A man, whose tuned humours be
A set of rarest harmonie?
Wouldst see blithe looks, fresh cheeks beguile   25
Age? wouldst see December smile?
Wouldst see a nest of roses grow
In a bed of reverend snow?
Warm thoughts, free spirits, flattering
Winters self into a spring?   30

In summe, wouldst see a man that can
Live to be old, and still a man;
Whose latest and most leaden houres
Fall with soft wings, stuck with soft flowres?
And when lifes sweet fable ends,   35
His soul and bodie part like friends:
No quarrels, murmures, no delay;
A kisse, a sigh, and so away?
This rare one, Reader, wouldst thou see?
Heark hither, and thy self be he.   40

Her garments, that upon her sitt
As garments should doe, close and fitt;   20
A well-cloth'd soul; that's not opprest
Nor choak't with what she should be drest.
A soul sheath'd in a christall shrine;
Through which all her bright features shine;
As when a peice of wanton lawn   25
A thinne, aeriall veil, is drawn
Or'e beauty's face; seeming to hide
More sweetly showes the blushing bride.
A soul, whose intellectuall beames
No mists doe mask, no lazy steames.   30
A happy soul, that all the way
To HEAVN rides in a summer's day.
Wouldst' see a man, whose well-warm'd blood
Bathes him in a genuine flood!
A man, whose tuned humors be   35
A set of rarest harmony?
Wouldst' see blith lookes, fresh cheekes beguil
Age? wouldst see december smile?
Wouldst' see nests of new roses grow
In a bed of reverend snow?   40
Warm thoughts, free spirits flattering
Winter's selfe into a SPRING?

In summe, wouldst see a man that can
Live to be old, and still a man?
Whose latest and most leaden houres   45
Fall with soft wings, stuck with soft flowres;
And when life's sweet fable ends,
Soul and body part like freinds;
No quarrells, murmurs, no delay;
A KISSE, a SIGH, and so away.   50
This rare one, reader, wouldst thou see?
Hark hither; and thy self be HE.

35 *humors:* i.e. the four physiological conditions.

VII

Secular Poems translated into English from Greek, Latin, and Italian

In this section, the Greek, Latin, and Italian originals are on the left-hand page, and Crashaw's English versions are on the right-hand page.

371   ΗΛΙΟΔΩΡΟΥ ΑΙΘΙΟΠΙΚΩΝ
(Heliodorus' The Æthiopians)

ΠΡΩΤΟΝ

Ἡμέρας ἄρτι διαγελώσης καὶ ἡλίου τὰς ἀκρωρείας καταυγά-

ζοντος, ἄνδρες ἐν ὅπλοις ληστρικοῖς ὄρους ὑπερκύψαντες, ὃ δὴ

κατ' ἐκβολὰς τοῦ Νείλου καὶ στόμα τὸ καλούμενον Ἡρακλεωτικὸν

ὑπερτείνει, μικρὸν ἐπιστάντες τὴν ὑποκειμένην θάλατταν ὀφθαλ-

μοῖς ἐπήρχοντο, καὶ τῷ πελάγει τὰς ὄψεις τὸ πρῶτον ἐπαφέντες,

ὡς οὐδὲν ἄγρας ληστρικῆς ἐπηγγέλλετο μὴ πλεόμενον, ἐπὶ τὸν

πλησίον αἰγιαλὸν τῇ θέᾳ κατήγοντο. καὶ ἦν τὰ ἐν αὐτῷ τοιάδε·

ὁλκὰς ἀπὸ πρυμνησίων ὥρμει τῶν μὲν ἐμπλεόντων χηρεύουσα,

φόρτου δὲ πλήθουσα· καὶ τοῦτο παρῆν συμβάλλειν καὶ τοῖς πόρ-

ρωθεν· τὸ γὰρ ἄχθος ἄχρι καὶ ἐπὶ τρίτου ζωστῆρος τῆς νεὼς τὸ

ὕδωρ ἀνέθλιβεν. ὁ δὲ αἰγιαλός, μεστὰ πάντα σωμάτων νεοσφαγῶν,

τῶν μὲν ἄρδην ἀπολωλότων, τῶν δὲ ἡμιθνήτων καὶ μέρεσι τῶν

σωμάτων ἔτι σπαιρόντων, ἄρτι πεπαῦσθαι τὸν πόλεμον κατηγο-

ρούντων. ἦν δὲ οὐ πολέμου καθαροῦ τὰ φαινόμενα σύμβολα, ἀλλ'

ἀναμέμικτο καὶ εὐωχίας οὐκ εὐτυχοῦς ἀλλ' εἰς τοῦτο ληξάσης,

ἀλεεινὰ λείψανα, τράπεζαι τῶν ἐδεσμάτων ἔτι πλήθουσαι.

371   *The beginning of* Heliodorus.

The smiling Morne had newly wak't the Day,
And tipt the mountaines in a tender ray:
When on a hill (whose high Imperious brow
Lookes downe, and sees the humble Nile below
Licke his proud feet, and hast into the seas   5
Through the great mouth thats nam'd from *Hercules*)
A band of men, rough as the Armes they wore
Look't round, first to the sea, then to the shore.
The shore that shewed them what the sea deny'd,
Hope of a prey. There to the maine land ty'd   10
A ship they saw, no men shee had; yet prest
Appear'd with other lading, for her brest
Deep in the groaning waters wallowed
Up to the third Ring; o're the shore was spread
Death's purple triumph, on the blushing ground   15
Lifes late forsaken houses all lay drown'd
In their owne bloods deare deluge, some new dead,
Some panting in their yet warme ruines bled:
While their affrighted soules, now wing'd for flight
Lent them the last flash of her glimmering light.   20
Those yet fresh streames which crawled every where
Shew'd, that sterne warre had newly bath'd him there:
Nor did the face of this disaster show
Markes of a fight alone, but feasting too,
A miserable and a monstrous feast,   25
Where hungry warre had made himself a Guest:
And comming late had eat up Guests and all,
Who prov'd the feast to their owne funerall, &c.

Beginning of Heliodorus. 46 (48).* Crashaw translates from the beginning of Heliodorus' ro-
mance *Æthiopicorum Libri Decem.* For a discussion of this Greek prose romance, see
"Upon the Faire Ethiopian," No. 363.
    6 *great mouth:* i.e. the Straits of Gibraltar, called the Pillars of Hercules.

372   ῎Ερως δραπέτης. (*Cupid's Cryer*)

This poem by Moschus, a Greek pastoral poet, provides a picture of the pagan Eros to contrast with Crashaw's many descriptions of sacred love. The first attribute, for example—"Her little fugitive"—will be found as the basis

ʽΑ Κύπρις τὸν ῎Ερωτα τὸν υἱέα μακρὸν ἐβώστρει·

ὅϊτις ἐνὶ τριόδοισι πλανώμενον εἶδεν ῎Ερωτα —

δραπετίδας ἐμός ἐστιν — ὁ μανύτας γέρας ἑξεῖς

μισθός τοι, τὸ φίλαμα τὸ Κύπριδος· ἢν δ' ἀγάγῃς νιν,

οὐ γυμνὸν τὸ φίλαμα, τὶ δ' ὦ ξένε καὶ πλέον ἑξεῖς.

ἔστι δ' ὁ παῖς περίσαμος· ἐν εἴκοσι πᾶσι μάθησῇ.

χρῶτα μὲν οὐ λευκός, πυρὶ δ' εἴκελος· ὄμματα δ' αὐτῷ

δριμύλα καὶ φλογόεντα· κακαὶ φρένες, ἁδὺ λάλημα·

οὐ γὰρ ἴσον νοέει καὶ φθέγγεται· ὡς μέλι φωνά,

ἐν δὲ χολὰ νόος ἐστὶν ἀνάμερος· ἠπεροπευτάς,

οὐδὲν ἀλαθεύων, δόλιον βρέφος, ἄγρια παίσδων.

εὐπλόκαμον τὸ κάρανον, ἔχει δ' ἰταμὸν τὸ μέτωπον.

μικκύλα μὲν τήνῳ τὰ χερύδρια, μακρὰ δὲ βάλλει,

βάλλει κεῖς ᾽Αχέροντα καὶ εἰς ᾽Αΐδεω βασιλῆα.

γυμνὸς ὅλος τό γε σῶμα, νόος δέ οἱ εὖ πεπύκασται.

καὶ πτερόεις ὡς ὄρνις ἐφίπταται ἄλλον ἐπ' ἄλλῳ,

ἀνέρας ἠδὲ γυναῖκας, ἐπὶ σπλάγχνοις δὲ κάθηται.

τόξον ἔχει μάλα βαιόν, ὑπὲρ τόξω δὲ βέλεμνον,

372   *Out of the Greeke* Cupid's *Cryer.*

of "[Non fugitivus Amor]," No. 117. The "Quiver Shafts and Bow" (line 70)
reappear in "In cicatrices Domini," No. 50.

Love is lost, nor can his Mother
Her little fugitive discover:
Shee seekes, shee sighs, but no where spyes him;
Love is lost; and thus shee cryes him.
O yes! if any happy eye,   5
This roaving wanton shall descry:
Let the finder surely know
Mine is the wagge; Tis I that owe
The winged wand'rer, and that none
May thinke his labour vainely gone,   10
The glad descryer shall not misse,
To tast the *Nectar* of a kisse
From *Venus* lipps. But as for him
That brings him to mee, hee shall swim
In riper joyes: more shall bee his   15
(*Venus* assures him) than a kisse;
But least your eye discerning slide
These markes may bee your judgements guide;
His skin as with a fiery blushing
High-colour'd is; His eyes still flushing   20
With nimble flames, and though his mind
Be ne're so curst, his Tongue is kind:
For never were his words in ought
Found the pure issue of his thought.
The working Bees soft melting Gold,   25
That which their waxen Mines enfold,
Flow not so sweet as doe the Tones
Of his tun'd accents; but if once
His anger kindle, presently
It boyles out into cruelty,   30
And fraud: Hee makes poore mortalls hurts,
The objects of his cruell sports.
With dainty curles his froward face

Out of the Greeke Cupid's *Cryer.* 46 (48).* *Cryer:* one who calls out public announcements,
here the description of a fugitive and the rewards for his arrest.
  5 *O yes:* i.e. Oyez, the call for attention.
  8 *owe:* own.

τυτθὸν μὲν τὸ βέλεμνον, ἐς αἰθέρα δ' ἄχρι φορεῖται.

καὶ χρύσεον περὶ νῶτα φαρέτριον, ἔνδοθι δ' ἐντί

τοὶ πικροὶ κάλαμοι, τοῖς πολλάκι κάμμε τιτρώσκει.

πάντα μὲν ἄγρια ταῦτα· πολὺ πλεῖον ἅ δ' ἀεὶ ἀυτῷ

βαιὰ λαμπὰς ἐοῖσα τὸν "Αλιον αὐτὸν ἀναίθει.

ἤν τις ἕλῃ τῆνον, δήσας ἄγε μηδ' ἐλεήσῃς.

κἤν ποτίδῃς κλαίοντα, φυλάσσεο μή σε πλανήσῃ.

κἤν γελάῃ, τύ νιν ἕλκε. καὶ ἤν ἐθέλῃ σε φιλῆσαι,

φεῦγε· κακὸν τὸ φίλημα, τὰ χείλεα φάρμακον ἐντί.

ἤν δὲ λέγῃ "λάβε ταῦτα, χαρίζομαι ὅσσά μοι ὅπλα,"

μὴ τι θίγῃς πλάνα δῶρα· τὰ γὰρ πυρὶ πάντα βέβαπται.

Is crown'd about; But ô what place,
What farthest nooke of lowest Hell 35
Feeles not the strength, the reaching spell
Of his small hand? Yet not so small
As 'tis powerfull therewithall.
Though bare his skin, his mind hee covers,
And like a saucy Bird he hovers 40
With wanton wing, now here, now there,
'Bout men and women, nor will spare
Till at length he perching rest,
In the closet of their brest.
His weapon is a little Bow, 45
Yet such a one as (*Jove* knowes how)
Ne're suffred yet his little Arrow
Of Heavens high'st Arches to fall narrow.
The Gold that on his Quiver smiles,
Deceives mens feares with flattering wiles. 50
But o (too well my wounds can tell)
With bitter shafts 'tis sauc't too well.
Hee is all cruell, cruell all;
His Torch Imperious though but small
Makes the Sunne (of flames the sire) 55
Worse then Sun-burnt in his fire.
Wheresoe're you chance to find him
Cease him, bring him, (but first bind him)
Pitty not him, but feare thy selfe
Though thou see the crafty Elfe, 60
Tell down his Silver-drops unto thee,
They'r counterfeit, and will undoe thee.
With baited smiles if he display
His fawning cheeks, looke not that way;
If hee offer sugred kisses, 65
Start, and say, The Serpent hisses.
Draw him, drag him, though hee pray
Wooe, intreat, and crying say
Prethee, sweet now let me goe,
Here's my Quiver Shafts and Bow, 70
I'le give thee all, take all; take heed
Lest his kindnesse make thee bleed.
  What e're it be Love offers, still presume
  That though it shines, 'tis fire and will consume.

58 *Cease:* i.e. Seize.

373   [Venus *putting on the Arms of* Mars.]

"Αρεος ἔντεα ταῦτα τίνος χάριν, ὦ Κυθέρεια,
ἐνδέδυσαι, κενεὸν τοῦτο φέρουσα βάρος.
αὐτὸν "Αρη γυμνὴ γὰρ ἀφώπλισας· εἰ δὲ λέλειπται
καὶ θεός, ἀνθρώποις ὅπλα μάτην ἐπάγεις.

374   *De* Pallade *Volente Certare Armis Cum* Venere.

Armatam vidit Venerem Lacedæmone Pallas.
Nunc certemus, ait, iudice vel Paride.
Cui Venus: Armatam tu me, temeraria, temnis,
Quæ, quo te vici tempore, nuda fui?

375   *In Faustulum Staturæ Brevis Anicii Probini*
           (*On little* Faustulus)

Faustulus insidens formicæ, ut magno elephanto,
Decidit, et terræ terga supina dedit.
Moxque idem ad mortem est mulcatus calcibus eius,
Perditus ut posset vix retinere animam.
Vix tamen est fatus: Quid rides, improbe livor?
Quod cecidi: cecidit non aliter Phæthon.

376   *CARMEN V. Ad* Lesbiam. (*Song V. to* Lesbia.)

Vivamus, mea Lesbia, atque amemus,

Rumoresque senum severiorum

Omnes unius æstimemus assis.

Soles occidere, et redire possunt:

Nobis, cum semel occidit brevis lux,

373   *Upon* Venus *putting on* Mars *his Armes.*

What? *Mars* his sword? faire *Cytherea* say,
    Why art thou arm'd so desperately to day?
Mars thou hast beaten naked, and o then
    What need'st thou put on armes aginst poore men?

374   *Upon the same.*

Pallas saw *Venus* arm'd, and streight she cry'd,
    Come if thou dar'st, thus, thus let us be try'd.
Why foole! saies *Venus*, thus provok'st thou mee,
    That being nak't, thou know'st could conquer thee?

375   *On* Nanus *mounted upon an Ant.*

High mounted on an Ant *Nanus* the tall
Was throwne alas, and got a deadly fall.
Under th' unruly Beasts proud feet he lies
All torne; with much adoe yet ere he dyes,
Hee straines these words; Base Envy, doe, laugh on.   5
Thus did I fall, and thus fell *Phaethon.*

376   *Out of* Catullus.

Come and let us live my Deare,
Let us love and never feare,
What the sowrest Fathers say:
Brightest *Sol* that dyes to day
Lives againe as blith to morrow,   5
But if we darke sons of sorrow
Set; ô then, how long a Night

Upon Venus putting on Mars his Armes. 46 (48).* The Greek epigram is attributed to Le-
onidas of Alexandria (Martin, p. 440).

Upon the same. 46 (48).* Crashaw omits the Latin reference to the judgment of Paris; a
closer translation of line 2 would read: "Now let us try . . . whether Paris was a [good]
judge." The Latin poem is by Ausonius, entitled "On Pallas, wishing to vie in arms with
Venus."

On Nanus mounted upon an Ant. 46 (48).* The Latin is by Ausonius.
   6 *Phaethon:* the son of the Sun who fell while driving the chariot of the sun.

Out of Catullus. 46 (48).* One of the most popular and most often translated of the Catullan
songs, Carmen v.

Nox est perpetua una dormienda.

Da mi basia mille, deinde centum,

Dein mille altera, dien secunda centum:

Dein usque altera mille, deinde centum:

Dein cum millia multa fecerimus,

Conturbabimus illa, ne sciamus,

Aut ne quis malus invidere possit,

Cum tantum sciat esse basiorum.

377   [*A prayer to* Venus.]

O dea, syderei seu tu stirps alma Tonantis,
Seu patrem factura Jovem, da numine dextro
Has movisse preces, placataque lumina flecte.
Ecce ignes jussitque pati, jussitque fateri.
Nil non ausus amor. Nec sortem despice nostram,
Nympha potens, Cælum cognataque numina cernis
Pauperibus votis & parco thure vocari,
Placarique tamen. Tibi jam sua stamina Parcæ
Concessere meæ. Vitam si forte negabis,
Da saltem Regina mori; da sydere flammæ
Nympha perire tuæ. Non dignius arserit ales,
Quæ super Eöos extincta renascitur ignes.

Shuts the Eyes of our short light!
Then let amorous kisses dwell
On our lips, begin and tell   10
A Thousand, and a Hundred score
An Hundred, and a Thousand more,
Till another Thousand smother
That, and that wipe of another.
Thus at last when we have numbred   15
Many a Thousand, many a Hundred;
Wee'l confound the reckoning quite,
And lose our selves in wild delight:
While our joyes so multiply,
As shall mocke the envious eye.   20

377   *Out of* Euphormio.

Bright Goddesse, (whether Jove thy father be;
Or Jove a father will be made by thee)
Oh crowne these praie'rs (mov'd in a happy hower)
But with one cordiall smile. for (loe) that power
Of Loves all-daring hand, that makes me burne,   5
Makes me confess't. Oh, doe not thou with scorn,
Great Nymph, o'relooke my lownesse. heav'n you know,
And all their fellow Deities will bow
Ev'en to the naked'st vowes. thou art my fate;
To thee the Parcæ have given up of late   10
My threds of life. if then I shall not live
By thee; by thee yet lett me die. this give,
High beauties soveraigne, that my funerall flames
May draw their first breath from thy starry beames.
The Phænix selfe shall not more proudly burne,   15
That fetcheth fresh life from her fruitfull urne.

10 *tell:* i.e. count up.
Out of Euphormio. MS.*
10 *Parcæ:* the Fates.

378   [*On Ælia's cough.*]

Si memini, fuerant tibi quatuor Ælia dentes:

Exspuit una duos tussis, & una duos.

Jam secura potes totis tussire diebus;
Nil istic, quod agat, tertia tussis habet.

379   [*On Taste.*]

 Ales Phasiacis petita Colchis,

 Et pictis Attagen opaca pennis,

 Atque Afræ volucres placent palato,

 Quod non sunt faciles: at albus anser

 Plebeium sapit. ultimis ab oris

 Attractus Scarus, atque arata Syrtio

 Siquid naufragio dedit, probatur.

 Mullus jam gravis est: amica vincit

 Uxorem: rosa cinnamum veretur:

 Quicquid quæritur, optimum videtur.

378   *Out of* Martiall.

Foure Teeth thou had'st that ranck'd in goodly state
    Kept thy Mouthes Gate.

The first blast of thy cough left two alone,
    The second, none.

This last cough *Ælia,* cought out all thy feare,
Th'hast left the third cough now no businesse here.

379   *Out of* Petronius.

The bird, that's fetch't from Phasis floud,
Or choicest hennes of Africk-brood;
These please our palates. and why these?
'Cause they can but seldome please.
Whil'st the goose soe goodly white,   5
And the drake yeeld noe delight,
Though his wings conceited hewe
Paint each feather, as if new.
These for vulgar stomacks be,
And rellish not of rarity.   10
But the dainty Scarus, sought
In farthest clime; what e're is bought
With shipwracks toile, Oh, that is sweet,
'Cause the quicksands hanselld it.
The pretious Barbill, now groune rife,   15
Is cloying meat. How stale is Wife?
Deare wife hath ne're a handsome letter,
Sweet mistris sounds a great deale better.
Rose quakes at name of Cinnamon.
Unlesse't be rare, what's thought upon?   20

Out of Martiall. 46 (48).*
Out of Petronius. MS.*
  1 *Phasis:* a remote river in Asia, regarded as the easternmost limit of navigation.
 11 *Scarus:* an exotic fish believed to chew the cud.
 14 *hanselld:* tasted first (OED).
 15 *Barbill:* a fish of great delicacy (barbel).

380 *[In praise of Spring.]*

Ver adeo frondi nemorum, ver utile sylvis;

Vere tument terræ et genitalia semina poscunt.

Tum pater omnipotens fœcundis imbribus æther

Conjugis in gremium læté descendit, & omnes

Magnus alit, magno commistus corpore fœtus.

Avia tum resonant avibus virgulta canoris,

Et Venerem certis repetunt armenta diebus.

Parturit almus ager: Zephyrique tepentibus auris

Laxant arva sinus; superat tener omnibus humor:

Inque novos Soles audent se gramina tutó

Credere: nec metuit surgentes pampinus Austros,

Aut actum cœlo magnis Aquilonibus imbrem:

Sed trudit gemmas, & frondes explicat omnes.

Non alios prima crescentis origine mundi

Illuxisse dies, aliumve habuisse tenorem

Crediderim: ver illud erat, ver magnus agebat

Orbis, & hibernis parcebant flatibus Euri:

Quum primum lucem pecudes hausere, virumque

Ferrea progenies duris caput extulit arvis:

Immissæque feræ silvis, & sidera cœlo.

Nec res hunc teneræ possent perferre laborem,

Si non tanta quies iret frigusque caloremque

Inter, & exciperet cœli indulgentia terras.

380   *Out of* Virgil, *In the praise of the Spring*

All Trees, all leavy Groves confesse the Spring
Their gentlest friend, then, then the lands begin
To swell with forward pride, and seed desire
To generation; Heavens Almighty Sire
Melts on the Bosome of his Love, and powres   5
Himselfe into her lap in fruitfull showers.
And by a soft insinuation, mixt
With earths large Masse, doth cherish and assist
Her weake conceptions; No loane shade, but rings
With chatting Birds delicious murmurings.   10
Then *Venus* mild instinct (at set times) yeilds
The Herds to kindly meetings, then the fields
(Quick with warme *Zephires* lively breath) lay forth
Their pregnant Bosomes in a fragrant Birth.
Each body's plump and jucy, all things full   15
Of supple moisture: no coy twig but will
Trust his beloved bosome to the Sun
(Growne lusty now;) No Vine so weake and young
That feares the foule-mouth'd Auster, or those stormes
That the Southwest-wind hurries in his Armes,   20
But hasts her forward Blossomes, and layes out
Freely layes out her leaves: Nor doe I doubt
But when the world first out of *Chaos* sprang
So smil'd the Dayes, and so the tenor ran
Of their felicity. A spring was there,   25
An everlasting spring, the jolly yeare
Led round in his great circle; No winds Breath
As then did smell of Winter, or of Death.
When Lifes sweet Light first shone on Beasts, and when
From their hard Mother Earth, sprang hardy men,   30
When Beasts tooke up their lodging in the Wood,
Starres in their higher Chambers: never cou'd
The tender growth of things endure the sence
Of such a change, but that the Heav'ns Indulgence
Kindly supplies sick Nature, and doth mold   35
A sweetly temper'd meane, nor hot nor cold.

Out of Virgil. 46 (48).* A translation of the *Georgics,* ii. 323–45. Ellrodt (I, 382) has called attention to this poem (and to "Veris descriptio") as an example of Crashaw's attraction to erotic themes even early in his career, "des amours printanières."
  5–6 *Melts . . . powres . . . showers:* the archetype of this metaphor is the union of Danaë with Jove, who fell into her lap in a shower of gold.
  19 *Auster:* hot southern wind.

381   *Ode* xiii.

[1] Ille et nefasto te posuit die,
        Quicumque primum, et sacrilega manu
            Produxit, arbos, in nepotum
                Perniciem, opprobriumque pagi.

[2] Illum et parentis crediderim sui
        Fregisse cervicem, et penetralia
            Sparsisse nocturno cruore
                Hospitis: ille venena Colcha.

[3] Et quidquid usquam concipitur nefas,
        Tractavit: agro qui statuit meo
            Te triste lignum, te caducum
                In domini caput immerentis.

[4] Quid quisque vitet, numquam homini satis
        Cautum est in horas. navita Bosphorum
            Pœnus perhorrescit, neque ultra
                Cæca timet aliunde fata.

381   *Out of* Horace.

[1] Shame of thy mother soyle! ill-nurtur'd tree!
    Sett to the mischeife of posteritie!
    That hand, (what e're it were) that was thy nurse,
    Was sacrilegious, (sure) or somewhat worse.
    Black, as the day was dismall, in whose sight   5
    Thy rising topp first staind the bashfull light.
[2] That man (I thinke) wrested the feeble life
    From his old father. that mans barbarous knife
    Conspir'd with darknes 'gainst the strangers throate;
    (Whereof the blushing walles tooke bloody note)   10
    Huge high-floune poysons, ev'n of Colchos breed,
[3] And whatsoe're wild sinnes black thoughts doe feed,
    His hands have padled in; his hands, that found
    Thy traiterous root a dwelling in my ground.

Out of Horace. English and Greek versions from MS.* Two translations of Ode xiii from Book ii.
    11 *Colchos:* a remote kingdom on Asia, the location of the Golden Fleece.

381   [*Out of* Horace]

[1] "Ὥρᾳ σε κεῖνος θῆκεν ἀποφράδι
     Ὁ πρῶτος ὅστις, χειρὶ τε βώμακι
     "Εθρεψε, δένδρον, τῆς τε κώμης
     Αἴτιον, ἐσσομένων τ' ἔλεγχος.

[2] Κεῖνος τοκῆος θρύψε καὶ αὐχένα,   5
     Κεῖνός γε (φαίην) αἵματι ξεινίῳ
     Μυχώτατον κοιτῶνα ῥᾶινε
     Νύκτιος, ἀμφαφάασκε κεῖνος

[3] Τὰ δῆτα Κόλχων φάρμακα, καὶ κακοῦ
     Πᾶν χρῆμα, δώσας μοι ἐπιχώριον   10
     Σὲ στυγνὸν ἔρνος, δεσπότου σε
     "Εμπεσον ἐς κεφαλὴν ἀεικῶς.

[4] Πάσης μὲν ὥρης πᾶν ἐπικίνδυνον.
     Τίς οἶδε φεύγειν; δείδιε Βοσφόρον
     Λιβὺς ὁ πλωτήρ, οὐδ' ἀνάγκην   15
     Τὴν κρυφίην ἑτέρωθεν ὀκνεῖ.

     Perfidious totterer! longing for the staines   15
     Of thy kind Master's well-deserving braines.
[4] Mans daintiest care, and caution cannot spy
     The subtile point of his coy destiny,
     Which way it threats. With feare the merchants mind
     Is plough'd as deepe, as is the sea with wind,   20
     (Rowz'd in an angry tempest); Oh the sea!
     Oh! that's his feare; there flotes his destiny:
     While from another (unseene) corner blowes
     The storme of fate, to which his life he owes.
     By Parthians bow the soldjer lookes to die,   25
     (Whose hands are fighting, while their feet doe flie.)
[5] The Parthian starts at Rome's imperiall name,
     Fledg'd with her Eagles wing; the very chaine
     Of his captivity rings in his eares.
     Thus, ô thus fondly doe wee pitch our feares   30
     Farre distant from our fates. our fates, that mocke
     Our giddy feares with an unlook't for shocke.
[6] A little more, and I had surely seene
     Thy greisly Majesty, Hell's blackest Queene;

[5] Miles sagittas, et celerem fugam
   Parthi: catenas Parthus, et Italum
      Robur: sed improvisa lethi
         Vis rapuit, rapietque genteis.

[6] Quam pæne furvæ regna Proserpinæ
   Et judicantem vidimus Æacum
      Sedesque descriptas piorum, et
         Æoliis fidibus querentem

[7] Sappho puellis de popularibus,
   Et te sonantem plenius aureo
      Alcæe, plectro dura navis,
         Dura fugæ mala, dura belli.

[8] Utrumque sacro digna silentio
   Mirantur Umbræ dicere: sed magis
      Pugnas, et exactos tyrannos
         Densum humeris bibit aure vulgus.

[9] Quid mirum, ubi illis carminibus stupens
   Demittit atras bellua centiceps
      Aureis, et intorti capillis
         Eumenidum recreantur angues?

[10] Quin et Prometheus, et Pelopis parens
   Dulci laborum decipitur sono:
      Nec curat Orion leones,
         Aut timidos agitare lyncas.

And Æacus on his Tribunall too,   35
Sifting the soules of guilt; and you, (oh you!)
You ever-blushing meads, where doe the Blest
Farre from darke horrors home appeale to rest.
[7] There amorous Sappho plaines upon her Lute
Her loves crosse fortune, that the sad dispute   40
Runnes murmuring on the strings. Alcæus there
In high-built numbers wakes his golden lyre,
To tell the world, how hard the matter went,
How hard by sea, by warre, by banishment.
[8] There these brave soules deale to each wondring eare   45
Such words, soe precious, as they may not weare

35 *Æacus:* a judge renowned for his justice and piety.
39 *Sappho:* a Greek poetess.
41 *Alcæus:* a Greek lyric poet.

[5] Πάρθων μάχημων Ῥωμάϊκος φυγήν,
Καὶ τόξα. Πάρθος Ῥωμαίκην βίαν,
Καὶ δεσμά· λάους ἀλλὰ μοίρας
Βάλλε, βαλεῖ τ᾽ ἀδόκητος ὁρμή.   20

[6] Σχέδον σχέδον πῶς Περσεφόνης ἴδον
Αὔλην μελαίνην, καὶ κρίσιν Αἰακοῦ,
Καλὴν τ᾽ ἀπόστασιν μακαίρων,
Αἰολίαις κινύρην τε χορδαῖς

[7] Σαπφὼ πατρίδος μεμφομένην κόραις,   25
Ἠχοῦντα καί σε πλεῖον ἐπιχρύσῳ,
Ἀλκαῖε, πλήκτρῳ σκληρὰ νῆος,
Σκληρὰ φυγῆς, πολέμου τε σκληρά.

[8] Εὐφημέουσαι δ᾽ ἀμφοτέρων σκιαὶ
Κλύουσι θάμβει, τὰς δὲ μαχὰς πλέον,   30
Ἀναστάτους τε μὲν τυράννους
Ὠμιὰς ἔκπιεν ὦσι λᾶος.

[9] Τί θαῦμ᾽; ἐκείναις θὴρ ὅτε τρίκρανος
Ακην ἀοιδαῖς, οὖατα κάββαλε,
Ἐριννύων τ᾽ ἡδυπαθοῦσι   35
Βόστρυχες, ἡσυχίων ἐχιδνῶν.

[10] Καὶ δὴ Προμηθεύς, καὶ Πέλοπος πατὴρ
Εὔδουσιν ἠχεῖ τῷ λαθικήδεϊ:
Ἄγειν λεόντας Ὠρίων δὲ
Οὐ φιλέει, φοβερὰς τε λύγκας.   40

Without religious silence; above all
Warres ratling tumults, or some tyrants fall.
The thronging clotted multitude doth feast.
What wonder? when the hundred-headed beast   50
Hangs his black lugges, stroakt with those heavenly lines;
The Furies curl'd snakes meet in gentle twines,
And stretch their cold limbes in a pleasing fire.
Prometheus self, and Pelops sterved Sire
Are cheated of their paines; Orion thinkes   55
Of Lions now noe more, or spotted Linx.

---

54 *Prometheus:* the god who was punished by being chained to a rock while an eagle devoured his liver daily. *Pelops sterved Sire:* i.e. Tantalus, who was punished by being starved ("sterved") in Hades, unable to reach food or water.
55 *Orion:* a great hunter, he once boasted he would clear the earth of all wild beasts.

382   *Musicks Duell*

This poem is one in a long poetic tradition of contests between nightingale and lutenist, nature and art, tracing from the middle ages. Strada's neo-Latin version published in 1617, here printed on the left-hand page, gave fresh impetus to the tradition and provoked at least a dozen English versions or re-tellings in the seventeenth century. Warren (p. 110): " 'Music's Duel' is the secular triumph of the Crashavian style, and it remains, of its kind, the most impressive achievement in English poetry." T. O. Beachcroft ("Crashaw—And the Baroque Style," *Criterion*, XIII [1933–34], 412–27, esp. 415–16): "This is the height of the baroque style in English poetry; throughout 'Musicks Duell' the most profuse luxury is formed with the most perfect art. It is a style at once formal yet enthusiastic, extravagant yet reasonable, fanciful yet systematic. . . . The intricate rise and fall of the rhythm, the exquisite refinements of detail in parenthesis and suspension, the luxurious elaboration of image, turn upon turn, must necessarily be likened to the temptestuously broken outline, the flashing movement, the impalpable effect given even in [baroque] sculpture. . . . Interdependent with this elaboration and deformation is a third feature

JAM Sol à medio pronus deflexerat orbe
Mitius è radiis vibrans crinalibus ignem.
Cum Fidicen propter Tiberina fluenta, sonanti
Lenibat plectro curas, æstumque levabat
Ilice defensus nigra scenaque virenti.

Audiit hunc hospes silvæ Philomela propinquæ
Musa loci, nemoris Siren, innoxia Siren.
Et propè succedens stetit abdita frondibus, alte
Accipiens sonitum, secumque remurmurat, & quos
Ille modos variat digitis, hæc gutture reddit.

Sensit se Fidicen Philomela imitante referri,
Et placuit ludum volucri dare. plenius ergò
Explorat citharam, tentamentumque futuræ
Præbeat ut pugnæ, percurrit protinus omnes

382   *Musicks Duell.*

. . . that of unity in the midst of complication. 'Musicks Duell' brilliantly ex-
emplifies that type of construction which consists of a weaving together of many
varying forms into one, rather than the exact balancing in self-contained parts."
W. G. Madsen ("A Reading of 'Musicks Duell,'" in *Studies in Honor of John
Wilcox* [Detroit, 1958], pp. 39–50) notes that while the voice of the nightingale
is melodic, the strings of the lute are harmonic, a distinction which is supported
by images of a river for the former and the sea for the latter. "The superiority
of the lute . . . lies in the fact that its 'full-mouth *Diapason*' can express that
sea of eternity . . . , the '*Empyræum* of pure Harmony' [the abode of
the Blest]." The contest in Crashaw—he finds it unique in the tradition—is
between nature and *grace* (pp. 45, 42). See further, Praz, pp. 245–48; J.
Jacquot, " 'Le Duel Musical' . . . et sa Source Italienne," *Revue de Littérature
Comparée*, XXV (1951), 232–40; R. Harrison, "Erotic Imagery in . . . 'Mu-
sicks Duell,'" *SCN*, xiii (1967), 47–49. *Musicks Duell* is in first position in the
1646 and 1648 *Delights of the Muses.*

Now Westward *Sol* had spent the richest Beames
Of Noons high Glory, when hard by the streams
Of *Tiber*, on the sceane of a greene plat,
Under protection of an Oake; there sate
A sweet Lutes-master: in whose gentle aires   5
Hee lost the Dayes heat, and his owne hot cares.
    Close in the covert of the leaves there stood
A Nightingale, come from the neighbouring wood:
(The sweet inhabitant of each glad Tree,
Their Muse, their *Syren*. harmlesse *Syren* shee)   10
There stood she listning, and did entertaine
The Musicks soft report: and mold the same
In her owne murmures, that what ever mood
His curious fingers lent, her voyce made good:
The man perceiv'd his Rivall, and her Art,   15
Dispos'd to give the light'foot Lady sport
Awakes his Lute, and 'gainst the fight to come
Informes it, in a sweet *Præludium*

Musicks Duell. 46 (48).*

Impulsu pernice fides. Nec segnius illa
Mille per excurrens variæ discrimina vocis
Venturi specimen præfert argutula cantus.

    Tunc Fidicen per fila movens trepidantia dextram,
Nunc contemnenti similis diverberat ungue
Depectitque pari chordas & simplice ductu:
Nunc carptim replicat, digitisque micantibus urget
Fila minutatim, celerique repercutit ictu.
Mox silet. Illa modis totidem respondet, & artem
Arte refert. Nunc ceu rudis aut incerta canendi
Proiicit in longum, nulloque plicatile flexu
Carmen init, simili serie, jugique tenore
Præbet iter liquidum labenti è pectore voci:
Nunc cæsim variat, modulisque canora minutis
Delibrat vocem, tremuloque reciprocat ore.
    Miratur Fidicen parvis è faucibus ire
Tàm varium tàm dulce melos: majoraque tentans
Alternat mira arte fides: dum torquet acutas,
Inciditque; graves operoso verbere pulsat,
Permiscetque simul certantia rauca sonoris,

Ceu resides in bella viros clangore lacessat.

Hoc etiam Philomela canit dumque ore liquenti

Of closer straines, and ere the warre begin,
Hee lightly skirmishes on every string   20
Charg'd with a flying touch: and streightway shee
Carves out her dainty voyce as readily,
Into a thousand sweet distinguish'd Tones,
And reckons up in soft divisions,
Quicke volumes of wild Notes; to let him know   25
By that shrill taste, shee could doe something too.
     His nimble hands instinct then taught each string
A capring cheerefullnesse; and made them sing
To their owne dance; now negligently rash
Hee throwes his Arme, and with a long drawne dash   30
Blends all together; then distinctly tripps
From this to that; then quicke returning skipps
And snatches this againe, and pauses there.
Shee measures every measure, every where
Meets art with art; sometimes as if in doubt   35
Not perfect yet, and fearing to bee out
Trayles her playne Ditty in one long-spun note,
Through the sleeke passage of her open throat:
A cleare unwrinckled song, then doth shee point it
With tender accents, and severely joynt it   40
By short diminutives, that being rear'd
In controverting warbles evenly shar'd
With her sweet selfe shee wrangles; Hee amazed
That from so small a channell should be rais'd
The torrent of a voyce, whose melody   45
Could melt into such sweet variety
Straines higher yet; that tickled with rare art
The tatling strings (each breathing in his part)
Most kindly doe fall out; the grumbling Base
In surly groanes disdaines the Trebles Grace.   50
The high-perch't treble chirps at this, and chides,
Untill his finger (Moderatour) hides
And closes the sweet quarrell, rowsing all
Hoarce, shrill, at once; as when the Trumpets call
Hot Mars to th' Harvest of Deaths field, and woo   55
Mens hearts into their hands; this lesson too
Shee gives him backe; her supple Brest thrills out

---

19 *warre:* the title of this poem in two manuscripts is *Fidicinis* [Strada's lutenist] *et*
Philomelæ Bellum Musicum (The Musical War of Fidicen and Philomela).
     24 *divisions:* elaborations on a melody made by dividing each note into several notes
of shorter duration.

Vibrat acuta sonum, modulisque interplicat æquis;

Ex inopinato gravis intonat, & leve murmur

Turbinat introrsus, alternantique sonore

Clarat, & infuscat ceu martia classica pulset.

Scilicet erubuit Fidicen, iraque calente,

Aut non hoc, inquit, referes Citharistria silvæ,

Aut fracta cedam cithara. Nec plura loquutus

Non imitabilibus plectrum concentibus urget.

Sharpe Aires, and staggers in a warbling doubt
Of dallying sweetnesse, hovers ore her skill,
And folds in wav'd notes with a trembling bill,   60
The plyant Series of her slippery song.
Then starts shee suddenly into a Throng
Of short thicke sobs, whose thundring volleyes float,
And roule themselves over her lubricke throat
In panting murmurs, still'd out of her Breast   65
That ever'bubling spring; the sugred Nest
Of her delicious soule, that there does lye
Bathing in streames of liquid Melodie;
Musicks best seed-plot, whence in ripend Aires
A Golden-headed Harvest fairely reares   70
His Honey-dropping tops, plow'd by her breath
Which there reciprocally laboureth
In that sweet soyle. It seemes a holy quire
Founded to th' Name of great *Apollo's* lyre,
Whose sylver-roofe rings with the sprightly notes   75
Of sweet-lipp'd Angel-Imps, that swill their throats
In creame of Morning *Helicon,* and then
Preferre soft Anthems to the Eares of men,
To woo them from their Beds, still murmuring
That men can sleepe while they their Mattens sing: 80
(Most divine service) whose so early lay,
Prevents the Eye-lidds of the blushing day.
There might you heare her kindle her soft voyce,
In the close murmur of a sparkling noyse.
And lay the ground-worke of her hopefull song,   85
Still keeping in the forward streame, so long
Till a sweet whirle-wind (striving to gett out)
Heaves her soft Bosome, wanders round about,
And makes a pretty Earthquake in her Breast,
Till the fledg'd Notes at length forsake their Nest   90
Fluttering in wanton shoales, and to the Sky
Wing'd with their owne wild Eccho's pratling fly.
Shee opes the floodgate, and lets loose a Tide
Of streaming sweetnesse, which in state doth ride
On the wav'd backe of every swelling straine,   95
Rising and falling in a pompous traine.
And while shee thus discharges a shrill peale
Of flashing Aires; shee qualifies their zeale

82 *Prevents:* i.e. comes before.

Namque manu per fila volat, simul hos, simul illos

Explorat numeros, chordaque laborat in omni,

Et strepit, et tinnit, crescitque superbius, & se

Multiplicat relegens, plenoque choreumate plaudit.

With the coole Epode of a graver Noat,
Thus high, thus low, as if her silver throat   100
Would reach the brasen voyce of warr's hoarce Bird;
Her little soule is ravisht: and so pour'd
Into loose extasies, that shee is plac't
Above her selfe, Musicks *Enthusiast*.

      Shame now and anger mixt a double staine   105
In the Musitians face; yet once againe
(Mistresse) I come; now reach a straine my Lute
Above her mocke, or bee for ever mute.
Or tune a song of victory to mee,
Or to thy selfe, sing thine owne Obsequie;   110
So said, his hands sprightly as fire hee flings,
And with a quavering coynesse tasts the strings.
The sweet-lip't sisters musically frighted,
Singing their feares are fearfully delighted.
Trembling as when *Appollo's* golden haires   115
Are fan'd and frizled, in the wanton ayres
Of his owne breath: which marryed to his lyre
Doth tune the *Sphæares*, and make Heavens self looke higher.
From this to that, from that to this hee flyes
Feels Musicks pulse in all her Arteryes,   120
Caught in a net which there *Appollo* spreads,
His fingers struggle with the vocall threads,
Following those little rills, hee sinkes into
A Sea of *Helicon;* his hand does goe
Those parts of sweetnesse which with *Nectar* drop,   125
Softer then that which pants in *Hebe's* cup.
The humourous strings expound his learned touch,
By various Glosses; now they seeme to grutch,
And murmur in a buzzing dinne, then gingle
In shrill tongu'd accents: striving to bee single.   130
Every smooth turne, every delicious stroake
Gives life to some new Grace; thus doth h'invoke
Sweetnesse by all her Names; thus, bravely thus
(Fraught with a fury so harmonious)
The Lutes light *Genius* now does proudly rise,   135
Heav'd on the surges of swolne Rapsodyes.
Whose flourish (Meteor-like) doth curle the aire
With flash of high-borne fancyes: here and there

110 *Obsequie:* it is to be noted that the lute, if defeated, would have received the same
fate as the bird.

Tum stetit expectans, si quid paret æmula contra.
Illa autem, quanquam vox dudum exercita fauces
Asperat, impatiens vinci simul advocat omnes
Nequidquam vires. nam dum discrimina tanta
Reddere tot fidium nativa & simplice tentat
Voce, canaliculisque imitari grandia parvis;
Impar magnanimis ausis, imparque dolori
Deficit, & vitam summo in certamine linquens
Victoris cadit in plectrum, par nacta sepulcrum.
USQUE adeò & tenues animas ferit æmula Virtus.

Dancing in lofty measures, and anon
Creeps on the soft touch of a tender tone: 140
Whose trembling murmurs melting in wild aires
Runs to and fro, complaining his sweet cares
Because those pretious mysteryes that dwell,
In musick's ravish't soule hee dare not tell,
But whisper to the world: thus doe they vary   145
Each string his Note, as if they meant to carry
Their Masters blest soule (snatcht out at his Eares
By a strong Extasy) through all the sphæeares
Of Musicks heaven; and seat it there on high
In th' *Empyræum* of pure Harmony.   150
At length (after so long, so loud a strife
Of all the strings, still breathing the best life
Of blest variety attending on
His fingers fairest revolution
In many a sweet rise, many as sweet a fall)   155
A full-mouth'd *Diapason* swallowes all.
        This done, hee lists what shee would say to this,
And shee although her Breath's late exercise
Had dealt too roughly with her tender throate,
Yet summons all her sweet powers for a Noate.   160
Alas! in vaine! for while (sweet soule) shee tryes
To measure all those wild diversities
Of chatt'ring stringes, by the small size of one
Poore simple voyce, rais'd in a Naturall Tone;
Shee failes, and failing grieves, and grieving dyes.   165
Shee dyes; and leaves her life the Victors prise,
Falling upon his Lute; o fit to have
(That liv'd so sweetly) dead, so sweet a Grave

168 *Grave:* in Marino's translation, the lutenist buries the bird in his lute.

383   [*Song.*]

Dispiegate
    Guance amate
    Quella porpora acerbetta;
    Che perdenti
    Che dolenti
    Fian le rose in su l' herbetta.

Deh scoprite,
    Deh partite
    Chiare stelle i vostri rai;
    Che partendo
    Che scoprendo
    Fia men chiaro il sol d' assai.

Deh togliete
    Quella rete
    Auree chiome, aureo thesoro;
    Ch'a toccarni
    Ch'a spiegarni
    Tornerà quest' aria d'oro.

Suela, suela
    Quel, che cela
    Dolce bocca il desir nostro;
    Ch'a suelarlo,
    Ch'a mostrarlo
    Perderan le perle, e l'ostro.

Apri o labro
    Di cinnabro
    Vu sorriso ancor tra 'l velo;
    Ch' ad aprirlo,
    Ch' a scoprirlo
    Ridera la terra, e 'l cielo.

383 *Out of the Italian. A Song.*

To thy Lover
Deere, discover
That sweet blush of thine that shameth
(When those Roses
It discloses)   5
All the flowers that Nature nameth.

In free Ayre,
Flow thy Haire;
That no more Summers best dresses,
Bee beholden   10
For their Golden
Lockes, to *Phoebus* flaming Tresses.

O deliver
Love his Quiver,
From thy Eyes he shoots his Arrowes,   15
Where *Apollo*
Cannot follow:
Featherd with his Mothers Sparrowes.

O envy not
(That we dye not)   20
Those deere lips whose doore encloses
All the Graces
In their places,
Brother Pearles, and sister Roses.

From these treasures   25
Of ripe pleasures
One bright smile to cleere the weather.
Earth and Heaven
Thus made even,
Both will be good friends together.   30

Out of the Italian. A Song. 46 (48).* Praz terms this a "masterly" rendering of Ceba's "d
lightful little song" (p. 238).

Tocca, tocca
   Bella bocca
   L'aria homai di qualch' accento;
   Che toccando,
   Che parlando
   Tacerà per l' aria il vento.

Ma se fuore
   Tant' honore
   Non sospinge il tuo sereno,
   Tua vaghezza,
   Tua bellezza
   La pietà mi mostri almeno.

E la dove
   Morte move
   A predarmi i suoi guerrieri,
   Lidia mia
   Tutta pia
   Volgi gli occhi lusinghieri.

Che se tocchi
   Co begli occhi
   Lo mio spirto fuggitivo,
   La tu' aita
   La tua vita
   Mel terran nel petto vivo.

384   *Foco d' Amore diviso* (*The fire of Love Divided.*)

Amor non hà più foco,

Che' l divise frà noi:

Diede l' arsura à me, la luce à voi

Donna gentil per Dio

Rendete il vostro lume à l' ardor mio,

The aire does wooe thee,
Winds cling to thee,
Might a word once flye from out thee;
Storme and Thunder
Would sit under, 35
And keepe silence round about Thee.

But if Natures
Common Creatures,
So deare Glories dare not borrow:
Yet thy Beauty 40
Owes a Duty,
To my loving, lingring sorrow.

When to end mee
Death shall send mee
All his Terrors to affright mee: 45
Thine eyes Graces,
Guild their faces,
And those Terrors shall delight mee.

When my dying
Life is flying; 50
Those sweet Aires that often slew mee;
Shall revive mee,
Or reprive mee,
And to many Deaths renew mee.

384 *Out of the Italian.*

Love now no fire hath left him,
We two betwixt us have divided it.
Your Eyes the Light hath reft him,
The heat commanding in my *Heart* doth sit.
O! that poore Love be not for ever spoyled, 5
Let my *Heat* to your *Light* be reconciled,

Out of the Italian. ("Love now no fire hath left him,"). 46 (48).* The Italian title is "The fire of Love Divided." ("Foco": in modern spelling "fuoco.") The Italian is by Marino, author of the "Sospetto," No. 87.
   5–6 *spoyled, reconciled*: a rhyming pair in Crashaw's time.

Onde chiaro, e lucente à gli occhi vostri

(Qual' è nel cor) si mostri,

O pur' in voi la fiamma mia prendete,

E com' io ardo ardete.

385   [Cupid *blind and naked.*]

Sapete, amanti, perché ignudo sia,
Perché fanciullo, e perché cieco Amore?
Perché mentre l'angelica armonia
Della mia bella donna intento udia,
Per gran dolcezza uscito di sé fuore
Perdé la veste, il senno, gl'occh' e 'l core.

So shall these flames, whose worth
Now all obscured lyes
(Drest in those Beames) start forth
And dance before your eyes.   10

Or else partake my flames
(I care not whither)
And so in mutuall Names
Of Love, burne both together.

385   *Out of the Italian.*

Would any one the true cause find
How Love came nak't, a Boy, and blind?
'Tis this; listning one day too long,
To th' Syrens in my Mistresse Song,
The extasie of a delight   5
So much o're-mastring all his might
To that one Sense, made all else thrall,
    And so he lost his Clothes, eyes, heart and all.

---

12 *whither:* i.e. whether, or which; the choice is between the expression of her light or of his flame—Crashaw's verb "partake" does not make the choice quite so explicit as does the Italian "in voi . . . prendete."

Out of the Italian. ("Would any one the true cause find"). 46 (48).* Presumably the Italian "senno" (*wisdom*) responds to "fanciullo" (*little boy*) and explains "How love came [to be] a Boy." Crashaw disregards the regular sequence in the Italian to provide his own—less satisfactory. The last words should be something like "Clothes, mind, eyes, and heart." The Italian is by Marcellini.

VIII

Secular Poems
in Latin

In this section, Crashaw's secular poems in Latin
are on the right-hand page, and the English prose
translations are on the left-hand page.

POLITICAL AND ROYAL

386   *On the birth of the Princess Mary.*

Spare, fierce winter, spare your fury.
Lay aside your wraths. O give the breath of a gentle breeze
that it may calm the harsh year with its more delicate blast.
Surely events and time deserve this. Let wicked Auster
rage and roll on with wild roar:
let the impatient Notus be inflamed with his rain-bearing wings.
Yet here, surely here now if you do not refuse it, wild one,
neither impatient Notus nor wicked Auster should be [here].
Surely was it fitting while such a shining
series of events exalts us, so much a common serenity
of joy and deep delight in the spirits of spring shines;
that now cruel battle lines and rough wars
pass and bring to ruin the year with their wintry storms?
Ah better that today, restored by the gleam of new youth,
winter itself should feel the life of spring and hasten
the purple wealth with a beautiful uproar; joyful may it pour forth all
its heart and wish the shining day
to go on forever in fragrant hours: with so great a profusion of flowers
around the blessed cradle may it arise
and greet and softly enfold the new limbs.
    Now she comes. Again the great hall echoes
with holy cries of a child. See a splendor comes, a sweet sister,
added to [her] rosy brother. She stretches, stretches her little arms to you,
Great Boy! and turns her open mouth with a charming smile
to you; for you she calms her sweet tears and tempers her noble cries
and hangs upon your neck.
Such a joy: just as in a woven wreath when one
makes his lilies shine next to the roses. Such
honor gleams when two stars in the midst of the heavens

386   *In Natales* Mariæ *Principis.*

Parce tuo jam, bruma ferox, ô parce furori.
Pone animos. ô pacatæ da spiritus auræ
Afflatu leviore gravem demulceat annum.
Res certè, & tempus meruit. Licèt improbus Auster
Sæviat, & rabido multùm se murmure volvat;   5
Imbriferis licèt impatiens Notus ardeat alis;
Hîc tamen, hîc certè, modò tu non (sæva) negares,
Nec Notus impatiens jam, nec foret improbus Auster.
Scilicet hoc decuit? dum nos tam lucida rerum
Attollit series, adeò commune serenum   10
Lætitiæ, vernisque animis micat alta voluptas;
Jam torvas acies, jam squallida bella per auras
Volvere? & hybernis annum corrumpere nimbis?
Ah melius! quin luce novæ reparata juventæ
Ipsa hodie vernaret hyems; pulchroque tumultu   15
Purpureas properaret opes; effunderet omnes
Læta sinus, nitidumque diem fragrantibus horis
Æternùm migrare velit; florumque beatâ
Luxurie tanta ô circum cunabula surgat,
Excipiatque novos, & molliter ambiat artus.   20
    Quippe venit. sacris iterum vagitibus ingens
Aula sonat. venit en roseo decus addita fratri
Blanda soror. tibi se brevibus, tibi porrigit ulnis,
Magne puer! facili tibi torquet hiantia risu
Ora; tibi molles lacrymas, & nobile murmur   25
Temperat, inque tuo ponit se pendula collo.
Tale decus; juncto veluti sub stemmate cùm quis
Dat sociis lucere rosis sua lilia. talis
Fulget honos; medio cùm se duo sydera mundo

In Natales Mariæ Principis. MS.* In connection with this and the following series of royal gratulatory poems see the comparable poems in English, Nos. 337–39. The Princess Mary, Princess of Orange, was born on November 4, 1631.
    4 *Auster:* South Wind.
    6 *Notus:* North Wind.
    22 *fratri:* Charles, born 1630; an earlier son had died at birth.
    24 *puer:* Charles.

weave themselves together with their sweet rays. Nor at one time did a
more worthy happy union of shining beauty gleam;
then when between her starry brothers, the most beautiful woman of all
first blushed and, Leda's eggshell broken,
Helen displayed the new joys of her young brow.
   O thus mingle your joint splendor, you, fair brother,
serene sister. O thus give joys to your father,
thus to your mother. Whenever at some time in the years to come he
wishes to move in glory among the triumphs proper to
his mighty shoulder and to prove his strength;
then too he will flatter you with full star and high
flower of your own and the more mature fire will touch your sweet eyes
with its divine nature and its beams of honor.
Then o how many times will deceitful Apollo swear
you are his Phoebe (except that you are lovelier than she)!
Then o how many times will foolish Mars swear
you are his Venus (except that you are purer than she)!
Ah happy man! Not Mars, not golden Apollo himself
will believe him equal to you! who, exalting in such a wife,
will be able to hasten to your lovely embrace and to take his sacred
delights and, alone, to call your eyes, your kisses
his own; and while he proves he is a god,
because of such nectar, [he will be able] to spurn the tables of the gods.

387   *On the face of the most majestic king recovered*
                    from the small pox.

Return muse; our propitious mother the University calls: lo our
Apollo returns, our Apollo returns before our eyes.
Still his face and the royal color in his face lives
a little and continues to love the mingled snows.
Do you violate those cheeks? do you, violent illness,
try to pass through that face with your pock marks?
Do you test the face of Phoebus, fool of fools? Our
Phoebe did not know how to regard her own spots.
The face itself, its own avenger, disdains the disease:
it sits o so safe, in its own rays:

Dulcibus intexunt radiis. nec dignior olim   30
Flagrabat nitidæ fælix consortio formæ,
Tunc cùm sydereos inter pulcherrima fratres
Erubuit primùm, & Ledæo cortice rupto
Tyndarida explicuit teneræ nova gaudia frontis.
   Sic socium ô miscete jubar, tu, candide frater,   35
Tuque serena soror. sic ô date gaudia patri,
Sic matri. cùmque ille olim, subeüntibus annis,
Ire inter proprios magnâ cervice triumphos
Egregius volet, atque suâ se discere dextrâ;
Te quoque tum pleno mulcebit sydere & alto   40
Flore tui, dulcesque oculos maturior ignis
Indole divinâ, & radiis intinget honoris.
Tunc ô te quoties (nisi quòd tu pulchrior illâ)
Esse suam Phæben falsus jurabit Apollo!
Tunc ô te quoties (nisi quod tu castior illâ)   45
Esse suam Venerem Mavors jurabit inanis!
Felix ah! et cui se non Mars, non aureus ipse
Credet Apollo parem! tantâ qui conjuge celsus
In pulchros properare sinus, & carpere sacras
Delicias, oculosque tuos, tua basia solus   50
Tum poterit dixisse sua; & se nectare tanto
Dum probat esse Deum, superas contemnere mensas.

387   *In faciem Augustiss. Regis à morbillis integram.*

Musa redi; vocat alma parens Academia: Noster
   En redit, ore suo noster Apollo redit.
Vultus adhuc suus, & vultu sua purpura tantum
   Vivit, & admixtas pergit amare nives.
Tune illas violare genas? tune illa profanis,   5
   Morbe ferox, tentas ire per ora notis?
Tu Phœbi faciem tentas, vanissime? Nostra
   Nec Phœbe maculas novit habere suas.
Ipsa sui vindex facies morbum indignatur;
   Ipsa sedet radiis ô bene tuta suis: 10

---

32 *fratres:* Castor and Pollux.
47 *Felix:* the happy man, i.e. her husband.
In faciem Augustiss. Regis. 46 (48).* Published first in the Cambridge volume congratulating
the King on the restoration of his health (1632); King Charles had had the smallpox
(Grosart, II, 337).

Indeed there is a god, an even holier star of the heavens.
Indeed all Apollo smiles under these cheeks.
That the king was unharmed in his face, that he was affected elsewhere:
in the latter the king showed he was a *man;* in the former, a *god.*

388   *The king's return.*

He returns, he returns. At this the people roll forth a mighty roar;
at this the public applause (do you hear?) reaches the stars:
at this a common repose settles on every face;
from this for all there is one expression of joy.
Our king, our light returns; England, joyous
in every expression, smiles on the face of the returned [king]:
Each one kindles his own eyes from those eyes
and takes a new day from that sacred face.
By chance you may ask what dangers worthy of such great acclaim
Charles escapes, what evils, or what fears:
whether the untrustworthy tides of the wandering sea
dared almost to refuse him [re-entry] to his own lands
or whether mindful again of too great a guest in him, the Spanish land
would scarcely give up this long-hoped-for head.
None of these things; for neither did the untrustworthy tides of the sea
nor the Spanish land see this sacred head.
True love, however, these false dangers fashions for itself:
(false dangers are often fashioned by true love)
but he who fears false [dangers] for Charles would not fear true dangers:
(true dangers are often spurned by true love).
Fearing false dangers for him, spurning true dangers for itself,
love not only is loyal but also is brave.
Meanwhile he is enough reason for our triumph
and (ah!) he was enough reason for our grief.
Charles was a cause of grief, although he was unharmed;
because England could truly say *He is away.*
And Charles is now enough reason for our triumph
because we can truly say, *He is returned.*

Quippe illic deus est, cœlûmque & sanctius astrum;
Quippe sub his totus ridet Apollo genis.
Quòd facie Rex tutus erat, quòd cætera tactus:
Hinc *hominem* Rex est fassus, & inde *deum.*

388 *Rex Redux.*

Ille redit, redit. Hoc populi bona murmura volvunt;
Publicus hoc (audin'?) plausus ad astra refert:
Hoc omni sedet in vultu commune serenum;
Omnibus hinc una est lætitiæ facies.
Rex noster, lux nostra redit; redeuntis ad ora   5
Arridet totis Anglia læta genis:
Quisque suos oculos oculis accendit ab istis;
Atque novum sacro sumit ab ore diem.
Forte roges tanto quæ digna pericula plausu
Evadat Carolus, quæ mala, quósve metus: 10
Anne pererrati male fida volumina ponti
Ausa illum terris pene negare suis:
Hospitis an nimii rursus sibi conscia, tellus
Vix bene speratum reddat Ibera caput.
Nil horum; nec enim male fida volumina ponti   15
Aut sacrum tellus vidit Ibera caput.
Verus amor tamen hæc sibi falsa pericula fingit:
(Falsa peric'la solet fingere verus amor)
At Carolo qui falsa timet, nec vera timeret:
(Vera peric'la solet temnere verus amor)   20
Illi falsa timens, sibi vera pericula temnens,
Non solum est fidus, sed quoque fortis amor.
Interea nostri satis ille est causa triumphi:
Et satis (ah!) nostri causa doloris erat.
Causa doloris erat Carolus, sospes licet esset;   25
Anglia quod saltem dicere posset, *Abest.*
Et satis est nostri Carolus nunc causa triumphi;
Dicere quod saltem possumus, *Ille redit.*

Rex Redux. 46 (48).* Published first in the Cambridge volume congratulating the King on
his return from Scotland where he received the crown and the loyalty of the Parliament in
1633. The references in lines 11–16 recall Charles's earlier trip out of the country, to Spain
("Ibera" line 14) in 1623.

389 *To a prince not yet born.*

Be born now; o now! indeed why do you delay, dear boy?
No sweeter hour will give a day to you.
So will you linger so many lagging months (slow poke!)?
The king returns. You come and say nicely *Welcome home.*
For what is our *Hail?* what are the words of our triumph?
You will have spoken better with that infant's cry of yours.
But yet you may stay: and a new cause for our triumphs
you will be later; but not a new cause:
for as often as a new son or daughter is born to Charles,
indeed so often Charles himself returns.

390 *To the Queen.*

But even now it was time for you, greatest mother,
to speed the day with these sweet eyes:
it was time that your caressing kisses should not be idle;
lest the burden should be less suited for your neck.
Clearly your child, the hope and fear of his parents,
your pride by whom you first became a happy mother,
even now bravely contemplates angry swords;
now he is more his father's, now more his own.
O goads of nature! while infancy has scarcely passed from him,
already he impatiently snatches manhood to him.
That restless boy even now says he does not go by his years:
now he is not yet a boy, and he is older than a boy.
If any lion brought to life in embroidered rages stands
in these halls, which the needle mimicked with its clever point,
O ho! he is an enemy; indeed he will honor no other enemy;
no lesser rage is really fit for such great hands.
Then the heavy spear rages against the foe (the spear is a rod);
soon the false breast gapes with a real wound.

389 *Ad Principem nondum natum.*

Nascere nunc; ô nunc! quid enim, puer alme, moraris?
Nulla tibi dederit dulcior hora diem.
Ergone tot tardos (ô lente!) morabere menses?
Rex redit. Ipse veni, & dic bone, *Gratus ades.*
Nam quid *Ave* nostrum? quid nostri verba triumphi?   5
Vagitu melius dixeris ista tuo.
At maneas tamen: & nobis nova causa triumphi
Sic demum fueris; nec nova causa tamen:
Nam, quoties Carolo novus aut nova nascitur infans,
Revera toties Carolus ipse redit.   10

390 *Ad Reginam.*

Et verò jam tempus erat tibi, maxima Mater,
Dulcibus his oculis accelerare diem:
Tempus erat, nè qua tibi basia blanda vacarent;
Sarcina ne collo sit minùs apta tuo.
Scilicet ille tuus, timor & spes ille suorum,   5
Quo primum es felix pignore facta parens,
Ille ferox iras jam nunc meditatur & enses;
Jam patris magis est, jam magis ille suus.
Indolis O stimulos! Vix dum illi transiit infans;
Jamque sibi impatiens arripit ille virum.   10
Improbus ille suis adeò negat ire sub annis:
Jam nondum puer est, major & est puero.
Si quis in aulæis pictas animatus in iras
Stat leo, quem docta cuspide lusit acus,
Hostis (io!) est; neque enim ille alium dignabitur hostem;   15
Nempe decet tantas non minor ira manus.
Tunc hasta gravis adversum furit; hasta bacillum est:
Mox falsum vero vulnere pectus hiat.

Ad Principem nondum natum. 46 (48). Presumably the prince was James, born October 14, 1633. Charles reached London (Greenwich), returning from Edinburgh, at the end of August.
Ad Reginam. 46 (48).* Published first in the Cambridge volume congratulating the Queen on the birth of James, the Duke of York, in 1633. The poem is chiefly concerned to praise the manliness of Charles; he was then three. See also No. 369.

The lion stands, just as if stunned, pierced through by such an enemy;
as if he should fear or love something in these eyes,
so fiercely so sweetly they flash: he professes not to know
whether *Mars* was behind these eyes or *Love*.
For in fact *Mars* was there, but one who could easily be loved;
and surely there is *Love*, but a Love to be feared.
Such a *Love*, such a *Mars* is there to see; like a
god either way whether as a boy or as a man.
This child now recognized by you succeeds to the kisses of his brother.
See! not a troublesome addition to your games.
Now your kisses may come however great the troop;
now with whatever muttering your love may play.
Lo! here you have soft and pliant material,
here you have enough wax for your charms.
Hail child, sweet excuse for so many little kisses,
sweet little employment for your mother's lips,
O hail! for at your birth, golden boy, there was born
to *Charles and Mary* a third eye.

391   *On the delivery of the fairest Queen in winter.*

Garlands, boy: (what garden would not offer flowers now?)
Weave garlands for me with your nimble fingers, boy.
Why do you tell me something or other about December, fool?
Why bother me with snows? give me garlands, boy.
Snow? Winter? No such words come from our mouths;
it is not: if it be, still it cannot be.
Spring is here: whatever mask makes December stern,
whatever fierce cold rages, spring is here.
Don't you see with what new shoots of vine the palace
decks itself, and on the sacred ridges what grape is sitting?
What winter usually smiles on clusters so fruitful?
What cheeks of winter does such radiance tinge?
O Mary! O child of the gods and mother of gods!
In this way will our seasons be your plaything?
Do you thus with your spring hold back the stars of winter

Stat leo, ceu stupeat tali bene fixus ab hoste;
 Ceu quid in his oculis vel timeat vel amet,   20
Tam torvum, tam dulce micant: nescire fatetur
 Márs ne sub his oculis esset, an esset *Amor.*
Quippe illìc *Mars* est, sed qui bene possit amari;
 Est & *Amor* certe, sed metuendus Amor:
Talis *Amor*, talis *Mars* est ibi cernere; qualis   25
 Seu puer hic esset, sive vir ille deus.
Hic tibi jam scitus succedit in oscula fratris,
 Res (eccel) in lusus non operosa tuos.
Basia jam veniant tua quantacunque caterva;
 Jam quocunque tuus murmure ludat amor.   30
Enl Tibi materies tenera & tractabilis hic est:
 Hic ad blanditias est tibi cera satis.
Salve infans, tot basiolis, molle argumentum,
 Maternis labiis dulce negotiolum,
O salvel Nam te nato, puer aurëe, natus   35
 Et *Carolo & Mariae* tertius est oculus.

391   *In Serenissimæ Reginæ partum hyemalem.*

Serta, puer: (quis nunc flores non præbeat hortus?)
 Texe mihi facili pollice serta, puer.
Quid tu nescio quos narras mihi, stulte, Decembres?
 Quid mihi cum nivibus? da mihi serta, puer.
Nix? & hyems? non est nostras quid tale per oras;   5
 Non est: vel si sit, non tamen esse potest.
Ver agitur: quæcunque trucem dat larva Decembrem,
 Quid fera cunque fremant frigora, ver agitur.
Nónne vides quali se palmite regia vitis
 Prodit, & in sacris quæ sedet uva jugis?   10
Tam lætis quæ bruma solet ridere racemis?
 Quas hyemis pingit purpura tanta genas?
O Marial O divûm soboles, genitrixque Deoruml
 Siccine nostra tuus tempora ludus erunt?
Siccine tu cum vere tuo nihil horrida brumæ   15

---

36 *tertius . . . oculus:* James, joining Charles and Mary; *oculus* is a strange word to choose—it has for Crashaw evidently here the same connotations as does "star" in the poem "Upon the Kings coronation" ("Sound forth"), No. 338.

In Serenissimæ Reginæ. 46 (48).* Published first in the Cambridge volume congratulating the Queen on the birth of the Princess Elizabeth on December 28, 1635. See also No. 339.

[that they are] not terrifying at all? and the south winds
[that they are] not rain-soaked at all?
Is it so in the middle of winter that your lilies will be able to rise
and know only their own snows?
Or thus with the snows opposing and the winds gnashing their teeth
will our kingdoms be able to produce new roses?
O good disturber of the year, who do not let the seasons travel
under their own signs on the well-known path!
O pious destroyer of winter, who hold the sad mutterings
of the universe under your dominion so sweet!
Continue, I pray, to impose your beautiful power on our calendar:
Continue, I pray, to count your months in this way.
Continue to seem unseasonable and unsuitable.
Thus take everything in fee of your womb.
Thus may we often see our winters
pass disinherited by your flowers.   [snows of roses because of you.
May these springlike winters and May-like Decembers often see these
Let another race count its changing year by the stars
and reckon its days by the wandering signs.
would it be proper for us to grant so much to so many clouds?
for the British climate to suffer such gloomy changes?
Nay rather we will give you our whole year:
pay it all out for your deliveries, Mary.
May your womb be the just arbiter of our year:
may every season pass to you in fee.
For what other names so sweet would a month assume?
or in what toga could it move so fair?
Janus would want this crown of laurel on each of his brows,
indeed May would buy it for himself [even if it cost] all of Chloris.
With spring exiled the whole state of the flowers
would want, as its queen, you or your child.
O happy fate of the year when all the months [are] in order,
one the month of Charles, the next the month of Mary.

Sydera, nil madidos sola morare notos?
Siccine sub mediâ poterunt tua surgere brumâ,
  Atque suas solùm lilia nosse nives?
Ergò vel invitis nivibus, frendentibus Austris,
  Nostra novis poterunt regna tumere rosis?   20
O bona turbatrix anni, quælimite noto
  Tempora sub signis non sinis ire suis!
O pia prædatrix hyemis, quæ tristia mundi
  Murmura tam dulci sub ditione tenes!
Perge precor nostris vim pulchram ferre Calendis: 25
  Perge precor menses sic numerare tuos.
Perge intempestiva atque importuna videri;
  Inque uteri titulos sic rape cuncta tui.
Sit nobis sit sæpe hyemes sic cernere nostras
  Exhæredatas floribus ire tuis.   30
Sæpe sit has vernas hyemes Maiosque Decembres
  Has per te roseas sæpe videre nives.
Altera gens varium per sydera computet annum,
  Atque suos ducant per vaga signa dies.
Nos deceat nimiis tantum permittere nimbis?   35
  Tempora tam tetricas ferre Britanna vices?
Quin nostrum tibi nos omnem donabimus annum:
  In partus omnem expende, Maria, tuos.
Sit tuus ille uterus nostri bonus arbiter anni:
  Tempus & in titulos transeat omne tuos.   40
Nam quæ alia indueret tam dulcia nomina mensis?
  Aut qua tam posset candidus ire toga?
Hanc laurum Janus sibi vertice vellet utroque,
  Hanc sibi vel tota Chloride Majus emet.
Tota suam (vere expulso) respublica florum   45
  Reginam cuperent te, sobolemve tuam.
O bona sors anni, cum cuncti ex ordine menses
  Hic mihi *Carolides*, hic *Marianus* erit.

---

34 *vaga signa:* the zodiac.
43 *Janus:* the two-faced god of doorways for whom January is named.
44 *Chloride:* the imaginary mistress of May.

392   *To the newborn princess, a sign*
                   of her mother's nature.

Grow, o [child] destined to be judged by the gentle gods,
o grow and hasten, little princess,
hasten to fill the roles of your mother.
And when a small pair of smaller thunderbolts
first Charles and then James,
ready to succeed to their father's glory,
will lead the fates in brilliant rage;
When a holy fear and the great murmur
of the name of England will rattle the whole
Bosporus from shore to shore and will shake
the Ottoman Moors with unfeigned fear;
then other battles will summon you, which peace will not have to fear.
Your power will lie in the flutter
of your modest eye, and you will scatter abroad
sweet deaths against a devoted enemy.
O when that tender flower which,
pressed from a new star, now plays about your face,
at some time grown more powerful will roll forth
a whole golden flank through swords of fire;
he, peaceful up to now, then adult,
will frolic in the pure fields of your cheeks,
mightier Cupid;
O what sure darts will fly
on haughtier wing, and sweet deaths
hither and yon in the rejoicing throngs,
wherever you command, quickly will fly!
O how many hearts of burning gods
will feel pleasant wounds at your hand!
O how many breasts of princes will become
an easy mark for your well-aimed arrows!
For through what battles will you not be able to be borne
for whom the workshop of great loves
opens the bosom of your mother and each star?

392   *Principi recèns natæ omen*
               maternæ indolis.

Cresce, ô dulcibus imputanda Divis,
O cresce, & propera, puella Princeps,
In matris propera venire partes.
Et cùm par breve fulminum minorum,
Illinc Carolus, & Jacobus indè,   5
In patris faciles subire famam,
Ducent fata furoribus decoris;
Cùm terror sacer, Anglicíque magnum
Murmur nominis increpabit omnem
Latè Bosporon, Ottomannicásque   10
Non picto quatiet tremore Lunas;
Te tunc altera, nec timenda paci,
Poscent prælia. Tu potens pudici
Vibratrix oculi, pios in hostes
Latè dulcia fata dissipabis.   15
O cùm flos tener ille, qui recenti
Pressus sidere jam sub ora ludit,
Olim fortior omne cuspidatos
Evolvet latus aureum per ignes;
Quíque imbellis adhuc, adultus olim,   20
Puris expatiabitur genarum
Campis imperiosior Cupido;
O quàm certa superbiore pennâ
Ibunt spicula, melleæque mortes,
Exultantibus hinc & indè turmis,   25
Quoquò jusseris, impigrè volabunt!
O quot corda calentium deorum
De te vulnera delicata discent!
O quot pectora Principum magistris
Fient molle negotium sagittis!   30
Nam quæ non poteris per arma ferri,
Cui matris sinus atque utrumque sidus
Magnorum patet officina Amorum?

Principi recèns natæ. 46 (48).* Published first in the Cambridge volume congratulating the
King on the birth of the Princess Anne, March 17, 1637.
   11   *Lunas:* ("moons") i.e. in crescent shape.
   27   *deorum:* i.e. suitors (she died December 8, 1640, aged three).

Hence may you take, o little princess
whatever you need for your quiver.
Take one hundred Cupids from one
eye of your mother, one hundred graces,
one hundred Venuses: there will still remain
one hundred thousand Cupids; there will remain
three hundred Venuses and Graces
left over forever in that pure spring.

393   *On the queen,*
  continually delivering both her own and the University.

Hither, o Muse, with the sacred company flying
around about, hither bring the regular beat
of the trochee trained by annual practice
to rock the royal cradle.
See noble Mary by another birth
calls forth your fruitfulness
and the excellent child demands for himself
the attendant offspring of the Muses.
Of course she never has been brought to bed
with a simple child or only for herself:
the birth is re-echoed, or far off,
it produces everlasting twins.
Of course she herself brings about these births
and adds strength to the verses
who gives the breath of life
at once to both princes and to muses.
The goddess in childbirth may be able to wear out
our Muses, not without divine inspiration,
and to dry up the whole spring
of Helicon with perpetual joys.
Nay, may you continue to endure and to vie
in turn on holy terms.
It is a pleasant contest to have been able
to be conquered thus in dust not ignoble.

Hinc sumas licet, ô puella Princeps,
Quantacunque opus est tibi pharetrâ.   35
Centum sume Cupidines ab uno
Matris lumine, Gratiásque centum,
Et centum Veneres: adhuc manebunt
Centum mille Cupidines; manebunt
Ter centum Venerésque Gratiæque   40
Puro fonte superstites per ævum.

393   *In Reginam,*
            Et sibi & Academiæ semper parturientem.

Huc ô sacris circumflua cœtibus,
    Huc ô frequentem, Musa, choris pedem
Fer, annuo doctum labore
    Purpureas agitare cunas.
Fœcunditatem provocat, en, tuam   5
Maria partu nobilis altero,
    Prolémque Musarum ministram
        Egregius sibi poscit Infans.
Nempe Illa nunquam pignore simplici
Sibíve soli facta puerpera est: 10
    Partu repercusso, vel absens,
        Perpetuos procreat gemellos.
Hos Ipsa partus scilicet efficit,
Inque ipsa vires carmina suggerit,
    Quæ spiritum vitámque donat   15
        Principibus simul & Camœnis.
Possit Camœnas, non sine Numine,
Lassare nostras Diva puerpera,
    Et gaudiis siccare totam
        Perpetuis Heliconis undam.   20
Quin experiri pergat, & in vices
Certare sanctis conditionibus.
    Lis dulcis est, nec indecoro
        Pulvere, sic potuisse vinci.

38–40   this sequence of numbers recalls Catullus' song which Crashaw translated, "Out of Catullus," No. 376.

In Reginam. 48.* Published first in the volume congratulating the Queen on the birth of Prince Henry, July 8, 1640; the volume contains also the long poem (second version) "A Panegyricke [upon the Royal Family]," No. 369, but the two poems are not associated in the volume.

3   *annuo:* not strictly speaking, but the many royal births must have made it seem so.

Nature devises the [light of] day and the darkness [of night] in
[alternation
becoming a mother first by a dark then by a light pledge of love.
A better Nature, you maintain your turns,
sweetest one, (but for what a different reason!)
Shining white, and always the same color as you is each child,
you give first a daughter then a son but each one is a day.

394   *The University commends its book*
                    to the fairest queen.

The poem was written to introduce to the Queen a volume celebrating the birth of a prince, i.e. either *Ducis Eboracensis Fasciae* for James in 1633 (to which Crashaw contributed "Ad Reginam," No. 390, and perhaps prepared "Upon the Duke of Yorke his Birth a Panegyricke," No. 369), or *Votes Votivae*

Take this also—unless we ask too much—in your hand like a mother
or at least like a grandmother, Mary.
This sweet little pink babe is newborn of its mother, the Muse,
and his father is a child of yours (who would think it?).
Even so far impatient love is in the virgin Muse:
already now she does not deny she is the mother by him.
How many grandchildren you may hope for from this son at some time
who at once both is a father and creates a father!

Alternis Natura Diem meditatur & umbras,   25
    Hinc atro, hinc albo pignore facta parens.
Tu melior Natura tuas, dulcissima, servas
    (Sed quam dissimili sub ratione!) vices.
Candida Tu, & partu semper Tibi concolor omni:
    Hinc Natam, hinc Natum das; sed utrinque Diem.   30

---

394   *Serenissimæ Reginæ librum suum*
            commendat Academia.

for Henry in 1640 (to which Crashaw contributed "In Reginam, Et sibi," No.
393, and "To the Queen, An Apologie," No. 369 A, and "To the Queen, Upon
her numerous Progenie," No. 369 B). On the whole, the earlier date seems the
likelier.

Hunc quoque maternâ (nimium nisi magna rogamus)
    Aut aviæ saltem sume, Maria, manu.
Est Musâ de matre recens rubicundulus infans,
    Cui pater est partus (quis putet?) ille tuus.
Usque adeo impatiens amor est in virgine Musâ:
    Jam nunc ex illo non negat esse parens.
De nato quot habes olim sperare nepotes,
    Qui simul & pater est, & facit esse patrem!

---

30 *Natam . . . Natum:* of seven children only one was of the same sex as its imme-
diate predecessor.
Serenissimæ Reginæ. MS.*

FUNERARY AND GRATULATORY

395 *Epitaph*
On the Rev. Dr. Brooke.

Beneath this earth (not heavy) he laid his head;
he, whom death itself scarcely dared to claim
but learned to fear and hesitated long
with blow upraised watching from afar
the shining features and that keen star of his face.
When fame in letters gave glory to him,
he accepted it and is the richer for his gifts.
His clear skill knew how to soften
harsh practices in his old age,
the youth of his fame and fortune flourished.
While his lifetime was short, yet he did not seem over hasty.
Although long, he did not seem tired. Do you even believe he is dead?

396 *On the death of the Venerable Rev. Dr. Mansell*
Master of Queens' College which followed very closely
the death of the Rev. Dr. Brooke.

Does death then again a second time with her tragic hand
order [us] to go into tears and moans of bitter lamentation?
Indeed that hand which now brings new shafts,
that hand still drips fresh with the former blood.
O you, whom Lachesis almost mingled in a common urn,
and [whom] the close-neighboring threads scarcely allowed to be two,
O go, whom the fellowship of our loss joins,
too equal through our tears, o go!
Go by a pleasant path through the Elysian vales

FUNERARY AND GRATULATORY

395
In reṽ. D.ʳᵈ Brooke.
Epitaphium.

Posuit sub istâ (non gravi) caput terrâ
Ille, ipsa quem mors arrogare vix ausa
Didicit vereri, plurimumque suspenso
Dubitavit ictu, lucidos procul vultus,
Et sydus illud oris acre prospectans.   5
Cui literarum fama cùm dedit lumen,
Accepit, atque est ditior suis donis.
Cujus serena facilitas graves mores
Mulcere novit; cujus in senectute
Famæque viguit, & juventa fortunæ.   10
Ita brevis ævi, ut nec videri festinus;
Ita longus, ut nec fessus. Et hunc mori credis?

396
In obitum Rev. V. Dʳⁱˢ Mansell Coll. Regin. Mʳⁱ
qui rev. D.ˢ Brooke interitum proximè secutus est.

Ergo iterum in lacrymas, & saevi murmura planctûs
    Ire jubet tragicâ mors iterata manu?
Scilicet illa novas quæ jam fert dextra sagittas,
    Dextra priore recens sanguine stillat adhuc.
Vos ô, quos sociâ Lachesis propè miscuit urnâ,   5
    Et vicina colus vix sinit esse duos;
Ite ô, quos nostri jungunt consortia damni;
    Per nostras lacrymas ô nimis ite pares!
Ite per Elysias felici tramite valles,

In reṽ. D.ʳᵈ Brooke. MS.* See "An Epitaph upon Dr. Brooke," No. 344. Brooke died September 16, 1631.

In obitum Rev. V. Dʳⁱˢ Mansell. MS.* John Mansel, President of Queens' College, Cambridge, died October 7, 1631.

    5 *Lachesis:* the Fate who assigns to a man his fate.

and unite your souls on common paths.
There mingle [your] mighty shades beyond,
and may the same joyful work demand you both.
At the same time go with varied conversations through nectareall hours,
may night continually carry on the alternate turns.
May one tree bear food [for you both] and summon you into its shade.
May one turf give easy couches to both.
Meanwhile it will be certain how much greater the friendship of death
must be considered than that which exists throughout life.

397   *Epitaph on Master Herris.*

Stop for a while, wayfarer, where you will have to remain for
a long time; of course you know that hither you are hastening
wherever you hasten. The reward for your delay will be your
tears, if you know that here lies William the brightest star of
the distinguished Herris family. When you have learned that such
a one has lived and lived so much, you may learn to what great hopes
mortality can rise, from what great hopes can fall. As an infant,
Essex saw him; as a youth, Cambridge; ah both unfortunate
because neither saw him as an old man. He was a pupil of Christ
College, a fellow of Pembroke Hall. Both had a great rivalry for
[his] love.

Et sociis animos conciliate viis.   10
Illic ingentes ultrò confundite manes,
   Noscat & æternam mutua dextra fidem.
Communes eadem spargantur in otia curæ,
   Atque idem felix poscat utrumque labor.
Nectareæ simul ite vagis sermonibus horæ: 15
   Nox trahat alternas continuata vices.
Una cibos ferat, una suas vocet arbor in umbras.
   Ambobus faciles herba det una toros.
Certum erit interea quanto sit major habenda,
   Quàm quæ per vitam est, mortis amicitia.   20

397   *Epitaphium in Dominum* Herrisium.

Siste te paulum (viator) ubi Longum Sisti
   Necesse erit, huc nempe properare te scias
      quocunque properas.
    Moræ prætium erit
    Et Lacrimæ,   5
    Si jacere hic scias
    Gulielmum
Splendidæ Herrisiorum familiæ
    Splendorem maximum:
Quem cum talem vixisse intellexeris,   10
    Et vixisse tantum;
    Discas licet
   In quantas spes possit
    Assurgere mortalitas,
    De quantis cadere.   15
Quem { Infantem, Essexia— / Juvenem, Cantabrigia } vidit
   Senem, ah infælix utraque
   Quod non vidit.
        Qui   20
   Collegii Christi Alumnus,
   Aulæ Pembrokianæ socius,
Utrique, ingens amoris certamen fuit.

Epitaphium in Dominum Herrisium. 46 (48).* See "Upon the death of Mr. *Herrys*," No. 345, for information about William Herrys. The "Epitaphium" forms the text of the memorial tablet for Herrys at Pembroke College.

Until God made vain the sweetest struggles and made
him fellow of the heavenly college whose pupil he always was, he
himself was the college in which all the muses and graces, nowhere
else more sisterly, united in a most steadfast fellowship under
their guardian religion.

Whom Oratory recognized as a poet, Poetics as an orator, and Both as a
philosopher, all men [acknowledged] as a Christian. Who in
Faith went beyond the world, in Hope the heavens, in Charity his
neighbor, and in Humility himself. Beneath his young brow, a
mature mind; beneath his ease of habits, a severity of character;
beneath his very great genius, a few years; beneath his greater
modesty, the greatest talents finally lay hidden so that you might
have called his life a beautiful and virtuous dissimulation:

nay indeed even his death, for see how he suffered himself to be
concealed even in his burial, under such a little gravestone
such a great guest; yet to the extent that the monument is too
large, so the grave is too small. He died on that very day on which
the Church of England reads at vespers: He was taken away lest
that wickedness should alter his understanding; namely 15 October, in the
year of Salvation 1631.

Donec

Dulciss. Lites elusit Deus,   25
Eumque cœlestis Collegii
Cujus semper Alumnus fuit
    socium fecit;
Qui & ipse Collegium fuit,
       In quo   30
Musæ omnes & gratiæ,
    Nullibi magis sorores,
    Sub præside religione
In tenacissimum sodalitium coaluere.

	Oratoria	Poetam		35
Quem	Poetica	Oratorem	Agnovere.	
	Utraque	Philosophum		
	Christianum	Omnes		

	Fide	Mundum		
Qui	Spe	Coelum	Superavit.	40
	Charitate	Proximum		
	Humilitate	Seipsum		

Cujus

Sub verna fronte senilis animus,
Sub morum facilitate, severitas virtutis;   45
Sub plurima indole, pauci anni;
Sub majore modestia, maxima indoles
    adeo se occuluerunt
      ut vitam ejus
Pulchram dixeris & pudicam dissimulationem: 50
    Imo vero & mortem,
    Ecce enim in ipso funere
    Dissimulari se passus est,
Sub tantillo marmore tantum hospitem,
    Eo nimirum majore monumento   55
      quo minore tumulo.
Eo ipso die occubuit quo Ecclesia
    Anglicana ad vesperas legit,
Raptus est ne malitia mutaret Intellectum ejus;
    Scilicet Id. Octobris, Anno S *1631*.   60

59 *Raptus . . . ejus:* the Vulgate text for Wisdom of Solomon 4:11, appointed to be
read for the first lesson at Evening Prayer on October 15 in the Book of Common Prayer
(1606).

60 *Id.:* the Ides; the Prayer Book (edition of 1636) in the calendar for October the
fifteenth calls that number "Idus."

398   *A Scazon on the same [Gentleman].*

It is not altogether certain what Crashaw intended this title to mean. A scanzon is a form of iambic trimeter verse having a spondee or trochee in the

> Hither, O guest, turn your eyes, but blind with tears,
> he reads these best whom weeping does not let read.
> Recently art and nature, beauty, and strength
> aflame with rivalry agreed
> to prove in one youth what they all could
> do. The world was unequal to [deciding] so great a case:
> Therefore here they await the Judge from heaven itself.

399   *Elegy.*

> Go my tears go, for I do not delay [you]. But I pray
> only do not bar the path of my sad voice.
> O may [my] words enliven my plaintive sorrows,
> and at the least may our love say he has died.
> See still they say no, see they say no and the rebellious tears
> press on and rush headlong on their unbridled way.
> O dear one, do you want our silences to call you?
> Do you want our silent love to weep with unceasing murmur?
> It will weep, and the dank urn will always drink its dews,
> and always, always will it have faithful waters.
> Meanwhile, whoever you are, do not think it strange
> if real tears have not learned to speak.

398   *In Eundem Scazon.*

last foot; it would seem in this title that Crashaw is using it to mean a series of lines of verse. The lines follow No. 345.

> Huc hospes, oculos flecte, sed lacrimis cœcos,
> Legit optime hæc, Quem legere non sinit fletus.
> Ars nuper & natura, forma, virtusque
> Æmulatione fervidæ, paciscuntur
> Probare in uno juvene quid queant omnes,
> Fecere. tantæ terra impar fuit liti,
> Ergo hic ab ipso Judicem manent cœlo.

399   *Elegia.*

> Ite meæ lacrymæ (nec enim moror) ite. Sed oro
>   Tantùm ne miseræ claudite vocis iter.
> O liceat querulos verbis animare dolores,
>   Et saltem ah periit dicere noster amor.
> Ecce negant tamen, ecce negant, lacrymæque rebelles   5
>   Indomitâ pergunt, præcipitantque viâ.
> Visne (ô care) igitur Te nostra silentia dicant?
>   Vis fleat assiduo murmure mutus amor?
> Flebit, & urna suos semper bibet humida rores,
>   Et fidas semper, semper habebit aquas.   10
> Interea, quicunque estis ne credite mirum
>   Si veræ lacrymæ non didicére loqui.

In Eundem Scazon. 48.*

Elegia. 48. In the reprint of this poem in the 1670 edition, it is described as referring also to Herrys and it follows his memorial epitaph.

400   *Epitaph.*

Whoever you are, joyous in an age of nectar
and shining with hope of golden youth,
you do not know that radiant suns go away,
you do not know chains and the ironclad night
of the deepest dungeon and bustling Dis
and you look at trembling old age far off,
from this you will learn tears and to this repay them.
Here ah too clearly here beneath this shallow cave
hope and a thousand, thousand joys have put on
the long night—alas too long.
The wave of the Stygian fen
has drowned the flaming torch of shining youth.
But if you deny the tears of grief,
surely hither you will bring tears of fear.

401   *To the most honorable Dr. Robt. Heath, chief Justice*
       of the Court of Common Pleas, Congratulations!

I congratulate you for your crimson stripe and sacred purple,
O love and great glory of your toga!
For I see. Look, Themis glows on those shoulders [of yours]
and rejoices to come wholly into your embrace.
O how well she reaches from that radiant star
and teaches her rays to abound here!
Indeed my golden Themis forever go in endless pomp!
O may she ever wish to have her star here!
Thus may it blaze and never may your purple grow pale.
O never may it be worthy to pass into your facial expressions.
May it drink no redness from innocent blood.
May it not profit from such cruel purple dye.

400   *Epitaphium.*

Quisquis nectareo serenus ævo,
Et spe lucidus aureæ juventæ
Nescis purpureos abire soles,
Nescis vincula, ferreamque noctem
Imi carceris, horridumque Ditem,   5
Et spectas tremulam procul senectam,
Hinc disces lacrymas, & huc repones.
Hic, ô scilicet hic brevi sub antro
Spes & gaudia mille, mille longam
(Heu longam nimis) induére noctem.   10
Flammantem nitidæ facem juventæ,
Submersit Stygiæ paludis unda.
Ergo si lacrymas neges doloris
Huc certè lacrymas feres timoris.

401   *Honoratiss° D? Rob?* Heath, *summo Justit.*
               de com. Banco. Gratulatio.

Ignitum latus, & sacrum tibi gratulor ostrum,
    O amor; atque tuæ gloria magna togæ!
Nam video. Themis ecce humeris, Themis ardet in istis,
    Inque tuos gaudet tota venire sinus.
O ibi purpureo quàm se bene porrigit astro!   5
    Et docet hîc radios luxuriare suos!
Imò eat æterna sic ô Themis aurea pompâ!
    Hîc velit ô sydus semper habere suum!
Sic flagret, & nunquam tua purpura palleat intus.
    O nunquam in vultus digna sit ire tuos.   10
Sanguine ab innocuo nullos bibat illa rubores.
    Nec tam crudeli murice proficiat.

Epitaphium. 48.*

Honoratiss° D? Rob? Heath. MS.* Sir Robert Heath, Recorder of London, Solicitor-General, Attorney-General, and on October 26, 1631, Chief Justice of the Court of Common Pleas. It is possible that during Crashaw's years in London he came to know Heath.
    2 *togæ:* apparently the robes of office are being here described; the color of the robe sets up the color conceit of the entire poem.
    3 *Themis:* goddess of Justice.
    10 *in vultus . . . ire:* i.e. never may you have occasion to be ashamed: the clauses that follow (lines 11–18) reflect the cases that Heath may have to judge.

May each shining virtue which is yours (and which is not yours?)
conduct your fortune without storms to the skies.
May your gravestone drip with the tears of no widow
nor may any home which calls upon you be broken.
May no pine cut down bewail its fate to you
as if it fell sadly amid the complaints of its master.
May fame spread its feathers underneath you as you go.
May she make you the charge of a louder praise.
May incense travel with your name wherever it goes
and may that lucky breeze which bears you bear [also] roses.
Live your whole life according to your prayers whatever
stars call you (for they are most just),
Until this purple of yours yields to the snowy shroud
where your robe will be a lily, which was here a rose.

Quæque tibi est (nam quæ non est tibi?) candida virtus
    Fortunam placidè ducat in alta tuam.
Nullius viduæ lacrymas tua marmora sudent.   15
    Nec sit, quæ inclamet te, tibi fracta domus.
Non gemat ulla suam pinus tibi scissa ruinam,
    Ceu cadat in domini murmure mæsta sui.
Fama suas subter pennas tibi sternat eünti;
    Illa tubæ faciat te melioris opus.   20
Thura tuo (quacunque meat) cum nomine migrent;
    Quæque vehit fælix te, vehat aura rosas.
Vive tuis (nec enim non sunt æquissima) votis
    Æqualis, quæ te sydera cunque vocant.
Hæc donec niveæ cedat tua purpura pallæ,   25
    Lilium ubi fuerit, quæ rosa vestis erat.

AMOROUS

402   *The treasury of evils is woman.*

What god, o who was it who fashioned you, wicked woman?
Bah! the crime of the gods, the shameful punishment of the gods!
What hand of the gods is still not pledged in friendship to the world?
Hand fit for our disaster.
Spare me; I have made a mistake: for indeed no holy divine wills can
be so cruel as to have willed such utter evil.
Piety is your handiwork. Harmony is your handiwork.
Indeed I do not at all suppose that you are such contrivers.
Alas you infernal band [of devils]! Recognize your brood.
Isn't it shameful that this [woman] can surpass your crime?
Applaud, Tartarean princes, powers of Hell
(it is not strange you could [fashion] such a great evil)
Now praise [the work of] your hands. If by chance you are silent,
this work of your craftsmen will speak praises abundantly.
How well do I observe you all in that mirror?
Into that one narrow breast is forced all evil.
Nay, sleep Pluto. Restrain the frenzied sisters,
our downfall does not require your help now.
Enough that this machine has been built against our walls,
human furies will make our hell.

AMOROUS

402   *Thesaurus malorum fæmina.*

Quis deus, O quis erat qui te, mala fæmina, finxit?
Proh! Crimen superûm, noxa pudenda deûm!
Quæ divùm manus est adeo non dextera mundo?
In nostras clades ingeniosa manus!
Parcite; peccavi: nec enim pia numina possunt   5
Tam crudele semel vel voluisse nefas.
Vestrum opus est pietas; opus est concordia vestrum:
Vos equidem tales haud reor artifices.
Heus inferna cohors! fætus cognoscite vestros.
Num pudet hanc vestrum vincere posse scelus?   10
Plaudite Tartarei Proceres, Erebique potentes
(Næ mirum est tantum vos potuisse malum)
Jam vestras Laudate manus. Si forte tacetis,
Artificum laudes grande loquetur opus.
Quàm bene vos omnes speculo contemplor in isto?   15
Pectus in angustum cogitur omne malum.
Quin dormi Pluto. Rabidas compesce sorores,
Jam non poscit opem nostra ruina tuam.
Hæc satis in nostros fabricata est machina muros,
Mortales Furias Tartara nostra dabunt.   20

Thesaurus malorum. 48.
   19 *machina:* a battering ram designed to break down the walls of a resisting town.

MISCELLANEOUS

403   *On the picture of the Right Reverend Bishop,*
Dr. Andrews.

See also "Upon Bishop Andrewes his Picture," No. 359. Perhaps at one time
it was thought to use a Latin rather than a vernacular poem for the volume of
the Bishop's *Sermons;* this poem is designed to be placed in a book (see

This picture shows one whom Fame shows better
but even fame itself does not yet show enough [of] him;
he, he alone enriched all eloquence,
alone mastered so many tongues, and achieved also
a retiring fame: the father of a fiery mind,
alert to the dancing ray of eternal light,
wandering invincibly through the deep considerations of knowledge,
he made haste with his unbridled spirit, for in fact he gallantly exhausted
nature itself by the skills of his many good works,
and by his many tongues he changed himself
into all far off peoples and was a kinsman
to the whole world at the same time: thus willingly he
inclined his sacred and unbroken brilliance
and heart full of heaven toward his father's fires: in this, in this picture,
Reader, you see him; look! O would that you might hear him too.

404   *On Bp. Andrewes's picture.*

This picture, the sacred face of which has divided to prosper,
is not to be seen except through your tears.
Of course you will say when you look at this face,
O, the holy father bore just such a face.
Thence, you will hope for his familiar voice, for his pious thunderbolts,
and for his holy sweetness to come by so sweet a path.
Just so was that hand, when he transmitted his winged [words] to Fame,
just so—you will say—was that hand on his pen.

MISCELLANEOUS

403　　　*In Picturam Reverendissimi Episcopi,*
D. Andrews.

"Lector," line 14) (—the following poem is not so certainly designed). Andrewes had mastered many languages and was a preacher of singularly impressive delivery.

Hæc charta monstrat, Fama quem monstrat magis,
Sed & ipsa nec dum fama quem monstrat satis.
Ille, ille totam solus implevit Tubam,
Tot ora solus domuit & famam quoque
Fecit modestam: mentis igneæ pater　　　　　　　5
Agilique radio Lucis æternæ vigil,
Per alta rerum pondera indomito Vagus
Cucurrit Animo, quippe naturam ferox
Exhausit ipsam mille Fœtus Artibus,
Et mille Linguis ipse se in gentes procul　　　　10
Variavit omnes et fuit toti simul
Cognatus orbi: sic sacrum & solidum jubar
Saturumque cœlo pectus ad patrios Libens
Porrexit ignes: hac eum (Lector) vides
Hac (ecce) charta O Utinam & audires quoque.　　15

404　　　　　　　*[In picturam Epis.* Andrewes.]

Hæc est, quæ sacrâ didicit florere figurâ,
　Non nisi per lachrymas charta videnda tuas.
Scilicet ah dices, hæc cùm spectaveris ora,
　Ora sacer sic, ô sic tulit ille pater.
Sperabis solitas illinc, pia fulmina, voces;　　　　5
　Sanctaque tam dulci mella venire viâ.
Sic erat illa, suas Famæ cùm traderet alas,
　Ad calamum (dices) sic erat illa manus.

In Picturam. 46 (48).*
[*In Picturam Epis. Andrewes.*] MS.* The idea seems to be that the Bishop has given life to each of the many copies of the engraving made for his *Sermons.*

And such was his breast, the lofty home of his towering mind,
such was his heart filled with his star.
O how beautiful are the falsities of this deceptive picture!
and the workmanship which lives in bronze so like [him].
Since you have given life to so many pictures, dear father,
this one picture justly gives life to you.

405   *When I had dedicated some of these*
            pieces to my most admired teacher,
            my dearest friend, R. Brooke.

Lo [my] Muse, most admired teacher, still timidly stretching her
wings for you, as if before your eyes, [those wings] which she acquired
from your lectures just as if from the workshop of Apollo.
Just as from the nest the bird, now resplendent in full-grown wing,
contemplates the stars and the beautiful paths
between the princes of the air; although he has never experienced
the heavens and for the first time puts forth on his awkward feathers to
climb the heights, still he trembles to go and, shaking his shoulders lightly
clad in their handsome cloak, and warbling and frolicking through the air,
he does not hesitate at all to hang his weak wing-motions upon the stars.
But indeed at the same time exhausted by the great distances
through the vast void, suspended beneath the empty heaven,
he sees the fields far off and his forests and far off all
that he usually sees: but then his spirit, overcome indeed, fails
and fearing his hopes and such great efforts, he looks fully
back at his mother and returns on the rushing winds.
The fact that I bring this to you, most cultured sir, is not the flattery
of one giving, but the justice of one returning: nor have I chosen you as
the patron of my little book so much as I recognize you as its master.
Clearly these pieces are yours and mine. Neither yet are they mine in
that if anything is good in them, it is wholly yours: nor meanwhile yours
such that whatever is bad in them is not wholly mine. Thus in a certain
middle way and shared prerogative, they belong to us both. Indeed not
that I would bring envy to myself until I rise to the society of your
praises or do an injustice to you in that I should try to bring you down
to the fellowship of my insignificance. Indeed I should not dare to recog-
nize in my heart, much less openly to acknowledge, anything good about

Tale erat & pectus, celsæ domus ardua mentis,
Tale suo plenum sydere pectus erat.   10
O bene fallacis mendacia pulchra tabellæ!
Et, qui tam simili vivit in ære, labor!
Cùm tu tot chartis vitam, Pater alme, dedisti;
Hæc merito vitam charta dat una tibi.

405   *Cùm horum aliqua dedicâram*
Præceptori meo colendissimo,
Amico amicissimo, R. Brooke

En tibi Musam, (Præceptor colendissime) quas ex tuis modò
scholis, quasi ex Apollinis officinâ, accepit, alas timidè adhuc,
nec aliter quàm sub oculis tuis jactitantem.
Qualiter è nido multâ jam floridus alâ
Astra sibi meditatur avis, pulchrosque meatus   5
Aërios inter proceres; licèt æthera nunquam
Expertus, rudibusque illi sit in ardua pennis
Prima fides; micat ire tamen, quatiensque decorâ
Veste leves humeros, querulumque per aëra ludens
Nil dubitat vel in astra vagos suspendere nisus.   10
At verò simul immensum per inane profundis
Exhaustus spatiis, vacuoque sub æthere pendens,
Arva procul, sylvasque suas, procul omnia cernit,
Cernere quæ solitus; tum verò victa cadit mens,
Spesque suas, & tanta timens conamina, totus   15
Respicit ad matrem, pronisque revertitur auris.
Quòd tibi enim hæc feram (Vir ornatissime) non ambitio
dantis est, sed justitia reddentis: neque te libelli mei tam
elegi patronum, quàm dominum agnosco. Tua sanè sunt hæc,
et mea. neque tamen ita mea sunt, quin si quid in illis boni est,   20
tuum hoc sit totum: neque interim in tantum tua, ut quan-
tumcunque est in illis mali illud non sit ex integro meum. ita
medio quodam, & misto jure utriusque sunt. ne vel mihi, dum
me in societatem tuarum laudum elevarem, invidiam facerem;
vel injuriam tibi, ut qui te in tenuitatis meæ consortium   25
deducere conarer. Ego enim de meo nihil ausim boni mecum
agnoscere, nedum profiteri palàm, præter hoc unum (quo

---

10 *sydere:* i.e. star, the inspiration of God.

Amico, R. Brooke. MS.* Robert Brook was Schoolmaster at the Charterhouse while Crashaw
was a student there (1629–31). See also the dedicatory poem to him in the Appendix,
"Ornatissimo viro . . . Magistro Brook."

my book besides this one spirit (than which even now nothing is better) obviously not thankless and in itself repaying the account of your kindnesses with most scrupulous loyalty. Before whatever witnesses, this [work] I throw into the face of heaven and of my conscience as my own. In this I rise above enduring a rival. But truly others of your pupils will honor you in more polished service (and I know they may honor you): no one will possibly be more sincere or honest than I. In short, finally, this praise will belong peculiarly to these little streams, however small and nameless, because *they have known without doubt their own Ocean.*

406   *On Apollo pining for Daphne.*

"This piece and the three following are modelled metrically on the lines 'Pasiphaes Fabula' to be found in . . . *Epigrammata et Poematia Vetera,* Paris, 1590, . . . p. 447. The twenty-two lines, each in a different metre, repro-

"Foolish Cupid,
what is your flame preparing?
Is it not true that under this very sun
[your] burning torches become pale?"
"But our torch is more powerful than those [rays],
it can inflame flames, [it can make] fire burn itself."
See the one with power over flames
groans under a greater flame.
Alas! what is this? See Apollo
with a silent lyre (lest he celebrate his sorrows);
the eternal beauty of his face is rough with hanging
hair. Lo! to please a woman more
he puts forth a sluggish radiance with a languid flame.
He terrifies the heavens with his pale face.
The eye of the heaven grows powerless with tears.
He pays his debt to the sea and what he has drawn with his fires,
he repays with his tears.
At nightfall he hastens to hide among the shadows
and he cherishes the dusky shades of the shadows,
for he hates and rejects his own rays, baneful light.
He hesitates whether to lurk in the shadows or lead forth the day;
on one side burning grief persuades [him to come forth], on the other
                                         [love repells [him].

tamen nihil melius) animum nempe non ingratum, tuorumque
beneficiorum historiam religiosissimâ fide in se reponentem.
hoc quibuscunque testibus coram, hoc palàm in os cœli,⁣ 30
meæque conscientiæ meum jacto. effero me in hoc ultra
æmuli patientiam. Enim vero elegantiore obsequio venerentur
te (& venerantur, scio) tuorum alii: nemo me sincero magis,
vel ingenuo poterit. Horum denique rivulorum, tenuium
utcunque, nulliusque nominis, hæc saltem laus erit propria,⁣ 35
quòd *suum nempe norint Oceanum.*

406⁣⁣⁣⁣⁣⁣⁣⁣⁣ *In* Apollinem *depereuntem* Daphnen.

duce the various lines employed by Horace" (Martin, p. 445). The poems are
evidently school exercises.
⁣⁣⁣⁣The story of Apollo's love for Daphne would seem to have been based on the
account in Ovid *Metamorphoses* i. 452–567.

Stulte Cupido,
Quid tua flamma parat?
Annon sole sub ipso
Accensæ pereunt faces?
Sed fax nostra potentior istis,⁣⁣⁣⁣⁣⁣⁣⁣ 5
Flammas inflammare potest, ipse uritur ignis,
Ecce flammarum potens
Majore sub flammâ gemit.
Eheu! quid hoc est? En Apollo
Lyrâ tacente (ni sonet dolores)⁣⁣⁣⁣⁣⁣⁣ 10
Comâ jacente squallet æternus decor
Oris, en! dominæ quò placeat magis,
Languido tardum jubar igne promit.
Pallente vultu territat æthera.
Mundi oculus lacrymis senescit,⁣⁣⁣⁣⁣⁣⁣⁣ 15
Et solvit pelago debita, quodque hauserat ignibus,
His lacrymis rependit.
Noctis adventu properans se latebris recondit,
Et opacas tenebrarum colit umbras,
Namque suos odit damnans radios, nocensque lumen.⁣⁣ 20
An lateat tenebris dubitat, an educat diem,
Hinc suadet hos luctus furens, inde repugnat amor.

In Apollo. 48.

407   *Aeneas, the bearer of his father.*

The walls of Troy
The enemy and the fire hold.
Between the enemy and the fires
Aeneas takes out the sacred spoils
and on his shoulders the venerable burden,
and now o now spare [him] savage flames.
Do not spare me (he shouts),
but look with favor on my sacred pack;
but if you refuse, I will not be able
to delight in life but I will delight in death:
and I shall become a pyre for my father and ashes for myself.
After these words he speeds through the enemy lines;
he rejoices, and with his rescued trophies, as it were,
leads the triumphs. For the fury of the enemy
is now benumbed, and by such great piety,
the victor is vanquished: nay even Troy dies more willingly
and rejoices in its funeral rites
and triumphant applies the torches lest there be concealed in the dark
shadows a mighty deed of piety.
Thus you pay your debts to your father, thus you repay your rightful
duty. He had given life to you, you return [life] to him.
Happy are you who will be said to be the father of your own father.

408   *On Pygmalion.*

He grieves for his art,
does Pygmalion, for his own art.
Because the work was happy,
the artist was unhappy.
He feels wounds but does not see the blow.
Who believes? flames come from the frozen marble.
Too thankless, the marble
burns its maker.

407   *Æn*æas *Patris sui bajulus.*

Mænia Trojæ
Hostis & ignis habet.
Hostes inter & ignes
Ænæas spolium pium,
Atque humeris venerabile pondus   5
Excipit, & sævæ nunc o nunc parcite flammæ,
Parcite haud (clamat) mihi,
Sacræ favete sarcinæ,
Quod si negatis, nec licebit
Vitam juvare, sed juvabo funus;   10
Rogusque fiam patris ac bustum mei.
His dictis acies pervolat hostium,
Gestit, & partis veluti trophæis
Ducit triumphos. Nam furor hostium
Jam stupet & pietate tantâ   15
Victor vincitur; imò & moritur Troja libentius
Funeribusque gaudet,
Ac faces admittit ovans, ne lateat tenebras
Per opacas opus ingens pietatis.
Debita sic parti solvis tua, sic pari rependis   20
Officio. Dederat vitam tibi, tu reddis huic,
Felix! parentis qui pater diceris esse tui.

408   *In* Pigmaliona.

Pænitet Artis
Pigmaliona suæ.
Quod felix opus esset
Infelix erat artifex.
Sentit vulnera, nec videt ictum.   5
Quis credit? gelido veniunt de marmore flammæ.
Marmor ingratum nimis
Incendit autorem suum.

*Æn*æas *Patris sui bajulus.* 48.* The story is based on the *Æneid* ii. 559–751.
In Pigmaliona. 48.* The story is based on Ovid *Metamorphoses* x. 243–98.
  3 *felix:* i.e. well done.

He conceived idle rages;
he admires and worships his work.
First his hand created, lo now it cherishes;
gently it applies the probing fingers;
the hard flesh deludes the gentle touches.
Whether the maid is real or ivory,
whether she returns the kisses which were given,
he does not know. But he doubts, he fears, he begs for a favor,
and mingles sweet words.   [triumphs
To you, wretched man, Venus wishes to give pains, and takes these
from you because you flee all love.
Alas why do you flee live women? a dead girl kills you.
She will not be harmless although you fashion her with your hand;
alas she will be too harmful whose statue does harm.

409   *Arion.*

On the scaly, living,
Slippery back of a raft
Now Arion climbed.
The fare paid is as strange
as is the boat boarded. That
fare is of the air and
the boat is of the water.
Men lost him
at a great fee, this saves him
for no fee, this fish: and thus
his fall costs him more than his rescue;
and hence he is saved for less than he is lost.
While [the fish] cuts the waves, he cuts the air:
by his course, the fish; by his fingers, Arion:
and [the fish] scatters the waves and he scatters the airs.
For this soothing trident of a song
now the wind abjures its roars and more gentle
to the ears changes its appearance.
He forgets its appearance and fears its faintest whispers.

Concepit hic vanos furores;
Opus suum miratur atque adorat. 10
Prius creavit, ecce nunc colit manus,
Tentantes digitos molliter applicat;
Decipit molles caro dura tactus.
An virgo vera est, an sit eburnea;
Reddat an oscula quæ dabantur 15
Nescit. Sed dubitat, Sed metuit, munere supplicat,
Blanditiasque miscet.
Te, miser, pœnas dare vult, hos Venus, hos triumphos
Capit à te, quòd amorem fugis omnem.
Cur fugis heu vivas? mortua te necat puella. 20
Non erit innocua hæc, quamvis tuâ fingas manu,
Ipsa heu nocens erit nimis, cujus imago nocet.

409 Arion.

Squammea vivæ
Lubrica terga ratis
Jam conscendit Arion.
Merces tam nova solvitur
Navis quàm nova scanditur. Illa 5
Aërea est merces, hæc est & aquatica navis.
Perdidére illum viri
Mercede magnâ, servat hic
Mercede nullâ piscis: & sic
Salute plus ruina constat illi; 10
Minoris & servatur hinc quàm perditur.
Hic dum findit aquas, findit hic aëra:
Cursibus, piscis; digitis, Arion:
Et sternit undas, sternit & aëra:
Carminis hoc placido Tridente 15
Abjurat sua jam murmura, ventusque modestior
Auribus ora mutat:
Ora dediscit, minimos & metuit susurros.

Arion. 48.* The story is told in *Herodotus* i. 24.
4 *Merces:* sailors on shipboard wished to rob Arion and take his life, but he sang so
sweetly that the gods provided the dolphin for his rescue; the fare is the song.
8 *Mercede:* they were punished.

(The other sound prevents this sound from [reaching] the men.)
The murmuring breeze silently encompasses the nearby [surface of the]
[sea with its wings
and encircles the face of the man, but here no sails fill with the winds;
the wind attends to this raft; it does not draw; it is drawn.

410   *Birth* and *Burial* } *of the Phoenix.*

Phoenix, child of death,
what a strange woman in labor you are!
You rise not from nests but fires;
as if prepared not to lay eggs but to die:
Death is the midwife and you yourself give yourself birth.
    You yourself are the mother to you,
      and you, the daughter to you.
Thus you, the fragrant harvest
of your funeral rites, arise,
restored to yourself by your fall,
you take your own place. O death
which is fecund! O blessed profits of a costly death!
    Live, sweet wonder, live
    and be sufficient unto yourself.

411   *Hymn to Venus.*
As the virgins pass to her guardianship.

Be at hand at your rites, dear Venus:
May you smile sweetly and kindly, Venus,
just as when you press and subdue
Mars with your golden eye.

May you smile. O then neither will his flame help
Phoebus nor her weapons Phoebe. Only that
Cupid of yours wields weapons adequate
against you.

(Sonus alter vetat, ut sit sonus illis)
Aura strepens circum muta it lateri adjacente pennâ,　　20
Ambit & ora viri, nec vela ventis hîc egent;
Attendit hanc ventus ratem: non trahit, at trahitur.

410　　　　　　　　Phænicis $\left\{\begin{array}{c}\textit{Genethliacon}\\ \textit{&}\\ \textit{Epicedion.}\end{array}\right.$

Phænix alumna mortis,
Quàm mira tu puerpera!
Tu scandis haud nidos, sed ignes.
Non parere sed perire ceu parata:
Mors obstetrix; atque ipsa tu teipsam paris,　　5
　　Tu Tuique mater ipsa es,
　　Tu tuique filia.
Tu sic odora messis
Surgis tuorum funerum;
Tibique per tuam ruinam　　10
Reparata, te succedis ipsa. Mors ô
Fœcunda! Sancta ô Lucra pretiosæ necis!
　　Vive (monstrum dulce) vive
　　Tu tibique suffice.

411　　　　　　　　*Hymnus* Veneri.
　　　dum in illius tutelam transëunt virgines.

Tu tuis adsis, Venus alma, sacris:
Rideas blandùm, Venus, & benignùm,
Quale cùm Martem premis, aureoque
　　Frangis ocello.

Rideas. ô tum neque flamma Phæbum,　　5
Nec juvent Phœben sua tela. gestat
Te satis contra tuus ille tantùm
　　Tela Cupido.

Phænicis. 48. The life cycle of the phoenix is narrated in Ovid *Metamorphoses* xv. 391–407.
Hymnus Veneri. MS.*

Often with a smile he placed his arrows in the
quiver of Diana herself. He even
dared burn the lord of fire with
his mastering flames.

The chorus of virgins begs you (they would
not wish to be virgins long) only to
increase your company of so many serving
doves and sparrows.

[These virgins] dedicate whatever the lips of roses
or the necks of lilies preserve for you;
they dedicate the whole spring of [their] cheeks and
the spring of [their] eyes to you.

Hence for your son you may take arms or new arrows
for these [virgins'] eyes; or he may
wish to blow the long-haired torches
with a keener flame.

Take [these virgins]. And o may they learn why you
are friendly; why the night is
kindly and sweetly guarded; what sweet madness
and a wanton lover demand.

Take them. By these hearts, so many, which
burn for you. By the mystery your
girdle breathes. By whatever your Adonis
once said or did to you.

412   *On Hope.*

Hail, thou goddess hope. Goddess prolonging the eager
need for your favor, conqueror of the
raging of fortune; the only safety in the midst of
disaster.

Sæpe in ipsius pharetrâ Dianæ
Hic suas ridens posuit sagittas. 10
Ausus et flammæ Dominum magistris
Urere flammis.

Virginum te orat chorus (esse longùm
Virgines nollent) modò servientûm
Tot columbarum tibi, passerumque au- 15
gere catervam.

Dedicant quicquid labra vel rosarum,
Colla vel servant tibi liliorum:
Dedicant totum tibi ver genarum,
Ver oculorum. 20

Hinc tuo sumas licet arma nato,
Seu novas his ex oculis sagittas;
Seu faces flamma velit acriori
Flare comatas.

Sume. et ô discant, quid amica; quid nox, 25
Quid bene, & blandè vigilata nox sit;
Quid sibi dulcis furor, & protervus
Poscat amator.

Sume. per quæ tot tibi corda flagrant.
Per quod arcanum tua cestus halat. 30
Per tuus quicquid tibi dixit olim, aut
Fecit Adonis.

412   [*In Spem.*]

Spes Diva, salve. Diva avidam tuo
Necessitatem numine prorogans;
   Vindicta fortunæ furentis;
      Una salus mediis ruinis.

---

11 **Dominum:** Hephæstus, husband of Venus (Aphrodite); the story of his fury on the discovery of his wife's adultery with Mars (Ares) is told in the *Odyssey* viii. 266–358.
[*In Spem.*] MS.* See also the joint English poem "On Hope," No. 68, by Cowley and Crashaw.

Although queen, you make your throne under the
fallen roof of a little hut; those lying
in the midst arise; there, more firm,
your kingdoms endure.

You fashion chants from chains, poems
from prisons, and joys from grief itself.
You are a living spark deep in the heart,
not fearing any storms at all.

You are a kingdom for slaves; plenty for
the poor: triumph for the conquered:
shores for the shipwrecked: and a patron for
the condemned themselves: an anchor in the midst of the sea.

Indeed I am your foster child myself. We cling to
your breast and draw therefrom our soul.
O, holy nurse, o open the nourishing folds of your
bosom. Athirst I struggle.

413   *To suffer loss often results in gain.*

Losses are profits of secret gain to many,
and they teach by lucky delay how best to hasten,
and thus the wise serpent redeemed the wanton living of the years by
shedding his skin and so moved on to new ages.
You see how that eternal bird comes to its own aid, its age rolled back,
and renews itself by much death.
Noble to itself, it springs up with abundant [life], through the tender
flames, through its own ashes, and through its death.
What [is the meaning of] its clever jettisoning [of life]? what is the
                                        [usefulness of its funeral?
[What is] the faith of the flames, [what is] the nature of the pyre?
Do you advance thus by deceiving? do you laugh at costly funerals?
do you undergo death lest you should die?
Happy is he who has such a great knowledge of healing death;
for whom the hand of the Fates is so busy.

Regina quamvis, tu solium facis   5
Depressa parvi tecta tugurii;
   Surgunt jacentes inter; illic
     Firma magis tua regna constant.

Cantus catenis, carmina carcere,
Dolore ab ipso gaudiaque exprimis.   10
   Scintilla tu vivis sub imo
     Pectoris, haud metuens procellas.

Tu regna servis; copia pauperi:
Victis triumphus: littora naufrago:
   Ipsisque damnatis patrona: 15
     Anchora sub medio profundo.

Quin ipse alumnus sum tuus. ubere
Pendemus isto; & hinc animam traho.
   O, Diva nutrix, ô foventes
     Pande sinus. sitiens laboro.   20

413   *Damno affici sæpe fit lucrum.*

Damna adsunt multis taciti compendia lucri
   Felicique docent plus properare morâ,
Luxuriem annorum positâ sic pelle redemit
   Atque sagax serpens in nova sæcla subit.
Cernis ut ipsa sibi replicato suppetat ævo,   5
   Seque iteret, multâ morte perennis avis.
Succrescat generosa sibi, facilesque per ignes
   Perque suos cineres, per sua fata ferax.
Quæ sollers jactura sui? quis funeris usus?
   Flammarumque fides, ingeniumque rogi?   10
Siccine fraude subis? pretiosaque funera ludis?
   Siccine tu mortem, ne moriaris, adis?
Felix cui medicæ tanta experientia mortis,
   Cui tam Parcarum est officiosa manus.

---

16 *Anchora:* the anchor is a Christian symbol for hope.
Damno affici. 48.
   3 *Luxuriem annorum:* the serpent is said to be a symbol of wanton living (Martin, p. 445). *positâ sic pelle:* the serpent regains a fresh appearance by sloughing off his skin; he is thus a symbol of the Christian putting off the old man.

414   *A description of human life.*

O life, or at least a certain fleeting madness
and the spoils of life! to be sure, the brief guest
of long error. O the error of mortals!
O certain error! which keeps wandering old age
in uncertainty through a thousand pitfalls of the fleeting
path, and lures the drunken steps
through the violent waves of the churning sea,
and leads the tangled days into nothing.
O fate! how much of this treacherous life which we may reckon
flies in shades and breezes, where
both shade and breeze play serious parts
and confuse the backdrops; we are tossed about by the mockery
of the wanton tide as across a trackless sea
our fragile bark nods over the violent waves.
And the very threads of life by which the spinning goddesses
weave in their hand the rough cloth of [our] life,
these very [threads] entangle our footsteps
and draw [us] back and forth until with one misstep
a mighty ruin brings down our wearied feet.
Happy the man who, greeting fleeing days,
sets his calm course and is not a prey to the snares
of his age; life will be borne to him
on gentle breezes and rarely will he falter
in a time of feebleness. He will unravel the whirlwinds
of the vagrant year, his own sober defender.

415   *Peace of mind, with a likeness drawn*
                from the captive bird still
                       singing.

Just as when the watchful wayfarer with his
doubtful skill recognizes, from above,
the pleasant delights and chattering
companion of the grove and the roving
muse: and the crude destroyer of the
countryside evilly with his treacherous trap (alas, cruel man) snatches

414   *Humanæ vitæ descriptio.*

O vita, tantum lubricus quidam furor
Spoliumque vitæ! scilicet longi brevis
Erroris hospes! Error ô mortalium!
O certus error! qui sub incerto vagum
Suspendit ævum, mille per dolos viæ   5
Fugacis, & proterva per volumina
Fluidi laboris, ebrios lactat gradus;
Et irretitos ducit in nihilum dies.
O fata! quantum perfidæ vitæ fugit
Umbris quod imputemus atque auris, ibi   10
Et umbra & aura serias partes agunt
Miscentque scenam; volvimur ludibrio
Procacis æstus, ut per incertum mare
Fragilis protervo cymba cum nutat freto.
Et ipsa vitæ fila, quêis nentes Deæ   15
Ævi severa texta producunt manu,
Hæc ipsa nobis implicant vestigia
Retrahunt trahuntque donec everso gradu
Ruina lassos alta deducat pedes.
Felix, fugaces quisquis excipiens dies   20
Gressus serenos fixit, insidiis sui
Nec servit ævi, vita inoffensis huic
Feretur auris, atque claudâ rariùs
Titubabit horâ: vortices anni vagi
Hic extricabit, sanus Assertor sui.   25

415   *Tranquillitas animi, similitudine ductâ*
      ab ave captivâ & canorâ
        tamen.

Ut cùm delicias leves, loquacem
Convivam nemoris, vagamque musam
Observans dubia viator arte
Prendit desuper: horridusve ruris
Eversor, malè perfido paratu   5
(Heu durus!) rapit, atque io triumphans

Humanæ vitæ descriptio. **48.**
Tranquillitas animi. **48.***

[the bird] and moves on in triumph; at once with a quick pressure
unfolding his fingers drawing his slender little
machine gently with practiced thumb,
he weaves a cruel arrangement of branches,
devising a narrow home for the bird.
    However, although she grieved
for her former haunts and the
familiar grove, far away the dark cool spots
of soft shade and sunny rays of bright sun
and the never silent peace
of her native forest where she, a little while ago
a free guest throughout the grove
and every tree, with unrestrained warbling
easily called forth a host of friends:
although the grove itself and the trees
invoke their child who fled and seek her
much loved chirpings and the lyric song
of her sweet throat and peaceful melody:
nevertheless, on the other hand, she now does not
recall at all her abandoned home (innocent[bird]) nor
does she think about the forests any more; but in her little cage
Ah too small herself with clipped wings,
ah without ceremony, only for herself,
alas a minstrel in private!—she sings, and keeping her warbling
home filled with a pervasive murmur,
she dupes the chains and makes sweet her prison;
nor fighting boldly does she rail against
the peaceful silence sadly, but hopping about
on the tiny circuit in her shrunken world,
she measures the dimensions of the hateful cage.
    Thus a pious mind confined in itself, remains alone highly secure;
nor does it burn outside
or is it wont to burn at any fate.
Although all may be in confusion,
it is not moved by the storm of its black lot:
it takes upon its calm back the madness
and the sorrowful weight of fortune no less
than the dove who carries Venus
accepts the miniature yoke on her soft neck.
If any fierce storm threatens,
if any rage and menace threaten, that [mind]
ignores [them], does not know [of them], and averts the fury
by her countering flatteries, and she loves and courts

Vadit; protinus & sagace nisu
Evolvens digitos, opus tenellum
Ducens pollice lenis erudito,
Virgarum implicat ordinem severum,   10
Angustam meditans domum volucri.
Illa autem, hospitium licet vetustum
Mentem sollicitet nimis nimisque
Et suetum nemus, hinc opaca mitis
Umbræ frigora, & hinc aprica puri   15
Solis fulgura, Patriæque sylvæ
Nunquam muta quies; ubi illa dudum
Totum per nemus, arborem per omnem,
Hospes libera liberis querelis
Cognatum benè provocabat agmen: 20
Quanquam ipsum nemus, arboresque alumnam
Implorant profugam, atque amata multùm
Quærant murmura, lubricumque carmen
Blandi gutturis & melos serenum:
Illa autem tamen, illa jam relictæ   25
(Simplex!) haud meminit domus, nec ultrà
Sylvas cogitat; at brevi sub antro,
Ah pennâ nimium brevis recisâ,
Ah ritu viduo, sibique sola,
Privata heu fidicen! canit, vagoque   30
Exercens querulam domum susurro
Fallit vincula, carceremque mulcet;
Nec pugnans placidæ procax quieti
Luctatur gravis, orbe sed reducto
Discursu vaga saltitans tenello,   35
Metitur spatia invidæ cavernæ.
Sic in se pia mens reposta, secum
Altè tuta sedet, nec ardet extrà,
Aut ullo solet æstuare fato:
Quamvis cuncta tumultuentur, atræ   40
Sortis turbine non movetur illa:
Fortunæ furias onusque triste
Non tergo minus accipit quieto,
Quàm vectrix Veneris columba blando
Admittit juga delicata collo.   45
Torvæ si quid inhorruit procellæ,
Si quid sæviat & minetur, illa
Spernit, nescit, & obviis furorem
Fallit blanditiis, amatque & ambit

the blow itself by which she might be harmed.
She will not voice her cares by any whisper;
grief does not flow by tears nor a troubled brow
reveal the clouds of her dark mind,
unless a willful tear breaks out,
[and] escapes in a rebel drop.
Tears are unwanted, grief is denied,
clear smiles play about her face.

416   *We do not receive a short life but we make it.*

Why do you mourn that too swift a life is
alloted by the hastening cycle?
Do you bemoan the niggardly gods when you yourself
are wasteful of your lifetime?

Do you complain that what you yourself lose dies?
Do you yourself drive [life] on, but also weep its passing?
Life is not your slave, is it? The slave himself
driven off will go.

The river of life is fleeting, I confess;
but swift flying desire may make the [usual] slope
more like a headlong stream, and it slips away on
a fleeing wave.

Sleep, that thief, steals a great part from this [life]
(closing the eyes); Pleasure, a highwayman carrying
off his loot, casts down a great part
of time.

You make a thousand deaths for yourself. Indeed the more
years you waste, the more you demand.

Ipsum, quo malè vulneratur, ictum.   50
Curas murmure non fatetur ullo;
Non lambit lacrymas dolor, nec atræ
Mentis nubila frons iniqua prodit.
Quod si lacryma pervicax rebelli
Erumpit tamen evolatque guttâ.   55
Invitis lacrymis, negante luctu,
Ludunt perspicui per ora risus.

416   *Non accipimus brevem vitam, sed facimus.*

Ergò tu luges nimiùm citatam
Circulo vitam properante volvi?
Tu Deos parcos gemis, ipse cùm sis
              Prodigus ævi?

Ipse quod perdis, quereris perire?   5
Ipse tu pellis, sed et ire ploras?
Vita num servit tibi? servus ipse
              Cedet abactus.

Est fugax vitæ (fateor) fluentum:
Prona sed clivum modò det voluptas,   10
Amne proclivi magis, & fugace
              Labitur undâ.

Fur Sopor magnam hinc (oculos recludens)
Surripit partem. ruit inde partem
Temporis magnam spolium reportans   15
              Latro voluptas.

Tu creas mortes tibi mille. & æva
Plura quò perdas, tibi plura poscis.

Non accipimus brevem vitam. MS.*

417   *Beauties are not lasting.*

Alas for the short and envied spring!
Alas for the days just blooming!
How you run. Your sweet beauty
which now lightens in a restless
glance alas will be mingled with the
grasping clouds—Alas!—
of blackest night. Deceitful
love, shadow of a dream!
Indeed you struggle. (Thus the
hated distaff directs, and the
spinning wheel of old time,
running in swift circle.)
O seize the fleeting
years; and the clear radiance
of the spring star and the
lightning bolts of the new flower,
which you owe to gentle loves,
do not expend on
murky shades and greedy chaos.
    Although the youthful
roses blaze on the starry
cheeks (which always flourish
in places unharmed by modest
snow) like the bud of a simple flower:
    Although with everlasting faith you
bring forth a thousand Cupids,
a hundred thousand Cupids
fed on a feast of nectar
in flattering luxury;
who, wandering in those regions,
drunk with their fill of games,
sweetly blessed with dewy moisture,
more than ten times in one
day rekindle their dormant
torches from those very eyes
of yours and renew their listless

417   *Pulchra non diuturna.*

Eheu ver breve, & invidum!
Eheu floriduli dies!
Ergò curritis. improbâ
Et quæ nunc face fulgurat,
Dulcis forma tenacibus   5
Immiscebitur infimæ
Heu! noctis nebulis; amor
Fallax, umbraque somnii.
Quin incumbitis. (invida
Sic dictat colus, & rota   10
Cani temporis incito
Currens orbe volubilis)
O deprendite lubricos
Annos; et liquidum jubar
Verni syderis, ac novi   15
Floris fulgura, mollibus
Quæ debetis amoribus,
Non impendite luridos
In manes, avidum & Chaos.
Quanquam sydereis genis,   20
Quæ semper nive sobriâ
Synceris spatiis vigent,
Floris germine simplicis,
Flagrant ingenuæ rosæ:
Quanquam perpetuâ fide   25
Illic mille Cupidines,
Centum mille Cupidines,
Pastos nectareâ dape
Blandis sumptibus educas;
Istis qui spatiis vagi,   30
Plenis lusibus ebrii,
Udo rore beatuli,
Uno plus decies die
Istis ex oculis tuis
Istis ex oculis suas   35

Pulchra non diuturna. MS.*
    10   *colus:* the distaff of the fates, spinning the thread of man's life.

darts with your sweet honey;
then nimble with new flames they
flit about like a playful
torch, then swollen with copious
threats, then indeed
they afright the stars
and the heaven and fickle Jupiter:
  Although beneath this lofty brow,
his eminent grandeur vigilant,
he firmly composes gentle rules
for the untamable loves:
  Although the whole frame sets
forth [the map of] heaven in all
its regions, even so the manifold
page written in the living book [of
your face] pointing out to the lands
the heavens and the paths of the stars:
alas, alas, perhaps tomorrow's death
will make cruel marks on these cheeks,
on these rosy cheeks,
on this blooming star of a face,
on the lovable realm of this brow, and
will condemn the lofty pride of nature
to the pit of the grave.

418   *A description of Spring.*

Now is the time when the new Sun increased in hours
is wont to caress the bright days, and with the star of spring,
blooming, to move through the heavens with noble mien,
the common love of nature; the golden hope of the world;
the glory of maidens; and the sweet jollity of the world,
the tender spring, the sweet spring advances; now the year more lovely
in its new youth and fresh in the bloom of rosy youth
exudes perfumes from its happy embrace and the [fragrance of the]
                                              [father is loosed
by his scented offspring [everywhere]. Through the waters, through the
                         [fields, through everything far and wide,
he wonders at his wealth and wonders at his honors.

Sopitas animant faces,
Et languentia recreant
Succo spicula melleo;
Tum flammis agiles novis
Lascivâ volitant face,   40
Tum plenis tumidi minis,
Tum vel sydera territant,
Et cælum & fragilem Jovem:
    Quanquam fronte sub arduâ
Majestas gravis excubans,   45
Dulces fortiter improbis
Leges dictat amoribus:
    Quanquam tota, per omnia,
Cælum machina præferat,
Tanquam pagina multiplex   50
Vivo scripta volumine
Terris indigitans polos,
Et compendia syderum:
    Istis heu tamen heu genis,
Istis purpureis genis,   55
Oris sydere florido,
Regno frontis amabili,
Mors heu crastina forsitan
Crudeles faciet notas,
Naturæque superbiam   60
Damnabit tumuli specu.

418   *Veris descriptio.*

Tempus adest, placidis quo Sol novus auctior horis
Purpureos mulcere dies, & sydere verno
Floridus, augusto solet ire per æthera vultu,
Naturæ communis amor; spes aurea mundi;
Virginëum decus; & dulcis lascivia rerum,   5
Ver tenerum, ver molle subit; jam pulchrior annus
Pube novâ, roseæque recens in flore juuentæ
Felici fragrat gremio, & laxatur odora
Prole parens; per aquas, perque arva, per omnia latè
Ipse suas miratur opes, miratur honores.   10

Veris descriptio. MS.* See also No. 380.

Now released by its own Zephyrs, the intoxicated earth swells
and drinks Jove in the abundant rain. Under the lofty boughs,
Flora sitting hears—o happy one!—with what a roar
the ancestral spring is threatened by gliding waters which from the
only look down and press on far off in noisy array.   [waving crest
And she hears whether any sighing breeze returning
chatters in the leafy branches; she hears with what whispers
the tree herself gives assent and murmurs back with bowed head.
Indeed she hears the warblings, she hears through the shadows whatever
the mournful nightingale tells in her tearful notes.
Then too especially Cytherea all over the land is spread out
with [her] soft commands; then increased in size, she keeps urging
and slapping her gentle reins, her girdle more fiery increases
the dews and girds her swelling bosom with more glitter.
She wanders more widely, in the crown of the nymphs and the graces
more splendid, and she fastens more swans to her chariot:
Indeed the fruitful mother also then sends forth her Loves
in the sunny fields and pours forth all her Loves from her lap.
A thousand sweet horsemen rush forth and a thousand wanton lines
of footmen as well: part leap on the backs of fleet beasts
and rejoice to prick them with their arrows;
part wishing to go twice as fast
climb on the horses of the air; leaping up, one makes a game of his
on a sweet sparrow; he moves quickly hither and yon   [journey
fickle in no fixed lodging and wandering in all the shadows:
but another rising larger with full reins
is busy with his mother's birds: that scamp of the same ilk
disturbs the sharp bee and recognizes himself in him;
they combine their paths or to go separate ways for short times.
Some wandering without care through the meadows
try to combine their lilies with stately roses; then the rank of flowers
comes in a fragrant design: the fruitful band frolics
in every seed: new glory is added to their shining feathers;
a golden harvest rests in this noble lap;
the pleasant hair rejoices to go 'neath the scented shadows.
They shake out their accustomed arrows (vengeful weapons)
and the smiling quivers are seen [filled] with other arms.
With a flower the hand, with a flower the bosom, with a flower
                              [everything glows.
Everywhere now is a flower. Inclined toward the glassy water one [Love]
admires the nature of the playful wave, the flowing springs,
and the moving reflection of [his] quivering beauty.

Jam Zephyro resoluta suo tumet ebria tellus,
Et crebro bibit imbre Jovem. Sub frondibus altis
Flora sedens, audit (fælix!) quo murmure lapsis
Fons patrius minitetur aquis, quæ vertice crispo
Respiciunt tantùm, & strepero procul agmine pergunt.   15
Audit & arboreis siquid gemebunda recurrens
Garriat aura comis. audit quibus ipsa susurris
Annuit, & facili cervice remurmurat arbor.
Quin audit querulas, audit quodcunque per umbras
Flebilibus Philomela modis miserabile narrat.   20
Tum quoque præcipuè blandis Cytheræa per orbem
Spargitur imperiis; molles tum major habenas
Incutit increpitans, cestus magis ignea rores
Ingeminat, tumidosque sinus flagrantior ambit;
Nympharum incedit latè, charitumque coronâ   25
Amplior, & plures curru jam nectit olores:
Quin ipsos quoque tum campis emittit apricis
Læta parens, gremioque omnes effundit Amores.
Mille ruunt equites blandi, peditumque protervæ
Mille ruunt acies: levium pars terga ferarum   30
Insiliunt, gaudentque suis stimulare sagittis;
Pars optans gemino multum properare volatu
Aërios conscendit equos; his passere blando
Subsiliens leve ludit iter; micat huc, micat illuc
Hospitio levis incerto, & vagus omnibus umbris: 35
Verùm alter gravidis insurgens major habenis
Maternas molitur aves: ille improbus acrem
Versat apem similis, seseque agnoscit in illo,
Et brevibus miscere vias, ac grangere gyris:
Pars leviter per prata vagi sua lilia dignis   40
Contendunt sociare rosis; tum floreus ordo
Consilio fragrante venit: lascivit in omni
Germine læta manus: nitidis nova gloria pennis
Additur; illustri gremio sedet aurea messis;
Gaudet odoratas coma blandior ire sub umbras.   45
Excutiunt solitas (immitia tela) sagittas,
Ridentesque aliis pharetræ spectantur in armis.
Flore manus, & flore sinus, flore omnia lucent.
Undique jam flos est. vitreas hic pronus ad undas
Ingenium illudentis aquæ, fluitantiaque ora,   50
Et vaga miratur tremulæ mendacia formæ.

Then, examining, he tests—with a nymph as judge—
[the best way to] arrange his beams, lest with not enough gamesome fire
they flicker on his face; and [his] new countenance teaches swift
[lightnings,
and orders [them] to flash more wantonly like his own star.

419   *The Bubble.*

An extraordinary *tour de force,* this trifle appeared first at the end of an edi-
tion of Daniel Heynsius' *Crepundia Siliana* (a volume of editorial notes on
Silius' *De Bello Punico*) in 1646. After the index in this long work Crashaw's
Bulla is appended, "ne datur vacuum" ("so there is no blank space"). The
editor justifies his whimsy: "Argumenti certe non ita dissimulis, seu crepundia

Why does my silly bubble offer its roundness to you?
   What does my worthless [toy] do for your seriousness?
A more noble toga awaits our shoulders: this
   is my bubble, see your right hand [holds] my lares.

           What are you? what new device
           that you hasten into a short life
           like such a bouncing ball?
           What sort of Venus still
           shaking her virgin curves,
           Venus so new, so fresh
           even in the midst of the
           foam, produced this
           shimmering side; you sparkle from
           native pearl and leap up with a beautiful rush
           at once filling your
           back with thousands of
           colors, you spin your plump

Inde suos probat explorans, & judice nympha
Informat radios, ne non satis igne protervo
Ora tremant, agilesque docet nova fulgura vultus,
Atque suo vibrare jubet petulantiùs astro.   55

419   *Bulla.*

respicias, seu Heinsii guttulam. Quid enim aliud Bulla, quam puerorum orna-
mentum, aut guttulae commentarius?" ("The 'arguments' of the works are not
so dissimilar, whether you consider the child's plaything or the editorial droplet
of Heynsius. For what is a Bulla other than an ornamental toy for boys or the
editorial commentary of a little drop?"). Fitting editorial modesty.

Quid tibi vana suos offert mea bulla tumores?
    Quid facit ad vestrum pondus inane meum?
Expectat nostros humeros toga fortior; ista
    En mea bulla, lares en tua dextra mihi.

        Quid tu? quæ nova machina,   5
        Quæ tam fortuito globo
        In vitam properas brevem?
        Qualis virgineos adhuc
        Cypris concutiens sinus,
        Cypris jam nova, jam recens,   10
        Et spumis media in suis,
        Promsit purpureum latus;
        Conchâ de patriâ micas,
        Pulchroque exsilis impetu;
        Statim & millibus ebria   15
        Ducens terga coloribus
        Evolvis tumidos sinus

Bulla. 48.*
Bulla: (1) a water bubble; (2) an amulet worn around the neck by young Roman children.
    3 *toga fortior:* when the boy grew up and put on the toga of manhood, he removed his
childish bulla which then often became a part of the household shrine (line 4, lares).
    7 *vitam . . . brevem:* Praz (p. 249): "a theme which was [in the seventeenth century]
familiar, the soap bubble, to which it was customary for moralists to compare human life."

sides in a whirling full
circle. Through your changeable
side, through your smooth sphere,
a shining Iris, coursing through
a hundred varied guises and shapes
of a painted dance, holds sway;
and on all sides the winged
goddess giddy with pleasant
attack and feigned dizziness
pursues her in playful
flight and beautifully hesitates.
So many times, so deceptive she
flows in new paths, so many
times a vein deceptive with
strange color spreads through
paths retraced and twisting mazes
and swims in a drunken display. In
such a war the shining line is split
by a foil. Nay, even in flying fields
and in the sea of a light field,
the frantic file
wandering about flees and
puts itself to flight everywhere, and
everywhere loses and finds.
Here lovely chaos is spread.
Here the lively wandering rivers
wander out of banks not their
own but mingle their common
paths and in a common channel
compress their delights.
The varying closeness of
these at such an uncertain interval
with such delicate marks
distinguishes the narrow juncture,
so that the blooming display
nowhere has clear paths; nor may
it glow in its own expression.
But a sweet mass, mingling
new purple coils, blazes with
its richness, rejecting its
own radiance with the flood
of a wandering flower and a
public star of a flower.

Sphærâ plena volubili.
Cujus per varium latus,
Cujus per teretem globum 20
Iris lubrica cursitans
Centum per species vagas
Et picti facies chori
Circum regnat, & undique
Et se Diva volatilis 25
Jucundo levis impetu
Et vertigine perfidâ
Lascivâ sequitur fugâ
Et pulchrè dubitat; fluit
Tam fallax toties novis, 30
Tot se per reduces vias,
Errorésque reciprocos
Spargit vena Coloribus;
Et pompâ natat ebriâ.
Tali militiâ micans 35
Agmen se rude dividit;
Campis quippe volantibus,
Et campi levis æquore
Ordo insanus obambulans
Passim se fugit, & fugat; 40
Passim perdit, & invenit.
Pulchrum spargitur hic Chaos.
Hîc viva, hîc vaga flumina
Ripâ non propriâ meant,
Sed miscent socias vias, 45
Communique sub alveo
Stipant delicias suas.
Quarum proximitas vaga
Tam discrimine lubrico,
Tam subtilibus arguit 50
Juncturam tenuem notis,
Pompa ut florida nullibi
Sinceras habeat vias;
Nec vultu niteat suo.
Sed dulcis cumulus novos 55
Miscens purpureos sinus
Flagrat divitiis suis,
Privatum renuens jubar.
Floris diluvio vagi,
Floris Sydere publico 60

Golden spring comes up
widespread and everywhere is
poured into the strength of
her forces. Of course
because every color is seen,
no color is seen here and the
stiff-necked neighborhood dashes against
the wandering shapes. There in neighboring waters
colorless torches faint.
Here the vein of a delicate
wave full of the nearest flames
learns the purple paths and leaps
from the red recess.
The milky rivers lap the
bloody splendor of purple;
at the behest of the azure sea
the golden field grows tame
and the pliable cheeks of
light grow numb at the deceptive
fogs; and beneath the little red
grapes the sober lilies blaze.
Next, the neighboring snows
keep watch over neighboring roses,
that they be snowy roses and also
that snows be rosy; and the
roses set the snow on fire
and the snows put out the fires of the roses.
There the face of the wanton dance
grows red with green,
and here grows green with red;
and whatever the fickle path
of its starry tail marks,
goes on into a beautiful revolution.
Here the labor of heaven is grasped;
the spheres meet the spheres.
Here the flock of golden fleece
is the gleaming flock of heaven,
which exhausts the black pasture
of night with its innocent
grazing. Here whatever shining and
moving shakes the small field of
heaven is painted as a gentle joke.
Here the young world encircles

Latè ver subit aureum,
Atque effunditur in suæ
Vires undique Copiæ.
Nempe omnis quia cernitur,
Nullus cernitur hîc color,   65
Et vicinia contumax
Allidit species vagas.
Illic contiguis aquis
Marcent pallidulæ faces.
Undæ hic vena tenellulæ,   70
Flammis ebria proximis
Discit purpureas vias,
Et rubro salit alveo.
Ostri Sanguineum jubar
Lambunt lactea flumina;   75
Suasu cærulei maris
Mansuescit seges aurea;
Et lucis faciles genæ
Vanas ad nebulas stupent;
Subque uvis rubicundulis   80
Flagrant sobria lilia.
Vicinis adeo rosis
Vicinæ invigilant nives,
Ut sint & niveæ rosæ,
Ut sint & roseæ nives,   85
Accenduntque rosæ nives,
Extinguuntque nives rosas.
Illîc cum viridi rubet,
Hîc & cum rutilo viret
Lascivi facies chori.   90
Et quicquid rota lubrica
Caudæ stelligeræ notat,
Pulchrum pergit in ambitum.
Hîc cœli implicitus labor,
Orbes orbibus obvii;   95
Hîc grex velleris aurei
Grex pellucidus ætheris;
Qui noctis nigra pascua
Puris morsibus atterit;
Hic quicquid nitidum et vagum   100
Cæli vibrat arenula
Dulci pingitur en joco.
Hîc mundus tener impedit

itself in its own arms, and
in the fold of the girded globe
it wanders through its own
glory. Here unexpected
torches gleam and make sport
of the tremulous day.
Soon they steal away and seek the shelter
of their gloom and hide their
impudent splendor and settle
down shamelessly. And all these
are deceits of how short a strategem!
Obviously all things run in a
sphere, indeed not glassy
(as once the Sicilian globe)
but more shining than glass,
more brittle than glass, more
glassy than glass.

    I am the brief nature of the
wind. To be sure, I am the flower of air,
the star of the sea, as it were,
the golden wit of nature,
the rambling tale of nature,
the brief dream of nature,
the pride of trifles and the grief,
sweet and learned aimlessness,
the golden daughter of treachery,
the mother of the quick smile:
only a drop is prouder and
the clay more fortunate.
    I am the prize of flowing hope,
one of the islands of the Hesperides,
a casket of a sort, clearly
the blind little eye of lovers,
and the light heart of empty glory.
    I am the glass of the blind goddess;
I am the die of fortune which she
gives to her soldiers;
I am the creed of fortune by which
she confirms the tenuous faith
of drunken mortals and seals
their documents.

Sese amplexibus in suis.
Succinctique sinu globi   105
Errat per proprium decus.
Hîc nictant subitæ faces,
Et ludunt tremulum diem.
Mox se surripiunt sui &
Quærunt tecta supercili;   110
Atque abdunt petulans jubar,
Subsiduntque proterviter.
Atque hæc omnia quam brevis
Sunt mendacia machinæ!
Currunt scilicèt omnia   115
Sphærâ, non vitreâ quidem,
(Ut quondam siculus globus)
Sed vitro nitidâ magis,
Sed vitro fragili magis,
Et vitro vitreâ magis.   120

Sum venti ingenium breve
Flos sum, scilicet, aëris,
Sidus scilicet æquoris;
Naturæ jucus aureus,
Naturæ vaga fabula,   125
Naturæ breve somnium.
Nugarum decus & dolor;
Dulcis, doctaque vanitas.
Auræ filia perfidæ;
Et risus facilis parens.   130
Tantùm gutta superbior,
Fortunatius & lutum.
   Sum fluxæ pretium spei;
Una ex Hesperidum insulis.
Formæ pyxis, amantium   135
Clarè cæcus ocellulus;
Vanæ & cor leve gloriæ.
   Sum cæcæ speculum Deæ.
Sum fortunæ ego tessera,
Quam dat militibus suis;   140
Sum fortunæ ego symbolum,
Quo sancit fragilem fidem
Cum mortalibus Ebriis
Obsignatque tabellulas.

I am charming, wanton, inconstant,
beautiful, gleaming and noble,
ornate, somewhat blooming, and fresh,
distinguished by snows, roses,
waves, fires, air,
painted, bejewelled, and golden,
O I am, of course, O nothing.

[boredom

If it is painful and long lasting to have drawn out this pomposity into
and my Bubble seems too old;
Lift your eyes and this light trifle will fly away.
A Fate, not busy with her agile hand, will cut it off.
Still it lived. Why did it live? Indeed [because] you read this far.
Indeed it was time then to have been able to die.

Sum blandum, petulans, vagum,   145
Pulchrum, purpureum, et decens,
Comptum, floridulum, et recens,
Distinctum nivibus, rosis,
Undis, ignibus, aëre,
Pictum, gemmeum, & aureum,   150
O sum, (scilicet, O nihil.)

Si piget, et longam traxisse in tædia pompam
   Vivax, & nimiùm Bulla videtur anus;
Tolle tuos oculos, pensum leve defluet, illam
   Parca metet facili non operosa manu.   155
Vixit adhuc. Cur vixit? adhuc tu nempe legebas;
   Nempe fuit tempus tum potuisse mori.

Appendix

NOTE

These pieces are assembled here from dedications and other preliminary matter in Crashaw's collections of poems. The Latin texts are by Crashaw, the English pieces are by his friends (see Introduction).

The first Epistle Dedicatory accompanied a manuscript collection of Crashaw's Sacred Epigrams, containing poems written before June 1634. It may well have been presented to Laney, the dedicatee, at that time, and it is not impossible that Crashaw, encouraged by Laney's response, then decided to publish the collection as the *Epigrammatum Sacrorum Liber* (1634). The second Epistle Dedicatory to Laney which introduced the published collection contains lines which may refer to such a decision: "exorandus es . . . ut quem sinu tam facili privatum excepisti, eum jam ore magìs publico alloquentem te non asperneris" (I must beg you . . . not to spurn him whom you received so graciously in private when speaking to you now in a more public guise). The two Epistles Dedicatory to Laney have enough in common to suggest that the second is a reworking of the first: the ideas of juvenile enthusiasm and rashness and of Laney as the original inspirer of the poems, the metaphor of the star to describe Laney's face, and Laney's work of restoration in the chapel. The prohibition not to praise the dedicatee—"negatam mihi provinciam; laudum tuarum" (a province denied to me, that of your praises)—may refer to an attempt by Laney (not too successful) to curb the fulsomeness of a young and over-fond enthusiast.

The second Epistle Dedicatory to Laney, the commendatory poems to Tournay and Brooke, and the long poem "To the Reader" preface the

Epistle Dedicatory to Epigrams

420   *To a gentleman of a most famous and honored name,
our most worthy Master, heavenly protection.*

See, most honored sir, how this little book has dared to introduce your most revered name; I know not whether into its light or into its shade. Nor does it have any excuse except that it needs an excuse; doubtless there is [in it] not so much the sturdy confidence of a bold muse as the almost frolicsome impudence of a still tender babe which without guile indeed and by the warmth of overpowering love drives it laughing, as it

Master: Benjamin Laney (1591–1675), Master of Pembroke College (1630–44).

published collection of sacred epigrams. The poems to Tournay and Brooke are what are to be expected from a young poet, well trained in the flowers of rhetoric by tutor and former headmaster—polite, artificial, whimsical, witty, and self-conscious. The poem "To the Reader" offers the traditional rejection of the pagan gods in favor of the Christian ones, specifically, Venus and Cupid, Mary and Christ. This rejection has interest, though, in its back-handed praise of Martial, who obviously served as a model for Crashaw's epigrams. The poem anticipates the maternal interests and the emphasis on moisture and liquids found in the later poems; the Magdalene is prominent already, as are the idea of abundance, the darts of Cupid to be transformed to the dart of St. Teresa's Seraph, the instruments of the passion, tears, and blood.

The preliminary matter to the published volumes of 1646 (reprinted in 1648) and 1652 is the work of Crashaw's admirers. The three pieces provide biographical material of no little interest, centering on Crashaw's intense religious devotion (his nightly vigils—"restlesse rest") and his brilliant and various mind. The preface to the volume of 1646 describes its aims as providing "Stepps for happy soules to climbe heaven by"; the "Epigramme" to the volume of 1652 describes its "holy . . . aymes" as "To wound, to burne the hart with heavenly fire." These two introductory documents define the change in emphasis and style between early and late Crashaw, the two ways to Heaven: reason and rhapsody, temperance and enthusiasm, classicism and baroque, Canterbury and Rome.

Epistle Dedicatory to Epigrams

420 *Amplissimi et ornatissimi nominis viro,*
     Custodi nostro dignissimo, custodiam cælestem.

Tuum ecce (vir amplissime) sacratissimum nomen aperire sibi ausus est libellus iste; in lucem suam magìs an in umbram nescio. neque vero habet quo se excuset nisi id quod & ipsum excusatione indiget; nimirum non tam esse audacis Musæ robustam fiduciam, quàm teneræ adhuc & infantis pænè lascivientem proterviam quæ illam sub oculos tuos ac si in quoddam augustissimi secreti adytum simplici quidem æstu officiosi

Amplissimi. MS.*

were, and rejoicing before your eyes as if into some sanctuary or other of a most sacred mystery. And hence, because of the fame of your praise indeed, it will surely have enough from which it can commend itself to posterity; because [that] furnished the themes to its inexperienced, clumsy, callow infancy, nevertheless suitable and not rising from a degenerate talent; because from it, doubtless, it learned how to return straight to its Apollo. Why not let me, with this child of mine, whatever it is, come into part of that public and most auspicious ray with which you shine so deeply into every corner of this family of yours; indeed nothing is so obscure and undistinguished in its own night that it does not know and confess you as its Phoebus. Meanwhile how blessed we are (for it is pleasant to enjoy our good fortune by boasting; it is pleasant for a little while to indulge ourselves in the envy of the world) o how blessed we are! Who dare call our very own that sweet but reverend star of your face full of you and your virtues (however, by the light of these virtues, casting the shadow of modesty, with a less burning but much more gentle beam, it distributes these [virtues] to us and spares our eyes from too much, as it were) that star, I say, by whose auspices our days are regulated in an always well controlled flood, nor do they experience Apollo's suns except temperately. But we, aware of so great fortune so presumptuous for us, cannot with certainty be unafraid for our joys. But both the world itself has long since resented and the ordinary situation of the states complains that your great genius is held in check by restrictions of your private virtue; nor indeed would [the world] have been patient this long while that you yourself are owed to it and to that dignity so long awaiting you were it not that some divine spirit next to Jove himself in wisdom and power had laid out your path on this way, and that you had already begun to reveal yourself in a sphere more capacious for you; whence at last the splendor of your virtues will lift you (however reluctant your modesty is) to a peak as small compared to your merits as it is great compared to your desires (—not in vain does Apollo make me a soothsayer). For indeed to whom did the very fact that that [splendor] transferred you from the care of familiar temples to greater altars not forbode that solemn assurance granted by the gods? Let those too pious and scrupulous men be pleased by the beauty of their own meanness with which they love some trifle or other of the sacred rites, and they do not blush to conduct the gods themselves (for shame!) and the high holy rites of the spirit into the fellowship of their own squalor (barbarous men!): let them continue to believe that they can make suitable sacrifices at those altars whose vows they themselves refuse to hear; they may wish to banish from themselves that horror of people

28:    *more capacious:* Laney was named Master in 1630, Vice-Chancellor for 1632-33.

amoris ludentem quasi & exultantem impulit. Et satis hinc habebit profectò, unde se istius saltem laudis nomine commendare posteritati possit; quòd simplicis utcunque, rudis, & implumis, legitimæ tamen nec degeneri indole exsurgentis infantiæ argumenta dederit; ex eo nimirum quòd rectà adeò se recipere norit ad Apollinem suum. Quidni verò liceat et mihi, cum hoc fætu meo qualicunque, venire in partem publici illius & auspicatissimi radii, quo intimè penetras in omnem hujus familiæ tuæ angulum; qui quidem nullus est tam obscurus suâque nocte ignobilis, quin suum te sentiat & fateatur Phæbum. O interim beatos nos (juvat enim fælicitate nostrâ ad jactantiam etiam frui. juvat orbis invidiæ tantisper indulgere) ô nos beatos! qui proprium audemus & nostrum dicere suave illud sed & verendum sydus oris tui te plenissimi & virtutum tuarum (quarum tamen luci umbram modestiæ offundens, minùs fervido quidem sed dulci multo magis radio nobis eas dispensat, et in tantum nostris quasi parcit oculis) sydus inquam illus cujus ab auspiciis nostræ influxu nunquam non pacatissimo temperantur dies, nec nisi serenos experiuntur & Apollineos soles. Nos verò tantæ & tam audacis felicitatis nobis conscii, non possumus profectò nostra non timere gaudia. sed et ipse jampridem indignatur orbis, communisque rerum publicarum status queritur sub angustiis privatæ virtutis castigari ingentem tuum Genium; neque vero patiens esset tam diu te sibi deberi fastigioque te jamdudum expectanti, nisi numen ipsi Jovi tam prudentiâ quam potentiâ proximum, viam tibi in hoc stravisset modò, teque in sphæra tui capaciore explicare jam nunc cæpisset; unde tandem te tuarum virtutum splendor (reluctante tuâ quantumcunque modestiâ) elevabit te in apicem meritis tuis tam minorem, quam majorem votis (—nec vanus vatem me finxit Apollo.) Enimverò hoc ipsum cui non spondebat omen illud divinitùs indultum, quod te a domesticorum sacrorum curâ ad aras majores transtulit? Placeant sibi suarum sordium pulchritudine, pii nimirum isti & religiosi homines, quo nescio quam sacrorum illuviem amant, ipsosque (proh pudor!) cælites, & sacro-sanctos numinis ritus deducere in consortium squalloris sui (barbari homines) non erubescunt: pergant credere se ad illas aras litare posse, quarum & ipsi quidem vota dedignantur exaudire; orantium scilicet, & quasi supplices manus (frustra) tendentium, velint a se horrorem illum abstergere, vultusque elegantes, lucidos, augustos, suos demum sibi reddere. apud nos interim sub tuis (vir sanctissime) auspiciis amæniori facie Religio se spectandam indulget. comit se pulcherrima dea; suosque jam ornatiore curâ distinguens radios, majestatem suam venustate etiam commendari quærit. nimirum ad oris tui exemplum, ubi severitatis reverentiam ita demulcet amænitas, ut pulcherrimo demonstret argumento, quàm bene possit amabile quid esse, praying and as it were stretching out their hands as suppliants (in vain) and to restore at last for themselves those faces, elegant, bright, haughty —their own. Among us meanwhile under your auspices (most holy man) Religion permits itself to be seen in a more pleasing aspect. It adorns itself as a most beautiful goddess; now decorating its beams with more embellished care, it asks that its grandeur be commended also for its beauty. Much by the example of your face where pleasantness so tempers reverence for severity that it shows by a most beautiful argument how readily something can be lovely and holy at the same time. See moreover while you restore to the holy houses their elegance, while you are engrossed in adorning things divine, a pleasing spirit has poured out on you that same splendor which you have brought back to its sacred things, and by the fairest turn, your honors reflected on you, as it were, you have returned from your altars yourself ennobled by these sanctuaries. Still the holy shrine of kings responds in kind to the increased ornaments of our little chapel; and you who have adorned the one most generously, most justly are decorated by the other in turn. But I do not wish to burden your modesty any more nor indeed my letter's: which long since I made ashamed while I seemed to want to be assigned to it these parts of your praises, which could indeed rouse the panting orator with the spirit of panegyric and even overwhelm him. May the most noble and greatest God increase [your days] for himself and for us and our happiness (honored sir), but may he preserve you forever for you and your happiness. Meanwhile by any sort of whisper of this infant Muse, allow your ears to be pleased, not as a critic's but as a father's. And may you deem worthy to commend hereafter and to encourage that beam which you have granted to one so insignificant as I from your ever setting star.

> The least of your least—
> Ri: Crashaw.

---

4 *more pleasing aspect:* Laney's high-church policies included an emphasis on the beauty of the divine services.

10 *restore . . . elegance:* Laney had restored the chapel at Pembroke.

& sanctum simul. ecce autem dum suum sacris sedibus nitorem restituis, dum in rebus divinis ornandis totus es; splendorem quem sacris suis attulisti modò, gratum numen in te refudit; et æquissimâ vice quasi repercussis in te tuis honoribus, rediisti ab aris tuis ipse excultus donariis. adeò res auctas nostri sacelli sacrarium rependit regium; et qui illud ornasti benignissimè, ab altero justissimè exornaris invicem. Sed tuam nolo ultrà onerare modestiam, nec etiam Epistolæ meæ: cui jampridem pudorem feci, dum has laudum tuarum partes ei viderer velle assignari, quæ quidem provocare possint anhelum Panegyrico spiritu oratorem, et etiam obruere. Augeat te sibi Deus optimus maximus diuque te (vir egregie) nobis nostræque, tibi verò tuæque felicitati æternum servet. tu interim hoc qualicunque murmure infantis Musæ patere tibi demulceri non quidem censorias, sed paternas aures. eumque quem prono semper sydere tantillo mihi indulsisti radium, ornare porrò et fovere digneris.

Tuorum minimorum minimus
Ri: Crashaw.

Preliminary Matter to volume of 1634.

421   *For the very reverend*
                          gentleman,
                      Benjamin Lany,
                Professor of Sacred Theology,
         Most honorable master of Pembroke College,
          the least of the least of his [*students*],
                          R.C.,
                         invokes
                  heavenly protection.

This is his and the fruit of his own flowers; which we enjoy, if not quite usefully, surely quite pleasantly. And indeed it is not remarkable that from the hope of spring, through its promising little flowers, as it were, we might require payment of the more mature year, even Autumn itself. Therefore, o most cherished sir, forgive the Muse hastening up to the gaze of her Apollo and rejoicing in the caprice of her youth. She bears the little flowers of a tender age, not the fruits of a late one: indeed to bring them to that late and judicious maturity we rightfully expect in our [ripe] fruits will be hard; perhaps indeed because of this very precocious rashness of theirs they will be more pleasing: Especially for you whom a fatherly spirit (as it is usually found) keeps intent upon every daybreak of its hope, by which you may promise yourself anything from the genius of your students. According to the custom of those who hastily, as a reward for their labor and the payment of their patience, of those [plants] which they themselves have sown and cherished, seize upon whatever little flower comes forth first, testing, as it were, with maiden modesty the airs and open [sky of] Jove, and affix a savor to it, not so much from its own birth and nature as from the affections of their own mind, which fosters in it their own cares and hopes. Therefore (reverend master) allow this little wreath of flowers of this same kind to be fastened upon you, surely festive: not otherwise will it endure the most auspicious star of your face except (how gracious even that is) by a softer light when it bends down and takes so much from itself. Nor clearly could anything be more suitable for theological repose than this kind of writing (when it has maintained sufficiently its own character) in which doubtless Theology itself described in poetic graces commends its majesty by beauty. In short, whatever this is, you still will be able to love it; and you will wish to, I know: not as something great, not as

Preliminary Matter to volume of 1634.

421

Reverendo Admodum
viro
Benjamin Lany
SS. *Theologiæ Professori,*
Aulæ Pembrochianæ *Custodi dignissimo,*
ex suorum minimis
minimus
R.C.
custodiam cœlestem
P.

Suus est & florum fructus; quibus fruimur, si non utiliùs, deli-
catiùs certé. Neque etiam rarum est quòd ad spem veris, de se per flores
suos quasi pollicentis, adultioris anni, ipsiúsque adeò Autumni exigamus
fidem. Ignoscas igitur (vir colendissime) properanti sub ora Apollinis
sui, primæque adolescentiæ lasciviâ exultanti Musæ. Teneræ ætatis flores
adfert, non fructus seræ: quos quidem exigere ad seram illam & sobriam
maturitatem, quam in fructibus expectamus meritò, durum fuerit; forsan
& ipsâ hac præcoci importunitate suâ placituros magís: Tibi præsertim
quem paternus animus (quod fieri solet) intentum tenet omni suæ spei
diluculo, quò tibi de tuorum indole promittas aliquid. Ex more etiam
eorum, qui in præmium laboris sui pretiúmque patientiæ festini, ex iis
quæ severunt ipsi & excoluerunt, quicquid est flosculi prominulum, primâ
quasi verecundiâ auras & apertum Jovem experientis arripiunt avidè,
saporémque illi non tam ex ipsius indole & ingenio quàm ex animi sui
affectu, foventis in eo curas suas & spes, affingunt. Patere igitur (reve-
rende Custos) hanc tibi ex istiusmodi floribus corollam necti; convivalem
veró: nec aliter passuram Sydus illud oris tui auspicatissimum nisi (quâ
est etiam amœnitate) remissiore radio cùm se reclinat, & in tantum de se
demit. Neque sanè hoc scriptionis genere (modò partes suas satìs
præstiterit) quid esse potuit otio Theologico accommodatius, quo nimirum
res ipsa Theologica Poëticâ amœnitate delinita majestatem suam venustate
commendat. Hoc demum quicquid est, amare tamen poteris; & voles,
scio: non ut magnum quid, non ut egregium, non ut te dignum denique,
sed ut tuum: tuum summo jure; utpote quod è tua gleba, per tuum
radium, in manum denique tuam evocatum fuerit. Quod restat hujus
libelli fatis, exorandus es igitur (vir spectatissime) ut quem sinu tam
facili privatum excepisti, eum jam ore magìs publico alloquentem te non
asperneris. Stes illi in limine, non auspicium modò suum, sed & argu-

Reverendo Admodum. 34.*

something unusual, not as something worthy of you finally, but as your own: yours according to the supreme law: inasmuch as this has been evoked from your soil, through your light, at last into your hand. Because the fate of my little book remains [unknown], I must beg you therefore (highly regarded sir) not to spurn him whom you received so graciously in private when speaking to you now in a more public guise. May you stand by him on the threshold, not only for guidance but also for his theme. Actually your countenance is either a sacred epigram or it explains what one should be; where doubtless the severe is tempered by the amiable and the holy is softened by the sweet. You see me bending to a province denied to me, that of your praises, I mean: since your modesty took these away from me, there is left to me only that I must necessarily be brief: nay indeed [I am] too long; inasmuch as that theme was cut out from this, on which only could I without tedium be prolix. Farewell, most polished of men, do not disdain the fact that so poor a suppliant as I dare to cherish the serenity of your spirit, and (since divine inspiration does not deny this for itself as well) even to love. But meanwhile grant your favor to the Muse who does to this extent not restrain herself, that she has dared—at least for this part of your praise, which is richly deserved by you because of your having adorned the sacred rites among us—to fly forth with the following song, whatever kind it may be:

Hail, sweet master of the Pierian flock:
through whom it breathes in learned repose;
whether it longs for the coolness of a damp cave
or [the sky of] Jove and the shining suns.

Not more beautiful [was that] master
[who] led the Aemonian flocks beneath the trackless shadows.
Not even Apollo himself was known to them
for better control of his flute.

If you should grant [us] a peaceful [and kindly] eye to enjoy,
we have the countryside, ridges, waters,
the lyres of the sweet sisters
(not known to me by another Phoebus [than yourself]).

Under your guidance, Religion arranged a neat dress,
under your guidance, she adopted observances; and [as is]
to be seen in her own face,
knows not dust and ashes.

Pierian: pertaining to Pieria, where the Muses were born; Laney is seen, in the pastoral tradition, as a shepherd; cf. "Lycidas," lines 23–36.
Aemonian: i.e. Thessalian.
the sweet sisters: the nine muses.

mentum. Enimvero Epigramma sacrum tuus ille vultus vel est, vel quid
sit docet; ubi nimirum amabili diluitur severum, & sanctum suavi demul-
cetur. Pronum me vides in negatam mihi provinciam; laudum tuarum,
intelligo; quas mihi cùm modestia tua abstulerit, reliquum mihi est neces-
sariò ut sim brevis: imò verò longus nimiùm; utpote cui argumentum
istud abscissum fuerit, in quo unicè poteram, & sine tædio, prolixus esse.
Vale, virorum ornatissime, neque dedigneris quòd colere audeam Genii
tui serenitatem supplex tam tenuis, & (quoniam numen quoque hoc de
se no negat) amare etiam. Interim verò da veniam Musæ in tantum sibi
non temperanti, quin in hanc saltem laudis tuæ partem, quæ tibi ex rebus
sacris apud nos ornatis meritissima est, istiusmodi carmine involare ausa
sit, qualicunque,

> Salve, alme custos Pierii gregis:
>   Per quem erudito exhalat in otio;
> Seu frigus udi captet antri,
>   Sive Jovem nitidósque soles.
>
> Non ipse custos pulchrior invias   5
> Egit sub umbras Æmonios greges;
>   Non ipse Apollo notus illis
>   Lege suæ meliore cannæ.
>
> Tu si sereno des oculo frui;
> Sunt rura nobis, sunt juga, sunt aquæ,   10
>   Sunt plectra dulcium sororum;
>   (Non alio mihi nota Phœbo)
>
> Te dante, castos composuit sinus;
> Te dante, mores sumpsit; & in suo
>   Videnda vultu, pulverémque   15
>   Relligio cinerémque nescit.

She stands, her beautiful head bound with a leafy crown:
through you openly confessing her God;
a Goddess, she gives natural order
to her hair and vestments.

Now, look, you seem grander and even larger to us.
What radiance flickers down on your face!
With what great labor of its own
your modest genius works!

Now He Who passes to you with a serene face
has His own star in a greater heaven;
the greater flower of the sceptred day
adorns your hair around your face.

The case rests. Indeed God himself, God,
the altar, beautiful through your efforts,
returns this day to you and comes
with glory to meet you, his worshipper.

Look, look! On the sacred threshold while you [touch]
the great earth on pious bended knee,
the altars nod approval from on high;
with outstretched wings [the boy] applauds you

and glowing from his lovely duty the boy
with the curly glory of his hair
and a face which does not bespeak the earth
runs about there as a rosy attendant.

And rightly so. For while the shrines lament so many
insuperable catastrophes and [Religion] herself (an unfit suppliant
should stretch forth praying hands)
asks for help, alas denied,

The Altar itself is bound to you by its vow;
and it will repay you. O how in the presence of that God
you always will officiate before whose altar
you yourself have heard prayers.

---

adorns your hair: shows special favor.
boy: a cherub; or perhaps a chorister.

Stat cincta dignâ fronde decens caput:
Suósque per te fassa palàm Deos,
   Comísque, Diva, vestibúsque
    Ingenium dedit ordinémque.   20

Jámque ecce nobis amplior es modò
Majórque cerni. Quale jubar tremit
   Sub os! verecundúsque quantâ
    Mole sui Genius laborat!

Jam qui serenas it tibi per genas,   25
Majore cœlo Sydus habet suum;
   Majórque circum cuspidatæ
    Ora comit tua flos diei.

Stat causa. Nempe hanc ipse Deus, Deus,
Hanc ara, per te pulchra, diem tibi   30
   Tuam refundit, obvióque
    It radio tibi se colenti.

Ecce, ecce! sacro in limine, dum pio
Multúmque prono poplite amas humum,
   Altaria annuunt ab alto;   35
    Et refluis tibi plaudit alis

Pulchro incalescens officio, puer
Quicunque crispo sydere crinium,
   Vultúque non fatente terram,
    Currit ibi roseus satelles.   40

Et jure. Nam cùm fana tot inviis
Mœrent ruinis, ipsáque (ceu preces
   Manúsque, non decora supplex,
    Tendat) opem rogat, heu negatam!

Tibi ipsa voti est ara sui rea.   45
Et solvet. O quam semper apud Deum
   Litabis illum, cujus aræ
    Ipse preces priùs audiisti!

422   *To the honorable gentleman, Master* Tourney
his highly esteemed tutor.

Now the fourth harvest has gilded the hair of Ceres,
Bacchus has a fourth garland from his vine,
since our Muse touched with the white of the first frost
on her plumage dared make her nest in your bosom.
Here the grove, here the suns, here the sky more gentle for her:
here [the home] which gave its shadow and sweet breath to the Muses.
There she sat free from caring why the wicked south wind raged
whose heavy wing troubled the wintry [sky of] Jove.
Somehow meanwhile she was well known to you by her whisper:
and, indeed, you could love even this whisper.
At last behold (alas giving birth from a similar stock)
she has become at last a tender mother of a tender child.
And now I ask what other embrace should hold this child of mine?
Who obviously had such warm feelings for me?
But too that naughty thing herself
(as soon as she could talk) said (of you) *He will be my very own tutor.*
I do not think these ignoble traits are known to my legal child,
not born under an unlucky star;
of course she knew to go to the arms of her father,
always so wide open, always so easy.
Therefore take your child to yourself: let her go under your wings:
receive this from us to protect also.
So may Suada who has made for herself a fountain in your mouth
pass forever in holy and carefree honey.
So may a Siren to whom your court gave approval
and its garland flatter no ears so. So, I pray,
may your Tagus either flow with no barrier or
(as before) be greater than every barrier.

Tourney: John Tournay, Crashaw's tutor at Pembroke.
fourth: Crashaw entered Pembroke in the summer of 1631; the *Liber* went to press
evidently in May of 1634; "fourth" is only admissible by poetic license.
Suada: the Roman personification of persuasion.
Tagus: a river in Spain famed for its golden sand.

422   *Venerabili viro Magistro* Tournay,
            Tutori suo summè observando.

Messis inauravit Cereri jam quarta capillos,
   Vitis habet Bacchum quarta corona suæ,
Nostra ex quo, primis plumæ vix alba pruinis,
   Ausa tuo Musa est nidificare sinu.
Hîc nemus, hîc soles, & cœlum mitius illi: 5
   Hîc sua quod Musis umbra vel aura dedit.
Sedit ibi secura malus quid moverit Auster,
   Quæ gravis hybernum vexerit ala Jovem.
Nescio quo interea multùm tibi murmure nota est:
   Nempe sed hoc poteras murmur amare tamen.   10
Tandem ecce (heu simili de prole puerpera) tandem
   Hôc tenero tenera est pignore facta parens.
Jámque meam hanc sobolem (rogo) quis sinus alter haberet?
   Quis mihi tam noti nempe teporis erat?
Sed quoque & ipsa *Meus* (de te) *meus,* improba, *tutor*   15
   (Quàm primùm potuit dicere) dixit, *erit.*
Has ego legitimæ, nec lævo sydere natæ
   Non puto degeneres indolis esse notas;
Nempe quòd illa suo patri tam semper apertos,
   Tam semper faciles nôrit adire sinus.   20
Ergò tuam tibi sume: tuas eat illa sub alas:
   Hoc quoque de nostro, quod tuearis, habe.
Sic quæ Suada tuo fontem sibi fecit in ore,
   Sancto & securo melle perennis eat.
Sic tua, sic nullas Siren non mulceat aures,   25
   Aula cui plausus & sua serta dedit.
Sic tuus ille (precor) Tagus aut eat objice nullo,
   Aut omni (quod adhuc) objice major eat.

423   *To the most learned man,*
      his highly esteemed Praeceptor Master Brook

O you who were never an unpleasant name to me,
even then when you were to be feared in the guise of a master!
I am he who at one time was the most unpunished member
of your kingdom, familiar with no labor of your rod,
I give to you this which will long complain of you
because I did not have to fear you too much:
because at your hands such a shameful boy as I withstood the lazy rule
of an inactive staff as much as the gentler dominance of your stick.
Of course something will be wrong in these pages,
which your rod at once may flog; that will be.
Therefore this page of mine may take your punishment for me.
Here much work for your rod is ready.
Therefore whatever in me the rod once spared too much,
let it take all its revenge on my child.
Here your finger will find enough in which it may go wild,
and which the editor's mark may cross through like a learned spit.
Obviously these are mine; these which are bad [most] obviously: o if
here there might be some better (which of course would be yours)!
Whatever they may be, these rivers know their own source.
(The Nile from an unknown source is haughty)
and surely there is something which is like its creator. Springs
are accustomed to be the fame and honor of their own river.
This book also so small (my times may speak of me)
was also the child of a mighty spring.
For this reason you yourself may wish to have said of me,
He was the least of my [pupils]. But he was mine.

Brook: Robert Brooke, the Headmaster of the Charterhouse while Crashaw was a student there (1629–31).

423 *Ornatissimo viro Præceptori sue colendissimo, Magistro* Brook.

O Mihi qui nunquam nomen non dulce fuisti
  Tunc quoque cùm domini fronte timendus eras!
Ille ego pars vestri quondam intactissima regni,
  De nullo virgæ nota labore tuæ,
Do tibi quod de te per secula longa queretur   5
  Quòd de me nimiùm non metuendus eras:
Quòd tibi turpis ego torpentis inertia sceptri
  Tam ferulæ tulerim mitia jura tuæ.
Scilicet in foliis quicquid peccabitur istis,
  Quod tua virga statim vapulet, illud erit.   10
Ergò tibi hæc pœnas pro me mea pagina pendat.
  Hîc agitur virgæ res tibi multa tuæ.
In me igitur quicquid nimis illa pepercerit olim,
  Id licet in fœtu vindicet omne meo.
Hîc tuus inveniet satìs in quo sæviat unguis,   15
  Quódque veru docto trans obeliscus eat.
Scilicet hæc mea sunt; hæc quæ mala scilicet: ô si
  (Quæ tua nempe forent) hîc meliora forent!
Qualiacunque, suum nôrunt hæc flumina fontem.
  (Nilus ab ignoto fonte superbus eat)   20
Nec certè nihil est quâ quis sit origine. Fontes
  Esse solent fluvii nomen honórque sui.
Hic quoque tam parvus (de me mea secula dicant)
  Non parvi soboles hic quoque fontis erat.
Hoc modò & ipse velis de me dixisse, Meorum   25
  Ille fuit minimus. Sed fuit ille meus.

424 *To the Reader*

Hail. And now farewell. For why would anyone go any further?
Will you go where playful jesting does not call? Obviously,
Reader, this is not the reason you will be ours; this book
does not aim at your pleasure. For neither does my page give
forth Acidalian dews nor does our breath favor Cupid's torch.
In vain will [Cupid] have promised to his wings anything from this:
in vain may [Venus] hope to depart with a
new heart from here. Better that he should ask for such favors
from his mother's myrtle, she from the heights of Ida. There
let her search out in which field her Adonis may rise that
may be a better home for her delicate violets. From there he
may fill his wings, she her bosom with the truths and the
wisdom of the whole Spring. My weed may crown me (still pure,
though it be rustic): my weed supports me (if it is rustic
let it be rustic). No cups of Circe, sweet and serviceable
for your lustful passion, overflow in my verse; no Lethe lies con-
cealed [in my verse], which the deceit of flowers pours out
for you, as the rose under false cheeks disguises itself; [here]
subtle poison counterfeits no sweets; no snare captures from
its ambush. Both anger and bitterness are well spared from
these pages. Ah poorly would either stand with these [pieces]
of mine. There is rarely a page that is funny; there is
never a page that is lewd:
there is nothing unsavory, if he could recognize good taste.
There are no nude Venuses: nor, if there is a joke, is it
wet [from wine]. Not too much was Bacchus our Apollo.
There is nothing whose suggestive leer should make anyone
cringe; there is nothing which should be read with a smirk.
These things are in the open, and [even] Lucretia could read

5 *Acidalian:* pertaining to Acidalia, a fountain in Boeotia associated with Venus.
Crashaw's writing will not please Venus or Cupid.
9 *myrtle:* a plant sacred to Venus. *Ida:* a mountain in Troas where Adonis died of a
wound received in a boar hunt.
13 *weed:* a garment, here associated with the poet's simple cloak.
15 *Circe:* a sorceress who transformed men into swine by giving them a potion to
drink.
16 *Lethe:* the personification of oblivion.
26 *Bacchus . . . Apollo:* i.e. few of these pieces were composed under the influence of
wine.
29 *Lucretia:* a notably chaste matron, who rather than face shame killed herself after
having been ravished.

424 *Lectori.*

Salve. Jámque vale. Quid enim quis pergeret ultrá?
   Quà jocus & lusus non vocat, ire voles?
Scilicet hîc, Lector, cur noster habebere, non est;
   Delitiis folio non faciente tuis.
Nam nec Acidalios halat mihi pagina rores;   5
   Nostra Cupidineæ nec favet aura faci.
Frustra hinc ille suis quicquam promiserit alis:
   Frustra hinc illa novo speret abire sinu.
Ille è materna meliùs sibi talia myrto;
   Illa jugis meliùs poscat ab Idaliis.   10
Quærat ibi suus in quo cespite surgat Adonis,
   Quæ melior teneris patria sit violis.
Illinc Totius Floræ, verísque, suíque
   Consilio, ille alas impleat, illa sinus.
Me mea (casta tamen, si sit rudis) herba coronet: 15
   Me mea (si rudis est, sit rudis) herba juvat.
Nulla meo Circæa tument tibi pocula versu:
   Dulcia, & in furias officiosa tuas.
Nulla latet Lethe, quam fraus tibi florea libat,
   Quam rosa sub falsis dat malè fida genis.   20
Nulla verecundum mentitur mella venenum:
   Captat ab insidiis linea nulla suis.
Et spleni, & jecori foliis bene parcitur istis.
   Ah malè cum rebus staret utrumque meis.
Rara est quæ ridet; nulla est quæ pagina prurit: 25
   Nulla salax, si quid nôrit habere salis.
Non nudæ Veneres: nec, si jocus, udus habetur:
   Non nimiùm Bacchus noster Apollo fuit.
Nil cui quis putri sit detorquendus ocello:

Lectori. 34.

with her righteous eyes: and modesty itself could go hence
with unblushing cheeks. For no purer breath of a chaste vow
comes bearing incense from the virgin dawn: girded with
garments with snowy folds, her temples gleaming with snow,
performing the cool rites with a bride's veil of snow on her
hair, poising her careful footprints step by step, at last
she stopped before the altars and trembled. And not the
solemn altar itself, which piously rejects impure hands,
breathes forth a more chaste [incense] to its own divinity.
So the too-golden Venus is not in our verse: so the fear-
some weapons of the boy god are not [in our verse]. Often
the boy had moved his fluttering wings around me and hurled
his fickle arrows before our face. Often that flatterer gave
me a quill from his own wing or from his mother's fairer swan.
Often he promised me garlands from the Dionaean crown; often
he said to me "You will be my bard." "Go far away, go with
your mother, wicked boy," I said: "you will not have any of
my verses. More gracefully you will go with the sparrow of the
Veronese [poet] or you may seek to be more fashionable in the style
of the Bilbilian one.
He will fix your hair in any style at all: at all points he
will be equal to your wickedness. Too much does that field
lie open to your battles (I said); Alas too much is he the
bard and too much yours. That soil (ah, how your adulterous
harvest [gathered from it] still burns) would have been how
greatly productive, [planted] with the seed of Idumaea! How
great a Boy would there press the breasts of how great a
Mother! And with a face not concealing his own heavens. In
that verse his eyes would be stars enough; how very safe in
his mother's star-studded embrace! How he would clasp both
his arms around his mother's neck and trace the shining curves
on her fair face! How she would kiss the cheeks of the boy
with her sweet lips and well might they bloom in his cheeks
like kindred roses! How would that moist gem which falls
so full of Mary learn there to swell under its own value!
The saintly Weeper would stand there before her Master. Per-

---

46 *swan:* one of the birds associated with Venus.
47 *Dionaean:* pertaining to Dione, the mother of Venus.
51 *Veronese [poet]:* Catullus, born in Verona, writer of erotic poems, famous for his poem on his mistress's sparrow; see "Out of Catullus," No. 376.
52 *Bilbilian one:* Martial, the most famous classical epigrammatist, born in Bilbilis in Spain; see "Out of Martiall," No. 378.
57 *Idumaea:* a region of Palestine, used here as a synonym for Judaea, or the Christian religion.
69 *Weeper:* St. Mary Magdalene.

Est nihil obliquo quod velit ore legi.   30
Hæc coràm, atque oculis legeret Lucretia justis:
    Iret & illæsis hinc pudor ipse genis.
Nam neque candidior voti venit aura pudici
    De matutina virgine thura ferens;
Cùm vestis nive vincta sinus, nive tempora fulgens,   35
    Dans nive flammeolis frigida jura comis,
Relligiosa pedum sensim vestigia librans,
    Ante aras tandem constitit; & tremuit.
Nec gravis ipsa suo sub numine castior halat
    Quæ pia non puras summovet ara manus.   40
Tam Venus in nostro non est nimis aurea versu:
    Tam non sunt pueri tela timenda dei.
Sæpe puer dubias circum me moverat alas;
    Jecit & incertas nostra sub ora faces.
Sæpe vel ipse sua calamum mihi blandus ab ala,   45
    Vel matris cygno de meliore dedit.
Sæpe Dionææ pactus mihi serta coronæ;
    Sæpe, Meus vates tu, mihi dixit, eris.
I procul, i cum matre tua, puer improbe, dixi:
    Non tibi cum numeris res erit ulla meis.   50
Tu Veronensi cum passere pulchrior ibis:
    Bilbilicísve queas comptiùs esse modis.
Ille tuos finget quocunque sub agmine crines:
    Undique nequitiis par erit ille tuis.
Ille nimis (dixi) patet in tua prælia campus: 55
    Heu nimis est vates & nimis ille tuus.
Gleba illa (ah tua quam tamen urit adultera messis)
    Esset Idumæo germine quanta parens!
Quantus ibi & quantæ premeret Puer ubera Matris!
    Nec cœlos vultu dissimulante suos.   60
Ejus in isto oculi satìs essent sydera versu;
    Sydereo matris quàm bene tuta sinu!
Matris ut hic similes in collum mitteret ulnas,
    Inque, sinus niveos pergeret, ore pari!
Utque genis pueri hæc æquis daret oscula labris!   65
    Et bene cognatis iret in ora rosis!

haps a light sigh would fly away or a sad tear would fall;
this the child of her eyes, that the offspring of her perfumed
heart. [In that verse] more beautifully would the flood
fall, more gently would the breeze blow. Finally whatever
seems dusky in these verses would gleam in those [of his].
Wicked one, is it not enough that he is still yours? Go, wicked
boy: for why do you flatter my songs? The songs from your
darts will be silent. Go, boy, where the reins of some saucy
maid [call] you; where the shameful scruples of a wanton
sweetheart call; where the lovely lies of miserable slime gleam
evilly;
where the white painted cheeks with counterfeit honor [lure];
where you will admire the roses, the stars of a foreign
spring; which the ransomed winter of snow not its own
cuts down. Go, boy (I said this, and I say it now), go
wicked mother. Another Cyprian holds us; another Love holds
us." Surely here is Love. Here too is the Mother of Love.
But the Mother is a virgin. And Love is not blind. "O Boy!
O Master! O the worship of the great Mother! sweet wonder
and piety of your embrace! O Love, who possess the sacred rites
of a harmless quiver, your arrow does not burn except
in a chaste heart. O Boy, pierce me whom you pierce with
a well-aimed arrow. O may your quiver become light because
of me. Thence also each thing thirsts and drinks, and drinks
and thirsts forever: forever may my heart thirst and forever
may it drink. Pierce this heart, Boy. You are present very
little in these *thorns*, much in the sharp point of *nail* or
spear, more with the whole *cross*, or most of all at last
you transfix this heart with your very presence. Pierce [me],
Boy. O may your bow have proclaimed this eternal aim: may
the heavier breath of your shaft whizz to this mark. O if
a fiercer wing should bear any dart for you, may it have this
path of the old wound to go. Whatever is the crowd, whatever
is the throng in your quiver, this nest will hold those
wounding birds well. O may you ever be so savage in this war
against me! Never may you enter this breast [as] a gentler foe.
How I wish I might lie well torn apart in this fight! How
very whole I will be with a torn heart!" These are my wishes.
These too are the wishes of my little book. May these be
yours, Reader; if you wish to be mine. If you wish to be
mine; to be mine (Reader) your eyes [should be] chaste, but

---

84   *Cyprian:* i.e. Venus, who was born near Cypris and was there worshipped.
104   *birds:* i.e. the feathered vanes of Cupid's arrows.

Quæ Mariæ tam larga meat, quàm disceret illîc
    Uvida sub pretio gemma tumere suo!
Staret ibi ante suum lacrymatrix Diva Magistrum:
    Seu levis aura volet, seu gravis unda cadat;   70
Luminis hæc soboles, & proles pyxidis illa,
    Pulchriùs unda cadat, suaviùs aura volet.
Quicquid in his sordet demum, luceret in illis.
    Improbe, nec satìs est hunc tamen esse tuum?
Improbe cede puer: quid enim mea carmina mulces?   75
    Carmina de jaculis muta futura tuis.
Cede puer, quà te petulantis fræna puellæ;
    Turpia quà revocant pensa procacis heræ;
Quà miseri malè pulchra nitent mendacia limi;
    Quà cerussatæ, furta decora, genæ;   80
Quà mirere rosas, alieni sydera veris;
    Quas nivis haud propriæ bruma redempta domat.
Cede puer (dixi, & dico) cede improba mater:
    Altera Cypris habet nos; habet alter Amor.
Scilicet hîc Amor est. Hîc est quoque mater Amoris.   85
    Sed mater virgo. Sed neque cæcus Amor.
O puer! ô Domine! ô magnæ reverentia matris!
    Alme tui stupor & relligio gremii!
O Amor, innocuæ cui sunt pia jura pharetræ;
    Nec nisi de casto corde sagitta calens!   90
Me, puer, ô certâ, quem figis, fige sagittâ.
    O tua de me sit facta pharetra levis.
Quódque illinc sitit & bibit & sitit usqué;
    Usquè meum sitiat pectus, & usque bibat.
Fige, puer, corda hæc. Seu *spinis* exiguus quis,   95
    Seu *clavi* aut *hastæ* cuspide magnus ades;
Seu major *cruce* cum totâ; seu maximus ipso
    Te corda hæc figis denique. Fige puer.
O metam hanc tuus æternum inclamaverit arcus:
    Stridat in hanc teli densior aura tui.   100
O tibi si jaculum ferat ala ferocior ullum,
    Hanc habeat triti vulneris ire viam.
Quíque tuæ populus cunque est, quæ turba, pharetræ;
    Hic bene vulnificas nidus habebit aves.
O mihi sis bello semper tam sævus in isto!   105
    Pectus in hoc nunquam mitior hostis eas.
Quippe ego quàm jaceam pugnâ bene sparsus in illâ!

not, I pray, too dry. For let this [book] of mine have met
you with damp wings (with blood or with its tears may it
flow). Everything opens with the tree and is closed with
nails and spear: will your fountain be idle in [filling]
the rivers? If this litttle [book] of mine has gone to you
on a great stream of blood, will you deny it your waters,
cruel one? Ah cruel man! Whoever does not want my loves,
except dry-eyed, let him deny there is here a cause for his
tears. Often here will he have loved either the waters of
Magdalene or the floods; I do not believe your mind prefers
Assyrian riches. I suppose that fire will rekindle at your
fires: and perhaps that wave will swim in your waters.
Here you will be near [His] cradle and [His] body scented
for burial: hence the passions of a witness arise and thence
my passions. Here will you seek my joys with me and with
His Mother: a grown man or a fool may wish to be Prince;
or if He is hidden by the cave of His tomb (now a temple):
the third dawn will give Him back (but that is slow): Ah
(you will say), I pray that the shadows [of Hell] be loyal
and easy; while my light demands the help of night (a new
thing!). Finally, whatever my writings may say of my Love

> However it fears him or weeps, (you will say)
> these [pieces] show too little joy but still they are sweet:
> and surely (you will say) this [man's] Love ought to be loved.

If it seems too much is promised you here, good reader, in behalf
of him to whom this little book shall be satisfying, you should know that I
look not only to these [pieces] which you have here in this book but also
to those which you will be able to have at some time (by encouraging
these meanwhile). For I did not wish (if up until this time I could not
disappoint my friends encouraging me to submit these [pieces], at the
risk of their own peril, even to such great partiality as yours), I did not
wish, I say, to give myself up to your discriminating criticism. You have
enough here either to banish to the schoolmaster's stick (for none of
these claim to have greater age) or to clasp to your bosom as the
promise of other more mature [efforts]. Choose yourself whichever one
of these you wish. Meanwhile what interests me [is that] my purpose has
not been unsuccessful. I had already reached the greatest peak of ambi-
tion then when this slight whisper from my almost speechless Muse
sounded not unpleasant to those ears, than which none more learned

122 *Assyrian:* emblematic of great wealth.
150 *those ears:* Laney's, evidently.

Quàm bene sic lacero pectore sanus ero!
Hæc mea vota. Mei sunt hæc quoque vota libelli.
Hæc tua sint Lector; si meus esse voles.　　　　　110
Si meus esse voles; meus ut sis, lumina (Lector)
　　Casta, sed ô nimiùm non tibi sicca precor.
Nam tibi fac madidis meus ille occurrerit alis,
　　(Sanguine, seu lacrymâ diffluat ille suâ:)
Stipite totus hians, clavísque reclusus & hastâ:　　115
　　Fons tuus in fluvios desidiosus erit?
Si tibi singuineo meus hic tener iverit amne,
　　Túne tuas illi, dure, negabis aquas?
Ah durus! quicunque meos, nisi siccus, amores
　　Nolit; & hîc lacrymæ rem neget esse suæ.　　　120
Sæpe hic Magdalinas vel aquas vel amaverit undas;
　　Credo nec Assyrias mens tua malit opes.
Scilicet ille tuos ignis recalescet ad ignes;
　　Forsan & illa tuis unda natabit aquis.
Hîc eris ad cunas, & odoros funere manes:　　　　125
　　Hinc ignes nasci testis & indè meos.
Hîc mecum, & cum matre sua, mea gaudia quæres:
　　Maturus Procerum seu stupor esse velit;
Sive per antra sui lateat (tunc templa) sepulchri:
　　Tertia lux reducem (lenta sed illa) dabit.　　　130
Sint fidæ precor ah (dices) facilésque tenebræ;
　　Lux mea dum noctis (res nova!) poscit opem.
Denique charta meo quicquid mea dicat amori,
　　Illi quo metuat cunque, fleátve, modo,
Læta parùm (dices) hæc, sed neque dulcia non sunt:　135
　　Certè & amor (dices) hujus amandus erat.

Si nimium hîc promitti tibi videtur, Lector bone, pro eo cui satis-
faciendo libellus iste futurus fuerit; scias me in istis non ad hæc modò
spectare quæ hîc habes, sed ea etiam quæ olim (hæc interim fovendo)
habere poteris. Nolui emin (si hactenus deesse amicis meis non potui,
flagitantibus à me, etiam cum dispendii sui periculo, paterer eos experiri
te in tantum favorémque tuum) nolui, inquam, fastidio tuo indulgere.
Satìs hîc habes quod vel releges ad ferulam suam (neque enim maturiores
sibi annos ex his aliqua vendicant) vel ut pignus plurium adultiorúmque
in sinu tuo reponas. Elige tibi ex his utrumvis. Me interim quod attinet,
finis meus non fefellit. Maximum meæ ambitionis scopum jamdudum
attigi: tunc nimirum cùm qualecunque hoc meum penè infantis Musæ

have I to fear from the public nor more kindly to hope; still I may be neither over-confident for your acclaim now (I shall speak simply and briefly) nor apprehensive for it in the future. First, my respect for you, whoever you are, Reader, of whose judgment I can have every high hope, prevents [this]; second, respect for those men, of whose perspicacity I cannot dissuade myself from having every high hope, does not allow [it]. O even so, how I wish I were of such great importance that my country would want to set aside its usual practice, so unworthy of its prophetic genius, that practice by which all its own things scorned, it rushes to kiss those things to which having crossed the Alps or being from across the sea alone gives merit. But these promises of too bold a hope abandoned, I shall turn to the Acygnian teachers; who, I know (although I name no one) have angrily abandoned me for my latest writings; but let them regulate their anger and let them confess that they owe (may they pardon an ambitious youth for such a strong word) I say they owe me this: that truly in so noble an argument in which they have needed to resort neither to fetid pretenses about their holy things nor to evil slander about ours, from this slender volume of mine I have given their great work something over which it may rise. But let it rise; (I speak seriously) and let them know that they will always find me, very peacefully contented, under that shadow which their great light shall have poured upon me.

---

162 *Acygnian:* anagram of Ignatian (Ignacyan), i.e. followers of St. Ignatius Loyola, the Jesuits (Martin); it is not known to what controversy Crashaw alludes here.
168 *ours:* those of the Anglican Church.

murmur ad aures istas non ingratum sonuit, quibus neque doctiores mihi de publico timere habeo, nec sperare clementiores; adeò ut de tuo jam plausu (dicam ingenuè & breviter) neque securus sim ultrà neque solicitus. Prius tui, quisquis es Lector, apud me reverentia prohibet; de cujus judicio omnia possum magna sperare: posterius illorum reverentia non sinit, de quorum perspicacitate maxima omnia non possum mihi non persuadere. Quanquam ô quàm velim tanti me esse in quo patria mea morem istum suum deponere velit, genio suo tam non dignum; istum scilicet quo, suis omnibus fastiditis, ea exosculatur unicè, quibus trajecisse Alpes & de transmarino esse, in pretium cessit! Sed relictis hisce nimis improbæ spei votis, convertam me ad magistros Acygnianos; quos scio de novissimis meis verbis (quanquam neminem nominârim) iratos me reliquisse: bilem verò componant; & mihi se hoc debere (ambitioso juveni verbum tam magnum ignoscant) devere, inquam, fateantur: quòd nimirum in tam nobili argumento, in quo neque ad fœtida de suis Sanctis figmenta, neque ad putidas de nostris calumnias opus habeant confugere, de tenui hoc meo dederim illorum magnitudini unde emineat. Emineat verò; (serius dico) Sciántque me semper se habituros esse sub ea, quam mihi eorum lux major affuderit, umbrâ, placidissimè acquiescentem.

Preliminary matter to volumes of 1646, 1648

The Preface to the Reader.

Learned Reader,

The Authors friend, will not usurpe much upon thy eye: This is onely for those, whom the name of our Divine Poet hath not yet seized into admiration, I dare undertake, that what *Iamblicus* (*in vita Pythagoræ*) affirmeth of his Master, at his Contemplations, these Poems can, *viz.* They shal lift thee Reader, some yards above the ground: and, as in *Pythagoras* Schoole, every temper was first tuned into a height by severall proportions of Musick; and spiritualiz'd for one of his weighty Lectures; So maist thou take a Poem hence, and tune thy soule by it, into a heavenly pitch; and thus refined and borne up upon the wings of meditation, in these Poems thou maist talke freely of God, and of that other state.   11

Here's *Herbert's* second, but equall, who hath retriv'd Poetry of late, and return'd it up to its Primitive use; Let it bound back to heaven gates, whence it came. Thinke yee, St. *Augustine* would have steyned his graver Learning with a booke of Poetry, had he fancied their dearest end to be the vanity of Love-Sonnets, and Epithalamiums? No, no, he thought with this, our Poet, that every foot in a high-borne verse, might helpe to measure the soule into that better world: *Divine Poetry;* I dare hold it, in position against *Suarez* on the subject, to be the Language of the Angels; it is the Quintessence of Phantasie and discourse center'd in Heaven; 'tis the very Outgoings of the soule; 'tis what alone our Author is able to tell you, and that in his owne verse.   22

It were prophane but to mention here in the Preface those under-

The Preface to the Reader. 46 (48). The Preface may have been written by a member of the Little Gidding community, by one of Crashaw's Cambridge friends (Joseph Beaumont being the likeliest), or by Crashaw's friend in Lincolnshire.

   3 *Iamblicus:* a celebrated Neo-Platonist (died ca. A.D. 330), author of a *Life of Pythagoras.* Martin observes, however (p. 432), that the correct reference is to Eunapius' Life of Iamblichus "where mention is made of the power of levitation attributed to Iamblichus."

   12 *Herbert:* George Herbert (1593–1633), Cambridge University Orator, Anglican priest, and author of a collection of sacred poems, *The Temple,* the basis of the title of this volume (*Steps to the Temple*); see "On Mr. G. Herberts Booke," No. 66.

   16 *Epithalamiums:* marriage poems.

   18 *Divine Poetry:* for Crashaw's justification see his poems in this Appendix.

   19 *Suarez:* Francisco Suarez (1548–1617), the chief theologian among the Jesuits and the author of a commentary on the *Summa Theologica* of St. Thomas Aquinas. The reference may be to Volume I, Part 2, Book 2, Chapter 26 of that work (Martin, p. 432).

headed Poets, Retainers to seven shares and a halfe; Madrigall fellowes, whose onely businesse in verse, is to rime a poore six-penny soule, a Subburb sinner into hell;—May such arrogant pretenders to Poetry vanish, with their prodigious issue of tumorous heats and flashes of their adulterate braines, and for ever after, may this our Poet fill up the better roome of man. Oh! when the generall arraignment of Poets shall be, to give an accompt of their higher soules, with what a triumphant brow, shall our divine Poet sit above, and looke downe upon poore *Homer*, *Virgil*, *Horace*, *Claudian*? &c. who had amongst them the ill luck to talke out a great part of their gallant Genius, upon Bees, Dung, froggs, and Gnats, &c. and not as himself here, upon Scriptures, divine Graces, Martyrs and Angels.   35

Reader, we stile his Sacred Poems, *Stepps to the Temple*, and aptly, for in the Temple of God, under his wing, he led his life in St. *Maries* Church neere St. *Peters* Colledge: There he lodged under *Tertullian's* roofe of Angels: There he made his nest more gladly then *David's* Swallow neere the house of God: where like a primitive Saint, he offered more prayers in the night, then others usually offer in the day; There, he penned these Poems, *Stepps* for happy soules to climbe heaven by.   42

And those other of his pieces intituled, *The Delights of the Muses*, (though of a more humane mixture) are as sweet as they are innocent.

The praises that follow are but few of many that might be conferr'd on him, hee was excellent in five Languages (besides his Mother tongue) *vid.* Hebrew, Greek, Latine, Italian, Spanish, the two last whereof hee had little helpe in, they were of his owne acquisition.   48

Amongst his other accomplishments in Accademick (as well pious as harmlesse arts) hee made his skill in Poetry, Musicke, Drawing, Limming, graving, (exercises of his curious invention and sudden fancy) to bee but his subservient recreations for vacant houres, not the grand businesse of his soule.   53

To the former Qualifications I might adde that which would crowne them all, his rare moderation in diet (almost Lessian temperance) hee never created a Muse out of distempers, nor with our Canary scribblers)

24 *Retainers to . . . halfe:* writers engaged to share-holders of theaters.
37 *St. Maries Church:* the Church of St. Mary the Less, which adjoins Peterhouse; Crashaw had evidently some official position there (Martin).
38 *Tertullian's roofe:* a reference presumably to the comments of the early Christian writer and apologist, Tertullian, who speaks of the presence of angels in church (Martin, p. 432).
39 *David's swallow:* compare Psalm 84.
41 *night:* the practice of night vigils was common at Little Gidding and was evidently followed by Crashaw at St. Mary's.
55 *Lessian:* pertaining to Lessius (Leonard Leys of Antwerp); see "Temperance," Crashaw's poem in praise of Lessius' regimen of health, No. 370.
56 *Canary scribblers:* poets drunk with Canary wine; compare "Non nimiùm Bacchus noster Apollo fuit" in "Lectori."

cast any strange mists of surfets before the Intelectuall beames of his mind or memory, the latter of which, hee was so much a master of, that hee had there under locke and key in readinesse, the richest treasures of the best Greeke and Latine Poets, some of which Authors hee had more at his command by heart, then others that onely read their workes, to retaine little, and understand lesse. 62

Enough Reader, I intend not a volume of praises, larger then his booke, nor need I longer transport thee to thinke over his vast perfections, I will conclude all that I have impartially writ of this Learned young Gent. (now dead to us) as hee himselfe doth, with the last line of his Poem upon Bishop *Andrews* Picture before his Sermons 67

> *Verte paginas.* 68
> —*Look on his following leaves, and see him breath.* 69

Preliminary matter to volume of 1652

CRASHAWE,
THE
ANAGRAMME.
HE WAS CAR.

Was CAR then Crashawe; or WAS Crashawe CAR,
Since both within one name combined are?
Yes, Car's Crashawe, he Car; t'is love alone
Which melts two harts, of both composing one.
So Crashawe's still the same: so much desired   5
By strongest witts; so honor'd so admired.
CAR WAS but HE that enter'd as a friend
With whom he shar'd his thoughtes, and did commend
(While yet he liv'd) this worke; they lov'd each other:
Sweete Crashawe was his friend; he Crashawes brother.   10
So Car hath Title then; t'was his intent
That what his riches pen'd, poore Car should print;
Nor feares he checke praysing that happie one
Who was belov'd by all; dispraysed by none.

---

66 *now dead to us:* referring presumably to the fact that Crashaw is no longer in England, possibly to the fact that he is no longer an Anglican.
68 *Verte paginas:* Turn the pages.
Crashaw, The Anagramme. 52. This and the following poem are the work of Thomas Car (born Miles Pinkney) (1599–1674), a Roman Catholic expatriate Englishman living in Paris.

To witt, being pleas'd with all things, he pleas'd all.   15
Nor would he give, nor take offence; befall
What might; he would possesse himself: and live
As deade (devoyde of interest) t'all might give
Desease t'his well composed mynd; forestal'd
With heavenly riches: which had wholy call'd   20
His thoughtes from earth, to live above in th'aire
A very bird of paradice. No care
Had he of earthly trashe. What might suffice
To fitt his soule to heavenly exercise,
Sufficed him: and may we guesse his hart   25
By what his lipps brings forth, his onely part
Is God and godly thoughtes. Leaves doubt to none
But that to whom one God is all; all's one.
What he might eate or weare he tooke no thought.
His needfull foode he rather found then sought.   30
He seekes no downes, no sheetes, his bed's still made.
If he can find a chaire or stoole, he's layd,
When day peepes in, he quitts his restlesse rest.
And still, poore soule, before he's up he's dres't.
Thus dying did he live, yet lived to dye   35
In th'virgines lappe, to whom he did applye
His virgin thoughtes and words, and thence was styld
By foes, the chaplaine of the virgine myld
While yet he lived without: His modestie
Imparted this to some, and they to me.   40
Live happie then, deare soule; injoye the rest
Eternally by paynes thou purchacedest,
While Car must live in care, who was thy friend
Nor cares he how he live, so in the end,
He may injoye his dearest Lord and thee;   45
And sitt and singe more skilfull songs eternally.

19 *Desease:* i.e. Dis-ease.
29 *What . . . thought:* compare Matthew 6:25–34.
31 *still:* always.
35–36 *dye . . . lappe:* Crashaw died at the shrine of the Blessed Virgin at Loreto; the metaphor used is erotic.
43 *Car . . . care:* a pun is intended on these words which were pronounced alike.

AN
EPIGRAMME

*Upon the pictures in the following Poemes which the Authour first made
with his owne hand, admirably well, as may be seene in his Manu-
script dedicated to the right Honorable Lady the L. Denbigh.*

Twixt pen and pensill rose a holy strife
Which might draw vertue better to the life.
Best witts gave votes to that: but painters swore
They never saw peeces so sweete before
As thes: fruites of pure nature; where no art   5
Did lead the untaught pensill, nor had part
In th' worke.
The hand growne bold, with witt will needes contest.
Doth it prevayle? ah no: say each is best.
This to the eare speakes wonders; that will trye   10
To speake the same, yet lowder, to the eye.
Both their aymes are holy, both conspire
To wound, to burne the hart with heavenly fire.
This then's the Doome, to doe both parties right:
This, to the eare speakes best; that, to the sight.   15

THOMAS CAR.

An Epigramme. 52.* The pictures in the volume of 1652 probably drawn by Crashaw are
those at the head of the poems "To the Noblest and best of Ladyes" and "The Weeper."
The others would seem to be standard printers' blocks; some of these are signed by other
artists. The "Manuscript" is not now known. See also poem No. 364.
    1 *pen and pensill:* writer's and drawer's tools.
    3 *that:* i.e. the pen.

SUPPLEMENTARY POEMS

Martin included in a section entitled "Supplementary Poems" (pp. 401–9), six poems "not included in previous modern editions":

> On the death of W^m. Henshaw
> An Elegy upon the death of Mr. Wm. Carre
> An Elegy on the death of the Lady Parker
> An Elegy upon the death of Mr. Christopher Rouse
> An Epitaph ("Heere in deaths closett")
> Epithalamium ("Come virgin tapers")

The first five of these poems have been shown to be very probably by Philip Cornwallis and are not included in the present edition (J. Yoklavich, "Not by Crashaw, but Cornwallis," *MLR*, LIX [1964], 517–18). The "Epithalamium" (No. 358) is accepted in the canon in this edition; Martin confesses more confidence in the ascription of this poem than in that of the other five. Martin also included five other poems (pp. 410–14) as "Probably Spurious." As there is no reason to question the condition of these poems, they have been dropped in the present edition.

Since the 1927 publication of Martin's edition, two other poems have been brought forward as worthy of inclusion in the canon. The first of these is "On the Translation of the House of Loreto" proposed by B. H. Newdigate ("An Overlooked Poem by Richard Crashaw," *London Mercury*, XXXII [May–October, 1935], 265–66); the second is a Latin elegy (untitled) on Edward King proposed by Miss Wallerstein (*Richard Crashaw*, p. 26). The opinion of the present editor based on his general impression of each poem and on diction, metaphor, tone, and idiom is that neither poem is by Crashaw.

I

["No poet but Crashaw would have so linked classical myth with pious tradition, paganism with Christian faith, earth with heaven itself, as the writer of these lines has done. We have too the figure of the Eastern Sun, which is found again and again in Crashaw's sacred poems" (Newdigate, p. 265). The poem is found in *Tixall Poetry* (1813), pp. 266–67.]

On the Translation of the House of Loretto.

When the misterious chamber first did move
From Jewry vales into the aire above,
   A quire of Angels held it downe,
   Or to the highest heavens 't had flowne.
     Gabriel led on before,   5
     Towards the Hesperian shore,
   Whence west winds breathed in their face,
   Not to resist, but to embrace.
Ore his owne seas then Dedalus might descry
A labirinth itself of wonders fly;   10
Rhodes' great Colossus durst not aske a stay,
For here imensity contracted lay.
   The virgin mother's spouse's roome
   At unchast Paphos would not come;
   Truth's selfe disclaim'd his seate   15
   Should dwell in lying Crete.
Delos in vain look'd up with hope awhile;
The flying house past ore the floating isle.
Unhappy easterne nations! dayly thus
Suns rise with you, but alwaise make to us.   20
   The never-erring chair is come
   From your Antioch to our Rome;
     Poore Nazareth's sole blis
     Now too translated is:
   On fair Loretto's hill it stands,   25
   Thither convey'd by angells hands;
Where the same roofe, that in our father's age
A pilgrim was, is now a pilgrimage.

II

["One such occasional poem, not written indeed, until Peterhouse days,
. . . touches our imagination by giving Crashaw a share in the most famous of all volumes of occasional verse . . . [The poem] signed R.C.
. . . is written in the style of verbal play and paradox thoroughly characteristic of Crashaw. . . . The probability that Crashaw should have written for this occasion is strengthened not only by the fact that so many other sons of Cambridge who were noted as poets contributed to the volume, but also by the fact that Crashaw's particular friend Joseph Beaumont was among them" (Wallerstein, p. 26). "The Latin verses
. . . may well be by Crashaw" (Martin, p. xcii). The poem is found in *Justa Edouardo King naufrago* (1638), pp. 23–24.]

> In liquido horrentis tumulati marmore ponti
>   Hoc solidum marmor nomen inane capit.
> Sed nec inane tamen: dum stat modò pontus & æther,
>   Flumina dum Chami leniùs ipsa meant;
> Et fluvius placidè surrepenti agmine lapsus   5
>   Exprobrat ipse fretis invidiámque facit.
> Infelix, quid agis? quid tecum Helicona remisces?
>   Casta quid in falsis fluctibus unda perit?
> Alpheum poteras facili transmittere ductu,
>   Nec magìs hinc rivos polluit ille suos.   10
> Ipse negabo meas posthac tibi ducere lymphas:
>   Ah! scelus unda tuum nulla piare potest.
> Nil agis, ô demens: non primùm hic æquore mersus
>   Est sophiæ princeps; sed neque mersus erit:
> Æternum Aoniis nomen superenatat undis,   15
>   Murmur aquæ titulos bulliet usquè meæ.
> Mota quidem est Thetis, & damnum sua crimina flevit,
>   Fluxit & in guttas noxia petra suas.
> Frustrá; namque virum evexit super æthera virtus:
>   Credite, naufragium nesciit illa pati.   20
> Suspensaque Deo mens est elapsa tabella,
>   Corporis & laceram despicit indè ratem;
> Et sedet in portu, sanctóque armata sereno
>   Tranquillum æterno lumine nacta diem est.
> Ite leves undæ, & nequicquam sæva procella,   25
>   Et bene vexati gratior ira maris.
> Vela dabat cœlo; liquidam facit unda curulem,
>   Qua jam tacturum sidera summa vehit.

                              R.C.

On the liquid marble of the tomb of the rough sea
this solid marble bears an empty name.
But still not empty: while still stand sea and air,
while the rivers of Cam themselves move so slowly;
and the stream gliding on its stealthy course
itself rails at its channels and shows its envy.
Unhappy [sea], what are you doing? Why do you mix Helicon with
Why does the guiltless wave perish in false floods?   [yourself?
You could have sent Alpheus over with an easy passage
and he would not have desecrated the waters any more from there.
I myself will deny that my clear waters lead to you:
Ah no wave can cleanse your sin.
You do nothing, foolish [sea]: the prince of wisdom is not the first
to have been drowned in the sea; but neither will he have been drowned:
[his] name eternally swims above the Aonian waves,
the sound of my [verse] will lift his fame from the water forever.
Indeed Thetis was moved and wept for him condemned for his sins,
and the hurtful rock flowed into its own tears.
In vain; for virtue has raised this hero above the heavens:
believe me, that [virtue] did not know how to suffer shipwrecks.
[His] spirit with a clean slate has been lifted by God
and looks down from there on the mangled raft of its body
and rests in harbor, and protected by a holy calm
has found the everlasting light of a peaceful day.
Go gentle waves, faithless is the savage storm,
even more pleasing than the anger of the vexed sea.
He set his sails for heaven; the wave makes a watery chariot
in which it bears him now about to touch the highest stars.

NOTES

TEXTUAL NOTES

Crashaw's poems were published in the seventeenth century in the following printed collections:

Epigrammatum Sacrorum Liber (Cambridge, 1634)
Steps to the Temple . . . with other Delights of the Muses (London, 1646)
Steps to the Temple . . . with other Delights of the Muses (London, 1648)
Carmen Deo Nostro (Paris, 1652)
A Letter to the Countess of Denbigh (London, [?1653])
Epigrammata et Poemata (Cambridge, 1670).

Each of these volumes adds some new poems to the canon, and each is therefore, to some extent a substantive edition. The first of the list is the only volume that Crashaw could have seen through the press; the others were all the care of friends. The two editions of the *Steps* were entrusted to the "authors friend" who may have been one of Crashaw's Cambridge associates, one of his Little Gidding associates, or a resident of Lincolnshire—or perhaps all of them (see Saveson, "Richard Crashaw," *TLS*, February 28, 1958, p. 115). This friend published the first collection two or three years after Crashaw had left England, describing him as "now dead to us." Similarly, Thomas Car published the *Carmen Deo Nostro* six years after Crashaw had left Paris, and three years after he was indeed dead. For the last two items listed, no information is available about an editor.

The relationships between these volumes is clear in some instances, murky in others. The *Epigrammatum Sacrorum Liber* was in effect reprinted in the *Epigrammata et Poemata* in 1670; to the later volume several new Greek and Latin epigrams were added, presumably from some manuscript sources not now known. The *Delights of the Muses* of 1646 was reprinted in 1648 with some new poems added in English and in Latin. The *Steps to the Temple* of 1646 was reprinted in 1648 with some new poems added in Latin and with major revisions in many of the poems now considered to be among Crashaw's most important ones (see J. C. Maxwell, "Steps to the Temple: 1646 and 1648," *PQ*, XXIX [1950], 216–20). The *Carmen Deo Nostro* prints a collection of Crashaw's major religious poems in a form generally like those revised versions of 1648, but deriving from a different manuscript containing different revisions.

It is commonly assumed that those poems which appear in the volumes of 1646, 1648, and 1652 in different versions show a continuing succession of revisions. This assumption is not necessarily valid. What is demonstrable is that there are two parallel lines of transmission for the revised poems, one line in England passing into the 1648 volume, another line in France (perhaps with another and later stage of authorial revision) passing into the 1652 volume. Further to complicate the matter is the difference in accidentals between the 1648 and 1652 editions; the English edition is spare and modern in typography, the French edition is lavish and obsolete in typography. Those accidentals in the French edition include also the illustrations, two of which are by Crashaw.

The *Letter* of 1653 is a revised version of one of the poems in the 1652 volume.

The copies of these volumes in the Henry E. Huntington Library have served as copy texts for this edition.

In addition, there are a good many poems which Crashaw published in various Cambridge collections in the 1630s and 1640s; all of these were collected in the 1646 and 1648 editions by the "friend." There are also several manuscript collections of Crashaw's poems, and many of the poems appear in manuscript books of the period.

In the preparation of the present edition all the substantive editions have been collated and the separately published poems whenever possible have been examined in their first printed forms. The appropriate manuscripts have been re-examined. In this examination I have followed the texts as printed in the editions of Grosart and Martin. The most useful of the manuscripts is "Tanner 465" in the Bodleian Library; it contains some 60 sacred epigrams in Latin (see the Table in the Index) and many secular poems from Crashaw's early period. Two other manuscripts at the British Museum include a few poems not elsewhere available. The Pierpont Morgan Library has a manuscript version of "An Apologie," No. 62, with a unique title in Crashaw's hand. Since the publication of Martin's second edition, another manuscript containing poems by Crashaw has been identified, the Loseley Manuscript at the Folger Shakespeare Library (see *ELN*, II [1964], 92–97).

The textual notes which follow give after the short title of the poem the publication year of the volume which is used as copy text. (This will usually be one of the volumes listed above, but for the separately published poems the number will refer to the year of their first publication if that is the copy text.) This number may be followed by another number in parentheses, this latter number referring to the presence of the poem in another volume. If the poem is merely reprinted in a later volume, the number of that reprinting is generally not given. For the poems in two versions, the two copy texts are given for poems on the left-hand pages and on the right-hand pages. The notes record all substantive departures from the copy text; they do not offer an historical collation of the later editions, as that collation is readily available in Martin's edition. The accidentals of the copy text have been preserved except where they are manifestly in error. Punctuation emendations have been introduced without record.

I. Sacred Poems in One English Version

2. PSALME 23. *46.*
    5 On] *48;* One *46.*   20 wooe] *48;* woe *46.*

3. PSALME 137. *46.*
    12 One] *48;* On *46.*

6. OUR LORD IN HIS CIRCUMCISION. *46.*
    10 but] *MS.;* both *46.*

15. SHE BEGAN TO WASH. *46*.

1 Her] *48;* Heer *46*.

30. THE BLIND CURED. *46*.

HEADING: Marc. 10.] Martin; Matthew. 10. *46*. [The Latin epigram (1634) was headed "Matth. 10.52", and from it the English (1646) evidently derived its error "Matthew 10." Martin emended the Latin error to "Marc. 10.52." and the English error to "Matthew 9." (in which text two men are cured).]

1 spak'st] *MS.;* speak'st *46* [the authority for this emendation lies in the Latin epigram ("loquutus eras")].

37. BUT NOW THEY HAVE SEEN. *46*.

3 thee] *48;* the *46*.

41. TO PONTIUS. *46*.

3 any can] *corrected in 46* [CSmH Copy; (?) B.M. Copy]; can] *uncorrected in 46* [Bodleian Copy].

43. UPON THE THORNES. *46 (48, 52)*.

HEADING: the Thornes] *46;* the Crowne of thornes *48, 52.* our Lords head] *46;* the head of our B. Lord *48, 52.* bloody] *46, 48;* all bloody *52.*
3–4 'Tis . . . Spring?] *omitted in 48, 52.* [It will be noted that this couplet is present in the Latin version, #267.]   5 an] a *48, 52.* could] did *48, 52.*   7 (thinke ye)] *omitted in 48, 52.* that] which *48, 52.*   8 Thornes] Thrones *52.*

44. ON OUR CRUCIFIED LORD. *46 (48, 52)*.

HEADING: On our crucified Lord] *46, 48;* Upon the body of our Bl. Lord *52.*
4 of] *46, 48;* in *52.*   5 bee found Garments] *46;* there be garment *48, 52.*
6 these] *46;* this *48, 52.*

45. ON THE WOUNDS OF OUR CRUCIFIED LORD. *46 (48)*.

6 too] *48;* two *46.*

46. UPON OUR SAVIOURS TOMBE. *46 (48, 52)*.

HEADING: Upon . . . laid.] *46, 48;* To our B. Lord upon the choise of his Sepulchre. *52.*

48. UPON THE SEPULCHRE. *46 (48, 52)*.

HEADING: Upon . . . Lord.] *46, 48;* Upon the H. Sepulcher. *52.*

55. HYMN TO THE NAME OF JESUS. *52 (48)*.

HEADING: To . . . Hymn.] On the name of Jesus. *48.*
7 you] the *48.*   24 World] word *48.*   50 hasty Fitt-] habit fit of self *48.*
73 Provinces] powers *48.*   74 your] *48;* yours *52.*   93 alowd] *48;* lowd *52.*
105 yeilds] yeild *48.*   106 Seraphim] Seraphins *48.*   107 joyfull] Loyall *48.*
115 from forth] forth from *48.*   133 Heaven] heavens *48.*   140 this] thy *48.*
186 spices] *48;* species *52.*   188 soul that] soules *48.*   203, 5 bore . . . wore] bare . . . ware *48.*   210 therein] *48;* them in *52.*   228 Or] Oh *48.*

56. HYMN FOR NEW-YEAR'S DAY. 52 (46, 48); 48 agrees with 52 except where noted.

HEADING: New . . . Day.] A Hymne for the Circumcision day of our Lord. 46, 48 [48 An Hymne . . .].

1 best and brightest] first and fairest 46. 5 that] of 46 [for "lace" as a verb see poems No. 339, line 51, and No. 358, stz. 10.3]. 7 Guilds] Guild 46. 10 strowes] 46, 52; showes 48. 13 thy] the 46. 14 best . . . rise] glorious beames 46. 16 These] 46, 52; Those 48. their] his 46. 18 Search . . . keep] Rob the rich store her Cabinets keep 46. 19 Rob . . . nest] The pure birth of each sparkling nest 46. 20 beds] bed 46. 21 embrave] embrace 46, 48 [for "embrave" as a verb see poems No. 70, line 48, and No. 87, stz. 61]. 23 those] them 46. 28 bright] faire 46. 29 this] the 46. 31 morn] Moone 46, 48. to] and 48. 32 her . . . neglected] the long adored 46. 33 Here . . . Beautyes] Thy nobler beauty 46. 37–38 omitted in 52.

57. EPIPHANIE HYMN. 52 (48). In 52 the prefixes are set off in parentheses in lines 1–6, 10–108; in brackets elsewhere. Usage is standardized in this edition.

HEADING: In . . . Hymn.] A Hymne for the Epiphanie. 48.

1 (1.Kinge.)] omit 48. 3 (2.)] omit 48. 5 (3.)] omit 48. 41 sphear] 48; spear 52. 48 (1.)] 48; (2.) 52. world's] 48; wold's 52. 52 kis't] hist 48. 83 this] thy 48. 98 (3.) Shall] Shall 48. But] (3.) But 48. 99 (Cho.) See] See 48. 100 And] Chorus. And 48. 103 (2.) Fly] Fly 48. As] 2. As 48. 111 witt] will 48. 122 his] 48; this 52. 133 (1.)] 48; [2.] 52. 143 clear] deere 48. 155 domestick] domesticks 48. 161 loves] love's 48. 163 (1.)] 48; [2.] 52. 181 their] the 48. 183 (1.)] 48; [2.] 52. 187 it] omitted in 48. 188 it] 48; in 52. 190 that] the 48. 196 what] 48; that 52. 197 his] 48; this 52. 207 Come] 3. Come 48. 208 (3.) And] And 48. 241 gorgeous] glorious 48. 244 (1.)] 48; [3.] 52. (2.) his] His (2.) 48. (3.) his] (3.) 48.

58. TO THE QUEEN'S MAJESTY. 52 (48).

HEADING: Majesty.] Majestie upon his dedicating to her the foregoing Hymne. 48.

6 dawn] down 48. 10 read] wade 48. Rare] deare 48. 13 Golden] Royall 48. 17 whole] 48; whose 52. 19 dread] great 48.

59. CHARITAS NIMIA. 52 (48).

1 thee] you 48. 2 thee] you 48. 20 thy] the 48. 25 ever-] omit 48. 33 thou] 48; you 52. 45 were] was 48. 47 thy] the 48.

60. THE TEARE 46 (48; not in 52).

4.4 it] 48; its 46. 5.1–6 this stanza reappears as st. 11 of The Weeper in 48, 52 (see collation there). 5.4 manly] MS.; watry 46, 48. 7.6 thee] the 48.

61. A HYMN TO ST. TERESA. 52 (46, 48; Pierpont Morgan Library MS. [PM MS.]).

The Pierpont Morgan Library has a manuscript of the Hymne and the Apologie (described by Martin, TLS, April 18, 1952, p. 272) for which Crashaw has prepared a new heading and in which he has made four marginal references to Teresa's Vida and biography; these are noted in the footnotes to the Hymne. There are also three textual corrections to the manuscript by

Crashaw; these have all been assimilated in the later printed editions. *48* agrees
with *52* unless noted.

HEADING: A Hymn to . . . The Hymne.] In memory of the vertuous and
Learned Lady Madre de Teresa that sought an early Martyrdome. *46, 48;* A
Hymn *to the name and honour of the renowned* S. Teresia Foundres of the
Reformation of the Order of barefoote Carmelites; *A Woman for* Angelicall
height of Contemplation, *for* Masculine *courage of* Performance, *more than a
woman. Who yet a Child outranne Maturity & durst plott a* Martyrdome; *but
was reserved by God to dy the* living death *of the* life *of his* love. *of whose great
impressions as her noble heart had most heroically exprest them, in her Spirituall
posterity most fruitfully propagated them, and in these her heavnly writings most
sublimely, most sweetly taught them to ye world. PM MS.*

3 Wee'l now appeal] Wee need to goe *46.*　4 Great] stout *46.*　5 Ripe . . .
Martyrdom,] Ripe and full growne, *46.*　8 into] unto *46.*　10 spatious Bosomes
spread] large breasts built *46.*　11 at . . . sweat] their Lord, glorious and great
46.　12 And] weell *46.*　13 Making] And make *46.*　15 has] hath *48;* had *46.*
the] a *46.*　21 has] hath *46, 48.*　25 has] hath *48;* had *46.*　27 has] hath *48.*
dares] dare *48.*　31 you] we *46.*　33 or] nor *48.*　37 thirsts] thirst *46.* dares]
dare *46.*　40 weake] what *52.*　43 at] *omit 48.*　44 travail] travell *46, 48.*
to] for *48.*　45 her] hers *52, 48.*　47 trade] try *48.*　49 she'l offer] she offers
46.　52 and] *omitted in 52.*　61 *omitted in 52.*　72 chast] soft *48.*　77 armes]
hand *46.*　90 sent] spent *46.*　93 sons] Loves *46.*　94 Seraphim] Seraphims
46, 48.　104 he . . . Dy.] he still may dy. *46.*　107 his] thine *48.*　117 resolv-
ing] disolving *46.*　122 thou shalt] you *52.*　128 for] on *46.*　129 reveal'd Life]
she *46.*　130 his] her *46, 48.*　133 joyes] joy *46.*　147 *omitted in 52.*　148 All]
And *46, 48.*　151 Deaths] *46, 48;* Death *52.*　152 that erst] which late *46.*
166 Thousands] Thousand *46.*　168 soveraign] *omitted in 46.*　175 keeps] keep
52.　178 shalt] shall *46.*　179 setts] sitts *46.*

62. AN APOLOGIE. *52* (*46, 48*); *48* agrees with *52* except where noted.

HEADING in *46:* An Apologie for the precedent Hymne. [*The Apologie* fol-
lows *The Hymn to St. Teresa* as in *52*].

HEADING in *48:* An Apologie for the precedent Hymnes on *Teresa.* [i.e. *The
Hymn* and *The Flaming Heart*].

HEADING: Hymne] Hymen *52.*

2 floud] sea *46.*　5 art] are *48.*　9 hopefull] heavenly *46.*　12 thy] the *48.*
here] there *46.*　16 a] one *46.*　20 come from] dwell in *46.*　25 the] a *48.*　26
feels] finds *46.* hatch'd] *46, 48; omitted in 52.*　29 enow] *46, 48;* now *52.*　34
too 'our] to our *48;* our *46.*　41 youth] youths *46.*　45 at] in *46, 48.*

63. THE FLAMING HEART. *52* (*48*).

HEADING: the seraphicall saint] *omitted in 48.*

3 too] so *48.*　11 Read] And *48.*　16 Showes] Shew *48.*　18 happy] hap-
pier *48.*　25 meant'st] mean'st *48.* paint] *48;* print *52.*　28 cheeks] *48;* checks
52.　30 found] form'd *48.*　31 What] But *48.* weares] wore *48.*　33 cheekes]
48; cheek *52.* [See line 66.]　36 Had] She *48.*　48 shaft] shafts *48.*　58 kindly
takes] *48;* gives *52.*　66 glistering] glittering *48.*　76 wounds] *48;* wound *52.*
85–108 *omitted in 48* [Martz writes: "The poem has a sense of completeness
without these lines, which may have been a later addition . . . ; on the other
hand . . . they may have been omitted in error or because of some theological
objection to the strong adulation of the saint" (*The Meditative Poem* [Anchor
Books, Garden City, N.Y., 1963], p. 545)].

64. A SONG. 52 (48).
> HEADING: A Song] A Song of divine Love. 48.
> SUB-HEADING: Second part] The second part 48.   13 loving] longing 48.

65. TO [MRS. M. R.] COUNCEL. 52 (48).
> HEADING in 1648 and 1652: To the Same Party Councel concerning her Choise.
> 4 may] 48; my 52.   30 follow] fellow 48.   35 more] most 48.

66. ON MR. G. HERBERTS BOOKE. 46 (48; not in 52).

67. UPON THE ENSUING TREATISES [OF MR. SHELFORD]. 1635 (46, 48; not in 52); 48 agrees with 46 unless noted. First published in Robert Shelford, *Five Pious and Learned Discourses* (Cambridge, 1635).
> HEADING in 46, 48: On a Treatise of Charity.
> 12 this] thy 48.   15 She'll] Sh'l 46.   17 Altars] offrings 46, 48.   30 A] Pure 1635 [compositorial anticipation].   59–68 *omitted in 46, 48*.

68. ON HOPE. 46 (48, 52); 48 generally agrees with 46 except where noted.
C. H. Miller ("The Order of Stanzas in Cowley and Crashaw's 'On Hope,'" *SP*, LXI [1964], 64–73) has argued persuasively that the likelihood of scribal error in the preparation of 46 and the lack of logical and poetic consistency in that version of the poem strengthen the possibility that the Crashaw stanzas are erroneously placed. He demonstrates that the sequence of the four first stanzas in 46 is correct but that the sequence of the last four in 46 is incorrect; he emends the latter sequence to the order as printed in the present edition (on the basis of his argument). He suggests further that the stanza "Faire *Hope*" (lines 41–50) should conclude the poem, but the metaphoric consistency between the two Crashaw stanzas "Thou art" and "Faire *Hope*" (lines 31–50) as responding to Cowley's stanza "Hope, thou bold" (lines 21–30) argues more strongly for the location as printed in the present edition. It is evident that Crashaw has provided one stanza more than Cowley's four anticipate; as the order of Crashaw's lines is the same in 46 and in 52, it would seem desirable to retain it and to fit the stanza in where it is consistent rather than where it is cumbersome.
Alternating stanzas in 46, 48; in 52 the stanzas of each poet are gathered into separate poems, Cowley first followed by Crashaw. The Crashaw stanzas are indented in the present edition so that the reader may follow the argument more easily. See further my "Order of Stanzas in . . . 'On Hope,'" *SB*, XXII (1969), 207–10.
> 41–50 *location*] this edition; *following line* 60 46, 48
> 61–70 *location*] Miller; *following line* 80 46, 48
> 81–70 *location*] Miller; *following line* 70 46, 48
The text of the Cowley stanzas in 52 follows Cowley's own publication of the poem in *The Mistresse* (1647), in many significant readings differing from the text in 46; in consequence the variants are omitted from this collation. This is the only one of the major poems printed in 46, 48, and 52 that was not revised for 48. The text of the Crashaw stanzas of 46, 48 is not "much altered" in the version of 52 (cf. Martin, p. 143). The poem presents therefore a unique situation in the transmission of the text.
> 14 hath] has 52.   15–16 Faire . . . Night] Substantiall shade! whose sweet allay / Blends both the noones of night and day 52.   19 thinne] lean

52.　20 like] as 52. at] from 52.　31 Thou art] Rich hope 52.　32 the . . . our] still spending, and still 52.　33 -lands lye] -land lyes 52.　38 thus steal'st] steal'st us 52.　39 kisse wrongs] stealth harmes 52.　43 Thy] 52; The *46, 48*.　44 need wee] does it 52.　45 head] growing head 52.　48 doth] does 52.　50 subtile] supple 52.　55 Thinne . . . eye] 52; Thine empty cloud the eye it selfe *46, 48*.　61 low warres] 52; law warres: *46, 48*.　62 kicks] walks; &c kickes 52.　63 our] these 52.　64 And *Fates*] Fortune's 52.　65–66 *omitted in* 52.　68 or] nor 52.　73 Child] 52; shield *46, 48*.　83 Temper'd] Temper 52. cold] chill 52.　89 Huntresse] hunter 52.　90 field] fields 52.

69. UPON THE POWDER DAY. *46* (*48*; not in *52*).

II. Sacred Poems in two English Versions

70. NATIVITY HYMN. First version *46*; second version *52* (*48*); *48* agrees with *52* except where noted.

HEADING: In . . . The Hymn.] An Hymne of the Nativity, sung as by the Shepheards *48*.

28 eyes'] eyes *48*; eye's 52.　30 eyes'] Eyes *48*.　32 Young] Bright *48*.　41 ye] *48*; the 52.　43 ye] *48*; the 52.　47 his own] all one *48*.　60 wings] *48*; wing 52.　64 I] we *48*.　69 we] I *48*.　85 nor to] not to *48*.　90–91 *48* follows *46* in supplying the stanza omitted in 52.　102 the] their *48*.

71. OFFICE OF THE HOLY CROSSE. First version *48*; second version *52*.

MATINS HYMN (*52*): Father's] Father' 52.

PRIME RESPONSOR (*52*) ii, 1: Convenant] *so 52 from Prime to Compline* [it is an obsolete form for 'covenant' as in Matins and is therefore possibly correct, but it is more likely a French error based on forms from the verb *convenir*].

PRIME PRAYER (*52*): God] Ood 52.

THIRD HYMN (*52*) 6: then] them 52.

THIRD RESPONSOR (*52*) ii, 2: world's] word's 52.

NINTH RESPONSOR (*52*) ii, 2: world's] word's 52.

EVENSONG PRAYER (*52*): &c.] &c. 42 [the page number of the complete prayer immediately preceding in 52].

The texts from the Prymer are from *The Prymer in Englishe and Latine* (London: Wayland, 1557), sigs. G.iij–L.iij^v, *passim*. Though the hymns are in rhymed verse, they are printed in the *Prymer* as prose.

72. SONG UPON THE BLEEDING CRUCIFIX. First version *46*; second version *52* (*48*); *48* agrees with *52* except where noted.

HEADING: wounds] *46*; body *48* [otherwise *48* follows *46*].

II.4 strives] streames *48*.

III.4 floud] blood *48*.

73. HYMN IN THE ASSUMPTION. First version *46*; second version *52*. *48* contains both lines 17–32 of *52* (not in *46*) and lines 29–40 of *46* (not in *52*). Martz (*The Meditative Poem*, pp. 314–16) prints the *48* version, eighty lines long. *48* agrees with *52* unless otherwise noted.

HEADING: On . . . Assumption.] *46, 48*.

17–32 *omitted in 46* (but not *48*).　18 wert] were *48*.　21 so] as *48*.　25 does] doth *48*.　29 tree] *48*; three 52.　30 heavy] leavy *48*.　40 sweet] great *48*. 31–40 (of *46*) *omitted in 52* (but not *48*).　68 best] *48*; brest 52.

74. THE WEEPER. First version *46;* second version *52* (*48* agrees with *52* except where noted).

HEADING: The Weeper] *46, 48.*

I. 2 footed] forded *46.* [In view of the significance Crashaw attaches to feet generally and in this poem specifically, the *52* "footed" is surely to be preferred. Martz (*The Meditative Poem,* p. 542) suggests that "The thought of rills with silver fords (quiet, shallow places) makes an effective image." It does, but "footed" makes a more relevant one. See "An Elegie on the death of Dr. Porter," No. 352, line 1, where the adjective appears.]

v. 6 this] his *48.*

IX. 1 There's] There is *48.* 13.2 (*46*) ease] case *46.*

XI this stanza is st. 5 of "The Teare" *46.* 2 purpling vine] wanton Spring *46.* 3 parent] *omitted in 48.* 4 at the bridegroome] *48;* at the bridegroomes *52;* on the watry *46.* 5 Blossom] Balsome *48.*

XII. 5 draw] *48;* deaw *52.* 6 Water] Waters *48.*

[XVI.] 5 While] White *48.*

XVII. 2 bosom] balsome *48.* thee] *48;* you *52.* 3 Can so] Cause *48.*

XVIII. 2 Vine] *48;* wine *52.* 3 the] that *48.* 4 these] those *48.*

XX. 2 rare] large *48.* 4 wealth] wrath *48.*

XXI. 2 calls't] blank space *48.*

XXII. 4 the] thy *48.*

XXIV. 2 faithfull] *48;* faith full *52.* 3 praire] *48;* paire *52.* 6 does] doth *48.*

XXVII. 3 fire] *48;* fires *52.*

XXVIII. 1 ye] *48;* the *52.*

XXIX. 4 your] *48;* their *52.*

75. ODE ON A PRAYER-BOOK. First version *46;* second version *52* (*48*); *48* agrees with *52* unless noted. Stanzaic divisions in *48* generally follow those in *46.*

HEADING in *48:* An ode which was prefixed to a Prayer booke given to a young Gentlewoman.

7 thy] *48;* the *52.* 17 your] *48;* their *52.* 18 (*46*) hands] hand *46.* 19 your] Martin; their *52;* the *46, 48.* foes] foe *48.* your part] *48;* their part *52.* 20 your] *48;* their *52.* 33 your] *48;* their *52.* 34 his] its *48.* 41 his] its *48.* bosom] *48;* besom *52.* 54 ith'] *48;* th' *52.* 56 Spheare] *48;* Spheares *52.* 62 Mean while] *omitted in 48.* 63 that] the *48.* 75 does] doth *48.* 118–19 lining in *48* as *46.*

III. Sacred Poems Translated into English

77. VEXILLA REGIS. *52* (*48*). The Latin text is from Daniel, *Thesaurus Hymnologicus,* I, 160–61.

HEADING: The . . . Crosse.] *omitted in 48.*

II 2 thy] the *48.*

IV 5 the] a *48.*

v 6 excellence] crueltie *48.*

VI 2 way'd] wag'd *48.* 3 Us . . . weighed'st;] Both with one price were weighed, *48.* 4 Our . . . payed'st;] Both with one price were paid, *48.*

VII 1–6 *omitted in 48.*

VIII 3 to'] for to *48.* 4 this Crosse] thy blessed death *48.* 5 Amen.] *omitted in 48.*

78. SANCTA MARIA DOLORUM. 52 (48). The Latin text is from Daniel,
II, 131–32.

    HEADING in 48: The Mother of Sorrowes.
    I 10 All,] Are 48. owne] 48; one 52.
    VI 3 loves] love 48.   7 in] to 48.   9 Me] Oh give me 48.
    VII omitted in 48.
    VIII omitted in 48.
    IX 1 sett] in sins set 48.   6 If] 48; Is 52. just] 48; soft 52 [soft is emended
in the present edition to just on paleographic similarity and on the analogy of
"just and solemn," "just and true" in Lauda Sion, iii and xiii].
    X 1 Rich Queen,] Lend, O 48.   9 him] thee 48.
    XI 3 the] thy 48.   7 Fold . . . life] Let my life end 48. lay't] lye 48.   8 My]
Thy 48. lord's] lost 48.   10 thy lord's in] in thy Lords 48.

79. ADORO TE. 52 (48). The Latin text is from Daniel, I, 255.

    HEADING in 48: A Hymne to our Saviour by the Faithfull Receiver of the
Sacrament.
    1 powres] Power 48.   33 my Faith] 48; omitted in 52.   37–38 omitted in
48.   57 Amen.] omitted in 48.

80. LAUDA SION SALVATOREM. 52 (48). The Latin text is from Daniel,
II, 97–98.

    HEADING in 48: A Hymne on the B. Sacrament.
    I 3 you] thou 48.   4 to] and 48.   6 ambition] Ambitions 48.
    III 3 the] their 48.
    IV 1 Lord] Law 48.
    VII 3 names] 48; name 52.   6 one] on 48.
    X 1 shall] shalt 48.
    XIV 3 lean] meane 48.   9 Amen.] omitted in 48.

81. DIES IRÆ. 52 (48). The Latin text is from Daniel, II, 105–8; Claydon,
pp. 4, 151.

    HEADING in 48: A Hymne in meditation of the day of judgement.
    I 1 what] 48; with 52.
    V 3 that] the 48.
    XVI 4 thy] the 48.

82. O GLORIOSA DOMINA. 52 (48). The Latin text is from The Prymer
in Englishe and Latin (London: Wayland, 1557), sigs. Fj–fjv (typography
modernized), but the same poem with minor variants may be found as the
concluding four stanzas of "De Beata Virgine," Daniel, I, 172–73.

    HEADING in 48: The Virgin-Mother.
    2 thy] the 48.   4 starres] 48; stares 52.   10 things] 48; thing 52. thee.] 48;
the. 52.   21 sprung] Spring 48.   26 their] your 48.   35 omitted in 52.
    In the Latin text, #2, line 4, facta es. is emended from facta est.; #3, line 4,
redemptæ is emended from redempte.

83. CHRISTS SUFFERINGS. British Museum MS Add. MS. 33219. The
Latin text is from Hugonis Grotij Poemata (Lugdun. Batav.: Cloquium, 1617),
pp. 467–69.

    A few minor emendations of punctuation have been made to the Manuscript.

84. ALEXIAS. *52* (*48*). The Latin text is from F. Remondi *Epigrammata et Elegiae* (Antwerp, 1606) reprinted in Martin, pp. 450–52.

HEADING: Sainte] *omitted in 48.*

FIRST 1 loud] *48;* lou'd *52* [i.e. loved]. 9 should] would *48.* 17 the way] *48;* way *52.* 23 his] its *48.* 25 where] when *48.*

SECOND 1 fleed] fled *48.* 10 beauteous] *48; omitted in 52.* 20 times] *48;* time *52.*

THIRD 7 by] with *48.* 11 Nor] Not *48.* 16 exile] exiles *48.* 17 O] *48;* Or *52.* 29 Queen of angels] Blessed Virgin *48.* 41 gaping] facing *48.* 50 have] hath *48.* 51 sweet] sweet's *48.* 54 thousands] *48;* thousand *52.*

85. IN AMOREM DIVINUM. Bodleian MS. Tanner 465. The Latin text is from *Pia Desideria Lib. iii* . . . Herm. . . . Hugone . . . Editio 6 . . . (Antwerpiae, M.DC.XXXII), p. 309.

86. DESCRIPTION OF A RELIGIOUS HOUSE. *52* (*48*). The Latin text is from Joannis Barclaii *Argenis* (Parisiis, M.DC.XXI), pp. 1093–94.

HEADING: And Condition . . . Barclay.)] *omitted in 48.*

3 sweeping] weeping *48.* 4 costlyer] costly *48.* 7 slippery] *48;* flippery *52.* 17 and sigh] *48;* &, & sigh *52.* 18 sphear] *48;* spear *52.* 19–20 Paines . . . themselves;] *48; omitted in 52.* 30 reverent] reverend *48.* 33 and] *omitted in 52.* make] keep *48.*

87. SOSPETTO D'HERODE. *46* (*48*). The Italian text is from Giovanni Battista Marino, *Strage de gli innocenti* (Venetia: G. Scaglia, 1633), pp. 5–27, verified by G. Pozzi, ed. *Dicerie Sacre e La Strage de Gl'Innocenti* (Torino: Einaudi, 1960), pp. 467–88.

28.1 dusty] Martin from Bodl. MS. Tanner 465; dusky *46, 48.*

29.3 now] Martin from Bodl. MS. Tanner 465; not *46, 48.*

39.8 out] Martin from *48;* our *46.*

48.3 ever.] Martin from Bodl. MS. Tanner 465; ever *46, 48.*

51.1 leige to Cesar] Martin from Bodl. MS. Tanner 465; *omitted in 46, 48.* 3 linage] Martin from Bodl. MS. Tanner 465; image *46.*

59.1 snake] Martin from *48; omitted in 46.*

64.4 Lord . . . delay.] Martin from Bodl. MS. Tanner 465; Lord: . . . delay *46.*

IV. Sacred Poems in Latin and Greek

88. PSALM 1. Bodleian MS. Tanner 465.

12 Quam] Martin; Quem *MS.*

90. ZACHARIAS MINÙS CREDENS. *34.*

HEADING: Luc. 1:18] Martin; Luc. 1:12 *34.*

91. BEATÆ VIRGINI. DE SALUTATIONE. *34.*

6 qui dicit] Martin; quæ dicit *34.*

92. BEATÆ VIRGINI CREDENTI. *34.*

HEADING: Luc. 1.] Martin; Luc. 2. *34.*

103. [IN CIRCUMCISIONEM.] *MS.*
　　47 Ah ferus] Martin; At ferus *MS.*

109. [DONA MAGORUM.] *MS.*
　　4 accipias] Martin; accipies *MS.*

110. IN NOCTURNUM & HYEMALE ITER. *34.*
　　82 sternit] Martin; sternet *34.*

115. [IN FELICES MARTYRES.] *MS.*
　　20 longa est. . . brevi.] Martin; longa . . . brevi est. *MS.*

138. PISCATORES VOCATI. *34.*
　　HEADING: 4.] Martin; 6. *34.*

161. MITTIT JOANNES. *34.*
　　HEADING: 7.] Martin; 17. *34.*

189. QUISQUIS PERDIDERIT. *34.*
　　2 mihi est] Martin; mea est *34.*

198. ONUS MEUM. *34.*
　　3 sit] Martin; est *34.*

199. BEATI OCULI. *34.*
　　3 oculos] Martin; oculus *34.*

213. QUIS EX VOBIS SI HABEAT. 70 (*MS.*)
　　HEADING: Luc. 15:4.] Luc. ix. *MS.*
　　1 O ut ego] O ego ut *MS.*   5 agebat] abegit *MS.*   9 Horum] Ex his *MS.*
10 De] Ex *MS.*

228. AD VERBUM DEI. *34.*
　　HEADING: Marc. 10.] Martin; Matth. 10. *34.*

241. ÆDIFICATIS SEPULCHRA. *34.*
　　HEADING: 23.] Martin; 25. *34.*

244. CÙM TOT SIGNA. *MS.*
　　HEADING: 37.] Martin; 19. *MS.*

250. UBI AMOREM PRÆCIPIT. *MS.*
　　HEADING: 34.] Martin; 14. *MS.*

255. EGO VITIS VERA. *MS.*
　　HEADING: 15.] Martin; 14. *MS.*

256. VIDÉRUNT, & ODERUNT. *MS.*
　　HEADING: 15.24.] Martin; *omitted in MS.*

299. AD JUDÆOS ("Quid datis"). *34.*
HEADING: 7.] Martin; 8. *34.*

300. S. STEPHANUS AMICIS SUIS. *34.*
HEADING: 7.] Martin; 8. *34.*

301. "ECCE TUOS LAPIDES." *MS.* 4 vols] Martin; nos *MS.*

317. IN ATHENIENSEM. *MS.*
4 at] Martin; et *MS.*

331. IN DRACONEM. *34.*
HEADING: 12.] Martin; 7. *34.*

334. VOTIVA DOMUS PETRENSIS PRO DOMO DEI. *48.*
34 faciat] Martin from *MS.;* nec faciat *48.*

335. EJUSDEM GEMITUS. *48.*
6 saltu] Martin from *MS.;* salutu *48.*

V. Secular Poems in One English Version

337. UPON THE KINGS CORONATION ("Strange Metamorphosis"). Bodleian MS. Tanner 465.

338. UPON THE KINGS CORONATION ("Sound forth"). Bodleian MS. Tanner 465.

339. UPON THE BIRTH OF THE PRINCESSE ELIZABETH. Bodleian MS. Tanner 465.

340. ON THE GUNPOWDER-TREASON. Bodleian MS. Tanner 465.

341. UPON THE GUNPOWDER TREASON. Bodleian MS. Tanner 465.

342. UPON THE GUNPOWDER TREASON. Bodleian MS. Tanner 465.

343. AN EPITAPH UPON MR. ASHTON. *46* (*48*).
13–14 For . . . repetition] British Museum Add. MS. 33219; *omitted in 46, 48.*

346. UPON THE DEATH OF THE MOST DESIRED MR. HERRYS. *46* (*48*).
71–72 Keepe . . . charmes] Bodleian MS. Tanner 465; *omitted in 46, 48.*

349. UPON THE DEATH OF A GENTLEMAN [MR. CHAMBERS]. *46* (*48*).
11–12 For . . . teares.] Bodleian MS. Tanner 465; *omitted in 46, 48.* 21–22 Leaving . . . dead,] Bodleian MS. Tanner 465; *omitted in 46, 48.*

350. AN ELEGY UPON THE DEATH OF MR. STANNINOW. Bodleian MS. Tanner 465.

351. DEATH'S LECTURE. *52* (*46, 48*). *48* agrees with *52* except where noted.

HEADING: Upon Mr. Staninough's Death. *46;* At the Funerall of a young Gentleman. *48.* At] *48;* And *52.*

8 ye] *46, 48;* the *52.*   14 self] bulke *46.*   15 Wild] Wide *48.*   16 leane] small *46.*   21 Proud . . . eyliddes] *omitted in 46.*   22 Your selves] Thy selfe *46.* your] this *46.*   24 (Though . . . painted)] Through all your painting *46.* true] own *46.*   26 lowd Boasts] proud hopes *46.*   27 These] Those *48.* retired] selfe-prison'd *46.*

352. AN ELEGIE ON THE DEATH OF D^R. PORTER. Bodleian MS. Tanner 465.

353. UPON THE DEATH OF A FREIND. Bodleian MS. Tanner 465.

354. AN EPITAPH UPON A YOUNG MARRIED COUPLE. *52* (*46, 48*). *48* agrees with *52* except where noted.

HEADING: An Epitaph Upon Husband and Wife, which died, and were buried together. *46.*

2 their] the *46.*   5 sunder] sever *46.*   6 'Cause] Because *46.*   10 knott] knot that *46.*   11–14 *omitted in 46.*   17 Till] And *46.*   19 wake into] waken with *46.* a] that *46, 48.*   20 dy] sleepe *46.*

355. WISHES. TO HIS (SUPPOSED) MISTRESSE. *46* (*48*).

27 commend] Martin from *MS.;* command *46.*

358. EPITHALAMIUM. British Museum MS. Harleian 6917.

Martin has argued convincingly for the addition of this poem to the Crashaw canon ("Crashaw's Branston Epithalamium," *London Mercury*, VIII [1923], 159–66; edition, pp. lxxvi–lxxviii, 462–63) on the basis of many verbal parallels to the canon and on the biographical connection between the poet and the addressee (see note).

359. UPON BISHOP ANDREWES HIS PICTURE. *32* (*46, 48*).

First printed (i.e. engraved) on the portrait page of L. Andrewes, *XCVI Sermons . . .* , the Second Edition, (London, 1632). The presence of a 1635 print (so dated) of the engraving pasted into the Cambridge University Library copy of 1631, E.8.23 (this copy microfilmed by University Microfilms, Inc., for the series *English Books 1475–1640*) has led to the belief that the poem was written in 1631. The second edition exists in two issues, 1631 and 1632; the later issue contains the frontispiece, presumably the cause for the new issue. HEADING as in *46: omitted in 32.*

1 *See heer a*] This reverend *46. from*] cast *46.*   2 *this*] our *46.*   3 *our*] this *46.*   5 *rare industrious*] faire illustrious *46.*   10 *'Midst*] Mongst *46.*   11 *a*] her *46.*   12 *Where still she reads*] There still to read *46.*

360. ON THE FRONTISPIECE OF ISAACSONS CHRONOLOGIE. *33* (*46, 48*).

The poem was first printed facing the "frontispiece," i.e. title page (engraved by Marshall), beside another description. Neither poem is attributed to an author, and though both appear in 1646, only this one is by Crashaw, the longer of the two being the work of Edward Rainbow (Martin, p. 463).

HEADING as in *46:* The Frontispiece Explained . . . Or Thus. *33.*
3 if] *omitted in 46.*

361. "AT TH' IVORY TRIBUNALL." British Museum. Add. MS. 33219.

362. "THOUGH NOW 'TIS NEITHER MAY NOR JUNE." British Museum.
Add. MS. 33219.

365. UPON TWO GREENE APRICOCKES. *48.*
2 chidd] Turnbull; chide *48.*

367. ON A FOULE MORNING. *46 (48).*
18 Two ever . . . beds] Martin from *MS.;* To every . . . Bed *46, 48.*

368. TO THE MORNING. *46 (48).*
20 rapture] *48;* raptures *46.*

VI. *Secular Poems in Two English Versions*

369. A PANEGYRICKE [UPON THE ROYAL FAMILY]. First version *46;*
second version *40 (48);* 48 agrees with *40* except where noted. See note to this
poem for history of the text. The publication of the first version in 1646, six
years after the second version had been put into print, provides an interesting
comment on the general nature of the copy that Crashaw's friend had for the
1646 volume. The present edition offers the anomaly of a "first version" printed
six years later than the "second version"; for this poem, the progressive states
of the text are opposite to the progressive dates of publication. The first version,
though split apart in the present printing, is printed continuously in *46,* with
the exception of blank lines after *(46)* lines 48 and 58. The subheads placed
marginally in *40,* are centered before the sections in *48.*
To the Queen.
7 to] for *48.*
Upon the Duke.
46 cherries mocke] Cherrimock *46.*

370. IN PRAISE OF LESSIUS. First version: "On taking Physicke" found
in British Museum Add. MS. 22118, printed here from the version of *46;* "To
the Reader" from *Hygiasticon* (1634). Second version: "Temperance" *52 (48).*
See note to the poem for the history of the text. Pasted to the flyleaf of the
Huntington Library copy of *Steps to the Temple* (1646) (DX C6836 102361)
is a manuscript version of this poem in a contemporary hand, entitled "To the
Reader, upon the intent of Lessius his booke concerning Temperaunce—", pre-
sumably copied from *34.*
On taking Physicke (46).
HEADING as in *MS.*] In praise of Lessius his rule of health. *46.*
4 treasures] *MS.;* treasure *46.* 12 'gainst] *MS.;* against *46.*
To the Reader 34 (46).
HEADING as in *34*] *omitted in 46.*
3 all] all, *46.* 4 musick] Physick *46.* 11 Whose soul's] A soule *46.* 20
rides in] hath *46.* 21 see] thou see *46.* 33–40 *omitted in 46.*

Temperance 52 (48).
HEADING: In praise of Lessius his rule of health. *46, 48.*
of] or *52.*
2 whilst] while *48.*   4 treasures] treasure *48.*   9 shalt'] shall *48.*   10–11 *no space in 48, 52.*   16 musick] Physick *48.*   36 set] *48;* seat *52.*

VII. Secular Poems Translated into English

371. THE BEGINNING OF HELIODORUS. *46 (48).* The Greek text is from Αίθιοπικῶν βιβλία δέκα. *Æthiopicorum libri X* (Heidelberg, 1596), pp. 1–2.

HEADING: Heliodorus] Helidorus *46, 48.*
7 they] *48;* thy *46.*

372. OUT OF THE GREEKE CUPID'S CRYER. *46 (48).* The Greek text is from *Theocriti Aliorumque Poetarum Idyllia* (n.p.: Stephanus, MDLXXIX), pp. 264, 266.

373. UPON VENUS PUTTING ON MARS HIS ARMES. *46 (48).* The Greek text is from *Anthologia Graeca* ([Parisiis]: Stephanus, MDLXVI), Book IV, p. 324.

374. UPON THE SAME. *46 (48).* The Latin text is from *D. Magni. Ausonii Opera* (Lugduni, MDLXXV), p. 12 (Epigram lxiii [xlii]).

375. ON NANUS MOUNTED UPON AN ANT. *46 (48).* The Latin text is from *D. Magni. Ausonii Opera* (Lugduni, MDLXXV), p. 28 (Epigram xx [cxxii]).

HEADING as in *48]* omitted in *46.*

376. OUT OF CATULLUS. *46 (48).* The Latin text is from *C. Val. Catulli Opera Omnia* (Lutetiæ, M.D.CIIII), p. 19.

377. OUT OF EUPHORMIO. Bodleian MS. Tanner 465. The Latin text is from *Euphormionis Lusinini . . . Satyricon* (Lugdun. Batavorum, 1637), Pars. II, p. 200.

HEADING in *MS.:* Ex Euphormione. R.Cr. O Dea syderei Seu tu stirps alma Tonantis &c.

378. OUT OF MARTIALL. *46 (48).* The Latin text is from *M. Valerii Martialis Epigrammatum Libri XV* (Parisiis, MDCVII), p. 15 (Epigram I, xix).

379. OUT OF PETRONIUS. Bodleian MS. Tanner 465. The Latin text is from *Satyricon Petronii Arbitri Vivi Consularis* (Lutetiæ Parisior, M.D.XXCV), pp. 31–32 (No. 93).

HEADING in *MS.:* Petronij Ales Phasiacis petita Colchis &c. R. Cr.

380. OUT OF VIRGIL. *46 (48).* The Latin text is from *P. Vergilii Maronis Georgica* (Parisiis, 1564), pp. 182–83 (II, 323–45).

381. OUT OF HORACE. English and Greek versions are from Bodleian MS. Tanner 465; the Latin text is from *Q. Horatius Flaccus* (Lugduni Batavorum,

M.D.IIIC), p. 113. The Greek text is reprinted from Martin (pp. 377–78); for support of his emendations see pp. 377–78, 456.

HEADING in *MS.:* Horatij Ille & nefasto te posuit die &c R. Cr. [above English]; Horatii Ode. Ille & nefasto te posuit die &c. Ἑλληνιςί. [above Greek].

382. MUSICKS DUELL. *46* (*48*). The Latin text is from *Famiani Stradæ Romani e Societate Jesu Prolusiones Academicæ* (Romae, 1617), pp. 363–65 (Book II, Prolus. vi).

69 whence] Martin from *MS.;* when *46.* 99 graver] Martin from *48;* grave *46.* 156 full-mouth'd] *MS.,* 1670, Turnbull, Grosart; full-mouth *46, 48.*

383. OUT OF THE ITALIAN. A SONG. *46* (*48*). The Italian text is from *Rime d'Ansaldo Ceba* (Anversa, M.D.XCVI), p. 256, reprinted from Martin, pp. 442–43.

384. OUT OF THE ITALIAN. *46* (*48*). The Italian text is from *La Lira, Rime del Cavalier Marino . . . Madrigali & Canzoni* (Venezia, MDCXV), p. 14 (Madrigal xi).

385. OUT OF THE ITALIAN. *46* (*48*). The Italian text is by Valerio Marcellini, set to music by Luca Marenzio and published in his *Il quarto libro de' madrigali a cinque voce* (Venezia, 1584), no. xviii, reprinted here from M. Praz, "Drummond and Crashaw," *TLS,* October 21, 1949, p. 681.

VIII. Secular Poems in Latin

386. IN NATALES MARIÆ PRINCIPIS. Bodleian MS. Tanner 465.
48 qui] Martin; cui *MS.*

387. IN FACIEM AUGUSTISS. REGIS. *46* (*48*); first published in *Anthologia in Regis Exanthemata* (Cambridge, MDCXXXII).
6 tentas] *32, 48;* tantas *46.*

388. REX REDUX. *46* (*48*); first published in *Rex Redux* (Cambridge, MDCXXXIII).
26 dicere] *33, 48;* discere *46.*

390. AD REGINAM. *46* (*48*); first published in *Ducis Eboracensis Fasciae* (Cambridge, 1633).
16 tantas] *48;* tantus *46.*

391. IN SERENISSIMÆ REGINÆ PARTUM HYEMALEM. *46* (*48*); first published in *Carmen Natalitatum Ad cunas . . . Principis Elizabethae* (Cambridge, 1635).

392. PRINCIPI RECÈNS NATÆ. *46* (*48*); first published in ΣΥΝΩιΔΙΑ, *Sive Musarum . . . Congratulatio* (Cambridge, 1637).

393. IN REGINAM, ET SIBI & ACADEMIÆ SEMPER PARTURIENTEM. *48;* first published in *Voces Votivae . . . Pro novissimo . . . Principe Filio* (Cambridge, MDCXL).
HEADING: In] *40;* Ad *48.* semper] *40; omitted in 48.*

394. SERENISSIMÆ REGINÆ LIBRUM SUUM. Bodleian MS. Tanner 465.

395. IN REV̄. D.ʳᵉ BROOKE. Bodleian MS. Tanner 465.

5 illud oris acre] Bensley *conj. apud* Martin; oris acre procul *MS.*   8 facilitas graves] Bensley; gravitas faciles *MS.*

396. IN OBITUM REV. V. Dʳⁱˢ MANSELL. Bodleian MS. Tanner 465.

397. EPITAPHIUM IN DOMINUM HERRISIUM. *46* (*48*); first published on the memorial monument at Pembroke College.

13 quantas] *48;* quantus *46.*   35 Oratoria] Martin from *MS.;* Oratoriæ *46, 48.*   60 S] Sal. *48.*

398. IN EUNDEM SCAZON. *48;* following the poem "Upon the Death of Mr. *Herrys*" ("A Plant of noble stemme").

2 fletus] Martin from *MS.;* flectus *48.*   6 Fecere] Martin from *MS.;* Fuere *48.* impar] Martin from *MS.;* nuper *48.*

400. EPITAPHIUM. *48.*

7 huc] Martin from *MS.;* hinc *48.*

401. HONORATISSᵒ Dᵒ ROBᵒ HEATH. Bodleian MS. Tanner 465.

16 fracta] Garrod *conj. apud* Martin; facta *MS.*

403. IN PICTURAM REV. EPIS. D. ANDREWS. *46* (*48*).

3 Tubam] *48;* Tubani *46.*   10 in gentes] Martin from *MS.;* ingentes *46, 48.* 11 et fuit] Martin from *MS.;* fuitq; *46, 48.*   15 Hac] Martin from *MS.;* Hæc *46.*

404. [IN PICTURAM EPIS. ANDREWES.] Bodleian MS. Tanner 465; in this manuscript these lines follow immediately the preceding poem "Hæc charta monstrat . . . ," No. 403, on the same subject. They are, however, not to be thought of as a continuation of that poem.

405. CÙM HORUM ALIQUA. Bodleian MS. Tanner 465.

407. ÆNÆAS PATRIS SUI BAJULUS. *48.*

1–4 4 lines in Martin from *MS.;* as two lines in *48.*   16–17 Victor . . . libentius / Funeribusque] Martin from *MS.;* Victor . . . moritur / Troja . . . Funeribusque *48.*   16 libentius] Martin from *MS.;* libenter *48.*

408. IN PIGMALIONA. *48.*

20 vivas] Martin from *MS.;* vivos *48.*

409. ARION. *48.*

19 vetat . . . sit] Martin from *MS.;* restat . . . fit *48.*   20 it] Martin from *MS.;* sit *48.*

411. HYMNUS VENERI. Bodleian MS. Tanner 465.

412. [IN SPEM.] Bodleian MS. Tanner 465.

415. TRANQUILLITAS ANIMI. *48.*

5 perfido] Martin from *MS.;* persido *48.*

416. NON ACCIPIMUS BREVEM VITAM. Bodleian MS. Tanner 465.

417. PULCHRA NON DIUTURNA. Bodleian MS. Tanner 465.

418. VERIS DESCRIPTIO. Bodleian MS. Tanner 465.

419. BULLA. *48;* first published in *D. Heynsii Crepundia Siliana* (Cambridge, 1646).

27 perfidâ] Martin; persida *48.* 56 purpureos] Martin from Heynsius; purpureus *48.* 57 Flagrat] Martin from Heynsius; flagrant *48.* 85 roseæ] Martin from Heynsius; rosæ *48.* 93 in] Martin from Heynsius; & in *48.* 102 en] Martin from Heynsius; in *48.* 157 Nempe] Martin from Heynsius; Tempe *48.*

Appendix

AMPLISSIMI ET ORNATISSIMI. British Museum Add. MS. 40176.
The dedication was printed for the first time by Martin (pp. 2–3).
28 ipsi] Martin; ipso *MS.* 61 indulsisti] Martin; indulsi *MS.*

REVERENDO ADMODUM. *34.*
25 evocatum] ink correction in several copies; evocata *34.*

AN EPIGRAMME. *52.*
9 no] Martin; wo *52.*

[Table of First Lines of Sacred Epigrams
in *Epigrammatum Sacrorum Liber* (1634).]

[Bracketed dates of composition from Milhaupt.]

Ecce tuus, Natura, pater! pater hic tuus, hic est 93
Frustra illum increpitant, frustra vaga saxa: nec illi 298
Exul, *Amor Christi* est: Christum tamen invenit exul 325
Fundite ridentes animas; effundite cœlo 112
Ah, redeas miseræ, redeas (puer alme) parenti [Jan. 8, 1632] 116
In tua tecta Deus veniet: tuus haud sinit illud 156
Nil ait: ô sanctæ pretiosa silentia linguæ! 264
Spésne meas tandem ergò mei tenuêre lacerti? 105
Sæpe Dei verbum sentes cadit inter; & atrum 166
Res eadem vario quantum distinguitur usu! 210
Christe, loquutus eras (ô sacra licentia verbi!) 228
Esse levis quicunque voles, onus accipe Christi: 198
Ecce vagi venit unda cibi; venit indole sacrâ 176
Aut Deus, aut saltem dæmon tibi notior esset 193
In gremio, quæris, cur sic sua lumina Virgo 96
O Frontis, lateris, manuúmque pedúmque cruores! 270
Ergò *istis* socium se peccatoribus addit? 147
Ipsum, Ipsum (precor) ô potiùs mihi (candide) monstra [April 1, 1632] 278
Lex jubet ex hominum cœtu procul ire *leprosos* [Easter] 218
Quicquid *spina* procax, vel stylo *clavus* acuto 283
Petre, tua lateam paulisper (Petre) sub umbra 297
En me, & signa mei, quondam mea vulnera! certè 281
Ferri non meminit ferrum: se vincula Petro 311
Imperiosa premunt morbos, & ferrea fati 318
En serpit tua, prupureo tua palmite vitis 253
Penè? quid hoc *penè* est? Vicinia sæva salutis! 321
Luce suâ venit ecce Deus, mundóque refulget 134
O Mihi si digito tremat & tremat unica summo 216
Dic, Phoenix unde in nitidos novus emicat annos 132
Ille jubet: procul ite mei, mea gloria, rami 236
Infantis fore te patrem, res mira videtur 90
Felix ô, sacros cui sic licet ire per artus! 121
In proprios replicata sinus quae repserat, & jam 207
Christe, malas fraudes, Pharisaica retia, fallis 240
O Mihi cur *dextram,* mater, cur, oro, *sinistram* 223
Ni se dejiciat Christus de vertice Templi 125
Discite vos miseri, venientes discite flammas 233
Istum? vile caput! quantum mihi gratulor, inquis, 220
Quae lucis tenebræ? quae nox est ista diei? 304
Cum Christus nostris ibat mitissimus oris 199
Ergóne tam subitâ potuit vice flebilis horror 160
Ergóne delitias facit, & sibi plaudit ab alto 196
Dicite, quæ tanta est sceleris fiducia vestri? 137
I Frustra truculente; tuas procul aurea rident 331
Miraris (quid enim faceres?) sed & hæc quoque credis 92
Post tot Scribarum (Christe) in te prælia, tandem 238
Vani, quid strepitis? nam, quamvìs *dormiat* illa, 172
Ludite jam pisces secura per æquora: pisces 138
Cuncta Deo debentur: habet tamen & sua Caesar 239
Ille igitur vilem te, te dignatur asellum 231
Immo *veni:* aërios (ô Christe) accingere currus 246
Impius ergò iterum clavos? iterum impius hastam? 284

[Table of First Lines of Sacred Epigrams in Bodleian Manuscript Tanner 465]

Hos quoque? an hos igitur sævi lacerabitis agnos?	*195*
Ergò ille, Angelicis o sarcina dignior alis,	*124*
Vox ego sum, dicis. tu vox es, sancte Johannes?	*127*
Monstrat Joannes Christum. haud res mira videtur:	*89*
Ad te sydereis, ad te, Bone Tityre, pennis	*100*
Arma, viri! (ætheriam quocunque sub ordine pubem	*330*
Ipsos naturæ thalamos sapis, imaque rerum	*317*
Credo quidem. sed & hoc hostis te credidit ipse	*255*
Ille abiit. jamque o quæ nos mala cunque manetis [May 18, 1634]	*291*
Quæ vehit auratos nubes dulcissima nimbos?	*292*
Quis malus appendit de mortis stipite vitam?	*307*
Jamque pates. cordisque seram gravis hasta reclusit,	*205*
Accipe (an ignoscis?) de te sata germina, Miles.	*267*
Nox erat, & Christum (Doctor malè docte) petebas,	*131*
O ego ut Angelicis fiam bona gaudia turmis!	*213*
Tantum habuit Baptista loqui, tot flumina rerum,	*120*
Mors tibi, & Herodes instant: cùm nuncius ales	*310*
Ad nutum Domini abjecisti retia, Petre.	*141*
Ergò tot heu (torvas facies) tot in ora leonum,	*128*
Quæ secreta meant taciti tibi retia verbi,	*186*
En caput! atque suis quæ plus satìs ora laborant	*248*
Quanta amor ille tuus se cunque levaverit ala,	*244*
O Nigra hæc! Quid enim mihi candida pectora monstrat?	*289*
Ergò meas spernis lacrymas, urbs perfida? Sperne.	*235*
Tu quoque dum istius miseri peccata fateris,	*221*
Ah, quis erat furor hos (tam raros) solvere somnos?	*169*
Cedit jo. jam, jamque cadet. modò fortiter urge.	*182*
Siccine fraternos fastidis, improbe, morbos,	*148*
Nuper lecta gravem extinxit pia pagina febrem:	*142*
Hanc, mihi quam miseram faciunt mea crimina vitam,	*324*
Ergò tuam pone; ut nobis sit sumere nostram:	*188*
Quae mella, o quot, Christe, favos in carmina fundis!	*261*
Quid non tam fœdè sævi maris audeat ira!	*268*
Ille ut eat tecum, in natique, tuique salutem?	*135*
Dum nimiùm in captis per te, Petre, piscibus hæres,	*140*
Vidit? & odit adhuc? Ah, te non vidit, Jesu.	*256*
Tu mala turba tace. mihi tam mea vota propinquant,	*225*
O quàm te miseri ludunt vaga tædia voti,	*237*
Falleris. & nudum malè ponis (Pictor) Amorem:	*171*
Tolle oculos, tolle o tecum (tua sydera) nostros.	*228*
Quid mortem objicitis nostro, quid vincla timori?	*320*
Oro, quis es? legat ista suo Baptista Magistro.	*162*
Ergò veni; quicunque ferant tua signa timores:	*245*
Felices! properastis jo, properastis. & altam	*115*
Ergò ut inultus eas? Sed nec tamen ibis inultus,	*326*
Ecce tuos lapides! nihil est pretiosius illis;	*301*
Ah ferus, ah culter! qui tam bona lilia primus [Jan. 1, 1635]	*103*
Ne, pia, ne nimium, Virgo, permitte querelis:	*117*
Accipe dona, Puer; parvæ libamina laudis.	*109*
Nec facta est tamen illa Parens impunè; quòd almi	*95*
Circulus hic similem quàm par sibi pergit in orbem!	*273*
Absint, qui ficto simulant pia pectora vultu,	*295*

List of Events, Miracles, Teachings, and Parables in the Sacred Epigrams

[The citations are the poem numbers.]

EVENTS IN THE EARLY LIFE OF CHRIST

Introductory Annunciations 89–92; Birth of Jesus 5, 93–100; Circumcision 6, 101–3; Presentation in the Temple 104–7; Visit of the Wise Men 108–9; Flight into Egypt 110; Slaughter of the Innocents 7, 8, 112–15; Visit to the Temple 9, 116–19; Ministry of John the Baptist 120; Baptism of Jesus 10, 121–22; Temptation in the Wilderness 123–25; John's Testimony before Priests 126–28.

EVENTS IN THE PUBLIC MINISTRY OF CHRIST

Calling of the Apostles 13, 138–41, 145–46. *Healing Miracles:* the Nobleman's Son 135; the Centurion's Servant 14, 156–58; the feverous Woman and the Dropsical Man 142, 208–9; Lepers 143, 217–18; the Lame 149; the Cripple 207; the Withered Hand 150–52; the Blind 30, 174, 202, 225–29; the Dumb 16, 21, 164, 184–85; the Dead 159–60, 172–73. *Other Miracles:* Changing water into Wine 11, 129–30; Stilling of the Tempest 18, 168–70; Feeding of the Multitudes 19–20, 175–79, 186; Walking on the Water 180. *Events and Teachings:* Visit of Nicodemus 12, 131–34; Eating with Publicans 147–48, 212; Sermon on the Mount 153–55; Delegation from John 161–62; Anointing by Mary Magdalene 15, 163; the Canaanitish Woman 181–83; Predictions 187–89; Transfiguration 190; Discourse on Humility and Freedom 22–23, 191–94; Mission of the Seventy 195–99; Visit to Mary and Martha 201; Pharisee and Publican 29, 219–22; Request for James and John 223–24; Zachaeus in Sycamore 230; Miscellaneous 136, 137, 171, 203, 206, 210, 212. *Parables:* Word among Thorns 17; Grain Field 165–67; Good Samaritan 24, 200; Good Shepherd 25, 204–5, 213; the Feast 211; Prodigal Son 26, 214; Dives and Lazarus 27, 28, 215–16.

EVENTS AT THE END OF CHRIST'S LIFE

Entry into Jerusalem and Weeping over the City 31, 231–35; Cursing of the Fig Tree 236; Conversations with the Pharisees 32, 33, 34, 237–41; Widow's Mites 35, 242; Jewish Rejection of Christ 243–44; Apocalyptic Vision 245–46; The Last Supper and the Farewell Discourses 36, 37, 38, 247–61; Peter Cutting off the Ear 39, 262; Christ before Caiaphas 40, 263–64; Pontius Pilate Washing his Hands 41, 42, 265–66; Christ Scorned by the Soldiers 43, 267–68; Crucifixion of Christ 44, 45, 71, 269–72; Burial of Christ 46, 273–74; Resurrection of Christ 47, 48, 49, 275–79; Appearances of Christ 50, 51, 280–86; Ascension of Christ 287–91.

WORKINGS OF THE HOLY SPIRIT

Descent of the Holy Spirit 292–95; Peter Healing the Sick 52, 296–97; Stephen the Martyr 298–301; Simon Rejected 302; Baptism of the Ethiopian 53, 303; Conversion and Work of Paul 304–7; James Executed 308; Peter freed from Prison 54, 309–12; Herod's Sudden Death 313–14; Paul at Lystra and elsewhere 315–17; Paul Healing 318; Paul Imprisoned and Preaching 319–22; Luke the Physician 323–24; John Persecuted 325–27.

All Saints Day 328–29.

War in Heaven 330–31.

Scriptural Index to the Sacred Epigrams

[Based on the texts to the translations; the citations are the poem numbers.]

The Table [of Contents to the Volume of 1646].

[The citations are the poem numbers.]

FINIS.

The Table [of Contents to the Volume of 1648].

[The citations are the poem numbers.]

FINIS.

[The Table of Contents to the Volume of 1652.]

[The citations are the poem numbers.]

Index

INDEX OF FIRST LINES AND TITLES

[The citations are the poem numbers.]